*f*P

Also by Tyler Anbinder

NATIVISM AND SLAVERY
*The Northern Know Nothings and
the Politics of the 1850s*

TYLER ANBINDER

FIVE POINTS

The 19th-Century New York City Neighborhood That Invented Tap Dance, Stole Elections, and Became the World's Most Notorious Slum

THE FREE PRESS

NEW YORK LONDON TORONTO SYDNEY SINGAPORE

THE FREE PRESS
Rockefeller Center
1230 Avenue of the Americas
New York, NY 10020

THE FREE PRESS and colophon are
trademarks of Simon & Schuster Inc.

For information about special discounts for bulk purchases,
please contact Simon & Schuster Special Sales:
1-800-456-6798 or business@simonandschuster.com

DESIGNED BY LISA CHOVNICK

Manufactured in the United States of America

Library of Congress Cataloging-in-Publication Data
Anbinder, Tyler.
Five Points : the 19th-century New York City neighborhood that invented tap dance, stole
elections, and became the world's most notorious slum / Tyler Anbinder.
p. cm.
Includes bibliographical references (p.) and index.
1. Five Points (New York, N.Y.)—History.   2. Five Points (New York, N.Y.)—Social
conditions.   3. New York (N.Y.)—History.   4. New York (N.Y.) —Social conditions.
5. Slums—New York (State)—New York—History—19th century.   6. Ethnic neighborhoods—New York (State)—New York—History—19th century.   7. City and town life—
New York (State)—New York—History—19th century.

F128.68.F56 A53   2001   2001033296
974.7'1—dc21

ISBN 0-684-85995-5

To Jacob and Dina,
with all my love

CONTENTS

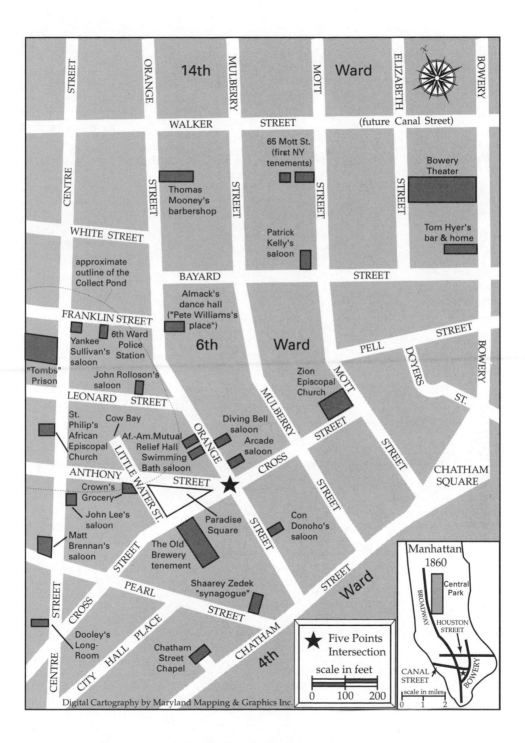

FIVE POINTS, 1830–1854

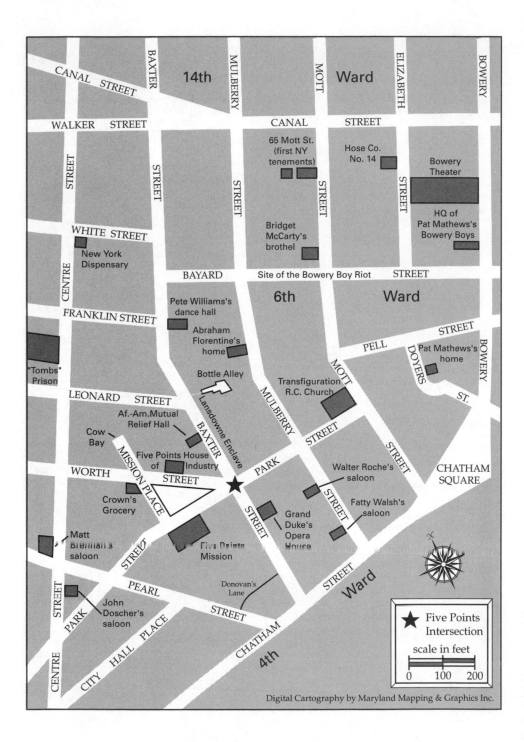

FIVE POINTS, 1855–1867

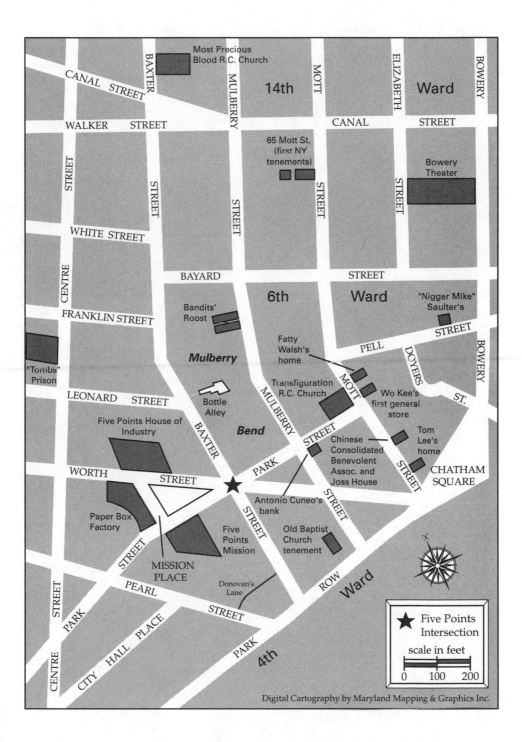

FIVE POINTS, 1868–1895

INTRODUCTION

"FIVE POINTS! . . . The very letters of the two words, which mean so much, seem, as they are written, to redden with the bloodstains of unavenged crime. There is Murder in every syllable, and Want, Misery and Pestilence take startling form and crowd upon the imagination as the pen traces the words. What a world of wretchedness has been concentrated in this narrow district!"

Frank Leslie's Illustrated Newspaper, August 16, 1873.

FIVE POINTS was the most notorious neighborhood in nineteenth-century America. Beginning in about 1820, overlapping waves of Irish, Italian, and Chinese immigrants flooded this district in what is now New York's Chinatown. Significant numbers of Germans, African Americans, and Eastern European Jews settled there as well. All but forgotten today, the densely populated enclave was once renowned for jam-packed, filthy tenements, garbage-covered streets, prostitution, gambling, violence, drunkenness, and abject poverty. "No decent person walked through it; all shunned the locality; all walked blocks out of their way rather than pass through it," recalled a tough New York fireman. A religious journal called Five Points "the most notorious precinct of moral leprosy in the city, . . . a perfect hot-bed of physical and moral pestilence, . . . a hell-mouth of infamy and woe."[1]

While Americans may have considered Five Points repulsive, they found it fascinating as well. Tap dancing originated in its raucous dance halls. The neighborhood was a playground for "Bowery B'hoys" and "sporting men," two of nineteenth-century America's most colorful street cultures. Its residents squared off in some of the most talked-about bare-knuckle prizefights of the century. Many of the city's most renowned gangs were headquartered there. It was also the epicenter of rough-and-tumble Tammany politics and some of the most infamous riots in early American history.

Touring Five Points became an international attraction, drawing such notables as Charles Dickens, a Russian grand duke, Davy Crockett, and Abraham Lincoln. "Londoners know it as well as St. Giles; and strangers ask to be shown to it before they visit Fifth Avenue or the Central Park," commented one authority. Indeed, the American concept of "slumming" was probably invented there.[2]

In its heyday, Five Points was very likely the most thoroughly studied neighborhood in the world. Journalists chronicled its rampant crime, squalid tenements, and raucous politics. Religious magazines detailed missionaries' efforts to "save" the district's residents from sin and perdition. Many of nineteenth-century America's best-known writers published accounts of their visits, and popular novelists from Ned Buntline to Horatio Alger set their stories there.

Yet those who saw Five Points firsthand believed that written words could never convey what life there was really like. "I have never seen any thing which has been written about this noted place, that gave any idea of it," observed one author in 1852. Nor could the dozens of prints of Five Points that appeared in *Harper's Weekly* and *Frank Leslie's Illustrated Newspaper* truly communicate the crowding, the suffering, and the crime that seemed so overwhelming in person. Jacob Riis's famous photos of the neighborhood from the late 1880s finally gave Americans some sense of the wretched conditions in its tenements and drove the city to raze a sizable portion of the neighborhood. Five Points, for generations one of the most talked-about districts of the city, quickly faded from public consciousness.[3]

Few historians devoted much attention to Five Points in the early years of the twentieth century. Academic historians concerned themselves primarily with politics and the law. Slums, immigrants, crime—none of these subjects seemed important enough to merit scholarly analysis. A few popular historians did study Five Points. The neighborhood figured prominently in Herbert Asbury's *Gangs of New York* in 1928 and Alvin F. Harlow's *Old Bowery Days* in 1931. But Asbury and Harlow were imbued with many of the same prejudices against the neighborhood's Irish, Jewish, Italian, and Chinese immigrants that had colored contemporary accounts of Five Points, and this led to many distorted depictions of the district and its inhabitants. In addition, they tended to accept as fact virtually anything found in nineteenth-century newspapers, even though the press of the day was hardly reliable. Many of the most sensational stories about Five Points in *The Gangs of New York* and *Old Bowery Days* are patently untrue.[4]

Thirty years ago, with the advent of "social history," academics began to pay more attention to Five Points, though few devoted more than passing interest to its fascinating story. Only recently has Five Points bubbled back into popular consciousness, in popular histories of the city such as Luc Sante's *Low Life* and prominent novels such as Caleb Carr's *The Alienist*. An archaeological dig commissioned by the federal government in 1991 led to significant media interest in Five Points, as did Martin Scorsese's screen adaptation of *The Gangs of New York*, which he set in Five Points and began shooting in the fall of 2000. Yet many of the recent accounts of Five Points continue to perpetuate the most egregious myths about the neighborhood. The two most important works on the history of New York published in the 1990s, for example—*The Encyclopedia of New York City* and *Gotham*—both misidentify something as simple as the streets whose confluence created the five-cornered intersection that gave the neighborhood its name.[5]

Five Points, it is hoped, will set the record straight by providing the first detailed history of this fascinating immigrant enclave. Drawing on bank ledgers, court records, real estate documents, government reports, marriage and adoption records, newspapers, diaries, and manuscript collections, I hope to show that Five Points was more than a degraded object of fascination. The Five Points story is the quintessential immigrant saga, full of striving and—contrary to the neighborhood's reputation—both misery *and* achievement.

Politics offers just one example. Five Pointers played a vital role in reshaping New York's political landscape. They were key players at virtually every turning point in nineteenth-century New York's electoral history. The district's residents were among the first working-class New Yorkers to snatch political power from the hands of the old elite that had governed the city for centuries. They perfected the rough-and-tumble style of politics that, when eventually adopted citywide, would make the city's Democratic machine, Tammany Hall, so infamous. In 1857, when state authorities attempted to hamstring Tammany by usurping many of its patronage prerogatives, Five Pointers made the city's most dramatic statement of protest by fomenting a bloody riot. In the late 1860s, when the Tweed Ring was at its height, many of its most audacious acts of electoral fraud were perpetrated in Five Points. Many Irish Catholic Five Pointers excused these excesses, viewing the political system as a route to prestige and financial security.

Yet this history in no way denies that squalor dominated the lives of most Five Pointers. Recent scholarship on the neighborhood has tended to argue that conditions there could not have been as awful as previous generations have insisted. The myriad prejudices that observers harbored toward Irish Catholics, Italians, and the poor generally, these critics argue, must have significantly colored their depictions of the neighborhood.[6]

These revisionists have vastly improved our understanding of Five Points, forcing us to recognize that much of what was written by contemporaries was simply not true. Yet in their well-intentioned efforts to identify prejudice, these writers have, I believe, lost sight of some unpleasant truths. Even if one considers only the statements of Five Pointers themselves, rather than the biased views of outsiders, one finds a neighborhood rife with vice, crime, and misery. Brothels were everywhere. Alcoholism was omnipresent. Habitually drunken men beat their wives and children. The neighborhood's many female alcoholics neglected their sons and daughters, producing some of the Five Points' most heart-rending tales of abuse and suffering. Upwards of 1,000 Five Pointers at any given time lived in filthy, overcrowded, disease-ridden, tumbledown tenements whose conditions are unimaginable to modern Americans. Previous generations of writers may have exaggerated certain aspects of life in Five Points, but the truth is that conditions there *were* quite wretched.

Nearly two centuries ago, New York City officials decided to extend Anthony Street east to the already-existing, X-shaped junction of Orange and Cross Streets, creating a five-cornered intersection that became known as Five Points. By the 1830s, it had become a concentration of vice, disease, crowding, and bloody conflict unparalleled in American history. But the neighborhood was far more than a collection of pathologies. Some Five Pointers were dragged down by the district's crime, poverty, and misery, but most survived and eventually thrived, establishing more prosperous lives for themselves and their families than would have been possible back in Ireland, or Poland, or Italy, or China. From their struggles to endure the neighborhood's brutal tenements, to their desperate efforts to find and keep work to support themselves and pay for the immigration of additional family members, to their eventual success in creating brighter futures for themselves and their children, Five Pointers' stories are as old as America itself, and yet as contemporary as the current waves of immigrants that continue to reshape our society.

1

PROLOGUE

THE FIVE POINTS RACE RIOT OF 1834

ON HIS WAY into the Laight Street Presbyterian Church on June 12, 1834, silk importer Lewis Tappan noticed a lone black man standing nervously outside the house of worship. Dozens of white parishioners stood by the doorway, chatting amiably among themselves, but casting suspicious glances at the man and then whispering to their friends. Incensed at the insensitivity of his fellow congregants, Tappan approached the man and recognized him as the Rev. Samuel E. Cornish, whom Tappan knew because both were active in the abolition movement. Cornish, who a few years earlier had co-edited the first African-American newspaper, had no congregation of his own. He had appeared at the door of the Laight Street Church that morning seeking a place for Sunday worship. Ignoring the looks of horror on the faces of the other parishioners, Tappan invited Cornish inside to attend the service and insisted that he sit in Tappan's own pew toward the front of the church.

Tappan's gesture was bound to create an uproar in 1830s New York, even within his relatively liberal congregation. Once inside, a number of parishioners complained loudly to Tappan and demanded that he never so embarrass them again. Observing the commotion, the church's own minister, Samuel H. Cox, decided to make it the subject of his sermon that day. Condemning the intolerance of his parishioners, Cox told them that the peoples of the Holy Land were dark-skinned and would be considered "colored" by American standards. Jesus himself, Cox asserted, was therefore probably dark-skinned as well. Americans should thus have sympathy for all people of color.

In the press the next day, Tappan's enemies seized upon Cox's sermon as a means to discredit the entire anti-slavery movement. Reporting that

New York Transcript.

MONDAY, JULY 14.

☞ Communications and advertisements, intended for the NEW YORK TRANSCRIPT, may be left at the Book Store and Circulating Library of A. GREENE, No. 1 Beekman street, where, also, *papers* can be obtained.

THE RIOTS.

At length we have time to breathe again. We have been for some days past so hurried about from point to point, to look after the mobs, in their various attacks, that it gave us little time to think of any thing else.

It had been hoped, that after the attack on Lewis Tappan's house, when most of its contents were burned and destroyed, that the rioters would have been satisfied, and have reposed upon the laurels of disgrace which they had won—thinking it sufficient glory to have so signally distinguished themselves against one who seemed to be the most prominent object of their resentment. But the event proved, what might indeed have been known from the history of other mobs, and the very nature of mobocracy, that they are never satisfied; that the more they do the more they resolve upon doing, and that like the horse-leech's daughters. they still cry, "Give! give!"

Coverage of the anti-abolition riot from the *New York Transcript*, July 14, 1834. Collection of the New-York Historical Society.

Cox claimed Christ was black, anti-abolitionists wrote that such radical ravings proved that the abolitionists were "amalgamationists," seeking intermarriage and social integration of blacks and whites. Two conservative journals, the *Commercial Advertiser* and the *Courier and Enquirer*, were especially vicious in their attacks, advocating violence to suppress abolitionism and the threat it posed to national unity.[1]

The incident at the Laight Street Church might not have had significant repercussions had not anti-abolitionists in general, and the *Commercial Advertiser* and the *Courier and Enquirer* in particular, been engaged in a long-running feud with Tappan and his brother and business partner Arthur, also an active abolitionist. The bad blood between the Tappans and the city's conservative press dated back to 1832, when the brothers leased the Chatham Theater, located just south of Chatham Square at the fringe of the Five Points neighborhood, and converted it into a chapel for the famed evangelist Charles G. Finney. According to Finney, the Tappans had selected the location because it was "in the heart of the most irreligious population of New York. It was not far from the 'five points,' and was a place of resort highly discreditable to the city." Although designated by its founders the Second Free Presbyterian Church because it charged no pew rent (in hopes of attracting the poor into the evangelical movement), the house of worship became universally known as the Chatham Street Chapel. Under the leadership of Finney and the Tappans, the chapel became a popular venue for abolitionist meetings.[2]

The movement to abolish slavery was still considered quite radical in 1830s New York. Most of those willing to admit that slavery was an evil did not support its immediate abolition, but instead promoted the colonization movement, which sought to send voluntarily emancipated slaves to Africa. The Tappans had once been active in the colonization movement, but around 1830 converted to the abolition cause. In order to discredit colonization, Lewis Tappan in May 1834 conducted a public interrogation of a man recently returned from Liberia, the African nation set up by American colonizationists. The man painted a picture of licentiousness, drunkenness, and sexual debauchery in the new African state. Embarrassed colonization advocates (especially the editors of the *Commercial Advertiser* and the *Courier and Enquirer*) responded with scathing attacks on the Tappans. But the Tappans remained determined to expose colonization as a subterfuge by which those who really hoped to protect slavery diverted attention and money from abolitionism.

The tensions between New York abolitionists and their adversaries had smoldered throughout early 1834. By early July, just a few weeks after Tappan had invited Samuel Cornish inside his church, they ignited into violence. And because both the Chatham Street Chapel and one of the city's largest concentrations of blacks were located in or near Five Points, the neighborhood became the focus of much of the bloodshed. On Independence Day, an angry mob disrupted an abolitionist lecture at the Chatham Street Chapel. Outnumbered and intimidated, the opponents of slavery canceled their meeting. According to the *Sun*, the rioters then proceeded to City Hall Park "to act out their patriotism in knocking down the blacks . . . [and] commanding every man of color they met to leave the Park. . . . On seeing this Alderman [James] Ferris interfered, and the rioters knocked him down also." Police eventually dispersed the mob and arrested six rioters.[3]

Three days later, violence erupted again as a group of African Americans gathered at the Chatham Street Chapel to celebrate the anniversary of the abolition of slavery in New York. When some members of the New York Sacred Music Society arrived for practice, not knowing that it had been canceled, they brusquely ordered the assembled blacks to leave. An argument flared, and the ensuing scuffle degenerated into a brawl that was "waged with considerable violence on both sides, and resulted in the usual number of broken heads and benches."[4]

When the *Courier and Enquirer* announced inaccurately on Wednesday, the ninth, that another anti-slavery meeting would take place at the chapel that evening, anti-abolitionists mobbed it once again. Finding the church closed, they broke in and held a meeting of their own. Led by George "Legs" Williamson ("a most desperate character [who] would cut and shoot when in a tight place"), the crowd then stormed Lewis Tappan's house at 40 Rose Street. Tappan and his family had gone to Harlem to escape the summer heat, so were not hurt by the flying glass when the rioters smashed some windows. The rioters' next target was Five Points' Bowery Theater, where the rioters forced the cast to abort a benefit performance for the playhouse's English-born stage manager, who had supposedly made anti-American remarks. Still burning with resentment, the mob returned to Tappan's house, broke in, smashed the crockery, tore down the blinds, and removed and burned all the furniture. Future Vice President Schuyler Colfax, then a boy of twelve, visited the scene the next day and later said that his disgust at the wanton destruction helped convince him to support the anti-slavery cause.[5]

On the following evening, Thursday, July 10, mobs seemed to be everywhere—at Tappan's house again, at his store on Pearl Street, at Reverend Cox's house, and at the Bowery Theater, among other places. And on the evening of the eleventh, the rioting degenerated into a full-scale racial pogrom, as crowds attacked African-American homes, businesses, and churches throughout the Five Points area. This time, the violence began at the Tappan store, where a mob of more than one hundred overwhelmed fifteen security guards and broke the shop's windows. The rioters moved up Pearl Street to Five Points, where they attacked two or three houses on Mulberry Street just north of Chatham Square. Word soon spread throughout the neighborhood that the rioters wanted Five Points whites "to exhibit lights in the windows," so the mob would know which houses not to attack. Meanwhile, most of the rioters moved northwest to the block of Orange Street just north of the Five Points intersection, where many Five Points blacks lived. There the mob attacked the African-American Mutual Relief Hall at 42 Orange Street, breaking all the windows and tearing down the sign. Around the corner at African-American John Rolloson's porterhouse at 157 Leonard Street, "the mob rushed in, tore down his bar, threw his kegs of liquor into the streets, and carried them off, broke all the decanters and glasses, and carried off a clock and what money was in the drawer." Rioters went upstairs and took almost two hundred dollars "in silver, 4 valuable watches, a set of silver spoons and jewelry to the amount of $100,—then destroyed the furniture in the basement," until they were driven away by the "watch." Still not satisfied, the mob crossed the street and burned all the furniture at 156 Leonard Street, including that of African-American Maria Willis, who "was robbed of everything she had in all the world." The poor woman, who had four children and was pregnant with a fifth, had been widowed just two weeks earlier.[6]

Back on Orange Street, still other rioters were smashing doors and windows near the Five Points intersection. According to the account in the *New York Transcript*, "they were about to pull down the Arcade," a saloon at 33 Orange, and the Swimming Bath bawdy house at 40 Orange, when a street inspector named McGrath "addressed them, and assured them that every negro should be out . . . by twelve o'clock the next day; they then gave three cheers, shook hands with the officer, and left . . . without disturbing a plank." Moving north, the rioters attacked 56 and 56½ Orange, where they "broke all the windows [and] furniture, abused the inmates, and carried off property to the amount of $100." Next, they stormed Thomas Mooney's barbershop at 87 Orange. But Mooney, armed in preparation for the onslaught, fired three times at the mob, injuring one person and convincing the rest to spare his business. The rioters then moved westward. They attacked St. Philip's African Episcopal Church on Centre Street around 11:00 p.m. "and demolished it almost entirely, including a fine organ." Up and down Centre Street the crowd attacked the homes of African Americans, smashing windowpanes and wrecking furniture. From some residences the mob even "took the clothes of gentlemen, which the colored people had taken in to wash." Finally, the mob arrived at Anthony

Street and broke the windows of the African Baptist church and a few other buildings, including those of the porterhouse operated by African-American Robert Williams. In anticipation of the violence, Williams had closed his saloon that afternoon and moved his valuables, "as did several other black families whose dwellings were attacked." Only after venting their rage at virtually every manifestation of African-American life in the neighborhood did the rioters disperse.[7]

In terms of wanton destructiveness, the Five Points anti-abolition riot was the most devastating in New York history to that point. "In thirty years' acquaintance with the city," insisted the *Post*, "nothing has ever happened to compare with it." Surveying the damage in the riot's aftermath, the *Sun* remarked that it appeared "as if the angel of destruction had swept his bosom over the land." Many black Five Pointers were "seriously wounded," and the casualty list would have been longer had many more not fled the city altogether. The riot left the Five Points African-American community devastated, both physically and emotionally. "It is enough to sicken the heart of every one not destitute of humanity," commented the *Sun*, "to see weeping fathers and mothers sobbing over the ruins of all they possessed, the effects of years of toil, with their little children around them crying for bread."[8]

What had motivated this tremendous outpouring of hatred? On one level, the mob undoubtedly sought to emphasize its opposition to the abolition movement and its implied message that blacks were the equals of whites. Yet the breadth and intensity of the attack against black Five Pointers indicate that members of the crowd, either consciously or unconsciously, harbored some deeper resentments. Signs of African-American economic independence clearly galled them, for while the black-occupied hovels of a particularly decrepit alley known as "Cow Bay" were left untouched, the few black-owned businesses in the neighborhood were devastated. Finally, by literally tearing the roofs off black-occupied buildings, the mob sent perhaps its most emphatic and unmistakable message. The rioters sought not merely to injure black-owned or -occupied property, but to make their homes and businesses permanently uninhabitable.[9]

The Five Points anti-abolition riots were not isolated incidents of violence in an otherwise peaceful community. In 1834 and 1835 alone, two other significant riots would rock the neighborhood. The scope, ferocity, and deadliness of these three episodes of unrest were unprecedented, not merely for Five Points but for the entire city. They revealed racial, ethnic, and religious fault lines that New Yorkers had previously recognized but preferred to ignore. Over the next sixty-five years, Five Pointers would often find themselves at the epicenter of these struggles—ones that would help shape modern New York.

CHAPTER ONE

The Making of Five Points

⟨⟨⟨⟩⟩

IVE POINTS, the lower Manhattan neighborhood named for the five-cornered intersection of Anthony, Orange, and Cross Streets, was originally verdant and bucolic, like everything else in America. A five-acre lake known as "the Collect" was its defining landmark. Just northeast of the Collect, Bunker Hill rose more than a hundred feet, providing picnickers with breathtaking views of both the wildlife that gathered at the Collect's shores and the expanding city to the south. But as New York spread northward, the Collect area became a favorite site for the city's most noisome industries. Slaughterhouses, banned from inhabited areas, clustered just east of the lake on what is now Bayard Street. By the mid-1700s, it was the only place in the city where one could lawfully kill livestock. Here meatpackers could butcher their cattle at a safe distance from the populace, transferring the meat south to the markets and the hides to the many nearby tanneries that concentrated on the shores of the Collect. The curing carcasses and the chemicals used to process them created a stench every bit as pungent as that produced by the slaughterhouses. The drovers who patronized the slaughterhouses spent their layovers at the famous Bull's Head Tavern on the Bowery, which provided pens where cattlemen could keep their herds while they drank or spent the night.[10]

By the end of the eighteenth century, contamination from the tanneries, slaughterhouses, and other industries had transformed the Collect from a lovely landmark into a putrid nuisance. Architect Pierre L'Enfant proposed cleaning the lake and surrounding it with a park so that the city might grow around a central recreation area, but landowners refused to sell and the project collapsed. A proposal to make the Collect part of a canal from the Hudson to the East River was also abandoned. With no alternative in sight and the city expanding rapidly northward, New Yorkers began to consider something other than water for the site. The Common Council in 1802 ordered the Collect filled with "good and wholesome earth" from Bunker Hill, which was leveled at the same time. By 1813, the Collect had been completely covered over, literally laying the ground for what would become the world's most notorious neighborhood.[11]

Once the Collect had been filled, the area changed rapidly. Although some of the local industries such as the Coulthardt Brewery and the Crolius pottery works remained, most of the tanneries moved. Some of the tanners shrewdly retained their real estate holdings in the area. The Lorillard family, for example, became tobacco merchants while they built and rented housing on the property that had once held their tannery. The Schermerhorns, whose rope works had once lined the east side of the Collect, retained property in the neighborhood, too, as did the Livingstons. German immigrant Heinrich Ashdor, who had purchased land around the slaughterhouses in 1785, maintained a significant interest in real estate there as well. His profits from the sale of sixteen lots on and behind the Bowery in 1825 helped establish the fortune of the family, by this point rechristened as the Astors.[12]

Prominent citizens made real estate investments in the Collect neighborhood, as it was still known for nearly two decades after the lake had disappeared, because a healthy return on their investments seemed assured. With the city's population expanding rapidly after the War of 1812, and the portion of Manhattan south of City Hall already densely populated, newcomers to New York were desperate to find new residential and commercial locations farther to the north in neighborhoods like Five Points. In one of their many efforts to meet these demands, municipal authorities in 1817 authorized the extension of Anthony Street east to the intersection of Orange and Cross.[13]

Landowners generally filled their lots with two-and-a-half-story wooden buildings, the half story an attic with low ceilings and dormer windows suitable for small workshops. Of the neighborhood residents who filled these houses, about half worked as artisans, with shoemakers, tailors, bakers, carpenters, and masons especially numerous. Merchants, shopkeepers, and professionals also scattered throughout the area. Businessmen housed their own families and often their clerks or journeymen

Photo of the Five Points intersection taken some time after 1867 from the south side of Worth Street (previously Anthony) looking toward the northeast. These two-and-a-half-story buildings dominated the neighborhood in the 1820s and 1830s. Collection of the New-York Historical Society.

and apprentices in the very same buildings where their businesses operated.

Although the mix of occupations in the Collect neighborhood did not differ dramatically from that of the rest of the city at this point, some distinctions quickly emerged. By 1825, immigrants accounted for at least 25 percent of the area's population, more than double their representation in the city as a whole. African Americans also concentrated in the district, comprising about 15 percent of its inhabitants, again double the city average. These immigrants and blacks were much more likely to be unskilled menial laborers than were other citizens. Perhaps as a result, the per capita income of the ward was the lowest in the city, about 40 percent below the average.[14]

Yet the Collect district in the 1820s was far from the "ulcer of wretchedness" that it would soon become. A number of factors, many complex and interrelated, contributed to the deterioration of the neighborhood that would soon become known as Five Points.* One was the declining economic status of the city's artisans. As the "market revolution" slowly transformed the nation, many of the goods once handcrafted on a small scale by local artisans were now mass-produced in parts of the city or country where it was most economical or efficient to do so. Shoemaking, for example, became concentrated in Massachusetts, where footwear could be shipped on the nation's increasingly thorough network of roads, canals, rivers, and coastal waterways. Shoe manufacturers took more and more business from independent, small-scale shoemakers, frequently hiring workers without a master shoemaker's thorough training. Although artisans whose skills could not be "bastardized" in this way (such as shipbuilders or masons) escaped much of the impact of these changes, most suffered a decline in income.[15]

In the old days, artisans had speculated in real estate by obtaining long-term leases on their houses, which served as both workplace and home, for themselves and their employees. If they decided to relocate their businesses before the lease expired, they might sublet or sell the rights to the lease. By the 1830s, however, most did not feel economically self-confident enough to continue such speculation. Instead, they leased houses for a few years at most. They were also less likely to rent enough living space for their employees, for in an economic slowdown they might need to lay off their workers and did not want to be stuck paying rent for unoccupied rooms. Because of these changes and the general decline of the home workshop, neighborhoods organized by trade began to disappear, and New York

---

* Defining the borders of a neighborhood is not easy. In 1873, *Frank Leslie's Illustrated Newspaper* asserted that "Five Points is bounded by Canal Street, the Bowery, Chatham, Pearl and Centre Streets, forming a truncated triangle about one mile square." Others conceived of the district as slightly larger or smaller. I came to my own conclusions about how Five Pointers would have demarcated their territory both by reading their own accounts of the enclave and by walking the neighborhood's streets to determine how the layout of the thoroughfares and buildings would have shaped their perception of their turf. In the end, my own sense of Five Points' boundaries matched that of *Frank Leslie's,* and those boundaries are the ones I have used throughout this book. See *Frank Leslie's Illustrated Newspaper* (August 16, 1873): 363.

began for the first time to divide into commercial and residential districts. Five Points became one such residential neighborhood.[16]

As these changes took place in the 1820s and 1830s, immigration and migration swelled the city's population, and as a result housing prices rose dramatically. Landlords discovered that it was significantly more profitable to subdivide their two-and-a-half-story houses into small apartments and rent each to a single family. Some tore down the small houses on their lots and put up taller brick buildings that could accommodate many more tenants. Most simply converted existing buildings. The owners of old decrepit buildings paid less in taxes than owners of sparkling new structures, providing landlords with additional incentive to subdivide old buildings into many small apartments and spend little or nothing to maintain them. Because so many unrelated tenants lived in these structures, they became known as "tenant houses," and by the 1840s as "tenement houses." Thus was born one of America's signature immigrant environments. Most Five Points landlords happily converted their small buildings into tenements and rented apartments in them to increasingly less well-to-do workers and their families, while employers and other prosperous citizens moved to neighborhoods populated by their peers.[17]

The proliferation of residential neighborhoods provided advantages for tenants as well as landlords. Under the old system, employers had closely monitored their workers' after-hours behavior. If the worker lived with his boss, the employer would know if the employee came home late, or drunk, or with a woman of ill-repute. Even if a worker merely lived in the same neighborhood as his boss, his after-work behavior was likely to be observed by his employer. This became an especially sensitive issue in the twenties and thirties, as evangelical ministers began to prod their employer parishioners to hold their workers to the same high moral standards to which they themselves aspired. New Yorkers who resented others dictating how they should spend their leisure time took offense at this meddling, and their animosity contributed to violence directed against Baptist and Methodist churches in New York. The Baptist church on lower Mulberry Street in the heart of the Five Points neighborhood was the target of attacks on a number of occasions in the 1820s.[18]

The new residential districts were more homogeneous than earlier New York neighborhoods. Five Points' prosperous merchants moved west to homes near Broadway. Successful artisans relocated to the Fourteenth Ward north of present-day Canal Street, where the quality of housing was superior. Some wealthier residents remained, but these were primarily grocers and saloonkeepers, who even though they could afford to live elsewhere found it more convenient to live where they worked or in buildings that they owned. Because the journeymen and laborers who came to dominate Five Points tended to have fluctuating incomes, the quality of the homes that they could afford varied from year to year, so they moved especially frequently, creating an impression of instability that made the neighborhood unattractive to better-off New Yorkers.

The very ground under Five Points was also a problem. Although civil engineers had succeeded in erasing all obvious traces of the Collect, the ground remained damp and unsettled, causing houses to shift and tilt dramatically just a few years after construction. The slightest rain or snowfall created basement floods throughout the neighborhood, especially in its western portion along Anthony and Orange Streets where the lake had once stood. Because so many diseases of the period were attributed to dampness and "vapours," few New Yorkers wanted to live in such a locale.[19]

The increasing association of the area with immigrants and blacks also played a role in its decline. Discrimination forced African Americans into certain occupations—especially those of chimney sweep, barber, and sailor—whose status and pay kept them in constant poverty. Many whites shunned such "degraded" workers. Immigrants sometimes faced similar bigotry. By 1830, an increasing proportion of newcomers settling in New York were Irish and Catholic. They usually arrived with less savings than other immigrants and sought the cheapest housing available, much of which was in Five Points. As Catholic immigrants became more numerous, native-born Protestants increasingly moved away.

Finally, it was Five Points' development into a center of prostitution that sealed its disreputable fate. Until 1820, the waterfront district around Water Street had housed the city's largest concentration of prostitutes and brothels. But by 1830, Five Points had become the center of New York's commercial sex industry, with more bordellos located on Anthony Street between Centre and Orange than on any other block in the city. It is difficult to determine why Five Points became the city's most popular red-light district. Perhaps it was the large population of rootless immigrant men. Prostitutes may have also selected the district because its central location, just a few blocks from Broadway and City Hall, made it convenient for customers from all over the city.[20]

There were other parts of New York that were just as impoverished. Both Corlear's Hook and the waterfront area around Water Street struggled with crime and poverty. Yet because Five Points was so central (no more than a twenty-five-minute walk from any significantly populated portion of New York), residents continued to cram into its houses well after the tenements had reached a point that most would have considered full. Crowding grew worse and worse, apartments got smaller and smaller, until finally Five Points became something new in America: a slum in the very center of a city.

"I WOULD RATHER RISQUE MYSELF IN AN INDIAN FIGHT THAN VENTURE AMONG THESE CREATURES"

Five Points' speedy decline can be traced in the newspapers of the 1820s and 1830s. Business publications such as the *Journal of Commerce*, party organs such as the conservative *Courier and Enquirer* (the voice of the Whigs), the more moderate *Evening Post* (Democratic), and even tabloids such as the *Sun* all began to mention Five Points with increasing frequency. The first known press comment about the alarming conditions in Five Points dates from 1826. In that year, a letter to the editor of the *New York Evening Post* demanded that the city address the neighborhood's increasingly shameful conditions. "CORNELIUS," as he signed himself, claimed inaccurately that "the Collect" acquired its name because of "the vast collection of houses of ill fame, tippling shops, drunken persons and other kinds of filth in which it abounds." His account nonetheless indicates a close familiarity with the area: "The houses generally are of wood from one to two and a half stories high and of no very attractive appearance; every fourth or fifth one, upon an average," sells liquor and "sundry" other goods

without particularly enquiring how they were obtained, a fact which our police records will fully substantiate. In and about these rum holes [live] both sexes, and almost every variety of age and colour, drinking, swearing and fighting. . . . I saw no less than four fights in as many minutes, conducted in the Kentucky style of rough and tumble, accompanied with a grand chorus of shouts and the most profane language. The different combatants, black and white, men and women, displayed admirable proficiency in the art of boxing and afforded amusement to the crowd, who formed rings for the purpose of betting on the victor. In short, the wretched appearance of the place, the immorality of the inhabitants, &c. would hardly be believed if not witnessed. Something ought to be done for the honour of the city, if for no other reason than to render the place less disgusting and pernicious, it being the resort of thieves and rogues of the lowest degree, and by its filthy state and "villanous smells" keeps respectable people from residing near it.[21]

In 1829, the press for the first time referred to the neighborhood as "Five Points." An editorial in the *Evening Post* directed police "to put an end to the crimes and outrages almost daily committed in this neighborhood, which has become the most dangerous place in our city." Even prominent citizens were not safe there, noted the *Post*, which reported that Assistant Alderman George D. Strong had been slashed in the nose with a knife.[22]

The same *Post* editorial also demanded that a small group of Five Points tenements be razed—one of the first recorded efforts at slum clearance in American history. In January 1829, a group of New Yorkers petitioned the Common Council to tear down a tiny triangular block of tenements created when city officials had demolished the surrounding buildings in order to extend Anthony Street eastward to the Five Points intersection. Most of the houses remaining in the 7,500-square-foot triangle had been sheared in half, lending them a tumbledown quality that frightened away most potential tenants. As a result, stated a committee of councilmen, the triangle's buildings were "occupied by the lowest description and most degraded and abandoned of the human Species."[23]

A year later, a letter writer to the *Post* complained about the lack of progress. New buildings were under construction all over town, but "in that place only which stands in most need of improvement—I mean the Five Points—nothing is done." The *Post's* correspondent condemned the whole area as a "nuisance" and asked for "the removal of Five Points," though by this comment he may have meant merely the triangular plot of buildings rather than the entire neighborhood. A subsequent petition to the Common Council suggested that the city build a new jail on the triangular site and widen some of the streets leading to the intersection by tearing down portions of other existing buildings. Supporters justified the plan on the grounds that the conditions in Five Points adversely affected businesses in other parts of the city. Citizens who might venture from the East Side to shop on Broadway were disinclined to do so because they feared having to pass through Five Points, while businesses on Pearl Street to the south and east of Five Points suffered similarly.[24]

But the Common Council balked at tearing down the triangle of tenements. It would be dangerous to locate a prison near the former site of the Collect, noted some of the lawmakers, because disease would spread uncontrollably in a prison built on such low, damp ground. The potential expense of the plan also worried them. Those proposing demolition had assumed that acquiring the property would cost the city little, because the wretched tenements on the triangle of land were almost worthless. Yet the land below the rotting buildings was actually quite valuable, the council discovered, because it produced "a great rent on account of its being a good location for small retailers of Liquor. . . . What may be considered as the Nuisance has in reality increased the Value of the property." Consequently, the Common Council refused to endorse any changes in Five Points. Continued pressure from the press and business owners in surrounding neighborhoods, however, resulted in the enactment of compromise legislation in January 1802. The city would acquire the triangle of tenements and tear them down, but rather than constructing the prison there would instead build a tiny park. It became known as Paradise Park. The legislation also provided for the widening of some of the streets (Cross, Little Water, and Anthony) leading to Five Points, in the hope that wider thoroughfares would seem less dark and forbidding. "The decent inhabitants in the vicinity of the Five Points," applauded the *Mirror*, "ought to give 'nine cheers' at the breaking up of that loathsome den of murderers, thieves, abandoned women, ruined children, filth, misery, drunkenness, and broils."[25]

The decision not to build a prison in Five Points because of the fear of contagious disease proved a wise one, for just a few months later, the cholera outbreak of 1832 ravaged the neighborhood. Cholera is a bacterial infection that spreads primarily through water contaminated by human feces. Symptoms include high fever and a ricelike diarrhea in which the "rice" is actually pieces of a victim's colon flaking away. Thousands of New Yorkers died during the 1832 epidemic, and the disease spread especially rapidly in tenement districts such as Five Points where outhouses and wells were located too close together. The tendency of cholera to run rampant in impoverished tenement districts led to the belief that it was the dissolute habits of the poor, rather than an inadequate sanitation system, which made one susceptible to the contagion. "The disease is now, more than before, rioting in the haunts of infamy and pollution," reported the *Mercury*. In Five Points, "a prostitute at 62 Mott Street, who was decking herself before the glass at 1 o'clock yesterday, was carried away in a hearse at half past three o'clock. The broken down constitutions of these miserable creatures, perish almost instantly on the attack." What worried more fortunate New Yorkers most about cholera in Five Points was the neighborhood's proximity to their own homes. In the past, the poor had lived on the periphery of town or were too widely dispersed to create a concentration of contagion. Yet with Five Points' "race of beings of all colours, ages, sexes and nations . . . inhabiting the most populous and central part of the city," complained a *Post* correspondent, "when may we be considered secure from pestilence? Be the air pure from Heaven, their breath would contaminate it, and infect it with disease."[26]

By 1834, the press began to publish lengthy exposés about the neighborhood. The first appeared in the *Sun* that spring. The reporter found that apartments in the worst parts of Five Points did not have "a table, chair or any other article of furniture, save a cooking utensil, a few plates, and knives, and bottles, with which to carry on the business of living. Few beds were found in any of these apartments, the inmates sleeping or lying on heaps of filthy rags, straw and shavings, the stench from which was almost insupportable." He described "white women, and black and yellow men, and black and yellow women, with white men, all in a state of gross intoxication, and exhibiting indecencies revolting to virtue and humanity. . . . The drunkards of both sexes, intermingled with scarcely any thing to hide their nakedness," lay "in a state of misery almost indescribable."[27]

Although the conditions inside Five Points apartments were bad, the *Sun*'s reporter was also horrified at how Five Pointers made public spectacles of themselves: "In the afternoon of each day, when drunkenness is at its height, the most disgusting objects, of both sexes, are exhibited to the eyes of the examiner. Indecency, squalid poverty, intemperance and crime, riot and revel in continued orgies, and sober humanity is shocked and horrified, at the loathsome spectacles incessantly presented." Evenings were no better: "At night the streets and sidewalks are literally blocked by swarms of sturdy vagabonds of both sexes; the grog shops are filled . . . horrid oaths and execrations burst upon the ear from every tipling house, and brothel, and the most abominable indecencies of every kind, by word and deed, are perpetrated and heard."[28]

According to the *Sun*, the drinking and carousing that took place inside was worse than that on the streets. Here neighborhood criminals hatched their larcenous plans, divvied up the loot after each heist, celebrated by drinking, dancing, and gambling, and procured prostitutes. The favorite haunts of the "rogues and vagabonds of the Five Points are the Diving Bell, Swimming Bath, and the Arcade, at Nos. 39, 40, and 33, in Orange street." The reporter also mentioned "the Archway" on Orange at the corner of Leonard (either 46 or 48 Orange) and "the Yankee Kitchen" on Cross Street just above Orange. The entire two-block length of Little Water Street was a gathering place for criminals. Both the portion north of Anthony, known according to the *Sun* as "Cow bay," and the block south of Anthony, which the reporter labeled "Squeeze Gut Alley," were described as "principally the resort and residence of white, black, and mulatto prostitutes, and the bullies and blackguards who keep and visit them, and are seats of vice, hotbeds of debauchery, wretchedness, and poverty, such as few eyes have witnessed."[19]

The reporter concluded that "if ever wretchedness was exhibited in a more perfect garb, if ever destitution and degradation were more complete, if ever immorality and licentiousness were presented in more disgusting forms, we confess we have never yet beheld them." He assured his readers that he had seen on the "frontiers . . . squatters . . . without any visible means of support," as well as "untutored Indians" in "the howling wilderness . . . and examined minutely the situation of the slaves, held to labor, in their most deplorable conditions; after seeing all these, we hesitate not

Five Points, by George Catlin, probably from 1827. Collection of Mrs. Screven Lorillard, Far Hills, New Jersey.

to say, that the colored, and some of the white tenants of the Five Points, are infinitely more degraded and debased, than these others we have named; and the border settler in his hut, the Indian in his wigwam, and the Southern slave in his cabin, is each a monarch in comfort, respectability, happiness and virtue, when compared to the wretched vagabonds, who inherit, as it were, poverty, vice and crime, in and near the Five Points. They endure literally, a hell of horrors, arising from their poverty and wickedness, such as few others on earth can suffer."[30]

One of the most fascinating documents available for the analysis of Five Points' early history is a painting of the intersection by George Catlin from about 1827. All the elements of Five Points' reputation are in evidence. Fights are breaking out everywhere; people are drunk; pigs roam the streets; whites and blacks are mixing; and prostitutes brazenly solicit customers (see the second-story window on the upper right). Even the abun-

dance of groceries portrayed would have been significant to 1820s New
Yorkers, as antebellum groceries were often little more than liquor stores,
generating most of their profits selling beer, ale, rum, and gin. That an
accomplished artist such as Catlin would bother to paint an impoverished
working-class neighborhood indicates that—by that early date—Five
Points was truly renowned.[31]

By the 1830s, Five Points' infamy was so well known that out-of-town
visitors went there to see its depravities. The first of these tourists to
record his impressions for posterity was frontiersman Davy Crockett. In
1834, Crockett toured the Northeast and soon after published *An Account
of Col. Crockett's Tour to the North and Down East.* Written in a style that
attempted to convey that Crockett's co-author was as much a backwoods-
man as the famous colonel (the ghostwriter was actually Pennsylvania
congressman William Clark), *An Account of Col. Crockett's Tour* listed
the visit to "Five-points" as one of the highlights of the frontiersman's
tour. "The buildings," noted Crockett and Clark, "are little, old, frame
houses, and looked like some little country village. . . . It appeared as if
the cellars was jam full of people; and such fiddling and dancing nobody
ever saw before in this world." The mixing of the races in these dance halls
was especially noteworthy: "Black and white, white and black, all hug-
emsnug together, happy as lords and ladies, sitting sometimes round in a
ring, with a jug of liquor between them: and I do think I saw more drunk
folks, men and women, that day, than I ever saw before. This is part of
what is called by the Regency the 'glorious sixth ward'—the regular Van
Buren ground-floor. I thought I would rather risque myself in an Indian
fight than venture among these creatures after night. I said to the colonel,
'. . . these are worse than savages; they are too mean to swab hell's
kitchen.'" The infamy of Five Points was now being conveyed to a
national audience.[32]

With their reference to Vice President Martin Van Buren, though,
Crockett and Clark added a new element to the discourse surrounding Five
Points. Five Points was part of the city political district known as the Sixth
Ward, and "Regency" was the term used by enemies to describe the Democratic party's statewide organization, then headed by Van Buren. "The regular Van Buren ground-floor" referred to the large Democratic majority the
district routinely polled—larger than that in any other ward. Crockett had

recently broken with the Democrats and thrown his support instead to their Whig opponents. Crockett and Clark were using the Democrats' popularity in Five Points to cast aspersions on the entire party.

"KEEP THOSE DAMNED IRISHMEN IN ORDER!"

The reference to Van Buren may have been inspired by a Five Points election riot in 1834. There were actually three riots there in 1834 and 1835—the first an election battle; the second the Lewis Tappan–inspired race riot; and the third an ethnic and religious fight between natives and Irish Catholics. The initial riot began on Tuesday, April 8, 1834, the first of three days set aside for voting in New York's municipal election. That year, for the first time, the various groups that opposed the policies of President Andrew Jackson and his Democratic party had unified in a single organization, just then becoming known as the Whig party. The Whigs were determined to unseat the Democrats, who had controlled New York's municipal government in recent years. Whigs believed that by emphasizing Jackson policies they considered unconstitutional (such as his removal of federal deposits from the Bank of the United States without the consent of Congress) and by vigilantly guarding the polls to prevent Democratic intimidation of voters in places such as the Sixth Ward, they could carry the election.

Each side blamed the other for the fighting. Whigs insisted that it started when a mob of a hundred or so Democrats, led by ex-Alderman George D. Strong (he of the slashed nose), invaded the Whigs' Sixth Ward committee rooms, tore down banners, destroyed Whig ballots, and assaulted those Whigs present. Democrats, on the other hand, asserted that peace had prevailed in the district until Whigs from the First and Second Wards arrived at the Sixth Ward polls. They had come ostensibly to prevent Democratic intimidation, but instead threatened peaceable Democrats with weapons, insulted them by repeating slurs from the Whig press, and vowed loudly to *"keep those damned Irishmen in order!"* Such confrontations led to polling place fights at which a number of participants were seriously injured.[33]

To highlight their claim that Jackson ignored the Constitution, the Whigs had constructed a huge model of the warship *Constitution* which, with the aid of four horses, they pulled through the streets. When the *Constitution* rolled into the Sixth Ward on the second morning of balloting, more fisticuffs ensued, though this time a heavy police presence prevented severe injuries. Voting proceeded relatively quietly until noon on the third and final day of the canvass, when violence erupted outside the Whig headquarters at Masonic Hall on Broadway, at the western edge of the ward. Democrats claimed that the trouble started when one of the "sailors" from the *Constitution* (then parked outside Masonic Hall) beat an Irishman, whose friends headed toward Five Points looking for reinforcements. Whigs claimed that no such beating took place and that they were simply, in the words of former mayor Philip Hone, attending to the "miniature frigate . . . when suddenly the alarm was given, and a band of Irishmen of the lowest class came out of Duane Street from the Sixth Ward poll, armed with clubs, and commenced a savage attack upon all about the ship and the hall. There was much severe fighting and many persons were wounded and knocked down. The Irishmen then retired and the frigate was drawn away, but in a few minutes the mob returned with a strong reënforcement, and the fight was renewed with the most unrelenting barbarity. The mayor arrived with a strong body of watchmen, but they were attacked and overcome." Each side had hundreds engaged in the rioting by this point.[34]

Determined not to be bested, the Whigs retreated into the Sixth Ward to the nearby city arsenal at the corner of Elm and Franklin Streets, where they broke in and began to arm themselves with muskets. The mayor, who a few minutes earlier had pleaded with the Democrats to desist, now implored the Whigs to leave the weapons alone before the riot turned murderous. "He begged them to consider the awful consequences of this movement" to introduce firearms, reported the *Sun*. "Civil war" was inevitable if they did not reconsider. "'Stop, for the love of heaven, stop,' said the Mayor, as the tear stood in his eye—'You are rash—you know not what you do.'" After this impassioned plea, the Whigs came out of the arsenal without the weapons and order was restored. Thus ended the ordeal.[35]

The rioting that day was unprecedented in the history of New York City—at least prior to July's race riot. "The extent and violence of the disturbance went well beyond any riot of the eighteenth century and far exceeded any previous political tumult in New York," writes historian

Paul Gilje. "Never before had an election pushed the city so near the brink. Never before had there been such anarchy." Both Democrats (such as the *Post*'s editors) and Whigs (such as Hone) blamed the heightened tension on ethnic animosity. Hone characterized it not as a fight between Democrats and Whigs, but "between the Irish and the Americans." The riot further hurt Five Points' reputation, convincing New Yorkers that the neighborhood's Irish threatened not only the health and morals of the city, but its peace as well.[36]

Just three months later, in July, the anti-abolition riot erupted. And eleven months after that, a third riot disgraced the neighborhood. Like the first, this one pitted Irish immigrants against native-born citizens. Since the election riot, tensions between natives and immigrants had increased alarmingly in many parts of the United States. In August 1834, a mob burned a Catholic convent near Boston. A few months later, Samuel F. B. Morse published a series of virulently anti-Catholic newspaper articles in New York charging the Catholic Church with a conspiracy to flood the United States with Catholic immigrants in order to assist in the overthrow of democratic government. The growing animosity between natives and Irish-Catholic immigrants manifested itself in New York as well, with street fights breaking out in September and October 1834 and January and March 1835.[37]

Hostility between the Irish and natives truly exploded in early June 1835, however, when word spread throughout the city that the Irish in Five Points were about to form an exclusively Irish militia company. Without a standing army of any significance, antebellum Americans relied upon volunteer militia units to defend the nation and at times quell domestic disturbances. Two decades had passed since the United States's last war, and because none seemed imminent, these militia companies had become primarily social organizations, with picnics and drinking occasionally interrupted for a bit of target practice or drilling. Because Irish immigrants tended to socialize with each other and probably felt unwelcome in units comprised either primarily or exclusively of natives, it was inevitable that they would form militia units of their own. Yet the nativist press vehemently objected. "No greater insult was ever offered the American people than the arrangements now being made to raise in this city an *Irish* regiment to be called the '*O'Connell Guards*,'" insisted the *Courier and*

Enquirer. "Such a corps would soon attempt to enforce with the bayonet what too many of the misguided and ignorant of the foreign voters already boast of—the complete subjection of the *Native* Citizens to their dictation." Similar diatribes in the *Courier and Enquirer* had helped foment both 1834 riots, so New Yorkers braced themselves for another outbreak of violence.[38]

Natives claimed that the trouble started on Sunday evening, June 21, 1835, when an Irishman upset the cart of a native-born apple vendor. The Irish insisted that it originated when natives insulted a drunk Irishman, perhaps concerning the propriety of drinking on the Sabbath. Others said the cause was a brawl between the O'Connell Guard and its neighborhood rival, the natives-only American Guard.[39] Whatever the cause, every observer agreed that a "most disgraceful riot" erupted between "natives and Irish" along Pearl and Cross Streets between 6:00 and 7:00 p.m. According to the *Sun*, "Ireland and America were the battle cry of the contending parties, and both sides found plenty of zealous friends. Bloody noses, bunged eyes, cracked craniums, and barked knuckles soon became the distinguishing marks of scores of combatants." At its height, several thousand were engaged in the melee, and dozens were injured.[40] Fighting also spread north of Five Points. On Grand Street, Irish rioters hit Dr. William McCaffery with a brick, "which broke his jaw bone." The doctor, after "being thrown down, was jumped on, and several of his ribs broken." McCaffery died a day later. The *Courier and Enquirer* claimed that the rioters had singled out McCaffery for such a malicious attack because he was an Irish Whig, and the paper set up a fund to assist his widow and children. This was the first fatality of the bloody year in Five Points.[41]

Rioting resumed Monday night, June 22, as both natives and immigrants gathered on Chatham Street near Orange and Pearl looking for trouble, though "the party claiming to be American" far outnumbered its adversary. Fighting spread across the neighborhood and from there both southward toward City Hall and northward above Walker Street, where the natives stoned the house of a "Mr. O'Brien" and "menaced" St. Patrick's Cathedral (on Mott Street north of Walker) as well. They also attacked the Green Dragons tavern on the Bowery and some twenty houses on Orange Street. The next evening, a large crowd that "seemed to cherish burning resentments against the adopted citizens" collected on Chatham Street near Orange. Meanwhile, closer to the Five Points intersection, "fire arms and clubs were seen" in the hands of immigrants, who vowed to use them against natives if attacked. Many Catholics assembled at the Cathedral to protect it from an expected onslaught, but none materialized. Although there were again many "broken heads" and bruises, the mayor, aldermen, and police finally managed to disperse the rioters and bring the violence to an end.[42]

In many ways, this riot was the least dreadful of the three. The neighborhood never seemed as close to anarchy in June 1835 as it had fourteen months earlier when the Whigs stormed the arsenal. There was no serious damage to property this time, in stark contrast to the rampant destruction during the anti-abolition violence of the previous summer. Yet the deaths of Dr. McCaffery and an English-born piano maker made the final melee the only one to result in fatalities, something virtually unprecedented in previous American rioting. The final unrest also helped lead to the creation of the city's first nativist political party.[43]

A subsequent incident, one that did not receive the attention of the riots, reflected the lingering ethnic and religious tensions in Five Points. In March 1836, the *Herald* reported that "the Bowery gang" was up to its old mischief again, invading the oyster bar at the North American Hotel at the corner of Bowery and Bayard and causing a commotion. Later that day, gang members threw snowballs and ice at the predominantly Irish-American city workers clearing snow from the streets. When the workers protested, the Bowery gang beat them unmercifully with the laborers' own shovels and pickaxes, injuring one badly. The reaction of the crowd when Alderman Ferris and some constables arrived at the scene revealed the ethnic tensions at the source of the attack. The offenders had long since disappeared, but the crowd defended the assailants and excoriated Ferris and the city workers, shouting "D__m the Irishmen, they ought not to have work—the Corporation always gives them work and not *us* Americans." Some of this animosity, of course, had a religious underpinning. Writing at about this time, New Yorker Asa Green reported that the city was brimming with anti-Catholicism and that he commonly heard it said that "the Pope of Rome is coming hither, with hasty strides, to take the land."[44]

From this point on, Five Points would be renowned as the most violent part of the "Bloody Sixth" Ward, where collective violence was the standard response to almost any grievance. The reputation was mostly unwarranted, at least at this point. Outsiders had instigated most of the violence in the anti-abolition riot, and much of the blame for the 1835 anti-Irish riot rested outside the community as well. Nonetheless, observers concluded that any neighborhood in which three major riots could take place in just fifteen months must be particularly brutal. Additional election riots, particularly one in 1842, would reinforce this impression.[45]

"LET US . . . PLUNGE INTO THE FIVE POINTS"

By the late 1830s, all the major elements of Five Points' reputation were well established in the minds of New Yorkers and many Americans. It was an Englishman, however, who brought that reputation to the world. Charles Dickens was not yet thirty years old when he embarked on a five-month tour of North America in 1841. He had become a celebrity a few years earlier for his *Pickwick Papers,* and the subsequent publication of *Oliver Twist* established his reputation as a severe critic of England's treatment of the poor. Consequently, one might have expected Dickens to portray Five Pointers with sympathy and compassion. But the young writer harbored a burning resentment of the United States, where inadequate copyright laws brought him little compensation for sales of his work. Dickens's account of his visit, the *American Notes,* brutally condemns nearly every aspect of American life.

His description of Five Points revealed its appalling conditions, already well known to New Yorkers, to readers all over the world:

> Let us go on again . . . and . . . plunge into the Five Points. . . . We have seen no beggars in the streets by night or day; but of other kinds of strollers plenty. Poverty, wretchedness, and vice are rife enough where we are going now.
>
> This is the place, these narrow ways, diverging to the right and left, and reeking everywhere with dirt and filth. . . . Debauchery has made the very houses prematurely old. See how the rotten beams are tumbling down, and how the patched and broken windows seem to scowl dimly, like eyes that have been hurt in drunken frays. Many of those pigs [previously described wandering the streets foraging for food] live here. Do they ever wonder why their masters walk upright in lieu of going on all-fours? and

why they talk instead of grunting? . . . . Here, too, are lanes and alleys, paved with mud knee deep; underground chambers, where they dance and game . . . hideous tenements which take their name from robbery and murder; all that is loathsome, drooping, and decayed is here.

Dickens described in detail his visits to some of the neighborhood's wretched tenement apartments. In one, what initially appeared to be piles of rags was in fact several African Americans sleeping in their clothes on rag-pile beds on the floors of their apartments. Although he had thought that no slum in America could match those of London, Dickens concluded that Five Points contained every bit as much misery as the "Seven Dials, or any other part of famed St. Giles."[46]

DECEMBER 5, 1885.] FRANK LESLIE'S ILLUSTRATED NEWSPAPER. 245

NEW YORK CITY. — "DOING THE SLUMS" — A SCENE IN THE FIVE POINTS.
FROM A SKETCH BY A STAFF ARTIST.—SEE PAGE 247.

Although this image dates from the 1880s, slumming parties had begun to visit Five Points as early as the 1830s. *Frank Leslie's Illustrated Newspaper*, December 5, 1885. Collection of the Library of Congress.

Dickens's visit to Five Points made it fashionable for well-to-do New Yorkers to go "slumming," visiting Five Points as Dickens had done, with a police escort, to marvel at its poverty and gawk at its displays of vice. Indeed, the term "slumming" may have been coined there to describe such tours. "I had never before any adequate idea of poverty in cities," admitted the writer and literary critic Nathaniel P. Willis after visiting Five Points in the mid-1840s. "I did not dream that human beings, within reach of human aid, could be abandoned to the wretchedness which I there saw." The writer, abolitionist, and reformer Lydia Maria Child toured Five Points in about 1844. "Morally and physically, the breathing air was like an open tomb," she wrote in *Letters from New York*:

> How souls or bodies could live there, I could not imagine. If you want to see something worse than Hogarth's Gin Lane, go there in a warm afternoon, when the poor wretches have come to what they call home, and are not yet driven within doors, by darkness and constables. There you will see nearly every form of human misery, every sign of human degradation. The leer of the licentious, the dull sensualism of the drunkard, the sly glance of the thief—oh, it made my heart ache for many a day. . . . What a place to ask one's self, "Will the millennium ever come!"

Such expeditions soon became a standard part of visiting tourists' itineraries. A Scandinavian writer, Fredrika Bremer, inspected the infamous district carefully, recognizing that conditions varied immensely within Five Points, sometimes even within a single tenement. Nonetheless, she concluded that "lower than to the Five Points it is not possible for human nature to sink."[47]

By the late 1840s, such descriptions had convinced Americans that Five Points was the nation's worst neighborhood. *New York Tribune* contributor George G. Foster wrote in 1849 that Five Points was to New York "the great central ulcer of wretchedness—the very rotting Skeleton of Civilization, whence emanates an inexhaustible pestilence that spreads its poisonous influence through every vein and artery of the whole social system, and supplies every heart-throb of metropolitan life with a pulse of despair." Others asserted that no slum in the world could rival its filth and misery. "We know of no place on the earth where there are more wretched beings congregated together than at the Five Points," contended the *New York Evening Post* in 1846. Minister Lyman Abbott concurred, writing in 1857 that Five Points "contains more squalid poverty and abominable wickedness than any area of equal size in the world."

Five Points had become so notorious that its very name became an adjective, a term used to describe something scandalously raunchy. The *Herald* jibed in 1842 that "if you desire to revel in the midst of Five Points literature, read the *Courier and Enquirer*, and the *New York American*," which daily "contain columns of the lowest, most vulgar, most black-guard, most ferocious libels against the President." The Methodist mis-sionaries who attempted to reform the area likewise found that Five Points had become "the synonym for ignorance the most entire, for misery the most abject, for crime of the darkest dye, for degradation so deep that human nature cannot sink below it."[48]

Five Points became so infamous that reference to it even became a staple of the southern defense of slavery. Northern abolitionists were hyp-ocrites to complain about slavery, insisted slaveholders, when they tacitly condoned such abject suffering in their own midst. A Kentucky doctor who had treated Five Points cholera victims in 1832 argued that its residents "are far more filthy, degraded, and wretched than any slave I have ever beheld, under the most cruel and tyrannical master. . . . They are in the lowest depths of human degradation and misery." Two decades later, a South Carolinian who visited Five Points contended that it contained more vice, poverty, and wretchedness than the entire South. Only "when the Abolitionists have cleared their own skirts," could they "hold up their hands in holy horror at the slave-holder, and the enormity of his sins." Even southerners who had not seen the slum firsthand began to cite it as proof of the superiority of their way of life. *The Southern Quarterly Review* asked "whether there is any negro quarter, from Mason and Dixon's line to the Rio del Norte, which could furnish a picture of vice, brutality, and degradation comparable to that drawn from the heart of London" or "the Five Points of New York?" Southerners also cited Five Points as proof that the anti-slavery Republican party was in favor of the "social equality of the negro." A slave state congressman described to the House of Representatives "a ball held at Five Points in the city of New

York, where white women and negroes mingled 'in sweet confusion in the mazy dance.'" Southerners felt certain that the life of a free person in Five Points, whether black or white, was infinitely worse than that of any slave.[49]

Opponents of slavery and its expansion also alluded to Five Points to justify *their* political organization, the Republican party. In reply to the previously quoted speech to the House of Representatives, Michigan congressman Francis W. Kellogg asserted that while his colleague's depiction of Five Points might be accurate, the ward in which the neighborhood was located "is the strongest Democratic ward in the city, and I doubt if a Republican vote was ever polled there." Those who endorsed or participated in the depravity described by Kellogg's colleague were in fact Democrats, and could in no way be linked to the Republican party or the anti-slavery cause. North Carolina Republican Hinton Helper elaborated upon this theme in his famous *Impending Crisis of the South.* Helper noted that at the "Five Points Precinct" in the 1856 presidential election, Democrat James Buchanan received 574 votes to only 16 for Republican John Frémont and 9 for Know Nothing Millard Fillmore. He then pointed out that Five Points, "with the exception of the slave-pens in Southern cities, is, perhaps, the most vile and heart-sickening locality in the United States. . . . The votes polled at the Five Points precinct, which is almost exclusively inhabited by low Irish Catholics," proved that the Democratic party appealed most to degraded slum dwellers and those too ignorant to resist the "Jesuitical" influence of the Catholic Church. Northerner and southerner, slaveholder and abolitionist, could all use Five Points to justify their political views.[50]

The reputation of Five Points, the "Five Points of the mind," one might say, was firmly and irreversibly established. But was the neighborhood really as bad as these writers claimed? After all, each of the groups that shaped its reputation had some incentive to make it look as horrible as possible. In fact, not too long after Dickens had published his description, New York journalists admitted that as bad as Five Points was, it was "not one half the pestilential hole he has represented."[51]

The truth is horrifying and yet simultaneously inspiring as well. There were many irredeemable individuals, yet the immigrants who dominated Five Points survived and eventually thrived in their new homeland. Five

Points had more fighting, drinking, and vice than almost anywhere else; but also more dancing and nightlife, more dense networks of clubs and charities, and opportunities both small and large for those who seized them. With its energy, brutality, enterprise, hardship, and constant dramas, Five Points was an extreme case, yet still a deeply American place.

2

PROLOGUE

NELLY HOLLAND COMES TO FIVE POINTS

IF FIVE POINTS was so famously wretched, why did so many immigrants settle there? Ellen Holland's tale provides one answer: it was far better than staying home. "Nelly" had been born and raised in southwestern Ireland in the County Kerry parish of Kenmare. There she grew up surrounded by jagged mountain peaks and lush green hills that sloped dramatically to the wide, majestic Kenmare River. Nelly and her family lived on the estate of the third marquis of Lansdowne—an English nobleman whose property was home to thirteen thousand of the most impoverished residents of nineteenth-century Ireland. Visitors to the huge estate commonly chose adjectives such as "wretched," "miserable," "filthy," "half naked," and "half fed" to describe the poor farmers and laborers who comprised the vast majority of its population.

Observers invoked such descriptions of Nelly's birthplace even before a mysterious potato blight began to wreak havoc with the staple of her diet in 1845. By late 1846, Kenmare residents began to succumb to starvation and malnutrition-related diseases that spread in the blight's wake. In early 1847, the death toll multiplied. An Englishman who visited Kenmare village wrote that "the sounds of woe and wailing resounded in the streets throughout the night." The following morning, nine of those sufferers lay dead. "The poor people came in from the rural districts [of the Lansdowne estate] in such numbers, in the hopes of getting some relief, that it was utterly impossible to meet their most urgent exigencies, and therefore they came in literally *to die*." Tens of thousands fled Ireland in 1847, hoping to start new and more prosperous lives in England or America. But almost none of the Lansdowne tenants could afford to leave Kerry. Few had emigrated from this isolated estate in the pre-famine years, so Kenmare residents were not receiving the remittances from abroad that enabled many famine victims to leave Ireland.[1]

When the fungus subsided in 1848, British officials in charge of famine relief declared the emergency at an end. But such decrees meant nothing to Holland and others suffering in Kenmare. Most of Lansdowne's tenants were by that point too weak to work or plant and too destitute to buy seed potatoes. And what few tubers they did cultivate in 1849 were again ravaged by the dreaded fungus. Kenmare once more became the center of suffering in the region, with people "dying by the dozens in the streets." Those on the brink of death crowded into the village workhouse, where, in return for giving up all of their worldly possessions, the starving received just barely enough food to keep them alive. By April 1849, the institution held 1,800 souls "in a house built for 500—without shoes, without clothes, in filth, rags and misery," wrote Kenmare's Roman Catholic archdeacon, John O'Sullivan. "The women squatted on the ground, on the bare cold clay floor and [were] so imprisoned for months . . . without as much as a stool to sit on." One of these poor souls was Ellen Holland. She and her three sons, thirteen-year-old James, nine-year-old Thomas, and four-year-old George, were almost certainly among the institution's inmates. Her husband Richard was probably one of the many men who remained outside the workhouse hoping to find work. Or he may have been one of the hundreds authorities turned away for want of space.[2]

Securing one of the coveted spaces in the Kenmare workhouse did not ensure survival. Hundreds died there during the famine from diseases such as dysentery and cholera that spread rapidly in the crowded, unsanitary conditions. The food supply was so meager that some inmates died of starvation just hours after being released from the facility. Nelly Holland probably remained at the workhouse throughout 1849 and 1850, wondering how her life might ever return to normal, or if she and her sons would also fall victim to the seemingly unending cycle of disease and death.[3]

Nelly must have been elated when Lansdowne's estate agent announced in December 1850 that the marquis would finance the emigration to America of all his workhouse tenants who wished to go. Holland and her sons were among the first to take advantage of the program. Yet trans-Atlantic voyages were challenging even for hearty souls, and Lansdowne's tenants were emaciated and totally ill-equipped for the crossing. Sailors were horrified when they first encountered the Lansdowne emigrants, reporting that in the half decade since the onset of the famine they had never laid eyes on such wretched beings. The emigrants continued to suffer as they made their way across the Atlantic. The rags they wore provided woefully inadequate protection from the elements aboard a North Atlantic sailing ship in the dead of winter. Nelly Holland's vessel, the *Montezuma*, had to detour around an iceberg and huge swaths of "field ice" during its voyage, giving some indication of the frigid conditions she and her shipmates endured. And although Lansdowne's agent had paid for the emigrants' tickets, he did not supply his charges with the foodstuffs that the typical Irish immigrant brought aboard a trans-Atlantic vessel. Holland was forced to subsist on the "ship's allowance," just one pound of flour or meal and thirteen ounces of water each day, during her thirty-nine days at sea.[4]

By the time Nelly arrived in New York in mid-March, hundreds of thousands of Irish men, women, and children fleeing the famine had arrived in the United States through this bustling port. Yet even jaded New Yorkers considered the condition of the Lansdowne immigrants shocking. A *New York Tribune* reporter found many of the *Montezuma*'s passengers dazed, disoriented, homeless, and starving in the streets near the waterfront days after their arrival. The *Herald* also singled out the Lansdowne immigrants for comment, characterizing their treatment as "inhuman." With three children in tow and no husband (he came on a later vessel), Nelly must have found those first weeks in New York extraordinarily difficult.[5]

Like most of the Lansdowne immigrants, Nelly and her family eventually settled in Five Points. Unable to afford anything else, the Hollands rented an apartment at 39 Orange Street, where they were surrounded by drunks, notorious saloons and brothels, and other Lansdowne immigrants. The Hollands' two-and-a-half-story frame building was set within one of the most notoriously squalid blocks of tenements in the world. A journalist visiting the building less than two years before the Hollands' arrival in New York had found 106 hogs residing on the premises.[6]

Despite these hardships, Ellen Holland and her family set to work rebuilding their lives. After years of unemployment, they must have been eager and delighted to take even the lowly jobs available to them. Ellen became a washerwoman. Richard found work as a menial day laborer. Their son James, fifteen years old when he arrived in New York in 1851, probably began doing day labor as well. But a laborer's life was a hard one, full of long hours and backbreaking work in all kinds of weather. Such strenuous exertion could take its toll on even the heartiest constitutions, especially those weakened by years of famine. Ellen Holland discovered this all too well. By July 1855, Richard and James were both dead. Still living in squalor at 39 Orange, Nelly now had to pay the rent and support two children on the few dollars a week she could scrape together by taking in laundry. But Nelly Holland was not a quitter. As bad as life in Five Points was, Kenmare had been far worse. Holland would live at least to age fifty-two. Not only would she survive in America—she would eventually thrive.[7]

CHAPTER TWO

Why They Came

∽〰〰〰〰〰∽

BY THE EARLY 1850s, the drama of life in Five Points so captivated Americans that tales of the famous neighborhood found their way into nearly every form of literary endeavor. Barnum's Museum featured a play about its most infamous tenement. A best-selling novel depicted dissolute immigrants engaged in lives of crime and orgies of incest in overcrowded, squalid tenement buildings. A poet lamented the struggles of its inhabitants for dignity. The new pictorial newspapers published exposés of tenement life there, featuring lurid portraits of gruesome, thieving thugs and wizened, pipe-smoking old hags as typical Five Points residents. When an entirely new form of literature—the book-length, nonfiction account of urban crime and debauchery—made its way from Europe to the United States, the "sins" of Five Points served as a featured attraction. Yet many of the stories in these publications were obviously fictitious, or exaggerated, or simply recycled versions of a few shockingly lurid tales. Not every Five Pointer could have been a thief, a prostitute, or a drunk. What kinds of people really lived in Five Points? And how did they end up there?[8]

"EVERY NATIONALITY OF THE GLOBE"

In order to answer these questions, it is important to understand how dramatically the population of both Five Points and the city as a whole had changed since 1830, when the neighborhood had first become notorious. Immigration increased enormously after 1830, with most of the newcomers who settled in New York coming from Ireland and the German states. The foreign-born population expanded from 9 percent of the city's total in 1830 to 36 percent in 1845. With the onset of the potato blight in Ireland, the pace of immigration accelerated further. By 1855, when the flood of immigrants had finally begun to subside, 51 percent of New Yorkers had been born abroad. The population of the city swelled tremendously in these years, more than doubling from 1825 to 1845 (from 166,000 to 371,000), and then increasing 70 percent more during the famine decade, to nearly 630,000 by 1855.[9]

Five Points became home to many of these newcomers. From 1830 to 1855, the population of the ward virtually doubled, from 13,570 to 25,562. The most dramatic increase came during the peak Irish famine years from 1845 to 1850, when it increased from 19,343 to 24,698. With immigrants pouring into the neighborhood and many natives leaving, the foreign-born accounted for 72 percent of Five Points' population by 1855. Even this figure understates the immigrant presence in the neighborhood, however, because the vast majority of "natives" were the young children of recent immigrants. If only adults (those eighteen years of age or older) are considered, the foreign-born constituted a full 89 percent of Five Points residents. No New York neighborhood could boast a higher concentration.[10]

Observers believed that immigrants from all over the world settled in Five Points. "All the nations of the earth are represented," stated the *Five Points Monthly*, a Methodist journal. A minister working there on the eve of the Civil War likewise found "a population that . . . represents every nationality of the globe." Yet this perception was somewhat exaggerated.

Nativity of Five Points Residents, 1855

Place of Birth	Percentage of 1855 Five Pointers Born There	Percentage of 1855 Adult Five Pointers Born There
Ireland	52%	66%
United States	28	11
German states	11	14
Italy	3	3
England	3	2
Poland	1	2
Scotland	1	1
Other	1	1

In comparison to some modern New York neighborhoods, antebellum Five Points seems relatively homogeneous, as 91 percent of its residents were born in Ireland, the United States, or the German states. Of the other groups, only Italians and Poles lived there in significantly greater numbers than in the rest of the city. Five Points was far from the Tower of Babel many perceived.[11]

Most Five Pointers did not arrive in New York alone, but instead made the journey to America with at least one other family member. Among married couples who had had children in Europe, about three-quarters emigrated together (though, like Nelly Holland, they may not have all come on the same ship). It is impossible to determine how many of those who arrived in Five Points before marriage came to the United States alone. But a sampling of all Irish immigrants disembarking at New York during the famine years indicates that 56 percent traveled with at least one family member.[12]

Whether one arrived in New York alone or with family members, the immigrant was usually expected to send money back to his or her native land to finance the passage of others—a process known as "chain migration." In cases in which a family with small children was divided, the husband typically went to America first and then brought the rest of his family over to Five Points. Laborer William Higgins, for example, emigrated from Ireland to New York in 1851. Only after two years of saving could he afford to bring over his wife Mary and four-year-old son James. Levi Abraham, a tailor, left his wife Amelia with their newborn son Abraham for four and a half years before they were reunited at the beginning of 1855. Sometimes, the emigrating husband brought a child with him and left his wife with the rest of their children.

In a surprising number of cases, husband and wife emigrated together and left the children behind. Michael and Bridget Conway left their four-year-old daughter Catharine in Ireland when they emigrated in 1850. She rejoined her parents two years later. John and Mary Hughes left four children—ranging in age from nine to one—in Ireland when they departed for America in 1850. They brought the middle children over a year later and the other two only in 1853. Their youngest child, Ann, by then four, undoubtedly had no memory whatsoever of her parents when they met her in New York. Even widows sometimes left children behind. When widow Margret McHugh embarked for America in 1849, she left five children ranging in age from twelve to two. She became a washerwomen in New York, and brought her twelve-year-old daughter Mary over in 1850, then two sons in 1852, and finally the two youngest girls, who she had not seen for four years, in 1853. It did not take most families this long to reunite completely, but even a relatively short period of separation brought anxiety to all involved and guilt to the immigrant who could not pay for the reuniting of the family as quickly as promised.[13]

The names of these immigrants reflect the Irish domination of Five Points. But other ethnic groups constituted nearly a quarter of the neighborhood's adult population. Most numerous after the Irish were natives of the German states. The important distinction within this group was religion. The German community in Five Points was almost evenly divided between Jews and Christians. The Jews in Five Points may not have considered themselves "German"; they emigrated from what was then often referred to as "Prussian Poland," the region of Poland annexed by Prussia in the eighteenth century. Yet if these Jews are counted as Prussian and therefore German, Jewish German families made up 53 percent of the neighborhood's German population.[14]

One might imagine that these Christian and Jewish "Germans" would have too little in common to consider themselves a "community." They do not, for example, seem to have come from the same regions of Germany. Most German states were represented in the Five Points population. But it appears that slightly more than half of the Christians were natives of two areas, Baden-Württemberg in the southwest and Hanover in the north. The remainder came mostly from Bavaria, Saxony, and Westphalia.[15] In contrast, the Jews in Five Points came overwhelmingly from a single place: Poznan. Referred to in the nineteenth century as "Posen" and located midway between Berlin and Warsaw, Poznan was a Polish duchy that Prussia had occupied since the eighteenth century. At least 70 percent of the Jews living in antebellum Five Points were natives of this single Polish region.[16]

After the Irish and the Germans, no other ethnic or racial group made up more than 3 percent of the Five Points population in 1855. The size of the Italian contingent is somewhat surprising, even at 3 percent, given that large numbers of Italians did not begin immigrating to New York until the late nineteenth century. At this point they were concentrated almost exclusively on two blocks—Anthony Street east of Centre and Orange

Street north of the Five Points intersection. A final group of Five Point-ers—African Americans—merits discussion because their presence in the neighborhood was declining rapidly in these years. In 1825, African Amer-icans constituted 14 percent of the Sixth Ward's population. In 1855, how-ever, only 4 percent of the ward's residents were black, and they made up only 3 percent of the neighborhood's population in that year. It is possible that the 1855 census undercounted the black populace. The 1855 census taker, for example, does not seem to have ventured into many of the infa-mous tenements in the part of Little Water Street known as "Cow Bay" (so called because the street was supposedly laid out over a path that stock-men once used to reach the Collect to water their cattle). As recently as 1849, one news report had claimed that six hundred blacks lived in Cow Bay, more than the census recorded in the entire ward in 1855. On the other hand, a black exodus had begun in the late 1830s after the anti-abolition riot. Observers noted blacks moving from Five Points to the West Side of Manhattan throughout the antebellum period. Those African Americans who remained had one thing in common with their white neighbors: few had been born in New York. Seventy-one percent of Five Points blacks were not native New Yorkers. Yet only a few—21 percent—were natives of slave states or island slave territories. Most had been born free in other mid-Atlantic states. So while Five Points still had "a full sprinkling of blacks" in the 1850s, it was no longer a focal point of the city's African-American community.[17]

IT IS POSSIBLE to re-create block-by-block, even house-by-house, an ethnic map of the neighborhood. Ethnic and racial groups concentrated on certain blocks, and sometimes even in certain buildings. Germans were especially numerous on Centre Street at the western edge of the district and on Mott and Elizabeth Streets in the northeast corner of the neighborhood. Jews congregated at the foot of Orange Street and on upper Mott Street. Although most of the African-American strongholds in the ward had become Irish by 1855, several large clusters still existed on Cross Street between Orange and Mott and on Little Water Street. The Irish lived every-where in the neighborhood, but especially dominated Orange Street above the Five Points intersection and Mulberry Street from Chatham Square all the way to Canal Street.[18]

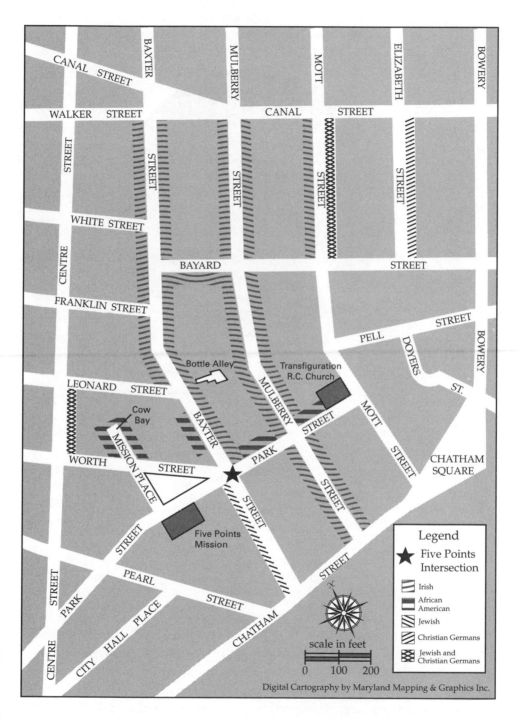

FIVE POINTS ETHNIC AND RACIAL ENCLAVES, 1850

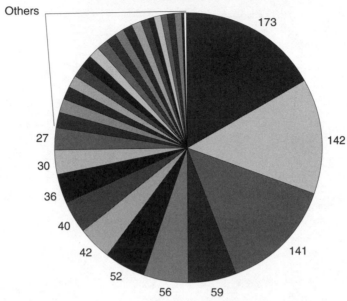

Irish counties and the number of Transfiguration Five Pointers born in those counties

Sligo	173	Others *(counterclockwise)*			
Cork	142	Dublin	19	Westmeath	12
Kerry	141	Tyrone	17	Cavan	12
Galway	59	Donegal	16	Monaghan	10
Limerick	56	Fermanagh	15	Carlow	7
Tipperary	52	Clare	15	Derry	9
Mayo	42	Longford	15	Kildare	8
Roscommon	40	Meath	14	Wexford	9
Leitrim	36	Louth	14	Armagh	9
Waterford	30	Queen's	13	Wicklow	3
Kilkenny	27	King's	12	Down	3

Source: Marriage Register, Church of the Transfiguration, 29 Mott Street, New York.

Immigrants from every part of Ireland lived in Five Points, but those from certain Irish regions settled there more often than others. More than three-quarters of the Irish Catholics, for example, came from the western half of Ireland, where the potato blight was especially severe. More surprising is that so large a proportion—44 percent of the Irish Catholic immigrants—came from just three of Ireland's thirty-two counties: Sligo, Cork, and Kerry. The presence of many Cork natives at Five Points is understandable. County Cork was the most populous in Ireland—its pre-famine population of 854,000 was almost twice that of the next most populous county, and its rate of emigration, even on a per capita basis, outpaced that from most Irish counties.[19]

Why natives of relatively tiny County Sligo—on the northwest coast of Ireland—significantly outnumbered the Cork immigrants in Five Points demands an explanation. Immigrants from Sligo seem to have congregated in the northern section of the neighborhood long before the Great Famine. Many Sligo natives had lived in New York since the 1810s and 1820s and had resided in Five Points since the 1830s. No other Irish Five Pointers had such long-standing ties to the United States. These connections had two consequences. First, because so many Sligo natives were already in North America when the famine struck, they could send money back to help during the crisis. Some of this money bought food, but County Sligo residents also used it to pay for tickets to America. And when these immigrants arrived in New York, many sought out their countrymen and settled with or near them in Five Points.[20]

Records kept by the neighborhood's Roman Catholic Church of the Transfiguration reveal that half the Sligo immigrants were natives of just two of the county's forty-one Roman Catholic parishes. These same records indicate that more than three-quarters of the other unusually large Irish contingent in Five Points—that from County Kerry—came from just three out of eighty-six parishes. It turns out that so many Irish men, women, and children emigrated from these five Sligo and Kerry parishes because the three landlords who owned them (Lord Palmerston and Sir Robert Gore Booth in Sligo and the third marquis of Lansdowne in Kerry) paid for six thousand five hundred of their starving tenants to go to America. In fact, even though these three estates occupied only one-half of 1 percent of the Irish landmass, by 1855 nearly one in five Irish Catholic Five Points immigrants was a native of one of these three properties.[21]

Most Irish immigrants did not receive emigration assistance from their landlords; only about 6 percent in the famine years received such aid.[22] Yet the Irish experiences of these Five Points immigrants are unusually well documented. Estate records for the three properties, used together with government documents, allow us to re-create in remarkable detail the ten-

ants' often miserable pre-famine lives and their struggles simply to survive
once the "Great Hunger" began. As with Nelly Holland, it is vital to appreciate the immigrants' experiences before they arrived in the United States
to understand the world they made in Five Points.

"THE MOST WRETCHED PEOPLE UPON THE FACE OF THE GLOBE"

By the 1820s and '30s, overpopulation, a dearth of affordable land, and a
lack of economic development made conditions for the small farmers and
laborers on the Palmerston and Lansdowne estates truly miserable. Like
those all over western Ireland, these workers could not find nearly enough
employment to support their families comfortably. A Protestant minister
on Palmerston's Ahamlish estate testified before the Irish "Poor Inquiry"
of 1836* that the average unskilled workman there could find only three
months of employment each year. "Fourteen years ago I could get as much
work in the fields as would maintain me and my family, without land,"
laborer Owen Casey told the same committee. By 1836, he could only find
work breaking stones on a road crew at a penny per barrel. Another laborer
remembered the days of constant employment, but "it now often happens
that I don't get more than a day in the week." Unemployment was just as
prevalent on the Lansdowne estate in County Kerry.[23]

As work became increasingly scarce, wages fell to incredibly low levels.
The most a laborer could expect to earn annually in wages was £1 10s. or
perhaps £2 5s. in a very good year. This was the equivalent, in 1845, of
about $8 to $13 per annum. Given their meager incomes, impoverished
laborers tried to conserve their cash by growing their own food (usually
potatoes) on small rented plots, but the scarcity of arable land and overpopulation drove rents to astronomical levels.

There were a number of ways a poor Irishman might pay for this land.
He might use a large portion of the rented land to grow corn or oats, which

---

* The British Parliament conducted hearings all across Ireland in 1836 in order to determine
the extent of poverty there for use in amending the British "Poor Laws." The testimony
recorded in these hearings provides the most complete record of life for the rural Irish laborer
and small farmer in the years before the Great Famine began in 1845.

he could sell to pay the rental fee. Or he could pay the rent in labor rather than cash, although he probably already worked three days per week to pay for his family's one-room cabin and an accompanying bit of land (or one day per week for a cabin without land). Selling pigs, butter, or eggs might also help to make ends meet. A laborer might, for example, buy a piglet for five shillings, feed it the family's "waste potatoes" (those unfit for human consumption), and then sell it fully grown for eighteen shillings, netting a significant sum. Butter production required the capital to acquire both a cow and grazing land. Eggs necessitated a smaller initial investment for the poultry, but also brought smaller returns. Women could generate a bit of income for the family through spinning.[24]

As rents increased and wages fell over the first half of the nineteenth century, the Irish were forced to alter their diets to glean the largest quantity of food from their meager resources. Though the potato had occupied a central role in the diet of the laborer and small farmer for generations even before low wages and high rents became so burdensome, the Irish had eaten other vegetables and grains as well. "But as rents got high, and the price of labour fell," explained one North Sligo farmer, "they gradually were compelled to reserve the grain" to pay their rent. On the tiny bit of land left for growing food, small farmers had little choice but to plant only potatoes because, as this farmer explained, "an acre of potatoes will feed at least five times as many people as an acre of corn." As a result, said another area farmer, "a very large proportion of the labouring classes never take any other food than potatoes."[25]

This was no exaggeration. Most residents of the Palmerston and Gore Booth estates ate nothing but potatoes for breakfast, potatoes for dinner (the midday meal), and potatoes for supper. Sometimes they prepared their potatoes with skimmed milk or a bit of butter, "but often salt is their only kitchen." The poor ate no other vegetables, no fruit, no bread or grain, and no meat, testified a North Sligo resident, "unless they make a struggle to procure a bit [of meat] on one or two set nights in the year," usually Christmas and Easter. A report from the Lansdowne estate concurred that "no groceries are used in a labourer's family except a very little at Christmas." Although many impoverished families had chickens that laid eggs, they never ate them, selling them instead to pay for tobacco. Given their proximity to the sea, one might imagine that these Irishmen could have eaten fish. But fishing required expertise and equipment that few laborers possessed. Professional fishermen caught plenty of seafood, but they sold it at prices far beyond the reach of the typical Irish peasant.[26]

While the diet of the average Palmerston or Lansdowne laborer may have been monotonous, it was at least filling. An adult laborer typically ate fourteen pounds of potatoes per day! As incredible as this may seem, contemporaries unanimously asserted that this was the daily diet of a working-man. When a laborer's wages included food, one testified in 1836, "a stone [fourteen pounds] of potatoes is laid out for each man." All agreed, noted an official of the Poor Inquiry, "that a man could not subsist upon less than one stone of potatoes in the day, and some thought that quantity would be hardly sufficient." Other family members ate less, but their consumption was still impressive. A North Sligo laborer stated that he, his wife, and four children consumed 2.5 stone (35 pounds) of potatoes each day.[27]

For all that, hunger was a fact of life in the west of Ireland before the famine. Escalating rental fees forced the poor to grow more and more corn and grains that they sold to pay their rent. Using more land for such cash crops left very little on which to sow potatoes to feed one's family. In order to stretch their food supplies to last the whole year, a Sligo laborer and his family typically ate only two meals a day during the first two summer months they waited to harvest the new potato crop. Even if one managed to grow enough potatoes to last the whole year, midsummer was still a season of suffering, because "from the middle of July to the latter end of August, the [old] potatoes are unfit for use." Even though the potatoes were stored in pits in order to preserve them as long as possible, they usually became rotten and inedible before the new crop matured. "The interval between the old crop becoming unfit, and the new crop becoming fit for food is often a season of great distress," stated one North Sligo farmer. According to George Dodwell, Gore Booth's Sligo estate agent, this hunger gap lasted at least two weeks each year, but "with many it extends to two months; and in proportion to its length is the distress that prevails." Lansdowne's tenants dreaded "Hungry July" as well.[28]

Many residents of western Ireland lived lives similar to those of the Palmerston and Lansdowne tenants. But Lansdowne's tenants were so desperately poor that they often nailed their cabins shut during the summer and walked one hundred miles or more through Counties Cork, Limerick, and Tipperary in search of work. "In autumn they go to the low country during the harvest," noted a Kerry resident, "and their wives then often shut up their houses and go begging with their families until their husbands come home" in time to harvest their potatoes. After digging up the tubers, some again went inland to find work before returning home for Christmas. Not all Lansdowne laborers needed to roam the countryside in search of work, but those who lived on mountainsides in the remote parishes of Tuosist and Bonane could rarely rent enough potato land to feed their families, and thus had no choice but to join in this migratory ritual.[29]

The cabins these migrant laborers returned home to were small, dark, and uncomfortable, and those in North Sligo were not much better. According to the testimony of one resident to the 1836 Poor Inquiry, "nine-tenths of the ordinary cabins are under 21 feet in length, and . . . none exceed 13 feet in breadth." The largest were divided into two rooms, "but the number of them, too small to be divided, is by far the greater. They are nearly all constructed of walls of loose stones, coated outside with a mixture of clay and mortar. . . . The roof is formed of branches of trees laid across the rafters and covered with '*scraws*,' *i.e.*, sods of turf, over which is laid a very thin and imperfect thatching of straw. None have ceilings, and the dirt and cobwebs which fall from the exposed and damp roof" constantly annoyed the inhabitants. Cabins had "no other flooring than the earth. The floor is generally uneven, and, being too often below the level of the external soil," puddles sometimes formed inside when it rained, an almost daily occurrence in western Ireland. "There are more cabins without chimneys than with them, and in many where they were originally constructed . . . the sides have subsided, and no longer permit the passage of smoke, which may be seen rolling in volumes through the door." Smoke could not escape through the single window in the typical cabin because the pane of glass—stuck directly into the wall during construction—did not open. Cabins generally had no well for water and no stove or even grate over which to cook one's food. Sligo housewives placed their potato pot directly on top of the burning turf they used for fuel. Such cabins had neither toilets nor outhouses of any kind. "Privies are absolutely unknown," another resident told investigators. The cabin dweller simply found a secluded spot at which to relieve himself. In short, Sligo cabins were dirty, damp, crowded, dark, smoke-filled, primitive dwellings.[30]

Cabins on the Lansdowne estate were apparently even more wretched than those in North Sligo. Until the mid-1830s, Lansdowne's tenants reputedly lived in some of the worst dwellings in all of Ireland. One visitor who traveled throughout Ireland in 1834 called these "as miserable cabins as I ever beheld." With walls made of dried mud, they were "beyond description, wretched abodes." Apparently embarrassed, Lord Lansdowne began financing the construction of stone homes to replace the mud hovels. By the eve of the famine, stone cabins predominated, but revolutionary Michael Doheny, who hid in Tuosist cabins after a failed uprising against the British in 1848, insisted that in many cases their "showy exterior is sadly belied by the filth and discomfort of the inside."[31]

Poor laborers and farmers could afford few possessions to add comfort to these miserable abodes. A North Sligo resident told the parliamentary inquiry that "a majority of cabins possessed nothing beyond a table, a few stools, and a large chest." Laborers did not have beds or mattresses either. At best they owned "rude bedsteads, but very frequently no other bedding than straw and hay, and a single quilt, or sheet, made of coarse sacking, in a condition of great filth." Many children lacked even these comforts, sleeping instead on "a litter of old hay, which during the day-time, was collected in a corner, and had been in use for months." North Sligo laborers slept in their clothes, but because they were "clothed very poorly and insufficiently," they were seldom warm at night. The few men who did "possess a good suit [did] not wear it except on Sundays, and on a few other occasions; the women and children are still worse off than the men, especially the latter, who are at all times in rags." Many, especially women and children, had neither socks nor shoes. Identical conditions prevailed on the Lansdowne estate. "Furniture miserable; bedding wretched," was how the recording secretary summed up testimony concerning the Lansdowne tenants.[32]

Who was to blame for this situation? Some faulted the landlords and their agents. But Kenmare archdeacon John O'Sullivan, who was no admirer of Lansdowne, admitted the marquis charged very reasonable rents and did not evict tenants even when they fell years behind in their payments. Those in North Sligo generally said the same for Palmerston and Gore Booth. The landlords' agents tended to blame the poor tenants for their own plight, insisting that they married too young, had too many children, and subdivided their land too frequently among their offspring. No matter who one faulted, all observers agreed that living conditions for most tenants were truly pitiful. "The tenantry are extremely wretched," said a North Sligo resident in summing up his testimony concerning the Palmerston and Gore Booth estates. Irish Poor Inquiry official Jonathan Binns concluded that Lansdowne's "poor cottagers are in a very distressed condition. . . . They are nearly half naked, and are but half fed. This is indeed a wretched state of things." Lansdowne's isolated tenants were even worse off than those in North Sligo, living in smaller cabins with less arable land and fewer personal possessions. The Lansdowne tenants, O'Sullivan asserted in 1844, were "the most wretched people upon the face of the globe."[33]

"FAMISHED AND SPECTRAL HUMAN BEINGS"

Given their precarious circumstances in 1844, it was no surprise that Lansdowne's tenants were devastated by the famine that began after a fungus infested and almost completely destroyed potato crops in 1845, 1846, and 1847. During the first year after the blight struck, from mid-1845 to mid-1846, the distress was relatively mild.[34] But with the second, more complete failure of the potato crop in the summer of 1846, the situation became dire. "I see nothing within the bounds of possibility that can save the people," wrote a relief official responsible for setting up public works projects on the Lansdowne estate in February 1847:

> On one road, on which I have 300 men employed, the deaths are three each day. This is in the parish of Tuosist. The people are buried without coffins, frequently in the next field. No noise or sign of grief for the dead; every thought is selfish and unfeeling. . . . I daily witness the most terrible spectacles. Men and women are discolored with dropsy, attacked with dysentary, or mad with fever, on the works—driven there by the terrible necessity of trying to get as much as would purchase a meal. . . . With most of these working is a mockery; they can scarcely walk to and from the roads, and how can they work! . . . When a respectable person passes the houses of these poor people, the saddest sights present themselves; women, children, and old men crawling out on all fours, perhaps from beside a corpse, to crave a morsel of any kind of food.

Conditions in Tuosist, agreed visitor William Bennett, were "utterly past
the powers of description, or even of imagination, without witnessing."[35]

The situation in the town of Kenmare was hardly better than in the
countryside. Archdeacon O'Sullivan recorded in his diary in early 1847
that there was "nothing more usual than to find four or five bodies in the
street every morning." The suffering of the living was almost as difficult to
bear as the sight of the dead. "The swollen limbs, emaciated countenances,
and other hideous forms of disease . . . were innumerable," wrote the
appalled Bennett. "In no other part of Ireland had I seen people falling on
their knees to beg. It was difficult to sit over breakfast after this." O'Sullivan wrote directly to Charles Trevelyan, permanent secretary at the Treasury in London and the man who single-handedly controlled most relief
expenditures, hoping that if Trevelyan understood the extent of the suffering, he might make more aid available. "The cries of starving hundreds
that besiege me from morning until night actually ring in my ears during
the night," O'Sullivan reported. "I attended myself a poor woman, whose
infant, dead two days, lay at the foot of the bed, and four others nearly dead
in the same bed; and, horrible to relate, a famished cat got up on the corpse
of the poor infant and was about to gnaw it, but for my interference. I could
tell you such tales of woe without end."[36]

Similarly horrifying conditions prevailed in North Sligo. "On the
Ahamlish Estate the [potato] disease was late in appearing," reported
Palmerston's agents to the foreign secretary in February 1846, "but in some
parts of the parish it has committed dreadful ravages. . . . [N]o doubt the
labouring class will be very badly off." No one appears to have perished
from hunger in late 1845 or early 1846, even though food was in very short
supply and hundreds went hungry. But many refused to pay their rents, the
agents noted, "under the plea of starvation & the failure of the Potato
Crop."[37]

As in South Kerry, it was only in late 1846 with the second consecutive
failure of the potato crop—"utterly and completely destroyed," said one
Sligo newspaper—that Palmerston and Gore Booth's already reeling tenants began to succumb to starvation. Victims often perished due to famine-
related illnesses rather than actual hunger. An Ahamlish doctor reported
that "a dreadful disease is breaking out amongst them. I allude to Dysen-
try with discharge of blood from the bowels." Another ailment, "sore

mouth," appeared as well, "which I think has been produced by the unwholesome food the poor were obliged to use in the early part of the season and which so injured the coat of their stomachs and bowels, that now they are not in a state to bear strong food and the consequence is the living membrane of the intestine is coming away." As in southwestern Kerry, a relief official in North Sligo wrote directly to Trevelyan to ensure that he understood the magnitude of the suffering. "I assure you that unless something is immediately done the people must die. . . . Pray do something for them. Let me beg of you to attend to this. *I cannot express their condition.*"[38]

Gore Booth labored tirelessly to compensate for the lack of governmental assistance to the starving. He imported large quantities of corn to his Drumcliff estate, which he sold to his tenants below cost. He also sold bread at less than half the market price and set up kitchens that distributed free soup. In addition, reported a local newspaper, Gore Booth provided "employment on an extensive scale," doling out jobs on his estate for as many as the government employed under the local public works program. Gore Booth was forced to mortgage his property in Lancashire to finance these expenditures, which amounted to thousands of pounds. These laudable efforts reduced but could not eliminate starvation in Drumcliff. "It is no exaggeration to affirm that . . . the people are dying from starvation by dozens daily," reported a relief official there in March 1847. "But for Sir Robert Booth they would be dying by scores—by fifties."[39]

Despite these efforts, conditions on the Gore Booth estate continued to deteriorate. A relief official reported pitiable scenes, even among those who had recently been well off:

> The first place I visited, was a wretched hamlet of three cottages, with outhouses, containing three families, numbering in all 32 persons, belonging to three brothers; the whole having lived on 12 acres for a period of [years]. . . . Last year, they thought themselves so well off, they refused to take £60 to give up the lease and depart. Now they are starving. . . . One of the brothers, and three others of the families, had died during the previous week. The widow was lying on the ground in fever, and unable to move. The children were bloated in their faces and bodies, their limbs were withered to

bones and sinews, with rags on them which scarcely preserved decency, and assuredly afforded no protection from the weather. *They had been found that day, gnawing the flesh from the bones of a pig which had died in an out-house. . . .* I saw the pig, I believe the fact.

The situation in Ahamlish, where Palmerston provided far less private relief to his tenants than did Gore Booth, was even more dire. Ahamlish is "barren and [has] now almost become a waste," reported the press. Of 1,800 Ahamlish families, stated another eyewitness, 1,700 were utterly "destitute," with "8500 individuals actually starving." The death rate in County Sligo during the famine years outpaced that of virtually every other county in Ireland.[40]

"I MAKE THIS RECOMMENDATION ON THE PRINCIPLE OF PROFIT AND ECONOMY"

Despite the thousands Gore Booth spent on relief for the suffering, his poor tenants were not much better off in early 1847 than Palmerston's "neglected" ones. Even had they been able to afford seed potatoes in the spring of 1847, most North Sligo farmers would have been too weak to sow them. "Pen cannot dictate the poverty of this country, at present, the potato crop is quite done away all over Ireland," wrote two County Sligo residents to relatives in Canada. ". . . Now, my dear parents, pity our hard case, and do not leave us on the number of the starving poor . . . if you knew what hunger we and our fellow-countrymen are suffering, if you were ever so much distressed, you would take us out of this poverty Isle." As if they had not made their desperation clear enough, the children added a postscript: "For God's sake take us out of poverty, and don't let us die with the hunger." But most of the starving in North Sligo did not have loved ones in America who could relieve their suffering.[41]

Unable to conceive how the crisis might be brought to an end, Gore Booth and Palmerston eventually began to consider mass emigration. The landlords were inspired to initiate a program of assisted emigration partly out of humanitarian motives and partly out of economic calculation. Under a new relief program to take effect in early 1847, landlords would have to pay a much larger share of the famine relief costs than they had before.

Palmerston's estate agent, Joseph Kincaid, informed the foreign minister that his tax bill under the new law "cannot fall much short of £10,000 [roughly equivalent to $900,000 today] for the next seven months. . . . This is awful to contemplate." Kincaid's employees had polled Palmerston's destitute tenants and found that hundreds would give up their leases and emigrate if they had the means. Considering how much Palmerston would have to spend in taxes should his starving tenants stay in Ahamlish, Kincaid advised Palmerston to send out *all* those willing to take passage to America. "I make this recommendation on the principle of profit and economy," Kincaid admitted, arguing that "your estate will be of more value in the course of a year or two with the population reduced by 1000 than if they remained[.] The cost of supporting these 150 families for the next 7 months would be at least £1500 and at the end of that time they are still upon the property as dead weights." Kincaid argued that Palmerston would more than recoup the costs of emigration in reduced poor taxes and be left with a "better class of tenants" as well. The emigrants, on the other hand, would make new, prosperous lives for themselves in North America. Everyone, concluded Kincaid, would benefit from assisted emigration.[42]

Palmerston saw the logic behind Kincaid's reasoning and by the end of 1847 had underwritten the emigration to Canada of about two thousand of his starving tenants. Gore Booth, who seems to have been motivated more by humanitarian impulses, sponsored the voyages of fifteen hundred destitute Drumcliff residents. The landlords chose Canada in part because passage there was a bit cheaper at that point than a ticket to the United States, but primarily because they did not want to be accused of depopulating the British Empire. Yet most of the Palmerston and Gore Booth immigrants moved to the United States soon after their arrival in Canada, and hundreds eventually settled in Five Points.

Although the first ship carrying Palmerston's assisted emigrants wrecked off the coast of Canada (killing three-quarters of the passengers), most of the early trans-Atlantic voyages went smoothly. The two landlords provided their passengers with generous allotments of food and water to supplement the daily pound of flour or meal and thirteen ounces of water they received from the ship's crew. But by summertime, conditions began to deteriorate. Contagious diseases—especially typhus, known popularly as "ship fever"—began to ravage whole shiploads of weary travelers. Because they were well provisioned and inspected by Gore Booth's private physician before boarding the ship, the death rate on the Palmerston and Gore Booth vessels (7.5%) was less than half that for other immigrants to Québec and St. John, New Brunswick (the two ports at which most of their emigrants landed), in 1847. Nonetheless, one in nine passengers from the *Numa* and one in eleven from the *Marchioness Breadalbane* (both chartered by Palmerston) perished during their midsummer voyages or soon after landing.[43]

To that point, there had been little if any criticism of Palmerston or Gore Booth for sending their tenants to America. That began to change by September. Because so many tenants wanted to emigrate, the landlords had trouble securing enough berths for all of them. Many of those promised passage in the spring only left Ireland in August or September, arriving in Canada when the weather was turning cold and jobs were very scarce in North America's seasonal labor market. And as the emigration bills mounted, Palmerston's agents began to skimp on supplies for the travelers, especially clothing.

Canadians noticed these changes. "This is the fifth season in which I have boarded vessels with emigrants arriving at this port," noted an immigration official in St. John after inspecting a shipload of Palmerston's immigrants, "but I have never yet seen such abject misery, destitution and helplessness as was exhibited yesterday on the decks of the 'Lady Sale.'" A story in the *New Brunswick Courier* called the passengers on a subsequent Palmerston vessel "a destitute and helpless set. . . . They are penniless and in rags, without shoes or stockings and lying upon the bare boards, not having even straw! Some of the men's attire were little more than shreds tied together with cords. Not one of them owned even a box." A Canadian politician equated conditions on the final Palmerston ships to those in the slave trade. Once lauded for his particularly humane treatment of his tenants, Palmerston was now accused in the press and by Canadian officials of cruelty bordering on murder.[44]

How could the assisted emigration from North Sligo, which just months earlier had seemed to be a winning proposition for tenant and landlord alike, have ended so badly? Palmerston's agents—and Gore Booth himself—were forced to appear before the House of Lords to answer the charges. Indeed, the landlords and their agents deserved some reproach. Rather than selecting for emigration those whose health and age made it most likely that they could endure the rigors of a five-week trans-Atlantic crossing, they tended to choose the weakest and most dependent. "I preferred to send out what might be termed the bad Characters," admitted Gore Booth—those who brewed illegal whiskey, caused trouble, or never paid their rents. Kincaid and his partner, James R. Stewart, likewise conceded that those chosen for emigration "were of the poorest class of farmers and their families, very little better than paupers." In letters to Palmerston, both Stewart and Kincaid insisted they had done nothing wrong, but between themselves they were more honest. "I dont know what to think of the St Johns Emigrants," Stewart confided to Kincaid. "I fear we did not inform ourselves enough of the circumstances of the place they were sent to & the suitable seasons."[45]

Palmerston must have found it ironic that his huge expenditures on behalf of his tenants prompted such scorn and censure, especially since the emigrants themselves seemed profoundly grateful. A committee of passengers from the *Aeolus* thanked Stewart, Kincaid, and Palmerston "for engaging such a fine ship as the above for our countrymen to America. The provisions, water and medicines were good and plentiful, and the Captain, his officers, and crew, treated us kindly and with every attention to our wants, for which we shall ever feel thankful." Gore Booth's emigrants wrote similarly grateful words of thanks to their landlord.[46]

"Spectres from the grave could not present a more ghastly, unearthly appearance"

While Palmerston's and Gore Booth's tenants were sailing to America in 1847, Lansdowne's continued to languish and die in southwest Kerry. With the death toll mounting, one wonders why the marquis did not follow the example of his political confidant Palmerston. Instead, most of Lansdowne's tenants were still in Kerry receiving meager relief rations paid for primarily by Lansdowne himself. Perhaps Lansdowne believed that his tenants could survive the blight without his having to expend such huge sums on emigration. If so, reports from Kenmare in the spring of 1848 must have pleased the marquis immensely. All signs indicated that suffering and privation were on the wane, and the potatoes his tenants planted in 1848 initially showed no signs of blight.[47]

But either because of illness or lack of seed potatoes, Lansdowne's leaseholders had not planted nearly enough to feed themselves for a whole year, and by February 1849 gruesome reports of starvation again began emanating from Kenmare. "I was shocked in Skibbereen, Dunmanway, [and] Bantry," wrote a visitor to Kenmare who had just come from those infamously destitute West Cork towns, "but they were as nothing to what was now before me. . . . Bad as the Bantry paupers were they were 'pampered rogues' in comparison to these poor creatures. . . . Spectres from the grave could not present a more ghastly, unearthly appearance. . . . The very thought of them to this moment sickens me." The emaciated once again crowded into Kenmare, "dying by the dozens in the streets." According to O'Sullivan, "theft and robbery and plunder became . . . universal" as some resorted to these desperate measures to stave off starvation. However obtained, food alone did not necessarily ensure survival. The cholera epidemic sweeping Europe and North America in the spring of 1849 also struck Kenmare, and due to the overcrowding in the workhouse, its inmates were particularly susceptible. Dysentery afflicted many as well, observed O'Sullivan, its victims so thirsty that they would barter their weekly one pound relief ration of cornmeal "for a half noggin of new milk to try and quench the burning thirst which invariably follows them." Despite government declarations that the famine was over, the death toll in southwest Kerry climbed steadily higher in early 1849. By the end of that year, after the blight again destroyed the 1849 crop, at least 1,000 (and perhaps as many as 1,700) of Lansdowne's 12,000 tenants had succumbed to the famine and the diseases spread in its wake.[48]

In 1850, Lansdowne hired a new estate agent, William Steuart Trench, in hopes that he might better administer relief to his suffering tenants. Trench, an experienced estate manager who probably knew about Palmerston's emigration program, made precisely the same recommendation to Lansdowne that Kincaid had made to the foreign secretary almost three years earlier:

> I showed him by the poor-house returns, that the number of paupers off his estate and receiving relief in the workhouse amounted to about three thousand. . . . [I]f left in the workhouse, the smallest amount they could possibly cost would be £5 per head per annum, and thus . . . the poor rates must necessarily amount, for some years to come, to £15,000 per annum, unless these people died or left—and the latter was not probable. . . . I explained to him fur-

ther, that . . . inasmuch as the poor rates were a charge prior to the rent, it would be impossible for his lordship to expect any rent whatever out of his estate for many years to come. The remedy I proposed was as follows. That he should forthwith offer *free emigration* to every man, woman, and child now in the poor-house and *chargeable to his estate*. . . . That even supposing they all accepted this offer, the total, together with a small sum per head for outfit and a few shillings on landing, would not exceed from £13,000 to £14,000, a sum less than it would cost to support them in the workhouse for a single year. . . . I plainly proved that it would be cheaper to him, and *better for them*, to pay for their emigration at once, than to continue to support them at home.

Lansdowne must have been predisposed to accept Trench's reasoning, writing him a check on the spot for £8,000 (roughly $650,000 today) to be used to initiate the project. By the end of 1851, Lansdowne had spent £9,500 (perhaps $760,000 today) on emigration.[49]

Trench later recalled that when he returned to the estate and announced the emigration offer, "it was considered by the paupers to be too good news to be true. But when it began to be believed and appreciated . . . they rushed from the country like a panic-stricken throng, each only fearing that the funds at my disposal might fail before he and his family could get their passage." Each week, Trench wrote in his memoirs, he chose from the poorhouse population two hundred "of those apparently most suited for emigration; and having arranged their slender outfit," put them in the hands of an employee, who led them on the sixty-mile journey to Cork. Some sailed from there directly to America. But most traveled first to Liverpool or London before boarding a trans-Atlantic vessel. Even the hardened Cork seamen who took the Lansdowne immigrants on board their ships were stunned by their condition. "They had seen human misery in every form," reported the *Cork Examiner*, but "anything like the spectacle presented by the emigrants in question, they never before beheld." Nonetheless, "two hundred after two hundred, week after week, departed for Cork," wrote Trench, "until the poor-house was nearly emptied of paupers chargeable to the Lansdowne estate." About three thousand destitute Lansdowne tenants—more than a quarter of the estate's population—took the free passage to America. The emigration program more than fulfilled

Trench's predictions. The Kenmare workhouse, which in 1850 had housed twenty-five hundred Tuosist and Bonane paupers chargeable to the Lansdowne estate, by 1853 contained only fourteen inhabitants from those parishes.[50]

At first Trench allowed the emigrants to select their destination. Nearly all chose New York. Estate records indicate that seventeen hundred Lansdowne tenants left Kenmare for New York from December 1850 through March 1851. From that point, perhaps in an effort to save money, Trench no longer offered a choice, instead requiring them to sail to Qúebec. By the end of 1851, another thirteen hundred had departed for that port, though many of them soon joined their friends and relatives in Five Points.[51]

Lansdowne's tenants continued to suffer during their journeys across the Atlantic. Estate records show that of the 1,700 emigrants sent to New York in 1851, Trench supplied clothing to at most 226, even though none would have owned a wardrobe suitable for a North Atlantic crossing in the dead of winter in an unheated ship. In addition, 1,350 of the 1,700 New York–bound immigrants were not provided with food for the passage. They were, in the words of one Irish journal, "obliged to subsist on the ship's allowance—an allowance which is scarcely sufficient to keep a full grown person from starvation. God help them!" Each of Palmerston's assisted emigrants, in contrast, had received each week, in addition to the meager ship's allowance, six pounds of biscuit, three and a half pounds of flour, one pound of pork or beef, one pound of sugar, one pound of rice, eight ounces of treacle, four ounces of coffee, and two ounces of tea. To the charge that he had not properly supplied the emigrants, Trench publicly denied any wrongdoing, but privately admitted that "this is to a certain extent true, but it would have cost thousands more to do it otherwise."[52]

Consequently, even jaded New Yorkers found the sight of the Lansdowne immigrants appalling. The *New York Tribune* singled them out for comment in a short story on March 19, 1851, noting that the Lansdowne immigrants "who arrived in this city a few days ago by the ship *Montezuma* [Ellen Holland's vessel], from Liverpool, were found Monday afternoon in the streets, in a starving condition." A few days after the *Tribune* story appeared, the *Sir Robert Peel* arrived in New York Harbor from London. The Lansdowne emigrants disembarking from that ship presented such a spectacle of wretchedness that it prompted an entire editorial in the *Herald*:

IRISH EMIGRANTS.—It is really lamentable to see the vast number of unfortunate creatures that are almost daily cast on our shores, penniless and without physical energy to earn a day's living. Yesterday, groups of these hapless beings were to be seen congregated about the [City Hall] Park and in Broadway, looking the very picture of despair, misery, disease and want. On enquiry, we ascertained that they had arrived here by the ship Sir Robert Peel, and that they had been, for the most part, tenants of the Marquis of Lansdowne, on his county Kerry estate—ejected without mercy by him, and "shipped" for America in this wholesale way. Among them were gray haired and aged men and women, who had spent the heyday of their life as tillers of their native soil, and are now sent to this country to find a grave. This is too bad—it is inhuman; and yet it is an act of indiscriminate and wholesale expatriation committed by the "liberal" President of the Council of her Majesty Queen Victoria's "liberal" ministry.[53]

Many of the Lansdowne immigrants were apparently so weakened by their voyage that they died soon after their arrival. In 1868, an anonymous critic in the *Dublin Review* charged that "in one of the principal hospitals of the city of New York there is a ward which is called the Lansdowne Ward; and the reason why it bears this name is that for months and months together [after they first arrived in New York], it was crowded by the emigrants from the Lansdowne estate, who left it commonly in their coffins." The author was probably the well-known journalist John Francis Maguire, who had recently returned from the United States researching his book *The Irish in America*. The Lansdowne family called the *Dublin Review*'s charge a partisan fabrication, but others wrote to Irish newspapers to verify it. Whether or not the "Lansdowne Ward" ever existed is impossible to confirm though deaths were undoubtedly common among these immigrants. It certainly seems plausible that patients or doctors could have bestowed such a nickname on a New York hospital ward, especially one in New York Hospital, which was located just two blocks west of the neighborhood where most of the Lansdowne immigrants settled.[54]

By the time the potato blight struck Ireland, Five Points was known throughout the English-speaking world as a veritable hellhole. Yet the Irish who settled there during the famine years had seen far worse, going months and sometimes years without work and watching friends and family starve before their eyes. The Irish did not come to Five Points expecting streets paved with gold. They simply wanted work—work that would enable them both to feed their families and to put a little something away so that someday, their children could have a better life.

3

PROLOGUE

"The Wickedest House on the Wickedest Street That Ever Existed"

If Five Points as a whole was infamous for its depravity, one of its buildings in particular became ground zero for wretchedness. Here is the story of the "Old Brewery," the most repulsive building of its day, a vast dark cave, a black hole into which every urban nightmare and unspeakable fear could be projected.

In the Old Brewery, Americans believed, lived the worst of Five Points' population—its most hardened criminals and destitute paupers. "No language can exaggerate its filth or the degradation of its inmates," insisted Five Points' Methodist missionaries. "Here is vice at its lowest ebb," agreed the *National Police Gazette,* "a crawling and fetid vice, a vice of rags and filth." Solon Robinson, a reporter for the more respectable *Tribune,* concurred with the scandal sheet's assessment, stating that "every room was a brothel or a den of thieves, or both combined." In short, concluded the *Police Gazette,* the Old Brewery was "the wickedest house on the wickedest street that ever existed in New York, yes, and in all the country and possibly all the world."[1]

As its name suggests, the Old Brewery had once produced beer, one of the many manufactories established in the eighteenth century by the shores of the Collect Pond to make use of its supply of fresh, pure water. Owned by the Coulthardt family, the brewery continued to brew beer until about 1837, when it was converted into a tenement. As part of the conversion process, the high-ceilinged floor that held the brew vats was divided in two, leaving four stories in all. Few residential buildings in antebellum New York were even half the size of the Old Brewery. Because the structure was so wide (it covered both 59 and 61 Cross Street) and so deep (it stretched back from the street at least one hundred feet on its irregular lot), it was filled with windowless apartments and pitch black, labyrinthine hallways. As a result, only the poorest Five Pointers seeking the cheapest rents took apartments there, creating a tenement so repulsive that it quickly became the most infamous in New York, "famed in song and story."[2]

The supposed depravities of the Old Brewery have taken on mythic proportions. In the 1920s, Herbert Asbury, a usually careful if somewhat overly dramatic chronicler of old New York, depicted the building as a Sodom reborn:

> Throughout the building the most frightful living conditions pre-
> vailed. Miscegenation was an accepted fact, incest was not uncom-
> mon, and there was much sexual promiscuity; the house swarmed
> with thieves, pickpockets, beggars, harlots, and degenerates of
> every type. Fights were of almost constant occurrence, and there
> was scarcely an hour of the day or night when drunken orgies were
> not in progress; through the flimsy, clapboarded walls could be
> heard the crashing thud of brickbat or iron bar, the shrieks of the
> unhappy victims, the wailing of starving children, and the frenzied
> cries of men and women, and sometimes boys and girls, writhing
> in the anguish of delirium tremens. Murders were frequent; it has
> been estimated that for almost fifteen years the Old Brewery aver-
> aged a murder a night.

When demolition crews eventually tore down the Old Brewery, insisted Asbury, the wreckers "carried out several sacks filled with human bones which they had found between the walls and in the cellars, and night after night gangsters thronged the ruin searching for treasure which rumor had it was buried there." A contemporary maintained that "the old brewer of all the world's misery, the Evil One himself, has dominion there at this day."[3]

Could the Old Brewery really have been this bad? The tenement certainly was crowded and most of its apartments were filthy. In 1850, the
New York Tribune found two and sometimes four families occupying
single rooms in some of its basement apartments. Another eyewitness

account described walls "once plastered, but now half the wall [falling] off, in some places mended by pasting newspapers over it, but often revealing unsightly holes." In the basement "in a lower room, not more than fifteen feet square, *twenty-six* human beings reside. A man could scarcely stand erect in it . . . women lay on a mass of filthy, unsightly rags in the corner— sick, feeble, and emaciated; six or seven children were in various attitudes in the corner . . . two women were peeling potatoes, and actually pulling off the skins with their finger nails; the smoke [from their fire] and stench of the room was so suffocating that it could not be long endured, and the announcement that, in addition to the misfortune of poverty, they had the measles to boot, started most of our party in a precipitate retreat from the premises." Others confirmed that dirt pervaded the building. In trying to describe the filth of one Old Brewery room used as a lodging house, upstate New Yorker Joel Ross wrote that "if you have ever seen farmers fix lodgings for their hogs, you will probably need no further explanation, except that the pigs have more *straw*, and less *bugs*." Nathaniel P. Willis, the writer and critic, who toured the Old Brewery with a police escort in the early 1840s, described the following scene in one apartment:

> The floor was covered by human beings asleep in their rags; and when called by the officer to look in at a low closet [i.e., bedroom] beyond, we could hardly put our feet to the ground, they lay so closely together, black and white, men, women, and children. The doorless apartment beyond, of the size of a kennel, was occupied by a woman and her daughter, and the daughter's child, lying together on the floor, and covered by rags and cloths of no distin- guishable color, the rubbish of bones and dirt only displaced by their emaciated limbs. The sight was too sickening to endure, but there was no egress without following close to the lantern. [In another apartment] six or seven black women lay together in a heap. . . . I had never before any adequate idea of poverty in cities. I did not dream that human beings, within reach of human aid, could be abandoned to the wretchedness which I there saw.[4]

Whether this crowding was typical is difficult to determine. The only thorough census of the building, taken in 1850, lists 221 people living in thirty-five apartments, an average of 6.3 persons per apartment. The census enumerator, who conducted his survey in late spring, did not find twenty-six persons inhabiting any room or apartment, but he did note sixteen in one, fourteen in a second, and thirteen in a third, numbers rarely found in other buildings in the neighborhood. It is not inconceivable that twenty-six could have squeezed into a basement lodging room at some point, especially in the winter, when the homeless were most likely to splurge on indoor accommodations.[5]

As with most legends, some staples of the Old Brewery story are obvious fabrications. In an era when fewer than thirty murders per year were committed in the entire city, Asbury's daily murder toll was ridiculous. Charges of rampant incest also are unfounded. Furthermore, at least some of the building's residents were not the depraved souls denigrated in the press. On his visit to the notorious tenement, Joel Ross met John Burke, who called himself the "Old Man of the Brewery and Father of Temperance." Burke, a fifty-four-year-old chair maker who had lived in the Old Brewery for thirteen years, took Ross upstairs from his shop to his apart-

This print of the Old Brewery dates from about 1850, when the Five Points Mission bought the building. The numbers in the first-story doorways identify certain particularly notorious parts of the building, such as "Murderer's Alley" (number 1) and the "Den of Thieves" (3, 4, and 5). Collection of the New-York Historical Society.

ment. Much to Ross's surprise, he found that "the floors were carpeted, the beds were tidy, the furniture clean, and on every face, a smile."

The Scandinavian writer Fredrika Bremer also found that the Old Brewery did not quite live up to its reputation. Although she and her female companion found much evidence of debauchery, "neither did we meet any instance of rudeness nor even of incivility. We saw young lads sitting at gaming-tables with old ruffians; unfortunate women suffering from horrible diseases, sickly children, giddy young girls, ill-tempered women quarrelling with the whole world, and some families, also we saw, who seemed to me, wretched rather through poverty than moral degradation. . . . Every grade of moral corruption, may be found festering and fermenting in this Old Brewery; filth, rags, pestilent air, everything is in that Old Brewery, and yet after all, I did not see anything there worse than I had seen before in Paris, London, and Stockholm."[6]

Bremer was right. Conditions in the Old Brewery were not uniformly squalid, nor were the tenants habitually murderous and dissolute. Yet dozens, perhaps even hundreds, of its residents lived in windowless, filthy, teeming apartments that were unfit for habitation. Everyone, from lawmakers to ordinary citizens, was aware of the conditions. But no government agency made the slightest effort to do anything about them. In an era of laissez-faire, decades before the country's first housing codes had been written, city officials could not control where or how people lived. Before mass immigration, when abject poverty was rare in America and its cities were relatively free from congestion, housing codes were not necessary. But the desperate newcomers who poured into New York in the famine years were willing to live in conditions unimaginable to previous generations of Americans. A charitable group, the Five Points Mission, eventually bought the Old Brewery, and in December 1852 had it torn down. But tenements with conditions nearly as bad would persist in Five Points for another half century.

CHAPTER THREE

How They Lived

〇〨〨〨〇

FROM HENRY ROTH to George Bellows, American writers and artists have made the tenement a central symbol of immigrant life in America. Today, even many city dwellers who walk by tenements every day would be hard-pressed to identify them by the name. Yet not long ago, the word fairly pulsed with meaning, conjuring visions of teeming, reeking, sweltering brick boxes bursting with hyphenated Americans.

Accounts of Five Points had not always focused on its tenements. In the 1830s, the press had concentrated on the supposed moral degradation of the neighborhood—the prostitution, the crime, the drunkenness. But the neighborhood's already inferior housing deteriorated significantly during the 1830s and '40s, due to lack of maintenance and overcrowding. By the 1850s, exposés of Five Points life increasingly concentrated on the tenements. These buildings—"worn out, . . . disgustingly filthy, and unhealthy beyond description"—became just as infamous as the Five Pointers themselves.[7]

"THESE TUMBLING AND SQUALID ROOKERIES"

There were two types of tenements found in Five Points—those of wood and those of brick—and they were in many ways dramatically different. Wooden tenements were generally two or two and a half stories tall. Most had been designed to hold an artisan's or shopkeeper's place of business, his family, and perhaps a few of his employees. These buildings, dozens of which still stood in the 1850s, generally measured about twenty to twenty-five feet wide and twenty-five to thirty feet deep. Other wooden structures had been built as workshops, stables, or for mixed commercial/residential use, and might be three stories tall and up to forty feet deep. Sometimes two or three of these were crowded into a single 25-by-100-foot standard lot. By the 1850s, landlords had carved most of them into tenements, creating in each building two to five apartments plus commercial space for a shop or saloon in the front of the house on the ground floor.[8]

Before the Civil War, these wooden tenements—"so old and rotten that they seem ready to tumble together into a vast rubbish-heap"—were considered Five Points' worst, "the oldest, most ricketty, wooden buildings" in the city. Many apartments in these structures consisted of a single room, which often had to provide shelter for an entire family. A Health Department investigation noted that in some dwellings, especially those in attics and basements, *"the ceilings . . . were too low to allow the inmates to stand erect."* The bedrooms were typically windowless, and the resulting lack of ventilation and air circulation created an "atmosphere productive of the most offensive and malignant diseases."[9]

The wooden tenements also typically failed to keep out the elements. They were so drafty that tenants commonly posted handbills on the walls, not for decoration but as insulation. "Open to the wind and the storm— and far less comfortable than the buildings used as *barns* or cattle-stalls," Five Points' "wretched dens" of wood were "exposed to all the rigors of inclement weather, and to every possible cause of wretchedness and suffering," complained the *Courier and Enquirer.* "We have known cases in which nearly a *dozen* persons were forced to live in one small room, less than ten feet square, immediately under an old, dilapidated roof, which let in a full tithe of the rain that fell upon it, and entirely destitute of any means of keeping warm." Visitors commonly found snow drifting in the entranceways, halls, and sometimes even the apartments themselves. Even if the snow could be kept outside, it might make its way inside in another form, for "most of the roofs were leaky, and the basements, after every rain were flooded with filthy water."[10]

Water was not the only thing that spilled into these tenements when it rained. Because their original owners had designed these small frame buildings for far fewer people, the hordes now occupying them severely overtaxed the backyard outhouses. A Health Department report noted that the commodes of these wooden tenements "were in a most filthy and disgusting condition; in several places there were accumulations of stagnant fluid, full of all sorts of putrefying matter, the effluvia from which was intolerable." Few of the wooden tenements were connected to sewers in the antebellum years, so heavy rains tended to wash outhouse "effluvia" into Five Points basements.[11]

By 1855, brick tenements outnumbered those of wood in Five Points by a ratio of about three to two. Much taller and deeper than frame structures, the brick buildings housed in that year 76 percent of the neighborhood's residents. Many brick tenements were just as offensive. In the four-story brick building at 17 Baxter,* for example, legislative investigators found "walls damp, rooms dark, passages filthy, and with no sort of ventilation." These brick tenements were built in one of two patterns. The most common design in the antebellum years called for a structure twenty-five feet wide by fifty feet deep. Such buildings generally reached three, four, or (especially after 1845) five stories in height. Each floor above the ground floor usually contained four two-room apartments; the front half of the ground floor generally housed a store or saloon. Apartment dimensions tended to be identical. The main room of each two-room apartment, which served as kitchen, living room, and dining room, usually measured about twelve feet square and typically had two windows, facing either the street or the yard. The second room, known as the "sleeping closet," was aptly named, for it was windowless and hardly bigger than a modern walk-in closet, usually about eight by ten feet. Thus the entire apartment covered just 225 square feet.[12]

In a triumph of efficiency over humanity, landlords often built a second brick tenement in the backyard behind the front building. These rear tenements generally measured twenty-five by twenty-five feet (precisely half the size of the front buildings) and were divided into two two-room apartments per floor. Anticipating that other rear tenements would be built adjacent to their own, landlords put no windows on the backs or sides of these structures. The only windows overlooked the outhouses in

---

* For reasons that will be discussed at the end of this chapter, city lawmakers in 1854 decided to change the names of Five Points' four most notorious streets. Orange became Baxter, Anthony become Worth, Cross became Park, and Little Water became Mission Place. Because most of the tenement descriptions in this chapter date from just after 1854, I will for the sake of consistency use the new street names throughout this chapter.

the yard, "thick with mephitic gases, and nauseous from the effluvia of decaying matter and pools of stagnant water." As a result, rear tenements were "suffused with the odor emanating from the cesspools." Rarely did enough fresh air reach them to allow these noxious odors to escape. "These tumbling and squalid rookeries," concluded an investigative committee, are ". . . the most repulsive features of the tenant-house system."[13]

Some landlords, not satisfied with two tenements, sought to cram even more dwelling space into their lots. "The crazy pigeon-holes of the Five Points," as *Harper's Weekly* described them, were legendary throughout the city. "Every inch . . . is covered by structures of various kinds and degrees of discomfort, into which is crowded the reeking, seething mass of poverty, vice, sickness, and wretchedness." Some property owners managed to fit a third tenement onto their lots. Others converted cellars, attics, and even storage areas into apartments. Still others erected tiny shacks in yards in order to squeeze a few extra dollars in rent from their property.[14]

Whether brick or frame, front or rear, most Five Points tenements were terribly overcrowded. Press reports described seven, ten, or even fifteen people living in a single room. But how typical were such horror stories? According to the census, the typical two-room dwelling held on average "only" five people per apartment. Yet 46 percent of these apartments housed six or more people, and one in six accommodated eight or more. With so many people per apartment, and so many buildings per lot, the population density of the Sixth Ward in the 1850s (310.4 per acre) exceeded that of any other district in the city. With the possible exception of one or two sections of London, antebellum Five Points was the most densely populated neighborhood in the world.[15]

Five Pointers adjusted to this crowding in a number of ways. Squeezing in enough beds for all the inhabitants always presented a challenge. Sometimes a bed doubled as a couch or was covered with a board for use as a table or countertop during the day. In many dwellings, the "beds" were merely piles of rags or straw covered with "bed clothes" (sheets), which could easily be pushed out of the way when the room was too crowded. Children especially slept on such bedding. In the apartment of one Italian family, one child slept "under the bed, another under the table, a third by the stove, and the fourth at liberty to roll over any of her sisters." Children lucky enough to have beds usually shared them with their siblings. One remembered sleeping head to toe with his four brothers and sisters so they could all fit in the single bed allotted to them. Sometimes squeezing an extra bed into the apartment to reduce such overcrowded sleeping arrangements meant partially blocking a door, which might prove deadly should fire break out. Beds that folded into the wall or stacked on top of each other would have significantly reduced such crowding, but such luxuries were beyond the means of most Five Pointers.[16]

Privacy in such conditions was virtually impossible. Families strategically hung curtains, prints, and handbills to create private spaces within the tiny apartments, especially around the parents' bed. But since these added to the clutter and often made the small spaces seem even tinier, not everyone bothered. Given that many of the immigrants, especially the Irish and the Italians, had lived in one-room huts in Europe, these conditions were at least familiar to them. But as they adapted to nineteenth-century American ideals of decorum and separation of the sexes, this lack of privacy must have been mortifying, especially for women.[17]

A crowded apartment was not necessarily a cluttered one. Visitors to Five Points usually found the dwellings rather bare by middle-class New York standards. One investigator asserted that each abode featured "the same bare floors, the same blank walls, the same pine tables, broken chairs and ragged bedding." For the most destitute, this certainly would have been the case. They often had to pawn their possessions to buy food and fuel. Impoverished widows with many children to support and families whose main breadwinner could not work for long periods due to illness were most likely to live in this state. Others kept possessions to a minimum because they moved so frequently, changing apartments once a year or even more often as their employment fortunes rose and fell.

But more often than not, Five Pointers did what they could to give their rooms a comfortable, homelike quality. An 1859 survey of tenement apartments in the *New York Times* found that most contained "lithographs, in high colors, of the crucifixion, Christ in the manger, Mary at the Annunciation, the Parting Lovers, and JAMES BUCHANAN." Many had "broad posters" bearing slogans such as " 'True Democrats meet here'; or, 'Friends of good oysters call in,' pasted over the bed," a reference to the free food offered at political rallies. The same reporter noted mantels filled with bric-à-brac in many apartments. An archaeological dig in Five Points in the 1990s uncovered toys of every description, commemorative cups and saucers, cologne and hair tonic, all indicating that the majority of the neighborhood's residents could afford more than the barest necessities. Five Pointers did not usually live in the utter destitution that most often attracted the attention of the press.[18]

"THE MOST REPULSIVE HOLES THAT EVER A HUMAN BEING WAS FORCED TO SLEEP IN"

Five Points' unusually high population density resulted not merely from landlords' greed but also from the custom of some tenement dwellers to sublet space in their apartments to non-family members. Twenty-eight percent of Five Points families took in boarders. Of those who did, two-thirds rented space to only one or two non-family members. But in the most decrepit parts of the neighborhood, such as Baxter and Mulberry Streets between Park and Bayard, boarders abounded. Three-quarters of the sixteen apartments at 31 Baxter Street, for example, had lodgers in 1855. Boarders lived in ten of the fourteen apartments in the rear building at 51 Mulberry in that same year. Those who rented space to outsiders generally offered two types of arrangements. A "boarder" paid for both food and a place to sleep, while a "lodger" paid for sleeping space only. Lodging and boarding allowed recent immigrants to save money while seeking work to pay for the emigration of other family members. But many who had no such obligations chose to board anyway. Young immigrants often lived in boardinghouses until they got married. For older bachelors, living in someone else's home was a convenient means to obtain both shelter and meals. Widows often could afford no other kind of living arrangement. All told, one in seven Five Pointers lived in a non-family member's apartment.[19]

Widows were most likely to take in lodgers; nearly two in five widows did so. Barbara Sullivan, a forty-six-year-old widow from the Tuosist portion of the Landsdowne estate in Kerry, lived in the rear tenement at 39 Baxter in the mid-1850s with her six children, who ranged in age from four to sixteen when they arrived in New York in 1851. In 1855, Sullivan, her children, and her son-in-law shared her apartment with six lodgers: a forty-year-old widowed ragpicker, her fifteen-year-old newsboy son, a forty-year-old widowed peddler, and the peddler's three children. Johanna McCarty, a forty-five-year-old widow with five children, took in eight lodgers in her three-room apartment at 31 Baxter in 1855.[20]

Many non-widows took in boarders as well. In the rear building at 51 Mulberry Street, Patrick Hogan and his wife Mary took in one boarder; the Fox family rented space to two lodgers; the Shields, McCormacks, Mullins, and McManuses had three lodgers each; the Kavans and Conways four lodgers each; the Hanlans eight lodgers and a boarder; and widow Mary Sullivan one lodger. Yet 51 Mulberry and 31 Baxter held many more boarders than average. The front and rear buildings at 65 Mott were more typical. Seven of the sixteen apartments did not house any lodgers in 1850. Of the nine that did, five had just a single boarder.[21]

Although most Five Points lodgers lived in private homes, some patronized commercial boardinghouses. In New York City, these ran the gamut from elegant establishments catering to professionals, to modest mechanics' boardinghouses that were crowded but clean and respectable, to basement flophouses overflowing with people and filth. Five Points, of course, contained none of the refined residences, only a sprinkling of the mechanics' abodes, and dozens of the worst class.

Most of the seediest boardinghouses were located in cellars, where rent was cheapest and there were few other uses for the space. Cellar dwelling peaked in the early 1850s, as desperately poor immigrants flooding into the city sought to save every possible penny in order to finance the emigration of spouses, children, parents, and siblings. A *New York Tribune* exposé at midcentury found that the Sixth Ward contained 285 basements with 1,156 occupants, meaning that approximately 1 in 17 residents lived in a basement. At least half that number probably lived in Five Points, many in cellar-level lodging houses.[22]

The overcrowding in Five Points boardinghouses was terrible. Even before the heaviest immigration had begun, a friend of minister Samuel Prime saw lodging houses in Five Points where the rooms were "as thickly covered with bodies as a field of battle could be with the slain." In many of these establishments, lodgers slept on two-tiered bunks, which often consisted of canvas stretched between two wooden rails. When business was brisk, proprietors created a third tier by placing other customers on the floor underneath the lowest bunk. Others slept on bed frames covered with straw. Cellar lodging rooms were both crowded and, with so many dirty lodgers squeezing into windowless bedrooms, filthy and smelly as well. "Without air, without light, filled with damp vapor from the mildewed walls, and with vermin in ratio to the dirtiness of the inhabitants," commented the *Tribune*, "they are the most repulsive holes that ever a human being was forced to sleep in. There is not a farmer's hog-pen in the country, that is not immeasurably ahead of them in point of health—often in point of cleanliness." Doctors who worked in the tenement districts could immediately spot the cellar dwellers among their patients. "If the whitened and cadaverous countenance should be an insufficient guide," explained one, "*the odor of the person* will remove all doubt; a musty smell, which a damp cellar only can impart, pervades every article of dress, the woolens more particularly, as well as the hair and skin." In a neighborhood filled with hardship and privation, the suffering of these cellar dwellers was perhaps the worst of all.[23]

Other dives in Five Points were mere flophouses for drunks and street people, charging as little as three cents for a bed or even one cent per night for a place on the floor. Beds pushed against the walls of saloons and dance halls also catered to the lowest of the low, men and women who paid two

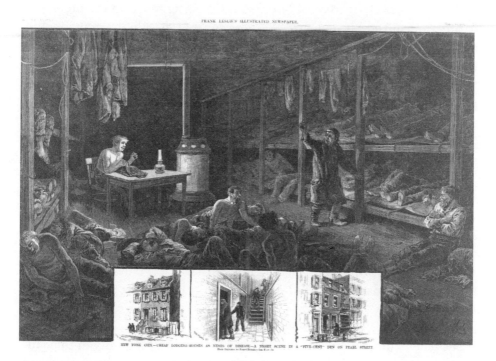

Basement boardinghouse at 508 Pearl Street, from *Frank Leslie's Illustrated Newspaper* (March 18, 1882): 56–57. Collection of the Library of Congress.

or three cents to sleep in full view of the other customers. A basement lodging house at 35 Baxter, "one of the filthiest, blackest holes" the *Times* reporter had ever seen, nonetheless charged six cents per night or "three shillings" (37½ cents) per week excluding food, a sure sign that it was at least a step or two above those catering to the most down-and-out.

There were cleaner, less crowded boardinghouses in Five Points too, but they received far less attention in the press. Many were large operations, occupying whole buildings and employing cooks and servants. In Five Points, these establishments especially catered to Christian Germans and tended to locate on Mott and Elizabeth Streets. One such boardinghouse was at 66 Mott, run by thirty-six-year-old Ignatz Kunz. Seventeen young German-speaking artisans boarded there in 1855, including carpenters, blacksmiths, gas fitters, and a goldbeater. Few had lived in the city long and none was married. They undoubtedly enjoyed flirting with the establishment's two young German "servant girls," Christiana and Presence, who had immigrated to New York in 1854. Kunz, who had himself emigrated from Germany in 1845, also ran a porterhouse on the premises. If Kunz organized his concern like most of its type, the boarders would have slept two to a bed, and four or six to a room. At breakfast and dinner, they could look forward to hearty meals. A British immigrant described the typical breakfast as consisting of "coffee, bread and butter, beefsteaks, pork or mutton chops, sausages, pickles, and buckwheat cakes with molasses. This is the boarding house mode of stuffing."[24]

"THE MOST SICKENING AND PESTILENTIAL STENCHES"

In the dozen or so years after 1845, when immigrants poured into Five Points, landlords quickened the pace of new construction, replacing more and more of the two- to three-story wooden tenements with four- to five-story brick buildings. Five Pointers might have been expected to applaud the change. But while reformers believed that brick tenements were an improvement, many of the buildings turned out to be just as miserable to live in.

Because brick tenements were so big (both taller and deeper than previous tenements), they tended to be very dark inside, especially in the hallways above the first floor. Either to save money or out of fear of starting a fire, landlords almost never provided gas lighting. Little light made its way up from the front door because in order to maximize living space, architects designed these buildings with extremely steep staircases. "No cave or dungeon was ever darker," complained one charitable worker about the stairway in a lower Mulberry Street tenement in 1867. A newspaper reporter encountered similar conditions climbing the stairs of a Baxter Street tenement in the 1890s, noting that "it was necessary to grope our way to the top by lighting matches on every landing." An antebellum investigative committee found these same conditions in both brick and wooden tenements, stating that "not only were the stairways crooked and inordinately steep, but they were so dark that faces could not be distinguished." Treacherously dark hallways were a consistent complaint of Five Points reformers and residents alike.[25]

The dark, steep stairways became more of an issue as tenements grew taller, for by the 1850s few landlords built front tenements of less than five stories. The thought of carrying young children, groceries, or pails of water up three, four, or even five flights of these steep, dark stairs filled many a housewife with dread. Some older women, especially those with bad backs or arthritic knees, rarely left their apartments for fear of falling, and stories of neighbors injuring themselves in stairway spills were a staple of tenement gossip.[26]

Curiously, the tallest tenement in nineteenth-century Five Points was apparently the very first New York building built specifically to serve as a tenement. This seven-story building, which still stands at 65 Mott Street, is a living monument to the evils of the tenement system. Historians have generally cited a building erected on the Lower East Side in 1833 by iron manufacturer James P. Allaire as the city's first designed tenement, basing this assertion on the late-nineteenth-century reminiscences of New Yorker Charles Haswell. But the building at 65 Mott almost certainly predates Allaire's structure by nearly a decade. According to an 1879 article in the building trades journal *Plumber and Sanitary Engineer*, 65 Mott Street "has been occupied some *fifty-five* years." This would date the building's construction to 1824. Its seven stories—a height then unprecedented for a dwelling place—dwarfed the surrounding two-story wooden homes and must have made quite a spectacle when it was first built. Even in the 1880s, half a century after its construction, the *Times* complained that the tenement "stands out like a wart growing on the top of a festering sore. It is the crowning glory of tenement-houses." Behind it stood a five-story rear tenement, meaning that at least thirty-four and probably thirty-six two-room apartments had been crowded onto this 2,450-square-foot property. Even by the end of the nineteenth century, no other landlord in Five Points had the nerve to squeeze so many families into so small a space. And like the other tall tenements in Five Points, their hallways were steeped in pitch black darkness even on the sunniest days.[27]

Just as infamous as Five Points' dark passageways were the layers of dirt that begrimed so many of its tenements. Describing a building on Little Water Street, a state investigative committee found that "the floors were covered with dirt, which had lain so long that, with occasional slops of water and continued treading on, it had the appearance of the greasy refuse of a woolen mill. There were sluggish, yellow drops pending from the low ceilings, and a dank, green slime upon the walls." The city inspector stated that the typical Five Points tenement contained walls "with the plaster broken off in many places, exposing the lath and beams, and leaving openings for the escape from within of the effluvia of vermin, dead and alive." Where the walls remained intact, they were "smeared with the blood of unmentionable insects, and dirt of all indescribable colours."[28]

Five Points tenements became so dirty in part because their residents invariably tracked in filth from the neighborhood's foul streets. New York streets were reputed to be the dirtiest in antebellum America. For decades citizens had thrown their garbage into the gutters, hoping that scavenging pigs would eat the mess or that rain would wash it away. Homeowners were supposed to sweep garbage into piles for the city to cart away, but the carts never came. As a result, street traffic mashed this household refuse together with the droppings of horses and other animals to create an inches-thick sheet of putrefying muck, which when it rained or snowed became particularly vile. Only when city fathers feared an outbreak of cholera in 1832 did the city properly clean its streets for the first time. When workers chopped and scraped the sludge off, revealing the paved streets below, an old woman who had lived in New York all her life purportedly asked: "'Where in the world did all those [paving] stones come from? . . . I never knew that the streets were covered with stones before.'"[29]

Although the city subsequently created a street-cleaning department, it did little to improve Five Points' thoroughfares. Because the district was so crowded, the garbage overwhelmed the new system. "The Sixth Ward can claim the preeminence of being the dirtiest Ward of the dirtiest City in the world," claimed one writer in 1848, citing Baxter and Worth Streets as the worst in the district. When the *Tribune* compiled a list of New York's filthiest thoroughfares two years later, it included virtually every block in the Five Points neighborhood. Not surprisingly, Baxter and Mulberry Streets, the most densely populated in the district, were the worst. "The latter street, from Canal to Chatham st., is a continual depository of garbage," noted the *Tribune* on a Tuesday in 1865, "and although it was cleaned on Friday, hundreds of loads have accumulated since that time, and the stench arising therefore is intolerable." According to another investigative report, "in the winter the filth and garbage, etc., accumulate in the streets, to the depth sometimes of two or three feet. The garbage boxes are a perpetual source of nuisance in the streets, filth and offal being thrown all around them, pools of filthy water in many instances remaining in the gutters." From this "decaying vegetable matter, and filth of every conceivable kind" emanated "the most sickening and pestilential stenches." These last two reports detailed conditions at the end of the Civil War when Five Points thoroughfares were much cleaner than they had been in the 1830s and '40s. One can hardly imagine how the streets had looked and smelled in those antebellum decades.[30]

With so much dirt and grime encrusting their neighborhood streets, Five Points tenement dwellers inevitably dragged much of that mess into their homes on shoes and clothes. Because Five Pointers did not usually own much clothing, they often had to wear their dirty clothes for quite some time. Clothing could not be washed on a whim since it might take days to dry. "Hard wash-days"—typically Mondays—provided some of the most unpleasant memories for tenement housewives such as those in Five Points. Mothers bribed children with candy money on wash day to keep them out of the house so they could devote their full attention and the entire space of the apartment to the arduous task at hand. They first made numerous trips up and down the stairs to haul water up from the yard. Then they heated the water on the stove and set to work scrubbing.

Drying the wash was actually the most dreaded task. There were many options, all involving some risk. The advantage of living on a low floor (with fewer flights of stairs to climb) became a disadvantage on wash day, because when hanging your laundry out to dry, "someone else might put out a red wash or a blue wash above it, and it drips down and makes you do

572   FRANK LESLIE'S ILLUSTRATED NEWSPAPER.   [August 2, 1879.

HOW THE STREET-CLEANING AUTHORITIES IN NEW YORK GUARD AGAINST SUMMER EPIDEMICS.

FATHER KNICKERBOCKER—"*Great heavens! is this all my descendants can do to keep this great city healthy!*"
REPRESENTATIVE OF THE STREET-CLEANING DEPARTMENT—"*Begorra, if yez think yez can scrape a mile of strate a day wid sich a brum better nor me, yez better thry it!*"

Though this was meant to be a humorous image, Five Points streets were often this dirty, especially in the pre–Civil War years. Street sweeping was hard work, but the jobs were much sought after, and were usually given as rewards to those who toiled faithfully for neighborhood political leaders. The "S.C.D." on this Irishman's hat stands for Street Cleaning Department. *Frank Leslie's Illustrated Newspaper* (August 2, 1879): 372. Collection of the Library of Congress.

your wash all over again." Similarly, "the women up over you shake their bedclothes and rugs over your clothes," complained one lower-level tenement dweller of the dust and dirt that would drop onto her briefly clean clothing.[31]

The perils of line drying applied to just half the tenement dwellers, because only those in apartments facing the yard had access to the clotheslines. "Those who live in the back have lines," testified an envious tenement resident before an investigative committee, "a luxury which can only be truly appreciated by those who must carry every bit of their wash up three or four flights of stairs to the roof, and on particularly cold winter days, it is almost enough to make people determine to wear their clothing longer." Roof drying avoided some of the problems of line drying, but it carried its own risks. If you hung your clothes on the roof, complained one tenement housewife, "you must watch them or they disappear. Only people who live in the back have pulleys, and even then one sheet and tablecloth fill the line." For some, roof drying was not an option. One housewife could not bring her clothes to the roof because climbing the stairs "makes my heart beat so." Children could be detailed to stand guard over the family's drying clothing, but they often abandoned their posts due to cold and boredom.[32]

Even if a housewife miraculously managed to cleanse the family wardrobe, the bodies underneath that clothing were bathed so rarely that they must have smelled awful anyway. No one in antebellum America bathed frequently. But tenement dwellers such as those in Five Points did so least of all, not out of any cultural aversion to cleanliness but because they had no access to bathing facilities. Tubs were not a standard tenement feature. They were expensive, and even if one could afford a tub, where would it fit? Those who did own tubs generally stored coal in them, limiting bathing to those days when the coal supply was nearly exhausted. Finally, drawing a bath was a laborious task, as water had to be hauled up from the yard, a bucket at a time, and then heated (again in small quantities) on the stove. This made bathing expensive as well, because coal was dear to a tenement family.

No matter how clean their clothes, bodies, or apartments might have been, the horrid stenches emanating from their backyards—and especially from the outhouses located there—would have made apartment life in Five Points an olfactory nightmare. There were essentially three types of toilet facilities in antebellum tenement yards. The most modern and sophisticated connected the outdoor toilets directly to sewer lines, flushing sewage directly and immediately away from the tenement yard. But very few Five Points tenements could boast such toilets by the Civil War, in part because few streets in the neighborhood were connected to the sewers. In 1857, only one-quarter of the city had sewer lines, and few of these were located in Five Points. Even in 1865, the only streets in Five Points with sewer lines were Centre, Pearl, and Worth, as well as Mott and Mulberry above Bayard. But just because a street had a sewer did not mean that landlords necessarily connected their buildings to it. Legislation enacted in 1867 required *new* buildings to tap into sewer lines, but did not require the same of existing structures. Few of the old wooden tenements on Worth, Baxter, and Park Streets would have been connected in the Civil War period.

Instead, most buildings had either cesspools or "school sinks." A cesspool in theory had to be emptied periodically. Judging by the complaints of tenants, such cleanings were rare. A school sink, in contrast, was a kind of cesspool connected to the sewers. Sewage collected below the commodes in a trough, which someone had to empty periodically by opening a sluice gate to the sewer lines. Property agents did not perform this task—which was nearly as unpleasant as emptying a cesspool—as frequently as necessary. In addition, the connection between the trough and the sewer line often became clogged. Raw sewage thus often sat festering in the backyards of the tenements for weeks or months at a time.[33]

The wooden outhouses above these pits were incredibly dirty, in part because their roofs and walls admitted too many of nature's elements, and in part because they were overused and undercleaned. The wooden seats were often rotting away. "To *look at the abominable water-closets that exist almost every where*" in Five Points, lamented one of the few publications willing to broach this delicate subject, "and then imagine that women and children are compelled to resort to them, is almost too much for human endurance." Tenants usually blamed one another for the mess, and were thus unwilling to clean the stalls. As a result, many resorted to chamber pots, which could be emptied into the outhouse when convenient, or out the window into the yard when it was dark.[34]

The yards in which these outhouses sat were thus revolting masses of mud, excrement, and garbage. Trash littered the yards both because it was stored there until put on the street, and also because tenants tossed it from their windows. They did so sometimes out of laziness, sometimes because it was too cold or rainy to go outside, and sometimes to avoid "climbing the dark stairs and running the risk of breaking one's legs," admitted one early-twentieth-century tenement dweller. "In some cases it is almost a necessity to throw it out, the premium on space is so high in their tiny kitchens . . . and just enough room to turn about." The combination of decaying and rotting animal and vegetable matter littering the yards attracted all sorts of vermin. In an attempt to cover up this filth, landlords often laid wooden boards over the ground in the yards, but the stench and effluvia still percolated up from beneath them. In one yard, for example, the boards when pressed yielded "even in dry weather, a thick greenish fluid." Not surprisingly, the Sixth Ward's sanitary inspector found that only 24 of the ward's 609 tenements were in "good sanitary condition" in 1865.[35]

Even if sewage made its way out of the tenement yard and into the sewer system, its odor continued to foul the neighborhood. Sewage was supposed to run through culverts under the street, but they were open to the air through grates at intersections. In addition, the Sixth Ward's culverts were "often choked up on account of the large amount of filth and garbage thrown into the gutters, and which is carried down the sewers." A mixture of sewage, trash, and "filthy water" might "stand several days before an outlet is cleared for it . . . in this pestilential locality." Even when the culverts were not blocked, the sewage did not flow very well, especially in low-lying areas such as Five Points. Early New York sewers were really "*one elongated cesspool*," insisted an 1859 report, "throwing out its noxious gases . . . at every opening on the corners of the streets, to fill and surround the dwellings and be inhaled with every breath." Every antebellum New York neighborhood was dirty by modern standards, but Five Points was the dirtiest. Newcomers never failed to comment upon the revolting smells of the neighborhood and the stench of its worst tenements.[36]

"The little ones cried and cried from cold"

The constant noise of tenement life probably bothered neighborhood residents just as much as the smells. The thin interior walls in both wooden and brick buildings blocked few sounds. The combination of wood floors and little carpeting meant that virtually no movement from above could escape the attention of those below. Children shouting, spouses fighting, and babies wailing all contributed to the cacophony, often making sleep impossible. A newspaper editor listed noise complaints as one of the most frequent causes of fights between tenement families. Street noise plagued those in the front apartments, while in the rear the sound from neighbors in buildings facing them (usually only twenty-five feet or less away) also caused distress. Windows that would not close properly as well as loose or missing panes exacerbated the problem, as did the universal practice of leaving apartment doors open for ventilation.[37]

Extremes of heat and cold—not outside but within the tenements—also afflicted Five Pointers. Immigrants from the temperate British Isles, especially those from Ireland, had never experienced freezing winters or sweltering, humid summers in their native lands. In the older buildings, cold posed the most serious problem. The exterior walls of wooden tenements were not insulated, and cold winds whistled relentlessly through their cracks, as well as through broken or improperly hung windows. Residents frequently lacked the fuel to heat these homes adequately. In Ireland, even the poorest peasant could usually find free turf to warm his cabin and cook his food. In New York, the Irish had to buy fuel (usually coal by the 1840s) to heat their stoves, and coal was expensive. As a result, tenement children were usually expected to scavenge for coal. The Irish-American journalist Owen Kildare remembered that as a destitute child in the Fourth Ward (just east of Five Points), his stepparents ordered him to find or steal ten pieces of coal each day. When scavenging failed to produce an adequate supply, desperately poor Five Pointers resorted to burning their doors, furniture, and bedding, especially on bitterly cold days and nights.[38]

Yet few froze to death. Neighbors usually intervened before suffering could turn fatal. "The kindness of these poor people to each other," commented the journal of a Five Points charitable group, "is frequently astonishing, but must be witnessed to be appreciated." Neighbors might bring cases of hardship to the attention of the Five Points Mission or the Five Points House of Industry after their establishment in the early 1850s. A House of Industry publication described an incident in which its missionaries found on Worth Street "a woman and five children in a room without a fire, and for the last two days they had had no food save a morsel given them by a neighbor almost as poor as themselves. . . . What little furniture they possessed had been burned for fuel, and when this last resource was gone, the little ones cried and cried from cold." Someone did freeze to death on Baxter Street in the winter of 1860–61, but such cases were rare. As a result, the *Tribune* could boast in 1864 that the woman who had "perished with cold and was eaten of rats on Mulberry-street is forgotten long ago." Nonetheless, the cold kept many a Five Pointer awake at night, made others sick, and was a source of constant worry for those of limited means.[39]

As tall brick tenements replaced small wooden hovels, heat became the greater issue. In order to support themselves, five- and six-story tenements were generally constructed with one-foot-thick exterior brick walls which kept out the cold fairly well, though these buildings were still not comfortably warm. But a brick tenement "in a hot spell becomes something little more tolerable than a sweat-box," noted *Frank Leslie's Illustrated Newspaper*. Poor ventilation and air circulation contributed to the oppressive temperatures. Open windows brought no relief to the stifling apartments, as cooler outdoor air stubbornly refused to flow inside. Those living on the upper floors suffered most in the summer, as the heat wafted persistently upward. During the day and evening, tenement dwellers poured into the streets to escape the indoor infernos, but at night there was little relief. Referring to the tiny windowless bedrooms that predominated in these buildings, a reporter from *Frank Leslie's* asserted that "the very idea of refreshing slumber in one of the seething little ovens which must usually shelter not one, but several persons, and sometimes a whole family, appears ridiculous." Many moved their beds near the living-room windows, but for half the tenement residents this meant confronting the stench emanating from the outhouses. Those lucky enough to have fire escapes slept on them during heat waves. Others sought relief on roofs, stoops, and even sidewalks, "until it is almost impossible to pass along without stepping upon a human body." Occasionally, newspapers would report an injury or even a death as a sleeping tenement dweller fell from a window ledge or fire escape.[40]

The fire escapes where so many Five Pointers spent sweltering summer nights were only erected at about the time of the Civil War. In 1860, the New York legislature enacted the first New York law mandating their installation, though the legislation stipulated only that landlords put them on new buildings housing eight or more families. A horrible Sixth Ward fire during the 1860 legislative session had helped convince the lawmakers to enact this limited statute. It broke out on the night of Thursday, February 2, just a block west of the Five Points neighborhood at 142 Elm Street. The blaze started in the basement wood bins of the four-year-old, six-story brick tenement and spread quickly up the steep stairwell, trapping many of those living in the uppermost apartments. Of the nine people killed in the blaze, one had lived on the third floor, two on the fourth, and five on the fifth. Many of those on the top floors survived only by jumping twenty-five feet from a fifth-floor apartment window down to the roof of a two-story building next door.[41]

As deadly fires continued to plague the city's tenement districts, the legislature in 1862 enacted a law mandating that *all* buildings housing eight or more families install fire escapes. By 1865, nearly half the Sixth Ward's tenements had them, although many landlords ignored the requirement, and smaller buildings were still exempted. One of these was the

Sleeping outdoors to avoid the tenement heat. *Frank Leslie's Illustrated Newspaper* (August 12, 1882): 392–93. Collection of the Library of Congress.

two-and-a-half-story wooden tenement at 15 Baxter Street, where in 1863 a fire killed three women and one child. The blaze started late at night and spread upstairs to the crowded attic, whose inhabitants "became frantic with fear, and rent the stillness of midnight with their piercing shrieks, rendering the scene one of horror and despair." Mrs. Collins and her lodgers, Mr. and Mrs. Sands, jumped safely to the street from their front attic room, though Mr. Sands suffered serious burns. In the other attic rooms, where Bridget Tierney kept eleven boarders, four died in the blaze. The dead included Alice Murphy, thirty-five, and her daughter aged four; Sarah Gray, thirty-five, and Mary Jane McMasters, about thirty, found dead in her bed. Gray's eleven-year-old son and McMasters's fifteen-year-old son survived by jumping to the roof of a rear building. The *Herald* reported that "Hugh Devier and his wife Catharine, who is blind, embraced each other and jumped from the window together, and miraculously escaped with only a few bruises." Tierney later testified that those who perished could also have jumped "had they not been under the influence of liquor." An African-American man living in a first-floor rear apartment and a female Irish immigrant living above him blamed each other for starting the blaze. Other tenants testified that both had been drunk and therefore could not be trusted to remember what had happened. Fire was a constant threat and concern to Five Points residents, one they knew could end their lives at any moment.[42]

"For misery, degradation, filth, and multitudes they cannot be exceeded"

The worst tenements in Five Points were the Old Brewery and those in Cow Bay. As one antebellum writer noted, the Old Brewery and Cow Bay together comprised "the two most famous spots in this dark region. For misery, degradation, filth, and multitudes they cannot be exceeded."[43] Cow Bay was the nickname of the portion of Little Water Street (later Mission Place) that ran north from Worth. It was actually a cul-de-sac, thirty feet wide at the entrance, but "narrowing, with crooked, uneven lines, back to a point about a hundred feet from the entrance," where the street abruptly ended surrounded by decrepit wooden tenements. Reputed to have once been a cow path used by local cattlemen to reach the Collect Pond, Cow Bay by the late 1840s rivaled the Old Brewery for "the extreme wretchedness which abounds on every hand." After the demolition of the Old Brewery in 1852, journalists could describe Cow Bay as "the very lowest and worst place in New-York."[44]

Saloons frequented by the most dangerous characters, even by Five Points standards, occupied the front ground-floor room of virtually every building in Cow Bay. In addition, the tenements were home to an especially heterogeneous mixture of races and nationalities. Blacks had originally dominated the infamous block, especially chimney sweeps, who constituted a significant portion of the city's African-American population. As late as 1849, one newspaper claimed that four hundred blacks lived in five Cow Bay tenements. While this was probably an exaggeration, it nonetheless indicates their long-standing presence there. At midcentury, journalist George Foster noted that Cow Bay "is chiefly celebrated in profane history as being the battle-field of the negroes and police. . . . Two memorable occasions, at least, have recently occurred in which 'Cow Bay' was rendered classic ground by the set fights which took place within its purlieus between the police and the fighting-men of the Ethiopian tribes." During the 1850s, however, the black presence at Cow Bay diminished rapidly. The number of African Americans recorded by census takers fell from one hundred twenty in 1850 to thirty-five in 1855. During the 1850s, Italians and Kerry Irish, "the poorest of the city poor," filled these "dens of misery" left vacant by the black exodus. The prostitutes, thieves, alcoholics, and interracial couples who concentrated in Cow Bay added to its scandalous reputation.[45]

Cow Bay horror stories abounded. The superintendent of the Five Points House of Industry led a tour of Cow Bay that found "a number of both sexes, huddled together like swine—some almost in a state of nudity. Not the slightest shame was apparent at their exposure before each other, nor before the visitors. The stench in this garret was most intolerable," caused by "a perfect cesspool of ordure, in a corner." Violent fights, sometimes ending in death, and typically alcohol-induced, were also common.[46]

The poor found Cow Bay equally offensive. Tom Nolan told those attending a Five Points temperance meeting that if they wanted to see the Cow Bay building he had lived in during his drinking days, "saturate your handkerchief with camphor, so that you can endure the horrid stench, and enter. Grope your way through the long, narrow passage—turn to the right up the dark and dangerous stairway; be careful where you place your foot around the lower step, or in the corners of the broad stairs, for it is more than shoe-mouth deep of steaming filth."[47]

Cow Bay may have been as crowded as the Old Brewery. Two married couples plus a female lodger who "sometimes has company" lived in the ten-by-twelve-foot back room of one three-room apartment. Five men and women lived in the front room, which measured eight by fourteen feet. The windowless middle room, a mere six by seven, was occupied by a lone woman. In the apartment above this one, with identical dimensions, the back room held a German widow with two boys, a black husband and wife, and a female lodger. The dark, tiny center room held a German woman, her black husband, and a four-year-old white "lodger," perhaps an orphan. Incredibly, these were not even the most crowded Cow Bay dwellings. An 1857 inspection found 23 families—179 people in all—living in just 15 rooms.[48]

Although they received far less publicity at this point than the Old Brewery or Cow Bay, the tenements along the east side of Baxter Street just north of the Five Points intersection were nearly as miserable. After demolition crews tore down most of the Cow Bay hovels to make room for an expanded Five Points House of Industry in the 1860s, this became the most notorious portion of the neighborhood. The block where these tenements were located, bounded by Baxter, Bayard, Mulberry, and Park Streets, would eventually become known as "Mulberry Bend." Mulberry Bend represented to postbellum Americans the same depravity and squalor that prewar New Yorkers associated with Cow Bay and the Old Brewery. But even in the 1850s, conditions in Mulberry Bend were already miserable. Bottle Alley, the courtyard at the rear of 47 and 49 Baxter Street that *Harper's Weekly* and Jacob Riis would make famous in the 1880s and 1890s, had a nasty reputation in the antebellum era. Longtime New Yorker Charles Haswell remembered that even in the 1840s, Bottle Alley had been a favorite haunt of murderers and thieves. No descriptions of the Bottle Alley tenements themselves survive from the antebellum period. We do know, however, that recent Sligo immigrants concentrated there.

Conditions deteriorated as one moved down Baxter Street from Bottle Alley toward the Five Points intersection. At 39 Baxter, whose front and rear wooden tenements were dominated by Lansdowne immigrants, an investigative committee in the mid-1850s found fifteen people living in a single room measuring fifteen by fourteen feet and with a ceiling only seven feet high. Yet that was an improvement over the late 1840s, when 106 hogs had lodged there along with the human tenants. One Lansdowne immigrant, laundress Barbara Sullivan, squeezed herself, six children, a son-in-law, and six boarders into a single apartment. Ellen Holland lived here as well.[49]

Next door, at 37½ Baxter, the legislative inspectors discovered the usual windowless bedrooms and destitute tenants. Particularly appalling were the circumstances of Honora Moriarty and her teenaged daughters Margaret and Mary, also probably Lansdowne immigrants. The "old dame of sixty" and her two daughters, the legislators reported in horror, "supported themselves by picking curled hair" out of city garbage barrels and then selling it to wigmakers or other manufacturers. By scouring the streets sixteen hours a day, they managed to find enough hair to earn five dollars per week.[50]

A few doors down, at 35 Baxter, the dreadful conditions continued. "Down half a dozen ricketty steps, the door was already open to one of the filthiest, blackest holes we had yet seen," wrote a *Times* reporter in 1859 of a nocturnal tour he took of the tenement's basement boardinghouse with a journalist from the *Express* and a police escort. The proprietor of this "damp and filthy cellar . . . with much loquacity, assured them that the bed-clothes were all 'clane and dacent sure,' that they were washed 'onst a week,' every Thursday, and that the place was quite sweet." Around the main room they saw "a number of wretched bunks, similar to those on shipboard, only not half as convenient, ranged around an apartment about ten feet square. Nearly every one of the half-dozen beds was occupied by one or more persons. No regard was paid to age or sex; but man, woman, and child were huddled up in one undistinguishable mass. . . . The most fetid odors were emitted, and the floor and the walls were damp with pestiferous exhalations. But this was not all. There were two inner apartments [i.e., bedrooms], each of which was crowded to the same capacity as the outer one. Not the slightest breath of air reached these infernal holes, which were absolutely stifling with heat." Inquiring about two small children sleeping soundly in one of the "hideous beds," the manager told the reporters that their older sister, who cared for them, "was out begging, even at this hour." The lodging house at 35 Baxter was actually superior to many others in the neighborhood. It charged six cents a night, far more than the worst dives. The landlord told the *Times* that he "lodged none under any circumstances but honest hardworking people—which statement the police received with smiles and without contradiction." "To do them justice," agreed the *Express* reporter, "such as were awake seemed to be quite sober." This was probably the establishment sarcastically referred to by the *New York Illustrated News* as "Mrs. Sandy Sullivan's Genteel Lodging-House on Baxter Street," operated by Lansdowne immigrants Sandy and Kate Sullivan. Former Lansdowne tenants occupied most of the other apartments in this wretched building and next door at 33 Baxter as well.[51]

Just before the corner, at 31 Baxter, one of the first five-story brick ten-

This 1859 view of Baxter Street above Worth shows the notorious tenements that lined the east side of that street. The large brick building at the center is 31 Baxter, whose three-room apartments were crammed full of Lansdowne immigrants and Italians. Sandy Sullivan's "Genteel Lodging-house" at 35 Baxter was in one of the two-story buildings just up the street, and 39 Baxter (where Ellen Holland lived) is the first three-story building visible. D. T. Valentine, comp., *Manual of the Corporation of the City of New York for 1860* (New York, 1860). Collection of the author.

ements in this part of the neighborhood towered over the surrounding wooden hovels. The investigators who detailed conditions in the neighboring tenements did not consider this relatively new building noteworthy, perhaps because it had not had much time to deteriorate. Yet the terrible crowding in its three-room apartments boggles the mind. Above the first two floors, most of the tenants were Lansdowne immigrants and Italians. Cornelius Shea and his wife Ellen, Lansdowne immigrants from Kenmare parish, shared their apartment with three children and four lodgers. Widow Johanna McCarty squeezed her four children (ranging in age from six to twenty) and eight lodgers into their three-room flat. McCarty's next-door neighbor, Italian widow Rose Ralph, took in only four lodgers. But another Italian, musician John Baptiste, housed his wife, five children, and four lodgers in a single three-room flat. Three other dwellings, including that of Tuosist native Daniel Haley, held nine persons each. Not all Lansdowne immigrants took in so many lodgers. Mary Shea of Kenmare and her husband Jeremiah, a Cork native, who had immigrated together in 1852, lived at 31 Baxter with their twenty-three-year-old servant daughter Margaret and just a single lodger. The combined incomes of father and daughter, plus the rent from the one lodger, allowed them to avoid the intense crowding endured by their neighbors. Laborer Daniel Hagerty, another Lansdowne immigrant from Kenmare, lived with his wife Mary and his younger brother Patrick, also a laborer. Their combined incomes allowed them to shun boarders altogether.[52]

The most notorious tenements in antebellum Five Points were not typical. Conditions varied enormously from block to block, and sometimes even from building to building. Some streets—such as White and Franklin west of Baxter, and Mott south of Pell—were rarely mentioned by

BACKGROUNDS OF CIVILIZATION.—MRS. SANDY SULLIVAN'S GENTEEL LODGING-HOUSE IN BAXTER STREET.—See page 202.

"Mrs. Sandy Sullivan's Genteel Lodging-House" at 35 Baxter Street was one of many boardinghouses in Five Points run by Lansdowne immigrants from County Kerry. *New York Illustrated News* (February 18, 1860): 216. Collection of the author.

investigators chronicling woeful tenement conditions. On some of these streets, a lone couple sometimes occupied a building that, if located just a block or two away, would have housed six or even twelve families. Still, with six or more people occupying nearly half the district's two-room, 225-square-foot apartments, along with a stove, a table and chairs, beds, clothing, food, and all the families' other worldly possessions, even the "average" Five Points apartment would have been a very unpleasant place to live.

"CONSIDERABLE REMAINS OF CLANSHIP AMONG THESE MOUNTAINEERS"

I have already noted the strength of the ethnic ties that drew certain groups to certain blocks of Five Points. Even more striking is that ethnic bands held together on a building-by-building basis. Few whole blocks were ethnically homogeneous. Each generally contained a clutch of almost exclusively Irish buildings and some others dominated by Germans. In five sample blocks, 82 percent of the buildings in which the Irish constituted a majority had no more than a single non-Irish family. And 90 percent of the buildings in which Germans made up the majority contained no more than one non-German family. In 78 percent of the tenements, one ethnic group made up 75 percent or more of the inhabitants.[53]

Though Irish and German tenements were often clustered together, the ethnic aggregation on one side of a street did not necessarily extend itself to the other. The most German "block" in the neighborhood, for example, was the east side of Mott between Canal and Bayard; the west side was predominantly Irish. Many Jews likewise lived on the west side of Baxter below Worth, but virtually none lived across the street.[54]

Racial segregation in Five Points was even more pronounced than ethnic clustering. Those African Americans who remained in Five Points tended to live in all-black tenements. Park Street between Baxter and Mott contained the largest proportion of such buildings, as several of the small houses on each of these blocks were boardinghouses that catered to blacks. African Americans also concentrated in Cow Bay, as well as in scattered houses on Baxter, Mulberry, and Pell Streets. If the census taker is to be believed, racial segregation in Five Points was almost absolute.[55]

Although ethnic and racial residential patterns are easiest to document, *intraethnic* housing patterns developed as well. The dominant Irish contingents in the neighborhood—those from Sligo, Cork, and Kerry—often concentrated in mini-enclaves. The Kerry immigrants were the most clannish, with 84 percent of them living in just two of the neighborhood's twenty blocks. These two blocks, Baxter from Worth to Leonard and Worth from Centre to Baxter (including Cow Bay), were two of the five blocks whose confluence formed the Five Points intersection. Kerry immigrants dominated those streets. Sixty-four percent of the Irish Catholic residents identified on these two blocks were Kerry natives; and 79 percent of these Kerry natives had emigrated from the Lansdowne estate. Callaghan McCarthy, a Catholic priest in the isolated Lansdowne parish of Tuosist, told a visitor to Kerry that "there existed considerable remains of clanship among these mountaineers" and "strong family attachments." These bonds remained potent in New York.[56]

Ethnicity of Five Points Tenement Dwellers
East Side of Mott Street from Canal Street to Bayard Street, 1855

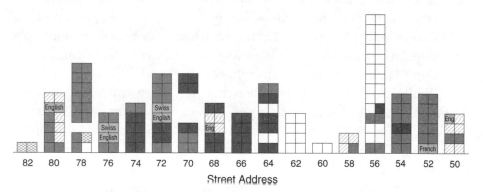

Street Address

The number at the bottom of each column represents a street address. The columns above each number represent tenements. Each row in a given column represents one apartment. The left-hand column of each address represents the male head of household; the right column, the female head of household. If there was only one household head, the entire row represents the ethnicity of that one person. Boarders are not represented. Blank space within a column represents the yard between front and rear tenements.

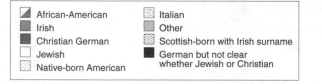

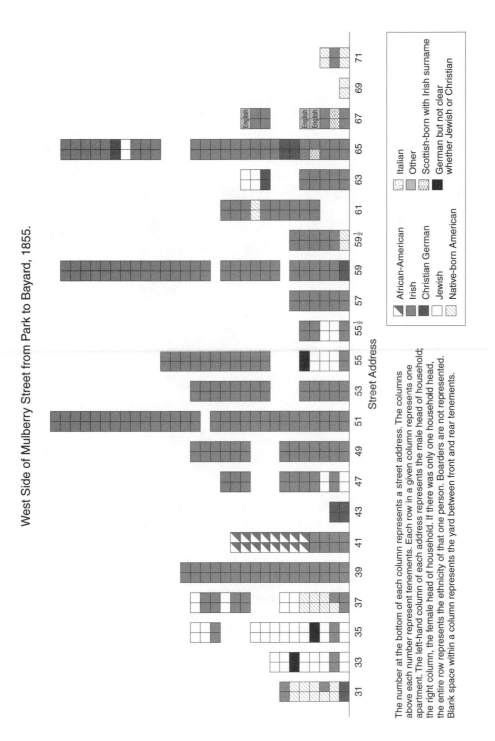

West Side of Mulberry Street from Park to Bayard, 1855.

Street Address

The number at the bottom of each column represents a street address. The columns above each number represent tenements. Each row in a given column represents one apartment. The left-hand column of each address represents the male head of household; the right column, the female head of household. If there was only one household head, the entire row represents the ethnicity of that one person. Boarders are not represented. Blank space within a column represents the yard between front and rear tenements.

African-American
Irish
Christian German
Jewish
Native-born American

Italian
Other
Scottish-born with Irish surname
German but not clear whether Jewish or Christian

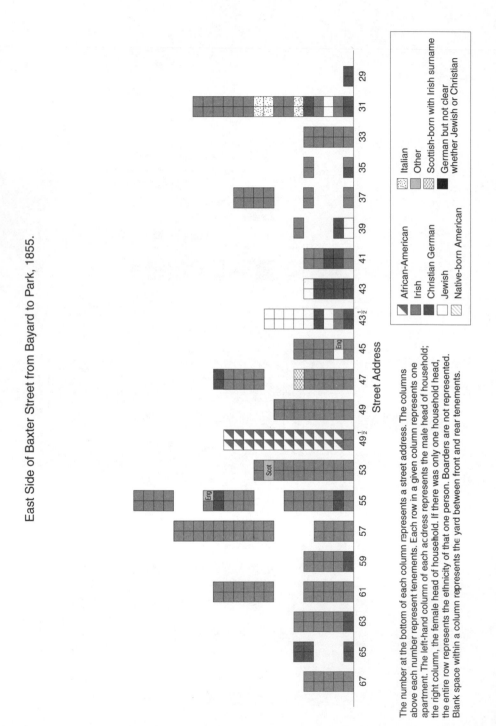

East Side of Baxter Street from Bayard to Park, 1855.

The number at the bottom of each column represents a street address. The columns above each number represent tenements. Each row in a given column represents one apartment. The left-hand column of each address represents the male head of household; the right column, the female head of household. If there was only one household head, the entire row represents the ethnicity of that one person. Boarders are not represented. Blank space within a column represents the yard between front and rear tenements.

East Side of Mulberry Street from Bayard to Canal Street, 1860.

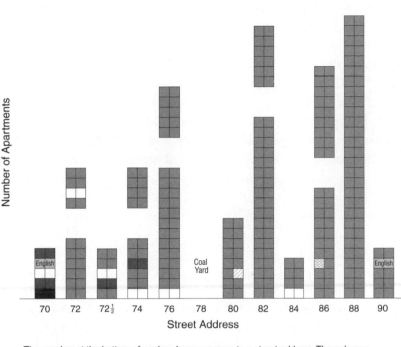

The number at the bottom of each column represents a street address. The columns above each number represent tenements. Each row in a given column represents one apartment. The left-hand column of each address represents the male head of household; the right column, the female head of household. If there was only one household head, the entire row represents the ethnicity of that one person. Boarders are not represented. Blank space within a column represents the yard between front and rear tenements.

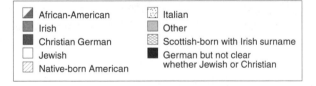

Source: 1855 New York State manuscript census; 1860 U.S. manuscript census; 1855 and 1860 New York City directories.

Sligo natives, in contrast, did not concentrate as compactly as did the Kerry immigrants. They settled primarily in the northern half of Five Points, but spread themselves out over a twelve-block area. The neighborhood's final large Irish contingent, that from Cork, was the least clannish of the three. Thirty percent of Five Points' Cork natives lived in the block bounded by Mulberry, Park, Baxter, and Chatham Streets, but otherwise emigrants from Cork spread out evenly across the neighborhood.

The smaller Irish subgroups clustered to some extent, but usually in single tenements rather than in specific blocks. Natives of Limerick concentrated in the connected buildings at 47 and 49 Mulberry Street, and at 7 and 9 Mulberry, 15 Baxter, and 64 Bayard Street. Mayo natives congregated at 84 Mulberry, Tipperary immigrants at 77 Mulberry, those from Waterford at 10, 11, and 12 Mulberry, and those from Cavan at 498 Pearl Street. But these cases were the exception. In most buildings, no single Irish county dominated.[57]

"THE PESTILENTIAL NUISANCE OF THE FIVE POINTS"

Newspaper editors, reformers, and government investigators were shocked not merely by conditions in Five Points tenements but also by how much tenants had to pay to rent them. Two-room apartments in the worst buildings generally rented for four to five dollars per month in the mid-1850s. Three rooms cost $5 to $6.50. In the rear wooden tenement at 37½ Baxter, a three-room apartment (two of which were windowless bedrooms) in the back of the building rented for five dollars per month. A front apartment that faced the yard, also with two tiny windowless bedrooms, cost $6.50. A two-room flat on the fifth floor of the infamous rear tenement at 9 Mulberry Street rented for $4.50. Some notorious addresses commanded surprisingly high rents. One three-room apartment in Cow Bay rented for ten dollars a month in the late 1850s, apparently because only one of the three rooms was a small windowless "sleeping closet." A single fifteen-by-fourteen-foot room with a seven-foot ceiling at 39 Baxter cost six dollars a month. Basements, in contrast, were the least-expensive dwellings. A cellar apartment in the rear of 9 Mulberry rented for three dollars per month. For that price one could also rent a shed in the backyard at 17 Baxter. But apartments in better buildings cost more. A two-room apartment in the new "model tenement" at 34 Baxter cost seven dollars per month. Figures compiled by the House of Industry also suggest that seven dollars was the typical rent for an average Five Points apartment.[58]

Because a three-room apartment in a decent working-class neighborhood only cost $8.50, reformers thought it unconscionable that Five Pointers were forced to pay nearly that much in a filthy, run-down district. "The old story of greedy capital," said the *Tribune*, motivated property owners to gouge even the most destitute tenants. Newspapers charged that Five Points landlords reaped huge returns on their investments, ranging anywhere from 17 to 26 percent per year, according to one estimate.[59]

Others insisted that "the merciless inflictions and extortions of the *sub-landlord*," rather than the actual property owner, were most responsible for the outrageous rents the immigrants paid. City Inspector John Griscom, author of the first detailed study of New York tenement conditions, noted that building owners often had no direct interaction with renters. They frequently leased an entire building to someone else, who then sublet the apartments on his own and took responsibility for maintenance of the property. These "sub-landlords" were often immigrants, sometimes proprietors of the saloon or grocery on the building's ground floor. Charles Loring Brace, who later founded the Children's Aid Society, described in 1853 a case in which the sub-landlord, rather than the property owner, reaped huge profits. According to Brace, a "notorious rum-seller" rented eight Five Points houses for $125 each per year from the property owner. "These he lets out to the prostitutes and negroes. They are filthy, broken-down, miserable, beyond any houses in the City." One of the buildings, in Cow Bay, brought in thirty dollars rent in one month, at which rate the saloonkeeper would clear "a profit of *nearly 300 per cent*" for the year. If landlords and sub-landlords would accept "a rational profit," argued Brace and other reformers, much of the suffering in New York's slums could be alleviated.[60]

Landlords and sub-landlords, of course, insisted that blame for the conditions and high rents in their buildings lay elsewhere. Samuel Weeks, a landlord who lived on Mott Street for almost all his life, complained that when he constructed new buildings at 47 and 49 Mott, the tenants immediately began taking in lodgers, overtaxing the buildings' facilities and making the tenements overcrowded and filthy. Weeks testified that he lowered the rents by 25 percent to discourage his tenants from taking in boarders, but they continued to do so anyway. Only when immigrants' wages improved, Weeks implied, would they be able to pay a reasonable rent and live in decent dwellings. Other landlords argued that high rents resulted from the city's seemingly perpetual shortage of housing, and could not be blamed on individual property owners who merely charged the market rate. In any case, surviving Five Points rent ledgers indicate that tenements did not typically generate outrageous profits for their owners.[61]

These ledgers also demonstrate that even scraping together four or five dollars in rent was a challenge for poor Five Pointers. Tenants rarely paid their rent on time. The tiny front and rear wooden houses at 70 Mott Street, for example, had five apartments whose rents ranged from four dollars to nine. Only the tenant in the cheapest apartment, Irish immigrant glass peddler Andrew McDermott, consistently paid his on time. Painter Robert Hall, a New York native who lived in the nine-dollar apartment with his wife and six children, was consistently six weeks behind on his payments. Carpenter Patrick Farmer paid his rent close to the due date in the spring and summer when construction work was plentiful, but in the winter tended to fall weeks behind. Furthest in arrears was an Irish-born menial laborer, William Trainor, who lived with his wife, three children, and a boarder. He too could rarely pay in the winter, falling four months behind in both April 1849 and April 1850. The property agents did not evict Trainor despite his consistent delinquency, indicating either that the expense involved did not justify such extreme measures or that they sympathized with his plight. The agents paid $13.56 in fees to evict a tenant in another Five Points building, a cost far greater than the interest lost allowing Trainor to pay his back rent at midyear when he could find steadier employment.[62]

Some argued that only governmental regulation could reduce rents and improve conditions in the city's decrepit tenements. "Tear down the rookeries," demanded the *New York Express*, "and let there be proper supervision, under authority of law, over the construction of whatever buildings may be erected in the future." But pervasive laissez-faire attitudes made tenement regulation seem radical to antebellum Americans. Supporters of regulation attempted to address this objection. "Why can the accommodations on a ship be regulated when they are only used for a few weeks," asked the *Tribune*, "but not for homes where people live for months or years?" Nonetheless, the movement for tenement regulation made little headway in the prewar years.[63]

Others offered solutions even more radical than regulation. Anticipating by more than five decades the eventual fate of the southern and western sections of the Five Points neighborhood, the *Herald* suggested that city officials raze "all that nest of drunkenness, roguery, debauchery, vice and pestilence, moral and physical, which lies between Centre street and Chatham Square—that is to say, the locality known as the Five Points and its dependencies." The city could then build a new post office as well as state and federal courts in its place. The *Herald* predicted that such a project would double property values in the surrounding area while allowing the city to "abolish the pestilential nuisance of the Five Points" once and for all. Yet such projects were considered too expensive and too intrusive on the rights of property owners to merit serious consideration. It would take another half century before New Yorkers would consent to use such drastic measures in the "battle with the slum."[64]

Unable to effect real change, civic leaders attempted to improve the neighborhood's image instead. At the end of 1854, city officials changed the names of the most infamous Five Points streets, in the hope that by simply expunging their notorious names from city maps they could initiate the revitalization of the district. The three streets whose confluence made up the Five Points intersection, as well a fourth nearby that ran up to Cow Bay, were all renamed. Cross Street became Park, Anthony was rechristened Worth, Orange was transformed into Baxter, and Little Water became Mission Place, named for the Five Points Mission which Methodists opened there in 1850. Yet "the shamelessness of Five Points" and the suffering of its "degraded denizens" remained all too much the same.[65]

Recognizing that new street names were not enough, those working in Five Points to aid the neighborhood's many destitute residents stepped up their efforts in the early 1850s. One of the first to devote himself full time to their plight was a minister, Lewis N. Pease. The Ladies' Home Missionary Society of the Methodist Episcopal Church hired Pease in 1850 to visit Five Pointers in their homes and convert them to Methodism. It was the lack of the moral compass provided by Protestant Christianity, Pease's employers believed, that led residents to dissolute lives of drunkenness, crime, and prostitution. Only a devotion to the teachings of Christ through Bible study could fortify Five Pointers to resist these temptations. But the Five Pointers themselves repeatedly told Pease that their problem was not a lack of morals, but a lack of work. "'Don't talk to us of death and retribution and perdition before us,'" they implored him. "'Tell us some way of escape! Give us work and wages!'"[66]

4

PROLOGUE

THE SAGA OF JOHNNY MORROW,
THE STREET PEDDLER

OF THE HUNDREDS of thousands of immigrants who passed through Five Points during the nineteenth century, precious few left written records. There are plenty of eyewitness accounts from reformers, journalists, law enforcement officials, and the like, but other than the occasional letter to the editor or affidavit describing a crime, working-class Five Pointers speak directly to us very rarely. A few have managed to narrate their own stories. Perhaps the most fascinating of these is the only one from the pre–Civil War years: a memoir, written by a teenager, of alcoholism, abuse, and life on the streets.[1]

His name was John Morrow, and he was born in about 1844 to Protestant parents in a village not far from Liverpool, England. He was the third of four children born to a Scottish father, an architect, and an English mother. John remembered his early years as carefree and happy, though when still a young boy he severely injured his left leg in a fall from a swing. The wound (perhaps a bad break) never properly healed, leaving his left leg lame for life. By the time he was full grown, it was three inches shorter than the right.

Far more traumatic to Johnny than his accident was the death of his mother when he was about five. His father remained single for quite some time, but finally remarried. Johnny recalled that his stepmother treated him and his three siblings quite well until she had children of her own, by which point she and his father were fighting a lot. "He would often spend the night away from home, carousing with a few companions, spending in this way much of his hard-earned money; and she would manage, while he was at his daily work, to drink a great deal of whiskey." Soon she "entirely neglected her household duties, left the table in disorder, the cow unmilked, the children uncared-for, and indeed often entertained carousing friends against father's will. Finally, in a fit of passion at her conduct, he declared that he would leave the homestead, and emigrate to America, in hopes that a change in circumstances would make things better." He sold everything they owned, left Johnny's two older brothers at a free boarding school in Dublin, and took the remainder of the family (including a servant girl whose passage they paid) to New York.[2]

That the Morrows could afford a servant girl indicates that they were still relatively well off. But in New York, Johnny's father continued to drink rather than work. After two months, as their nest egg dwindled, he took Johnny out of school so the boy could scavenge firewood and coal to reduce the family's fuel expenses. After about six months in New York, despite having left England with substantial savings, Johnny's father was broke.[3]

Finding it impossible to work as an architect, he took a lowly seventy-five-cent-per-day job in a cabinetmaker's shop on Chatham Street on the outskirts of Five Points. Johnny's stepmother earned a few cents per day sewing shirts for garment manufacturers, as did his younger sister Annie. After work, his parents would drink away most of their earnings and beat the kids in frustration. After about a year in New York, Johnny's father found relatively high-paying work as a house carpenter, but his drinking kept him from holding any job for very long. To cut their expenses, he moved the family uptown to a one-room basement apartment at the corner of Tenth Avenue and 40th Street, a run-down district that would soon become known as "Hell's Kitchen."

Meanwhile, Johnny continued to scavenge for fuel. At times his father ordered him to steal nails from construction sites instead, because he needed the two cents a pound they brought from the neighborhood junk dealer to pay for his brandy. "He soon became an almost helpless drunkard," wrote Johnny, "got out of work, out of money, and, consequently, out of bread. STARVE, was the word!" Time and again Johnny's father would take an oath of sobriety, but he always fell off the wagon. He pawned most of the family's possessions to help pay their mounting expenses, which continued to increase as they had more children. By the time Johnny was eleven, in about 1854, he and Annie slept head to toe in a single bed with their half siblings William, Jane, and Margaret Ann. Little Jonathan slept in his parents' bed.[4]

At about this point, Johnny was caught stealing lumber. Because of his lameness, he could not run fast enough to escape, and as a result was severely beaten. He came home and insisted he would steal no more, but suggested an alternative. During his days on the streets, he often came across children selling matches door to door. He had learned that the tiny peddlers would buy seventy-two boxes of matches wholesale for twenty-four cents. They took some matches out of each box and wrapped them with string into twenty-five additional bundles, selling the boxes and bundles for a penny a piece. His father consented to let Johnny try match peddling. On his first day he sold his entire stock, and returned home triumphantly with ninety-seven cents. His father spent most of the proceeds on brandy.[5]

Because of Johnny's success, his father stopped feeding him breakfast and lunch, insisting that he beg for meals from charitable customers. Soon his older brothers James and Robert, aged seventeen and fifteen, arrived from Dublin. They tried to make it on their own, but shortly moved into the one-room apartment with the rest of the family. Eventually they fought with their father over his drinking, moved out, and were never heard from again. Johnny continued to peddle matches, though he branched out into children's "picture-books" as well. Willie and Jane entered the profession too. Johnny would work one side of the street, Willie and Jane the other. But their father and mother continued to beat them if they did not come home with enough money to satisfy their addiction.

"My own position was now fast becoming unendurable," Johnny wrote. "I was liable at any time to be knocked about the room and beaten by my parents, and we children had to work very hard to earn money while they stayed in idleness at home, and drank away a large portion of our earnings." Johnny and Willie ran away, but three days later, their father found them and beat them "with a piece of clothes-line till the blood came trickling down." They ran away a second time a few weeks later, but a neighbor told their father where they were and he again dragged them home. When a kind man gave Johnny a $2.50 gold piece, he gave it to his father, hoping their sudden windfall would win his approval. The next morning, his father used it to buy a gallon of brandy. His father and stepmother spent the entire day in bed drunk.[6]

Johnny and Willie ran away once more, this time for good. To ensure that they would not be caught, they headed downtown to the Sixth Ward and its Newsboys' Lodging House. The lodging house had been set up in the early 1850s by Charles Loring Brace's Children's Aid Society as a refuge for the hundreds of homeless newsboys, bootblacks, and child peddlers who lived on New York's streets. Before the house opened, these children generally slept in doorways and coal bins; now they could find shelter in a warm, spacious dormitory for just six cents a night.

When Willie and Johnny checked in, they told the superintendent that they were orphans. Johnny felt guilty, though, and the next day told their true story. He was shocked that the society did not inform his parents or try to convince them to return home. But there were dozens of boys in the lodging house who could have told virtually identical stories. The superintendent did mention Johnny's tale to a reporter, who published it in a religious newspaper, the *Independent,* under the title "The Boy Who Confessed His Sin." When Johnny's Sunday school teacher read the article and recognized his pupil, he insisted that Johnny come live with him in his rooms at the Union Theological Seminary on University Place. Johnny went back to school and supported himself by peddling to the seminarians and on the streets after class. Willie remained at the lodging house.

Remained there, that is, until about a month later when the police picked him up on the street late one night and took him to the House of Refuge, the city's orphan asylum on Randall's Island. Johnny begged the authorities to release Willie, but was told that he would stay until someone found him a proper home. Johnny's Sunday school teacher suggested that they find him one out west through the adoption program run jointly by the Children's Aid Society and the Five Points House of Industry. About three weeks later, in 1856, Willie boarded a train for Iowa.[7]

While Willie was at the House of Refuge, their father died and was buried in an unmarked grave in the city's Potter's Field. Not long afterward, after Willie had left for Iowa, Johnny's sister Annie came to the seminary, complaining that her stepmother was mistreating her. Johnny brought her to Rev. W. C. Van Meter, who managed the adoption program run by the Five Points Mission. He sent her to an adoptive family in Iowa City. Johnny tried to help his half sister Jane by setting her up once again as a peddler, but when he saw his stepmother beat her one day because she could not account for all of her merchandise, he decided to have her adopted as well. On the pretense of taking her to get new shoes, he brought her to the Five Points Mission to meet Reverend Van Meter. She told him she would like a new home, and a few weeks later she was adopted by a family in Canton, Illinois. Her mother went to court to try to regain custody of the child, but was rebuffed.

Having lived at the seminary for some time, Johnny developed an ambition to go to college, Yale in particular. He moved to New Haven, where he lived at the Divinity School while supporting himself peddling to the students. In the summer of 1858, after about a year in New Haven, Johnny decided to go out west and find Willie, whom he had not heard from in almost a year. He traveled with Van Meter as far as Chicago, and then continued to Iowa City, where he found Annie living in a comfortable home. On a farm near "Fort Desmoines" he found Willie, who had been passed around to many families in the two years since he left New York. Johnny decided to bring him back to New Haven. On their way back they stopped in Illinois to visit Jane, who, like Annie, had found a good home.[8]

Willie eventually went back to the West with Van Meter, "to try his fortune again in some kind of family." The last he and Johnny saw of their stepmother, she was asleep on the bare floor of her apartment on West 17th Street with five-year-old Jonathan. Her only furniture was a pair of chairs. They took the little boy to New Haven, where they eventually put him up for adoption at the New Haven Orphan Asylum. Johnny remained in New Haven, still aspiring one day to study at Yale. With the help of some friends there, while only sixteen, he published his memoir in the hope that the proceeds might someday fund his college education.[9]

Johnny Morrow's story may seem extraordinary. Yet at any one time in Five Points there were dozens of boys who could tell similar tales. Over the course of the nineteenth century, thousands of neighborhood children went hungry, were abused by alcoholic parents, and were forced to work on the streets to support themselves or their families. Johnny Morrow's first sixteen years had been especially harrowing. But in the context of Five Points, what was unusual about his childhood was not his life on the streets but simply that he was given the opportunity to record it for posterity.

Johnny never did enroll at Yale. Just a year after he published *A Voice from the Newsboys*, he was dead. The cause was "[em]pyema," an accumulation of pus in the lungs probably associated with a bronchial infection. He was buried on May 26, 1861, in Evergreen Cemetery, Brooklyn.[10]

CHAPTER FOUR

How They Worked

⌒☡☡⌒

PEDDLER. RAGPICKER. Junk dealer. Seamstress. Teamster. The New World offered a much wider array of jobs than had the Old. Yet most immigrants heading for Five Points would have disembarked from the emigrant vessel with little savings. They needed work desperately and could not be choosy. Some newcomers simply continued with the same vocation they had followed in Europe.[11] Others arrived in North America brimming with ambition and a determination to improve their occupational status. Owen Healy was one of the first starving tenants sent by Lord Palmerston to America in 1847. Upon his arrival in New York, the twenty-eight-year-old worked as a laborer, but was soon selling fruit. In 1853, when Healy opened an account at the Emigrant Savings Bank, he described himself as a "dealer in bottles." By 1855, the Five Pointer had reached what many Irish immigrants considered the pinnacle of success— the opening of his very own saloon. Healy must have possessed some business acumen, for in a few years he amassed in his bank account more than $700 (equivalent to about $11,000 today),[12] a princely sum to one who had been on the verge of starvation just eight years earlier. Few Five Pointers soared to financial success this quickly. Many found themselves locked in the lowest-paying occupations, such as laborer, tailor, shoemaker, or seamstress. But despite the hardships of such work and frequent unemployment, most Five Pointers found better work, higher pay, and more consistent employment than they had had before they came to America.[13]

"IN SUMMER THE MEN HAVE MOST WORK"

Five Pointers worked at an extraordinary variety of jobs, from actor to xylographic printer. There were few New York occupations that were not followed by at least one or two of the neighborhood's inhabitants. An analysis of their occupations in 1855, however, reveals certain distinct patterns:

Employment by Occupational Category, 1855[14]

	Percentage of Five Points Men	Percentage of New York Men
Professionals	0.4%	2%
Business owners	4	14
Petty entrepreneurs	2	1
Lower-status white-collar workers	4	9
Skilled manual workers	49	47
Unskilled workers	40	22
Difficult to classify	1	5

	Five Points Women	All New York Women
Needle trades	48%	21%
Household servants	25	67
Laundresses	8	5
Boardinghouse keepers	13	4
Miscellaneous	6	3

A Five Pointer was much less likely than the average New Yorker to work in a profession or own a business and far more likely to toil as an unskilled worker. There was an underrepresentation of Five Points men in lower-status white-collar work (mostly clerks), which is understandable, given that many immigrants lacked the reading, writing, and math skills necessary for such employment. Among women, there were fewer servants (who generally lived where they worked) because few Five Points families could afford live-in help. Instead, Five Points women concentrated in the needle trades (the lowest-paying work for women), primarily as seamstresses sewing shirts, but also as dress, cap, and vest makers as well.

Perhaps the most surprising of the employment figures is that for skilled male workers. The stereotypical image of the Five Points immigrant is of a menial laborer digging ditches with his pickax. Yet in Irish-dominated Five Points, a majority of men worked in higher-status occupations, albeit the lowest-paying ones. Five Points' skilled workers were disproportionately represented in such low-paying crafts as tailoring, shoemaking, and glass repair, and significantly underrepresented in the highest-paying ones, such as shipbuilding, woodworking, food preparation, and the construction trades. The same pattern is evident in the unskilled labor category. Eighty percent of Five Points' unskilled workers were menial manual laborers, compared with only 59 percent in the entire city. The remainder of the city's unskilled workers held jobs as carters, drivers, hostlers, sailors, waiters, and watchmen, occupations with better working conditions, superior pay, and less seasonal unemployment.[15]

There were ethnic differences among Five Points workers as well. More than half the Irish were unskilled workers, compared to only one in twenty-five Germans. Most of the unskilled workers among the American-born population were African Americans or the children of Irish immigrants. Many of the skilled workers among the American-born, however, held relatively prestigious and high-paying jobs. Five Points butchers tended to be American natives. A disproportionate number of the printers and building tradesmen were also native-born. In contrast, skilled Jews toiled overwhelmingly as tailors and glaziers, the latter mostly wandering repairmen rather than highly paid construction workers.[16]

It is hardly surprising that Irish immigrants held lower-paying, lower-status jobs than their native- or German-born counterparts. Yet the Five Points Irish were even more likely to work as menial day laborers than other Irish New Yorkers. Five Points Irish male workers were almost twice as likely to toil as laborers, but only half as likely to hold positions in the high-paying construction and food-service trades. Similarly, Five Points Irishwomen were three times more likely to work as miserably paid seamstresses than Irishwomen throughout the city. The same pattern held for other ethnic groups. Five Points German men were twice as likely to be tailors as Germans citywide, and significantly less likely to work in the lucrative building and food-service industries.

So many clothing workers lived in Five Points because the cheap retail clothing business centered upon Baxter and Chatham Streets. Five Points was also the home of a large proportion of the city's Jews, particularly Polish Jews, who were especially likely to work in the garment trade. The German and Polish Jewish immigrants who settled in New York tended to come from cities or towns where they had plied urban trades and saved significant sums of money before leaving for America. Most of the Irish, in contrast, had toiled as rural agricultural workers and thus brought no job skills with them to the United States.

The need for expensive tools also contributed to Five Pointers' inability to work in better-paying trades. Tailoring, in contrast, required very little equipment before the widespread use of the sewing machine, and may have therefore attracted many Five Pointers. Immigrants also had trouble breaking into some trades because native-born workers conspired to keep foreigners out. Butchering and shipbuilding, for example, were generally closed to the Irish. Such discrimination cost the Irish dearly, for a day laborer generally earned about a dollar a day in the 1850s, and Five Points' tailors and shoemakers made little more. In comparison, a carpenter could command eight to nine dollars a week, a baker nine to ten dollars, a cabinetmaker as much as ten dollars, and a ship's carpenter twelve to fifteen dollars per week.[17]

Five Pointers must have found this pay disparity especially galling because many higher-paying industries were located right in their neighborhood. Manufacturing of almost every variety flourished in the Sixth Ward, especially on Chatham Square and Chatham Street. Many small-scale manufacturers were also located on Doyer, Bayard, and Elizabeth Streets in the 1850s. Small factories produced silverware, jewelry, billiard tables, umbrellas, lightning rods, false teeth, patent medicines, and firearms. There were even four piano factories. Carriage and inexpensive furniture manufactories abounded as well on Chatham Square. Yet relatively few Five Pointers worked for these businesses.[19]

Five Pointers' jobs were especially prone to seasonal layoffs. A day laborer could expect to work no more than four days in a typical six-day workweek. Employment was usually scarce in the winter and especially brisk in the spring and summer, but a spell of cold or rain could bring unemployment at any moment. Employment in the garment trade also varied seasonally. In the dressmaking business, for example, jobs for women fell 75 percent after the autumn rush each year. This was probably an extreme case, but observers agreed that needleworkers suffered significant under- or unemployment in the slack winter months.[19]

The bank accounts of Five Pointers clearly reflect these seasonal highs and lows. Aside from a spike in January (the result perhaps of New Year's savings resolutions or the bank's dividend payment schedule), deposits during the summer and early fall ran far ahead of those in the rest of the year. Five Pointers made almost three times as many deposits per month in July and August as they did in February, March, and April. Although the "transportation revolution" of the 1830s and 1840s ended New York's reliance on potentially frozen waterways for the importation of raw materials and the distribution of finished products, seasonal employment swings continued to define the economic lives of Five Pointers throughout the nineteenth century.[20]

These seasonal fluctuations rippled throughout the economy. A survey of the "china business" (the selling of earthenware cups and plates) found that citywide, trade was most brisk in the spring "when people go to housekeeping" and at Christmas when they bought presents. But a Five Points china dealer sold the most in the summer, said the report, "because her patrons are poor people, and in summer the men have most work, and their expenses are lighter—consequently the women have more money." Merchants usually had savings to fall back on when business dried up, but the most poorly paid manual workers often had none. "Mechanics and laborers lived awhile on scanty savings of the preceding Summer and Autumn," recalled *New York Tribune* editor Horace Greeley in his memoirs, "then on such credit as they could wring from grocers and landlords, till milder weather brought them work." The unemployed might look for work at the "Labor Exchange" run by the New York Commissioners of Emigration, located first at the northern edge of Five Points on Canal Street and later at its western fringe on Worth Street, but few workers other than domestic servants found employment there. There were also commercial employment agencies, but immigrants balked at paying their fees. Consequently, despite improvements in the nation's transportation network that helped mitigate some of the ups and downs of the seasonal economy, Five Points' charitable workers reported well into the 1850s that chronic unemployment made winter the "annual season of sorrow and dread."[21]

During the lean winter months, the entire family often pitched in to help make ends meet. "If [the husband is] discharged from labor, and in actual want," reported the New York Association for Improving the Condition of the Poor, "the wife can wash and scrub, [while] the children pick up fuel, and beg cast-off clothing and broken victuals." Struggling Five Points families could also secure loans from pawnshops. There were no more pawnshops in Five Points than in other portions of the city, perhaps due to the strict and expensive licensing involved. Yet the neighborhood's dozens of "second-hand" and junk shops located on Baxter Street served as informal pawnshops, buying whatever objects of value (such as empty bottles or scrap metal) area residents might find or steal. With the whole family helping out, most Five Pointers managed to scrape by each winter, though many suffered terribly until employment picked up in the spring.[22]

When they could find work, Five Pointers generally labored for ten hours each day, six days per week. The antebellum workday typically began at 7:00 a.m., was suspended for a one-hour "dinner" break at noon, and then continued until 6:00 p.m. Because seasonal unemployment was so common, scheduled days off were rare. Other than Sundays, work ceased only on New Year's Day, the Fourth of July, and Christmas (and for only some, Thanksgiving as well).

Long work days were nothing new to European immigrants, but they were startled by the productivity Americans expected. A British mechanic exaggerated only slightly when he commented that "there is no allowable cessation from labour during any part of this time—no lunching or watering time, or interval of any description; nothing but one round of work without the slightest intermission." Another English immigrant agreed that "'hurry up' is a phrase in the mouth of every person in the United States." German bricklayers found that while laying 1,000 to 1,200 bricks was an acceptable day's work in their native land, contractors expected 1,500 bricks per day in New York. When an English visitor, John White, told a New York Irish American that he should be happy earning "three times the Irish wages," the laborer complained that "he did six times the Irish work."[23]

"So great an amount of work for so little money"

It is very difficult to re-create the employment experiences of Five Points laborers and tradesmen. The tiny number of workingmen and -women who wrote extant memoirs and diaries did not hail from Five Points. But contemporary descriptions of the most widely followed neighborhood occupations do exist.

Tailoring, for example, was a family affair, most of the work being done in the tailor's tenement home. "Before we had sewing machines," recalled one immigrant garment worker decades later, "we worked piece-work with our wives, and very often our children. . . . We worked at home in our rooms. We had to buy fuel to heat the irons for pressing, and light in winter." Men did the most difficult work, such as sewing buttonholes and cutting the fabric, while wives and children completed tasks requiring less experience and training. Some Sixth Ward boardinghouse keepers subcontracted garment work from clothing manufacturers and then farmed it out to their tenants at a profit. Others came from outside the neighborhood to work in small clothing manufactories there. Mulberry Street was the headquarters for the neighborhood's needleworkers; 47 percent of them lived there during the early 1850s. In fact, a full third of the neighborhood's tailors lived on just one of Five Points' twenty blocks—Mulberry between Park and Bayard.[24]

The increasing tendency during the late antebellum period to farm out needlework to those who could toil at home, cooped up for long hours in sweltering apartments, led observers by 1850 to refer to such home workers as "sweaters" or "sweated labor." One such worker described "the miseries of New-York tailors" in a letter to the *New York Tribune*, stating that most in his trade were "half-paid" and "half-starved." Discussing immigrant weavers, who lived in circumstances similar to those of the tailors, the *Tribune* noted that miserable wages "compel them to exercise the most rigid economy and self-denial; and those who are burdened with large families find it *tight squeezing to keep the pot boiling.*"[25]

Because there were so many tailors in Five Points, the Journeymen Tailors' Protective Union held its weekly conclaves at the Sixth Ward Hotel—making it one of the city's few labor organizations to meet there. The tailors organized their union in mid-1850, calling a citywide general strike for higher wages in July. According to the *Herald*, they succeeded in winning "the moderate advance" they sought, though not every employer was willing to abide by the new rates. In Five Points, an angry mob of tailors attacked a needleworker taking garments from a Jewish clothing dealer on Chatham Street because he refused to accept the new pay scale. The tailors tried to take the unmade coats from the union buster, and police reinforcements were needed to subdue the irate mob. In subsequent years, the union was successful in organizing periodic strikes against individual employers, such as one who in 1853 refused to pay the "standard wages on California goods." None of the tailors' union officers were Five Points residents (though its longtime secretary, Joseph Mathers, lived just across Chatham Square at 5 Dover Street), and it is impossible to determine how many neighborhood residents joined the organization. Nonetheless, so strongly did New Yorkers associate the garment trade with Five Points and vicinity that after its demise, labor leaders referred to the defunct union as "the old Sixth Ward Society."[26]

After tailoring, the next most popular skilled trade with Five Pointers was shoemaking. Like tailors, Five Points shoemakers were terribly underpaid. "There is no class of mechanics in New York who average so great an amount of work for so little money as the journeymen shoemakers," observed the *New York Tribune*. They "are the worst paid and live the least like . . . men who have spent years in learning trades." Most observers cited the competition of ready-made shoes and boots from New England as the cause of the shoemakers' woes. Like the tailors, the shoemakers tried to organize to improve their pay. Although the Boot and Shoemakers' Association met uptown, one of its subsidiary societies, the leather crimpers' union, met in Five Points at 9 Elizabeth Street. As long as hundreds of desperately impoverished immigrant tailors and cobblers continued to pour into New York, their unions would have little power to improve their wages significantly. By 1855, the foreign-born constituted 96 percent of both New York's 12,600 tailors and its 6,700 shoemakers.[27]

Tailoring and shoemaking were the skilled trades employing more New Yorkers than any other. Yet the third most popular skilled trade in Five Points—window glazing—was practiced by very few New Yorkers. Jews, mostly Polish natives, constituted more than 90 percent of Five Points' glaziers. Many Russian Jews, who began coming to New York soon after their Polish counterparts, spent time in London before continuing on to America, often learning the glazier's trade there. Some of Five Points' Polish Jews also resided in England before sailing for New York, but other Polish Jews must have learned the craft in Manhattan. Glaziers did not have shops, but instead walked the streets crying "Glass put in!" in order to drum up business. Wandering Jewish glaziers were a common sight all over pre–Civil War New York, and many of them lived in Five Points.[28]

Glaziers operated very much like peddlers, another favorite Five Points occupation. Although the stereotype of the period associated Jews with this trade, Irish peddlers actually outnumbered Jewish ones in the neighborhood. By the 1850s, the peddler was a ubiquitous sight in the city, hawking anything that would bring a profit, including "suspenders, fiddle-strings, razor-strops, buttons, thread, dumb watches, pinchbeck jewelry, and pocketbooks." Ethnic specialization existed even among peddlers. African Americans sold buttermilk and straw for bedding. The Irish peddled seafood, crying, "Fresh sha-a-d!" or, "My clams I want to sell to-day; the best of clams from Rock-away." Some peddlers earned surprisingly good incomes. James Churchill, a Mayo native who had immigrated to New York in 1850 and lived on Baxter Street at the Five Points intersection, opened a bank account in 1852 with $90 and in a year had increased his savings to $160 (roughly $2,600 today). Those who enjoyed less success sometimes ventured out into the countryside with their wares. Jews who chose this strategy returned to their families only for Passover, Hanukkah, and the Rosh Hashanah/Yom Kippur High Holidays. Although peddlers enjoyed a modicum of independence, constant rejection by potential customers, harassment by children on the street, and miles of trudging through all sorts of weather made their lives especially hard.[29]

It was said that the aspiration of every peddler was to save enough money to open his own second-hand clothing store. Many of the neighborhood's peddlers specialized in old clothes, which they bought from indigent Five Pointers (especially those with a recently deceased family member) and resold to other district residents too poor to buy new garments. With enough success selling clothes door to door, many peddlers were able to settle down to ply their trade from storefronts. Given the number of second-hand stores and junk shops in Five Points, there must have been dozens of successful peddlers in the neighborhood. In 1850, nearly half of the hundred or so lots on Orange Street below Canal held a second-hand or junk shop. Below the Five Points intersection, Jews owned 80 percent of the Orange Street second-hand stores. Above it, more than 75 percent of the proprietors had obviously Irish surnames.[30]

Many of these dealers were notorious as "fences," those who bought stolen goods. Their shops "are generally second-hand stores and pawnbrokers' shops combined, where a little money is lent on a good deal, and where anything is purchased without the asking of impertinent questions," reported one journalistic exposé. "These shops are of course kept entirely by Jews," asserted another, "and are situated in a row, in Orange street, near the Points." George Washington Appo, a professional thief, remembered that just after the Civil War "at No. 14½ Baxter St., was a second hand clothing store owned by a man named Cohen who was a 'fence' and where all the crooks used to get rid of their stolen goods." The *New York Evening Post* in 1854 accused second-hand dealer Mayer Rosenthal of 6 Mulberry of fencing half the stolen calico, muslin, shawls, silk, and thread in New York. There were Irish fences as well. One named Grady posed as a peddler, carrying his purloined property in a box suspended from his shoulders. When possible, fences altered stolen goods to make identification more difficult, relining coats and melting down jewelry.[31]

In contrast to peddlers and second-hand dealers, almost nothing is known about the work lives of Five Points' largest single occupational group: its menial day laborers. Construction work probably provided most of the employment for day laborers, who comprised four in every ten male Five Points workers. Menial laborers could dig foundations, carry heavy hods full of bricks and mortar to masons, and haul away work-related debris. Municipal projects employed many laborers, especially for the digging of sewer lines and the paving of streets with cobblestones. When outdoor work slowed a bit in midsummer, a laborer might find a job along the waterfront, loading or unloading sacks and crates from the hundreds of ships that arrived and departed each week. Laborers' work was often very dangerous; newspapers overflowed with reports of hod carriers falling from ladders, longshoremen crushed by falling cargo, and laborers buried by the collapsing walls of unfinished buildings.

As dangerous as a laborer's work might be, his greatest fear was probably not death but unemployment. On days too cold or wet to work, the laborer did not get paid, because "a storm stops his work and wages." Some might find steady employment at a single construction site; others had to look for a position each day. Sudden sickness or a job-related injury could also throw one out of work at any time. Employers would not hold a laborer's position for him while he recuperated. Even in perfect health, observed the *Tribune*, only "an energetic and lucky man . . . can make more than two hundred and fifty days' work as an out-door laborer in the course of a year, while the larger number will not average two hundred." During recessions, many laborers could not secure more than one or two days of paid work per week. Unemployment could wreak havoc on family finances, because laborers had to fall back on summer savings to get by during the lean winter months. "A month's idleness, or a fortnight's sickness, and what misery!" observed an Irish journalist. Increasing the laborers' typical wage of a dollar a day would have helped, but given the vast numbers of impoverished laborers, they had little bargaining leverage. The Laborers' Union Benevolent Association concentrated its efforts on sickness and death benefits. In return for a two-dollar initiation fee and 12½ cents monthly dues, members in 1850 received two dollars per week when too sick to work and fifteen dollars for burial. The organization was not particularly popular, however, with no more than one in eight New York laborers joining. The laborer's life was one of the hardest, most dangerous, and most financially precarious in Five Points.[32]

One might imagine that the Irish would resent the extent to which they were forced to toil as laborers, but at least one Five Pointer found the Irish concentration in manual labor both natural and appropriate. "What a laughable sight it would be to see a German Jew or Dutchman mount a ladder with a hod of brick or mortar to a five- or six-story house," wrote Michael Coogan of Mulberry Street to the editor of the *Irish-American* in 1853. "No, they follow pursuits more congenial to their taste and capacity. One takes to his bag, basket and crook, rag-picking and bone-gathering; the other to glazing, peddling, and swopping old clothes." Given what they had been paid in Ireland, argued Coogan, Irish Americans should be happy to work as laborers in New York.

Finding themselves frequently unemployed, Irish-born laborers in New York responded as they often had in Ireland—they tramped into the countryside looking for work. Just as Lansdowne's poor tenants had walked hundreds of miles in search of employment in the autumn and early winter, New York's laborers sometimes ventured to the South during slow winter months hoping to find construction work there. Others went to upstate New York or even the Midwest looking for canal or railroad jobs. These workers suffered great hardships living in labor camps, and the families they left behind in Five Points endured equally severe burdens. Often, money left to support the family ran out before the worker returned. On Mulberry Street in an attic garret, a charity worker found a woman whose "husband had gone to the country in search of work, six months before, since which time she had heard nothing from him. How she had managed to live, we could not imagine. . . . There were four children, one an infant at the breast," all dressed "in rags." They would have starved but for meals provided by the Five Points House of Industry. A "Mrs. B." on Mulberry Street had a fifteen-month-old and a newborn baby. Her unemployed husband had left six months earlier looking for work outside New York, but she had heard nothing from him since and the money he left had run out, leaving her totally destitute. A Five Pointer whose sailor husband had not been heard from in nearly a year likewise appeared at the door of the Five Points Mission one day with three children who were "nearly naked. . . . To pay her rent, she had sold and pawned her furniture till nearly every article was gone; to get bread she had parted with her clothing and her children's clothing, till they were altogether in the deepest distress." Some of these missing men had undoubtedly died of disease or work-related injuries. Margaret Connor, for example, was left with a two-year-old son to care for when her husband drowned in 1855 while working for the Erie Railroad. But others had simply abandoned their families.[33]

"THE MOST APPALLING SCENES OF DESTITUTION"

Abandoned women had to find work to support their families; many became seamstresses. "There are none who are more poorly paid for their work, or who suffer more privation and hardship" than seamstresses, wrote a *New York Herald* reporter in 1853. In order to document his assertion, the journalist went to Five Points, where he ventured into a decrepit rear tenement on Mulberry Street to interview a shirt sewer, the lowest-paid type of needleworker. The mistress of the house, a widow, had supported herself and her children this way for seven years. She earned four cents per shirt, she explained to the reporter, and "some days, by working from seven in the morning till twelve at night, I have made five shirts." Working at that furious pace, the most she had ever earned in a week was a dollar.

One could not support a family on such a pittance. This seamstress supplemented her income by renting most of her tiny two-room apartment to three boarders, who paid $4 of her $4.50 rent. Her nineteen-year-old daughter had recently moved out to work as a domestic servant, and some of her salary helped support her mother and younger siblings. Sometimes, this seamstress got "washing and scrubbing to do, and then I make more than I could at the shirts." She was also lucky to have a relatively generous employer. Although many garment industry contractors were renowned for their heartlessness, her employer was "very good to me, and when I am in want of a dollar [he] always advances it to me."

Even after supplementing her income by these various means, the seamstress and her children led a very difficult life. Of the few possessions in her spare apartment—"four chairs, a rickety table, a looking glass, some cups, saucers, plates, a pot and a kettle, [and] a few other kitchen utensils"—many belonged to the lodgers. They could not afford beds, so they slept on the floor. Sometimes, all she could afford to feed her family was bread and molasses, though "on Sundays we generally get a piece of meat, and live more comfortably than on any other day."

About half the women in Five Points who did paid work had jobs in the garment trades. Not all seamstresses were as impoverished as this Mulberry Street shirt sewer, but such conditions were not uncommon. In the 1850s, in fact, what the *Tribune* called "the wretchedness of needlewomen" became something of a *cause célèbre* in New York. Newspaper exposés documented their pathetic lives, reformers held meetings to organize relief for them, and charitable organizations chronicled their struggles to support themselves and their families. Some female garment workers toiled merely to supplement the incomes of husbands, fathers, or brothers. But the hundreds who had no choice but to support either themselves or whole families with the needle, said the *Times*, inevitably led lives of "misery, degradation, and wretchedness."[34]

Some seamstresses in Five Points labored in workshops run either by clothing retailers or their suppliers. The needleworkers who received the most notoriety, however, were those who labored at home. Widows with children to care for and those supporting sick siblings or infirm parents usually sewed in their tenements. Widow Mary Ann Dwyre of 52 Mulberry Street, for example, turned to the needle to support herself and daughter Charlotte when her husband Laurence Muldoon passed away. A childless Lansdowne immigrant, Mary Sullivan, likewise sustained herself as a seamstress in New York after the death of her husband, Ned.[35]

Not all Five Points seamstresses were widows. Mary Twomey, also a Lansdowne immigrant, did needlework to supplement the income of her peddler husband, Cornelius. Others were single women who needed to earn money but did not want to become domestic servants, who were constantly on duty and worked virtually every day of the year. In contrast, noted the

Tribune, a seamstress "enjoys considerable personal independence as to hours, locations, &c." Others took to needlework because, having once lived in better circumstances, "they cannot bring themselves quite down to kitchen-work in the basements of those who . . . were yesterday their equals . . . so they shrink into a garret and stitch, stitch, until they wear out or starve out and are taken to the hospital, the poor-house or the grave."[36]

One of the factors that drove seamstresses to the grave was the way they were paid. Not only did they earn mere pennies for their labor, but they usually had to post a one-dollar deposit with their employer to get work at all. One "can have no idea of the sacrifices, hardships and humiliations to be passed through before sufficient means can be raised to enable them to make the necessary deposit," stated the *Tribune.* Some employers used the threat of confiscating the deposit to keep their workforce docile. Despite promising five cents per shirt, they would criticize the quality of the sewing when the finished shirts were returned and pay only four cents, threatening to keep the deposit if the needlewoman complained. Or the employer might return the deposit but refuse to pay for the work, claiming the shirts had been ruined. "No serf in the middle ages," concluded the *Tribune,* "was ever more helplessly under the absolute control of his superior lord as are the needle women to the employers."[37]

Some seamstresses fought back. When shirt manufacturer John Davis of 48 William Street would neither pay two seamstresses for their work nor return their deposit, they sued him. The court ordered Davis to pay the workers the promised six cents per shirt, return their deposits, and reimburse the seamstresses for time lost in pursuing the lawsuit. Still, many employers continued to cheat their workers. Five years later, Davis again found himself in court, sued by another group of seamstresses for the same offense. One can only imagine how many defenseless women Davis had managed to cheat in the intervening years. Another seamstress asked her employer for work that paid better than shirts and was given pillowcases, but failed to ask exactly how much she would earn. When she returned a day later with the finished cases and received only fifteen cents, she told the *Herald* in 1853, "my heart was nearly ready to break."[38]

Sensing their virtual helplessness at the hands of unscrupulous employers, a group of needlewomen and reformers in March 1851 organized the Shirt-Sewers' Association of the City of New-York. Its primary function was to establish a "Shirt Depot" at 9 Henry Street (just east of the

Five Points neighborhood) so that "mechanics and others" could order shirts directly from the sewers, thus putting the seamstresses "beyond the caprice of employers" and directing all profits to the needlewomen. The organization seemed at first to hold some promise of success. *Tribune* publisher Horace Greeley and Rev. Henry Ward Beecher endorsed it, and by the end of its first year the association employed as many as one hundred seamstresses. But their made-to-order work apparently could not compete with the convenience of choosing a ready-made shirt from a merchant's stock. By June 1853, only forty or fifty needlewomen worked at the association's shop. The overwhelming majority of seamstresses continued to labor under the grueling conditions that would characterize the needle trades into the twentieth century.[39]

As in other occupations, a seamstress's work life had seasonal swings. According to the *Tribune,* winter was the worst time for seamstresses because they had less work to do but had to pay more in fuel and lighting expenses. Yet summer was hardly better. The *Tribune* referred to late summer as "'the hurrying season'" because garment wholesalers rushed to complete orders for the retailers, who sold large quantities of clothing as the weather turned colder. A seamstress could count on plenty of work at this point, and perhaps even a penny or two more per shirt. But the stress was overwhelming, as each needleworker strained her eyes and muscles to complete as many shirts as possible in order to squirrel away funds for the winter. It was during these late summer months that the life of the seamstress most resembled that of the fictional needlewoman in the English poet Thomas Hood's "Song of the Shirt":

> . . . Work, work, work,
> Till the brain begins to swim,
> And work, work, work,
> Till the eyes are heavy and dim.
> Seam and gusset and band,
> Band and gusset and seam,
> Till o'er the buttons I fall asleep
> And sew them on in my dream.[40]

Many Five Points seamstresses who lived with brothers, parents, or husbands did not have to work this hard. They sewed to supplement the family income, not to support an entire household. But the suffering of those who had no other means of support cannot be exaggerated.[41]

While half the employed women in antebellum Five Points worked in the needle trades, another quarter toiled as domestic servants. Most domestics lived in the neighborhood with their employers, but one-third commuted to work. The proportion of Five Points women who would eventually work as domestics was probably much higher than the 25 percent indicated in the census, as many daughters would leave the neighborhood to take live-in positions as domestics when they turned nineteen or twenty. Significant numbers of Five Points housewives also may have worked as domestic servants before finding their mates.

In a material sense, the live-in domestic servant lived far better than the seamstress. Some were "thrust into noxious dark bed-rooms or unventilated garrets and lofts," but even these were far better than the typical Five Points "sleeping closet." Domestics also ate well and lived in safer, cleaner neighborhoods than other immigrants. Although their pay was as low as that of a seamstress ($4 to $8 per month depending on experience), they received free room and board, and could therefore either send virtually all their income to relatives back in Ireland or place it in a savings account. Margaret Naylan, a County Cork native who had emigrated to America in 1848, managed in seventeen years of work as a domestic to save nearly $500, the equivalent of about $7,000 today.[42]

Yet there was a heavy psychological toll involved. "The relationship between the servant girl and her employer, is nearly the same as that of master and slave," wrote a southerner commenting on life in New York. "The duties expected and exacted are precisely the same. The respect, and obedience, and humility required, are also nearly the same." Unlike slaves, however, employers felt no obligation to care for a sick servant and might simply fire her. Servants also had very little free time. The typical servant got every other Sunday off, alternating with the cook, chambermaid, or laundress, "so that the house shall never be 'left alone.'" This meant little if any social life, making the young Irishwoman's already difficult task of finding a mate even more worrisome.[43]

Observers constantly praised the "Irish servant girl" for her propensity to send her meager salary to loved ones back in Ireland. "The great ambition of the Irish girl is to send 'something' to her people as soon as possible after she has landed in America," observed a visiting Irish journalist, John

Francis Maguire, in 1868. ". . . Loving a bit of finery dearly," he continued, "she will resolutely shut her eyes to the attractions of some enticing article of dress, to prove to the loved ones at home that she has not forgotten them; and she will risk the danger of insufficient clothing, or boots not proof against rain or snow, rather than diminish the amount of the little hoard to which she is weekly adding, and which she intends as a delightful surprise to parents who possibly did not altogether approve of her hazardous enterprise. To send money to her people, she will deny herself innocent enjoyments, womanly indulgences, and the gratifications of legitimate vanity." Men scrimped and saved to send bank drafts to Ireland as well. Maguire noted that even hardened New York criminals who might spend much of the year in jail practiced self-denial around Christmas and Easter so they could send a remittance to their old father or mother in Ireland. But of the $120 million (according to Maguire's estimate) that Irish Americans had remitted to Ireland from 1845 to 1865, a large portion came from the purses of domestic servants.[44]

Some servants found it difficult to be surrounded by all that wealth and material comfort while their families suffered back in Ireland or Five Points. In 1859, for example, thirty-two-year-old Irish immigrant Ann Kelly of 54 Mulberry Street was accused by her employer of theft. Asked by the District Attorney's Office what had happened, the servant replied that "I got drunk, and went into the lady's wardrobe and helped myself pretty freely." For those who could resist such temptations, however, work as a domestic servant offered poor Irish immigrants the chance to wield more leverage with their employers than most Five Points workers. "Whenever one thinks she is imposed upon, the invariable plan is to threaten to leave the situation at once," noted the *Tribune*, "instead, as in other kinds of employment, of being fearful of losing it." This could translate, especially for an experienced servant, into better pay, more time off, and other benefits.[45]

In other parts of New York, young women found work in fields such as paper box making, type founding, book folding and binding, and umbrella and artificial-flower making. But virtually no Five Points women secured jobs in these better-paying occupations in the 1850s. These employers instead hired native-born women, mostly the young daughters of artisans and mechanics seeking to earn some money before marriage. Those who did hire immigrants, such as milliners, primarily employed English and French natives. By the 1890s, poor immigrant women would dominate most of these trades, in part because natives abandoned such work but also because employers sought a cheaper workforce. Until then, these lucrative trades would remain virtually off-limits to Five Pointers.[46]

Even in the sphere of domestic service, the Irish faced significant prejudice and discrimination. An 1853 advertisement in the *New York Sun* read: "WOMAN WANTED—To do general housework; she must be clean, neat, and industrious, and above all good tempered and willing. English, Scotch, Welsh, German, or any country or color will answer except Irish." A notice in the *Herald* two days later likewise specified "any country or color except Irish." The *Irish-American*—organ of the Irish community in New York—condemned such prejudice, vowing to "kill this anti-Irish-servant-maid crusade" and hiring a lawyer to sue the advertisers and newspapers involved. Although the *Irish-American*'s crusade did halt the appearance of specifically anti-Irish advertisements, employers simply modified their wording slightly. About one in ten continued to specify "Protestants" or "Americans" (though ads seeking male employees were remarkably free of such overt discrimination). While the *Irish-American* might boast by 1857 that "no Irish need apply" stipulations had virtually disappeared, thinly veiled prejudice against hiring Irish Catholics, especially as domestic servants, continued to be a staple of New York life.[47]

One way to escape such discrimination was to run one's own business. Five Points women usually got this opportunity only by taking over an enterprise after a spouse died. Twenty-nine-year-old Bridget Johnston, for instance, who had immigrated to New York from County Galway in 1840, operated a boardinghouse and liquor store at 8 Elizabeth Street after her husband disappeared. Forty-five-year-old widow Bridget Giblin, who had emigrated from Ireland in 1841, began to run the family's liquor store after her husband passed away. Grocer Ann McGowan at 55 Park Street, junk dealer Mary Hynes next door at 57 Park, and second-hand dealer Jane Wilson at 68 Baxter also seem to have been widows who took over family enterprises. Women who owned their own businesses sometimes earned relatively sizable incomes. Johnston, for example, had saved nearly $300 in her bank account by 1853, equivalent to about $5,000 today. If they chose to remarry, widows were expected to put family first. Eleanor Quinn, an old-clothes dealer on Baxter Street, told a neighborhood policeman that she planned to "get married and give up the business."[48]

Because few Five Pointers of either sex ever managed to start a business, very few women of an entrepreneurial bent got the opportunity to run one. A more typical pursuit for these women was to peddle fruit. The "Irish apple woman," with her pipe in her mouth and a small pile of fruit balanced on a folding table, was an omnipresent sight on the sidewalks of New York in the Civil War era. These peddlers sold whatever fruit was in season, but because apples could be kept without spoiling for many months and made a convenient snack for pedestrians, they were the favorite. Widows often sold apples to support themselves after their spouses died. Catherine Norris of 32 Baxter Street and Catherine McCall of 64 Mulberry both worked as fruit peddlers after their husbands passed away. Some married women peddled fruit if their children were old enough to be left alone. County Limerick native Johanna Baggott of 15 Mulberry Street, for example, became a "fruiterer" when her son Edward turned fourteen and began learning to manufacture walking canes. Working on the streets was not easy, but the flexible hours and independence fruit peddlers enjoyed must have often inspired envy in Five Points' hundreds of seamstresses and servants.[49]

"THEY . . . HAVE THEIR OWN LAWS AND CUSTOMS"

American society frowned upon street work by women, especially young women who might attract the attention of male passersby. Children, however, could work on the streets without breaking any sexual taboos. Consequently, hundreds of Five Points children plied "street trades" in order to supplement their families' incomes, or, in the cases of orphans, to support themselves. One of the best known street trades for girls was selling freshly cooked ears of sweet corn. " 'Here's your nice Hot Corn, smoking hot, smoking hot, just from the pot!' " cried dozens of girls on the streets of New York when corn was in season. Attorney George Templeton Strong noted in 1854 that he "heard the cry [of the hot-corn girls] rising at every corner" on August and September nights and was often "lulled to sleep by its mournful cadence in the distance." Young corn vendors were so closely associated with impoverished New York neighborhoods that when *Tribune* reporter Solon Robinson published a collection of his essays on "life scenes" of poor young New Yorkers, he entitled it *Hot Corn*.[50]

The most heartrending tale in Robinson's book was that of a Five Points hot corn vendor known as "Little Katy." He described her as "an emaciated little girl about twelve years old, whose dirty shawl was nearly the color of rusty iron, and whose face, hands, and feet, naturally white and delicate, were grimed with dirt until nearly of the same color." Asked why she stayed out so late selling corn, Katy replied that she was afraid to go home until she had sold it all because her alcoholic mother would beat her if she did not earn a certain sum each day. According to Katy, her mother used the money from her corn sales to buy rum. A few weeks after meeting Robinson in the autumn of 1853, Katy fell ill, supposedly from staying out too late in the chilly autumn air. Her ailment, wrote Robinson, was aggravated by a beating her mother gave her for not earning enough money. Soon after the thrashing, Little Katy died. Contributions to the Five Points House of Industry soared after publication of Robinson's story, as New Yorkers sought to support its efforts to take such children off the streets and away from abusive parents. Robinson's book sold 50,000 copies, more "than any since *Uncle Tom's Cabin*," according to Strong.[51]

Many of the young girls who sold corn in August and September became street sweepers during the winter. These children swept intersections so pedestrians could cross the street without dirtying their boots with mud. Given the filth of the New York streets and the quality of their brooms, a sweeper could do little to remove the muck from a street corner. Nonetheless, the tips they received in the rain and snow—when they did a "brisk business"—could be quite substantial. A street sweeper could earn a dollar a day, and twice that on a very busy and snowy Saturday, scurrying about at crowded intersections offering her services to the well-dressed passersby. But if the weather was good, a street sweeper might return home with twenty-five cents or less. Dozens of Five Points children supplemented their families' incomes by sweeping intersections in the winter months.[52]

Young girls were best known for selling corn and sweeping street corners; boys tended to work as bootblacks and newsboys. It was especially easy for Five Pointers to become newsboys because most of the city's newspapers were produced just south of the neighborhood at the southern end of the Sixth Ward. Newsboys, generally ten to thirteen years old, earned half a cent for every daily paper sold during the 1850s, paying 1½ cents for each two-cent journal. Some bought their papers directly from the publisher, but most purchased them from wholesalers, men in their late teens or early twenties who had once been newsboys themselves. Unsold newspapers could not be returned for a refund, so it was vitally important not to buy too many and be stuck with unsold inventory. In order to estimate sales, a newsboy would scan the contents of the paper—if he could not read, he would ask a friend to do it for him—before choosing how many to purchase. He would scream out the headlines at the top of his lungs in order to attract the attention of pedestrians on busy streets such as Broadway. Often he tailored his appeal to each passerby, emphasizing business news for a strolling merchant and cultural reports for a potential female customer. Newsboys typically earned from twenty-five to fifty cents per day, though sixty cents to a dollar was not unheard-of for the best and most energetic salesmen. On a day when the paper featured news of an execution, revolution, or disaster, a newsboy might take home two or three dollars, and on a particularly brisk Sunday, even more. With these substantial sums at stake, newsboys organized to protect their interests. In 1850, New York ministers sought to preserve the dignity of the Sabbath by banning the boys "from crying and selling papers on Sunday." The newsboys responded with a protest meeting in City Hall Park and successfully fended off the proposed law.[53]

Like the street sweepers and hot corn girls, most of the city's newsboys took their earnings home to help support their families. But many newsboys were orphans or runaways who lived on the streets. Owen Kildare was seven years old when, in 1871, his stepfather kicked him out of their Catherine Street home. Kildare went to Park Row (where most of the city's newspapers had their offices), took up with a gang of newsboys who slept on the streets, and soon began selling newspapers himself. During the summer, these waifs slept in City Hall Park, on courthouse steps, or in coal boxes under building stairwells. In the winter, they huddled over steam grates outside the newspaper pressrooms or in the doorways of unlocked buildings.

Despite these hardships, the newsboys relished their freedom and independence. On a typical day, they bought their morning papers at the crack of dawn and worked until they had exhausted their supply, usually around nine o'clock. They would then eat breakfast at an inexpensive restaurant, and afterward go to a ferry terminal hoping to earn tips carrying passengers' packages to the hacks and omnibuses. After their midday dinner, newsboys purchased their supply of afternoon papers and sold them into the evening. Many then went to the working-class theaters on the Bowery

or Chatham Street, after which they could often be found at midnight in a
"'coffee and cake' cellar" taking their supper, smoking a cigar, or sipping a
cup of coffee. Although Children's Aid Society founder Charles Loring
Brace started the Newsboys' Lodging House during the 1850s to take these
children off the streets, hundreds chose to continue living on their own.
Newsboys came from all over the city, but poverty drove an especially
large number of Five Points boys to this vocation. One was Tim Sullivan,
later the Tammany Hall boss "Big Tim" Sullivan. The son of Lansdowne
immigrants Daniel Sullivan and Catherine Connelly, Tim was living at 25
Baxter Street when, at age seven, he began hawking newspapers to help
support his family.[54]

The other trade most popular with Five Points boys was shoe shining,
universally known in the Civil War era as "boot blacking." Many newsboys had once been bootblacks. Tim Sullivan, for example, had shined
shoes at the Fourth Ward police station house before peddling newspapers.
Bootblacks typically ranged in age from ten to sixteen, though some (like
Sullivan) started work much younger. "The headquarters of this class are
in or near the Five Points district," noted one reporter in 1868. "They form
a regular confraternity, and have their own laws and customs." Like the
newsboys, the bootblacks were well organized, operating an informal trade
union. "The 'Order' establishes a fixed price for labor, and takes care to
protect its members against the competition of irregular intruders. . . . The
affairs of the society are managed by a 'Captain of the bootblacks,' whose
word is supreme, and who wields his power as all arbitrary rulers do." Like
street sweepers, bootblacks depended on bad weather to improve business,
though the filth of Manhattan's thoroughfares kept their services in constant demand. Those with regular followings set up shop in certain high-
traffic locations. Others, with small wooden foot stands slung over their
shoulders, chased potential customers up and down the sidewalks of the
busiest streets, lamenting the embarrassing appearance of a gentleman's
footwear in an effort to win his business. Earning about the same amount
as the newsboys, bootblacks who lived on their own were likewise
renowned for their lavish spending on food, drink, tobacco, and entertainment. But those who lived at home would have turned most of their earnings over to their parents. Although most bootblacks were the sons of Irish
immigrants, dozens of Five Points Italian boys were also working as bootblacks by the eve of the Civil War.[55]

For every child who worked full time as a bootblack or newsboy, there were five or ten who helped support their families in more informal ways. The most common was to scavenge for coal, looking for chunks of the shiny, black rocks on the street near coal yards or by the docks where it was unloaded from barges. Some children collected scrap wood, which could be burned in the family stove or sold for kindling. Still others prowled the streets looking for (or stealing) scrap metal, glass, or anything that could be sold to Five Points' many junk dealers.

Children could scavenge for fuel or scrap metal or glass while playing in streets, alleys, and yards. Yet as the Civil War approached, it seemed that increasing numbers of New York children devoted *all* their energy to work. Boys bought matches wholesale and sold them door to door. Girls peddled flowers on street corners in all but the winter months. In 1860, the Children's Aid Society found the increasing number of poor girls employed in factories especially alarming, noting that its inspectors regularly observed children making "hoop-skirts, artificial flowers, boxes, mantillas, caps, envelopes, and especially ready-made clothing." Adolescents had been almost unknown in these fields fifteen years earlier. Although cases in which children worked to support alcoholic parents garnered the most coverage in the press, the vast majority worked out of economic necessity. Children in Sixth Ward households headed by widows were three and a half times more likely to hold steady jobs than those in homes in which an adult male worked full time. Given Five Points' preponderance of widows, it is no wonder that so many youngsters there were forced to devote the bulk of their childhoods to street work.[56]

"Hard times"

Many Five Points workers lived in precarious circumstances even in the best of economic times, and when the American economy took one of its periodic downturns, living conditions became especially bad. In November 1854, the press began to note "hard times" for city workers that far exceeded the usual seasonal slowdown. "This winter, unlike any of the fifteen preceding it, has seen thousands of able and generally industrious men and women reduced to distress and beggary by the sudden and wholesale failure of their accustomed work," commented the *Tribune*. Record numbers of journeymen found themselves discharged from factories and workshops, while "even clerks" lost their jobs because so many "mercantile establishments are closed or out of business." Thousands of laborers "hitherto employed in the vast building operations of our City, now almost wholly suspended," found themselves destitute. Even many of those most steadily and reliably employed of immigrant workers, the "servant girls," had been "thrown out of place by the collapsing fortunes or the vanishing of incomes."[57]

As a result, New Yorkers flocked to the city's soup kitchens in unprecedented numbers. Relief statistics confirm the extent of the suffering. The New York Association for the Improvement of the Condition of the Poor, which dispensed food or fuel only to the most desperate paupers, aided nearly three times as many indigent New Yorkers in January 1855 as it had a year earlier. Many Five Pointers were among them. "The past year has been particularly marked by general pecuniary pressure, and excessive suffering among the poor," remarked the annual report of the Five Points Mission for 1855. "The wretchedness and degradation of this locality have been made *more manifest* than ever before. . . . [T]he multitude . . . seemed in many instances to be on the very verge of starvation." The mission distributed so much food in the winter of 1854–55 (providing foodstuffs to nine hundred families daily) that it teetered on the brink of bankruptcy by mid-February.[58]

Just three years later, the Panic of 1857 again threw thousands of Five Pointers out of work. "The past winter [1857–58] has been one of unparalleled suffering among the poor at the Five Points," reported charitable workers there. "Want of work has caused multitudes to ask for bread who never begged before." This depression seemed to have a particularly devastating impact on the needle trades. The *Herald* estimated that half the tailors, seamstresses and cutters were unemployed and that only one in ten wholesale clothing establishments was giving out work. "It was really afflicting yesterday and the day before to see the large number of poor working women who crowded many of the down town stores early in the morning, eagerly seeking for work, and each in turn pleading their and their families circumstances, and begging for some thing to do, even at half price, or on half or quarter time." Unable to save money due to their pitiful pay, the seamstresses were "in many instances already entirely destitute of the actual necessaries of life, although they, in some instances, have not been over a week or ten days out of employment." The Association for Improving the Condition of the Poor agreed that "there were probably none whose condition was more pitiable than that of the sewing women . . . who were suddenly deprived of work. . . . Their slavish labor and scanty compensation afforded them no reserved fund on which to fall back in time of need." Other Five Points workers found themselves in similarly desperate straits during the Panic of 1857.[59]

Such suffering must have sometimes made Five Pointers wonder if they would have been better off staying in Ireland. It *was* probably easier to ride out hard times (though not actual famines) in Ireland, where winters were warmer, fuel in the form of turf was often available for free, and one could grow one's own food. According to the *Irish-American*, "the 'hard times' and want of employment" actually drove some immigrants to return.[60]

"This is the best Country in the world"

Still, return migration was exceedingly rare in the Civil War era, even though observers on both sides of the Atlantic debated whether reports of Irish success in America were exaggerated. One such debate took place on the Lansdowne estate. "The most cheering accounts are daily reaching us of their success in New York," claimed Lansdowne's estate agent in 1851, soon after the emigrants had left Kerry. "Every letter which arrives brings new accounts of how well they fare and urging others to come over if they can." A few years later, Trench reported that some of the emigrants had returned to Kerry sporting gold chains. Whether or not the Lansdowne emigrants wrote glowing accounts of their new homes cannot be verified, as none of their correspondence is known to have survived. Kenmare archdeacon John O'Sullivan later complained that Trench should have been "ashamed" at the way he exaggerated the successes of "the victims of your ill-advised extermination." Yet according to Trench, the emigrants claimed that they were "now living as well as Father McCarthy himself."[61]

The few surviving letters written by Palmerston's and Gore Booth's North Sligo emigrants indicate that they had few if any regrets about having moved to North America. "I can not say that I am sorry that I left home, except that my heart aches now and again, to see those faces which I loved and yet left them behind me," wrote one Gore Booth emigrant. "Tell Mary I still feel hurt at her leaving me to come alone, altho' I am very glad that I did come, for I do feel most happy and content here, so much so that I sometimes forget Old Ireland for a time." Nineteen-year-old Eliza Quin, also a Gore Booth emigrant, wrote from the fringe of Five Points to her parents back in Ireland that "i am verry glad for leaving there and coming to this Country."[62]

These immigrants insisted that others should join them at their earliest opportunity. We "are fed everyday like on Christmas at home," boasted one Palmerston emigrant living with her employer near Toronto, "& the man and master are at one table—if a man is honest he is as well thought of as if he was worth thousands." Anyone willing to work hard could not only find employment but earn far more than in Ireland. Palmerston emigrant Pat McGowan wrote from New York that "I would advise [my brother] Mick McGowan to come out to this country & all the youngsters to come too if they are able. Let . . . them come as quick as possible."[63]

Not everyone was suited to life in America, warned the newcomers. McGowan recommended that those prone to drunkenness should stay behind. "Any person that does not think to mind himself let him stop at home for the whiskey is so cheap that it encourages the Irish fool to take it," he advised. He would have liked his friend "James Quin to come to this country but he would be too fond of the whiskey it is so cheap." Few of the immigrants regretted having left Ireland, and this was especially so for those who relocated to the United States. "This is the best Country in the world," exulted Quin, despite living in New York's most impoverished district. McGowan agreed that life in New York was far superior. Comparing his old life to his new one as he proudly sent his parents $20 (the equivalent of about $320 today) just months after arriving in New York, he could only wonder "how did we stand it so long a time?"[64]

Some observers nonetheless questioned the wisdom of emigrating, given that the Irish faced discrimination and were virtually forced into low-paying manual labor. Reading such charges in the *Irish-American*, Five Pointer Michael Coogan felt compelled to reply. Although it was true that Irish Americans worked primarily as laborers, he wrote, the Irish were especially well suited for the work. Besides, the County Wicklow native argued, manual labor paid well compared to the options available in Ireland. "*Don't they get good value for their time and labor,*" Coogan asked. "They can eat good beef, and pork, and butter, and eggs, and bread—not so at home in the old country," even though "an Irish laborer had to work harder there than here."[65]

Those familiar with the standard version of Irish-American history might be surprised by these letters. A deep pessimism pervades this literature, assuming that the famine immigrants were a kind of lost generation fated to be victims of disease, nativism, and overcrowded tenements in America.[66]

If any group of Five Pointers was going to fit this stereotype, it ought to be the Lansdowne immigrants. A full 90 percent of the Lansdowne men toiled as lowly paid menial laborers, and they lived with their families in the most filthy and overcrowded tenements. But account ledgers from the Emigrant Savings Bank suggest that these immigrants did far better than we have previously imagined. Lansdowne immigrants living in Five Points opened 153 accounts in the bank's first six years of operation (through August 1856). In fact, about half of the Lansdowne families living there had opened accounts by mid-1855. The bank records provide a rare glimpse into the economic fortunes of a very significant number of the Lansdowne immigrants.[67]

The bank ledgers suggest that even while living in Five Points, the Lansdowne immigrants were able to save far more than one might have imagined given their wretched surroundings and low-paying jobs. Take the case of the Tuosist natives who visited the bank together to open accounts on July 2, 1853. The first, Honora Shea, had been one of the earliest Lansdowne-assisted immigrants to arrive in New York, landing in March 1851 with her daughter Ellen Harrington, described by the bank secretary as "an illegitimate child, aged 14 yrs." Although Honora apparently could not depend on a male breadwinner for her support, and lived in the decrepit tenement at 35 Baxter Street, she was able to open her account with an initial deposit of $160, the equivalent of more than $2,500 today. The next account was assigned to laborer Patrick Murphy and his wife, Mary, who lived next door to Shea at 33½ Baxter and had also arrived in New York in March 1851. They made an initial deposit of $250, a sum worth roughly $4,000 in contemporary terms. Bank officials also gave an account to "washer" Barbara Sullivan, whose cramped apartment filled with her six children, son-in-law, and six boarders was described earlier. Sullivan, who at this point also lived at 33½ Baxter, made the smallest opening deposit of the three, $135 (roughly $2,200 today). Later in the day, a fourth Lansdowne immigrant, Judy O'Neill, also opened an account. O'Neill lived at 33½ Baxter as well and had arrived in New York in May

1851. She started her account with a deposit of $148 (about $2,400 today). These four Lansdowne immigrants, who had probably arrived in New York virtually penniless, had quickly managed to squirrel away substantial savings.[68]

Although the Lansdowne immigrants opened their accounts with an average deposit of $102, a significant sum, many of them started with just a few dollars and closed them a few weeks later, either because they needed the money or because they did not believe that their savings were safe. Only 51 percent of the Lansdowne immigrants ever managed to increase their initial balance by 50 percent or more. It appears that most Lansdowne immigrants saw the bank as a place to safely keep (and draw interest upon) nest eggs they had already managed to accumulate before opening their accounts. This would explain why so many Lansdowne immigrants did not add substantially to their initial deposits, even when they did keep their accounts open for extended periods. Bonane native Mary Flynn, for example, was in her early sixties when she opened an account in August 1853 with $45, though in less than a year she had doubled her money. During the recession winters of 1855 and 1858, she withdrew as much as half her savings, but always worked her way back to the $90 level within a year. That was the balance, give or take $5, at which her account remained into the late 1860s. Flynn undoubtedly saw $90 (about $1,500 today) as the appropriate size for her family's emergency fund.

Yet in 28 percent of the Lansdowne accounts, the immigrants accrued quite substantial financial resources—at least $250 ($4,000 in modern terms). Consider the three Tim Sheas. The first, along with his wife, Johanna, had accumulated $495 (more than $7,900 today) by 1860. A second Timothy and Johanna Shea, who arrived in New York in 1853, a year after their namesakes, had amassed $592 (roughly $9,500 in contemporary terms) by July 1857. A third Timothy Shea (sometimes called "O'Shea"), who had emigrated from Tuosist at age forty-eight in 1851, managed along with his wife Honora to save $658 (about $10,500 today) in three accounts by July 1857, the highest sum attained by any of the Lansdowne immigrants who had opened an account by mid-1856.[69]

One might argue that these Lansdowne immigrants were especially fortunate—that they must have found especially steady jobs and not had to deal with the financial crises caused by the death of a spouse or a long-term illness. But this does not seem to be the case either. Recall the story of

Lansdowne immigrant Ellen Holland. Her husband and eldest son both died, leaving Nelly a widow with two children to support. One might have expected her to dip into her savings to help make ends meet during such trying times, because she could not have earned much money as a "washer." But Nelly did no such thing. In fact, despite losing her family's two primary breadwinners, by 1860 she had increased her bank balance to $201.20 (more than $3,200 today), quite a feat for a widow who, just eight years earlier, had been on the brink of starvation. Nor were the Lansdowne immigrants more financially successful than other immigrants. Non-Lansdowne Five Pointers typically saved even more money.[70]

What accounts for this surprising financial success? Perhaps the privation these immigrants had experienced in County Kerry had conditioned them to practice extraordinary frugality. Living in Five Points they could pay among the lowest rents in New York, and taking in so many of their countrymen as lodgers enabled them to recoup a significant proportion of their housing expenses. Having so many of their kinsmen and former neighbors with them in New York also undoubtedly helped the immigrants. Virtually overnight, they created a large, intricate network that could be used to help find jobs, housing, even spouses. Their arrival in whole family units may have benefited the Lansdowners as well. Children could be set to work blacking boots or selling newspapers, while women could add to the family income by taking in boarders and laundry. And if someone through sickness, injury, or death became unable to work, there were plenty of relatives around to help out. There were also many Lansdowne immigrants who did not fare as well as the three Tim Sheas. For widows with young children, life was particularly hard. But the noticeable absence of Lansdowne surnames in the relief records of the Five Points Mission suggests that the Lansdowners took care of one another—helping widows find new mates and unemployed men and women new jobs.

It appears that once the Lansdowne immigrants got settled in Five Points and found work, they focused all their energies on saving money to establish nest eggs for their families, choosing to stay in Five Points even after they could afford to move to more spacious apartments in cleaner and safer neighborhoods. Inasmuch as many of them were undoubtedly also sending money to loved ones in Ireland, either to help support aged parents or to pay for relatives' emigration, the typical Lansdowne immigrant's ability to squirrel away $100 or more in just a few years is truly remarkable.

Some undoubtedly moved out of Five Points or to less squalid blocks within the neighborhood once they had established these competencies. But many, despite their substantial savings, decided to stay in the Lansdowne enclave, either because they enjoyed being surrounded by so many fellow Kerry natives or because they sought to continue saving as much money as possible by paying low rents. That so many of the Lansdowne immigrants' account balances remained relatively constant indicates that once they reached their savings goal, they began to raise their standard of living by spending more of their income. "If they do not get milk and honey in abundance," noted one Civil War–era immigrant, referring to the Irish, "they are able . . . to exchange . . . their 'male of potatoes' for plenty of good substantial food; their mud cabins and clay floors with fires on the hearth for clean, comfortable dwellings with warm stoves and 'bits of carpits on their flures.'"

Through a concerted scheme of hard work and self-sacrifice, then, the Lansdowne immigrants managed to improve their lives significantly, from both the misery of County Kerry and the initial privations of Five Points. So while natives may have considered Five Points "a hell-mouth of infamy and woe," most of the immigrants who arrived there from Ireland would have concurred with Quin's judgment that "this is the best Country in the world."[71]

5

PROLOGUE

"We Will Dirk Every Mother's Son of You!"

THE ELECTION DAY scene was typical of nineteenth-century New York. Hundreds of men thronged the street outside the polling place, dressed in long, rough overcoats and tall hats to ward off the November cold. Many were in a boisterous mood, having fortified themselves at neighborhood saloons for the anticipated rushing and shoving, fighting and brawling— what were popularly referred to as "election sports." At booths outside the polls, campaign workers handed out ballots and harangued the crowd with exhortations to vote for their candidates. Some in the crowd milled around these stands, harassing the speakers and arguing loudly with supporters of their political rivals. Others jostled their way into the line that wound from the ballot box far out into the street.

Suddenly a loud cry pierced the air, and all eyes turned to a "a lithe, dark, handsome man" standing atop a packing crate. *"I am Isaiah Rynders!"* he shouted, knowing that his name alone would strike fear into the hearts of many within earshot. "My club is here, scattered among you! We know you! Five hundred of you are from Philadelphia—brought here to vote the Whig ticket! Damn you! If you don't leave these polls in five minutes, *we will dirk every mother's son of you!"* New York voters, whether longtime residents or temporary Philadelphia transplants, knew that "Ike" Rynders did not make idle threats. Within five minutes, wrote an eyewitness, "five hundred men left the polls, . . . and went home without voting, for fear of assassination."[1]

This was just one episode in a life story that, as the *Times* noted without exaggeration years later, "forms one of the most romantic of histories." Born in 1804 near Albany to a German-American father and a Protestant Irish-American mother, Rynders earned his lifelong title of "Captain" when as a young man he commanded a sloop on the Hudson that carried produce and merchandise between New York and upstate river towns. By 1830 he had moved to the South, acquiring some notoriety there as a riverboat gambler. In 1832, after allegedly killing a man in a knife duel over a card game in Natchez, Mississippi, Ike fled to South Carolina. There he became "superintendent of the . . . racing stables" of General Wade Hampton, grandfather of the future U.S. senator of that name. After Hampton died and the Panic of 1837 set in, Rynders returned to New York and settled in Manhattan.[2]

In New York, Rynders became "a thorough-going sporting-man." Sporting men did not hold steady jobs, but instead devoted themselves to gambling, politics, boxing, and horse racing. An entire sporting subculture developed in New York, with its own saloons, own patois, even its

Isaiah Rynders as he appeared in the post–Civil War years. *Frank Leslie's Illustrated Newspaper* (January 24, 1885): 380. Collection of the Library of Congress.

own newspapers. One, the *Clipper*, reminisced years later that Rynders throughout his life had "a strong love for the card-room and the race-track." Another admiring journalist noted that the Captain was often found dealing faro or "presiding at one of those suppers of oysters, canvas-back ducks, and champagne with which the gamblers of New York nightly regale their friends and customers."[3]

Many sporting men were muscular bruisers, but young Rynders was a man "of medium size and sinewy form, with a prominent nose, and piercing black eyes—a knowing smile, and a sharp look altogether. He was cool and enterprising in his manners, and fluent and audacious in his speech." Unlike others in the "sporting fraternity," Rynders was not an especially skillful pugilist. A tough country minister, Sherlock Bristol, boasted in his autobiography that he fought Rynders to a draw on a Hudson River steamer after defying Rynders by signing an anti-slavery petition. But as a *leader* of fighters, Rynders was unsurpassed.[4]

It was in this capacity that Rynders rocketed to prominence in 1844. Realizing that Democrats needed to form an organization to rally the faithful during that year's tight presidential contest between their candidate, James K. Polk, and Whig Henry Clay, Rynders established the Empire Club. With a membership dominated by sporting men and prizefighters, the group began to whip up support for Polk. Political veterans believed that whoever captured New York's electoral votes would carry the presidency, and Rynders worked feverishly to turn out the Democratic vote. Led by Rynders on a "white charger," one thousand Empire Club members marched at the head of a Polk parade on the eve of the election, with "music, and thousands of torches, Roman candles, rockets, and transparencies, with never-ending hurrahs for Polk and Dallas, Texas, Oregon, Fifty-four-forty-or-fight!"* The following day, Rynders and his club used intimidation and outright violence to prevent Whigs from casting ballots. New York swung to Polk by just 5,100 votes out of 486,000 cast. Had he lost New York's thirty-six electoral college votes, he would have lost the

---

* The most important issues in the campaign were whether or not the United States should annex Texas, and how the country should conduct its negotiations with Great Britain regarding the disputed Oregon Territory, which both nations claimed. The Democrats' slogan "Fifty-four-forty-or-fight" referred to their promise to insist upon all of Oregon, up to the 54° 40' latitudinal line (at what is now central British Columbia) that marked its northern boundary. The Whigs were less bellicose in their demands.

election. Whigs and Democrats alike gave Rynders a significant share of the credit for Polk's razor-thin margin of victory. In gratitude, the new president rewarded him with a lucrative no-show job as a "measurer" in the New York Customhouse, allowing him to devote his full attention to gambling and politics.[5]

After 1844, Rynders and the Empire Club became real powers in New York politics, dominating primaries and disrupting political gatherings of their opponents. Rynders was feared not only outside the Democratic party but within it as well. In early 1845, for example, Rynders and his Empire Club compatriots attended a Tammany Hall meeting organized to discuss the possible annexation of Texas. "Aided by a crew of his noisy associates," complained the *Evening Post*, Rynders "took the resolutions prepared by the committee of arrangements and reformed them to suit his own ideas of public policy." His men shouted down speakers and bullied the meeting into adopting resolutions that suited him. No man before Rynders had ever so boldly and impudently dominated Tammany's public meetings. Yet Rynders was not an ignorant thug. His election night speeches at Tammany Hall, which became something of an institution, were "a mixture of terrible profanity with liberal quotations from the Scriptures and Shakespeare." He could recite entire scenes from memory.[6]

By midcentury, Tammany leaders made sure never to enter a meeting or convention without first trying to secure Rynders's support. But the ambitious Captain wanted to become one of those leaders himself. His strategy for advancement involved turning Five Points into his political fiefdom, something its emerging Irish Catholic political leaders were bound to resist. The outcome of this struggle would define the political future of the infamous neighborhood.

CHAPTER FIVE

Politics

༄༅

L IKE ALL NEW YORKERS in the early nineteenth century, Five Pointers deferred to their elite neighbors in political matters. Prominent
merchants and manufacturers held most important elective offices. With
the adoption of universal white male suffrage, however, this deference
began to wane. The election of the uneducated and uncultured Andrew
Jackson as president in 1828 and his raucous inauguration the following
year helped inspire this political revolution. The Five Points election riots
of 1834 marked its climax on the local level, as the neighborhood's Irish
immigrants rose up to seize power. Because the well-to-do in these years
were already rapidly abandoning the Sixth Ward for more prestigious
neighborhoods, few of the old political elite bothered to contest this transfer of power to the brawling multitude. Five Pointers were consequently
among the first New Yorkers to experience the new style of mass politics.

"A ZEALOUS, FIRM, HARD-FISTED
DEMOCRAT OF THE OLD SCHOOL"

Prominent Five Pointers still held the majority of political offices in the
years after the 1834 riot, but the political elite now comprised saloonkeepers, grocers, policemen, and firemen rather than manufacturers and
wealthy merchants. The political power of these four groups resulted from
their particular ability to influence voters. Saloonkeepers were the most
respected men in Five Points and other low-income neighborhoods. "The
liquor-dealer is their guide, philosopher, and creditor," commented *The*

Nation in 1875. "He sees them more frequently and familiarly than any-body else, and is more trusted by them than anybody else, and is the person through whom the news and meaning of what passes in the upper regions of city politics reaches them." Saloonkeepers could thus earn the gratitude and confidence of large numbers of tenement dwellers, gratitude that could be repaid as votes on election day. The liquor dealer also had the name recognition and financial resources to bid successfully for political office. Because many groceries sold little more than alcohol, grocers were as well positioned as saloonkeepers for political advancement.[7]

Another route to political prominence ran through the volunteer fire department, one of old New York's most colorful institutions. A well-drilled fire company was just as likely to turn out in force to support a particular electoral slate as to extinguish a fire. Intimidation was an important weapon in the rough-and-tumble world of Five Points politics, and the renowned fighters of the Sixth Ward fire companies frequently determined the outcome of a primary meeting or general election, often through a brawl with a competing company. Most companies admitted at least a few members to their exclusive ranks specifically for their fighting skills.

The popularity and respect that carried a Five Pointer to leadership within a fire unit were the same qualities political kingmakers sought in their candidates. Future Five Points political leaders such as Matthew T. Brennan, his brother Owen, Alderman Thomas P. Walsh, Assemblyman Michael Fitzgerald, and Police Justice Joseph Dowling all began their political careers in Engine Company No. 21. Because of its role as a means of political advancement, competition for places in No. 21 was fierce. As a result, some of its members created an auxiliary unit, the Matthew T. Brennan Hose Company No. 60, named in honor of No. 21's most prominent and politically powerful alumnus and dominated by his political allies. Its first foreman, John Clancy, became president of the board of aldermen and city register. Other early members included future alderman Morgan Jones, future county supervisor Walter Roche, and future city councilman Michael Brophy. Indeed, most Five Points politicians first came to prominence as foremen of the ward's fire companies, as did Tammany "Boss" William M. Tweed.[8]

Another path to political power wound its way through the police department. "There is no patronage . . . that a district leader desires so much and seeks so eagerly as places on the police force," noted the postbellum attorney and reformer William M. Ivins. Politicos usually reserved positions in the police department for young men who had demonstrated party loyalty through previous campaign efforts. In return for such a high-paying and secure job (about $12 per week in the mid-1850s), the officer was expected not only to continue laboring for the party at election time, but to contribute a portion of his salary to party coffers, and use his influence to assist party members who might run afoul of the law. In this "unobtrusive and quiet way," Ivins recognized, a policeman could render "valuable ser-vice" to both the political benefactor who secured him his job and the party as a whole. Such "service" enabled many a Five Points policeman to rise out of the ranks to both party leadership and elective office.[9]

A few Sixth Warders managed to claw their way to political promi-nence without first working in the police and fire departments or owning a saloon. A Five Pointer might, for example, approach a neighborhood political leader and promise to deliver the votes of a pair of large tenements or of those immigrants from a certain Irish county. Or he might offer the services of his gang to intimidate the leader's opponents at a primary meet-ing or on election day. Whether he offered voters or fighters, this political aspirant would expect something in return. Some gang leaders asked for money; but the more politically ambitious sought patronage—jobs with the local, state, or federal government—either for themselves or for their allies. Patronage was one of the keys to increasing one's political clout, especially for those who could not count on the support of a fire company or saloon customers. The aspiring politician who could deliver jobs to sup-porters was in the best position to increase his strength. This was espe-cially the case in Five Points, where steady jobs were so hard to come by.

By the end of the Civil War, these paths to political power had been systematized into a relatively well-defined hierarchy. At the top sat the city's party "boss." His lieutenants each controlled one of the city's assem-bly districts, and they in turn relied upon the ward leaders. Every ward was divided into election districts, headed by a single leader or a committee of ward captains or "heelers." In the postbellum years, the subdivisions con-tinued until every block (and sometimes even single buildings within a block) had its designated party leader. But before the Civil War, the situa-tion was far more fluid. No "boss" anointed a ward or district captain in those years. Instead, factional leaders and their supporters fought (often lit-erally) for control of each ward.[10]

The battles for the political supremacy of Five Points were always waged among Democratic factions. In the twenty years before the Civil War, Whigs and their Republican successors won only a single Sixth Ward political contest, and that only because the Democrats in that year split their votes among three different candidates. By the late 1850s, Republican candidates had trouble garnering even 15 percent of the district's vote. Five Pointers' overwhelming support for the Democratic party resulted from a number of circumstances. Democratic opposition to both the anti-slavery movement and to laws that would restrict the sale of alcohol drew many Five Pointers. So too did the party's reputation as the friend of the immigrant and opponent of nativism. But substantive issues were rarely discussed during Five Points political contests. Platforms and policy statements are conspicuously absent from neighborhood political campaigns, even the few covered thoroughly in the press. Instead, political struggles were usually decided by the personal popularity of the individual factional leaders; their ability to deliver patronage to their followers, and their skill at wielding violence and intimidation at primary meetings and on election day to secure power and maintain it thereafter.

The career of Constantine J. Donoho, the first Five Points political leader to emerge in the tumultuous new world of mass politics, exemplifies many of these rules of political life. What little we know about Donoho's career comes from the memoirs of Frank "Florry" Kernan, a self-described "sporting fireman" whose colorful reminiscences provide some of the most vivid depictions of political and cultural life in Five Points. Kernan remembered Donoho as "a zealous, firm, hard-fisted Democrat of the old school," who emerged as "king of the politicians of the sixth ward" during "the reign of Felix O'Niel [sic]." O'Neil served as Sixth Ward alderman in 1841–42, which made him the titular leader of the district's Democrats, but Donoho's role as kingmaker gave him every bit as much, and perhaps more, influence and power.[11]

Donoho's political support rested on the twin foundations of liquor sales and patronage. "Con" (as he was universally known) operated a grocery at 17 Orange Street, a half block south of the Five Points intersection. "The steps that led to the barroom from the street, although wide," recalled Kernan, "afforded only room for one customer at a time, as upon each step a barrel stood containing two or three brooms, another with charcoal, another with herrings nearly full to the top, while upon its half-open head lay piled up a dozen or two of the biggest, to denote what fine fish were within." Inside was "a bar quite ornamental," well stocked with liquor, pipes, and tobacco. "Seats there were none, as Con kept no accommodations for sitters, unless they found it on a half-pipe of gin, 'Swan brand,' that lay on its side near the counter, or a row of Binghamton whisky-barrels, interspersed here and there with barrels of pure spirits, much above proof, that told the fact that Con Donoho was a manufacturer of ardent spirits as well as ardent voters."[12]

The bulk of Donoho's power derived not from his status as barman but from his position as Sixth Ward "street inspector," a post he had held since at least 1839. In this capacity, Donoho hired men to clean, pave, and repair the ward's streets, giving him more patronage power than any other man in the ward. Con filled these dozens of positions not merely with loyal Democrats, but with "all the roaring, fighting, brawling heroes of his locality" who could be trusted to battle for whichever party faction he chose to support. Donoho also rewarded men who could deliver the votes of a particular tenement or of an ethnic or regional constituency within the neighborhood. Con would be sure to stretch his hiring budget to the limit in the month or so before an election, in order to ensure that influential Democrats and their friends and families had received a share of the proverbial "loaves and fishes." Donoho's status as street inspector benefited his grocery business as well. Those hoping for a job were sure to visit Con's establishment to remind him of their willingness to labor (both physically and politically) upon his behalf. Five Pointers whom he had favored with the coveted patronage posts would likewise show their gratitude by patronizing his bar. Rainy days in particular were "Con's harvest-time, for then the streets could not be swept, and knights of the broom, hoe, and shovel kept holiday at their chieftain's rendezvous."[13]

The support of Con Donoho and other local men of influence was the most important asset an aspiring politician could acquire to position himself for a nomination at the ward's annual Democratic primary meeting. As a prerequisite to running for alderman, a liquor dealer had to not only establish himself as one of the most powerful Democrats in his own election district, but earn endorsements from party leaders in others as well. This would take years of service on behalf of the party, along with building popularity in the neighborhood, and doling out patronage to influential neighborhood residents. In advance of the primary, the would-be alderman would treat potential voters in the ward's saloons and make deals with other party leaders to obtain their support. Endorsements might be offered in return for a promise of patronage, the pledge of a reciprocal endorsement in the future, or an up-front cash payment. Sixth Ward Democrats were generally divided into two factions, so in most cases the aldermanic hopeful would canvass support from just one and then hope to rally that faction to victory at the primary.

The leaders of each faction drew up a slate of candidates in advance of the primary meeting. By the 1850s, it was said that most candidates for significant offices such as alderman had to bribe these leaders to be assured a realistic chance at a nomination. The faction leaders also chose nominees for the minor ward offices (such as assistant alderman, constable, and school board member) and candidates to represent the ward at nominating conventions for city, state, and federal posts. With this ticket set, faction leaders had barely enough time to mollify disappointed officeseekers before the ward primary meeting, which typically took place three to four weeks before election day.

"A point of utmost consequence is the determination of the place at which the primary is to be held," Ivins noted in the 1880s, explaining that "the voting is usually done at that liquor store, cigar store, livery-stable, or other place where the contestant favored by the [party's ward] leader can best control the house, its exits and entrances, and can most easily and speedily gather his voters together." Before about 1858, the situation in the Sixth Ward was somewhat different. Until then, all Democratic factions had agreed that the ward primary meeting should be held in the neutral territory of "Dooley's Long-Room," the large barroom in the Sixth Ward Hotel on Duane Street near Centre and Cross. Kernan wrote in 1885 that in Dooley's Long-Room "there has come off more Irish jollifications, benefit balls, raffles for stoves, primary meetings, and political rows than in any other public place in the city." In the antebellum years, Dooley's Long-Room "was as famed in politics as was ever Tammany Hall. To hold a meeting there made it orthodox and regular. The ticket that was indorsed at that famed political head-quarters" almost always carried the ward. Consequently, all factions "struggled hard, even to bloody rows, to obtain an indorsement" at the annual primary meeting held there.[14]

In a city that became renowned for its rough and bloody primary meetings, those in the Sixth Ward were the most violent of all. "Regularity in the old Sixth was ofttimes only won by black eyes, torn coats, and dilapidated hats," recalled Kernan. "The knowing politicians of the ward never went well dressed to a caucus meeting at Dooley's Long-Room." The meeting's very first vote was the most crucial, because the faction that managed to elect the convention chairman controlled the proceedings and could, with official sanction, use its fighters to "maintain order," the typical excuse given for expelling the weaker faction's supporters from the building. If its strongmen failed to appear promptly, disaster loomed for even the most popular and seemingly invincible clique. "Once," Kernan remembered, "when John Emmons was the candidate [for alderman, in either 1843 or 1844], nothing gave him the victory but the fact that Bill Scally [a noted pugilist], with Con Donoho and his men, arrived just in the nick of time to save the chairman from going out of the window, and the secretary following him; but their timely arrival changed the complexion of things, and sent the opposition chairman and officers out through the same window." Candidates for even the most prestigious Sixth Ward office could not sit idly by while hired bullies did the rough work for them. Kernan noted that those nominees who did not "take a hand with their friends in battling for their cause" in Dooley's Long-Room would be derided as cowards and "lack votes on election days."[15]

The ticket that emerged victorious could claim to be the official slate of the Democratic party, its "regular" nominees. Supporters of the winning ticket would boast of their primary meeting heroics and gloat whenever they encountered the defeated faction's adherents. In contrast to most of the rest of the city, however, the losing side in a Sixth Ward primary did not usually agree to work dutifully for the party's official nominees. Because Democrats there so outnumbered their opponents, they could split their votes between two slates of candidates and still be relatively sure that one or the other would carry the ward. Consequently, a few days after the convention, the defeated faction typically announced that because of treachery at the primary, or the demands of the "true Democrats" of the ward, it would field its own set of candidates in the general election. Candidates running "on the split" (as this practice was called) hoped to convince voters that they would better represent their constituents' interests than would the nominees of the ruling cabal.

But there was also an ulterior motive for remaining in the race. By threatening to make a deal with the ward's Whigs or Republicans and thereby possibly defeating the regular nominees, the renegade Democrats were often able to extract concessions from the leaders of the ruling faction. Those running on the split might receive the promise of a certain share of the ward patronage for withdrawing from the race. Or the aldermanic candidate defeated at the primary might be promised that nomination the following year. Such concessions were most common in presidential or gubernatorial election years, especially when party unity was considered crucial for victory in an important state or national contest. But in most cases, the ascendant faction refused to make any concessions to the renegades, knowing full well that having won the nomination at Dooley's Long-Room, success on election day was usually assured.

One of Con Donoho's most important tasks was to ensure that the "regular" nominees outpolled those running on the split. To this end, he employed every means at his disposal. According to Kernan:

When Con was away on business, his good woman, Mrs. Donoho, stood behind the counter to attend to all customers; and an able helpmate was she to just such a rising man and politician as Con gave promise to be. Should Mrs. Conlan, or Mrs. Mulrooney, or the wife of any other good voter of the old Sixth, come for her groceries, or with a milk pitcher for a drop of good gin, or a herring to broil for the good man's twelve o'clock dinner, she would avail herself of the opportunity to have a bit of a talk with her concerning how her James, Patrick, or Peter would vote on the approaching aldermanic election . . . and heaven help the customer if she talked up in favor of John Foote on the split, or hinted that her man believed in Bill Nealus. If she did, the smallest herring or potatoes to be found in the barrel would be dealt out with a jerk, and a wink with it, that said when she had sense, and wanted to see her old man with a broom in his hand and ten shillings a day, work or no work, and pay from Con's own hand on Saturday nights, she had only to make her husband send the Nealuses to the devil, and hurrah for Felix O'Niel! In this way, Mrs. Con Donoho made many a convert to the banner of her liege lord, the bold Con Donoho.[16]

Although they could not vote, women like Mrs. Donoho could help determine the outcome of a close election.

The boisterous scene at the ticket booths outside a New York City polling place on election day 1856. The names on the booths are those of the presidential candidates. *Frank Leslie's Illustrated Newspaper* (November 15, 1856). Collection of the New-York Historical Society.

Even if defections to candidates running on the split had been kept to a minimum, party leaders such as Donoho had plenty of work to do on election day. If renegade Democrats used their fighters to gain control of the polling places, they might discourage many voters from casting ballots and carry the election by intimidation. One such struggle for the polls occurred in 1848, when Democrat Frederick D. Kohler challenged incumbent Thomas Gilmartin in the race for Sixth Ward alderman. Although it is not evident which candidate was the party's "regular" nominee, Gilmartin clearly held the upper hand at the "First District poll" located on the second floor of the Sixth Ward Hotel. According to the *Tribune*, "Gilmartonians . . . occupied the staircase for the purpose of exercising a wholesome supervision over the ballots of democratic voters. As soon as a man came up to vote they demanded to see his tickets, and if he refused[,] snatched them out of his hand for examination. If a Whig, he was suffered to go up and vote; but if a Kohlerite" he was thrown down the stairs. Around four-thirty, a large contingent of Kohlerites arrived at the hotel to remove the obstacle to their voting, "when all of a sudden the Gilmartonians brought forth a store of stout and heavy bludgeons, all ready for fight." The similarly armed Kohlerites initially routed their opponents, but the

Gilmartonians soon returned with bricks. "The struggle now became really fearful; hard blows were given, heads broken and blood flowed freely.—Several men were cut severely."

Police finally arrived to disperse the fighters, but the combatants regrouped at the second district polls near the Tombs (the city jail located on Centre Street between Leonard and Franklin) "and there attempted to renew the melee" before the authorities again subdued them. Kohler's success in the first district helped him carry the election. Such gory struggles, which made the Sixth Ward "notorious for the free indulgence of election privileges," were especially common from 1834 to 1856.[17]

"BLOODY AND HORRIBLE IN THE EXTREME"

On occasion, polling place fights in the Sixth Ward escalated into full-scale riots. One such melee—that of 1834—was described earlier. Another erupted in 1842, when the already violent world of Sixth Ward politics was convulsed by the volatile "school question," the controversy surrounding the role of religion in New York's public education system. Until 1842, public schools in New York City were run by a private Protestant organization, the Public School Society. Its schools featured readings from the Protestant King James Bible, the singing of Protestant hymns, and textbooks that—according to Catholics—presented "the grossest caricatures of the Catholic religion, blaspheming its mysteries, and ridiculing its authority." As immigration increased their numbers, New York Catholics complained bitterly about the overtly Protestant curriculum and asked that either religion be removed altogether from the schools or that the state fund Catholic schools to complement the overtly Protestant ones run by the Public School Society.

In April 1842, the New York legislature, attempting to mollify both dissatisfied Catholics and Protestants who felt threatened by Catholic demands, passed the Maclay Act, which created a new city-run public school system while leaving the Public School Society and its schools intact. Policy in the new schools on issues such as Bible reading would be set by school boards popularly elected in each ward. Neither side was completely satisfied with the Maclay Act. Catholic leaders such as Bishop John Hughes of New York were disappointed that the legislature would not finance Catholic schools and believed that the Catholic minority would not receive fair treatment from the new boards. Protestants, who perceived any changes to the prevailing system as capitulation to Catholics, were even more unhappy. Walt Whitman, the young editor of a Democratic organ called the *Aurora*, condemned the new law as a "statute for the fostering and teaching of Catholic superstition."[18]

Given the Democratic party's subsequent reputation as the organization most sympathetic to the city's Irish Catholic immigrants, Whitman's comments may come as a surprise. But city Democrats actually split over the school question, with Protestants generally supporting the Public School Society and Catholics endorsing the Maclay Act. Whitman argued in the *Aurora* that city Democrats should not submit to a "coarse, unshaven, filthy, Irish rabble" that did the bidding of the city's Catholic leaders. Describing Catholic priests, Whitman asked, "shall these dregs of foreign filth—refuse of convents—scullions from Austrian monasteries—be permitted to dictate what Tammany *must* do?" No, the young editor insisted, because if Democrats yielded to "the foreign riffraff . . . in this case . . . there will be no end to their demands and their insolence." Whitman asserted that he had "no prejudice against foreigners, because they are such," but felt that "they are becoming altogether too domineering among us." The best way to teach the newcomers to respect American institutions, Whitman argued, was to resist Catholic educational demands.[19]

The school question would have made the municipal election of April 1842 a contentious one in any event, but passage of the Maclay Act just two days before that contest threw city politics into virtual anarchy. The Sixth Ward, with its unusually high concentration of Irish Catholic voters, was especially volatile. "All the discordant and jarring elements and bones of contention seemed to have been concentrated in the unfortunate Sixth Ward, of bloody and riotous and immortal memory," lamented the *Herald*. In the race for alderman, William Shaler (the incumbent assistant alderman) apparently captured the "regular" Democratic nomination, though a second Democratic ticket headed by former alderman James Ferris entered the fray as well. It was not unusual to find two Democratic candidates vying in a Sixth Ward aldermans' race. But as the *Herald* pointed out, "all this quarrel arose out of the School question also. For Con Donohue [Donoho], the former Collector of the ward, was turned out by the Common Council for the part he took in the School Question. . . . When the nominations were made, Donohue was sacrificed and thrown overboard; on this his Irish friends rallied, made a new ticket, with Ferris at the head, to run it against Shaler, who had become very unpopular by his crusade against the little boys for crying Sunday newspapers." The late entry into the race of a third Democratic candidate, Shivers Parker, whom the *Herald* described as "the Bishop Hughes' candidate," further complicated matters, raising the real possibility that the Whig candidate, Clarkson Crolius Jr. (whose family had made a fortune manufacturing earthenware in the Sixth Ward), might win the contest.[20]

Tension in the Sixth Ward was thus palpable as voters went to the polls on April 12. Balloting progressed with no more than the usual fisticuffs until late in the afternoon, when the "Spartans" arrived at the Sixth Ward Hotel polls. The Spartans were a violent Democratic gang that had become renowned in the previous few years for its use of intimidation at primary meetings and general elections. Although membership in the gang was not limited to any particular locale, its leader, Mike Walsh, and most of his adherents lived outside the Sixth Ward. The inimitable Walsh, a self-styled "subterranean" radical who advocated workingmen's rights and Democratic independence from Tammany Hall, had in recent years led his troops into election day battles against the Whig "Unionist" Club. But on this occasion, Walsh decided to devote his energies to his Democratic foes.

Accompanied by noted pugilists "Yankee" Sullivan and Bill Ford, as well as dozens of less well known but equally tough Spartans, Walsh and his men picked a fight with the Ferris supporters distributing ballots outside the hotel. A phalanx of Unionists stood by "urging on the quarrel." When the Unionists realized that the Spartans considered this a fight between "Americans" and the Irish Catholics over the school question, they joined in on the Spartan side, attacking Irishmen up and down Centre Street. "Here the Irish got the worst of it, from the Americans" reported the *Herald,* as the Spartans and Unionists attacked them with both fists and bricks. The Irish initially retreated toward the Five Points intersection, but soon returned with reinforcements armed with sticks and clubs, "driving everything before them; and then the fight was bloody and horrible in the extreme." Police officers led by the mayor finally arrived on the scene and made many arrests, mostly of Irishmen, "and many who were taken to the Tombs were so beaten about the head that they could not be recognized as human beings."[21]

Yet the savagery was far from over. As soon as the police had departed, the Spartans and their allies returned to Centre Street with their own clubs, vowing to punish what Whitman (an ardent admirer of Walsh) called "the outrageous insolence of these foreign rowdies." As the Spartans inflicted "the most savage violence" upon the Irish Catholics, several of the immigrants took refuge in the Sixth Ward Hotel. The Spartans pursued them inside, reported the *Herald*, "and gutted the place, as completely as if there had been a fire there." Many of the Irish fled to their homes in Five Points, wrote Whitman, but the Spartans "burst in the doors, dragged out their antagonists, and cracked their heads."[22]

The rioters chose their targets carefully. They attacked the Orange Street residence and grocery of Con Donoho "and injured it considerably; they also attacked several other houses of Irishmen in Orange street, destroying furniture and breaking windows." The mob then moved uptown to Bishop Hughes's home, where rioters broke windows, doors, and furniture before authorities dispersed them. "Had it been the reverend hypocrite's head" that had been smashed, snarled Whitman, "instead of his windows, we could hardly find it in our soul to be sorrowful." The divisions among Sixth Ward Democrats allowed Crolius to carry the election for alderman, giving the Whigs a one-vote majority on that board. In those races in which the Democrats were more united, however, they emerged victorious. Donoho, for example, was elected to a spot on the new ward school board. Although a Democrat, Whitman rejoiced at his party's defeat in the contest for alderman, asserting that it would teach Tammany to resist Catholic demands concerning the school question.[23]

New York newspapers described the election riots of 1842 as a clash between Americans and Irishmen, but in retrospect the roots of the conflict were far more complicated. After all, Walsh himself was a native of County Cork (though he had immigrated to New York as a small child) as was his chief pugilist, Yankee Sullivan. Philip Hone blamed the troubles on religious rather than ethnic tensions. "The combatants in this scrimmage," he asserted, "consisted of two factions of Irish who, to keep up a pleasant recollection of their interesting amusements in their own country, retain the designations which they had there of Catholics and Orangemen, or as the terms are softened down here, 'Spartans' and 'Faugh-a-ballaghs.'" Walsh was in fact the child of Irish Protestants (whether he was himself religiously affiliated is not known), so there was some basis for Hone's conclusion that "the cause of all this trouble" was passage of the purportedly pro-Catholic

Maclay Act. Yet it seems unlikely that religion was the sole motivating factor either, because when Walsh ran for Congress twelve years later against a devout Irish Catholic Democrat, "Honest John" Kelly, the predominantly Catholic Sixth Ward voted overwhelmingly for Walsh.[24]

"I HAVE OFTEN SAID THAT THE ALDERMAN OUGHT TO BE LOCKED UP"

For the rest of the 1840s, Sixth Ward politics remained in a state of flux, as a slew of men jockeyed to become the district's Democratic leader. John Foote and Thomas Gilmartin, for example, successful running mates for alderman and assistant alderman respectively in 1846, fought a bitter battle for the top ward office a year later. Gilmartin succeeded in ousting the incumbent Foote, but the following year, Gilmartin's running mate from the previous contest—Frederick Kohler—challenged Gilmartin for the alderman's post, defeating him in the bloody contest described earlier. The details of these power struggles are impossible to reconstruct. Apart from a brief press announcement concerning which ticket had captured the "regular" nominations at the primary meeting and descriptions of the Sixth Ward polling places on election day, newspapers did not cover these local contests. All that changed in November 1849, however, when for a variety of reasons the entire city focused its attention on the contest for Sixth Ward alderman. A close look at this election reveals a great deal about the workings of Five Points politics.

The November 1849 contest became a *cause célèbre* because of the outrageous conduct of the incumbent, Patrick Kelly. Kernan recalled that Kelly, who lived above his saloon at the corner of Mott and Bayard Streets, had been "very anxious to be an alderman." But Kelly did not get along with Con Donoho, making his political ascent through normal channels impossible. According to Kernan, Kelly therefore "set himself up as a reformer who would knock the controlling power that was all to smash, and oppose the interest of old Tammany." Yet after spending liberally in unsuccessful attempts to win the regular nomination for assistant alderman in both 1847 and 1848, Kelly was close to bankruptcy. Kelly then "sued for peace on any terms," recalled Kernan, "and, in sympathy, was taken into friendship by the regulars and made an alderman" at the municipal election of April 1849.[25]

That "friendship," if it ever really existed, did not last very long. Because the city had decided to switch its municipal elections from April to November in order to match the state and national electoral calendars, Kelly was forced to run for reelection just seven months after taking office. Although few Sixth Ward aldermen served consecutive terms, Kelly believed that he deserved a second due to the unusually short duration of his first. A serious challenge to Kelly's reelection, however, was mounted by ex-alderman Foote, who had the backing of Yankee Sullivan, ward police captain John Magnes, and Matthew T. Brennan, an increasingly influential twenty-seven-year-old fire company foreman and saloonkeeper.

The source of the animosity between the Kelly and Foote factions is no longer apparent. Yet authorities were so certain that the upcoming Sixth Ward primary meeting would be even more violent than usual that they ordered the police from the First Ward to attend and preserve the peace (those from the Sixth would be in attendance with Magnes, fighting for Foote). According to the *Herald*, the First Ward officers "were ordered to wear their fire hats to ward off bricks and stones." Early reports from the tumultuous scene gave Foote the advantage, but when it became clear that a majority of the men in attendance were casting their votes for Kelly, "the Foot[e] party, under their leader, 'Yankee Sullivan,' endeavored to carry off, or break, the ballot box, but did not succeed in the attempt." Kelly and his supporters celebrated their primary victory at his saloon and all up and down Bayard Street, and according to the *Herald*, "every man they met of the Foote party they beat most unmercifully. One young man, a barkeeper of Mr. Brennan, of the opposite party, was severely handled; and in the Bowery, several of the voters for Foote were well 'licked.'" However, the primary battle was destined to be repeated in the general election, as Foote and his ticket vowed to run on the split.[26]

Because the contest in the Sixth Ward was so acrimonious, the press followed it closely, even taking the unusual step of publishing each of the sixty or so names on each faction's primary ticket, and providing a rare opportunity to determine exactly who Five Points' political activists really were. Of the men whose occupations could be determined, 53 percent were liquor dealers—either saloonkeepers or grocers. But a significantly higher proportion of the Foote delegates sold alcoholic beverages, while Kelly's advocates were twice as likely as Foote's to be blue-collar workers (artisans and unskilled laborers). These occupational distinctions make some sense given that Kelly positioned himself as a "reformer" in a district whose politics were dominated by saloonkeepers. The only other identifiable distinction between these Kelly and Foote supporters was geographic—Foote backers were much more likely to live in the western portion of the ward, while Kelly's partisans resided primarily in the eastern election districts. Foote advocates outnumbered Kelly's seventeen to four on Centre and Elm Streets (the two largest thoroughfares on the west side of the ward), while Kelly delegates exceeded Foote's by twenty to eleven from Mulberry Street east to the Bowery. This trend may reflect that Foote, Brennan, and Sullivan all resided in the western portion of the ward, while Kelly lived in its northeastern election district.[27]

Tensions between the two sides were still running high when, just after midnight on Friday, October 12, an inebriated Kelly stopped in at John Lee's Centre Street porterhouse for a drink. It took nerve for Kelly to visit Lee's establishment, inasmuch as Lee was a well-known Foote supporter and his saloon was a gathering place for Kelly's opponents. Indeed, when Kelly arrived, Yankee Sullivan and a number of "Mat. Brennan's boys" were drinking at the bar. According to eyewitnesses, Kelly and Sullivan soon began "using very coarse and vulgar language together." Fearing a brawl, Sullivan's friends took him outside, but the infuriated prizefighter soon rushed back in and struck Kelly a glancing blow to the forehead. Kelly then ordered a policeman who was present to arrest Sullivan. Sometime after 1:00 a.m., the alderman and his political lieutenant John Layden (a printer whom Kelly's friends had roused from bed when they learned that the alderman was quarreling with a slew of Foote supporters) left Lee's saloon to accompany Sullivan and the officer on the two-and-a-half-block walk to the Sixth Ward police station on Franklin Street.

Another person who had come to Lee's porterhouse when word of the confrontation spread through the ward was coal dealer and politico Frederick Ridaboek. Unlike Layden, Ridaboek did not travel to Lee's establishment to protect Kelly, but instead sought him out in order to have the alderman discharge two prostitutes—"'Big Maria' and Johannah Buckly"—who were being held at the station house. When the group arrived there around 1:45 a.m., Layden (himself once the ward's assistant police captain) convinced Kelly not to press charges against Sullivan. Tempers flared, however, when Kelly, Layden, and Ridaboek entered the station house and found it filled with prominent Foote supporters, including both Brennan and Captain Magnes. Magnes was especially incensed that Kelly had brought Ridaboek with him. Earlier that evening while drinking at a grocery on Orange Street, Ridaboek and the captain had engaged in a fierce argument over Ridaboek's claim that Magnes had caused the falling-out between Kelly and an influential ex-alderman, James Ferris.

When Kelly began writing the discharge papers for the two prostitutes, Magnes insisted that Kelly should not act in a judicial capacity while intoxicated. But Kelly ignored him and with Ridaboek's assistance continued drafting the release papers. The chagrined Magnes responded by ordering Ridaboek removed from behind the desk reserved for police and judicial officials. The two men and their associates hurled increasingly vicious slurs at each other, and when Magnes refused to remove a Foote supporter from behind the same desk, Kelly began screaming at the captain. Magnes then arrested Kelly for drunkenness and ordered him placed in a cell. Layden got another alderman out of bed to discharge Kelly, but the obstinate and still intoxicated Kelly refused to leave the cell unless the board president himself came to free him. The dutiful Layden fetched James Kelly from his Second Ward home, and at dawn Pat Kelly returned to his apartment on Bayard Street.[28]

News of Kelly's arrest for drunkenness caused a sensation in the Sixth Ward and throughout the city. His trial, which began on October 16, captivated New Yorkers for more than a week. The proceedings did not reveal any details not already well known within hours of Kelly's arrest, but did expose the extent of the animosity between the two political factions and the weapons those in power could use to punish their enemies. One witness for the prosecution admitted under cross-examination that he might harbor bitterness toward Kelly because the alderman had fired his brother-in-law from his post as ward lamplighter. Patrolman Edward Riley testified that he had been told that Kelly would dismiss him from the force if he won reelection. Rumor also had it that Kelly would replace Magnes with Layden if Kelly won a second term. Virtually every prosecution witness conceded having spoken disparagingly of Kelly in public at one time or another. Brennan, for example, admitted that "I have often said that the alderman ought to be locked up." After more than a week of testimony, attorneys for both sides rested their cases, and the judge announced that he would not render his verdict until after the election. The *Irish-American* hoped that the city would now concentrate on matters more important than "this supremely ridiculous affair."[29]

Meanwhile, Kelly's arrest became a campaign issue. Within hours of the alderman's release from jail, Foote's adherents posted handbills headed in large, bold type: "AN ALDERMAN IN CUSTODY," containing both a history of "the affray" and copies of the affidavits taken at the time of Kelly's incarceration. Kelly quickly responded with a letter to the editor of the *Herald*, insisting that his arrest and the fuss over it "was made up for the shop, by the 'stars' [police] and their underlings, to suit the present electioneering times, and prejudice the minds of the community against me." Each faction could also rely on newspaper allies to publish propaganda on its behalf. The *Sun*, one of the city's first "penny dailies," advocated the Foote cause, while a campaign sheet known as the *Clarion* rallied Kelly's supporters. The *Clarion* reminded voters that in his first term on the Common Council, Kelly had proposed to establish "a FREE BATHING AND WASHING HOUSE for the poor" and to increase the pay of laborers working for the city to $1.25 per day in the summer when demand for such employees was at its peak. Kelly's supporters also emphasized his status as a political outsider. According to the *Herald*, one speaker told Sixth Warders that the alderman "was none of your high-stiffened aristocracy. He did not live upon chicken for dinner, but his fare was just as homely as their own. And when he found any of the boys in a scrape he let him out of the Tombs."[30]

Both factions understood that spectacle was just as important as propaganda in an antebellum election, so as election day approached, each organized public demonstrations to inspire a groundswell of support for its candidates. On October 30, Kelly's advocates held a "ratification meeting" at the Sixth Ward Hotel, concluding with a torchlight parade in which the marchers bombarded Brennan's and Sullivan's saloons with bricks as they passed by. Later, Foote's supporters outfitted a Broadway omnibus with a "huge cap of liberty" and a "large placard" promoting the ticket. Inside the vehicle, someone lustily beat a drum while the other passengers chanted and sang of their allegiance to Foote. On the evening of November 2, his adherents organized an "open air meeting" which, according to the *Herald*, featured "bonfires, sky-rockets, torches, and bands of music . . . but no clubs, brick bats, or stones. Wonders will never cease."[31]

As election day dawned on November 6, the whole city braced for extraordinary violence at Sixth Ward polls. "In expectation of a riot," noted the *Herald*, men from all over town collected in the district "to witness the sports." But these enthusiasts were ultimately disappointed. "The election was one of extraordinary quiet," remarked the *Herald* in surprise. Merchants and saloonkeepers in the vicinity of the polls kept their establishments shuttered in anticipation of a riot, and as a result, the scene "bore the appearance of a Sabbath day, instead of a hotly contested election." According to the *Herald*'s reporter, the ward's only election day excitement was

> a negro hunt. A colored voter in the forenoon having made his appearance at one of the polls, some of the "bhoys" took it into their heads to give him a licking. . . . He took to his heels in beautiful style, and never was there a rarer hunt. Through Centre street, and the streets adjoining, he ran for his life, amidst shouts and yells, while his pursuers chased him most vigorously, still keeping close on his track, till at length he gave a short double round the corner of a street, and "earthed" himself in a friendly house.

As evening fell, the suspense became unbearable as each side waited to learn which ticket had polled the most votes. Kelly was finally announced the winner, having captured 892 votes to Foote's 707. The unusually low Whig turnout—just 98 votes—suggests that one of the factions may have consummated a last-minute deal with that party's leaders. The *Herald*, no great admirer of Kelly, insisted that the alderman had secured Whig support by placing the name of the Whig candidate for sheriff on some of his ballots. But it is also possible that Whigs stayed home (the total number of votes cast was well below normal) rather than risk bodily harm should they arrive at the polls as rioting erupted. In any event, after the results became known, Kelly's supporters "shouted and paraded around the ward," throwing stones at "Footites" they encountered, firing off an occasional pistol, and holding "really uproarious" celebrations in neighborhood saloons.[32]

In a fitting denouement, Police Justice Mountfort handed down his verdict on November 30. Issuing a stinging indictment of Kelly's behavior, Mountfort observed that had the alderman "not gone to the station house for an illegal purpose, that of discharging from confinement two prostitutes . . . his other delinquencies might have passed unnoticed." Mountfort reminded Kelly that an alderman could lawfully discharge a prisoner only after taking testimony and examining other evidence, not merely because a political ally asked him to do so. The judge pronounced Kelly guilty of drunkenness as charged, upbraided him for abuse of his judicial authority, but waived a fine, perhaps concluding that the embarrassing publicity and judicial tongue-lashing were penalty enough. In large part because aldermen such as Kelly so often abused their judicial powers, state lawmakers rescinded them when they reorganized the city's legislative bodies a few years later. As for Kelly, his haughtiness and penchant for making enemies doomed his political future. He ran unsuccessfully on the split for three more offices—alderman in 1851, Congress in 1852, and councilman in 1854—and thereafter quickly faded from the political scene.[33]

"THE BONE AND SINEW OF THE WARD"

Kelly's political demise cleared the way for Brennan's emergence as the undisputed leader of the Sixth Ward Democratic party. Brennan was born in New York in 1822 and grew up in impoverished Irish enclaves in the First and Fourth Wards. His father, Timothy, a porter, was supposedly "one of the political refugees driven from Ireland to escape the fury of the British Government after Lord Edward Fitzgerald's rebellion" in 1798. He died at about the time Matthew was born, forcing Matthew's mother, Hannah, who as a child had emigrated from County Donegal, to run a vegetable stand at the Franklin Market to support the family. After attending primary school, Matthew helped his mother at the vegetable stand and was briefly apprenticed as a molder. In the mid-1830s, his older brother Owen, eight years Matthew's senior and active in Whig political circles, opened Monroe Hall, a Sixth Ward saloon at the northwest corner of Pearl and Centre Streets, and the teenaged Matthew became a bartender there.[34]

Perhaps out of a desire to emerge from Owen's shadow, Brennan soon moved downtown and sold "coffee, cakes and oysters" from a small storefront at 89 Cedar Street near Broadway. According to the *Herald*, Brennan "remained there for four or five years and gained considerable custom." But by this point, recalled the *Tribune* years later, "running to fires" had become "the ruling passion" of Brennan's life. Although a childhood accident had left him with a perceptible limp, Brennan was "fleet of foot, and . . . possessed of extraordinary strength," precisely the traits of the ideal fireman. Emulating both Owen and his eldest brother, Timothy, Brennan entered the fire department. He spent a few years with Engine Company No. 11 before joining Owen in the Sixth Ward's Engine Company No. 21.[35]

Brennan's transfer to Engine No. 21 probably coincided with his move back to Five Points. The twenty-three-year-old Brennan had relocated there in 1845 when Owen turned over control of Monroe Hall to him. While Owen ascended in Whig circles, "Matt" (as he was universally known) began establishing a base in the ward's Democratic ranks. The ideal location of his saloon at the intersection of two heavily trafficked thoroughfares ensured brisk business and made Brennan a well-known neighborhood liquor dealer. But it was his election in the late forties as foreman of the politically powerful Engine No. 21, noted the *Times* years later, that served as Brennan's "stepping-stone to political preferment."[36]

Brennan exuded an air of confidence, strength, and congeniality that made him a natural leader and helped him achieve his prestigious position as company foreman. And in a neighborhood in which fighting and toughness were prerequisites to political power, Brennan's imposing physical presence also helped him. A friend and newspaper editor described Matthew Brennan at age forty as "a large and robust man, with spreading shoulders, large and arching chest; throat muscular and massive; face singularly open, strong and honest; black hair curling closely round his forehead; a dark brown imperial dropping down from his lower lip, and merging into a small black growth of throat-beard; hazel gray eyes, full of kindly humor and penetration, set under eyebrows rather slight and short; immensely broad round the base of the forehead; and with a nose, not long, but prominent and indicative of energy and courage." Brennan possessed both the physical and personal traits necessary to ascend through the rough world of Irish-American ward politics.[37]

As fire company foreman, Brennan commanded a gang of forty or so tough young men who could be counted on to fight at primary meetings and on election day. Such influence had its rewards. In January 1848, he received his first patronage plum—appointment as one of the two ward residents to whom chimney fires were to be reported. Modest though this might seem, city newspapers covering Kelly's arrest in late 1849 agreed that Brennan was an up-and-coming power in Sixth Ward politics.[38]

Despite Brennan's apparently rapid advancement, his political career seemed in jeopardy at midcentury. His support of Foote's unsuccessful bid to unseat Kelly in 1849 was potentially damaging to his political future, because city Democratic leaders looked disdainfully upon those who failed to fall in line behind the "regular" nominees. Yet a graver threat to Brennan's ambitions materialized in 1850 in the form of Isaiah Rynders, a political fighter feared even more than Con Donoho or Yankee Sullivan.

The colorful Rynders had reached the peak of his influence after Polk's election in 1844. He had become even more notorious in 1849 and 1850, helping to incite the bloody Astor Place Riot. Rynders bought dozens of tickets so that his men could attend the theater there in order to harass William Macready, the controversial English actor. He also paid for the printing and distribution of inflammatory handbills that helped whip the crowd surrounding the theater into a fury. A year later, Rynders again received national attention, this time for disrupting an abolitionist convention organized by William Lloyd Garrison and Frederick Douglass.

Despite these exploits, Rynders could not advance as rapidly within Democratic ranks as he would have liked. Because the most powerful positions within Tammany were chosen by delegates elected from each ward, Rynders needed to establish a base of power in one of these political districts. Given his penchant for violence and intimidation, political weapons that were both accepted and respected in the "bloody Sixth," his decision to concentrate his political operations there made perfect sense. That no leader or faction had managed to seize control of the ward's politics in the late 1840s also undoubtedly motivated Rynders. He therefore bought a Sixth Ward saloon (well south of Five Points on Reade Street), rented a house on Pearl Street just a block west of Monroe Hall, and according to Kernan, "quietly awaited an opening."[39]

Rynders made his move in the autumn of 1850, announcing his intention to take the district's nomination for state assembly. Yet Rynders's move "did not suit the bone and sinew of the ward," recalled Kernan years later, because Donoho, Brennan, and their allies saw Rynders and his Empire Club thugs as "squatters." Not easily deterred, Rynders arrived at Dooley's Long-Room for the primary meeting accompanied by noted fighters Bill Ford, Tom Maguire, John McCleester, and "Hen" Chanfrau—"men who seldom met defeat"—as well as hundreds of other supporters. But Brennan, Donoho, and the rest of Five Points' Irish-American leaders were not about to cede control of the ward without a fight. "When the hour came to name the chairman," Kernan recalled, "the fierce onset of Rynders's friends to defeat [Donoho's candidate] was met with a bold response. The ball opened and the strife commenced, and ere ten minutes passed away, the hall was cleared of all who stood in opposition to the regular voters of the ward. Rynders and his men met defeat."

He did not give up. When city Democrats met at Tammany Hall to choose their legislative candidates, Rynders captured the nomination anyway, probably due to support from the Third Ward, which made up the other half of the assembly district. But disgruntled Five Points Democrats had the last laugh. Many refused to vote for the Captain on election day, and as a result he received 350 fewer votes in the Sixth Ward than the other Democratic candidates. This proved to be decisive, as Rynders lost to his Whig opponent by 200 votes. Realizing that Sixth Warders would not accept him as their political leader, Rynders's "ambition to get a foothold in the glorious old Sixth was quieted ever after." He soon moved across the Bowery to the Seventh Ward, and stung by his embarrassing defeat, never again ran for elective office. He remained a power in Democratic circles throughout the 1850s, and for his continuing loyalty to the party President James Buchanan made Rynders a U.S. marshal in 1857. But Rynders never again dominated New York politics with the swagger and impudence that had marked his early career. His political comeuppance had been engineered in large measure by the increasingly influential Irish Catholic Democrats of the Sixth Ward.[40]

"A SERGEANT OR CAPTAIN IS A REAL POWER IF HE TAKES ANY INTEREST IN POLITICS"

With Rynders no longer a threat to dominate the Sixth Ward, Brennan could concentrate on his own advancement. In the November 1851 race for alderman, Kelly was opposed by his ambitious former protégé, Thomas J. Barr. Unlike Kelly, Barr was far too smart a politician to make an enemy of the up-and-coming Brennan. The two probably came to some sort of understanding before the election, because just a few weeks after Barr's victory, the alderman-elect helped secure Brennan an appointment to succeed Magnes as Sixth Ward police captain.[41]

Brennan used his new post to increase his already strong position in

Sixth Ward political affairs. "A sergeant or captain is a real power if he takes any interest in politics," noted Ivins, and Brennan certainly proved this to be the case. He used his authority as captain to appoint a number of his most trusted allies to places on the force. At the end of 1854, these supporters established the M. T. Brennan Hose Company No. 60, both to demonstrate their gratitude to their patron and to rally support for his candidates at primaries and on election days. To ensure control of the polling places (and to discourage the turnout of his adversaries), Brennan moved some of the voting stations from neutral sites to locations associated with his supporters. By 1856, Five Pointers in the ward's second electoral district had to cast their ballots inside the Brennan Hose Company's club room at 123 Leonard Street (Brennan lived next door at 121 Leonard). Voters in the fifth district were required to venture inside the "low rum-shop" of Brennan loyalist Walter Roche at 19 Mulberry. Another polling site was located in a "hair-dresser's saloon" at 6 Franklin Street, across the road from the ward's police station at 9 Franklin, enabling Brennan's allies on the force to maintain control. Brennan also probably engineered the transfer of the ward primary contest from Dooley's Long-Room in the Sixth Ward Hotel, where it had been held for decades, to the friendlier confines of Elm Street's Ivy Green saloon, another haunt controlled by his supporters.[42]

In 1854, after nearly three years as police captain, Brennan made his first run for elective office, seeking the influential post of police justice. Although police justices were the first judicial authorities before whom all those accused of misdemeanors and minor felonies were brought, legal training was not considered a prerequisite for the post. The judicial district in question covered not only the Sixth Ward but also the Fourth and Fourteenth, each a heavily Irish-American district. Although these demographics might appear to favor Brennan, Democrats in the other wards nominated their own candidates for the highly prized office. On the eve of the vote, these opponents attempted to blame Brennan for the police department's role in the arrest of an Irish patriot wanted by the British. Nonetheless, Brennan carried the election by a comfortable margin.[43]

Brennan had built up an effective electoral machine, but he also succeeded in politics because he was a likable man who made few personal enemies. He was "looked up to by all the poor of his ward and district as a protector and friend," reported his allies at the Leader. The Herald agreed that "he took a special and personal interest in the poor of his district, and always lent a willing ear to their grievances." Brennan was also a hard worker, and devoted to "his fireside and family"—he married Margaret Molony in about 1850 and by 1860 they had five children. Unlike some of his fellow politicians, Brennan "lived a temperate life in all things. . . . His habits of living were of the old fashioned type, early to bed and early to rise, up at five o'clock in the morning, winter and summer, and in his office . . . hours before any of his subordinates thought of stirring." Though a native New Yorker, Brennan and his entire family "spoke Irish and took a pride in it," a devotion to Gaelic culture that undoubtedly impressed the many recent Irish immigrants among his constituents. Brennan's popularity was such that state Democrats nominated him for the post of state prison inspector in 1856. Although Brennan and his Democratic running mates were defeated in the November election, the nomination of a Five Points Irish Catholic for statewide office was unprecedented.[44]

Brennan had a small coterie of especially loyal allies who played an important role in advancing his political career. One of the most important was Joseph Dowling. Dowling was one of the few successful Five Points politicians who had lived in Ireland long enough to remember it, having emigrated at age twelve. Upon arriving in New York in 1838, his family settled in Five Points, where Dowling's father worked as a shoemaker on Centre Street. Like many immigrant children, young Joseph augmented the family income as a newsboy. Soon he was employed "in the office of old Major Noah's *Times and Messenger*, . . . running errands, delivering papers, collecting bills, sweeping out the office and making paste." Later he worked as a paper folder for the *Herald*.

By his late teens, Dowling was a regular at Brennan's saloon, which the *Times* accurately described years later as "a resort for all the young and rising politicians of the period." Like most Five Points politicos, young Dowling "was robust and rugged in physique. He wrestled like a professional and his blow from the shoulder might have felled an ox." He was brave as well; as a teenager he supposedly challenged the renowned Yankee Sullivan to a fight in Brennan's saloon. Impressed by these qualities, Brennan made Dowling a runner with Engine Company No. 21. According to the *Times*, "this proved his starting point in political life." Allying himself with Brennan, Dowling "gradually gained notice as a shrewd and indefatigable worker in ward politics." In August 1848, Dowling was appointed to the ward's police force as a reward for his loyal service to the Democratic party. When Brennan became captain, Dowling as sergeant served as his mentor's right-hand man. And when Brennan became police justice, he made sure that Dowling succeeded him as captain.[45]

Even more important to Brennan's success than Dowling was another loyal ally, John Clancy. Clancy was born in the Sixth Ward on March 5, 1829, the son of "an Irish patriot, who had fought against England on several bloody fields." Other than this familiar refrain, however, Clancy's early years were very different from those of Five Points politicians such as Brennan and Dowling. Most Five Pointers left school to help support their families; Clancy was such a gifted student that his parents allowed him to attend "the grammar school of Columbia College" well into his teens. After working for a number of years as the junior associate of a "commercial merchant" on Water Street, Clancy moved to Savannah, where he wrote essays for several journals. He soon returned to the Sixth Ward and studied law in the office of attorney (and future Tweed Ring insider) Peter Barr Sweeny, who became Clancy's "dearest friend and most intimate associate."[46]

Sweeny's uncle, Sixth Ward Alderman Thomas J. Barr, must have facilitated Clancy's entry into Five Points politics, because he had few of the qualities one usually associates with the neighborhood's politicians. Whereas the biography of virtually every Sixth Ward politician emphasizes the subject's fighting prowess, Clancy's stressed that he had a "slender figure" and "blue eyes, soft as a woman's in their affectionate expression." Other Five Points politicos were known for their street smarts, but Clancy was bookish (though he never did complete his legal studies), erudite, and "a graceful and polished writer." Clancy did serve in the fire department, demonstrating his leadership skills by becoming foreman of Engine Company No. 28. This may have helped him win the respect of the neighborhood's rougher element. Whatever the case, Clancy's advancement in Sixth Ward politics was unprecedented. In 1853, without holding any of the usual minor patronage posts, or serving in the ward's police or fire departments (Engine No. 28 was located elsewhere), the twenty-four-year-old Clancy was elected to one of the ward's seats on the new board of councilmen, a body created to replace the board of assistant aldermen. He was reelected in November 1854, and was elected ward alderman in 1855. After his reelection in November 1856, Clancy's colleagues made him president of the board of aldermen, a great honor for a twenty-seven-year-old who four years earlier was literally unknown in city political circles.

Clancy's remarkable rise to prominence was facilitated by his involvement with the *New York Leader,* a weekly newspaper that became the Tammany organ in 1855. Clancy began contributing to the *Leader* as soon as it became affiliated with Tammany, and his work on the paper made him a well-known figure to all the city's Democratic strongmen. In February 1857, weeks after the aldermen chose him as their president, Clancy became one of the paper's editors. But just as important to Clancy's success was his alliance with Brennan. Founding members of the M. T. Brennan Hose Company No. 60 elected Clancy as their inaugural foreman.

In their capacities as police justice, president of the board of aldermen, and Tammany editor, the thirty-four-year-old Brennan and the twenty-seven-year-old Clancy had climbed further in Tammany's ranks by the beginning of 1857 than had any previous Sixth Ward Irish Catholics. Their accomplishments would have been almost unimaginable to the previous generation of Five Pointers. Only in the 1830s had Irish Catholics wrested control of the ward's politics from the old elite. Even after they had succeeded in overturning the old order, a Catholic Five Pointer of Con Donoho's day could at best aspire to a term as ward alderman. Tammany was still firmly in the hands of leaders who were happy to take the Irishmen's votes, but refused to give them major offices either in the party or in citywide government. But the new generation of Irish Catholic politicians refused to accept such limitations. Led by Brennan and Clancy, these Five Pointers would play a major role in reshaping the dynamics of political power in Civil War–era New York.[47]

6

PROLOGUE

"This Phenomenon, 'Juba'"

CHARLES DICKENS WAS NOT impressed by New York during his 1841 tour. He found the streets filthy, the buildings insubstantial and unimpressive, and his hosts coarse and unsophisticated. Dickens's published account of the trip, *American Notes*, overflows with sarcasm and condescension. But there was one part of his tour that Dickens loved: his visit to a Five Points dance hall.

Victorian Englishmen such as Dickens might sneer disdainfully at most American arts and letters, but they were fascinated by African-American culture. Dickens's introduction to black American dance took place on Orange Street at Almack's, one of the many black-run dance emporiums then operating in Five Points. He was enthralled from the moment he walked in and descended into the narrow, low-ceilinged basement dance room. "Heyday! the landlady of Almacks's thrives!" Dickens declared, describing her as "a buxom fat mulatto woman, with sparkling eyes, whose head is daintily ornamented with a handkerchief of many colours."

Dickens initially found the dance exhibition staged by five or six black couples unimpressive. But then a teenager, described by Dickens as "the wit of the assembly, and the greatest dancer known," dashed onto the floor. "Instantly the fiddler grins, and goes at it tooth and nail; there is a new energy in the tambourine; new laughter in the dancers; new smiles in the landlady; new confidence in the landlord; new brightness in the very candles," wrote Dickens as he thrilled to the dancer's multitude of steps and dance styles. "Single shuffle, double shuffle, cut and cross-out, snapping his fingers, rolling his eyes, turning in his knees, presenting the backs of his legs in front, spinning about on his toes and heels like nothing but the man's fingers on the tambourine; dancing with two left legs, two right legs, two wooden legs, two wire legs, two spring legs—all sorts of legs and no legs—what is this to him? And in what walk of life, or dance of life, does man ever get such stimulating applause as thunders about him, when, having danced his partner off her feet, and himself too, he finishes by leaping gloriously on the bar-counter and calling for something to drink . . . ?"[1]

The sixteen-year-old who mesmerized Dickens that night was William Henry Lane, one of the most influential dancers of the nineteenth century. Despite his fame, only the barest outlines of Lane's biography are known. Born in Providence, Rhode Island, Lane apparently honed his dancing skills with tutelage from black jig-and-reel dancer Jim Lowe. Moving to Five Points, Lane became known professionally as "Master Juba," though whether this was a nickname chosen by African-American friends or a stage name dreamed up by a white promoter is unclear. As would become a tradition in African-American dance, Master Juba first demonstrated his prowess by imitating the best moves of his competitors before wowing audiences with his own innovations.

According to the *Herald*, crowds squeezed into "Pete Williams' place," as Almack's later became known, to see "this phenomenon, 'Juba,' imitate all the dancers of the day and their special steps. Then Bob Ellingham, the interlocutor and master of ceremonies, would say, 'Now, Master Juba, show your own jig.' Whereupon he would go through all his own steps and specialties, with never a resemblance in any of them to those he had just imitated." When Lane performed in London in 1848, the British also found his combination of speed and grace astounding. "How could he tie his legs into such knots," asked the *Illustrated London News*, "and fling them about so recklessly, or make his feet twinkle until you lose sight of them altogether in his energy?"[2]

Although the *Illustrated London News* insisted that Juba and his African-American counterparts were the only original dancers in the world, white working-class New Yorkers took pride in their own dance styles. Young Walt Whitman noted that when butchers in their market stalls "have nothing else to do, they amuse themselves with a jig, or a break down." Describing another style of dance popular with native-born whites, the author and critic Cornelius Mathews asserted that there was "more muscle expended in one shuffle than in a whole evening of [dance at] a fashionable party." Irish immigrants brought their own forms to Five Points, including reels, jigs, and doubles. This last step, wrote one visitor

Master Juba performing in London, *Illustrated London News* (August 5, 1848). Collection of the author.

to Ireland, "consists in striking the ground very rapidly with the heel and toe, or with the toes of each foot alternately. The perfection of this motion consists, besides its rapidity, in the fury in which it is performed." All these styles could be found on display in Five Points' famous dance halls.[3]

Just as boxing promoters purposely pitted Irish versus American or, in later years, white versus black boxers to increase interest in their bouts, theatrical agents organized dance contests between Juba and his "greatest white contemporary," Irish-American John Diamond. Born in New York

City in 1823, Diamond has been called "one of, if not the greatest jig dancers that the world ever knew." Competing near Five Points at both the Chatham and Bowery Theaters beginning in 1844, the contestants were each paid the enormous sum of $500, indicating that such competitions must have attracted huge crowds. "No conception can be formed of the variety of beautiful and intricate steps exhibited by him with ease," stated one contest handbill advertising Master Juba's appearance. "You must see to believe." The "winner" of these competitions is not recorded. But we do know that such contests, as well as the friendly rivalries between native-born whites, Irish immigrants, and African Americans within Five Points' dance halls, had a profound influence on the direction of American dance. Each group incorporated favorite steps from their competitors' dance idioms into their own. In Juba's case, he adopted some of the high-stepping, foot-stomping style of the jig into his own footwork. It was from this inter-action between African Americans dancing the shuffle and the Irish danc-ing the jig that "tap dancing" developed. Lane, the "most influential single performer of nineteenth-century American dance," was the key figure behind the emergence of tap. A dance historian reported in 1948 that "the repertoire of any current tap dancer contains elements which were estab-lished theatrically by him." The 1995 Broadway dance production *Bring in Da Noise, Bring in Da Funk* included an homage to Juba.[4]

The melting pot of dance found in Five Points contributed enormously to Master Juba's innovations. But like many of the neighborhood's resi-dents, Juba left Five Points after becoming a star, joining an English dance troupe by 1848. Yet also like many Five Pointers, Juba did not live long enough to enjoy his success fully. Still in London, he died suddenly in 1852 at the age of twenty-seven.[5]

CHAPTER SIX

Play

⌒ᴍᴍᴖ

GIVEN THAT FIVE POINTERS lived hard, worked hard, and fought hard political battles, it should come as no surprise that they played hard, too. They joined volunteer fire companies that often seemed more determined to battle each other than to fight fires. Their favorite sport was bare-knuckle boxing. They also loved the theater, but even their passion for drama led to rioting. They gambled late into the night. They danced with abandon, until all hours. Although elite New Yorkers might disdain Five Pointers, working-class New Yorkers came from all over the city to join in the neighborhood's rowdy, carefree style of fun.

"THE CHEAPSIDE OF NEW-YORK; THE PLACE OF THE PEOPLE"

Residents or visitors in search of a good time might find entertainment on virtually any block in Five Points. But the neighborhood street most associated with amusement—for Five Pointers and all working-class New Yorkers—was the Bowery. The Bowery began at the eastern edge of Five Points at Chatham Square and continued northward for several miles. Cornelius Mathews called the Bowery "the greatest street on the Continent, the most characteristic, the most American, the most peculiar." Walt Whitman loved the Bowery because it presented "the most heterogeneous melange of any street in the city: stores of all kinds and people of all kinds are to be met with every forty rods." In contrast to Broadway, with its fashionable shops and well-heeled merchants, the Bowery was "the Cheapside of New-York; the place of the People; the resort of mechanics and the laboring classes; the home and the haunt of a great social democracy. . . . You may be the President, or a Major-General, or be Governor, or be Mayor, and you will be jostled and crowded off the sidewalk just the same." The variety of shops and amusements prompted one writer to call the Bowery "a city in itself," while a South Carolinian marveled that it "looks like a vast holiday fair two miles long."[6]

A number of features contributed to the carnival atmosphere. Bowery merchants were among the first to use brightly lit signs and displays to attract customers. In addition, most of the best known Bowery businesses in the Five Points vicinity were raucous bars. Two cavernous beer halls, the Atlantic Garden and the Volks Garden, faced each other between Bayard and Canal Streets. The Atlantic (on the Five Points side of the street) was the better known of the two, sporting several bars, a shooting gallery, billiard tables, bowling alleys, and an orchestra. Octogenarian Charles Haswell remembered its "dense clouds of tobacco-smoke, and hurry of waiters, and banging of glasses, and calling for beer." A few doors south of the Atlantic Gardens—at the southwest corner of Bayard and Bowery—was Paddy Worden's saloon, the Worden House. People came from miles around to see the carved black walnut ceiling in its bar, though it attracted its regular customers primarily from the East Side's "old sports," fighters and gamblers. Across the street at the northwest corner of Bowery and Bayard stood the North American Hotel, which housed another popular bar and hosted many Five Points political gatherings.[7]

Even if one had neither the money nor the inclination to patronize one of lower Bowery's famous watering holes, there was plenty to see, do, and buy out on the sidewalks. Street vendors thronged the boulevard, peddling oysters, hot yams (generally sold by African Americans), freshly roasted peanuts, hot corn in season, and sweet baked pears that one lifted by the stems out of syrup-filled pans. "Coffee and cake saloons" beckoned those seeking a respite from the throng or some warmth in colder weather.[8]

Other street activities could be found off the Bowery, especially around Paradise Square at the Five Points intersection. "Punch and Judy" shows (said to be the first ever performed in the United States), street singers, and an Englishman who swallowed swords "clean up to their hilts" could all be found on the sidewalks in the 1830s and '40s. Tumblers and jugglers would also appear, recalled Florry Kernan, "and throw somersaults, spin plates and eat live coals of fire, and afterward spin a hundred yards of ribbon from their mouths." Musicians were everywhere, including bagpipe players in kilts and a "dark-skinned Savonyard, with organ and monkey, who would grind out 'Moll Brooks,' a Dutch waltz, and the 'Fisher's Hornpipe'" while his monkey in red coat and hat collected money.[9]

By the late 1840s and 1850s, however, the Bowery had overtaken Paradise Square as the most popular Five Points location for fun and entertainment. Working-class New Yorkers from all over the city went there. Young men with their dates, as well as large, single-sex groups of journeymen and shop girls, cruised up and down the famous street simply to see and be seen.

Many of these young men were known as "Bowery B'hoys," members of one of the most colorful subcultures in the city's history. The precise origin of the "Bowery B'hoy" is unclear. Americans had used the term "b'hoy" as early as 1834 to describe a working-class fellow who loved fun, adventure, hard drinking, and a night out with his pals (Bowery regulars pronounced the term "buh-hoy," prompting the unusual spelling). But by the 1840s, the New York b'hoys, especially those who hung out on the Bowery, had developed a unique style of their own. The Bowery B'hoy dressed to be noticed. He wore a

> black silk hat, smoothly brushed, sitting precisely upon the top of his head, hair well oiled, and lying closely to the skin, long in front, short behind, cravat a-la sailor, with the shirt collar turned over it, vest of fancy silk, large flowers, black frock coat, no jewelry, except in a few instances, where the insignia of the engine company to which the wearer belongs, as a breastpin, black pants, one or two years behind the fashion, heavy boots, and a cigar about half smoked, in the left corner of the mouth, as nearly perpendicular as it is possible to be got. He has a peculiar swing, not exactly a swagger, to his walk, but a swing, which nobody but a Bowery boy can imitate.

The Bowery B'hoy was not a dandy, however. The "heavy boots," for example, were not worn for the sake of fashion but "for service in slaughterhouses and at fires." Yet the Bowery B'hoy did want to dress well and look sharp.[10]

"The Soap-Locks" by Nicholas Calyo gives some sense of the appearance of Bowery B'hoys dressed up for a night on the town. The posters advertise the typical amusements they favored. It is not clear what the "People's albais" pouring from the can at the bottom right refers to. Collection of the New-York Historical Society.

The Bowery B'hoy's attitude was just as important as his wardrobe. According to George G. Foster, who studied him closely, "the governing sentiment, pride and passion of the B'hoy is independence—that he can do as he pleases and is able, under all circumstances, to take care of himself. He abhors dependence, obligation." The B'hoy's "thorough dislike of . . . aristocracy" drove him to be something of a political radical, as Foster found him typically "on intimate terms with men like [Mike] Walsh and [William] Leggett," radical Democrats who sought to abolish the perks of privilege in the city's political and economic life. Despite this love of autonomy and independence, the Bowery B'hoy did not shirk his commitments to friends and family. He prided himself on "his constancy and faithfulness to his domestic duties and responsibilities—his open abhorrence of all 'nonsense'—the hearty manner in which he stands up on all occasions for his friend, and especially his indomitable devotion to fair play." The Bowery B'hoys' love of adventure even extended to the martial realm, with Foster noting that "many of the coolest as well as most daring acts of courage during the late Mexican war were performed by these men." Bowery B'hoys were also among the first New Yorkers to leave for California when the gold rush began. Yet while the B'hoy might live anywhere in New York, and travel far and wide in search of adventure and glory, he felt most at home on the Bowery.[11]

The Bowery B'hoy's feats of bravery and glory were often inspired by a desire to impress his "G'hal." According to Foster, "the g'hal is as independent in her tastes and habits as [the B'hoy] himself. Her very walk has a swing of mischief and defiance in it, and the tones of her voice are loud, hearty and free." Like her male counterpart, the G'hal dressed flamboyantly in brightly colored clothing which one New Yorker remembered as "a cheap but always greatly exaggerated copy of the prevailing Broadway mode; her skirt was shorter and fuller; her bodice longer and lower; her hat more flaring and more gaudily trimmed; her handkerchief more ample and more flauntingly carried; her corkscrew curls thinner, longer, and stiffer, but her gait and swing were studied imitations of her lord and master, and she tripped by the side of her beau ideal with an air which plainly said, 'I know no fear and ask no favor.'"[12]

Although it may be easy to reconstruct the appearance of the Bowery B'hoy and G'hal, determining exactly which New Yorkers were attracted to this subculture is much more difficult. "Who are the b'hoys and g'hals of New York?" asked Foster in 1850. "The answer to this question, if it could be completely efficient, would be one of the most interesting essays on human nature ever written." According to Cornelius Mathews, the B'hoy was "sometimes a stout clerk in a jobbing-house, oftener a junior partner in a wholesale grocery, and still more frequently a respectable young butcher with big arms and broad shoulders, in a blue coat, with a silk hat with a crape wound about its base, and who is known familiarly as a 'Bowery Boy!'" Charles Haswell agreed that the "Bowery Boy . . . was not an idler and corner lounger, but mostly an apprentice, generally to a butcher." The G'hal tended to work "in the press-room, the cap-sewing or the book-folding establishment."[13]

These trades were dominated by native-born workers. That the Bowery B'hoys were primarily American-born is confirmed by the only statement we have from a self-described B'hoy. Recalling the Astor Place Riot of 1849, John Ripley remembered years later that "I was at that time what was known as a 'Bowery Boy,' a distinct 'gang' from either the 'know-noth-ing' or 'Native American' parties. The gang had no regular organization, but were a crowd of young men of different nationalities, mostly American born, who were always ready for excitement, generally of an innocent nature." Ripley implies that although the Bowery B'hoys were not nativists per se, patriotic chauvinism was part of their persona. Given that at least some were Irish immigrants, Ripley's more nuanced account of the Bowery B'hoy subculture rings truer than Alvin Harlow's assertion in *Old Bowery Days* that "the Bowery Boy gang was . . . anti-Irish, anti-Catholic, anti-British, anti-anything that was exotic or unfamiliar."[14]

Nonetheless, this subculture does appear to have appealed primarily to the native-born. Playwright Benjamin Baker gave his wildly popular B'hoy and G'hal characters the names "Mose" and "Lize" (short for Moses and Eliza), names one could never mistake for Irish Catholic. Inasmuch as 90 percent of adult Five Pointers were foreign-born by 1855, not many could have perceived themselves as B'hoys or G'hals. But many Five Pointers of the previous generation probably did see themselves in that mold before they moved out of the district. Frank Chanfrau, who portrayed Mose so convincingly that the B'hoys would accept no other actor in the role, was a former ship carpenter born in Five Points at the corner of the Bowery and Pell Street. It was also said that he and Baker based "Mose" in part on a grocer, Moses Humphrey, who lived on Mulberry Street from about 1827 to 1842. So while the Bowery B'hoy subculture probably had relatively few followers in Five Points by the time it became well known in the early 1850s, the neighborhood did contribute significantly to its formation.[15]

The Bowery B'hoy was a relatively fleeting phenomenon—recognized only in the late 1840s and virtually extinct by the Civil War (though Hol-lywood created its own 1940s version with such films as *Pride of the Bowery, Bowery Blitzkrieg,* and *Bowery Battalion*). But a second subcul-ture with adherents in Five Points—that of the "sporting men"—flour-ished into the early twentieth century. Sporting men spent most of their time gambling, drinking, and fighting in saloons that catered to their ilk. Whereas Bowery B'hoys held regular jobs, consistent employment was anathema to the self-respecting sporting man. Isaiah Rynders, as we have seen, earned a living at various times through gambling, training race-horses, and intimidating voters. But most sporting men did not achieve

Rynders's fame or political status. More typical was Owen Kildare, who supported himself by working occasionally as a bouncer, fighting a sparring match, or teaching uptown dandies how to box. Although forgotten today, the "old sports" of New York formed a subculture as colorful and well known as that of the Bowery B'hoy.[16]

The most famous of the sporting men's hangouts were located just south of Five Points on Park Row facing City Hall Park. The best known of these was the Arena, at 28 Park Row, a saloon in which Rynders eventually bought an interest. But many of the sporting men's haunts, especially before 1850, were located in Five Points. Two of these, "Boss Thompson's" and "Vultee's old corner," faced each other on the west side of Chatham Street at the corner of Orange. In addition, "Big Jerry Tappen" had a place on Pearl near Elm, where, according to the *New York Clipper,* a sporting men's newspaper, "considerable sport could be obtained if necessary, in the way of muscular development. It was here that Country McClusky and Dave Scanlon had one of the hardest rough-and-tumble muddy fights that was ever seen. There was also a place on the Collect, or Five Points, kept by one Pete Rice, where many of the best sporting men assembled to participate with 'pasteboard'" (playing cards). Kernan, himself an old sport, recalled years later in the sporting man's patois that among the "good fighters who hailed from this locality" in its early days was "Eleck Fannin, at one time quite notorious to the city as a buffer. Joe Moon was some in his day, so was Siege Spears and Big-head Mat."[17]

Although we know that sporting men drank, fought, and gambled in Five Points, the extent to which they lived there is not clear. In a list of 275 or so "Old Sports of New York" published by the *Clipper* in 1860, there is a dearth of Irish surnames, leaving the impression that the "sporting" subculture, like that of the Bowery B'hoys, primarily attracted the native-born. Nonetheless, we know that some Irish Americans linked to the Five Points, such as Yankee Sullivan, James E. Kerrigan, and (much later) Owen Kildare, were perceived as sporting men. In general, sporting men were far less concerned about ethnicity than the Bowery B'hoys. The ultrapatriotism that characterized the Bowery B'hoy did not seem to motivate the sporting man, who above all prized one's ability to fight, drink, and avoid regular employment. Sporting men loved a good time, and as Kernan noted, "all jovial, free, generous stripes of mankind would have their frolic[s] and sprees at the Points in preference to any other place."[18]

"THE SPORTING FIREMAN IS IN A CERTAIN CIRCLE A MAN OF CONSIDERATION"

While the prominence of sporting men and Bowery B'hoys in Five Points may have declined as Irish immigrants came to dominate the neighborhood, the favorite pastime of both groups—service in volunteer fire companies—remained a staple of life. Firemen were the heroes of most lower-income New York neighborhoods. Young boys idolized and imitated local firefighters, while women swooned at their gallantry. "Roman gladiators and the Olympian games are brought to our mind," wrote the young Walt Whitman after seeing firemen race by pulling their pumping "machines." Although only volunteers, they took their responsibilities very seriously. Irish immigrant Matthew Breen recalled that "a fireman would sleep with his bedroom window partly open," no matter what the weather, in order to hear a summons to duty. When a nocturnal alarm did sound, the fireman could be found "rushing from his bed at midnight, snatching at his clothes, tumbling down stairs, and in a half distracted condition pulling foot for the engine-house, tearing open its door, hustling out the machine, and seizing the rope, hurrying away at the rate of ten miles an hour, shouting himself hoarse by the way, 'Fire—F-i-r-e—Fire! Fire! Fire!'—throwing himself like a salamander into the very thickest of the raging element—and in a couple of hours walking home to bed, sweating like a porpoise." In crowded tenements full of lamps and candles, fires were common and disastrous.[19]

In the antebellum years, only one fire company—Hope Hose Company No. 50 at 10½ Mott Street—was consistently located in the neighborhood. Others came and went. But Five Pointers did join nearby units, especially Fulton Engine Company No. 21 and Brennan Hose Company No. 60, located in 1858 just west of Five Points on Worth and Elm Streets respectively.[20]

Curiously, not a single laborer, tailor, or shoemaker (the three most followed occupations in Five Points) belonged to one of the neighborhood's fire companies in 1858 when the city published a thorough survey of the department's membership. The Five Pointers in Hope Hose Company No. 50 instead included a hatter, a saw maker, a baker, a fruit dealer, a carpenter, a picture-frame maker, a silversmith, a gas fitter, and two merchants. Why poorer Five Pointers did not join fire companies is unclear. The fire companies may have levied dues on members that precluded its less prosperous inhabitants from becoming members, or firemen may have required the job security to allow them to leave work on a minute's notice to fight a blaze.[21]

If so, these firemen need not have been financially secure for very long. Hope Hose Company's two "merchants," James Tucker and Edward Henry, had only recently achieved their relatively elevated occupational rank. Henry, a County Sligo native, had immigrated to New York in 1850. By 1852, the bachelor worked as a sailor and lived in a boardinghouse in the large brick tenement at 472 Pearl Street. Henry was a very disciplined saver, and by 1855, at twenty-seven, he had clawed his way up the economic ladder to become a clerk. He soon thereafter became a rag dealer, and by early 1857 had amassed savings of $511 (equivalent to more than $8,000 today). Like Henry, fireman Tucker had emigrated from County Sligo. Having arrived in New York in 1846 at age fourteen, he had undoubtedly worked in an unskilled capacity in his first years in New York. By 1855, when he lived in the heart of the Five Points Sligo enclave at 64 Mulberry Street, the twenty-three-year-old had snared one of the highly prized places on the city's police force. Work as a policeman offered high pay ($12 per week at that point) without seasonal layoffs. Tucker used the money he was able to save while working as a policeman to become a "paper dealer" after he left the force in 1857.[22]

Despite their relative prosperity, firemen were known as brawlers. In fact, it seemed at times that firemen had more to fear from their fellow firefighters than from the burning buildings they routinely entered. Firemen from different companies regularly clashed on the way to a blaze or at the hydrant nearest to it, because whichever unit reached the fireplug first had the right to pump its water. "A stranger upon witnessing the exciting races and savage howling of contending brigades . . . would immediately conclude that the town was at the mercy of an infuriated mob," commented an English immigrant. But competing companies sometimes fought even without the impetus of a dispute over a hydrant, or even of a fire. Five Points policeman William Bell recorded in his diary that he had to remain on duty one July evening until 11:15 p.m. "in consequence of a riot being anticipated between the members or runners of Engine Co. No. 21 & 22." This hostility may have developed out of a neighborhood or ward rivalry. Although both companies housed their engines in the Sixth Ward near Elm Street, most members of Protector Company No. 22 lived east of the Bowery in the Fourth Ward, while Five Pointer Matthew T. Brennan's political allies dominated No. 21. Firemen also had to battle neighborhood gangs not affiliated with the department. Chief Alfred Carson reported in 1850 that "not long since, a Five Point club took engine No. 44 from the company, beat some of the company dreadfully, run it down to the Points, upset it, broke the engine, and ran away." The same gang stole "hose carriage No. 34" while at a fire near the Bowery Theater in retaliation, said the chief, for the attack of William M. Tweed's Engine Company No. 6 on hose company No. 31.[23]

Mention of the young "Boss" Tweed (then twenty-seven years old) highlights the fire companies' important role in politics. A French visitor to New York in the 1840s learned that "the sporting fireman is in a certain circle a man of consideration. He plays an important part sometimes in the election, and is both throne and oracle in the public-houses." Tweed used the notoriety, respect, and friendships he earned as foreman of No. 6 to launch his political career in his native Fourth Ward.[24]

Although the fire department was the most prestigious voluntary organization they could join, many Five Pointers were also attracted to the neighborhood's militia units. In the days before the United States maintained a large standing army, the nation depended on volunteer militia companies to defend it against attack. The threat of foreign invasion was increasingly remote by the late antebellum period, so in most militia companies picnics and drinking became more important than drilling. Mathews described another motive for forming a militia company. "To acquire steadiness in aiming the pipe [i.e., hoses] at fires, the Firemen often form themselves into target companies," he reported. Others simply enjoyed "parading the streets in a half-uniform, with a target borne aloft . . . pierced to the very centre with holes."

Although Five Points could boast its share of militia companies, they are much more difficult to trace than the well-documented fire units. We know that in early 1850, forty Sligo natives formed the Sarsfield Light Guards (named for Patrick Sarsfield, one of the commanders of the defeated Catholic army at the Battle of the Boyne), which drilled in Five Points at 502 Pearl Street in a room above the saloon operated by its first captain. Another Irish-American military company in the neighborhood was the "Brennan Guards," named after ward heeler Matthew Brennan and commanded by his friend and fellow fireman Joseph Dowling.[25]

Irish immigrants seemed especially interested in forming militia companies when events in Europe indicated a weakening of British ability to maintain control over Ireland. In 1853, for example, when the Crimean War brought the prospect of a reduced British military presence in Ireland, the New York Irish flooded into militia organizations, demonstrating that these groups perceived themselves as more than merely protectors of the United States. "You and I will be called to the rescue" of our native land, predicted one Irish American as he described the community's militia companies before a gathering of New York Sligo natives, "and deadly will be our vengeance on the seven hundred year oppression of old Ireland."[26]

"TO MAINTAIN AND ESTABLISH THEIR CHARACTER AS MEN"

Of course, there were other, less political options for leisure. Some men chose athletics. Organized sports did not dominate men's social lives in the nineteenth century as they would later on, but the existence of a "Kenmare Hurlers" club indicates that some of the Lansdowne immigrants must have enjoyed that old Irish game on occasion. More prevalent were fraternal orders. Fraternal lodges were wildly popular in nineteenth-century America, with millions becoming Masons, Odd Fellows, Sons of Temperance, and Red Men. Five Pointers joined such groups, though they left few records behind. Some undoubtedly joined the Order of Ancient Hibernians, an outgrowth of one of the largest agrarian secret societies in Ireland. On the opposite end of the spectrum, the neighborhood's nativists probably enrolled in fraternal lodges such as the Order of United Americans. Young Tweed presided from 1848 to 1849 over one of these lodges, which met weekly at the foot of the Bowery.[27]

Five Points' African Americans had their own fraternal organization, the New York African Society for Mutual Relief. Founded in 1808 to aid members "whom the vicissitudes of time or the freaks of fortune might reduce to want," the society moved to Five Points in 1820, purchasing the tenement at 42 Orange Street as an investment while using the rental income to pay benefits to members who were unable or too ill to find work. Members erected a wooden building behind the tenement for their meetings. They installed a trapdoor in the floor to hide runaway slaves headed north on the Underground Railroad. Religious services and social events for the Five Points African-American community were held there as well. According to the reminiscences of fireman Florry Kernan, these activities continued until "the respectable residents of Orange Street, mostly negro families, began to move away" after the race riot of 1835. Then "the bell that each Sabbath morning tolled out a call for its congregation to assemble within its walls, that stood back in the rear from Orange Street near Leonard, was hushed; and that, too, moved to another spot to ring a welcome."[28]

The best documented Five Points fraternal group was the Sligo Young Men's Association. Formed in September 1849 by thirty men, "mostly all natives of Sligo, Ireland," the Sligo Young Men's Association was the first Irish fraternal order in New York to base its membership on county of origin. Its founders organized the group, they explained, for "Mutual Benefit and Protection, and for the purpose of maintaining a friendly intercourse with each other, and to maintain and establish their character as men." After nearly one year of operation, however, only seventy of the several thousand Sligo natives living in New York had joined.[29]

Perhaps the dues were too high. The semiannual "ball" organized by the society was not—at one dollar per person—outrageously expensive, though those wishing to attend did need formal attire. The society held the first of these gala events at Tammany Hall in February 1850, and the second six months later at "McCarthy's Hoboken Chateau." Many nonmembers seem to have attended these events, which received glowing reviews in the *Irish-American*. Its editor argued that the conspicuous consumption practiced at these events actually served a noble purpose, for it proved false "the calumnious statement that our position in America was 'one of poverty and shame.'. . . [T]hose who spend a delightful evening in the ball room, and combine for social and intellectual improvement, testify that they not only possess position and means, but have the spirit to keep pace with their fellow citizens in this regard."[30]

Although newspapers described the Sligo association's balls in great detail, little is known about its weekly meetings. The group did have its own song, and the officers undoubtedly organized their "well filled treasury" for the "mutual benefit and protection" of the members in case of illness or death. The society also organized the Sligo Light Guard (as the Sars-field Guard later renamed itself), and hoped "to amend the social condition of the poorer classes of their brothers, here and in Ireland." To this end, the Sligo association may have loaned money to members hoping to start businesses, as did the home-town societies created by subsequent Five Points immigrants from Italy and China. Five Pointers made up a significant proportion of the association's members. Nearly one-third of the members organizing the group's January 1851 ball lived or worked in the neighborhood. In the postbellum years, other county organizations (such as the Kerry Men's Society, which must have attracted some of the many Five Pointers from that district) were eventually formed as well. By the 1870s, at least eighteen Irish county societies operated in New York.[31]

The high costs of dues and balls may have discouraged many Five Pointers from joining one of these county societies, yet all but the most destitute could afford an occasional night out at one of the moderately priced theaters on the Bowery or Chatham Street. Bowery B'hoys and G'hals, and even bootblacks and newsboys, were devoted to the theater. They loved both lowbrow melodramas and classics such as Shakespeare. The best known of the city's inexpensive playhouses in that era was the Bowery Theater, located on that famous thoroughfare between Bayard and Canal Streets. Working-class New Yorkers flocked to the playhouse, even though the *Herald* in 1836 called the theater "the worst and wickedest that ever stood a month in any city under heaven." Foster agreed with the *Herald*'s assessment, remarking that its upper galleries were "filled with rowdies, fancy men, working girls of doubtful reputation, and, last of all, the lower species of public prostitutes, accompanied by their 'lovyers' or such victims as they have been able to pick up."[32]

Yet working-class men and women loved the raucous atmosphere of the Bowery Theater. A description of a performance in the 1870s gives a sense of the atmosphere. The featured attraction, noted Charles Haswell in his memoirs, was

> a stock Irish play, in which a virtuous peasant girl and a high-minded patriot with knee-breeches, a brogue and an illicit whiskey-still, utterly expose and confound a number of designing dukes, lords, etc. . . . We idled about behind the seats of the balcony, with audible steps among the thick-strewn peanut-

shells. . . . I saw but two gloved women in the audience. . . . [B]eside the proper and prevailing peanut, the spectators refreshed themselves with a great variety of bodily nutriment. Ham sandwich and sausage seemed to have precedence, but pork chops were also prominent, receiving the undivided attention of a large family party in the second tier, the members of which consumed the chops with noble persistence through all of the intermissions. . . . The denuded bones were most of them playfully shied at the heads of acquaintances in the pit . . . if you hit the wrong man, you have only to look innocent and unconscious.

The audience frequently interrupted those on stage with comments about the plot. Actors expected this, and after an important line they would turn to the audience and ask, " 'Is that so, boys?' or 'Don't you, boys?' and then the outcry and acclaim were so loud and long that all babies in the house cried out, which caused another terrible din." Patrons at least got their money's worth. When Haswell left at eleven forty-five, a third "piece" (probably a one-act play or vaudeville routine) was just beginning.[33]

These theaters catered to their customers' interests and prejudices. In 1843, the Chatham Theater (a few blocks south of the Bowery Theater) premiered the first "blackface" musical troupe, the Virginia Minstrels. Portrayals of "Jim Crow" likewise drew big crowds at the Bowery. In the postbellum period, the Bowery staged a life of Custer in which Sitting Bull died at Little Bighorn.[34]

But working-class theatergoers most loved to see themselves portrayed on stage. In 1848, actor and Five Points native Frank Chanfrau strode on stage with a fireman's red jacket, tight pants, and "soap locked" hair. The role was "Mose, the fire b'hoy," part of a short sketch of Bowery life meant to serve as an interlude between the full-length melodramas. The audience watched in rapt silence as Chanfrau's Mose took the cigar from his mouth, spit, and speaking of his fire company, defiantly declared that "I ain't a goin' to run with dat mercheen no more!" The crowd roared its approval. The sketch was such a hit that its author, Benjamin Baker, expanded it into an entire play, *A Glance at New York*. Like the real-life B'hoy, Mose was a loyal fireman ("I love that ingine better than my dinner") and was always pining for a fight ("if I don't have a muss soon I'll spile"). The play was so popular that Chanfrau once performed in it at midday at the Olympic

Theater, in midafternoon at the Chatham, and in the evening across the Hudson in Newark. Numerous sequels followed, and dramas featuring Mose and his G'hal Lize dominated working-class theater throughout the 1850s.[35]

Newsboys and bootblacks were especially avid theatergoers, so much so that they founded their own theater in a Five Points tenement basement. The tiny playhouse on Baxter Street just south of the Five Points intersection attracted little notice until late 1871, when the Russian grand duke Alexis visited the neighborhood during an American tour. His "slumming party" stopped at the youths' theater, bringing it to the attention of the general public and inspiring the lads to christen it "The Grand Duke's Opera House." "It is emphatically a boys' theatre, owned, built and managed by boys," commented *Frank Leslie's Illustrated Newspaper* in 1874. "Boys are the stage-carpenters, actors, musicians, scene-shifters, money-takers, and the audience is, for the most part, composed of boys." An accordionist "accompanied by a bone-player" provided the music. Though the theater was supposed to hold only fifty, three times that number (mostly

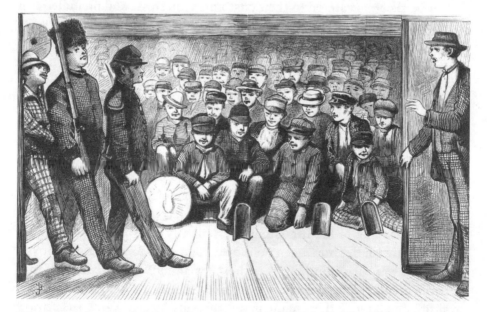

"Interior of the Grand Duke's Theatre—The Audience during the Performance of the Thrilling Spectacle of the March of the 'Mulligan Guards,'" *Frank Leslie's Illustrated Newspaper* (January 17, 1874): 316. Collection of the Library of Congress.

"bootblacks and newsboys") had crowded in when a reporter from the *Herald* visited in February 1874. The theater became so famous that Horatio Alger included a chapter entitled "The Grand Duke's Opera House" in his novel *Julius the Street Boy* (1904).[36]

"The most redoubtable stronghold of wickedness on Five Points, if not in New-York"

Though Five Pointers, like all working-class New Yorkers, were passionate about the theater, they spent the bulk of their leisure time drinking and socializing at one of the neighborhood's bars. In nineteenth-century New York, both saloons and grocery stores sold alcohol by the glass, and Five Pointers had dozens of such establishments to choose from. In 1851, there were at least 252 saloons and groceries in Five Points' 22 blocks, or about a dozen per block. The more impoverished a street's residents, the more watering holes they had to choose from. Relatively affluent Mott and Bayard Streets contained only sixteen and eighteen liquor sellers respectively (and these were mostly grocers). Mulberry Street, in contrast, could boast forty-six "groggeries" while Orange Street had fifty-three (63 percent of which were saloons). The short block of Orange just north of the Five Points intersection, one of the most squalid in the neighborhood, had sixteen liquor sellers on its twenty lots.[37]

The groceries in Five Points were mostly dark, dirty, depressing-looking establishments. Because the neighborhood's inhabitants did not generally have much money for discretionary spending, Five Points grocers specialized in "that class of commodities usually in demand where cheapness is the substitute for quality," wrote the *Clipper*. They stocked virtually everything a tenement resident might need—food, fuel, soap, candles, crockery, pipes, and tobacco. Grocers typically stored food in barrels and other items "behind the counter [in] tin boxes, devoid of their original laquer from wear of age and use. . . . At the end of the grease coated counter, furthermost from the door, a portion is railed off and constitutes the inevitable bar," behind which "are ranged some score of tall-necked bottles. A beer barrel stands in the extreme corner, and in these articles we have the most lucrative portion of the grocer's trade, for no purchaser enters the murky store without indulging in a consolatory drink, be their sex as it may." Some groceries were equipped with billiard tables to encourage customers to tarry and drink awhile. Prostitutes often loitered in them as well, reported Foster, looking for customers and "fortify[ing] themselves with alcohol for their nightly occupation."[38]

"Crown's Grocery" was the best known in Five Points. Located since about 1840 at 150 Anthony Street (at the southwest corner of Little Water facing Paradise Park), Crown's was a neighborhood institution and, according to one of the Protestant charitable organizations working in the district, "the most redoubtable stronghold of wickedness on Five Points, if not in New-York." Situated a few steps below street level in an "old dilapidated" three-story frame building, Crown's "combined groggery and grocery" did a thriving business. According to George Foster, a cornucopia of sights and smells overwhelmed the Five Pointer who descended the stairs and entered Crown's emporium:

> It is not without difficulty that we effect an entrance, through the baskets, barrels, boxes, Irish women and sluttish house-keepers, white, black, yellow, and brown, thickly crowding the walk, up to the very threshold—as if the store were too full of its commodities and customers, and some of them had tumbled and rolled outdoors. On either hand piles of cabbages, potatoes, squashes, eggplants, tomatoes, turnips, eggs, dried apples, chesnuts and beans rise like miniature mountains round you. At the left hand as you enter is a row of little boxes, containing anthracite and charcoal, nails, plug-tobacco, &c. &c. which are dealt out in any quantity, from a bushel or a dollar to a cent's-worth. On a shelf near by is a pile of fire-wood, seven sticks for sixpence, or a cent apiece, and kindling-wood three sticks for two cents. Along the walls are ranged upright casks containing lamp-oil, molasses, rum, whisky, brandy, and all sorts of cordials (carefully manufactured in the back room, where a kettle and furnace, with all the necessary instruments of spiritual devilment, are provided for the purpose). The cross-beams that support the ceiling are thickly hung with hams, tongues, sausages, strings of onions, and other light and airy articles, and at every step you tumble over a butter-firkin or a meal-bin. Across one end of the room runs a "long, low, black" counter, armed at either end with bottles of poisoned fire-water, doled out at three cents a glass to the loafers and bloated women

who frequent the place—while the shelves behind are filled with an uncatalogueable jumble of candles, allspice, crackers, sugar and tea, pickles, ginger, mustard, and other kitchen necessaries. In the opposite corner is a shorter counter filled with three-cent pies, mince, apple, pumpkin and custard—all kept smoking hot—where you can get a cup of coffee with plenty of milk and sugar, for the same price, and buy a hat-full of "Americans with Spanish wrappers" [cigars] for a penny.[39]

Crown profited handsomely from his business acumen. After fewer than ten years in business on Anthony Street, the Irish immigrant could afford to establish a "drygoods" outlet on Division Street as well. Crown apparently could not resist the very spirits he peddled, however—he supposedly "died of intemperance" in late 1857. Reformers hoped that Crown's death would lead to the demise of his "rum shop." Instead, his wife Susan became the proprietor, and it became known as "Mrs. Crown's." Two years later, upward of a thousand Five Pointers continued to patronize it daily.[40]

Most Five Pointers chose to do their drinking in saloons rather than groceries. Though temperance advocates perceived little difference between the two, the atmosphere in a saloon varied from that of a grocery in many ways. While German grocery proprietors outnumbered their Irish counterparts by about two to one, Irish Americans were four times more likely than Germans to operate a Five Points saloon. The interior of a saloon also bore little resemblance to that of a grocery. In contrast to the crowded grocery, a saloon was a long, narrow open space, with a long bar running down one wall and an empty floor opposite it to accommodate the crowds that might visit at lunchtime and in the evening. Sawdust covered the floors to sop up spit tobacco juice and spilt beer, and a large stove stood at the center of the room to provide warmth during the winter. Only saloons catering specifically to Germans offered their patrons tables and chairs. Five Points saloons lacked seats primarily because there was no space for them. But drinkers did not linger long in a single bar anyway. After a glass or two (enough to treat and be treated), the drinker and his friends generally went up the block or around the corner to another favorite watering hole. Finally, unlike the grocery, the New York saloon was an overwhelmingly male domain. Women could drink in groceries, but were rarely found in Five Points saloons.[41]

Many nineteenth-century New Yorkers associated Five Points with saloons. The earliest descriptions of the neighborhood give prominent place to its "grog shops" and "tippling houses." One writer, Luc Sante, even credits Five Points with the invention of the American saloon, insisting that "the saloon, as it came to be known, loved, and reviled, was born . . . in the area of the Five Points." No evidence exists to substantiate this claim. Saloons evolved from pubs and taverns, a feature of New York life long before Five Points' streets were even laid out. Yet saloons did occupy an important place in the social life of the typical male Five Pointer. Newspaperman and politico Mike Walsh noted that saloons were so popular in neighborhoods such as Five Points because the immigrants had "scarcely room enough to turn around" inside their tenements. Charles Loring Brace agreed that in comparison to the depressing conditions facing the immigrant at home, in a saloon "he can find jolly companions, a lighted and warmed room, a newspaper, and, above all, a draught which . . . can change poverty into riches, and drive care and labor and the thought of all his burdens and annoyances far away. The liquor shop is his picture-gallery, club, reading-room, and social *salon*, at once. His glass is the magic transmuter of care to cheerfulness, of penury to plenty, of a low, ignorant, worried life, to an existence for the moment buoyant, contented, and hopeful." The saloon also offered more tangible attractions, such as free lunches, bowling, billiards, raffles, card games like poker and faro, and even cockfights.[42]

The saloonkeeper himself frequently drew patrons to his establishment through his popularity or prominence. Many a Five Pointer must have found it exciting to sidle up to Yankee Sullivan's Centre Street bar and share a drink with the famous prizefighter, or hobnob with the neighborhood's leading politicos at Matt Brennan's Monroe Hall. Even in the absence of a celebrity proprietor, Irish Five Pointers, like their countrymen everywhere in America, preferred "the bar-keeper whose name has in it the flavour of the shamrock."[43]

But most Five Pointers respected their barkeepers primarily for their palpable power within the neighborhood. The saloonkeeper "was a social force in the community," remembered one self-proclaimed "son of the Bowery," Charles Stelzle, of his postbellum youth in the Five Points vicinity:

Often he secured work for both the workingman and his children. . . . [A]s a young apprentice, when I was arrested . . . the first man to whom my friends turned was the saloon-keeper on the block. And he furnished bail gladly. He was doing it all the time. He had close affiliation with the dominant political party; he was instrumental in getting the young men of the neighborhood on the police force and into the fire department, the most coveted jobs in the city among my young workmen friends. He lent money . . . [and] no questions were asked as to whether or not the recipient was deserving.

As a result of such kindness, immigrants deferred to their saloonkeepers in virtually every arena, even making them "officials in the church societies, marshals in church processions, [and] chairmen in church meetings." Matthew Breen summed up the feelings of most Irish immigrants when he stated that "there is no more charitable man living on the face of the earth than the New York liquor dealer."[44]

Gambling attracted many Five Pointers into the local saloons. Many competed at poker, but at midcentury the most popular card game was faro, a kind of card version of roulette in which players must bet on which card will be turned over next. Bars that featured these games of chance were some of the most infamous in the district. "Regular gambling-holes, they are; the dens of the Five Points!" exclaimed a shocked French actor who paid a policeman for a tour of the worst dives. "The frequenters of these dens play cards with shabby coats, sleeves rolled up, a pipe in their mouths, a loaded revolver by their sides, and a well-sharpened knife under their hands." Despite the hyperbole, there was some truth to his statements. Stabbings—some even fatal—were a staple of the Five Points gambling den. But a neighborhood resident would have had little to fear from merely entering one of the district's gaming saloons.[45]

Although no longer associated with wagering, bowling (probably the version now referred to as "duck pins") was also a gambler's sport in nineteenth-century New York, and many Five Points saloons featured the game. On his tour of New York in 1841, Dickens often saw at the top of cellar stairs "a painted lamp [which] directs you to the Bowling Saloon, or Ten-Pin alley; Ten-Pins being a game of mingled chance and skill, invented when the legislature passed an act forbidding Nine-Pins." Foster reported that "there are not less than four hundred of these fruitful sources of corruption in our city, plying their detestable trade with an activity that would do honor to a better calling. . . . On Saturday nights they are usually most crowded, and often keep in hot blast until the morning bells of the Sabbath compel their frequenters to slink away to a less noisy kind of dissipation." An 1880 insurance map shows that Five Pointers bowled in the alleys behind the saloons at 51 and 63 Baxter Street, whence the origin of the term "bowling alley." Boys often became acquainted with bowling by working in saloons. "They wait upon the players, setting up the pins, returning the balls, fetching a light for their segars, supplying them with liquor when thirsty," and received in return a small sum from the saloonkeeper and tips from lucky bowlers. One such "pin boy" was Timothy Harrington, a Lansdowne immigrant who came to New York with a brother and three sisters in 1851. Two years later, fourteen-year-old Timothy lived with his seventeen-year-old brother John in the heart of the Lansdowne enclave at 155 Anthony Street and supported himself setting up pins in a "bowling alley."[46]

Not all Five Points gambling took place in saloons. In fact, the neighborhood's most popular form of wagering was "policy gambling," private lotteries in which players tried to guess which numbers would be selected in a daily drawing. The more numbers guessed correctly, the more the player won. "The evil of all other modes of gaming sink[s] into insignificance in comparison with this," opined the *National Police Gazette* in an 1845 exposé on policy gambling, "as it is the only one which extends its havoc to the poor, and its corrupting mania to the females of that class." Some made their wagers by visiting policy offices. Others placed their bets with runners who, according to the *Gazette*, "penetrate into their very dwellings, and dog them to their places of work, for the last few pennies which a latent sense of prudence had reserved for food." For help in selecting their numbers, players often turned to "policy dream books," which explained how a gambler's dreams revealed his or her daily lucky numbers. The so-called father of the policy business, Moses Baker, based his operations at the eastern end of Five Points at 1 Chatham Square. That "prognosticators of lucky numbers were held in high repute with the denizens of the Points" also reflected the popularity of policy in the neighborhood.[47]

Gambling attracted many Five Pointers to the district's saloons; music and dancing enticed other customers into dance halls. The Five Points dance halls were concentrated on Anthony Street between Centre and Orange. Kernan remembered that they "were all fitted up in the same way; that is, there was the clean sanded floor, its red bombazine curtains at the shop-windows and doors, its whitewashed walls and ceiling, from which hung a hoop chandelier, which daily was replenished with new candles." Of course, the many dance halls located in cellars usually had no head-room for chandeliers. House of Industry founder Lewis Pease visited a dance hall in Cow Bay housed in "a low, damp, dingy basement, twelve feet wide by thirty long." Its ceiling was so low that taller customers had to duck to avoid hitting the floor joists. "The place was jammed so full, as not to leave room for the musician to sit, or even to draw his bow standing, without hitting some one," reported Pease, "while the steam and stench that issued therefrom was perfectly stifling." Kernan recalled that because these dance halls were so tiny, "a long bench on each side of the room was all the seats you could find, the object being to leave as much room for the dancers as possible. Away in one corner was a small bar, or counter, from which you could purchase ale, porter, or spruce beer by the glass publicly, ardent spirits by the half-pint slyly."[48]

Five Points dance halls attracted a wide variety of customers, from both within and outside the neighborhood. According to Foster, sailors and "the b'hoys, members of rowdy clubs and those who 'run' with the engines," were especially loyal customers. Kernan concurred, recalling that "it was a jubilee, indeed, to the landlords of the Points when the crew of a United States ship-of-war got paid off." Blacks and whites danced in the same basements, some wearing coats and boots while others went shirt-sleeved and barefooted. Dance halls did an especially brisk business when a favorite musician was scheduled to perform. "Jack Ballagher, the black musical wonder," was Five Points' "famed fiddler," recounted Kernan. He drew a throng of dancers whenever he rosined his bow. Dancing establishments also thrived during cold weather. "The homes of the poor in the Points are not fit places in which to spend an evening pleas-antly," commented the *Tribune* in explaining this surge in business, "for in most of them there are from four to a dozen individuals—the rooms are dirty and unventilated, consequently the inhabitants are forced into the streets to find either pleasure or comfort. But in cold weather the streets are too bleak, therefore to find what they seek they are in many cases com-pelled to resort to the theater, the dance-house, or the gambling or drink-ing saloon." As long as Five Pointers continued to inhabit overcrowded tenement apartments, concluded the *Tribune*, it would be impossible to keep them "from these wicked and degrading amusements."[49]

Of the many dance halls, one—Pete Williams's place—became by mid-century a virtual city landmark. A tourist believed that he "had not seen New York city unless he had visited Uncle Pete's," located at 67 Orange Street just south of Bayard. The establishment's fame dated back to 1842, when Charles Dickens featured the saloon—then called Almack's—in *American Notes.* Yet frustratingly little is known about Pete Williams himself. Foster described him as "a middle-aged, well-to-do, coal-black negro, who has made an immense amount of money from the profits of his dance-house—which, unfortunately, he regularly gambles away at the sweat-cloth of the roulette-table as fast as it comes in. He glories in being a bachelor . . . is a great admirer of the drama," and owned a team of fast horses that he loved to race. While virtually nothing else is known about him, Williams was remembered well after his death as "a great mogul on the Points."[50]

Pete Williams's basement differed little in appearance from other neighborhood dance halls. Despite its scandalous reputation, commented Nathaniel Willis, "really it looked very clean and cheerful. It was a spacious room with a low ceiling, excessively whitewashed, nicely sanded,

BACKGROUNDS OF CIVILIZATION.—BALL-ROOM OF MR. PETE WILLIAMS, DECEASED, AT PRESENT CONDUCTED BY MR. PHITTIES.—See page 200.

Pete Williams's Dance Hall, 1860. *New York Illustrated News* (February 18, 1860): 217. Collection of the author.

and well lit, and the black proprietor and his 'ministering *spirits*' (literally fulfilling their vocation behind a very tidy bar) were well-dressed and well-mannered people." But it was the mixing of blacks and whites on the dance floor that shocked well-to-do visitors. "Several very handsome mulatto women were in the crowd," Willis noted in the early 1840s, "and a few 'young men about town,' mixed up with the blacks; and altogether it was a picture of 'amalgamation,' such as I had never before seen." The *New York Clipper* agreed that at Pete Williams's place, "amalgamation reigned predominant, if we may judge from appearances." Outsiders viewed the mixing of the races—especially in the close, sweaty, and sexually charged context of the dance hall—as one of the most scandalous features of such Five Points establishments.[51]

Visitors' descriptions of the dancing at Pete Williams's place combined this moral indignation with prurient fascination. As the dancing commenced, the proceedings seemed innocent enough. According to Foster, "each gentleman, by a simultaneous and apparently preconcerted movement, now 'drawrs' his 'chawr' of tobacco, and depositing it carefully in his trowsers pocket, flings his arms about his buxom inamorata and salutes her whisky-breathing lips with a chaste kiss, which extracts a scream of delight from the delicate creature, something between the whoop of an Indian and the neighing of a horse. And now the orchestra strikes up 'Cooney in de Holler' and the company 'cavorts to places.'" But as the dancing progressed and the musicians picked up the pace, the passion of the dancers became far too palpable. "The spirit of the dance is fully aroused," observed Reverend Pease. "On flies the fiddle-bow, faster and faster; on jingles tambourine 'gainst head and heels, knee and elbow, and on smash the dancers. The excitement becomes general. Every foot, leg, arm, head, lip, body, all are in motion. Sweat, swear, fiddle, dance, shout, and stamp, underground in smoke, and dust, and putrid air!" The fiddler compelled the dancers to quicken the tempo further, observed Foster, until "all observance of the figure is forgotten and every one leaps, stamps, screams and hurras on his or her own hook. . . . The dancers, now wild with excitement . . . leap frantically about like howling dervishes, clasp their partners in their arms, and at length conclude the dance in hot confusion and disorder."[52]

AS THIS NEARLY OVERT SUGGESTION of orgasm implies, most middle- and upper-class New Yorkers found Five Pointers' modes of entertainment shocking and depraved. Although gambling, the theater, the fire and militia companies, the dance halls and saloons, and the subcultures that flourished in them were hardly illegal, it seemed to many New Yorkers that each of these licit activities led inexorably to others that were illicit. The fire companies brawled and rioted; the dance halls encouraged lewdness and promiscuity; the saloons and gambling dens fostered public drunkenness and crime; the sporting men promoted illegal prizefighting; and the working-class theaters (as well as the dance halls and the Bowery) were filled with prostitutes. Despite the neighborhood's vibrant and multifaceted cultural life, these vices would come to dominate Americans' perception of Five Points.

7

PROLOGUE

THE BARE-KNUCKLE PRIZEFIGHT BETWEEN
YANKEE SULLIVAN AND TOM HYER

FIVE POINTERS loved a good fight. Their propensity to riot was notorious. Election day in the neighborhood rarely ended without blackened eyes and bloodied lips. When fights broke out on the street, passersby typically circled round and egged on the combatants rather than break them up. Five Pointers often agreed to settle their grudges with fights. In 1856, for example, two well-known brawlers, Jim Moroney of the Fourth Ward and Tim Connolly of the Sixth, decided to resolve their ongoing feud with a boxing match in Weehawken, New Jersey, where Aaron Burr and Alexander Hamilton had settled their differences a half century earlier. The Irish were not the neighborhood's only brawlers. When one well-known Five Points boxer put on an exhibition in 1848, the "very promising New York novices" on the undercard included a few "Chatham street Jews." But the greatest Five Points fight of all, one of the most famous prizefights in American boxing history, a match that until the 1880s or '90s was the most talked about fight of the nineteenth century, was the 1849 battle between Tom Hyer and Yankee Sullivan.[1]

Yankee Sullivan was born Frank Ambrose in Bandon, Cork, in about 1807. At the age of twenty-three, the "freckled-face, ginger-haired, pug-nosed" young man with the "close-cropped, bullet-like head," already a renowned fighter in Liverpool, was arrested for an unknown felony and punished with transportation to Australia. He escaped in 1839 and sailed for America, landing at Sag Harbor, Long Island. Returning to England in 1840 to resume his boxing career, he took the name Jim Sullivan to avoid detection by the police, adding the nickname "Yankee" (whether of his own invention or that of his fans is unclear) to stress his purported American roots.[2]

Sullivan was not a big man. He stood five feet ten inches tall and had a wiry physique. Upon his return to England, he issued a public challenge to pay £100 to anyone weighing less than one hundred fifty-five pounds who could defeat him. He fought and won a number of bouts, including one in February 1841 against Johnny "Hammer" Lane that made Sullivan the English middleweight champion. Warned that the police suspected his true identity, Sullivan returned to the United States a few months later. He won a bout in Philadelphia and then secured a match against one of the best American boxers, Thomas Secor. The two squared off in January 1842 on Staten Island (the isolated location selected because bare-knuckle prizefights were illegal), with Sullivan eventually prevailing in sixty-seven hard-fought rounds.* Sullivan's victory, according to the nineteenth-century boxing historian Ed James, forced native-born New Yorkers to "cast their eyes round the pugilistic circle to find a man capable of holding up the honor of the Stars and Stripes against the encroachments of the Green Flag of the Emerald Isle."[3]

Five Pointers of Irish descent must have cheered the news of Sullivan's victory. In fact, as he became settled in New York, Sullivan increasingly identified himself with Five Points. His first exhibition sparring match in New York supposedly took place at Owen and Matthew Brennan's Monroe Hall saloon. Sullivan soon opened watering holes of his own, first just east of the Five Points district on Walker and Madison Streets, then slightly south of the neighborhood on Chatham Street, and finally in Five Points itself in 1849 at 110 Centre Street (at the southeast corner of Centre and Franklin). Sullivan also joined the fire department, according to James, becoming "identified with No. 15 Engine, known as the Spartan Band, and located in [the Five Points neighborhood on] Pell street, off the Bowery. In those days the do-as-you-please racket characterized the New York fire laddies, and every company had its fighter, and Jim Sullivan was installed bully of No. 15." Through the fire department, Sullivan became involved in local politics as well, playing a major role (as we have seen) in both the

---

* A round in the mid-nineteenth century did not last three minutes, as it does today, but instead ended when either combatant fell to the ground. In the bare-knuckle fights of this period, rounds rarely lasted more than a minute.

Sixth Ward election riot of 1842 and the wild race for Sixth Ward alderman in 1849.[4]

Meanwhile, Sullivan's ring exploits added to his fame outside Five Points. Boxing promoters had cannily paired him against "American" opponents so that each fight could be billed as one pitting Irish versus American pride (James noted that when Sullivan fought Irish-American John Morrissey in 1853, their "both being Irish rather mixed the gang up"). When Sullivan dispatched these American-born rivals, fight organizers imported Englishman Bob Caunt, to whom "the American boys gave their sympathies." In a fight staged in Harpers Ferry, Virginia, Sullivan whipped Caunt in just twelve minutes.

Sullivan's victory over Caunt left only one other top boxer for him to vanquish: Tom Hyer. Born in New York City in 1819, the one-time butcher established himself as America's premier fighter with just one victory. In 1841, the previously unheralded Hyer defeated John McCleester, the "pride of Chatham Square," in an epic three-hour battle that lasted 101 rounds and is still considered one of the greatest fights of all time. Sullivan, who had served as one of McCleester's "seconds" in this contest, sought to fight Hyer soon after, but the American refused because Sullivan could not raise his half of the unprecedented $6,000 Hyer insisted upon as prize money. Seven years later, with Sullivan having defeated every other available challenger, supporters of the two pugilists insisted that "they *must* fight." Sullivan finally managed to raise the required sum ($5,000 by this point) and began preparing for the bout.[5]

Despite Sullivan's bragging that no punch from Hyer could bring him down, experts made the Irishman the heavy underdog. Hyer stood four inches taller than Sullivan, weighed thirty pounds more, and had a much longer reach, all vital factors working against the Cork native, though these were not necessarily insurmountable handicaps under the permissive boxing rules of the day. Handicappers also speculated that at age forty-one, Sullivan was too old to keep up with a rival twelve years his junior. On the other hand, Sullivan did have far more experience than Hyer. The Irishman had never lost a bout, defeating a dozen top boxers over the course of his career, while Hyer still had only the one major victory to his credit. Sullivan was also an expert at the wrestling holds and throws then permitted in boxing matches, and his backers believed he could use these skills to compensate for Hyer's height and weight advantage.

In order to evade any law enforcement officials who might try to prevent or interrupt the contest, the combatants initially exercised the
utmost secrecy about the date and location of the contest. On the eve of
the fight, however, word of the impending clash leaked out. When news
spread that the day of the fight was finally at hand, it created a "perfect
frenzy of excitement" throughout the nation, and especially in New York.
"Nothing has been heard of or talked about for several days past but the
fight," marveled the *Herald*. "Urchins in school could not be kept at their
lessons, but insisted upon their right to talk of what the whole town talked
about. . . . At the courts, in the public offices, at steamboat landings, at
hotel dinner tables, in counting rooms, and even in the sick chamber,
everybody talked about the prize fight." Both men narrowly escaped Maryland law enforcement officials who sought to arrest them on the eve of the
bout—Sullivan climbed out a window and hid in a tree to avoid detection.[6]

The contestants finally squared off before just one hundred witnesses

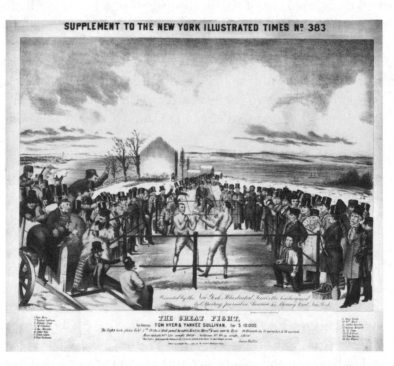

The 1849 prizefight between Yankee Sullivan (left) and Tom Hyer. Collection
of the Maryland Historical Society, Baltimore, MD.

on a snow-covered field overlooking the Chesapeake in the late afternoon on February 7. Playing the ethnic angle to the hilt, Sullivan chose green and white as his colors, while Hyer, the hero of the "native boys," chose red, white, and blue. In the first round, Sullivan charged at Hyer, who was able to use his superior reach to land the most damaging blows. Seeing that he could not fight Hyer at arm's length, Sullivan tried to crowd his opponent, but this was ineffectual as well. Sullivan then "rushed in at the body," wrote James, "and after two or three ineffective exchanges clinched his antagonist with the underhold and struggled for the throw," a reference to Sullivan's vaunted "tumble-down tactics." "This was the great point on which was to depend the result of the fight," explained James. "Sullivan relied mainly for success upon his superior wrestling, and it was calculated by his friends and backers that a few of his favorite cross-buttocks would break his young antagonist . . . and not only render him limpsey with weakness, but stun him with the falls." From the clinch, Sullivan attempted to lift Hyer and throw him to the ground. "Two or three times did Sullivan knot his muscles with an almost superhuman effort," but to no avail. He could not budge Hyer. When Sullivan had thus "spent his power by these terrible impulsions," Hyer used an "upper-hold" maneuver to throw his antagonist to the ground, falling heavily on top of the prone Irishman.[7]

Virtually every subsequent round was a repeat of the first: Sullivan attacking but taking more punishment than he could mete out; Sullivan moving in to fight at close range yet unable to land any damaging blows; Sullivan clinching and attempting in vain to throw Hyer; Hyer tossing Sullivan to the ground and "falling upon him, as before, with his entire weight." After a half dozen such rounds (each one lasted about a minute), Sullivan began to show the effects of the beating. His legs became weaker. His eyes began to swell shut. Blood flowed profusely down his face. His punches began to lose their sting. After sixteen rounds, Sullivan was reeling and staggering, and his second, McCleester, refused to let him continue. "Thus ended a contest," wrote James, "which had, up to that time, excited more interest than any other pugilistic encounter that ever took place in this country; but which, though it engaged thousands of minds for a period of six long months, was done up when once begun in [just] seventeen minutes and eighteen seconds."[8]

Despite Sullivan's ignominious defeat, the Hyer-Sullivan contest went down in boxing history as one of the most memorable and important fights of the century. "The result . . . has become as familiar as the Declaration of Independence," remarked the *Clipper* fifteen years later. Even a half century after the contest, Tammany ward boss George Washington Plunkitt said of the saloons in his Upper West Side district that "the only ornaments is a three-cornered mirror nailed to the wall, and a chromo of the fight between Tom Hyer and Yankee Sullivan." Even today, memorabilia of the Sullivan-Hyer fight circulate and recirculate, including whiskey mugs, playing cards, and prints.[9]

In the aftermath of the contest, the two fighters became close friends. Hyer became proprietor of the bar at the Branch Hotel at 36 Bowery (where he had also lived before the contest) while Sullivan opened his saloon at 110 Centre Street. By 1852, Sullivan had abandoned his Democratic allies and began lending his support to Hyer's Unionist Club, the pro-Whig organization that used its influence and muscle to counterbalance the efforts of Isaiah Rynders's Empire Club. Hyer, who refused to consider another bout for less than $10,000, never fought again. He did, however, impress Whig leaders with his intelligence and political savvy. Though he turned down many requests to run for office, he eventually became a confidant of the most powerful Whig and Republican politicians in the state. In 1864, he died of heart disease in New York at age forty-five.

Sullivan, in contrast, continued his brawling ways. He joined many of his fellow sporting men in California in 1850, but not satisfied there, soon returned to the East Coast. He fought John Morrissey in Boston in a much-anticipated bout, and though he apparently whipped his opponent, he was declared the loser for refusing to continue the fight when pandemonium broke out at ringside. He went back to California, where he quickly became involved in San Francisco politics. But the authorities there would not countenance the political tactics that Sullivan had perfected in Five Points. In 1855, they arrested him for ballot box tampering and other, more violent crimes. Threatened with a long prison term, the despondent Sullivan slashed his wrists in his cell and bled to death.[10]

CHAPTER SEVEN

Vice and Crime

ꟼ▬▬◗

Ｆ OR MOST AMERICANS, Five Points was the epitome of vice and lawlessness. The neighborhood "was, for years, the synonym for wretchedness, vice, and crime," wrote a superintendent of the Five Points House of Industry. The *Herald* labeled the district a "nest of drunkenness, roguery, debauchery, vice and pestilence." "If there is a spot in our city where vice reigns unchecked, and moral pollution is the unmixed atmosphere of immortal souls," agreed a magazine writer in 1853, "surely all will admit it to be in that vicinity." Could Five Points really have been so crime-ridden? Could prostitution, robbery, murder, and drunkenness—the crimes and vices for which Five Points was renowned—really have been so common? An analysis of the historical record reveals that some facets of the stereotype have been grossly exaggerated. But others, such as those concerning the pervasiveness of drunkenness and prostitution, were far closer to the truth than not.[11]

"EVERY HOUSE WAS A BROTHEL, AND EVERY BROTHEL A HELL"

There was no vice more synonymous with Five Points than prostitution. The reputed pervasiveness of the sex trade, the conditions under which the prostitutes supposedly worked, and the purported extent to which the young and innocent were forced into the business appear absurd to the modern reader. "Every house was a filthy brothel, the resort of persons of every sex, age, color, and nationality," wrote a nineteenth-century historian of Five

Points. George Foster agreed, writing in 1849 that "nearly every house and cellar is a groggery below and a brothel above," while House of Industry founder Lewis Pease remembered that at his arrival there, "every house was a brothel, and every brothel a hell." Bordellos were believed to be family-run businesses in every sense. "[I]t is no unusual thing," insisted Foster, "for a mother and her two or three daughters—all of course prostitutes—to receive their 'men' at the same time and in the same room—passing in and out and going through all the transactions of their hellish intercourse, with a sang froid at which devils would stand aghast and struck with horror." The tender age of Five Points' courtesans also consistently shocked New Yorkers. The *Evening Post* reported that girls of thirteen, fourteen, and fifteen were commonly "enticed" from their homes and taken to Five Points "dens, where they are kept until they are become so in love with the sin, that they can neither be persuaded nor forced to leave their wretched abodes."[12]

The evidence reveals that many of these charges were not so far-fetched. The New York District Attorney's indictment records reveal that for the blocks radiating from the Five Points intersection, nearly every building *did* house a brothel. Bordellos operated in thirty-three of the thirty-five dwellings on Anthony Street between Centre and the Five Points intersection at some point during the 1840s and '50s. Brothel proprietors were likewise prosecuted in twelve of the fifteen houses on Cross Street between the Five Points intersection and Mulberry, and in thirteen of the seventeen residences on Orange Street from the Five Points intersection to Leonard Street. In other sections of the neighborhood, prostitution was far less pervasive. In the same two decades, there were only two prosecutions for commercial sex in the eighty or so houses on Mulberry below Bayard, only two indictments for the sixty buildings on Bayard from the Bowery to Orange Street, and none on Mott below Bayard.[13]

Evidence also confirms the *Post*'s charge that young teenagers sometimes worked in Five Points brothels. In 1834, one charitable organization recorded the case of fifteen-year-old streetwalker Catharine Wood, who picked up customers on thoroughfares such as the Bowery and took them to Five Points houses of assignation (bordellos where women could bring men without prior arrangement). In 1849, police supposedly found an eleven-year-old girl working as a prostitute in Bridget Mangin's brothel. Some of the cases of young prostitutes also involved family members of

Worth Street (formerly Anthony) looking west from the Five Points intersection toward Centre Street, c. 1868. The appearance of the block had not changed much since the 1840s and 1850s, when virtually every building on the block housed a bordello. In the house at the corner on the left, Crown's Grocery operated on the ground floor for many years, while Bridget Mangin ran the brothel upstairs. Collection of the New-York Historical Society.

different generations working together, as Foster had described. County Tipperary native Bridget McCarty prostituted both her fourteen-year-old niece and a fourteen-year-old boarder at her homes at 57 Mott Street and 76 Mulberry. Henry Hoffman prostituted his own daughter in his Sixth Ward bawdy house. Fifteen-year-old Elizabeth Dayton worked as a street-walker, bringing customers back to the family bordello on Orange Street, where her mother also sometimes consorted with customers. By 1855, Mangin's two daughters (age unknown) prostituted themselves at their mother's brothel, then located above Crown's Grocery at 150 Worth Street. Such cases were undoubtedly not the norm. A survey taken just before the

Civil War found that the majority of prostitutes ranged in age from seventeen to twenty-two, and it seems unlikely that many mother-daughter
teams could have worked in the neighborhood's brothels. Nonetheless, the
seemingly outlandish charges made by the press concerning such practices
at Five Points "disorderly houses" were not entirely figments of their over-
active imaginations.[14]

Children did not often work as prostitutes in brothels, but they did
more frequently live in bordellos run by their parents. "I found that the
children lived in the brothels, and that as soon as the school was out the
children returned to their residence," reported an alarmed minister in
the 1840s. In fact, a survey on the eve of the Civil War found that nearly
half of New York prostitutes had children. Even more disturbing were the
cases in which young children were put to work in such places. At 37
Baxter Street, Thomas Laughlin posted his seven-year-old stepdaughter
Elizabeth upstairs late into the night to collect the prostitutes' pay (or perhaps his cut if it was a house of assignation) while he minded the bar
below. He became furious one evening in 1855 when she fell asleep and, in
her words, "I did not watch the girls . . . that go out for company." Having
previously been struck in the head with a bottle by Laughlin, little Elizabeth feared a similar punishment and ran away to the House of Industry.[15]

The charge that Five Points brothel keepers forced young women into
prostitution against their will is also borne out by contemporary evidence.
The *Times* reported in 1859 the case of a woman who took a position to
live and work as a "tailoress" at 82 Centre Street. After she moved in, she
was given nothing to sew but asked to have a drink with a man, clearly for
prostitution. She fled, but her "employer" would not return her trunk
unless she paid five dollars for room and board during her brief residence.
Only with the assistance of the police did she retrieve her valuables. Similar cases were constantly reported in the city press.[16]

The case of Mary O'Danicl illustrates the manner in which young
women could be tricked or pushed into prostitution. The thirteen-year-old
emigrated from County Waterford after the death of her father (her mother
was evidently dead already). Arriving in New York in January 1851, she
sought out her aunt, Bridget McCarty, a thirty-four-year-old widow living
at 57 Mott Street with her six-year-old daughter. To her chagrin, Mary discovered that her aunt and cousin shared the one-room flat with three other
"girls" who, according to Mary's subsequent deposition, "had men come to

see them, and . . . had sexual intercourse." When one girl brought a man back to the studio apartment for sex, the others went outside until the couple had finished. Much to Mary's relief, her aunt asked the other girls to leave about a month after her arrival. But McCarty then asked her niece "to go to bed with" a man, telling Mary "she would have a good life of it, and fine clothes, and plenty of money." After what one might imagine were days or weeks of pressure, during which her aunt undoubtedly reminded Mary of how grateful she ought to be for having been taken in, Mary had sex with a man procured by her aunt, for which he paid McCarty ten dollars. Mary subsequently had intercourse with the man again, earning her aunt from one to two dollars per session. Soon Mary began going to bed with other men her aunt brought home. Before the end of the year, with the income generated by her niece, McCarty was able to transfer her household to a larger, two-room flat at 76 Mulberry Street.

In early December, a fourteen-year-old, Ellen Cable, moved into McCarty's Mulberry Street apartment. Ellen had lived in the Fourth Ward on Roosevelt Street until her mother sent her to find work as a domestic servant. According to the girl, McCarty (who had once been Cable's neighbor) asked her "to go to her house to do house work." After a few days, McCarty began pressuring Ellen to sleep with one of her customers, telling her, as she later testified, that the sex trade "would give me a good living." Ellen stated that she initially refused to prostitute herself, but was eventually "compelled" to do so. She got into bed with a man that first night but would not have intercourse with him, even though he promised her ten dollars (apparently the going rate for a virgin). The persistent customer nonetheless stayed in bed with her all night. The next evening, he returned, and McCarty helped undress him and put him in bed with the girl. This time he "succeeded in having sexual intercourse with Deponent and seduced her." He paid Ellen four dollars, which McCarty then confiscated. The next day, a friend of the previous night's customer came to the house and McCarty locked him in the bedroom with Ellen, "and said man forced Deponent to undress herself and go to bed with him, and staid with her all that night and had sexual intercourse with her four times that night." In the morning he paid McCarty one dollar.

Ellen then went to the police, claiming that McCarty had forced her to have intercourse with these men against her will. McCarty denied the charges. "I work on shirts for a living," she stated in her deposition, main-

taining she had never had any female boarders or men come to her residences for sex. The combined testimony of Cable and O'Daniel effectively
refuted McCarty, and she might have been convicted had Ellen not admitted under cross-examination that she had managed to tell her mother
about the attempted seduction, and that her mother had told her to come
home. Cable testified that she had nonetheless returned to Mulberry Street
out of a determination to finish out her month of housework and receive
the three dollars per month pay that McCarty had promised. After Cable's
mother confirmed this, Prosecutor A. Oakey Hall asked the judge to
instruct the jury to acquit McCarty. The judge did so, and McCarty went
free. Brothel keepers such as McCarty understood that although prostitution was illegal, they could avoid prosecution so long as they did not keep
prostitutes in the bordellos against their will and did not disturb their
neighbors.[17]

Bridget McCarty seems to have specialized in procuring young virgins
for her clients. Five Points brothels varied enormously and featured a
number of special attractions to lure customers. "Parlor houses" were the
most expensive. These bordellos replicated the atmosphere of private residences, protected their clients' anonymity, only accepted known customers or those with references from known clients, and charged as much
as five dollars for a typical visit. They often limited their business to a particular type of customer, such as southerners, German Americans, or even
visiting Philadelphians. Although few if any parlor houses remained in
Five Points by the 1850s, a significant number probably operated there at
one time. The bordello at 3 Franklin Street was a parlor house, situated on
a relatively upscale block just three doors down from the ward's police station. Helen Jewett, a highly paid twenty-three-year-old courtesan who
became New York's most famous prostitute after her grisly murder in
1836, resided in "Mrs. Cunningham's" seraglio at that address until just
three weeks before her violent demise.

Much more common in Five Points, however, was the "public house,"
a relatively inexpensive establishment that did little to hide the nature of
its business and opened its doors to anyone. Whether public or private,
brothels did their best to satisfy their customers' tastes and predilections.
Some featured mulatto women (said to be preferred by all black and some
white men), while others offered only Irish paramours. The brothel at 62
Mott Street featured "ropes and braces." Still other Five Points sex estab-

lishments had no women actually in residence at all. Such "houses of assignation"—sometimes rooms behind or above saloons, in other cases apartments in tenements—were used by streetwalkers who did not have a steady clientele or did not want to pay a madam.[18]

One notorious form of brothel, the "panel house," used the lure of sex as a mere subterfuge for robbery. The prostitute would lead her target to a windowless room with only a bed and a single chair and make sure he saw her lock the door. Once they were in bed and otherwise occupied, her accomplice, waiting in the next room, would slide a panel in the wall, reach into the bedroom to the man's clothing on the chair, and empty his wallet while the prostitute made plenty of noise. When she subsequently asked for her payment, and the man discovered his money gone, he would claim to have been robbed, to which the prostitute would reply that this was impossible given the windowless room and the locked door. She and her partner would then chase the dupe from the brothel, threatening to have him arrested for refusing to pay for the sex if he should ever show his face in the neighborhood again. African-American Charles Quin, who was said to have lived in Five Points, operated panel houses in various parts of town, including one on Elizabeth Strreet. The *Herald* reported in 1841 that another "negro rascal" known as "Butcher Bill" and his partner Jenny Jones had robbed a man of $68 "by the stale trick of touch house." Panel thieves tried to choose targets with lots of cash (out-of-town merchants visiting New York to buy wholesale goods or farmers who had recently sold agricultural products), those who appeared too upstanding to risk the embarrassment of complaining to authorities about having been robbed at a Five Points brothel.[19]

One oft-noted aspect of Five Points prostitution was the brazen manner in which the prostitutes openly solicited business. "As evening sets in," reported Foster in *New York by Gas-Light*, "the inmates of the house, dressed in the most shocking immodesty, gather [and] the door is flung open wide, if the weather will permit it; and the women, bare-headed, bare-armed and bare-bosomed, stand in the doorway or on the side-walk, inviting passers-by, indiscriminately, to enter, or exchanging oaths and obscenity with the inmates of the next house, similarly employed." The Boston author and lawyer Richard Henry Dana Jr. toured Five Points in 1844 in the dead of winter, but he too observed that "at almost every door were girls standing, & whispering loud to me as I passed, 'Come here,'

'Come here, dear,' 'Good evening,' 'Where are you going?' & the like."
Nathaniel P. Willis also found that "women stood at every door with bare
heads and shoulders . . . showing a complete insensibility to cold" and
even quoting their prices.[20]

Those who ventured inside one of these bawdy houses found little variation from one to the next. Because they were not written expressly to
shock the public, Dana's diary entries (one written in 1843 and the other a
year later) provide the most reliable portrait of a Five Points brothel interior and thus deserve to be quoted at length. Looking for a little excitement
after an evening spent with New York social luminaries Theodore Sedg-
wick and William Cullen Bryant, the twenty-eight-year-old Dana put on
his "rough coat & cap," left his luxurious room at the Astor House, and
walked to "that sink of iniquity & filth, the 'Five Points.'" Heading east on
Anthony Street, Dana found that "the buildings were ruinous for the most
part, as well as I could judge, & the streets & sidewalks muddy & ill
lighted. Several of [the] houses had wooden shutters well closed & in
almost [each] such case I found by stopping & listening, that there were
many voices in the rooms & sometimes the sound of music & dancing. . . . Grog shops, oyster cellars & close, obscure & suspicious looking
places of every description abounded." He peeked inside one saloon and
saw "a dozen or so men & two women, the women cursing & swearing
most dreadfully & using the most foul language I ever heard come fr.
human lips." Successfully working up the courage to enter one of these
dives, Dana walked in and found "an old harradan [sic], with fat cheeks &
a quick, sharp, devilish eye, standing at the door, & four girls, all young, &
three of whom must have once been quite handsome." None appeared
older than seventeen. "There was only one man in the room, who had a
girl in his lap"; "obscene prints" hung "about the walls to help excite [sic]
passions of the young who should drop into the house. Some sailors came
in swearing & calling for drink, & I slipped out."

On his second visit to Five Points, Dana found a brothel "removed
from sight & in an obscure place, where no one seemed in sight." Inside, he
discovered two women,

> one apparently old, probably the "mother" of the house, & the
> other rather young, as well as I could judge from her voice & face.
> They invited me to walk in & just say a word to them. . . . The

room had but little furniture, a sanded floor, one lamp, & a small bar on which there were a few glasses, a decanter, & behind the bar were two half barrels. The old woman did not speak, but kept her seat in the door way. The younger one, after letting me look round a moment, asked me in a whisper & a very insinuating air, putting on as winning a smile as she could raise, & with the affectation of a simple childish way, to "just step into the bed room: it was only the next room."

Dana feared that the woman might have an accomplice waiting to rob him, but was too curious to refuse her invitation:

The bed room was very small, being a mere closet, with one bed & one chair in it, the door through wh. we came & a window. There was no light in it, but it was dimly lighted by a single paine of glass over the door through which the light came from the adjoining room, in wh. we had been. The bed stead was a wretched truck, & the bed was of straw, judging from the sound it made when the woman sat upon it. Taking for granted that I wished to use her for the purposes of her calling she asked me how much I would give. I said "What do you ask?" She hesitated a moment, & then answered hesitatingly, & evidently ready to lower her price if necessary, "half a dollar?" I was astonished at the mere pittance for which she would sell her wretched, worn out, prostituted body. I can hardly tell the disgust & pity I felt. I told her at once that I had no object but curiosity in coming into the house, yet gave her the money from fear lest, getting nothing, she might make a difficulty or try to have me plundered. She took the money & thanked me, but expressed no surprise at my curiosity or strangeness.[21]

What circumstances could force women into such degrading lives? Foster contended that "female prostitution is the direct result of the inadequate compensation for female labor." What little evidence exists on the subject seems to confirm his observation. In a survey of two thousand New York prostitutes conducted on the eve of the Civil War, Dr. William Sanger—chief physician at the hospital/prison complex on New York's Blackwell's (now Roosevelt) Island—found that most courtesans had tried to support themselves through other means before turning to the sex trade. They reported earning $1.50 a week as a "tailoress," $2 a week as a cap maker, or a dollar a week sewing shirts, and that only when they could find work. A domestic servant–turned–prostitute told Sanger that she had sent all her earnings to her mother, so that when she lost her position she quickly became destitute and turned to prostitution as a last resort. A police captain told Sanger that he saw many impoverished women live on bread and water in the streets before becoming prostitutes.

Sanger estimated that the average full-time prostitute earned ten dollars per week, though whether he meant net or gross income is unclear. Even if half of these earnings went to pay room and board to a madam or rent at a house of assignation, this still left a weekly income far above what a woman could expect to receive at needlework, domestic service, or any of the other "women's trades." Of the "wretched females" who work as New York prostitutes, the directors of the House of Industry asserted accurately that "a majority are dragged down or bred from birth to their trade of death by inexorable WANT; victims, not of guilty choice, nor of treacherous lust, but of absolute starvation and despair."[22]

Destitution, however, was not the only factor driving women to prostitution. Although more women cited that cause than any other when asked why they had become prostitutes (525 of 2,000), the variety of answers provided by the others is both surprising and illuminating. Nearly as many women (513) attributed their circumstances to "inclination," 282 reported being "seduced," 181 cited "drink," 164 ill-treatment by their parents, 124 called it "an easy life," 84 blamed keeping "bad company," and 71 were "persuaded by prostitutes" to take up the trade. One must read such evidence with caution and skepticism, yet certain revealing trends are apparent. Sanger noted, for example, that many of the cases of "inclination" involved women who left their husbands because their spouses refused to give them liquor or were abandoned by their husbands because they drank to excess. These cases, combined with those who specifically cited drink as the cause of their plight, suggest that liquor played a significant role in driving many women to prostitution. Some might argue that crushing poverty may have induced these women to drink, and that it all circles back to destitution, but as is the case today, many nineteenth-century women became prostitutes in order to finance an addiction to stimulants.[23]

Mary O'Daniel and Ellen Cable would have classified themselves among the next largest group, those claiming that they were "seduced" into the sex trade. But most women using this term referred to a different experience—that of having been impregnated and then abandoned by a boyfriend or fiancé. Foster contended that the "great source" of New York prostitutes was young women from the countryside who came to the city "to escape infamy" after becoming pregnant out of wedlock. The immigration experience also provided ample opportunity for young women (especially those traveling alone) to be seduced. Of the 282 women who attributed their lives as prostitutes to "seduction," 16 specified that they were "corrupted" on immigrant ships and another 8 in New York's emigrant boardinghouses (where newcomers stayed before finding a permanent home).[24]

Dr. Sanger found that nearly half of New York's prostitutes had been so employed for one year or less, indicating that few courtesans spent years in the trade. In fact, contemporaries reported that many women worked only sporadically as prostitutes when all other means of earning a living were exhausted. Sanger found that many were "women whose trades are uncertain, and who are liable at certain seasons of the year to be without employment. Then real necessity force[s] them on the town until a return of business provides them with work." Seamstresses, poorly paid and frequently unemployed, were often associated with casual prostitution, but Sanger found that many more former servants worked in the sex trade than did needleworkers.[25]

Over the course of the antebellum years, the ethnic background of the district's sex workers changed. In the 1820s and '30s, most of the neighborhood's prostitutes were native-born. By the 1840s, however, native-born courtesans (and their madams) had abandoned Five Points, moving either uptown or west across Broadway. Adeline Miller, for example, ran brothels at 32 Orange in 1822, 85 Cross in 1826, and 44 Orange in 1835, but by 1838 had relocated to the West Side, where she continued to operate bordellos until 1859. Brothel keeper Phoebe Doty, proprietor of establishments on Anthony and Orange Streets in the twenties and thirties, had likewise moved west of Five Points by the forties, as had Sarah Tuttle. As was often the case in Five Points, the Irish filled the vacuum left by the departing natives.[26]

The gender of the typical brothel keeper began to change as well. In the

1820s, women ran more than three-quarters of all Five Points bordellos; in the 1850s, in contrast, they operated just 37 percent. This transformation seems to have resulted primarily from changes in the Five Points population rather than in the sex trade itself, for in neighborhoods where native-born prostitutes still predominated (such as the area between Canal and Houston Streets and the Lower West Side), madams outnumbered male brothel keepers by a margin of more than five to one. As Five Points became more heavily Irish, men managed to capture an increasing share of the profits from prostitution.[27]

Despite the omnipresence of prostitution, residents did not hesitate to complain about a brothel when it disturbed the peace, especially when the bordello was located away from the Five Points intersection. In 1842, for example, neighbors filed a complaint about the brothel at 168 Leonard Street, where "dancing singing and carousing" went on "at late and improper hours of the night." A year later, Robert Gordon of 10 Orange Street and Edward Blackall of 12½ Orange pressed charges against John Donaho for keeping a house of prostitution in the basement of 12 Orange, where "persons of ill name & fame . . . are in the nightly practice of resorting until late and improper hours of the night to the great disgrace of the neighbourhood." That same year, Thomas Flynn of 87 Mulberry, William Murkitrick of 85 Mulberry, and Bernard Kennedy of 76 Mulberry secured the conviction of John Jack for keeping a disorderly house of prostitution at 83 Mulberry. The "premises are a great nuisance and annoyance to the neighbours," the complainants testified, "disturbances occurring there at late, and all hours of the night, persons complaining of being robbed in there, fighting and quarreling and disturbing the neighbourhood." Prostitution may have been grudgingly tolerated by Five Pointers, but disturbing the peace was not.[28]

The penalties for those convicted in such cases—the charge was usually "keeping a disorderly house"—varied enormously. When in 1843, Five Points police officer William Nealis arrested seventeen "females of the Five Points, prostitutes and vagrants," the judge sentenced each to four months in the penitentiary. A decade later, the *Herald* published a list of people, "mostly residents of the Sixth ward," who had been convicted of operating unlicensed saloons that also served as "dens of prostitutes" and "resorts for thieves and vagabonds." Their sentences ranged from two months to fifteen days in jail (the latter for the aforementioned Henry

Hoffman for prostituting his own daughter) to fines of fifty dollars or less. But these were exceptionally severe punishments. The overwhelming majority of those found guilty of keeping a disorderly house of prostitution received just a judicial slap on the wrist. When Osman and Margaret Cutter were convicted of operating a disorderly house at 7 Elizabeth Street, the judge suspended their sentence on the condition that they vacate the premises. Likewise, when landlord John Devins of 24 Elizabeth Street was found guilty of the same crime (Devins lived in the basement while the prostitutes leased the upstairs), the magistrate suspended his sentence provided that Devins evict the prostitutes. Many other brothel keepers simply vacated their places of business when indicted, which they correctly surmised would lead to a dismissal of the charges. Ordinarily, only habitual offenders or those who tried to avoid paying their liquor license fees suffered a significant criminal penalty operating a Five Points house of prostitution.[29]

"Crimes and Outrages Almost Daily Committed in This Neighborhood"

The first known press description of Five Points, from 1826, called the district "the resort of thieves and rogues of the lowest degree." Another early newspaper account asked authorities "to put an end to the crimes and outrages almost daily committed in this neighborhood, which has become the most dangerous place in our city." Antebellum police reports confirm that crime was endemic to the neighborhood. Hardly a day went by without the press announcing a number of arrests.[30]

One of the most common crimes was petty thievery. In contrast to the penalties for prostitution, those for theft could be quite severe. Mary Hoy of 83 Bayard Street, for example, charged her neighbor Margaret McCasken with stealing "some saucers and other crockery, worth fifty cents." The judge found her guilty and sentenced her to two months in the penitentiary. Sometimes it seemed that the defendant's status as a lowly Five Pointer motivated magistrates to impose particularly stiff punishments. Irish immigrant Mary White worked as a "housekeeper" for Ann Francis, "a negro woman, who keeps a sailors' boardinghouse at No. 94 Park-street." Francis supplemented her boardinghouse income by taking in clothes to wash, but after hiring White in 1857, she often found clothing missing. Her suspicions were confirmed when she noticed White wearing a frilled petticoat that had disappeared a few hours earlier. "I guess she stole the clothes," declared the judge in rendering his verdict. "She's no great shakes anyhow, to be housekeeper in a sailors' boarding house kept by a nigger. We sentence her to the Penitentiary for two months."[31]

Harsh sentences did little to deter many of Five Points' more hardened criminals. In 1850, Peter Meehan caught Patrick Murphy coming down the stairs of the tenement at 6 Mulberry Street carrying clothes, cash, and other items from Meehan's own apartment. Authorities had released Murphy from jail only two days earlier for a previous crime. Professional burglars such as Murphy often made Five Points their home. The Old Brewery and Cow Bay were especially renowned as dens of thieves, but police found criminals congregating throughout the district. In 1851, a "tail diver" (pickpocket) caught by Five Points policeman William Bell admitted during his interrogation "that N⁰ 7½ Elizabeth Street upstairs was a resort for small thieves—a number of them lodged there." On another occasion Bell discovered that "No. 15 Orange St. is the residence of a Gang of Thieves."[32]

Juvenile thieves abounded as well. "I went in Orange St. to look for a piece of blue pilot cloth that was stolen from the express wagon of Charles Croft of 70 Maiden Lane," Bell recorded in his logbook in February 1851. "On Wednesday evening last while standing in front of No. 11 Orange St. I learned that it was stolen by a boy and taken into a house in the neighborhood." When the husband of a woman whose bracelets were stolen placed a newspaper advertisement seeking information about the crime, he received word that a Five Points boy living in the basement of the rear tenement at 74 Mulberry Street had taken them. For the most part, such thefts seem to have been crimes of opportunity, in which children stole items they found unguarded, but some Five Pointers actually trained children to pilfer. Thirteen-year-old George Appo, for example, learned to pick pockets from two thieves who posed as newsboys.[33]

Five Points adult thieves especially targeted naive visitors carrying large sums of cash. In 1847, a pickpocket stole $45 (the equivalent of about $720 today) from an English sailor patronizing a brothel at 156 Anthony Street. Police in 1849 arrested Caroline Goldsmith for luring "greenhorn" Francis Oschatz into the "house" (brothel?) of Mrs. Cook at 81 Bayard and robbing him of $33 (more than $500 today). Sometimes criminals could reap substantial sums by doping their targets. An Illinois merchant passing through New York on his way to Boston with a load of butter claimed to have visited Five Points so that he could write about it to his friends back home. While at the corner of Cross and Orange, a woman asked him to treat her to a glass of gin. He did. But she drugged his drink and when he regained consciousness the woman had disappeared with his coat and a hundred dollars. Although he might have recovered his money by reporting the crime to the police, the man refused to do so and risk his reputable standing back home, where he served as a steward in his Methodist church.[34]

Tough New York juries had little sympathy for out-of-towners robbed after overindulging in Five Points saloons. In 1850, "three Five Point thieves" lured Reuben Knox into "John Orpen's [public] house, corner of Centre and Anthony streets," where they got him drunk playing cards and then stole his watch and thirty dollars. Knox complained to the police, who arrested the crooks, but Officer Denis Dowdican found Knox "so intoxicated that I deemed it my duty to take him to the station house for protection." At the trial, the defendants' attorney seized upon this last remark, arguing that the drunken Knox had lost the money and watch in the card game. The jury returned a verdict of not guilty. The chagrined judge released the prisoners, lamenting that the habitual criminals had been lucky to escape conviction. One of the three—Patrick Murphy—was the one caught a few days later robbing Peter Meehan's Mulberry Street flat.[35]

Some stolen goods, such as crockery and frilled petticoats, could be used by the thieves themselves. Coats and pocketwatches were disposed of through fences, many of whom operated in the locale. Patrolman Bell constantly sought leads on Five Points fences. By "pumping" Joe Hancock, a recently arrested criminal, Bell "ascertained that Meyer Blas [of] 36½ Orange St. was a fence." A few months later while interrogating an accessory to murder, Bell learned of three more fences, including one in "a little rum hole in Cross St. near Orange." Despite Bell's detective work, prosecutors found it difficult to win convictions against fences who ran secondhand shops, because the storekeepers could claim ignorance as to the origins of the goods. When police investigating the theft of forty-one silk parasols questioned Polish immigrant Harris Solomon at his second-hand clothing shop at 9 Orange Street in 1852, the thirty-year-old claimed to have none in his stock. In a search of his house, however, police found four of them in a bureau under some old clothes. Although Solomon claimed to have purchased those umbrellas in California, skeptical prosecutors charged him with possession of stolen goods. The outcome of Solomon's case is not known, but the paucity of such indictments in the district attorney's records suggests that few fences were punished for their crimes.[36]

Some Five Points robberies could be quite violent. Police in 1849 arrested African-American William Peterson who, along with "two other darkies," knocked William Everson (also black) senseless in Cow Bay with a missile from a slingshot and then robbed him of a "five franc piece and a shilling." Prosecutors in 1847 charged two other African Americans, Sam Rice and George Morgan, with assaulting a man from New Jersey while he walked on Orange Street, dragging him into an alley, and robbing him of eight dollars, his coat, and boots. Women could use violence to perpetrate crimes as well. Frances Wilson, a "colored woman," lured a man into a building on Little Water Street, then knocked him down and took his coat and a five-dollar bill. The man tried to hide his sterling silver pocketwatch, but Wilson "bit his clenched fist to get it out of his hand." The trial judge sentenced her to ten years in Sing Sing prison, probably because of the violence involved and her status as a repeat offender. In contrast, when Ann Gannon assaulted Bridget Fitzpatrick in front of 49 Mott Street and "knocked some of her front teeth out," she merely received a suspended sentence.[37]

Violence against women seems to have been especially common in Five Points. James Adams stabbed fellow African-American Margaret Turner in the back at her home at 76 Orange Street in 1853 because he was jealous of the attention she paid to other men. In 1872, a drunken Bayard Street man shot to death his live-in "lover" of two weeks because she went out with friends despite his objections. The *Times* described the murderer as a habitual thief while the victim was a twenty-year-old "waitress in a low concert saloon on Chatham-street." Their tenement at 61 Bayard was "a resort for the vilest type of low people."[38]

Marriage provided no guarantee of safety from the opposite sex. Spousal abuse was apparently common, though it was almost never reported to the police. In one of the few such cases described in the press, the *Tribune* noted the arrest of both Lewis Vatty Sr. and Jr. Police found the son "beating the father without mercy" because he had discovered his father "beating the wife." One Five Points girl insisted on leaving midway through Sunday school class each week to be sure her drunken father was not battering her mother again. He was finally jailed. A more common situation was probably the one a *Times* reporter found in the basement lodging house at 35 Baxter Street in 1859. The keeper of the establishment "had been 'banging his wife, and hit [a lodger] a lick sideways that almost killed her.' The wretch had kicked another girl so severely that she had gone to bed early in the day and not got up since." Despite the violence directed against her, the man's wife defended her husband, saying her "old man was a little wild when he was in liquor" but was otherwise a good mate. Given the utter dependence of Five Points wives (especially those with children) on the incomes of their husbands, most would have hesitated to press charges.[39]

Rape was another violent crime against women that was rarely recorded. Perhaps the close-knit nature of the Five Points community discouraged such a crime. Or, like spousal abuse, it may have gone unreported. The only two cases from Five Points found in a survey of antebellum New York newspapers and a sampling of indictment records both involved the rape of Irish-American women by non-Irish men. One involved Bridget Heney, a recently arrived Irish immigrant residing at 13 Mulberry Street. Heney had just lost her position as a live-in domestic servant and could not have been very happy as she tried to find her way back to Five Points on a Sunday evening in late January 1852. Her husband Patrick was still in Ireland, expecting her to earn money to pay for his passage to New York. According to her subsequent deposition, she was on Centre Street between Broome and Grand when she asked a passerby for directions to Mulberry Street. The young man, butcher John Holberton, convinced her to come inside and warm up before completing her journey. Holberton led Heney up a flight of stairs to the Centre Street Market militia drill room, where he threw her to the ground and raped her, telling her that he had plenty of cash and "would let her have some of the money" afterwards if she did not resist. When Holberton had finished, Heney (according to her own account) asked for the promised money. Holberton asked how much she wanted. Heney demanded two dollars, but Holberton refused to give her more than one. Holberton said he would give her the money downstairs, but before he could do so four or more of Holberton's friends arrived, forced Heney back inside, and raped her as well, one after the other. The men then literally dragged her outside and left her on a doorstep.

Police made little progress in apprehending Heney's assailants until a week later, when she told then that "she had received information" enabling her to identify five of them. The police immediately arrested the men and charged them with rape. They were native-born Americans ranging in age from seventeen to twenty-three, and all worked at the Centre Street Market (four as butchers and one as an oyster seller). Two of the five, twenty-three-year-old Jacob Evans and seventeen-year-old John Quitman, eventually pleaded guilty to lesser charges of assault and battery. Prosecutors dropped charges against a third. In late February, the *Herald* reported that Holberton and the fifth suspect would soon stand trial, but none was ever described in the New York press, and the indictment papers do not indicate a resolution.[40]

In rare cases, women were the perpetrators of serious crime. Incidents of infanticide, for example, occurred sporadically in Five Points throughout the antebellum period. In 1841, passersby found a newborn baby dead on Anthony Street. In 1849, the *Herald* reported the case of a lifeless baby girl discovered "in the sink at the dwelling house No. 6 Doyer street. From the appearance of the child when found, it was evident that foul means had been used, as, around the neck of the little innocent, a cord had been tied tight, causing strangulation." The building's residents told police that the mother was probably Eliza Rafferty, a thirty-year-old Irish immigrant with a husband and child living in Liverpool. On entering her apartment, the officers found Rafferty "sitting very composedly in a chair in her room, making a dress, that being her profession." After first denying that she had given birth to the child, she then admitted it, but insisted that "the child was dead before it was thrown into the sink." Police took Rafferty to jail to await an autopsy by the coroner, who ruled that the baby had been born alive and subsequently strangled to death.[41]

Much more common was child abandonment. In 1867, the Five Points Mission took in a one-month-old baby whose mother had asked a neighbor to watch it "for a few minutes" while she went to the store. The mother never returned. Three years later, a mother offered to buy kindling and food for an old woman if she would watch her baby while she shopped. This mother disappeared as well. In rare cases, parents even abandoned older children. Mary and Maggie Sherman were abandoned by their father at Mary McCarty's boardinghouse at 54 Mulberry Street in June 1860. After hearing "nothing of him," McCarty gave the children to the mission. In September 1856, a Five Points woman brought another abandoned child, eleven year-old William Morton, to the mission. He had lived in the rear tenement at 38 Baxter until the previous spring, when his parents had moved to California and left young William behind. Since his abandonment, William had "got his food by picking papers in the street and selling them at the junk shops. Slept in entries and carts." Cases such as William's were not common. For every child or infant abandoned in Five Points, there were dozens brought for adoption to the Five Points Mission and House of Industry by tearful mothers.[42]

Despite oft-told stories to the contrary, murder was—like infanticide and child abandonment—another rare crime at Five Points. The murder rate did rise dramatically in the prewar decade, however, as handguns became more widely available. As many New Yorkers were convicted of murder from 1852 to 1854 as had been found guilty of homicide in the entire 1840s.[43]

A significant number of murders involved the drunkenness of either the murderer or his victim. On June 12, 1853, for example, Patrick McNulty of Bayard Street and a number of fellow Five Pointers decided to go "skylarking," a drinking binge in which the inebriated participants insult, harass, and create mayhem wherever they go. The group had already been drinking heavily, first at a saloon on Bayard Street, then at another on Mulberry, and then at a third on Centre before entering the bar of Herman Doscher, also on Centre Street. McNulty and his companions stood atop the bar demanding drinks and threatening the other customers. They also chased Doscher's wife into her residence in the back of the house, forcing her to lock herself in a room and eventually to climb out the window to escape them. While the group ran amok, the least drunk among them announced that this was all innocent skylarking and promised to pay for everything the others drank and destroyed.

Doscher finally succeeded in chasing the rowdy gang out of his watering hole, at which point the revelers proceeded south to the Jenny Lind saloon, an oyster cellar at 48 Centre run by Doscher's brother John. Although the establishment ostensibly specialized in mollusks, a neighbor testified that its proprietor primarily "sold liquor and kept girls." The skylarkers arrived at John Doscher's den around midnight, started a fight, and invaded the bedrooms in search of courtesans and their lovers. Apparently fearing for his safety and that of his wife, John Doscher found his pistol, and when the revelers refused to desist, he shot McNulty three times— once in the head. The hearty Irishman survived, leaving the hospital after only four days, but he began complaining of headaches a few weeks later and died soon thereafter. Doscher was charged with murder, but despite the testimony of McNulty's friends that they had merely been engaged in some harmless fun, the jury found him not guilty.[44]

Although alcohol played a role in many Five Points murders, other killings involved love-related jealousies. When African-American Charles Thomas "saw his paramour in close conversation with another black man called Henry Ford" behind the tenement at 53 Orange Street in 1846, Thomas ran up and stabbed Ford, killing him "instantly." Two decades later, twenty-one-year-old iron molder William Connell was accompanying two women into the Live and Let Live Saloon on the Bowery at Bayard when Richard Casey of 80 Mott Street shook some money under their noses, apparently in an attempt to embarrass Connell for consorting with prostitutes. When Connell complained of the insult, Casey knocked his hat into the gutter and then shot him as he stooped to pick it up. A jury found Casey guilty of second-degree murder, and the judge sentenced him to life in prison.[45]

Some Five Pointers needed little justification to kill a man, as the 1851 case of Aaron Stookey demonstrates. Stookey "kept a drinking cellar in Anthony street" near Little Water that was frequented, according to the *Herald*, "by the lowest grade of the male and female residents" of Five Points. On the night of April 17, Stookey and another man were passing in front of Crown's Grocery when African-American Edward "Teddy" Moore of Broome Street bumped into Stookey's friend. According to the testimony of one of Moore's companions (an African American who lived in Cow Bay), Moore begged his pardon but Stookey exclaimed to his friend, "'why don't you kill the black son of a b——?'" Not waiting for a response, Stookey drew his own knife and stabbed Moore in the side. Moore died minutes later.

Given that Stookey had also pulled a knife on a black man a few days before, prosecutors today might label Moore's killing a hate crime. But in the trial that took place just fourteen days after the slaying, Stookey's attorney tried to play upon the presumed prejudices of the all-white jury, pointing out that all four prosecution witnesses—each a Five Points

African American—were convicted criminals. The most damning testimony, the attorney noted, had come from a witness who had told the district attorney that he had never been in prison, when in fact he had served three terms on Blackwell's Island and one at Sing Sing. The defense also suggested that Moore had bumped against Stookey to pick his pocket. A policeman testified that bumping was not a common pickpocket's device, but he did admit that Moore was a known thief and "a very bad character." To their credit, however, the jurors were not swayed by the defense tactics and returned a guilty verdict in just fifteen minutes. Stookey was hanged in the Tombs courtyard.[46]

Ethnicity, prostitution, and politics each played a role in the most talked about antebellum Five Points murder, the killing of brothel keeper Wilhelm Decker by aspiring politico John Glass. The twenty-three-year-old Glass was well known in the Sixth Ward, having served in 1858 as one of the district's constables (an elected post equivalent to that of a ward sheriff) and as foreman of Engine Company No. 21. On the evening of January 16, 1859, just days after relinquishing his post as constable, Glass rang Decker's doorbell at 21 Elm Street (now Lafayette). Accompanying Glass were twenty-four-year-old James Higgins (the *Herald* described the two of them as "active politicians"), twenty-two-year-old Constable James Loftus, and Glass's brother James, who ran the saloon next door at 19 Elm. When Decker opened the door, the four men burst in and began smashing lamps and furniture. The assailants then rushed out, but when Decker closed the door, John Glass fired a shot through it, killing him. Meanwhile, Richard Owens, a Brooklyn resident passing by the crime scene, began scuffling with Higgins on the street, prompting James Glass to shoot Owens. Like Decker, Owens died at the scene.

"The excitement in the Sixth ward was intense," commented the *Herald*, as word of the murders spread through the neighborhood. Yet despite the feverish speculation and various trials, no clear motive for the slayings ever emerged. Testimony established that John Glass had frequently visited the Decker house in the past, apparently in the company of prostitutes, and one witness implied that Glass attacked the house because Decker had turned him away earlier in the evening. Although such a rebuff hardly seems to justify murder, Glass was also known to have a violent temper. Prosecutors had previously charged him with assault on several occasions, which may have accounted for his expulsion from Engine Com-

pany No. 21 a few months before the murders. Or Glass and his accom-
plices might have been punishing Decker for failing to pay protection
money for his brothel. Whatever the case, John Glass and James Higgins
were convicted of manslaughter in the death of Decker and sentenced to
twenty-year jail terms. James Glass, also found guilty of manslaughter,
received a life sentence. Yet due to the Glass brothers' political connections, John served only five years and James only six before receiving par-
dons from the governor.[47]

As the Glass case demonstrates, law enforcement officials were sometimes no more law-abiding than the criminals they were paid to pursue.
Some policemen refused to search for stolen property without a prepaid
reward. Others demanded payoffs from the owners of brothels and dance
halls. A number of policemen were "said to have been engaged in a regular
system of levying contributions on the keepers of disorderly houses in the
districts they represent," threatening indictment or arrest if they did not
"fork over" a fifty- to hundred-dollar monthly payment. Officers became
so brazen in their demands, reported the *Tribune* in 1855, that despite the
risks of publicly airing their grievances, bordello operators in the Fourth
Ward complained about the shakedowns to Mayor Fernando Wood. Some
corrupt policemen must have extorted protection money from Five Points
bawdy-house keepers as well.[48]

Police corruption resulted in part from the character of the men on the
force. Some earned the coveted posts through party loyalty, but others
snared a spot by bribing local political leaders. One Sixth Warder promised
around midcentury that he could deliver a police appointment for twenty-
five dollars, which he would convey to the appropriate aldermen. As a
result, complained the head of the fire department, "convicts, freshly
emerged from the dungeon cells of Blackwell's Island, are appointed by
Aldermen as policemen." Others used elected law enforcement positions
to extort graft. Writing in 1860, a newspaper columnist recalled the Fourth
Ward's infamous constable, "Porgie Joe," who spent liberally to assure his
nomination by all the district's Democratic factions. "It would be a bad go
for a dance house to refuse to send up to Joe his weekly allowance," stated
the reporter, "as a failure would quickly be followed up by an indictment,
or a midnight arrest." Although Joe's authority ostensibly ended at the
Fourth Ward's borders, "on the Points he had his tools and spies" as well,

"and I have no doubt, his receipts per day were often more than a hundred dollars." The writer remembered, for example, a gang of young thieves with a "rendezvous . . . in Mulberry street, near Cross." They robbed empty apartments while the inhabitants were at work, taking money and jewelry out of locked bureaus. If police captured one of the crooks, the gang summoned Joe, who would put "the officer making the arrest to sleep with a fifty," receiving his quid pro quo "in a rake with the first good swag."[49]

The extent of police corruption in Five Points is impossible to determine. The countless press accounts of neighborhood officers sustaining serious injuries attempting to apprehend crime suspects indicate that many (and probably most) took their work seriously, especially when violent offenders were involved. An 1849 *Herald* story reported that a Sixth Ward policeman, while taking a prisoner into custody, "was violently attacked by a Five Points thief, nicknamed Monkey, who gave him a blow with a sling shot in the mouth, displacing some of his teeth, and otherwise injuring him severely." Yet after Five Points native Joseph Dowling rose through the Sixth Ward's police ranks to become the district's police justice, he complained from the bench that too many petty thieves escaped prosecution due to police payoffs, a charge a department veteran would not have made lightly. Police corruption—especially involving the vice industry—would remain a significant problem both in Five Points and citywide throughout the nineteenth century.[50]

One might imagine that the press exaggerated the extent of crime in Five Points in order to sell papers. But arrest records confirm that Five Points was particularly crime-ridden. Excluding the three downtown commercial wards, where there were few inhabitants and many warehouses to be robbed, the Sixth Ward led the city in per capita arrests. The arrest rate there was two to three times higher than in most other wards. Yet the rate for violent crime in Five Points was not drastically higher than in other parts of the city. Much of the Sixth Ward's elevated arrest rate derived from three misdemeanors: public intoxication, vagrancy, and disorderly conduct. Some of those arraigned on the latter two charges must have been prostitutes, but women were arrested as often as men for all three crimes. Even in 1869, when the bulk of the sex trade had moved uptown, the Sixth Ward was still the only place in the city where police arrested virtually as many women as men.[51]

"IF YOU LIVED IN THIS PLACE YOU WOULD ASK FOR
WHISKEY INSTEAD OF MILK"

From Hogarth's "Gin Lane" in Georgian London to the crackhouses of late-twentieth-century American ghettos, the abuse of stimulants has plagued the Western world's impoverished souls. Five Points was no different. Alcoholism destroyed the lives of hundreds of residents, impoverishing some, driving spouses and children away from others, leading many to jail, and countless others to their deaths through alcohol-related illnesses, injuries, or crimes. Given our appreciation of the anti-Irish bigotry harbored by so many Five Points charitable workers, it is tempting to disregard their many stories of drunkenness. Yet descriptions of alcohol-related crimes and tragedies appear throughout the documentary record—in sources written by Protestants and Catholics, by outsiders as well as Five Pointers themselves. The pervasiveness of alcoholism in Five Points played a significant role in shaping life there.

Drunkenness was everywhere. George Appo remembered that in the alley between the front and rear buildings at 14 Baxter Street where he lived as a boy, "it was a common sight to see every morning under the wagon sheds at least six to ten drunken men and women sleeping off the effects of . . . five cent rum." Many of the neighborhood's basement boardinghouses were filled with inebriates. When the wooden tenement across the street at 15 Baxter burned down in 1863, tenants stated that the three residents who perished could have escaped the burning building "had they not been under the influence of liquor." As to who started the fire, the tenants' list of suspects consisted of the drunken African-American couple on the ground floor and the drunken Irishwoman who lived above them, all of whom survived. Five Pointers' complaints about their neighbors' habitual drunkenness could be repeated ad infinitum. It is impossible to determine the exact extent of alcohol abuse, but it seems clear that hundreds of Five Points residents found it painful to go a day without a drink.[52]

Some area alcoholics asked workers at the mission and the House of Industry for help sobering up. "Harriet Bertram came in and said she wanted to reform," wrote one of the mission's employees in the group's logbook in 1856. The thirty-five-year-old Indiana native "was in a state of intoxication at the time, and after being sent up to bed, had a very severe attack of the horrors." After two weeks without liquor, the mission found her work as a domestic servant in Brooklyn. Others with similarly noble intentions left the charitable groups after a day or two, unable to cope with the physical and emotional symptoms of withdrawal.[53]

Children often suffered terribly due to their parents' alcohol abuse. "Last winter, my father drank so hard that we [ran out of money and] had to leave our room and move into a stable just before the heavy snow fell," eight-year-old Mary Jane Tobin told officials at the mission. The stable roof had large holes in it, "so the snow came down on us and we were almost frozen; but we wrapped us up in an old blanket and tried to keep warm the best we could." Mary Jane's older brother eventually took her to live with an aunt on Mulberry Street. Children without older siblings to care for them might fare even worse than poor Mary Jane. House of Industry agents found a small child starving to death in a rear tenement on Worth Street in 1859 because her mother spent almost every penny on liquor. The mother had pawned all the family possessions except a broken table. The House of Industry agents fed the girl and returned her to her mother, but a few weeks later a policeman brought her back because the neglect continued. A New York street urchin recalled frequently seeing "little children starving to death for something to eat, while their parents [were] lying dead drunk."[54]

Alcohol abuse by adults forced their offspring to take on responsibilities no child should have had to bear. An eight-year-old Five Points boy once went as long as three days with only a bit of bread to eat as his alcoholic mother became increasingly ill. Each day, she sent him to pawn another piece of furniture or clothing so he could buy her more brandy. By the time she died, she was completely nude. The House of Industry magazine reported in 1857 that two youngsters living next door to Crown's Grocery "came crying to the school—for mother was dead." The two adult boarders sharing the apartment with them ought to have summoned the authorities, but one lay on the floor in a drunken stupor, while the other had recently been sent to prison for habitual public drunkenness. As to the deceased woman, she had died "from the effects of long-continued intoxication." Some children paid the ultimate price for their parents' alcoholism. One little girl was forced to steal to pay for her mother's drinking habit. Police caught her one day, and while awaiting trial in the Tombs, where prisoners often had to build their own fires to keep themselves warm, the helpless girl apparently froze to death.[55]

Even children drank to excess in Five Points. The House of Industry discovered children drinking liquor to such an extent that it organized a temperance club exclusively for youngsters. "Little boys of eight have been found intoxicated in the infant class," reported mission workers a decade later. Many children got their introduction to alcohol when asked to "rush the growler" for their mothers or fathers. This chore involved bringing a pail (the "growler") downstairs to the nearest saloon and returning it filled with beer. Youngsters growing up in Five Points (especially in Irish families) were constantly surrounded by the sights, sounds, and smells of drinking and drunkenness.[56]

When a health official asked an inebriated rear tenement dweller why she drank, she replied that "if you lived in this place you would ask for whiskey instead of milk." But such a response tells only part of the story. The Germans, Polish Jews, and Italians who lived in Five Points in equally squalid conditions did not suffer from alcoholism to the extent that the Irish did. Citywide statistics from later in the nineteenth century suggest that Irishmen in New York were 75 percent more likely to die of alcohol-related illnesses than their English and Welsh counterparts, while for women the ratio was three to one. There must have been cultural or genetic factors at work. The Irish were certainly aware of their propensity to alcoholism before they arrived in America, even though many had been too poor in Europe to afford liquor except on rare occasions. Recall that Palmerston immigrant Pat McGowan had warned in one of his first letters back home to County Sligo that because liquor was so cheap and plentiful in America, his countrymen who could not resist the temptation to drink should not join him in New York. The Irish journalist John F. Maguire likewise attributed the Irish propensity to drunkenness to the omnipresence of liquor in the United States.[57]

But circumstances other than Five Points' concentration of Irish immigrants also account for the high rate of alcoholism there. Many alcoholics probably *chose* to live in Five Points. Its seedy saloons and groceries undoubtedly sold some of the most inexpensive liquor in town. Cheap rents in its run-down tenements allowed drinkers to devote every possible cent to buying liquor. Indigent inebriates could also probably find quiet, out-of-the-way alleys to sleep off binges more easily in Five Points than in other neighborhoods, where police would be more likely to awaken or arrest sleeping drunks. In addition, while newcomers without a propensity to drink could save money and move to better neighborhoods, alcoholic immigrants who could not work regularly were doomed to remain in Five Points indefinitely.

Five Points' reputation as a hotbed of vice and crime gradually changed over time. In 1828, the city's grand jury singled out the neighborhood as "a rendezvous for thieves and prostitutes." A generation later, New Yorkers had begun to reconsider their perceptions of the notorious district. George Foster wrote in 1850 that Five Points was much safer than it had been ten or twenty years earlier. Many of his contemporaries agreed. When South Carolinian William H. Bobo toured the Points with a police escort a year or two later, the guide told him that there was no danger visiting the neighborhood anymore and that "the larger lights, in the way of stealing and other concomitant evils, have generally gone out [of the district], and are now hanging about Water-street." Yet in the same year, the district attorney complained that more muggings occurred in Five Points than in any other portion of the city.[58]

It appears certain that in the 1820s and '30s, lawlessness plagued Five Points as virtually no other section of the city. Fighting, prostitution, and violent assaults were rampant. By the 1850s, however, public demands that the police suppress blatant lawbreakers, combined with an increased neighborhood presence by religious groups, helped reduce the crime rate significantly. Five Points probably continued to outpace most other portions of the city in what would today be termed "quality-of-life crimes," such as public drunkenness, public solicitation of prostitution, and petty theft. But in the category of violent crime—such as assault, rape, and murder—Five Points by the eve of the Civil War was no better or worse than other working-class New York neighborhoods.

Religious groups deserve much of the credit for the reduction in crime and suffering. Ever since the 1820s, religious activists had attempted to convert Five Points' worst "sinners," passing out tracts in saloons and tenements and even conducting Bible readings in front of the neighborhood's most notorious brothels. Yet few Five Pointers had responded. Beginning in 1850, however, Protestant reformers tried a new approach. In addition to religious counseling, they would offer struggling Five Pointers job training and placement, hot meals and clothing, instruction in hygiene and disease prevention, and even a place to stay when the money ran out or an abusive spouse became too much to bear. The institutions these reformers created

could not eliminate poverty in Five Points, and some of their methods—
such as taking hundreds of indigent Five Points children from their parents
to be placed in adoptive homes in the Midwest—seem heartless and cruel
by today's standards. Nonetheless, these innovative Protestant efforts, as
well as the Catholic countermeasures they precipitated, significantly
reduced suffering and crime in Five Points and played the key role in
ending the neighborhood's long reign as the city's leading center of vice and
lawlessness.

8

PROLOGUE

"I Shall Never Forget This as Long as I Live":
Abraham Lincoln Visits Five Points

In February 1860, Abraham Lincoln was invited to visit to New York. The Young Men's Central Republican Union, a group organized to expose prominent New Yorkers to the views of leading Republicans from around the nation, had asked him to deliver an address to its members, and Lincoln jumped at the chance. He was already well known in the Midwest, but if he was going to satisfy his steadily growing presidential ambitions, he would need to win support in the East as well. Lincoln spent weeks preparing the speech, working harder on it than on any he gave before or after.[1]

Lincoln was scheduled to appear at the Cooper Union auditorium on Monday evening, the twenty-seventh, and he arrived in New York on Saturday. The wide-eyed tourist strolled down Broadway, had his portrait taken at Mathew Brady's photography studio, and on Sunday morning attended services at the Brooklyn church of Henry Ward Beecher, renowned as "the greatest orator since St. Paul." But that afternoon, Lincoln chose to pass the time at a more unusual tourist attraction—the charitable institution known as the Five Points House of Industry.[2]

Living conditions in Five Points had improved markedly by the eve of the Civil War, but Lincoln nonetheless found the neighborhood's abject poverty shocking. When he arrived at the House of Industry, Lincoln was undoubtedly given a full tour of the organization's new six-story brick headquarters, which towered over the surrounding wooden hovels on the north side of Paradise Square just west of the Five Points intersection. It had spacious dormitories where dozens of abused, neglected, or homeless boys and girls lived until they found adoptive parents. His hosts would also have shown him the large chapel where religious services were held and the workshops where neighborhood teens and adults learned a variety of trades.

As Lincoln peeked in on one of the Sunday school classes, a teacher asked the tall, skinny lawyer to say a few words to his students. Lincoln at first declined, insisting that he could offer no words of advice to such destitute children. But his companion, Illinois congressman Elihu B. Washburne, insisted that Lincoln speak, suggesting that he describe the hard times of his own youth. Lincoln reluctantly consented, telling the students, as Washburne later recalled, that "I had been poor; that I remembered when my toes stuck out through my broken shoes in winter; when my arms were out at the elbows; when I shivered with the cold. And I told them there was only one rule. That was, always do the very best you can. I told them that I had always tried to do the very best I could; and that, if they would follow that rule, they would get along somehow." By now, Lincoln's eyes had filled with tears and he could not continue. When Washburne later told Lincoln that his little speech had inspired the children, Lincoln replied, "No, they are the ones who have inspired me—given me courage. . . . I am glad we came—I shall never forget this as long as I live."[3]

It is tempting to attribute Washburne's moving description of this poignant scene to the reverence for Lincoln that developed after his assassination. Yet even before Lincoln's death, a House of Industry teacher reported that his words were "strikingly beautiful, and his tones musical with intensest feeling." The children's faces "would droop into sad conviction as he uttered sentences of warning, and would brighten into sunshine as he spoke cheerful words of promise."[4]

That Lincoln chose to visit Five Points reflects the neighborhood's continuing notoriety on the eve of the Civil War. But his decision to tour the House of Industry, rather than the dives and dance halls as Dickens had done two decades earlier, shows that Americans' perception of the district had begun to change. The innovative efforts of the House of Industry to improve the lives of Five Pointers had become, by the end of the 1850s, as well known as the neighborhood itself.

The story of Lincoln's visit to the Five Points House of Industry also speaks volumes about how the institution had achieved its fame. One of Lincoln's guides that morning was Rev. Samuel B. Halliday, who had worked with the poor in Five Points for more than two decades. By the late 1850s, Halliday headed the American Female Guardian Society and Home for the Friendless, an uptown charity that sought to prevent destitute girls and women from becoming prostitutes, but he also continued to work closely with the House of Industry. Before Lincoln left Five Points, Halliday presented him with a copy of his recently published book *The Lost and Found; or Life Among the Poor.* Many of the work's heartrending accounts of poverty in Five Points and the House of Industry's efforts to alleviate it had already appeared in the *Times* and other city newspapers, as well as in the charity's own magazine. In fact, reporters often turned to Halliday for guided tours of the famous slum. He was known far and wide as "a gentleman having a speciality for the exploration, night and day, of the purlieus of city life."[5]

Of all the moving stories Halliday had collected during these explorations, the one that most touched New Yorkers' hearts was that of nine-year-old Mary Mullen. After her parents died, Mary was taken in by a Five Points couple who operated a small saloon. Their circumstances were relatively comfortable, especially by Five Points standards, yet they did not allow Mary to attend school. Instead, they forced her to work as a street sweeper at the intersection of Park Row and Beekman Street, clearing the mud and puddles from the crosswalks in exchange for tips from pedestrians. The worse the weather, the more Mary's guardians insisted that she must sweep, because on days of driving rain or windblown snow, passersby would especially pity the inadequately clothed girl and more readily reward her with their pocket change. Alerted to Mary's pitiful plight, Halliday found her at her intersection, with her dress "fastened up about the waist, after the fashion of the 'Emerald Isle'; short petticoat; legs, feet, face, and arms spattered with mud." Though it was late in the afternoon, all she had eaten that day was "hard bread and buttermilk." Mary informed Halliday that she had already collected "six shillings" (seventy-five cents) in tips that day, and that her income could vary from two shillings to as much as two dollars daily depending on the weather and the pedestrian traffic.

When Halliday told Mary that he would take her off the streets and find her a new home, she resisted on the grounds that her guardians would beat her if she did not return with her earnings. Despite her protests, Halliday dragged her to City Hall, where the mayor gave him official custody of the young girl. Mary's guardians attempted to win her return, but

according to Halliday, the mayor "was inexorable." After Mary had stayed
at Halliday's uptown institution for a few months, the minister found her
a "country home" with a new set of adoptive parents. By the time of Lincoln's visit, charitable organizations such as the House of Industry wielded
virtually unchecked power over the fate of Five Points children.[6]

Halliday was a true innovator in his field. He made extensive use of the
relatively new medium of photography, recording the appearance of children he found begging on the street and then using these images to persuade judges that he should be awarded custody of the kids. Halliday also
gave copies of these photos to wealthy New Yorkers to inspire donations to
organizations such as the House of Industry. In fact, historians of photography cite Halliday's photos as the first known use of the medium for char-

Mary Mullen, the street sweeper, c. 1859. Thomas
Walther Collection, New York (original image rephotographed by D. James Dee).

Tattered Maggie, the orphan, c. 1859. Thomas Walther
Collection, New York (original image rephotographed by
D. James Dee).

itable fund-raising. Halliday reported in 1859 that as a result of such
efforts, his photograph of Mary Mullen was "becoming distributed somewhat extensively. Entering the parlor of a wealthy family a few days since,
in a conspicuous place among most elegant paintings and engravings was
the form in photograph of my little street-sweeper." Another of his most
heart-wrenching photos was that of a girl he called "Tattered Maggie." Halliday had found this six-year-old barefoot orphan wandering the streets
after her mother, an alcoholic, had died in jail following her arrest for
public drunkenness.[7]

Lincoln's Cooper Union speech helped his campaign enormously. He
did not initially make a good impression with his high-pitched voice and
ill-fitting suit, but he soon won over his audience with his careful argu-

ments, homespun humor, and elegant prose. At the conclusion of the address, he received a thunderous standing ovation. "Mr. Lincoln is one of Nature's orators," said the *Tribune* approvingly the next day. Reprinted in newspapers across the nation, the Cooper Union speech helped make Lincoln a legitimate presidential contender. At the Republican National Convention in Chicago three months later, Tom Hyer led the cheering in the gallery for Lincoln's principal rival, New York senator William H. Seward, but the Illinois rail-splitter prevailed, and was soon headed for the White House.[8]

After Lincoln's victory in the general election, Halliday sent the first family an album filled with "before" and "after" photographs of children aided by the House of Industry. The president's album contains the only extant set of these arresting images.

CHAPTER EIGHT

Religion and Reform

◇▥▥◇

BY 1850, the most common explanation for the widely perceived "moral corruption" in Five Points was the lack of religious influence in the neighborhood. "No church edifice lured the besotted denizens of the Points from their reeking, . . . filth-streaming rookeries," commented one journalist as he looked back at the antebellum years. A minister in 1853 labeled Five Points an "idolatrous, Church-forsaken district." The number of religious institutions that had abandoned Five Points in the years before 1853 was indeed shocking. As recently as 1846, the neighborhood had served as home to a Baptist church on lower Mulberry Street, an Episcopal house of worship on Mott Street, a Swedenborgian church on Pearl Street, as well as an African-American congregation on Orange Street and a Welsh Baptist chapel on upper Mott. By 1855, each had abandoned Five Points. Neighborhood inhabitants "have already, by their peculiar repulsiveness, driven several of our most respectable Christian churches out of their borders," commented one minister in explaining the exodus. They "have never read or heard the Bible read, and know as little of its teachings as the most degraded heathen."[9]

"NO MAN CAN BECOME A MEMBER HEREAFTER WHAT WAS A RUSSIAN SUBJECT"

Of course, "Church-forsaken" was in the eyes of the beholder. If the Protestant churches abandoned ship, at least for a while, their Jewish and Catholic counterparts jumped aboard. For a time in the pre–Civil War period, more Jewish congregations met in the vicinity of Five Points than in the entire remainder of the city. The second, third, fourth, and fifth synagogues established in New York operated in the Sixth Ward during the 1820s, '30s, and '40s. The early history of the fourth, Shaarey Zedek, sheds light both on the tensions within New York's early Jewish community and the difficult choices Eastern European Jews faced as they wavered between loyalty to their religious traditions and assimilation in a predominantly Christian nation.[10]

Shaarey Zedek was founded in 1839 by Polish Jews who felt uncomfortable in the city's other synagogues, which were dominated by Jews of Western European origin. The congregation initially held services in an apartment on the top floor of the tenement at 472 Pearl Street, but within a year moved to a more spacious room above the New York Dispensary, a free medical clinic at the corner of Centre and White Streets.[11]

Shaarey Zedek was at first more receptive to intermarriage than New York's other synagogues. When the city's second oldest congregation, Bnai Jeshurun, refused to convert one member's non-Jewish wife to Judaism, he tried to complete the process himself by sneaking her into its *mikvah*, a ritual bath for women. He was caught and expelled from the congregation. He joined Anshe Chesed, the city's third synagogue, but it also refused to recognize his wife as Jewish. The desperate man then became a founding member of Shaarey Zedek. Its leaders declared his wife (as well as the non-Jewish wives of other founding members) officially converted and full congregation members. Yet even Shaarey Zedek's relatively liberal congregation apparently felt pangs of guilt about its decision. Thereafter, the synagogue's board declared, Shaarey Zedek would only certify conversions approved by a rabbi.[12]

The congregation also struggled with the observance of the Sabbath. Many of its members operated their businesses on Saturdays, a prime shopping day for most New Yorkers. The temple's leaders tried to encourage members to keep the Sabbath holy, decreeing in 1841 that no member could become an officer of the congregation "if he keeps open his Shop on Sabbath." But the Five Pointers who dominated Shaarey Zedek apparently valued business over religious fidelity, as a few years later the rule was no longer enforced. In fact, Shaarey Zedek had trouble attracting men to services at all. Like other New York synagogues, it resorted to hiring "*minyan* men," Jews paid to attend synagogue to ensure that ten men—the minimum required under Orthodox law—appeared at each service. But not all men were welcome. In 1844, its board of trustees declared "that no man can become a member hereafter what was a Russian subject except which are members at present—they the Russians are allowed to be seatholders only."[13]

New York synagogues relied so heavily on *minyan* men in part because ethnic rivalries and liturgical controversies continually prompted secessions from the existing congregations. In 1843, a group left Shaarey Zedek to form Beth Israel. In 1845, those seeking to exclude all Sabbath breakers from their midst created Shaarey Tefilah at 67 Franklin Street. Another splinter group founded Beth Abraham in the tenement at 63 Mott Street in 1850, the same year that Shaarey Zedek moved across Chatham Square to 38 Henry Street. In 1852, a dozen Russian Jews formed their own Five Points congregation, Beth Hamidrash, in an apartment on the top floor of the tenement at 83 Bayard Street. A year later, as membership increased (including German and Polish Jews), the congregation moved to 514 Pearl Street, paying twenty-five dollars per month to lease the top floor of Monroe Hall, Matthew Brennan's saloon. Beth Abraham already occupied space in the same building. The last Five Points congregation created in the prewar years was founded in 1853, when Polish members of Beth Hamidrash seceded to form Beth Hamidrash Livne Yisrael Yelide Polin ("House of Study for the Children of Israel Born in Poland"), located by 1860 at 8 Baxter Street among the Jewish-run second-hand clothing shops. Though a number of congregations would remain in Five Points until the end of the nineteenth century, most Jews were beginning to settle east of the Bowery on the Lower East Side, and they brought their synagogues with them.[14]

"THIS IS EMPHATICALLY '*MISSION GROUND*'"

The rise of Judaism in Five Points did not herald a burst of reform, because these congregations were devoted to worship. "Reformers," in those days, were almost always Protestants, especially members of proselytizing denominations. Beginning in the 1830s, a variety of evangelical Christian groups attempted to win converts in Five Points. The New York City Tract

Society distributed its literature there, while members of the American Female Moral Reform Society handed out tracts, read Bible passages on the streets, and urged those entering brothels to repent.[15]

Almost from the start, a split between spiritual and worldly assistance rent the reformers. The American Female Moral Reform Society began giving out food and clothing in 1839, with their missionary, Samuel B. Halliday, sometimes seeking jobs for the unemployed and shelter for the homeless. But the Tract Society, in order to differentiate clearly between its religious and temporal work, in 1843 created a separate organization, the New York Association for Improving the Condition of the Poor (AICP), to distribute aid to the needy. The AICP quickly became the most important and influential organization of its kind in nineteenth-century New York. Its executive secretary, Robert H. Hartley, believed that "the chief cause of [pauperism's] increase among us is the *injudicious dispensation of relief.*" According to Hartley, "the most clamorous and worthless" beggars secured the lion's share of New Yorkers' charity, while "the most modest and deserving" received none. Consequently, he instituted an elaborate system for the equitable distribution of relief. Hartley divided the city into hundreds of relief districts, each with its own "visitor." Anyone seeking charity from his organization had to submit to an investigation by a visitor, who would inspect the applicant's home and query the neighbors about his or her employment history and drinking habits. Those passing muster would then be added to the association's register of "worthy" poor, who could receive food, clothing, or fuel from one of its distribution centers. Hartley asked that any New Yorker hoping to relieve poverty should not give one cent to beggars on the street, but instead donate to the association, which would distinguish the frauds from the truly needy. Hartley's methods were adopted by most charities in the Civil War era.[16]

Soon several charities emerged that focused their efforts solely on New York's most infamous slum. Like the Tract Society and the Female Reform Society, these groups believed that religious renewal was the key to any temporal improvement in Five Pointers' lives, and that any distribution of food or clothing should be rigorously rationed. The first was the Five Points Union Mission, so called because a coalition of Protestant denominations funded and operated it. Founded in the 1840s and located at 42 Orange Street, the Union Mission opened its doors for only a few hours each week.[17]

Recognizing that the Union Mission could not effect significant change in Five Points, the New-York Ladies' Home Missionary Society of the Methodist Episcopal Church established in 1848 a continuously operating mission with a resident staff to offer religious services and seek conversions. The married middle- and upper-class women who ran the society did not live in their missions—paid "missionaries" assumed that role. But the "ladies" did occupy all the positions on the institution's board of directors, serve as "managers" of their various missions, visit neighborhood residents in an effort to convert them to Methodism, and administer the various philanthropic programs eventually organized by the society.[18]

Although the society originally intended to locate its mission on Centre Street, it ultimately rented a former "gin shop" in the heart of Five Points at 1 Little Water Street, directly across from the Old Brewery and Paradise Park. "This is emphatically '*mission ground*,'" exclaimed the society optimistically when it announced its intention to create the Five Points Mission, which began operations in May 1850. During the mission's first weeks of operation, its organizers were shocked by the neighborhood's poverty, public drunkenness, and prostitution. One mission "lady" present at the group's first Sunday service said of the motley adults and unruly children in attendance that it was "a more vivid representation of hell than [I] had ever imagined." One year later it was proudly noted that the churchgoers could now be kept orderly "without the aid of the Police."[19]

Luckily for the mission, its organizers had selected as resident missionary Lewis M. Pease, an innovative and persevering minister who was willing to go to almost any lengths to improve life in Five Points. Thirty years old in 1850, when he arrived in New York with his wife, Ann, and two-year-old adopted daughter, Pease had previously served as minister of a Methodist church in Lenox, Massachusetts. A year after his arrival, when Pease and the Ladies' Home Missionary Society were feuding bitterly, its "presiding Elder" nonetheless conceded that "Mr. Pease is one of the most indefatigable and daring missionaries I have ever seen."[20]

The dispute between Pease and the Missionary Society arose from a disagreement over the mission's goals. The mission's organizers sought merely to convert sinners to Methodism and expected Pease to utilize, in his words, only "the instrumentalities . . . ordinarily used in the awakening and conversion of sinners." These included visiting potential converts, explaining to them the "errors" of Catholicism and the superiority of

Methodism with its emphasis on the biblical "Word of God," praying with them, cajoling them, even shaming them. Yet Pease found that these traditional methods of proselytism had little impact on Five Pointers. "When a Tract or a Bible was offered to these unfortunates, they would ask for bread," Pease recalled two years later, "and when warned of the consequences of their lives, and urged to return to the path of honesty, sobriety, and virtue, they would reply: 'We do not live this life because we love it, but because we cannot get out of it.'" Pease informed the society's board that he could not convert Five Pointers unless the mission found some way, in the words of Pease's subsequent benefactors, "to remove the compulsory alternative of vice or starvation, and make a virtuous life by honest labor possible." The mission board replied that if Pease wanted to offer Five Pointers non-spiritual aid, he would have to do so on his own time and at his own expense.[21]

The headstrong Pease was determined to try. Locating a clothing manufacturer willing to supply him with material if he would vouch for its safe return, Pease hired destitute Five Points women to sew shirts for him. According to the ministers who later financed Pease's efforts, the first thirty or so women appeared for work in the mission chapel "in all the filthiness and raggedness of their every-day condition, and what was worse, in the disorderly, drunken, profane and savage habits which none had ever taught them to lay aside." Pease consequently established strict ground rules for his employees. He required them to come to work sober, to pledge to abstain completely from the use of alcohol while employed by him, and to "attend regularly some place of worship on the Sabbath."[22]

Even with these restrictions, Pease later recalled, his workers' "first efforts at the use of the needle were truly discouraging. Many of the shirts were so poorly made that the slightest force would pull them to pieces; others had to be ripped and re-made." In order not to humiliate his workers, Pease paid for the ruined shirts himself. Meanwhile, the mission board became increasingly resentful of all the time and effort involved, complaining, as he later recalled, that "it illy comported with the dignity of a minister, to be found in his shirt-sleeves, superintending a workshop—giving to such characters shirts and buttons." But Pease pressed on, expanding his operation within just a few weeks to employ one hundred indigent women.[23]

Pease's employees found it hard to abide by his rules when they returned home each evening to their saloon-infested tenements, so Pease next decided that the only way to isolate his charges from these degrading influences was to rent an entire building in which to lodge his workers and to exclude from it the bordellos and grog shops that flourished elsewhere. Finding no large tenements available, Pease secured the assistance of the district attorney and two police court justices, who agreed to arrest and evict the brothel keepers in two houses on Little Water Street adjoining the mission. In late August 1850, Pease chose thirty of his female employees— "mostly women of bad repute"—to live in the two houses, charging them $1.25 per week for room and board. The mission board refused to finance any of it. In the winter and spring of 1851, Pease's personal financial burden increased still further when he rented additional houses (increasing his "family" of tenants to 120) rather than allow brothel keepers to occupy the three-story wooden tenements surrounding his own.[24]

He was a one-man employer and landlord—and school superintendent. Another dispute between the Missionary Society and Pease developed over the issue of a mission school. The mission operated a Sunday school, but Pease told the board in August 1850 that his efforts to uplift Five Pointers would fail unless the mission operated a non-denominational school on weekdays as well. Otherwise, argued the minister, destitute women with small children would not be able to work, while the older offspring of those who did work would succumb to the district's immoral influences when left unattended. The mission's board replied that it could not afford to operate a "day school," which, in any case, lay outside its purview of pro-moting religion. Pease then sought outside funding, returning to the board a month later to ask if the city's other denominations could have a voice in the operation of a mission day school if these outsiders financed it. Again, the board rejected his proposal, so the infuriated Pease started the school on his own. In late September, just as he was about to open a bare-bones classroom, Pease discovered an Episcopal woman who had raised $700 to start a school in Five Points but had never carried her plans to fruition. He used the money to buy slates, maps, a stove, furniture, and a much-needed new coat of paint. Sensing that Pease would succeed despite them, the Missionary Society members begrudgingly hired a "female assistant mis-sionary" to work within the school, though after six months Pease financed her salary as well. He could soon boast an attendance of one hun-dred students each day.[25]

By this point, Pease and the mission had manifestly different agendas. In March 1851, when asked at the Missionary Society's board meeting how many Five Pointers he had won over to Methodism, he could not cite a single conversion. But Pease did excitedly report that he planned to combine his various charitable projects into a single enterprise, to be called the "Industrial House for the Friendless, the Inebriate, and the Outcast." When the National Temperance Society agreed in mid-1851 to finance it, Pease resigned his mission post to devote himself to his humanitarian endeavors, which his new backers renamed the Five Points Temperance House. The mission could save souls; he would provide schools, shelter, and employment opportunities. Only ten months later, however, a philanthropic takeover threw his work into jeopardy. The New-York City Temperance Alliance assumed control of the National Temperance Society and immediately withdrew its financial support for his operations. By then, he was so well known within reform circles that supporters were ready to step forward; the Rev. Gregory T. Bedell of the Episcopal Church of the Ascension (which had been financing Pease's day school) mobilized New York's philanthropic community to save his fledgling organization. Bedell found businessmen and ministers willing to fund Pease's efforts and act as an informal board of trustees. In May 1852, they renamed his organization the Five Points House of Industry.[26]

Not wanting their former minister to upstage them, the mission's leaders in early 1852 announced to the press their own bold plan—to buy the infamous Old Brewery tenement and make it the society's headquarters. Sixteen thousand dollars seemed a small price to pay to eliminate from the neighborhood that "great landmark of vice and degradation, the haunt of crime and the home of misery." After taking possession, however, mission officials found that the building could not be renovated economically, and instead decided to demolish it. Criminals from all over the city supposedly visited the deserted structure in the weeks before the wreckers arrived, hoping to find bulging sacks of stolen booty hidden by neighborhood thieves in the floors and walls. Thousands of law-abiding New Yorkers came to see the Old Brewery as well before its destruction, lighting their way with candles and torches provided by the mission. "Though the inmates had departed," wrote one of the mission ladies, "the very 'stones in the wall seemed to cry out'" with the "echoes of wailings and wild revelry" that had once occurred there. A number of artists recorded the scene for posterity.[27]

Though few city residents lamented the Old Brewery's demise, controversy developed over the city's financing of the project. In October 1852, the board of aldermen voted 13 to 1 to provide $1,000 of the $36,000 the mission would eventually spend to purchase the property, raze the Old Brewery, and construct a new building. A leading Catholic newspaper, the *New York Freeman's Journal*, bitterly condemned the proposed expenditure, complaining that the need to improve living conditions in the neighborhood did not justify "establishing *Methodism* as the religion of the Five Points, at the public expense." The *Times* replied that Pease's work with the poor justified the municipal appropriation. "They have converted what has always been the very den of thieves and murderers and prostitutes,— the very fountain of every imaginable abomination and every form of vice and crime,—into a house of industry and order," noted the *Times*. ". . . Can a sincere and right-minded Catholic so grudge them the chance of making a possible convert to their faith, as to denounce and oppose the unquestioned good they have done?" *Journal* editor James A. McMaster retorted that Pease was no longer associated with the mission, leaving it with only a religious function. Calling the mission "a proselyting-trap," McMaster predicted that its operatives "will try to convert the degraded classes of the Points by the *animal excitements* of Methodism;—that is, by the preachings, prayings, roarings, rantings, cantings, groanings, yellings, and other yet more obscene fooleries and indecencies of this ignorant, degraded, irrational and unpatriotic sect." When the *Times* discovered that Pease had indeed severed all ties with the mission, it reluctantly admitted that a city contribution to the project would not be appropriate. City fathers agreed. By a vote of 9 to 8, the board of assistant aldermen tabled the motion to grant funds to the mission.[28]

On June 17, 1853, the Missionary Society celebrated with pomp and circumstance the opening of a grand new, privately funded Five Points Mission building. The four-story facility covered three large lots and included a chapel that could seat five hundred worshippers, a parsonage for the missionary and his family, two schoolrooms, and twenty three-room apartments. All this on the very spot, boasted the mission, where a year earlier hundreds of the most degraded denizens of Five Points had lived amid wretched squalor and sin. "What no legal enactment could accomplish—what no machinery of municipal government could effect," bragged the mission "ladies" in the book they published to commemorate the event, "Christian women have brought about, quietly but thoroughly and triumphantly." By the time the new mission headquarters opened, the House of Industry had secured control of all seven of the three-story buildings on Little Water Street facing Paradise Park. Several years later, it relocated to its own large new headquarters on Worth Street directly across the park from the mission. In just a few years, the mission and the House of Industry had become an imposing presence in Five Points.[29]

Wary Catholics such as McMaster might claim that "there is not . . . a copper's difference between the rivals at the Five Points," yet they embraced two very different approaches to charity. The Missionary Society's first annual report stated that until its workers could bring about "clear, undoubted conversions, we have no sure footing." Catholics from the neighborhood were told that the Bible was the "'one Mediator between God and man' . . . the only guide to eternal life." Typical of these proselytizers was a "Mrs. Cameron, a most indefatigable Bible Reader. She visits the people at their houses, makes herself their friend. She reads to them, talks with them, knows them by name. She exercises great watchfulness over them, questions them closely, and urges them with great success to persevere in the way of self-denial and industry."[30]

Pease's organization, by contrast, was much more radical. "Its object is the physical, social and moral reformation of its members, and likewise of the immediate community in which it is located," he explained in 1852. "It aims, too, at the suppression of houses of infamy, and of the open lewdness of action, even in the Five Points. . . . Its instrumentalities for securing these objects are a bath-tub, a wardrobe . . . , a workshop, morning and evening devotion, prayer meeting, singing-school, a Bible-class, a Sabbath-school, and a regular Sabbath preaching. Likewise a Temperance meeting on Friday evenings." The House of Industry clearly did teach that religion ought to play an important role in every American's life, and its residents too were required to attend religious services. But whereas mission boarders were required to attend mission services, Pease allowed his tenants to go to other churches (or, in theory, synagogues) if they preferred. The "inmates of this Institution," he pledged in 1853, "shall have the privilege of worshipping God according to the dictates of their own consciences, without being interfered with by any."[31]

It is difficult to appreciate how radical Pease's approach appeared to most antebellum Americans. Pease had not coined the phrase "House of

Industry" and he was not the first to open one. *New York Tribune* editor Horace Greeley had suggested in the early 1840s that the city start a "House of Industry" to teach job skills and thrift to the indigent. Like Pease, Greeley advocated protecting clients from their own intemperate tendencies by forcing them to reside within the institution. But nothing ever came of Greeley's proposal. By early 1848, Episcopal minister Stephen H. Tyng and public health pioneer John H. Griscom had opened their own "House of Industry and Home for the Friendless" a few miles north and east of Five Points, but in its early years it functioned primarily as a shelter for homeless girls. Pease's House of Industry was thus the first to implement Greeley's ideas on a large scale. Charles Loring Brace, who founded his Children's Aid Society a few years after the House of Industry was established, recalled that the change from a religious to a material emphasis in charity initially "met with great opposition. To give a poor man bread before a tract, to clean and feed street-children before you attempt to teach them religiously, to open work-shops where prayer-meetings used to be held . . . to talk of cleanliness as the first steps to godliness,—all this seemed then to have a 'humanitarian' tendency, and to belong to European 'socialism' and 'infidelity.'" These were in fact the terms resentful Methodists used in condemning Pease and his innovations, calling those who advocated his ideas "rationalists, Socialists, Fourierists, &c." Enmity between the two institutions would continue for many years.[32]

"The children open the door for us"

The House of Industry and the mission profoundly altered life in Five Points. In the realm of job training, Pease quickly expanded beyond the sewing work that had launched his enterprise. By early 1851, before his split with the mission, Pease had added baking, shoemaking, and corset making to the vocational instruction offered. Basket weaving and hatmaking eventually became part of the curriculum as well. More than five hundred people worked at these trades in the House of Industry in 1854. Pease paid his workers for the products they produced during their training. "Dextrous" sewers, for example, could earn $2 to $2.50 per week—not much, but more than many needlewomen earned, and at least the work was steady. In about 1870, the mission opened its own sewing school. By the end of the seventies, the mission also trained its inmates for domestic service. "Moving harmoniously to the accompaniment of the piano," noted the mission's annual report with pride, "they wash and scrub, wait at the door, set the table, wash dishes, make beds, and sweep the floors." The House of Industry's extensive vocational training operation helped many Five Pointers find good jobs. In the twelve months ending in March 1857, for example, the House of Industry placed six hundred thirty of its trainees in workshops, factories, and homes all across the city.[33]

The "day schools" operated by the two Five Points charitable institutions also changed the lives of countless neighborhood residents. At first, it took quite some time for the teachers and students at the House of Industry school to adjust to each other's needs. "The room so stank from their filth," recalled Pease's financial backers of those first students, "that bathing facilities for each sex had to be established." Many children were distracted from their studies by hunger, so Pease opened a "soup-room" where the "poorest of the children" could eat. He eventually provided a hot lunch for all the children in the expanded facility's dining hall. One might wonder why Five Points' predominantly Catholic and Jewish parents would send their children to Pease's school when public ones already operated there. Brace found that some children were "so ill-clothed and destitute that they are ashamed to attend" the public schools. Others may have chosen to send their children to a charitable day school because it provided its needy pupils with clothing and food. Still others may have selected Pease's academy because it kept children later each day, operated year round, and accepted small kids too young to attend the public schools.[34]

The House of Industry and mission attracted even more students to their Sunday schools than their weekday classes. "The school is very full," the mission board was told in 1856, so much so that "many sit on the desks." Yet because of their more overtly religious nature, the Sunday schools came under sharp attack by Five Points Catholic leaders. Soon Catholics started their own neighborhood Sunday school, but when this failed to stem the flow of children into the two Protestant institutions, Catholics (sometimes "several hundreds") began to congregate in front of the House of Industry on Sunday mornings in September 1853 to encourage Catholic children to attend Catholic religious schools instead. Protestant mobs soon began appearing to defend their institutions. Tensions mounted and tempers flared each Sunday until the *Times* feared that a "bloody riot" might ensue.[35]

The *Freeman's Journal* claimed that Protestants in Five Points prevented Catholic teachers "from gathering up the children of Catholics to take them, according to the wish of their parents, to Catholic Sunday Schools. This kind of interference has been going on for some time." Pease insisted that no children attended the House of Industry Sunday school "in opposition to the will of their parents." He pointed out that "Catholics as well as Protestants are permitted to teach and preach the great common principles of our common Christianity in this Institution, if they will abstain from their peculiar dogmas." Pease complained that Catholics had organized "to have our public services wantonly disturbed . . . our visitors stoned and beaten, and one of them . . . threatened with having his brains knocked out, and the *regular* children of our school driven from our door with horrid oaths and imprecations. If this be controversy then we have had it."[36]

Pease had hoped that publicity would help prevent additional confrontations, but the situation deteriorated even further the following Sunday, October 9. According to a House of Industry Sunday school worker named Stonelake, "a prominent Catholic" confronted a child about to enter the charity, took a newly bound Bible from the youngster's hands, tore out a page, ignited it, and lit both his cigar and the rest of Bible with it. He then gave the burning Bible to some boys, who threw it into the street and "commenced the work of kicking it about amidst curses, language the most blasphemous, obscene shouts of brutal laughter, and riotous conduct of the worst description." Stonelake rescued the Bible in the gutter in front of Donnelly's coal yard and brought it to Pease, "who still has it should anyone doubt the story." When later that same morning Bartholomew Smith of the St. Andrew's Roman Catholic Church Sunday school tried to stop a teacher from bringing a Catholic child who lived in the House of Industry into its Sunday school, he was arrested for assault. The *Journal* claimed that the child was being forced into the House of Industry against his will.[37]

Tempers calmed after the Bible burning. Even the *Times*, which generally supported Pease, called the behavior of both Five Points groups "disgusting" and "disgraceful." Sunday school attendance at both the House of Industry and the mission dipped for a while as Catholics organized and publicized alternatives. Yet charity continued to attract many Five Pointers to the Protestant institutions' schools despite the scolding of their priests. When a local priest asked an Italian bootblack to come to his Sunday school, the boy's response was: "Say, Boss, d'ye give clothes and shoes for goin' to Sunday School same as at Five Poin'?"[38]

Initially, only those who either lodged in the House of Industry and mission or attended their schools were eligible to receive food or clothing from them. But soon the charities began to distribute these items more widely. The severe recession in the winter of 1854–55 seems to have first prompted the change. Pease set up a soup kitchen to meet the urgent demand for sustenance in the neighborhood and in just four months served 39,267 meals. The mission did not distribute food in such quantities, but instead complemented Pease's efforts by collecting second-hand clothes for the poor. During a twelve-month period ending in early 1856, the mission gave away 17,569 pieces of clothing, 922 pairs of shoes, 355 quilts, 250 caps, and 150 bonnets, as well as 25 tons of coal.[39]

The mission characteristically scaled back its charity once hard times had receded, while the House of Industry continued to expand its operations. The *Times* reported in May 1866 that the House of Industry had served an astounding 422,461 meals during the previous twelve months, an average of 1,157 per day. Eventually, the mission's largesse matched that of its neighborhood rival, as its workers by 1882 gave away 517,834 "rations" of food and 11,806 pieces of clothing to a total of 5,146 persons.[40]

There were limits, however, to the charities' generosity. A destitute Jewish glazier asked a mission employee for "some clothes to make me look so as people will like me, and give me work." The employee would not consider the request until after "first interrogating him on whether he believed that Jesus was his savior." The employee did not record the man's answer, but he did give him the clothes.[41]

In a similar case, a seven-year-old girl came to the mission one day asking for a quilt. According to the mission newspaper, "she was thinly clothed, and was accustomed to suffer from cold and hunger. The following conversation took place: 'What is your name?' 'Mary.' 'Where does your mother live?' 'She is dead.' 'Where do you live?' 'With a woman.' 'What street and number?' 'I have forgot it.' 'What is your father's name?' 'John.' 'Where do you go to school?' 'Nowhere.' 'Do you know your letters?' 'No.' Of course we could not give her the quilt." The missionaries did not send Mary away completely empty-handed. They gave her "a 'boiling' of potatoes" and told her they could give her additional assistance if she would attend the mission school. Otherwise, they would do little more to help her.[42]

The two charities generally did not assist children who did not attend school, and gave no food or clothing to adults who did not pledge to give up liquor. Both institutions made temperance efforts a cornerstone of their work. They held outdoor meetings in Paradise Park to attract attention to their movement and visited Five Pointers in their homes to check on their progress. The House of Industry also operated an "Inebriate's Retreat" where alcoholics could seek shelter and assistance in "the cleansing and cooling process" that might lead to permanent sobriety.[43]

Most of the funds the Five Points charities used to finance their work came from private donations. Through press reports, their own monthly newsletters, and benefit concerts, the two groups raised the thousands of dollars necessary to support their myriad operations. Collectively, the publicity worked wonders. Although a resident of Ohio, the teenaged John D. Rockefeller nonetheless gave 12 cents from his $4 a week salary to the Five Points Mission. Children from all over the United States joined the mission's "shoe club," making small contributions earmarked for the purchase of footwear for Five Points youngsters.[44] The House of Industry, especially, was the darling of the New York press, particularly during Pease's tenure as its superintendent. "Mr. Pease is certainly in his way one of the 'remarkable men' of the City," maintained the *Times* at the end of 1852. "He has the rather uncommon union of business talent and reforming talent. . . . There is a certain heartiness and manliness in him also," which helped him win over "the class with whom he deals." The House of Industry, the editorial concluded, was "one of the most carefully sustained and benevolent enterprises our City has ever beheld." Photojournalist Jacob Riis proclaimed almost forty years later that the House of Industry nursery was "one of the most touching sights in the world." But Riis lauded the mission as well, calling the two institutions "pioneers in this work of moral and physical regeneration."[45]

Some New Yorkers were less pleased with the charities' work. "I hate these canting scoundrels of the 'Five Points Mission' as much as I do the Inquisition," wrote one correspondent to the *Irish-American* in 1854, "and I regard their 'reformation' of the most abandoned as even worse than the destruction from which they affect to save them." The paper's editors agreed, condemning the "bigotry and attacks on the religion of the Roman

Catholic" found in the mission's publications: "We cry shame upon the ladies of the 'Five Points Mission' who are not satisfied with the charities of the heart, but must cram down the throats of the relieved religious opinions to which they are averse!"[46]

Catholics criticized the Five Points charities, and the mission in particular, because their prejudice toward Catholicism was so palpable. Of a drunkard asking for assistance, a mission worker wrote that "he is a Catholic of course; But 'doesn't know the way to the priest's house now'?" In contrast, when a Protestant mother of three whose husband was usually too drunk to work asked the mission for assistance, the secretary took pity on the "poor woman! She is 'no five-pointer,' but seems to have some intelligence." The mission records constantly boast of the assistance offered to "Protestants and Americans," as if Catholics, Jews, and immigrants were less deserving.[47]

"WE WOULD LIKE A LITTLE GIRL FROM THREE TO FIVE YEARS OLD"

Catholic leaders became even more hostile toward the Five Points Mission and the House of Industry when the two charities went into the adoption business. Hoping at first merely to expose Five Points children to life in the country, Pease in 1853 had the House of Industry purchase a sixty-four-acre farm sixteen miles north of Manhattan near the Westchester County village of Eastchester. He believed that the "quiet and beautiful country, with its pure air, wholesome food, and invigorating work, would do more toward reforming the vicious . . . than almost anything else." The farm could accommodate only a few dozen youngsters and adults at a time, yet there were hundreds, even thousands, of Five Pointers who in Pease's view would have benefited from temporary or permanent residence in the countryside.[48]

The charities began to consider adoption for Five Points' children in part because they were giving up on their parents. "Living in filth, and the extreme of poverty, addicted to drunkenness and its kindred vices, sunk in ignorance and superstition, they seem inaccessible to any good influence," lamented the House of Industry journal. "A large majority of these are Catholics, ignorant of the truth as it is in Jesus, and unwilling to listen to the teachings of any ministers but those of their own faith." Whereas adults had comprised two-thirds of the institution's "inmates" in 1854–55, by 1864 four-fifths were children.[49]

Why the mission and House of Industry began to put so many of these children up for adoption is not clear. We know that as word of the institutions' work began to spread, Five Pointers and others began to bring abandoned and orphaned children to them. Believing that such children would be better off with a family rather than in an institution, the organizations started to seek adoptive parents for them on an ad hoc basis. Soon after its founding in 1853, the Children's Aid Society had begun sending the dozens of children left in its charge to homes in the rural West, and this work may have inspired the two Five Points charities. Even without that precedent, most Americans in the antebellum period—even city dwellers—conceived of rural living as spiritually and physically superior to life in a congested urban center. After years of frustration, the charities' workers became convinced that growing up amidst crime, alcoholism, and prostitution doomed the neighborhood's children to fall prey to these vices as well. By the eve of the Civil War, finding adoptive homes in the countryside for Five Points children had become the two institutions' top priority.[50]

Initially, prospective parents came forward voluntarily. Some were New Yorkers who could not bear children of their own. Others had lost a child to illness. Soon, out-of-towners began to look to the New York philanthropies as a source of adoptive children as well, both for family and charitable reasons. The House of Industry newsletter noted in 1857 that an Indiana merchant planning a business trip to New York "looks round among his customers to see who 'wants' to do good by taking a homeless boy or girl." Some were grateful for any new addition to their family. A man in Wisconsin, in contrast, wrote to Halliday that "we would like a little girl from three to five years old, good-looking, light complexion, no freckles, darkish red or brown hair, with dark blue eyes or black, high forehead, pleasant disposition, smart and active, and an American child." Halliday, who at that point in the late 1850s ran his own orphanage uptown, did not have a match, but found one for his picky correspondent at the House of Industry.[51]

Hoping to place more of their children in the West, the charities eventually transported children at their own expense. In November 1856, the House of Industry and the Children's Aid Society sent an Iowa minister westward with thirty children in search of homes.[52] The mission also organized its own western journeys for children needing adoption, placing Rev. W. C. Van Meter in charge. On days when Van Meter headed west, large crowds gathered outside the mission to see the children off. A former newsboy who accompanied Van Meter to Iowa on one of these journeys wrote that at each railroad station, the children would sing a song for those gathered to meet the train. At each stop, one or two of the children would be adopted, and Van Meter would continue westward until all his wards had been taken. The sense of rejection felt by the last children to remain in each of Van Meter's groups must have been excruciating. Hundreds of neighborhood youngsters were transported to new homes outside New York as a result of the charities' adoption efforts.[53]

Some of the orphans were brought to the charities by neighbors. Just after the Civil War, neighbors alerted mission workers to the case of three little girls, none older than ten, found in their "deep cellar on Baxter Street. The mother lay dead on the floor." The woman had remained there since her death a day earlier because her children had not known what to do. Their father had passed away a few years earlier. The mission paid for the mother's burial and found the children adoptive homes. Others asked to be adopted. An older sister brought nine-year-old Elizabeth Cline to the mission for adoption in November 1856. Their mother had died in 1849 and their father in 1853. Around the same time, Mary Ann Barr rang the mission's doorbell. The Cow Bay resident, about twelve years old, had never known her mother and had not seen her father in two years. The mission sent her to a family in Burlington County, New Jersey.[54]

Yet the majority of children put up for adoption by the Five Points charities were not actual orphans; at least 60 percent put up by the mission had living parents. Anecdotal evidence from the *Monthly Record of the Five Points House of Industry* suggests that most of the children it sent to adoptive homes also had at least one living parent.[55] A variety of circumstances prompted parents to give their children up for adoption. Alcohol abuse frequently played a role. One mother reeking of liquor brought her four-year-old daughter Mary Anne to the House of Industry, telling the workers there that she could barely support herself, much less a child. The mission in 1856 recorded the case of "Mary Hare—aged 9 years . . . brought to us by a drunken mother, and given up to the mission." They had apparently been living in a brothel (the mission's secretary called it "a bad-house") for more than a year. The mother claimed, however, that she went out begging rather than prostitute herself. "She declares she is undefiled, though she has passed through the *mire.*" The mission sent Mary to live with a newspaper editor in upstate New York.[56]

The most famous adoption case from the two Five Points institutions also involved alcoholic parents. In 1853, the *Tribune* published a story by Solon Robinson entitled "'Wild Maggie,' of the Five Points." Pease had apparently bestowed this nickname on a disheveled little girl named Margaret Reagan who lived in a basement on Centre Street near Anthony. Maggie came to Pease's attention because of the way she relentlessly taunted and berated him. In a typical tirade, Maggie called Pease an "old Protestant thief. . . . I heard Father Phelan tell what you want to do with the poor folks at the Points; you want to turn them out of house and home, . . . and make them all go to hear you preach your lies." After many attempts to lure Maggie into the House of Industry, Pease finally succeeded by offering to let her lay out the sewing work for the women he trained, a task she agreed to undertake only if he left the door open so he could not steal her and send her to "the Island." She asked for more tasks of this sort and the apparently neglected girl soon began living at the House of Industry. At Pease's urging, she convinced her parents to attend the organization's temperance meetings. Despite their promise to reform, Pease convinced Maggie's parents to allow her to remain at the House of Industry. They eventually consented to her adoption by a farming family living near Katonah in Westchester County. Her story touched New Yorkers deeply.[57]

The vast majority of non-orphans given up for adoption had lived not with alcoholics but with widowed mothers who simply could not earn enough to support their children. Elizabeth Welland, for example, had managed to sustain herself and her son Henry through needlework for four years after her husband, a painter, died of "painter's colic." But after a six-week hospital stay prevented her from working, she became destitute and gave Henry to the mission. Twenty-three-year-old Irish immigrant Mary Harrison became a widow just a month after the birth of her first child. Quickly "finding all means of support exhausted," she asked the mission to locate an adoptive family for her infant.[58]

Some gave their children up to the mission soon after settling in New York because they found that earning a living there was much more difficult than they had expected. The widowed mother of twelve-year-old

Hugh Reilly turned her son over to the mission just eight weeks after they arrived in America because she found that she could not support them both. A woman from Albany likewise moved to New York after both her husband and brother died because she thought she could earn more money downstate. Finding that seamstresses earned less than she had imagined, she brought her son James to the mission.[59]

Catharine Donahue managed to find a new spouse after her first husband died, but he "treated her so ill that she was obliged to leave him." With no means available to support herself, she gave her eight- and five-year-old daughters to the mission for adoption. These women did not part with their children until absolutely forced to do so. The House of Industry newspaper described the case of one woman who, made a virtual widow by her husband's ten-year sentence to the penitentiary at Sing Sing, surrendered her baby for adoption rather than "see it starve to death before my face." When the widowed mother of ten-year-old George Leon left her son at the mission for adoption, "he did not wish to stay and his mother had to slip away slyly from him; he cried for an hour afterwards and had to be held and compelled to stay until his fretting was over."[60]

Most adoptees were given up voluntarily by desperate parents. But when charity workers found children's treatment or living conditions abhorrent, they sometimes took the youngsters forcibly. Pease usually tried to cajole these parents into parting with their offspring by describing the fresh air and material comforts their children would have in new homes. In one such case, Pease went to a tenement to determine why three sisters had stopped attending his day school. He discovered that their widowed mother had sent them out begging. The minister convinced the mother to let her two eldest daughters, Eliza and Maggie, live at the House of Industry, but she would not part with little Jane. "We felt that we could not give her up to a life of beggary and shame," reported a House of Industry publication; so when a man came to the House of Industry a few weeks later looking to adopt a girl Jane's age, Pease returned to see her. He found Jane eager to go, and because her mother that day was in the "state of inebriation characterized by good nature," she granted her permission, swayed in part because the adopting father gave her "a bonus" which "kept her in good humor." Pease saw no harm in brokering such deals if they removed youngsters from such miserable circumstances.[61]

On other occasions, Pease withheld assistance from desperate women and their children to force reluctant mothers to part with their offspring. His newsletter described one such mother whose husband had abandoned her "for the companions of the grog-shop." After selling all her possessions to sustain herself and three children, she was evicted from her apartment, at which point she appeared at the House of Industry seeking shelter. She was told she could stay only if she would allow Pease to put her children up for adoption. At first she agreed, but as the day of their departure approached she changed her mind and took them away, insisting "she would sooner beg, or even starve with them, than be parted from her innocent babes." Pease had once taken in and trained such women. By 1857, however, he had apparently concluded that the prospects for unmarried women with young children were so dismal that adoption was the best solution for both generations.[62]

In at least some instances, children initiated their own adoptions without the consent of their parents. The teenaged street peddler John Morrow took his repeatedly beaten half sister from his alcoholic stepmother and brought her to the mission for adoption. The woman went to court to try to have her daughter returned, but the justice ruled that her abuse of the child invalidated her claims. Van Meter sent her to adoptive parents in Illinois. Morrow's full sister, tired of supporting her stepmother's drinking habit, also put herself up for adoption at the mission.[63]

Another case in which a child chose to leave living parents involved seven-year-old Elizabeth Laughlin. Elizabeth was the little girl who ran away to Pease because she feared her stepfather would beat her after she fell asleep and failed to collect money from the prostitutes who used the rooms above his saloon. When Elizabeth's father came for her the next day, Pease refused to release her. Laughlin returned with a note from the district's police justice demanding that Pease hand her over, but he again demurred. The judge then summoned Pease to his courtroom, where the pastor once more insisted that he would not return Elizabeth to such a father. The infuriated police justice (possibly Matthew Brennan) called Pease's conduct "one of the most high-handed, barefaced outrages I ever met with! I command you to deliver up the body of that child to her friends." Pease asserted that only a higher court and a writ of habeas corpus could compel him to do so. The irate judge ordered his clerk to detain Pease and take a complaint against him from Laughlin, but the clerk said he had no right to do so, and Pease left.

The minister then consulted with District Attorney A. Oakey Hall, who advised Pease to take Elizabeth out of the city in case Laughlin bribed a judge to issue a summary ruling. The next day, a court officer served Pease with a writ of habeas corpus, claiming that he had seized Elizabeth from the street "for the purpose of *proselytism*, she being a Catholic." In response, Pease provided evidence indicating that Laughlin had previously struck Elizabeth in the head with a bottle and that he regularly forced her to stay awake far into the night collecting fees from prostitutes. When the judge asked Elizabeth whether she would rather live with Pease or return to Laughlin, she chose Pease, and the judge consented. Pease eventually found her a permanent home in upstate New York.[64]

The handful of other cases in which Pease refused to return children to living parents who opposed their being adopted are more difficult to justify by modern standards. In one, he temporarily sheltered a twelve-year-old girl named Katy while her mother spent a night in jail for throwing bricks through the windows of the house inhabited by Katy's father, who had abandoned Katy, her sister, and her mother, and moved in with another woman. When the father and his mistress left for California, Katy's mother had trouble feeding her children and from time to time boarded Katy and her sister at the House of Industry. When Katy's father returned from the West and reconciled with his wife, he demanded her back, but Katy (according to Pease) refused to go. Although the family hired a lawyer and sued for Katy's return, Pease cited the husband's behavior as evidence of the parents' lack of morals. The judge ruled in Pease's favor, and the minister eventually sent Katy to live with adoptive parents.[65]

An even more shocking case was that of "Lizzie D." In 1854, Pease had found Lizzie's widowed mother one of the most-coveted live-in domestic service positions—one in which the employer allowed the servant to keep her children with her. Despite her apparent good fortune, Lizzie's mother appeared on Pease's doorstep three years later, clearly having been unemployed for some time. She asked Pease to let Lizzie stay at the House of Industry and promised to return for her and pay her board once she found new employment. "The dirty and degraded appearance of the woman," wrote Pease, "made me mentally resolve that she should never again have possession of the child, to which, as I suspected, and afterwards learned, she had forfeited all moral right." Saying she had found a job, Lizzie's mother came back for her a few days later, but Pease said he would not give

Lizzie to her until she had been employed steadily for a month. Pease then sent an investigator to the mother's Cow Bay home. He found that the apartment "had but two occupants, a [male] negro and Mrs. D." This was all the proof Pease needed of her lack of fitness as a mother, and he immediately put Lizzie up for adoption. On the day set for her departure to Illinois, Lizzie cried that she did not want to go, but Pease sent her to the West anyway. The minister reported that "Mrs. D. made a great show of sorrow for the loss of her child, and sent a lawyer to threaten legal measures if she was not restored. We told him of the scene in Cow Bay, and he quietly took his departure." Although interracial liaisons—especially between Irish-American women and African-American men—were not unusual in Five Points, most whites considered them so repugnant that even Mrs. D.'s own attorney concluded that such a relationship would make it impossible for Mrs. D. to win the return of her daughter.[66]

Not surprisingly, New York's Irish Catholic community condemned the entire adoption system. The *Irish-American* insisted in 1859 that these "nominally religious and charitable" organizations were "really proselytising 'societies' . . . sinks of infamy, filth and corruption." Noting that their adoption activities had become "more extended, more energetic and more successful," the paper estimated that "at least five hundred children, the offspring of Irish Catholic parents, are proselytised, corrupted, and morally speaking, debauched, yearly, in New York, through their instrumentality." The editors denounced all the Protestant agencies that engaged in adoptions for the purpose of proselytizing, but complained especially about "a fellow named Halliday at the head of the gang." Considering himself a "special patrolman," Halliday "prowled, like a reformation fox to kidnap children." To prove its charges, the *Irish-American* described the case of a Fourth Ward woman named McInerny who was "not very careful or particular." Halliday, "hearing that she was in the Tombs, strayed down to Cherry street . . . where he found one of [her] children on the stoop and gave him a penny, whereupon, having thus acquired a property in him, he took him all the way up to Judge Kelly, and there satisfied the judge by competent testimony, that the child 'begged,' whereupon Kelly . . . consigns the child to the affectionate care of 'Patrolman' Halliday." The *Irish-American* claimed that the judge granted custody of the child to Halliday without the legally required advance notice, and that when the father attempted to win the child's return, various magistrates used flimsy excuses to uphold the illegal proceedings. At each of these hearings, the newspaper noted ruefully, the "smirking" Halliday "appeared with two [photographic] portraits of the boy, one taken when in rags, and the other when clothed by the hand of charity," which helped sway the judge to grant him custody. Most Catholic Five Pointers viewed the adoption programs with similar contempt.[67]

By the mid-1860s, Irish Catholics came to believe that the Five Points Mission and House of Industry sold orphaned children into virtual slavery. In November 1863, the *Irish-American* reported that Father Edward O'Flaherty, while visiting the Indiana State Fair several years earlier,

> was horrified by the spectacle of thirty or forty children, boys and girls, all evidently of Celtic origin, penned up like so many cattle, *for sale.* Yes, the term is only too weak to express the reality of this outrage on humanity. . . . They were "children of the poor," picked up in the lanes and streets of New York, congregated in a "Mission," petted and supported by the canting admirers of African ebony, and finally, with altered names, and every clue by which their identity might be traced carefully destroyed, deported to the West, and, for sums varying from ten dollars to thirty-five, disposed of to non-Catholic buyers until . . . by reaching their maturity, they should become free from the bondage into which they had been sold. The same system is still at work.

Six months before the *Irish-American* leveled its charges, the *Freeman's Journal* had announced that Catholics had retained attorney James M. Sheehan "to abolish the kidnapping and enslaving" of Irish children. Van Meter "has been bound over to answer, and is sure to be indicted, on the charge of kidnapping children for the purpose of reducing them to slavery. Mr. Sheehan is also putting a Mr. Barlow, of the Five Points House of Industry, into water of a most uncomfortably high degree of temperature" (Benjamin R. Barlow served as superintendent of the House of Industry from 1857 to 1864). Sheehan's advocacy of Catholic children's rights, the *Freeman's Journal* bragged, would force such ministers to limit their mischief to "setting the negroes loose to become vagabonds." The remarks in both journals tying the supposed enslavement of Irish Catholic orphans to the wartime emancipation of southern bondsmen suggest that rumors of children's enslavement sprang largely from Irish Americans' resentment of Republican efforts on behalf of African Americans. Yet stories of Irish slavery in rural America persisted into the 1870s.[68]

Others objected to the charities' adoption programs for different reasons. In the post–Civil War decades, westerners came to believe that their reform schools and jails overflowed with juvenile delinquents from New York. By the 1890s, many western states had responded by enacting laws limiting, restricting, or regulating the importation of orphans.[69]

In New York, meanwhile, the threat posed by the Protestant charities had forced previously apathetic Catholic leaders to devote significantly more energy and attention to Five Points. Archbishop John Hughes's decision to establish a parish there in 1853, even though two Catholic churches outside the neighborhood were not very far away, must have been intended at least in part as a defense against the proselytizing activities of the mission and House of Industry. Rather than undertake the time-consuming task of building a new church, Hughes purchased the recently vacated Zion Protestant Episcopal Church at the corner of Mott and Cross Streets. On May 14, he officially rechristened it the Church of the Transfiguration. The new parish quickly became one of the busiest in the city. By 1865, only six of the city's thirty-two Catholic churches conducted more marriages and baptisms than Transfiguration. According to a leading historian of American Catholicism, it was "the most flourishing Irish parish on the American continent."[70]

The New York Catholics also eventually began their own adoption service. It was launched in 1863—when mounting Civil War casualties began leaving hundreds of New York Catholic children without fathers to support them. In May of that year, Levi Silliman Ives established the Catholic Protectory, which sought to avoid sending children west by finding them adoptive Catholic parents within the city. But the number of children needing homes far exceeded the number of Catholic foster parents who stepped forward to claim them, so after Ives's death, the Protectory began sending its charges to Catholic homes in the Midwest. Another organization, the New York Foundling Hospital, became an even more important force in the Catholic community. Founded in 1869, it transferred children who could not be placed in New York homes to predominantly Catholic communities in the Midwest.[71]

"THE TRANSFORMATION THAT HAS OVERTAKEN THE 'FIVE POINTS' [IS] REMARKABLE"

Religious, humanitarian, and competitive forces all combined in the upsurge of Five Points charity work. The impact on the neighborhood was unmistakable, and nearly every commentator attributed the positive changes to the work of the Five Points Mission and the House of Industry. The demolition of the Old Brewery in 1852, most agreed, had marked the start of this transformation. "Perhaps in the entire annals of organized philanthropy," maintained the *Evening Post* concerning the Ladies' Missionary Society, "no more interesting incident can be found than the change by which the Old Brewery and its abominations yielded to the beneficent influences which these ladies have brought to bear." "The day of its demolition deserves to be distinguished as a red letter day in the annals of our city's history," concurred a mission publication.[72]

By the end of the decade, the changes to the neighborhood seemed even more remarkable. The New York Association for Improving the Condition of the Poor asserted that the district had undergone a "social and moral renovation." "The Five Points is not what it used to be," agreed *Harper's Weekly* in 1857, noting that "with its vice its romance has vanished. It has become Peasey and prosaic, and the old leaven of iniquity has nearly died out. . . . One has now to search for the bad places, whereas formerly the Five Points was one universal sore." The *Times* also agreed. "Who shall persuade us hereafter that any condition of humanity is desperate beyond redemption," it asked in reference to the House of Industry's accomplishments as the charity prepared to dedicate the new wing of its headquarters. "The transformation that has overtaken the 'Five Points,'" wrote the influential newspaper, was absolutely "remarkable."[73]

How were the charities able to effect such apparently far-reaching changes in the notorious neighborhood? The imposing presence of their large brick buildings at the Five Points intersection scared away many of the thieves, prostitutes, and drunks who had previously concentrated there. Others found inspiration in the organizations' home visits, temperance drives, and religious revivals, deriving the motivation they needed to stay sober, find work, or take better care of their families. Most of the tangible improvements, however, probably resulted from the unprecedented amounts of material assistance these charities distributed to neighborhood residents. For the first time, significant numbers of hungry, cold, and homeless Five Pointers could find food, clothing, fuel, and shelter. Some unskilled workers could even learn trades.

The *Times* noted in 1870 that Pease, by offering such services in his House of Industry, had adopted a "new principle" for helping the poor—one that emphasized "residence, sympathy and cooperation with 'the miserables.'" In this sense, the House of Industry was the nation's first "settlement house." Chicago's Jane Addams made settlements famous by establishing Hull House in the 1890s. Yet Pease's House of Industry pioneered most of her standard operating procedures—including job training, distribution of food and clothing, and instruction in health and hygiene—decades earlier. There were differences between the two, of course; women with college degrees in nursing and social work did not staff the antebellum House of Industry. And though the mission was a female-run institution, its "ladies" did not live in the slums with their clients as typical settlement house workers eventually would. Still, the House of Industry was progressive before the word came to stand for an era.[74]

The Five Points Protestant charities, and especially the House of Industry, can also be credited with having organized the city's (and perhaps the nation's) first modern welfare program. Unlike New Deal– and Great Society–era government assistance programs, Five Points charities did not entrust their clients with direct cash payments. The institutions also required religious devotion as a condition for most forms of aid. Yet virtually all the hallmarks of the modern welfare system—food, shelter, job training and placement, substance abuse counseling, and foster care—were offered by the Five Points charities.

Historians commonly cite the private welfare system established by "Boss" William M. Tweed and Tammany Hall in the late 1860s as the earliest precursor of the modern welfare state; but House of Industry efforts (eventually subsidized by the state government) predate Tweed's work by fifteen years. In fact, Tammany probably created its system in response to programs such as Pease's. Throughout the 1860s, Catholics complained bitterly that the state subsidized the House of Industry while denying aid to their own charitable efforts (legislators justified this on the grounds that the House of Industry was non-sectarian whereas Catholics preached a specific variety of Christianity). When Tweed extended his power to the state level, he reversed this policy officially in some areas, such as education, delivering state funds to parochial schools such as the one at Five Points' Church of the Transfiguration. In other realms, such as the distribution of coal and food, he instead used Tammany Hall as the conduit, in part to ensure that grateful voters thanked him and his organization on election day. While Tweed undoubtedly saw Tammany's private welfare system as a means to attract voters, he must also have been motivated by the desire to placate New York Catholics who wanted alternatives to Protestant aid programs such as those offered in Five Points.[75]

Harper's Weekly proved to be wrong in its nostalgic complaint that Five Points' charities had brought a permanent end to its mystique. The "romance" of its dark-alleyed crime and misery would return with the next wave of immigrants. Meanwhile, the drama of Five Points politics became the talk of the town, first because its Irish-American citizens took the lead in fighting Republican and Know Nothing efforts to usurp important parts of the city government, and later because the neighborhood played a pivotal role in the electoral frauds that made the Tweed Ring possible.

9

PROLOGUE

"He Never Knew When He Was Beaten"

"Fatty" Walsh was livid. Republicans had escalated the New York spoils war to a new level, disbanding the city's Democrat-dominated police department in July 1857 and replacing it with a Republican-controlled, state-run squad. Irish immigrants like Walsh often used positions in the police department as stepping-stones to political advancement. The New York Democratic party also relied on the money policeman kicked back to the party from their salaries to finance political campaigns. The Republicans' maneuver would seriously hamper the careers of aspiring spoilsmen such as Walsh.

But what particularly incensed Walsh was that when he and his Democratic Five Points friends went to the Bowery to harass and assault the new policemen just after midnight on the Fourth of July, a gang known as the Bowery Boys—led by Irish-American Democrats from the northeast corner of Five Points—had the audacity to defend the *Republican* police! The Bowery Boys and Walsh's "Mulberry Boys" had been engaged in an intra-Democratic feud for some time, but that did not justify aiding and abetting their Republican enemies. Adding injury to insult, the Bowery Boys later that day ventured well off their Bowery turf and onto Walsh's to protect the police from further attacks. When Walsh's gang fought to defend the Mulberry Street area against this incursion, the outnumbered Bowery Boys resorted to pistols and rifles. In the ensuing gun battle, they picked off Mulberry Boys with frightening ease despite the huge barricades of overturned carts and old furniture that both sides had erected on Bayard Street for protection.

Walsh was not about to let a bunch of Bowery toughs humiliate him and his gang without a fight. He knew Five Pointers looked to him as a leader. A few months earlier, they had made the twenty-two-year-old the assistant foreman of Engine Company No. 21, the very same politically prominent unit that had launched the political career of Walsh's idol, Matthew T. Brennan. Brennan had never backed down from a fight, no matter how tough the opponent, and neither would Tom Walsh.

So Walsh found a musket and boldly jumped in front of the Mulberry Boys' barricade. He may have been the "great strapping Irishman in a red shirt" described by one riot witness. But when Walsh squeezed the trigger, nothing happened. He tried again, but still the weapon would not fire. While he examined the gun in an attempt to diagnose the problem, a shot rang out from the Bowery Boys' side. The lead slug tore into Walsh's leg, shattering a bone near the knee. "The injury was very severe," reported the *New York Tribune* the next day. ". . . There is a chance that he will be maimed for life by the amputation of his leg." Walsh's fruitless bravery inspired many of his friends. By the end of the day, a dozen New Yorkers—mostly Mulberry Boys like Walsh—lay dead.[1]

Inciting one of the deadliest riots in New York history would doom the political careers of most men, but Five Pointers did not judge their leaders by the same standards as other New Yorkers did. In fact, the illiterate Walsh went on to become perhaps the most beloved politician in nineteenth-century Five Points. His career epitomized a momentous transformation in New York City that began with Five Points in the mid-1850s: the Irish took control of city politics.

Thomas Power Walsh was born in County Limerick, Ireland, in 1834. When he was three, his parents immigrated to New York with Tom and his one-year-old brother William. They settled on the West Side between Canal and Houston Streets, a district with relatively few immigrants. In their teens, Tom was apprenticed to a goldbeater, while William began learning the bookbinder's craft. Little else is known about their youth, though according to a later biographical sketch, it was in these years that Tom "developed the fighting tendencies which later made him somewhat famous."[2]

Tom continued to live on the West Side on Greenwich Street into his early twenties. But his social circle increasingly revolved around Five Points. He must have been well known in the Sixth Ward, especially in its political ranks, in order to have been elected assistant foreman of a fire company there. Walsh would have previously demonstrated his loyalty to the Democratic party and won the trust of Brennan or one of his key lieutenants. As assistant foreman, Walsh became intimately familiar with and personally involved in Five Points political disputes. This explains why Walsh, an Eighth Warder, leaped in front of the barricade and took a bullet in the leg for his Five Points friends.[3]

Despite the initially gloomy reports, Walsh did not lose his leg. The *Tribune's* announcement that his brother William was killed by a shot to the head also proved untrue. Perhaps the praise the brothers received for defending Mulberry Street from the Bowery interlopers finally convinced them to become Five Pointers themselves. In early 1859, they quit gold-beating and bookbinding and opened a saloon in the heart of Mulberry Boy territory at 7 Mulberry Street. The three connected buildings at 5 and 7 Mulberry were among the most crowded in Five Points. The rear tenement, a converted Baptist church, was fast becoming one of the most squalid in the city. But the Walsh brothers chose the location primarily out of political rather than business considerations. This was the block where most of the Mulberry Boys lived, and the Walshes were determined to become their standard-bearers.[4]

The move paid immediate dividends. In November 1859, twenty-two-year-old William was elected to the state assembly. Two years later, Sixth Warders made him their alderman. Tom, meanwhile, stayed out of the limelight. He did wield influence behind the scenes, however, first in Con Donoho's old (and very powerful) post as Sixth Ward street inspector and in 1864 as the city's superintendent of markets. Tom also took full control of the Mulberry Street saloon, while William opened his own on Centre Street. By the Civil War years, Tom's watering hole was a neighborhood institution, characterized by one critic as "a great resort for low politicians, prize-fighters, bounty-jumpers and tough men." William's political career continued to soar during the war. In 1863, he became president of the board of aldermen and a member of the influential Tammany Society general committee as well.[5]

But soon all that changed. One man, "Boss" William M. Tweed, increasingly controlled affairs in Tammany, the city's dominant Democratic organization. The Walshes refused to cooperate with Tweed and found themselves political pariahs as a result. William became a leader of the anti-Tammany movement in the Democratic party, running unsuccessfully for county clerk in 1867 and the state assembly in 1870. The Walshes' careers seemed doomed.[6]

Yet when Tweed was arrested in late 1871 and his Ring collapsed soon thereafter, well-known enemies of the Boss such as the Walshes were perfectly positioned to fill the resulting power vacuum. William was elected county clerk in 1873 and became one of the two or three most powerful Democrats in New York. Tom continued to work behind the scenes. He ran his saloon and secured a patronage post at the Tombs prison on nearby Centre Street. By this point, Tom had moved to a house at 36 Mott Street, on a block where many of the most affluent Five Pointers lived. It was there, in 1873, that Walsh's wife Armenia gave birth to their only child, Blanche.[7]

After William died in 1878, Tom began to seek elective office himself. Voters sent him to the state assembly in 1881, but he broke with Tammany again in 1882 and was not renominated. Running for alderman a year later on an insurgent Democratic ticket, the popular Walsh lost to the Tammany nominee by just 16 votes. Though he blamed his defeat on electoral fraud, in the end he was glad that he lost because many of the aldermen elected that year were indicted in a bribery scandal. "God is good to the Irish," he said afterward. "If I had been in the Board, where would I be now?" The following November, he won the race for alderman.[8]

By this point, Fatty Walsh was an influential member of the "County Democracy," the anti-Tammany Democratic organization. But he knew how to work with Tammany when it suited his interests. In return for his support during the 1886 campaign, Mayor Abram S. Hewitt appointed Walsh warden of the Tombs. Because Hewitt had a reputation as a reformer, many New Yorkers were outraged that the new mayor would name "a pothouse politician of a low type," one who "had no respectable occupation," to guard the city's criminals. After all, continued the *Times* in another story, Warden Walsh would "inevitably become the custodian of many of his former associates in lawbreaking."[9]

Yet according to the *Times*, it was his life as a typical Five Points politician, rather than any specific crime, that disqualified Walsh from the office of warden. Referring to him in terms that applied to virtually every neighborhood politico, the *Times* condemned Walsh because "he is the product of the roughest elements of the Sixth Ward. . . . For years he was not only a gambler and a keeper of gambling dens, but a ward heeler of the lowest type, an associate of thieves and blacklegs, spending his life in gin-mills and a congenial associate of lawbreakers and law defiers." Whether due to his background or not, Walsh soon lost his sinecure. Accused of having levied excessive fees on Tombs inmates (they had to pay for many services in those days), Walsh was forced to resign in April 1888 after little more than a year in office.[10]

Now in late middle age, Walsh could at least console himself with the success of his daughter. Blanche was both a beauty and a gifted actress, and in 1888 at fifteen she made her professional stage debut. By age twenty-two she was one of Broadway's leading ladies, and over the course of the subsequent decade she became one of the best known actresses in the United States. With her fame and substantial income, Blanche wanted to put Five Points behind her. She and her mother begged Tom to move the family uptown, but he steadfastly refused, "and declared that there he would live and die." Fed up with his intransigence, Blanche and her mother moved anyway.[11]

Walsh knew that leaving the neighborhood would have ended his political career. He had no base of support uptown, while in the Sixth Ward he remained a force to be reckoned with. He could still rally large blocs of the Five Points electorate, even though Italians far outnumbered Irish Americans there by this point. "Mr. Walsh had a wonderful control over the voters, particularly the Italians, in his district," noted one biographical sketch. "It is told of him that he had only to stand on a barrel and cry, 'Who is the truest friend of Italy in New York?' to receive from the Italians the answer, 'Fatta Walsha alla de time-a.'" In 1893, anxious to retain his support, Tammany leaders rewarded Walsh with a sinecure as a dockmaster.[12]

Walsh still held this post when he died in 1899 at age sixty-five. Five thousand New Yorkers came to pay their respects at his funeral service. "He was a man of remarkably good nature," said the *Times* in its obituary, "generous in disposition, and noted especially for his steadfastness to his friends and his pugnacity in political battles. He never knew when he was beaten." This was the epitaph to which every Five Points politician aspired.[13]

CHAPTER NINE

Riot

⟨ᴍᴍᴏ⟩

"As Ready with His Pistol as His Fisticuffs"

B Y THE MID-1850s, saloonkeeper and police court justice Matthew Brennan had established substantial control of Five Points politics through his dominance of the police department and two ward fire companies. He maintained that power with the help of a loyal cadre of supporters, most notably Councilman John Clancy and Captain Joseph Dowling. Yet Brennan's power was by no means absolute. In 1853, while Brennan was still a police captain and a year before he ran for his first elective office, there appeared on the political scene another young Five Pointer—one whose popularity and disdain for the dictates of the party did not bode well for Brennan or Clancy.

Like Clancy, James E. Kerrigan was twenty-four when he captured the 1853 Democratic nomination for councilman from the thirteenth council district (Clancy represented the eleventh). Kerrigan was also, like Clancy, relatively well educated, having studied at Fordham University. But there the similarities ended. Whereas Clancy was calculating, deliberate, and somewhat dull by Five Points standards, Kerrigan was colorful, brash, and unpredictable. Kerrigan had left Fordham after a few months to enlist, at age seventeen, in the Mexican-American War, where he was said to have "displayed marked gallantry in battle" in the assault on Monterrey. Upon his return, Kerrigan became a member of Hose Company No. 14. He first came to public attention just weeks before his nomination for council, when the press reported that he was one of the "short-boys" (political thugs) hired by city Democrats to overawe delegates at the state nominating convention in Syracuse. Tammany leaders hoped to use the intimidation tactics perfected by Con Donoho and his men in Dooley's Long-Room to seize control of the party statewide. That Kerrigan had recently been made a letter carrier—a much sought after patronage appointment—indicates that by 1853 he had already labored extensively for the party.

Kerrigan did not look like the typical Five Points politician. Although born in New York, his appearance was that of "the ideal Southerner. He was tall, graceful, swarthy, wore his jet-black hair long and wavy, and it fell in a cascade of curls upon his shoulders." Kerrigan was also "a natural-born fighter, and was as ready with his pistol as his fisticuffs. He shrunk from no antagonist." Among his antagonists were the leaders of his own party. No sooner had Kerrigan captured the council nomination than he spearheaded the successful effort of an insurgent Democratic to beat out the party's regular nominee in the race for the ward's third council seat. On election day, the popular Kerrigan easily won his council race, as did the insurgent candidate he supported. Aspiring ward leaders such as Brennan and Clancy knew they would have to monitor closely the temperamental Councilman Kerrigan.[14]

When he chose to do so, Kerrigan dominated council proceedings by the sheer force of his personality. Even outside the legislative chambers, Kerrigan constantly drew the attention of the press. After winning reelection to the council in November 1854, he made headlines in early 1855 for his involvement in the celebrated murder of sporting man Bill "The Butcher" Poole. In late February 1855, Poole, a Whig and an American native, got into a bitter argument in a Broadway saloon with another prominent old sport, Irish-born Democrat John Morrissey. A few hours later, Morrissey's friend Lew Baker shot Poole, and Bill the Butcher died two weeks later. The *Times* called Kerrigan one "of the principle [*sic*] accessories to the murder of Poole and the flight of Baker," apparently because Kerrigan, himself an Irish-American sporting man, helped Baker flee the country. Kerrigan spent several days in jail while authorities investigated his role in the affair, but in the end they did not indict him.[15]

Throughout the 1850s, freelance American adventurers known as filibusters staged periodic raids in the Caribbean and Central America, usually in the hopes that they could turn a profit by annexing the captured

territory to the United States. When news of William Walker's filibuster-
ing campaign in Nicaragua reached New York in 1856, Kerrigan rushed to
claim some of the glory, despite administration policy prohibiting any
American assistance. Describing the sailing of a steamer for Nicaragua in
early January 1856, the *Herald* noted that "among the most conspicuous of
those on board was Councilman Kerrigan." He told the *Herald*'s reporter
that "he had about fifty men with him, and that he was their captain [he
was actually a second lieutenant], and that he was going to Nicaragua to
assist General Walker." As the steamer pulled away from the dock, the
ever-flamboyant Kerrigan "ascended the paddle box, and was greeted with
nine tremendous cheers." Kerrigan "will be a better soldier than states-
man," predicted the *Herald* a few weeks later, but military glory eluded
him in Central America. Kerrigan returned quietly to New York that
autumn.[16]

During Kerrigan's absence, another brawler and sporting man—Pat
Mathews—attempted to assume Kerrigan's mantle as the dominant politician in the northeast portion of the ward. Born in Ireland, Mathews had
emigrated with his sister and mother to New York in 1841 when he was
about ten years old. He first gained notoriety in December 1852 when he
and a few others invaded a Tammany Hall meeting of the Democratic general committee. During the brawl, Mathews struck acting committee
chairman Augustus Schell over the head with "a large arm chair," knocking him unconscious and leaving him with a severe concussion. Mathews
used the incident both to settle a factional score within the party and for
personal financial gain. As coal dealer Frederick Ridaboek (one of the individuals at the center of the Kelly imbroglio three years earlier) prepared to
enter the meeting, Mathews told him not to go in because he "would get
licked." The next morning, Mathews visited Ridaboek and insisted that
because he had saved Ridaboek from harm, he was owed something. Asked
what he wanted, Mathews replied, "My mother is poor, and I'll take two
tons of coal." Ridaboek gave him one ton. Meanwhile, Mathews's conviction for assaulting Schell did not seem to affect his political career. He was
one of the "short-boys" who accompanied Kerrigan to Syracuse in the
autumn of 1853 to bully the other delegates. By 1855, when the census
taker found him residing at 8 Doyer Street with his widowed sister and her
two young children, Mathews had secured a patronage post in the customhouse. After Kerrigan sailed for Nicaragua in 1856, the twenty-five-year-

old Mathews decided to run for his council seat. Kerrigan, who returned to the city before the November balloting, did not stand for a fourth term himself, but refused to endorse Mathews. He instead threw his support to fruit dealer Martin Gilmartin.[17]

On election day, the two antagonists and their allies engaged in one of the most violent polling place melees of the antebellum years. The *Times* described the "desperate fight" as one "between the Bowery boys, headed by MATHEWS, and the Molly Maguire boys led on by JIM KERRIGAN—between whom and MATHEWS a feud has long existed." By nine in the morning, the antagonists had thrown the voting station at 3 Elizabeth Street into chaos as they engaged in "a regular running street fight . . . with the usual accompaniment of knock-downs, drag outs, damaged eyes and skinned noses." This was the first Sixth Ward election skirmish in which firearms played a significant role. Kerrigan brandished his revolver on several occasions, and as many as thirty or forty shots were fired by the various combatants. Most of the injuries, however, were inflicted with more traditional Five Points riot weapons. "About a dozen persons were wounded from blows received by axes and clubs," reported the *Herald*, "while two or three were severely stabbed." Toward the end of the day, commented the *Times*, "scarcely any person could vote at [any of] the Sixth Ward polls on account of the rioting about them." At one point, Brennan's toughs ventured to the Elizabeth Street voting station, apparently in an attempt to discourage balloting by supporters of both his cross-neighborhood rivals. Kerrigan's and Mathews's men momentarily put aside their differences to defend their turf against these "Mulberry St. Boys." But after the interlopers had been repulsed, the temporary allies once again turned their blows upon each other. Kerrigan's men finally bested Mathews's supporters, allowing Gilmartin to carry the council race by a wide margin.[18]

"THE OLD SIXTH REMINDED ONE OF A HOUSE IN MOURNING"

The 1856 rioting between the Mathews and Kerrigan loyalists involved more than a personal feud and a council race. Many of the newspapers covering the fracas noted that mayoral politics was involved as well. Two factions of New York Democrats had for some time been engaged in a struggle for control of the party at the citywide level. Mayor Fernando Wood headed one clique; the other had no single leader at this point but would eventually become identified with Tammany stalwarts such as William M. Tweed.

Wood was the most dynamic New York political figure of the 1850s. Although he was a Protestant and native-born, the dapper, charming mayor was especially beloved by the city's impoverished Irish Catholic immigrants, who appreciated his efforts to create jobs and distribute food during the severe recession winter of 1854–55. Such voters also lauded Wood's efforts to obstruct enforcement of state-imposed laws limiting the sale of alcoholic beverages. Yet despite his personal magnetism and popularity with voters, Wood's refusal to follow the dictates of Tammany's internal leadership outraged many Democrats. Whigs and Republicans soon came to despise Wood as well, fuming that his personal popularity did not diminish even as he broke promises to reform government and enforce temperance legislation. By the autumn of 1856, the city was firmly divided into pro- and anti-Wood camps. The animosity between the two sides had contributed to the Sixth Ward election rioting of 1856—Mathews's supporters were pro-Wood, Kerrigan's anti-Wood. When Mathews lost his customhouse position just weeks before the 1856 election, the *Leader* identified his "offense" as "*Wood Fever.*"[19]

After Wood won reelection in 1856, anti-Wood Democrats combined forces with Republicans to enact a slate of legislation designed to punish the mayor. Although some of the bills passed by state lawmakers sought to reform municipal government, others enacted in the winter of 1857 were designed primarily to strip Wood of his official responsibilities and patronage power. Two of these measures caused particular consternation in Five Points. One, a "license law," raised the cost of a liquor license to levels beyond the reach of many of the neighborhood's small saloonkeepers and completely banned the sale of alcoholic beverages on Sundays. The other, the Metropolitan Police Act, was the one that had so incensed Fatty Walsh. It mandated the disbanding of the city's police department and its replacement with a force administered by a state-appointed board of commissioners rather than the mayor.

The *Irish-American* condemned the Police Act for its "partisanship, odiousness, and tyranny. . . . It virtually disfranchises the people" by taking control of municipal institutions away from the city's duly elected leaders. Even many Republicans found the legislature's actions embarrassing. Diarist George Templeton Strong admitted that the legislature enacted the police bill "in order to take power out of the paws of Mayor Wood and get it into those of the other scoundrels at Albany." The Republican *Times* agreed that rather than making the police apolitical, as it ought to, the legislature had merely taken the police "from one political party and hand[ed] it over to another."[20]

Two aspects of the new legislation especially infuriated Five Pointers. One was the sense that the new laws were part of a nativist plot against the Irish. Know Nothings had long called for liquor restrictions, and in cities where they had gained power—such as Philadelphia and Chicago—Know Nothing mayors had created natives-only police forces because they believed immigrants could not be trusted to enforce temperance laws. Know Nothings had also sought to restrict saloons because they understood that most immigrant political activity centered in neighborhood taverns. The Know Nothing movement was fading by the spring of 1857. But most Irish Catholics believed that the "Black Republicans," so-called by Democrats because of their purported obsession with the plight of African Americans, had adopted much of the nativist platform. Sixth Warders cursed the Police Act as "'a Know-Nothing and Black Republican scheme,' the design of which was to disfranchise foreign-born citizens, and oust them from all political rights."[21]

Five Pointers also believed that the act was part of a continuing conspiracy to deny the Irish their fair share of the patronage. In 1856, an Irish-American journal noted that despite Know Nothing claims that "Irish citizens get all the offices," only 10 percent of the seven hundred fifty customhouse employees in New York were natives of Ireland, and that the Irish held the lowest-paying jobs. "The cosy sinecures with large emoluments are reserved for 'those to the manor born,'" agreed the *Irish-American*. The police department was one of the few government institutions that hired the Irish in significant numbers for non-menial jobs—Sixth Ward immigrants constituted 64 percent of the district's force in 1856.

Led by Wood, many city Democrats fought the new Police Act. In the spring of 1857, when the state set up its new "Metropolitan" police department, Wood refused to disband the old "Municipal" force. For more than a month, the city witnessed the spectacle of rival police departments. Criminals sometimes escaped as members of the two squads fought for the right to make arrests. On one occasion, the two units engaged in a full-scale riot on the steps of City Hall. The farce finally ended on July 2 when the state's highest court ruled that the disbanding of the old force was constitutional. Wood reluctantly dissolved the Municipal Police the next day. The stage was set for Fatty Walsh's riot.[22]

According to the *Tribune*, "the old Sixth reminded one of a house in mourning," as word of the mayor's capitulation spread across Five Points on Friday, July 3. Reports that the Metropolitan Police Board had not appointed any Irishmen to the new force, except for the occasional Irish Republican, confirmed Five Pointers' fears, and rumors flew that "the Know Nothings & Black Republicans were coming down to burn the [Transfiguration] Catholic Church in Mott St." With the typically raucous Fourth of July celebrations about to begin, Clancy offered the Metropolitan commissioners the services of Captain Dowling and his old Sixth Ward police force free of charge over the holiday weekend, so long as the men remained under Dowling's command. The commissioners wanted the extra manpower, but only if the men took orders from the Metropolitan commanders, something Dowling and his men refused to consider. Vowing to "lick" any Metropolitan foolish enough to show his face in the district, Five Pointers braced for a bloody Fourth of July in the bloody old Sixth.[23]

A "RATHER EXTRAORDINARY SIXTH WARD MUSS"

What transpired on the Fourth, not just where Walsh was involved but before, after, and elsewhere, exceeded even the most dire predictions, as the ward degenerated into what one historian has termed "the most ferocious free-for-all in the history of the city." Contemporaries agreed that the ensuing Sixth Ward riot threw the entire city into "a state of anarchy." No sooner had the clock struck midnight on the morning of the Fourth than the anticipated violence began. Shouting "Kill the G–d d——d Black Metropolitan Police s–n of a b——," a mob of Five Pointers beat and stoned a new policeman making an arrest after a street fight at the corner of Mulberry and Chatham Streets. The officer died several days later of injuries sustained in the brutal attack.[24]

About an hour later, a large crowd of Five Pointers appeared on Chatham Street, determined "to beat all the new policemen they could find." The rowdies moved north from Chatham onto the Bowery, "hooting & cheering Fernando Wood & making very noisy demonstrations." North of

Bayard Street, the Five Pointers found Metropolitan Abraham Florentine Jr. of Mulberry Street. The mob wrestled Florentine's club from him, but before it could harm him seriously he ran up the street and ducked into the saloon at 40 Bowery, known throughout the neighborhood as headquarters of Pat Mathews and his "Bowery Boys." Though the tavern was relatively deserted, the occupants barricaded themselves in as the rioters bombarded it with rocks and bricks. Meanwhile, the mob noticed another Metropolitan attempting to slip away undetected. With seventy-five to a hundred men at his heels, the officer ran inside Henry McCloskey's "coffee and cake saloon" at 36 Bowery. According to the establishment's baker, Richard Quinn, the crowd smashed the windows and hurled missiles inside at the occupants, who returned fire "with tumblers, bottles and other things that we could seize upon." After about ten minutes, a gang of Mathews's Bowery Boys arrived to repel the assault. The rioters then retreated down Bayard into the heart of the Five Points neighborhood, giving "three cheers for Fernandy Wud" as they made their escape. The Bowery Boys did not pursue them, "not desiring to penetrate too far into the enemy's camp." The two gangs clashed once more just before dawn.[25]

It was wholly appropriate that the rioters had vented their frustrations on Abraham Florentine, because he epitomized everything Five Pointers resented about the new force. Florentine, a thirty-year-old undertaker, was one of the very few white adult native-born citizens living on Mulberry Bend, the densely populated block bounded by Mulberry, Bayard, Baxter, and Park. In fact, until the 1855 census enumerator reached Florentine's house at 59½ Mulberry, he had not recorded a single native-born adult white male among the previous 928 residents. Florentine's selection for the Metropolitan force (albeit as a temporary officer) seemed to verify the Five Pointers' charge that the Republicans were discriminating against adopted citizens in their appointments to the new police department.

Florentine's hiring also lent credibility to the Irish charge that the new department was dominated by Know Nothings. Florentine's father, Abraham Senior, had been a leader of the anti-Catholic American-Republican party in the Sixth Ward, serving on the organization's "general executive" and finance committees in the 1840s. Abraham Junior had followed his father into the nativist political ranks. An 1854 *Herald* advertisement listing "Sixth Ward Reform Nominations" featured young Florentine as the candidate for one of the ward's three city council seats. This "reform" slate was actually the Know Nothing ticket—the initially secretive nativist party used this ploy throughout the United States to advertise its nominees in 1854. Another Sixth Ward Know Nothing candidate for councilman in 1854, Joseph Souder, was made a Metropolitan sergeant. A large proportion of the rioters harassing the Metropolitans lived on lower Mulberry Street, and some of them undoubtedly knew of Florentine's affiliations. The sight of their nativist neighbors in Metropolitan uniforms must have both infuriated them and confirmed that the Police Act was part of a Know Nothing conspiracy to humiliate the Irish and destroy their burgeoning political power.[26]

After so much predawn violence, the morning and afternoon of the Fourth of July were eerily quiet. But late that day, the violence recommenced. Learning that some of their Seventh Ward officers were under attack, Metropolitan commanders in the Sixth dispatched about two dozen patrolmen to assist them. The Sixth Ward policemen had remained in their barracks for most of the day, but at 5:00 p.m. they headed east from their White Street station house, planning to turn south on Baxter and then east onto Bayard, which would carry them across the Bowery to the Seventh Ward.[27]

Meanwhile, Five Pointers were thronging the streets, escaping from their crowded tenements and enjoying the district's holiday celebrations. Just before the phalanx of Metropolitans set out from White Street toward the Seventh Ward, a fight broke out on Bayard between Baxter and Mulberry, and an enormous crowd gathered to witness the excitement. "The belligerent parties had just been separated," the *Tribune* later reported, "when the cry was heard, 'The Metropolitans are coming.'" Suddenly gripped by a combination of panic and outrage, some dashed into their tenements, while others stood their ground determined to prevent the Metropolitans from making arrests in a harmless street fight.

When the police turned into Bayard Street moments later, they were set upon by the rabid crowd. The patrolmen's attempts to create a wall of defense were hampered by "the shower of stones, bricks, oyster-shells, fragments of ironware, and in some instances whole pots and kettles" that rained down upon them from the surrounding tenement windows and rooftops. The assault had been in progress no more than a few minutes when the cry rang out that "the Bowery Boys are coming." Indeed, two hundred or so men and boys were streaming westward on Bayard in an attempt once again to defend the police from attack. The Metropolitans dashed eastward to take cover behind the advancing Bowery Boys, who took over the fighting; the policemen continued toward the Seventh Ward. The Mulberry Boys, initially shocked at the sudden appearance of their Bowery foes, quickly regrouped and drove the Bowery Boys back to a construction site on the south side of Bayard between Mott and Elizabeth. The retreat proved fortuitous, as the Bowery Boys were able to lay in a new and superior supply of ammunition by helping themselves to the huge pile of bricks meant for construction of a new tenement. Using the brickbats as bludgeons and missiles, the Bowery Boys were able to drive their enemies back to Mott Street.[28]

At this point, about six o'clock, thirty to forty Metropolitans arrived on the scene in the rear of the Mulberry gang's line, prompting most of the Mulberry Boys to take cover inside nearby tenements. "Again the bricks and stones were showered from the housetops and windows by the hundred," commented the *Tribune*, "many of which struck the officers, causing severe injuries." The patrolmen—many "with blood streaming over their faces"—were nevertheless able to make about a dozen arrests before they retreated back toward White Street. Once the police had abandoned the front, the full force of Mulberry Boys returned to Bayard to defend against the Bowery Boys' incursion. They managed to dislodge the enemy from the brick pile and force a retreat to Elizabeth Street.[29]

The fight was primarily between Mathews's and Kerrigan's adherents on the one hand, and Brennan's on the other. The *Morning Express* reported that one side was composed of "the Bowery Boys, under the leadership of Pat Matthews [*sic*], a well known Custom House officer, and having headquarters at a drinking house No. 40 Bowery." The *Tribune* added that "many of the members of Hose Company No. 14 in Elizabeth street," the unit associated with Kerrigan, also "belong to the party." As used by the press, the term "Bowery Boy" now referred not to the colorful subculture that had flourished in the late 1840s and early 1850s, but primarily to the political adherents of Kerrigan and Mathews. The Bowery Boy of 1857 seems to have been more of a sporting man than a "B'hoy." Stories about the "old sports" of New York described both Mathews and Kerrigan as prominent sporting men. The image of the Bowery Boy published in *Frank Leslie's Illustrated Newspaper* after the riot closely resembles a typical sporting man and has little in common with the "soap-locked" and clothes-conscious Bowery B'hoy of 1849. Yet one does find some traces of the "B'hoy" persisting in the 1857 Bowery Boys, especially the strident nationalism, which accounts in part for Kerrigan's volunteering for action in Mexico, Nicaragua, and the Civil War. Most of the 1857 "Bowery Boys" lived on Elizabeth Street and the Bowery, but many resided on the far side of the Bowery in the Tenth Ward as well.[30]

Reporters covering the riot stated that the Bowery Boys' opponents in this struggle were members of a Five Points gang known as the "Dead Rabbits," and historians have consequently dubbed this conflict the "Dead Rabbit/Bowery Boy Riot." Yet the neighborhood residents who supposedly composed the ranks of the "Dead Rabbits" were unanimous in their insistence that no gang by that name existed. Instead, they claimed that the group the police initially referred to as the Mulberry Boys was actually the "Roach" or "Roche" Guard, a combination political/social club founded at the beginning of the 1850s in honor of prominent neighborhood saloon-keeper Walter Roche, an 1848 immigrant from County Carlow who at that point operated a popular saloon at 19 Mulberry Street. Marcus Horbelt, a twenty-one-year-old shoemaker residing at 25 Mulberry Street, wrote angrily after the riot to all the major New York dailies to complain about their pejorative depictions of the Roche Guard or "Dead Rabbit Club" as "a gang of Thieves, Five-Pointers, Pickpockets, &c. Now, if your reporter wished to earn $25, I hereby offer to give him, or any other one, that sum of money who will prove, satisfactorily, that a single member of the Guard (by the way, there *is* no such club as the Dead Rabbits) is a Five-Pointer, a thief or a pickpocket. . . . I say that the young men who compose that Guard are, 1st, honest; 2d, industrious; 3d, young men who follow some lawful occupation for a living." And another Five Pointer, Harry Molony, informed the *Herald* that a club called "the 'Dead Rabbits' . . . does not nor never did belong to the Sixth ward, to the personal knowledge of one resident in it for twelve years."[31]

The press nonetheless persisted in referring to the Bowery Boys' adversaries as the "Dead Rabbits." Some reporters stated that the Dead Rabbits were an offshoot of the Roche Guard. Divisions within the Roche Guard's ranks, they said, had led to a secession of some members, who to spite their former allies threw a dead rabbit into one of their meetings, thus earning the secessionists their gruesome nickname. In fact, the most likely source of the term lies elsewhere. One eyewitness to the riot, Metropolitan

A "DEAD RABBIT." SKETCHED FROM LIFE.

Frank Leslie's depiction of a typical Roche Guard supporter. *Frank Leslie's Illustrated Newspaper*, (July 11, 1857). Collection of the Library of Congress.

Thomas Harvey, later testified that "the thieves of the Five Points" were referred to in neighborhood slang as "the 'dead Rabbit party.'" In an attempt to cast aspersion on their antagonists, the Bowery Boys probably referred to their opponents by this name during the struggle (Horbelt's letter demonstrates that he and his allies were very sensitive about being associated with the criminals who concentrated at the Five Points intersection). Because most reporters used the Bowery Boys as sources for their stories on the riots, the scribes probably got the term from them. The

name so captured the imagination of New Yorkers that the press continued
to use it despite the abundant evidence that no such club or gang existed.
The *Morning Express,* for example, initially reported that mourners at one
rioter's funeral wore satin badges inscribed with the words "Dead Rabbit
Club," but the next day admitted that they had actually read "Roach
Guard. We mourn our loss." For more than a decade, "Dead Rabbit"
became the standard phrase by which city residents described any scandalously riotous individual or group. But there seems to be no justification
for referring to the Bowery Boys' adversaries by this name.[32]

While the origin of the term "Dead Rabbit" is uncertain, it is clear that
the Five Pointers referred to by that name were all loyal adherents of
Matthew Brennan. When Brennan became police justice in 1854, he put
Roche in charge of his Monroe Hall saloon. Roche also served as assistant
foreman of Brennan Hose Company No. 60 in 1858. Horbelt was a member

SCENE AT THE FIVE POINTS RIOT.   WOMEN AND MEN THROWING BRICKBATS DOWN ON
THE POLICE.

Five Points women helped defend the neighborhood against the incursions of the police and
the Bowery Boys. *Frank Leslie's Illustrated Newspaper* (July 11, 1857). Collection of the
Library of Congress.

of the same fire company. He was also appointed an election inspector for the lower Mulberry Street district for the November 1857 canvass (the polling place was in Roche's saloon there) and was elected a ward constable in that contest—honors he could not have achieved without Brennan's approval. The extent to which Roche or Horbelt participated in the actual rioting cannot be determined, though we do know that Fatty Walsh, one leader of the rioters, was affiliated with Brennan as well. The riot was clearly a political fight between the adherents of Brennan on the one hand, and those of Mathews and Kerrigan on the other.[33]

Despite the political overtones of the fighting, men were not the only participants. Women and children allied with the Roche Guard were "busily engaged in gathering and breaking up stones, brickbats, &c., in their aprons and handkerchiefs . . . and carrying them to those on the housetops to fire down on the crowd." By late afternoon, in order to protect themselves from the continuing rain of rocks, bottles, and bricks, the Bowery Boys at the corner of Elizabeth and Bayard erected a barricade from carts, wagons, and construction materials left on the street. Their adversaries soon followed suit.[34]

In order to penetrate these defensive fortifications, the rioters around

View from the "Dead Rabbit" barricade on Bayard Street, at the corner of either Mulberry or Mott. *Frank Leslie's Illustrated Newspaper* (July 11, 1857). Collection of the Library of Congress.

6:00 p.m. began to take up firearms for the first time, though the Bowery
Boys had far more pistols and rifles than did the Roche Guard. "A frightful
scene of riot and bloodshed ensued," reported the *Morning Express*. "A
large number were wounded, and some mortally." According to the
Herald, the scene became one "of indescribable confusion. The crowding,
fighting mass in the streets—the howling, shrieking women and children
in the upper floors busily engaged in showering every description of missile on the heads of those below, hitting indiscriminately friends and foes—
the explosion of firearms, amid the shrieks of the wounded and dying,
rendered the scene one of horror and terror."[35]

By this point, people from all over the city had flocked to the Sixth
Ward to witness the riot. Minister Lyman Abbott rented a room on an
upper floor of a boardinghouse at the corner of Bayard and the Bowery in
order to observe the spectacle. Richard Henry Dana Jr., who since his visits
to Five Points brothels had published *Two Years Before the Mast*, was also
there. When he asked who was engaged in the battle, an onlooker told
Dana that the struggle was "between our chaps & the Bowery boys." Dana
noted in his diary that "the fight was chiefly with fire-arms, tho' there
were occasional rushes & retreats, assaults and repulses of large bodies,
armed with bricks & clubs, & here & there a strong man made long bowls
with pieces of brick. On the side walk not far from me, was a pool of blood,
as if a hog had been killed, & a lad of 16 came out of a house with a bandage
over his face, & a long-nine [cigar] in his mouth, swaggering off with the air
of a hero." Observing the conflict was almost as dangerous as participating
in it. A stray bullet struck and killed a young spectator at a Bayard Street
window near Abbott's.[36]

Despite the escalating casualty rate, the Roche Guard and its allies
fought on in defense of their turf. "The recklessness of some of the men
seemed almost unaccountable," exclaimed the *Tribune*. "One of the Dead
Rabbits stood for [a] full fifteen minutes on the top of the brick pile throwing bricks at the Bowery boys, while at the same time the bullets were
whistling by in a fearfully ominous manner. . . . A woman displayed
remarkable bravery at this time" as well. "Several times she came out of
Mott street to the brick pile, filled her apron with bricks and carried them
into Mott street." Bowery Boys called on her to stop but when she returned
for more, they threw bricks at her. When she came back yet again, they
shot at her. She only stopped when a man "came out and carried her

forcibly into Mott street." After the shooting tapered off momentarily around seven o'clock, Isaiah Rynders made an effort to broker a truce. Both sides jeered the Captain, however, "and seeing a boy shot down beside him, he acted the wiser part and retired."[37]

The riot finally ended around eight o'clock. According to most press accounts, a former policeman from the Nineteenth Ward named Shangles convinced each side to cease and desist by telling them (inaccurately) that the militia was on its way to restore order. Clancy later insisted, however, that he, Dowling, and Brennan had persuaded the rioters to go home. Whatever the case, "each faction then slowly dispersed—the Atlantic Boys to the Bowery and the 'Dead Rabbits' to their haunts in Mulberry and the streets in the lower part of the Ward."[38]

As news of the cease-fire spread, Five Pointers swarmed out of neighborhood tenements and into district pharmacies—the de facto medical clinics of the day—to see if their loved ones were among the dead or wounded. "So great was the anxiety to obtain this information," reported the *Times*, "that the windows of several of the drug stores were broken and the doors forced. Women and children rushed forward frantically for their husbands, fathers, and brothers, and their cries and lamentations made this the gloomiest portion of the day." Twelve New Yorkers lay dead. Thirty-seven of the wounded were admitted to New York Hospital, but the *Times* estimated that two or three times that number were treated in their homes out of fear the authorities might prosecute the injured for their part in what a number of newspapers called the Sixth Ward's "civil war." "The greatest injury was done . . . to the Mulberry-street 'crowd,' as they were not so well armed as their Bowery antagonists," noted the *Times*. "Not one of the Bowery boys was fatally injured," concurred the *Tribune*, ". . . nearly all of the killed being of the Dead Rabbit crowd."[39]

Despite having inflicted the overwhelming majority of the serious injuries, the Bowery Boys were not the ones prosecuted for rioting. Authorities may have justified this bias on the grounds that the Bowery Boys initially had entered the fray in defense of the police. Prosecutors indicted only the six men arrested by the Metropolitans when the new police made their second foray into Bayard Street during the initial stages of the riot. Police had observed them throwing bricks into the crowd or attacking officers attempting to make arrests.

None of the men indicted for rioting hired an attorney and all presented the same defense: that they had merely been watching or passing by when apprehended. Barney Gallagher, a tailor who like all his codefendants could not sign his name to his statement, told the court that "I'm a poor man and han't had money to fee a lawyer nor anybody else. I was going through the street peaceably to my family with my little week's earnings, and didn't do nothin to nobody." Only Clancy appeared on behalf of the defendants, peppering the prosecution witnesses with questions in an attempt to poke holes in their cases. The New York press condemned the aldermen for taking the side of the riot's instigators, but Clancy insisted to the *Times* that he acted "from motives of charity, only, to help those men who were without friends." The alderman's efforts were in vain, however, as the judge found all the defendants guilty. Clancy did win a suspended sentence for a sixteen-year-old rioter, but the remaining five received the maximum permissible punishment—six months in prison. New York's Irish-American community perceived the verdicts and sentences as evidence of both selective prosecution and prejudice. "The principle evidence against some of those who have been sentenced to six months' imprisonment and hard labor was, that they had unmistakably Irish names," complained the *New York Citizen*, "and happened to be in the street, and perhaps wounded while the riots were going on!" Those responsible for the deaths of the Roche Guard members and its allies, in contrast, went unpunished.[40]

The Bowery Boy Riot still ranks as one of the deadliest episodes of civil unrest in the history of New York. To that point, only the Astor Place Riot of 1849 had resulted in more loss of life, and in that case most of the twenty fatalities had come when the military fired upon the crowd surrounding the opera house there. Never before the events of 1857 had New York civilians taken the lives of so many of their fellows.[41]

Many historians, including Mike Wallace and Edwin G. Burrows in *Gotham*, have portrayed the riot as one between nativists and the Irish. Given that the Bowery Boys aided the Metropolitans, and that most Five Pointers perceived the new police as part of a Know Nothing conspiracy against them, this interpretation has seemed perfectly plausible. Yet an examination of both the contemporary evidence and the subsequent careers of the Bowery Boy leaders suggests otherwise. No contemporary observer portrayed the conflict as a struggle between nativists and Irish Catholics. Mathews was a native of Ireland, and although his religious affiliation (if any) is not known, his given name Patrick and that of his sister Mary suggest a Catholic background. Kerrigan was a native New Yorker, but must also have been at least a nominal Catholic, having attended a Catholic university. His later career also indicates a devotion to Irish independence incompatible with significant anti-Catholicism. In 1866, Kerrigan raised a brigade for the invasion of Canada organized by the Irish freedom fighters known as the Fenians. A year later, he served as "brigadier general" for a force of thirty-eight men that sailed to Ireland with a shipload of weapons in the hopes of fomenting an uprising against the British.[42]

Recognizing the riot as an intraethnic rather than an interethnic battle, the Irish-American *Citizen* condemned the rioters as an embarrassment to Irishmen everywhere. It is "idle to deny that a portion of the Irish working classes are far too ready, when intoxicated, to engage in a row." Of all the evils associated with Irish drunkenness, the editor asserted, "the faction fights at home and abroad are undoubtedly the most to be regretted. . . . Riots are bad under any circumstances; but they are peculiarly detestable when got up by compatriots against each other in a foreign land. Thus Irishmen come to this free country to improve their condition; and because one party came from a different province [from] another, or perhaps only from a different county they attack each other like tigers whenever they get together and drink." Yet the Five Points riot was not a "faction fight" in the strictest sense of the term—a battle inspired by Irish regional pride. Although the Roche Guard drew an especially large proportion of its recruits from lower Mulberry Street, a stronghold of immigrants from County Cork in southern Ireland, its hero Brennan traced his roots to County Donegal in the far north.[43]

The real cause of the riot was not regionalism in Ireland so much as politics in New York, mixed with a good old-fashioned local turf battle. The *Herald* rightly attributed the hostilities to a long-standing feud between Five Points political factions. "The whole thing was an ordinary, or rather extraordinary Sixth ward muss," the *Herald* concluded, "rendered more disastrous by the appearance of the police force, against which the residents of that locality have an undoubtedly strong prejudice."[44]

The reason why Mathews, a prominent Wood supporter, would defend the Metropolitans alongside Kerrigan's men, well-known adversaries of the mayor, is that in the world of Five Points politics, defending one's turf trumped consistency on a controversial issue such as the Police Act. Mathews and Kerrigan might adhere to different factions within Tammany, but could unite in their determination to defend their territory against an incursion by Brennan's followers—even if that encroachment was for the harassment of the Metropolitans, something Mathews ought to have condoned. Kerrigan himself told the *Tribune* that the riot started because in their pursuit of the police to the Bowery, "the Dead Rabbits were on forbidden ground, the Bowery Boys claiming exclusive control over that part of the Ward." More than just the bragging rights over certain neighborhood blocks inspired this territorial jealousy. Brennan's followers realized, according to one riot witness, that "if they could lick the Bowery men they would have all of the 6th ward." This ongoing battle to stave off absorption into Brennan's sphere of influence helps explain why Mathews would aid the Metropolitans in their struggle with Brennan's supporters.[45]

Dana recorded in his journal that "one of the more respectable Irishmen" present at the uprising told him the riot had started because "the New police could not go into the 6th Ward,—that the men of the 6th Ward had vowed to kill them all, if they came there." When Dana reminded the Five Pointer that the police were backed by the authority of the entire state, he replied that "'the Sixth Ward, Sir, is the strongest power on earth.' He repeated this, & fully believed it. Nor is it strange that he should. It has given the great[est] Democratic Majority every year," and as a result its inhabitants "have enjoyed almost an impunity in their violences & wickedness." The result was one of the bloodiest riots in the city's violent history.[46]

"THESE DEMANDS OF THE IRISH"

In the immediate aftermath of the Bowery Boy Riot, it appeared that the police and license laws would irrevocably alter Five Points life. The police department, for years a bastion of Democratic patronage, was now firmly in the control of Republicans and Know Nothings. The Metropolitans made sure that the portion of the license law mandating the Sunday closing of saloons was strictly enforced. "Old residents declared that never before had they seen such a quiet Sunday in the Sixth Ward," reported the *Times* a few weeks after the riot. "The stoops and side-walks were never so crowded with men, women and children, seeking dubious air and conversation away from their narrow apartments up crooked alleys and lofty buildings. Their sports were somewhat rough and boisterous, but it was all good-natured and peculiar."[47]

Yet Five Points Democrats soon reasserted themselves, both in the ward and, for the first time, citywide as well. Brennan was so popular and respected as police justice for the Fourth, Sixth, and Fourteenth Wards that neither Democrat nor Republican opposed him when he stood for reelection in November 1857. About a half year later, in June 1858, the Metropolitans asked Dowling to return to the Sixth Ward as police captain. Whether Dowling received this invitation due to Brennan's influence, or because the Metropolitans came to appreciate Dowling's skill at keeping the peace in the unruly neighborhood, cannot be determined. But Dowling was thrilled to return to the force and seemed to consider it a vindication of sorts—his certificate of reappointment, dated June 24, 1858, hung on his bedroom wall until the day he died. In October, Dowling managed to get his former right-hand man, Sergeant John Jourdan, reinstated as well. Jourdan had returned to his teenage vocation as a *Herald* paper folder when the Metropolitans dismissed him.[48]

Even the men whose names were prominently linked to the 1857 rioting prospered politically. Kerrigan secured a patronage post as an assistant clerk in Brennan's own police court (whether in Brennan's courtroom or that of his fellow justice James Steers is unclear), indicating that the two foes had agreed upon some sort of truce. He would later serve in Congress. Those Five Pointers associated with Brennan and the Roche Guard found political success as well. When the city's new Board of Supervisors was created in 1858, Roche was elected to serve on it.[49]

The politician associated with Brennan who advanced furthest was John Clancy. A few months after the riot, at the end of November 1857, Clancy bought a controlling interest in the *Leader*—Tammany's official organ—and became its editor in chief. Clancy had already increased his visibility within Democratic ranks as the journal's junior editor. Now in complete command of the influential weekly, the ambitious and talented Clancy utilized his new influence and prestige in pursuit of citywide office. No Irish Catholic Sixth Warder had ever held such a post, but Clancy was determined to be the first.[50]

Clancy set his sights on the November 1858 contest for county clerk. Surveying the field and discovering that his main competition came from another rising Democratic star, Seventh Ward supervisor William M. Tweed, the twenty-nine-year-old Clancy unabashedly utilized the pages of the *Leader* to explain why he deserved the nomination. An editorial in early October noted that Tweed had spent a lot of money distributing "pasteboard cards" touting his candidacy. Yet despite the "herculean efforts" of the "'gay Supervisor,'" the *Leader* insisted that the nomination should go to Clancy. The editorial noted sarcastically that the "small sprinkling of Democratic voters" in the Sixth Ward "have never, within memory of any man connected with Tammany Hall . . . received an acknowledgement of their existence since Cornelius W. Lawrence [a Sixth Ward resident] was elected Mayor some twenty-three years ago." Harry Howard (Kerrigan's patron) had once been appointed receiver of taxes, but served only for a short period until he resigned

> for a *Seventh* ward man, and in the distribution of patronage, both federal and municipal, the Sixth Ward seems to have had a back seat. There is an end to all things, and the idea of working every election to elevate other people and then get no thanks for it, is pretty well played out in the 6th Ward. For the past twenty years the democracy of that district have never been recognized as they should be, except on election day, when they are of some impor-tance to county candidates; and during the several democratic administrations at the Custom House and in this city, up to the present time not one important place has ever been tendered to the 6th Ward. The whole of the departments of the county and city governments are filled with people from other wards, with whom we have no fault to find except to make a clear case why some-thing should be done for the 6th Ward at the coming county con-vention.

Clancy did not rely on the *Leader* alone to promote his candidacy. He used advertising and other means to whip up support, including "a gorgeous banner" strung across Third Avenue.[51]

The year 1858 was actually a watershed for Irish-American politicians all over New York, as they began an unprecedented push for a fair share of the nominations. The *New York Dispatch* noted that summer that "there is beginning to be a good deal of grumbling among the American and German Democrats, in consequence of these demands of the Irish." Such discontent became evident at the Tammany nominating convention. Clancy's opponents argued that because Irish-American John Kelly was the

THE VOTING-PLACE, NO. 460 PEARL STREET, IN THE SIXTH WARD, NEW YORK CITY.

The scene in a Five Points bar on election day 1858. The polls were located through the doorway in the back of the saloon. Note the large posters advertising the candidacies of Clancy and Kelly. Few Five Pointers would have agreed with those who complained that the ticket was "entirely too Irish." *Harper's Weekly* (November 13, 1858): 724. Collection of the author.

consensus choice to head the ticket as the candidate for sheriff, Clancy's nomination for clerk would mean that "the ticket would be entirely 'too Irish.'" Clancy spoke on his own behalf to rebut this argument, however, and the convention nominated him on the first ballot. "Mr. Clancy's nomination," explained the *Irish-American* afterward, "was generally conceded to the claims of the Sixth Ward."[52]

Clancy's triumph in the general election marked the climax of a remarkable quarter century in Five Points politics. The election riots of 1834 had dramatically signaled the end of deference as the hallmark of neighborhood politics, as Five Points' Irish-American residents demonstrated their determination to take their destiny into their own hands. In the alternative system that developed, violence, patronage, and party loyalty were the keys to advancement, as was the ability to command the support of fire companies, police officers, and liquor dealers. As the city became increasingly Irish with the flood of famine immigrants in the late 1840s, and as the violent tactics of Five Points politicians became standard throughout the city, Sixth Ward Irish Catholics for the first time discovered opportunities to advance their political careers beyond the ward's boundaries. Brennan was the first Five Points Catholic to become an important player in the Tammany hierarchy, and his influence was quickly matched by his protégé, Clancy. Clancy's victory in the race for county clerk ensured that, for the foreseeable future at least, Tammany leaders would no longer be able to take Five Points Democrats for granted. By the time the Tweed Ring had seized control of city politics at the end of the Civil War, Five Pointers would have the dubious distinction of being counted among the most influential of those leaders.[53]

10

PROLOGUE

"The Boy Who Commands That Pretty Lot Recruited Them for the Seceshes"

IN MID-DECEMBER 1860, as South Carolina prepared to secede from the Union, a strange advertisement appeared in the *New York Herald*:

> The captains of all the Volunteer [militia] Companies of the City of New-York [are requested] to send a communication to the undersigned, at No. 74 Mott-st., stating the name of the Company and the number of men under their command, for the purpose of perfecting a Military Organization to protect the municipal rights of the city and the constitutional rights of the citizens of the country, in the event of a revolution.

For the few New Yorkers who did not understand the code words, the *Herald* offered a translation. One object of the proposed corps, it explained, was to protect the city "from further republican encroachments" such as the Metropolitan Police Act of 1857. The reference to "constitutional rights" indicated that the organization "will be pro-slavery in principle, and will take prompt action in case of secession." In other words, the ad was a call for New York militia units to fight for the Confederacy should the country descend into Civil War. The ad was signed by the city's best known Bowery Boy, Five Pointer James E. Kerrigan.[1]

Kerrigan's story reflects the competing loyalties tugging at many New York Democrats during the War Between the States. He had laid relatively low since helping to incite the bloody Bowery Boy Riot in 1857, drawing a salary as a police court clerk while undoubtedly devoting most of his energy to gambling, fighting, and politicking with his fellow sporting men. He reemerged in the fall of 1860, however, running for Congress as the candidate of "Mozart Hall," the organization created by Mayor Fernando Wood as an alternative to Tammany. Discussing Kerrigan's qualifications for office, the *Herald* noted that his chief talent was as "a strong man to head crowds at political meetings. . . . If he should happen to be elected and there should be a disposition in the American Congress to break the thing up in a row, Councilman Kerrigan may be relied upon to do yeoman service in the cause of his country."[2]

Though the thirty-one-year-old might lack the résumé of the typical congressional candidate, his appearance and bearing were bound to impress Five Points voters. "He is tall, slim and graceful, though possessed, it is said, of a remarkable physical strength," commented the *Herald* on the eve of the election. "His face is long, thin and pale, free from mustache or beard, except [for] a delicate imperial, copied from the style of the old masters." Kerrigan's long, jet-black hair curled about his shoulders, but he was not burly like many of his fellow sporting men. "He has more the appearance, in gentility and grace, of one of Mr. Brown's dancing young men, than of the warlike and indomitable hero which he is known to be," observed the same reporter. "A gleam, which shoots out of his light, cold gray eyes, however, indicates the spirit which is within."[3]

Kerrigan entered the congressional contest at a distinct disadvantage. The Tammany nominee could rely on his organization's vast network of district leaders and ward heelers to assist him in his bid for office. Kerrigan, in contrast, had no such machine. But the demographics of the congressional district—comprising the Fourth, Sixth, Tenth, and Fourteenth Wards—must have encouraged him. According to the *Herald*, the constituency had "more of the active element of young America in it than any other, and, necessarily, Kerrigan is the leader and chief." Sure enough, Kerrigan pulled off the upset, one of several Mozart congressional victories that year.[4]

After the election, as the South began preparations for secession, New York swirled with rumors of conspiracy and intrigue. An attack by saboteurs on the Brooklyn Navy Yard was said to be imminent. Ships were said to be sailing from New York wharves laden with weapons and ammunition for the Confederacy. Given the city's overwhelming Democratic majority and close economic ties to the South, speculation that New York City might secede from the Republican North and join the Confederacy did not seem far-fetched. Kerrigan's advertisement in the *Herald* was thus especially provocative.[5]

Some New Yorkers did not take Kerrigan's announcement seriously, calling it another of his self-aggrandizing attempts to attract public attention. The *Tribune* interpreted it as a political gesture designed to draw recruits to a new Democratic political organization that would be independent of both Tammany and Mozart Halls. Nonetheless, rumors persisted throughout the winter of 1860–61 that Kerrigan's followers would join the Confederate ranks or attack the Navy Yard. He was even called before a grand jury to explain his intentions. After South Carolinians launched the attack on Fort Sumter in April 1861, northern opinion—even in New York—swung decisively against the South. If he had ever seriously entertained thoughts of fighting for the Confederacy, Kerrigan now abandoned them, and began seeking a command in the Union ranks. Although he lacked West Point training, he was able to parlay his political clout and his experience in Mexico and Nicaragua into a colonel's commission in May 1861. In early July, his unit of 777 soldiers, designated the Twenty-fifth Regiment of New York Infantry, left the city to join the forces defending Washington.[6]

As long as it remained under Kerrigan's command, the Twenty-fifth never fully reconciled itself to war with the South. When the troops assigned to the defense of the capital marched in review for Lincoln and General George B. McClellan on August 26, 1861, Kerrigan's unit refused to give a cheer for the president and the Union. A soldier from another command explained the regiment's attitude to the English journalist William H. Russell, telling him that "the boy who commands that pretty lot recruited them for the Seceshes in New York, but finding he could not get them away he handed them over to Uncle Sam." The unit's lack of enthusiasm for the war effort also manifested itself in the recruits' appearance. Russell described Kerrigan's soldiers as "miserable scarecrows in rags and tatters."[7]

Despite warnings that such embarrassing displays would not be tolerated in the future, Kerrigan and his men continued to treat their superiors with disdain while stationed in Arlington, Virginia. When Kerrigan's commanding officer, Brigadier General John H. Martindale, came to review the regiment in mid-October, he found the soldiers untrained, unkempt, and uncooperative. Martindale upbraided Kerrigan, but the colonel refused to listen and stomped away. He ignored a subsequent order to return for an additional inspection the next day, so Martindale had the Bowery Boy arrested. The charges against him included "habitual neglect of duty" for failing to train his men; "conduct to the prejudice of good order and military discipline" for allowing the soldiers to "engage in loud and unseemly disputes and brawls," to appear at inspection "in a dirty and slovenly condition, with their pants partially unbuttoned in front," and to keep their weapons and gear "in great filth and disorder"; leaving the inspection without permission; disobeying the order to return for the subsequent inspection; leaving camp at night without permission of his superior officer; "drunkenness on duty"; and "communicating with the enemy" while drinking at a roadhouse called Bailey's Cross Roads.

Kerrigan admitted leaving his post without permission but pleaded not guilty to the other charges. He also spared no expense in assembling a defense team, hiring Senator Reverdy Johnson of Maryland, a former U.S. Attorney General, as his counsel. Johnson convinced the court-martial tribunal to acquit his client of the final two charges, but it found him guilty of the others. Kerrigan could have been sentenced to a long prison term, but was instead merely mustered out of the army on February 21, 1862. He remained in Washington to complete his term in the House of Representatives, but as the *Herald* had predicted, the style of politics practiced in the Capitol did not suit Kerrigan's talents. He was arrested on the House floor when he repeatedly tried, after the time for debate had ended, to speak against a bill that would fund the abolition of slavery in Missouri. He never held elective office again.[8]

After the war, Kerrigan found other outlets for what the *Times* described as his "dare-devil" impulses. When word reached New York in June 1866 that several hundred Irish freedom fighters known as the Fenians had attacked Canada as revenge for the continuing British occupation of Ireland, "General" Kerrigan announced that he would raise a brigade of five thousand soldiers to assist in the assault. By this point, however, the invasion had been repulsed, and Kerrigan never made it to Canada.[9]

Kerrigan could not have been deeply involved with the Fenians before their attack on Canada, otherwise he would have been with them at the border, rather than in New York City, when they crossed into Ontario and Québec. But in 1867 Kerrigan did become a central figure in an even more daring Fenian military operation: an attempt to invade Ireland itself to spark an uprising against the British. On April 13, the *Jacmel Packet* left New York Harbor carrying "Brigadier General Kerrigan" and his force of thirty-eight Irish freedom fighters. Once at sea, they patriotically rechristened the vessel *Erin's Hope*. Despite the small size of its invasion force, the group believed it could succeed because the ship's arrival in Sligo Harbor would coincide with an uprising by indigenous revolutionaries, who could make use of the five hundred rifles the Americans brought with them. On the evening of May 23, the crew sighted the Sligo coastline, but remained safely in the bay while awaiting the sign to attack.

The signal never came. Apparently fearing that informants would compromise their plans, the Sligo Fenians had launched their uprising two months early, before Kerrigan and his men had even left New York. The revolt was a dismal failure, as the British quickly rounded up and imprisoned the leaders. At their contact's suggestion, the Americans sailed southward, hoping to return when their Irish allies had regrouped. But the ship soon began running low on supplies. Some on board insisted that they had come too far not to strike a blow at the British, even a futile one. A majority, however, demanded they set sail back to New York. A couple of daring souls did go ashore in Sligo with their cache of weapons, but authorities quickly arrested them. Kerrigan returned with the bulk of the force to New York.[10]

Given Kerrigan's Irish roots, one would imagine that he had risked his life on the *Erin's Hope* out of dedication to the Irish cause. But he seemed willing to take adventure wherever he could find it. In 1870, the lifelong Democrat served as a mercenary of sorts for the South Carolina Republican party. Looking for a way to counterbalance the terror tactics of the Ku Klux Klan that prevented both black and white Republicans from voting, South Carolina's Republican governor, Robert K. Scott, brought in Kerrigan and a band of his New York rowdies to fight back. After all, no one was more experienced than Kerrigan in the use of violence and intimidation at the polls. Whether or not Kerrigan actually came to blows with the Klan during his months in South Carolina is not known.[11]

How Kerrigan supported himself in these years is a mystery. He probably filled his days with the usual sporting men's pursuits, but he was no longer a significant player in city politics. Always the adventurer, he observed many battles during the Franco-Prussian War and toured Turkey in the mid-1880s as well. Later, he moved to Brooklyn. Even in his seventies, Kerrigan could not resist an exciting opportunity, traveling with another old-time Five Pointer to the Yukon Territory "as representative of a syndicate." Kerrigan fell ill during the trip and had to have surgery upon his return. Tough to the end, he supposedly "refused to take an anaesthetic and never uttered a moan while the surgeons were at work." He died a few weeks later, on November 1, 1899.[12]

CHAPTER TEN

The Civil War and the End of an Era

"No Coercion, No Civil War"

It is impossible to precisely gauge Five Pointers' views of slavery. Except for the occasional reference to the issue by a Sixth Ward candidate for political office, we have no means of judging how the average neighborhood resident perceived the "peculiar institution," except to suggest that Five Pointers' views on the subject probably mirrored those of the city's Irish, Catholic, and Democratic press. These papers consistently argued that both abolitionism and the more moderate movement to prevent the creation of additional slave territory threatened the survival of the nation. "We are totally opposed to Abolitionism in every shape;—not because we desire to perpetuate slavery, but to preserve the Union," announced the *Irish-American* in 1853. "That slavery is inconsistent with the Declaration of Independence and our Republican Constitution we will not affect to deny," its editors admitted four years later. But they argued that Americans had been "forced to accept the 'Institution' of slavery" as part of the compromises that created the nation, and that those pledges could not subsequently be broken.

Many New York Democrats insisted that slavery was beneficial to blacks and whites alike. The *Day Book*, a Democratic paper aligned with Mayor Fernando Wood, asserted that "'slavery,' or negro subordination to the will and guidance of the superior white man, is a law of nature, a fixed truth, an eternal necessity, an ordinance of the Almighty, in conflict with which the efforts of human power sink into absolute and unspeakable insignificance." Free blacks such as those in New York had been better off as slaves, maintained the newspaper's editors, because now they were still subordinate to whites but were not guaranteed the subsistence of food, clothing, and shelter that slaveowners provided.[13]

Catholic newspapers usually expressed their opposition to the anti-slavery movement in somewhat less repugnant ways. "None of us, North or South, pretend to think Slavery a blessing," contended the *New York Freeman's Journal*, a Catholic weekly edited by a non-Irishman but perceived in the antebellum years to be the organ of Archbishop John Hughes. "Its warmest defenders, if they are rational, say no more for it than that it is unavoidable in the nature of things; all would be rejoiced to see it abolished to-morrow, *if it could be done safely, or consistently with a due regard for the rights and interests of all classes.*" However, the *Journal* insisted that abolishing slavery would never be safe. To those who argued that good Christians must oppose slavery, the *Journal* retorted that not a single Catholic bishop in the United States had endorsed the abolition movement. Though nominally a non-partisan periodical, the *Journal* endorsed the Democratic opposition to Republican Abraham Lincoln in the 1860 presidential race. "The Democratic doctrine is not that there is no moral right or wrong about slavery, but that it is not the business of the political power to settle moral questions," the *Journal* noted approvingly, adding that only when a majority of Americans North and South could be brought by "moral suasion" to oppose slavery would it be appropriate for politicians to interfere with the institution.[14]

Irish Americans frequently justified their opposition to abolitionism on the grounds that it would hurt the movement to liberate Ireland. Daniel O'Connell, who fought to repeal the Act of Union that had bound Ireland politically to the United Kingdom, spoke out against American slavery in the early 1840s. "The black spot of slavery rests upon your star spangled banner," O'Connell wrote, "and no matter what glory you may acquire beneath it, the hideous, damning stain of Slavery remains upon you; and a just Providence will sooner or later, avenge itself for your crime." After O'Connell's repeal movement fizzled, many Irishmen cited his diversion into abolitionism as the cause. The *Irish-American* claimed that his statements on slavery "WERE THE FIRST—THE VERY FIRST—CAUSES OF THE DIVISIONS" which fractured the repeal forces. "American sympathy

Thomas Nast's "This Is a White Man's Government" perfectly captures the image most Americans had of Five Pointers. Nast, who supported Republican Ulysses S. Grant for the presidency in 1868, depicts what he believes to be the three main sources of support for Grant's Democratic rival. On the right is August Belmont, representing the greed of Fifth Avenue financiers and other unscrupulous capitalists. In the center is Nathan Bedford Forrest, a leading Confederate cavalry officer during the Civil War and self-proclaimed founder of the Ku Klux Klan afterward. On the left is a Five Points Irishman drawn with simian features. The burning building just behind the Five Pointer is the New York Colored Orphan Asylum, burned by the predominantly Irish-American rioters during the 1863 New York Draft Riots. *Harper's Weekly* (September 5, 1868): 568. Collection of the Library of Congress.

was a 'mighty fact' before then," but subsequently, "division, disunion, distrust, contention, [and] personal bitterness" doomed the repeal movement to failure. Besides, argued many Irish Americans, the Irish were as much slaves to the English as African Americans were to their masters in the South. Abolitionists ought to focus their attention on the 6 million white slaves in Ireland, insisted the *Irish-American*, before interceding on behalf of the 3 million black slaves in the United States.[15]

Irish Catholics also frequently alluded to abolitionists' prejudice against them to justify their refusal to endorse the anti-slavery movement. "Irishmen have no [more] bitter enemies, Catholics no fiercer foes, than are nine-tenths of the American Abolitionists," insisted the *Freeman's Journal* in 1843. "Dark, sullen, ferocious bigots as they are, they abhor the name of Ireland and Catholicity." In the mid-1850s, when the Know Nothing party scored major electoral victories in the Northeast where abolitionism was strongest, the *Irish-American* asked why "the citizens of New England, who spend their money, their time, their talents, in endeavoring to make the negro free, are so opposed to the 'foreigner'?"[16]

One factor that the antebellum Irish never mentioned when explaining their opposition to abolitionism was economic competition from African Americans. It is a staple of writing on the Irish that their opposition to the anti-slavery movement was based on a fear that freed slaves would take their jobs or drive down their already low wages. Yet not a single New York Irish or Catholic periodical surveyed for this study mentioned such a fear. Given the strict segregation of African Americans in the New York antebellum workplace, it really was not an issue. Five Points African Americans worked primarily as chimney sweeps, sailors, waiters, or street peddlers. Even in this last field, the only one populated by significant numbers of antebellum Irishmen, African Americans typically traded items such as buttermilk that whites did not usually sell.

The extent to which Five Pointers discussed the slavery issue is impossible to determine. By the late 1850s, Congress and the entire Democratic party were divided over the issue of slavery in Kansas, with the Buchanan administration supporting the "Lecompton constitution" that would allow slavery there, while another faction led by Illinois senator Stephen A. Douglas opposed it. The *Irish-American* admitted in early 1858 that Kansas, Douglas, and Lecompton "engage thought, talk, and writing, North and South. . . . Few sounds are uttered without these all-absorbing names being heard." This was undoubtedly the case even in the Sixth Ward, because whether one supported Buchanan or Douglas on this question determined party nominations and even many patronage appointments. Five Points politico John Clancy could often be found at the Sixth Ward's Ivy Green saloon regaling patrons with his enthusiasm for the "little giant" from Illinois.[17]

As the 1860 presidential election approached, sectional issues continued to loom large in Five Points political discussions. The attack on Massachusetts senator Charles Sumner by South Carolinian Preston Brooks in 1856, the *Dred Scott* decision of 1857, and Buchanan administration support for slavery in Kansas in 1858 all helped convinced most northerners to support Lincoln and the Republican party in 1860. Yet Five Pointers cast few votes for the rail-splitter from Illinois. Despite his visit to Five Points earlier in the year, Lincoln captured just 12 percent of the Sixth Ward vote in 1860, and an even smaller proportion of the ballots cast in the Five Points election districts.[18]

Five Pointers were deeply ambivalent as southern states began preparing to secede after Lincoln's victory. Most of the neighborhood's Irish-American residents probably opposed the breakup of the Union, yet Five Pointers were very reluctant to go to war to stop it. The *Irish-American*'s editors, for example, did "not believe that this Confederation can be held together by armed force. Even if it could be, it would not be worth the trouble." Clancy, still in control of the *Leader*, echoed a similar theme, recommending "no coercion, no civil war." After the attack on Fort Sumter, when most New Yorkers felt it their patriotic duty to defend the Stars and Stripes, neighborhood residents were distinctly unenthusiastic. When the New York state assembly voted to approve the enlistment of thirty thousand New York volunteers to defend Washington and resist southern aggression, only 6 of the 108 assemblymen opposed the measure. One of the six was Five Points' representative, William Walsh.[19]

The secession winter and first months of the war played havoc with the New York economy. Business ground nearly to a halt as anxious merchants and manufacturers cut back on orders and production. The *Herald* described the suffering of the unemployed poor as "unprecedented." "Thousands of persons, both male and female, were suddenly deprived of employment," concurred the New York Association for Improving the Condition of the Poor. Sectors of the economy that had once traded heavily with the South (such as the garment industry) were especially hard hit. The war also crippled the relief work of local charities. "Our wardrobes are empty," complained the journal of the Five Points Mission in August 1861. Donations of new and used clothing plummeted as northerners instead hoarded garments or directed their castoffs to organizations assisting veterans and their families.[20]

By the second half of 1861, employment began to pick up, especially after the Confederate victory at the first battle of Bull Run in July convinced northerners that the war would not be a short one. But by 1862, prices skyrocketed while wages for the poor remained relatively stagnant. The retail price of tobacco and whiskey tripled. Food prices also jumped. Tenement rents fell, however, as the precipitous decline in immigration combined with the departure of so many for the battlefields reduced demand.[21]

It is impossible to determine precisely how many Five Pointers enrolled in the military during the first years of the war. Enlistment records do not record the recruits' street addresses, and few residents had names unique enough to make their identification possible among the thousands of New York soldiers. Subsequent reports that elections in the Sixth Ward were quiet because those usually engaged in "tipping over ticket boxes . . . are now off to the war" indicate that some of the more rowdy Five Pointers must have enlisted. By the middle of the war, recruitment bonuses became quite substantial, in some cases equaling what a Five Points laborer might earn in six months or more. Irish pride also probably drew some into the army. The all-Irish Sixty-ninth New York Regiment overflowed with volunteers when famed Irish patriot Michael Corcoran became its commander. One, thirty-year-old Johnny Stacom, was an Ivy Green bartender and aspiring politician allied with Brennan and Clancy. He enlisted after the bombardment of Sumter. On April 23, 1861, after receiving a blessing from Archbishop Hughes at St. Patrick's Cathedral on Mott Street, the unit marched proudly to the ferries that conveyed the soldiers on the first leg of their journey to Washington. Thirty-eight members of the regiment were killed at Bull Run. Having completed their three-month tour of duty, the Sixty-ninth returned to New York for a heroes' welcome. Some members reenlisted in a new "Irish Brigade." Others had had enough of army life. Stacom waited until 1864 before volunteering for another three-month stint in the Irish unit, spending his entire uneventful ninety days besieging Lee's forces at Petersburg, Virginia.[22]

"I AM AS GOOD A DEMOCRAT AS YOU ARE"

During the war years, an era in New York politics would come to an end. The violence of sporting men and Five Points brawlers would be overshadowed by a new electoral tool: corruption. In the meantime, the war had dramatic effects on several key individuals. After completing his term as county clerk at the beginning of 1862, Clancy secured an appointment as "Volunteer Aid" to General Francis B. Spinola. Clancy's main contributions to the war effort came not in this largely ceremonial post, however, but in keeping Tammany from adopting an anti-war stance. Prominent Democrats such as Wood, Isaiah Rynders, and Governor Horatio Seymour publicly advocated compromise with the South, and even pragmatists like Tweed were tempted to adopt such a platform for the sake of Democratic unity. But Clancy insisted through the *Leader* that Tammany nominate only candidates who fully supported preserving the Union without capitulating to southern demands for the spread of slavery. By 1864, even Republican journals such as the *Tribune* commended Clancy for almost single-handedly preventing Tammany from adopting a pro-peace policy that would have seriously impeded the prosecution of the war.[23]

With Clancy no longer in municipal office, Sixth Warders once again lacked a representative in citywide government. Brennan, seen at the outset of the war as one of the most prominent city Democrats, was rarely mentioned in discussions of the most powerful Tammany leaders by 1862. All that changed, however, with the unexpected announcement on November 20 that Democrats had nominated Brennan for the highest office on that year's municipal election slate—that of city comptroller. This post was far more important than the relatively insignificant and invisible office of city register he had sought unsuccessfully two years earlier. The *Leader* had called the comptrollership "the most powerful office in the State next to that of Governor—locally and in point of patronage far greater" because of the many "subordinate departments, bureaux, clerkships, and offices of every description" that the incumbent could distribute to party members and factional allies. The huge municipal expenditures associated with the war made the comptrollership especially consequential.

Journalists handicapping the race for the Democratic nomination never considered Brennan, not even as a long shot. Yet factionalism both within Tammany and between it and Mozart Hall created a deadlock. All sides could accept Brennan, though, because he was not too closely linked to any clique and was not perceived as a threat to the future ambitions of the various factional leaders. According to the *Times*, even Brennan himself must have been surprised when Democratic leaders announced his nomination.[24]

With Democrats united behind a single slate of candidates for the first time since 1858, Brennan stood little chance of defeat. Yet the influential *Herald*—which generally supported Democratic candidates—endorsed Brennan's Republican opponent instead, stating that "we do not believe that Brennan is at all qualified for the office, or fitted for so important a position." A significant number of Democratic voters apparently found such arguments persuasive, but Brennan still won a large majority of the popular vote on election day, capturing 60 percent citywide and an unprecedented 95 percent in the Sixth Ward.[25]

When Brennan began his four-year term in January 1863, Five Pointers had achieved political power almost unimaginable a generation earlier. With Republican George Opdyke serving as mayor, Brennan was now the city's highest-ranking Democratic officeholder. Furthermore, when the two chambers of the city's legislative branch organized that same month, both elected Five Pointers to preside over their proceedings. Former "Dead Rabbit" William Walsh, just twenty-six years old, became president of the board of aldermen, while the councilmen chose Morgan Jones as their president. Jones, a thirty-three-year-old London native, had emigrated to New York as a small child and became a Centre Street plumber and active Democrat as an early member of Matthew T. Brennan Hose Company No. 60. Jones's links to Brennan undoubtedly helped him earn his prewar sinecure as "corporation plumber." Jones had served twice previously as council president before regaining the honor in 1863. Clancy, meanwhile, continued to use his control of the *Leader* and his status as a Tammany chieftain to influence Democratic policy throughout the city and state.[26]

Other Five Points politicos increased their influence in the war years as well, none more so than Brennan lieutenants Joseph Dowling and John Jourdan. When Brennan became comptroller, Dowling was appointed to complete his mentor's term as police justice, and Jourdan succeeded his best friend Dowling as Sixth Ward police captain. Jourdan by this point had already gained citywide fame as a detective, so much so that wealthy New

Yorkers regularly sent for him when uptown officers failed to recover their stolen property. Refusing to let anything stand in the way of their crime solving, Dowling and Jourdan (with the connivance of the District Attorney's Office) established in these years what the *Times* later called "'The Police Ring,' which held a reign of terror over all the criminals. . . . Their power was almost absolute, and instances are known where men arrested secretly at night by Jourdan and his detectives were locked up in the dark cells of the Franklin Street Station for weeks and absolutely starved into confessing their crimes and disgorging their plunder." Despite these excesses, Dowling ran unopposed for police justice in 1863 when his temporary appointment expired. Even the Republican *Times* lauded the Democrat Dowling, praising "his integrity of character, his fine capacities and a personal popularity seldom attached to any man." By mid-war, Dowling and Jourdan were nearly as well known to New Yorkers as Brennan and Clancy.[27]

Yet Five Points' ascent in New York politics came at a time when interest in local politics was waning. Residents who had once followed the factional infighting of New York politicos with intense interest now "generally seemed to regard their movements as of very little consequence," remarked the *Herald*. It was the war, of course, that had come to monopolize New Yorkers' attention. As the bloody conflict dragged on and the death toll mounted, Five Pointers—like most Manhattanites—became increasingly ambivalent about the struggle. This was especially the case after Lincoln announced in September 1862 his plan to promulgate the Emancipation Proclamation at the start of the new year. Many Democrats saw the proclamation as proof of what they had suspected all along—that the war was really being fought to end slavery. New York Catholics "will turn away in disgust," predicted Archbishop Hughes, if forced to fight for emancipation.[28]

After Lincoln's emancipation plans became public, Irish-American New Yorkers became more openly disdainful of the war effort. At a meeting of anti-war Democrats in April 1863, one Irish Catholic judge, John H. McCunn, complained about expending millions of dollars in a war against slavery. According to a newspaper that paraphrased his speech, "he had seen the negro at the mouth of the Congo River, and the Slavery of the South was a paradise in comparison. The negro was a prince in the South compared to his situation at home." Although the *Irish-American* and

Leader never criticized the proclamation, Clancy's journal called all interaction with African Americans "repulsive to the white man's instincts,"
and the *Irish-American* often referred to the Republicans pejoratively as
the "Abolition party" and "Abolition fanatics."[29]

Emancipation also raised the specter that ex-slaves might one day
come north and compete with the Irish for the lowest-paying jobs in the
city. Irish Americans feared that the freedmen, accustomed to working for
nothing, would accept ridiculously low pay and thus drive down the wages
of Irish menial laborers. But again, historians have overestimated economic fears as a source of Irish/black tension. For generations it has been a
staple of writing on Civil War New York that in early 1863, employers
replaced hundreds of striking Irish longshoremen with African-American
scabs, fueling Irish animosity toward emancipation. The historian Edward
K. Spann described three thousand strikers in June being "forced to watch
as black men, under police protection, took their jobs on the docks." In
fact, white army deserters and convalescents, not black scabs, loaded the
ships under police guard. A racially charged clash did take place in April,
but there were only two to three hundred strikers, and they too were not
replaced by a phalanx of black workers. The wildcat strikers, frustrated
that their demand for higher pay had not been met despite the wartime
shortage of workers, merely wandered the riverfront looking to vent their
frustration on the tiny handful of black dockworkers *already* employed
citywide. Blacks might pose a long-term threat to the job security of Irish
Americans, but the wholesale replacement of Irish-American workers by
African Americans during the war simply never took place.[30]

Most Irish criticism of emancipation focused on the racial interaction
it would necessitate. The *Day Book* opposed the use of African Americans
in the Union armies, for example, because "equality as soldiers means
equality at the ballot-box, equality everywhere," which would result in the
Irish being "degraded to a level with negroes." When in late June an Irish-
American mob in Newburgh, New York, lynched an African American
accused of assaulting an Irishwoman, the *Irish-American* blamed Republicans, whose emancipation policy had "sedulously placed the negro, with
all his drawbacks of character and condition, in opposition to the white
man." Republicans, complained the *Irish-American*, had "thrust the negro
again in their [whites'] faces," even though whites were already "smarting
under the reverses" brought about by the war.[31]

These tensions manifested themselves with deadly results during the 1862 political campaign. Locked in a close battle for reelection, First Ward alderman Henry Smith (a pro-war Democrat also endorsed by the Republicans) hired Five Points ropemaker Denis P. Sullivan to post handbills promoting his candidacy. With 2,500 bills to post, the thirty-three-year-old Sullivan rounded up some Five Points friends to assist him, and the nine men headed downtown with a ladder and two pails of paste on the evening of November 28. Pleased at having completed their work, the boisterous young men were heading home across Greenwich Street at 2:00 a.m. when Sullivan was approached by a gang led by First Ward politico "Big Tom" Byrnes, father-in-law of Smith's opponent, anti-war Democrat John Fox. When Byrnes and his friends learned that Sullivan was posting bills for Smith, they upbraided and threatened him. "You are working for a nigger and you are a nigger yourself," one of them shouted at Sullivan, adding that "the man you are working for hires nothing but niggers on the dock." Sullivan responded, according to his subsequent testimony, that "I am no nigger—I am as good a Democrat as you are." The former policeman flashed a pistol inside his coat, saying he would not use it if attacked by one man but would if set upon by the entire gang. Undaunted, Byrnes and his mates rushed Sullivan, vowing to "shove the pistol——." When they threw Sullivan to the ground and struggled for his weapon, Sullivan shot Byrnes dead. The policemen who witnessed the entire quarrel (but apparently feared to intervene) immediately arrested Sullivan for murder.

News of Byrnes's killing caused a sensation, especially in Democratic circles. Friends of both the accused and the victim immediately attempted to shape the public perception of the case. Just hours after the incident, Sullivan's companions wrote a letter to the *Herald* insisting that their friend had acted in self-defense. Councilman John Hogan replied the following day that Sullivan's comrades could not be trusted, as they were all "residents of that well-known locality, the Five Points," who had gone to the First Ward "with the intention of provoking a quarrel with the friends of Mr. Fox." At his February 1863 trial, Sullivan appeared with what the *Times* called "an able array of counsel" retained by Alderman Smith, who in the intervening weeks had won reelection. To the prosecution's implication that Sullivan would not have carried a pistol had he not intended to pick a fight, Sullivan's attorney retorted that the defendant armed himself that night because it "was a well known, though a lamentable fact, that any man who had the temerity to post Republican bills in the First Ward did so at the peril of his life." Given that Sullivan was lying on the ground surrounded by Byrnes and his men when he fired the fatal shot, the jury reasoned that Sullivan had indeed acted in self-defense and found him not guilty.[32]

"FOR MANY YEARS THIS LOCALITY HAS BEEN A MODEL OF GOOD ORDER"

The racial and political pressures that had been building up in New York during the first two years of the war exploded in the spring of 1863, when Congress instituted a draft to supplement dwindling voluntary enrollments. Now Five Pointers who disdained the war might be dragged into it against their will. New York's Irish Americans were especially angry when the Lincoln administration announced that some non-citizens—those who had declared their intention to become citizens or had voted in an American election—would be eligible for the draft. Many also complained about the conscription clause that allowed a draftee to pay $300 in lieu of enrolling. Low-income New Yorkers such as those from Five Points believed, according to the *Herald*, that "the draft was an unfair one, inasmuch as the rich could avoid it by paying $300, while the poor man, who was without 'the greenbacks,' was compelled to go to the war."[33]

When federal officials began choosing the first draftees in mid-July, New Yorkers responded with the bloodiest week in their entire history. The predominantly Irish-American mobs lynched a dozen or more African Americans and terrorized thousands. Hundreds of fires were set. Rioters fought pitched battles with the police and the militia for control of uptown avenues. The homes and businesses of prominent Republicans were looted and ransacked. Symbols of federal power in the city also drew the wrath of the enraged populace in what the *Irish-American* called "a saturnalia of pillage and violence."[34]

New Yorkers assumed that Five Pointers must have played a major role in the Draft Riots' carnage. A few months after the unrest, when Republican leader Charles Spencer announced the November election results at his party's city headquarters, he described the Sixth Ward as one populated by that "class of individuals who would like to murder, steal, and burn *ad libitum*," an obvious reference to the Draft Riots. Many modern writers have made the same assumption. According to Luc Sante, "the core of the participants unquestionably came from the Five Points."[35]

The two most scholarly studies of the riots, in contrast, do not mention a single act of violence occurring in the Sixth Ward, and found few acts of violence uptown that can be traced to Five Pointers. Contemporaries agreed. Clancy seized upon the apparent lack of bloodshed in Five Points to remind New Yorkers that the neighborhood no longer lived up to its violent, dangerous reputation. "While nearly every portion of the city has been the scene of tumultuous outbreak," asserted Clancy, "the Sixth Ward has maintained its usual uninterrupted quiet. For many years this locality has been a model of good order, and its citizens have much cause for congratulation on having passed through the fearful scenes of the week without a single evidence of excitement. . . . Let us hear no more the libelous epithet 'Bloody Sixth.'"[36]

The truth, it turns out, lies somewhere in between the overwrought charges of Sante and the equally exaggerated claims of innocence propounded by Clancy. Of the hundreds of rioters arrested, primarily in uptown wards where the rioting was most fierce, only two of those whose residence could be established lived in Five Points. Instead, most of those indicted lived, as one might expect, in the northern neighborhoods where the disorder was concentrated.[37]

Nonetheless, Clancy's claim that the Sixth Ward witnessed not "a single act of disorder" is also patently false. Although the bloodshed and destruction in Five Points were relatively mild compared to the mass murder and wholesale devastation found uptown, the rioting there was terrible nonetheless and terrorized the neighborhood's African-American residents. The unrest began in Five Points on Monday, July 13, the first day of violence citywide. That afternoon, police discovered that "the negro shanties in Baxter Street were being fired" and that the nearby tenement and meetinghouse at 42 Baxter belonging to the New York African Society for Mutual Relief were also under attack. Captain Jourdan and his men "were soon at the spot, and after a severe fight, in which the force was boldly opposed, the rioters were dispersed, many of them badly injured." A mob also descended upon "the saloon of Mr. Crook on Chatham St." to attack the black waiters he employed, but the prompt arrival of police prevented any significant injuries there. Around five-thirty, more anti-black violence erupted, this time in the northeast corner of the neighborhood.

According to one account, "some three hundred men, women, and boys attacked the dwellings of colored people in Pell, near Mott Street." One of the African-American residents, fifty-seven-year-old Elizabeth Hennesy, was severely injured when hit by a flying brick. Meanwhile, at about six o'clock, "upwards of six hundred rioters" near the corner of Leonard and Baxter Streets "attacked a house . . . occupied by some twenty colored families, stoning in the windows, [and] attempting to break in and fire it." When police arrived, "a severe fight ensued; the rioters were effectively handled, and dozens lay senseless on the street; ultimately they fled."

The violence continued into the evening. Around 8:00 p.m., "a mob of six hundred" terrorized 104 and 105 Park Street, African-American boardinghouses located near the corner of Mott. In order to disperse them, the police "made a charge; had to fight hand-to-hand, [and] using locusts [billy clubs] effectively, beat and scattered the rioters." The final melee that night was "a riot in . . . a locality known as Cow Bay," where for thirty years the largest concentration of African Americans in the neighborhood had lived. Police again successfully scattered a crowd menacing the three-story tenements there. Rumors that the rioters torched the nearby Five Points Mission—repeated to this day—were totally unfounded.

The bloodshed subsided considerably in the Sixth Ward on the following day, though sporadic attacks on Five Points African Americans continued. That morning, a mob gathered on Leonard Street "assaulting and beating colored people." The police rescued six African Americans from the rabid throng "and brought them in safety to the station." On Wednesday morning, police again had to disperse "a mob in Centre, near Worth Street, who were assailing every colored person they met." In the evening, rioters returned again to the block just north of the Five Points intersection, where "there were many demonstrations against the dwellings [at] Nos. 38 and 40 Baxter Street, occupied by colored people." Police once more managed to subdue the mob, "sometimes with and sometimes without a battle." This was apparently the last of the violence, though it raged on uptown for three more days.[38]

The draft rioting in Five Points resulted in the almost complete abandonment of the district by New York African Americans. The neighborhood's black population—once numbering well over one thousand—had declined dramatically and steadily ever since the race riot there nearly thirty years earlier, so that by the eve of the Civil War fewer than five hun-

dred African Americans were left, even though the ward's overall population had doubled. All but a handful of these now decided to leave. Under a
headline proclaiming the "Exodus of Blacks from the Five Points," the
Herald reported on Thursday, the seventeenth, that "the fear which has
seized the colored population in nearly every part of the city has extended
to the blacks of the Sixth ward." Three days of violence aimed against
them convinced Five Pointers of color that "their only safety is in flight."
As a result, "there seems to have been a general exodus of Africans from
the Five Points, and the whites are in possession of the whole field." Some
eventually returned. The 1870 census records 132 "colored" Five Points
residents, mostly sailors whose ties to the community were tenuous.
African Americans from all parts of the city fled to Long Island and other
safe havens during the riots, and most of the Five Pointers among them
decided never to move back.[39]

After a one-month delay caused by the riots, the draft for the Sixth
Ward finally took place on August 25. Of the 161 Five Pointers drafted, 59
were exempted from service. They received their exemptions either
because they were not American citizens, too old or young, physically
unfit, no longer lived in the congressional district, or the sole supporters of
widowed mothers or other dependents. Eleven of the 161 draftees hired
substitutes, an option available only to the neighborhood's more prosperous residents. Two of the eleven, Caspar Grote and Herman Schilling, were
successful Baxter Street grocers. Another, James Nealis, was a scion of one
of the ward's most powerful families. His father and uncle had at various
times served as ward policemen, operated a Mulberry Street grocery, and
actively participated in ward politics. James himself had spent three years
in college "out West" and was one of the men posting bills with Denis
Sullivan the night he shot "Big Tom" Byrnes. Two of the other drafted Five
Pointers avoided service by paying the $300 commutation fee.[40]

The most popular way to avoid military service, however, was simply
not to show up at the enrollment office after one's name was called. Fully
88 of the 161 Five Points draftees "failed to report." Draft dodgers could be
arrested, but the understaffed provost marshals did not have the means to
track down many evaders. Only a handful of the Five Pointers who failed
to report for duty were subsequently arrested; all proved themselves
exempt from duty and were released.

In the end, then, only a single Five Points resident was compelled to go to war as a result of the draft. This lone conscript was Hugh Boyle, a twenty-seven-year-old laborer who lived at 24 Mott Street. The blue-eyed, brown-haired Boyle put off enlistment as long as possible after the August 1863 conscription; but in December 1864, he finally claimed his $100 bounty and was mustered in for three years' duty with the Eighteenth New York Cavalry Regiment. Boyle joined his unit at Gainnie Landing, Louisiana, in January 1865. Five months later, when the war was over but his regiment was preparing to leave for Texas to serve as part of the Union occupation force there, Boyle deserted, absconding with his Remington revolver and a holster.[41]

"So lately nothing but a Ward politician"

One reason that New York's Irish Americans reacted so violently to the prospect of a draft was that they were increasingly distrustful of the Tammany leaders who claimed to represent them. When independent Democrat C. Godfrey Gunther defeated the Tammany candidate, Francis I. Boole, in the mayoral contest of 1863, it exposed the organization's continuing woes. The *Irish-American* explained Gunther's victory by observing that "the people, who, for a long while, have not been content with the manner in which the political 'machines' have been run for the exclusive profit of a score or two of political dictators, *voted* for the only candidate who appeared to be running without any machinery at all, and elected him." Brennan, the top Tammany officeholder, was now perceived as one of those "dictators."[42]

Those maligning Tammany increasingly singled out Brennan for condemnation. The most vitriolic attacks came not from Republicans but from the *Irish-American*. Throwing aside ethnic pride, the journal condemned "the ruling clique of Tammany—which is as much to say, Comptroller Brennan and Peter B. Sweeny," for nominating for sheriff another Irish American, the Fourteenth Ward's John Kelly, "without making even a pretence of consulting the wishes of the people. . . . Comptroller Brennan aspires to *command* the city Democracy; armed with the immense patronage of his position, he rules in Tammany Hall and dictates the course of that organization and the men to whom its support is to be given." Tammany, insisted the *Irish-American*, was an "organization which he thus practically *owns*. . . . The question to be decided in this nomination is whether the people are to have any voice in the management of their own affairs, or whether Comptroller Brennan is to be henceforth the autocrat of the city Democracy, dictating the candidates, and dividing, in undisturbed sovereignty, the spoils amongst his followers."[43]

Brennan should have expected, and undoubtedly could withstand, such complaints. One faction or another was always griping about the distribution of the patronage, and the *Irish-American*'s charge that Brennan "has been using Tammany Hall . . . for his own aggrandizement and the advancement of his own family" was a staple of campaign rhetoric. What may have embarrassed or insulted him, though, was the newspaper's assertion that Brennan's ascent through Tammany reflected the utter debasement of a once proud and distinguished organization:

> It is but a very few years since Matthew T. Brennan was simply Captain in the Sixth Ward Police—a very respectable office, but one not sought for by politicians with lofty aspirations. Mr. Brennan was looked upon as an efficient officer, and his fellow Democrats, believing him to be devoted to their own principles, deemed it but right to give him a further step; and he was, accordingly, made Police Justice. During the years in which Mr. Brennan was passing through these minor offices, the character of Tammany Hall underwent a complete revolution. [Soon it was run by] a clique of venal, selfish political charlatans [who] maintained themselves there by fraud and trickery. . . . Under such a parvenue regime, it was not surprising that Matthew T. Brennan,—so lately nothing but a Ward politician, glad to accept the small crumbs of local patronage distribution dispensed from the public table,— should be able to procure for himself the nomination for the Comptrollership, the richest and most important office in the gift of the citizens of New York. Here, again, he was aided by his former reputation, circumscribed as it was . . . and his fellow-citizens, trusting to the general belief in his integrity and the soundness of his Democracy, elected him. That trust Matthew T. Brennan has in every way betrayed.[44]

Because the intra-Democratic truce that had brought about his nomination had collapsed by 1866, Brennan stood no chance of gaining renomination when his term expired at the end of that year. Yet with great fanfare, he disingenuously announced his refusal to run for reelection, complaining in a long, self-aggrandizing letter that he would not remain in office at a time when every public official was assumed to be corrupt. Although his renomination had been considered unlikely, Brennan had accrued enough power in Tammany by that point that the *Herald* characterized his decision not to fight to retain his post as an "earthquake" for the city's Democratic party.[45]

Brennan might have been better able to maintain his elevated position within the Democratic ranks had he still been able to rely on John Clancy to promote his interests. But Clancy had died suddenly on July 1, 1864, at age thirty-five. All agreed that Clancy's premature death was a tragedy. Just before his death, he had been elected a sachem of the Tammany Society, the most sought after office within the Democratic organization and an honor that reflected his ascent to the very pinnacle of power there. The *Herald*'s obituary called Clancy "one of the most influential democrats in the state." Even his political enemies sincerely mourned his death. "Under his management," commented the Republican *Times*, "the *Leader*, though thoroughly partisan in politics, became one of the most able, brilliant and readable weeklies ever published in this City."[46]

By this point, Sixth Ward primaries were no longer the wild and raucous affairs of Con Donoho's day. Tammany leaders now dictated the Democratic nominations, so that in most cases, as the Republican attorney and reformer William M. Ivins put it, "the primary is usually only a gathering of the clans to get a drink, and incidentally vote the ticket put into their hands." In unusual circumstances, however, the primary could revert to rough-and-tumble tactics. New York politico Matthew P. Breen recalled one such postwar primary after Brennan had become comptroller and had moved far uptown. Dowling believed that because Brennan no longer lived in the ward, he ought to cede him control of the district, while Brennan, who continued to maintain a residence on White Street inhabited by his mother, had no intention of giving up his authority. The quarrel reached a climax at the ward primary. "I don't believe there ever was another such primary held in the City of New York," recalled Breen years later. "That primary is worth a prominent place in history." The day before the contest was to be held, adherents of both factions took up positions on all the approaches to the polling place in order to intimidate the other side's voters and prevent them from reaching the ballot boxes; but because both sides were skilled in such tactics, "the line was made up alternately, or very nearly so, of Brennan and Dowling men." Despite various fights and arrests for assault and battery, the opposing forces remained in place all night and all the next day until the polls opened on the evening of the second day, with sandwiches and beer provided for each man at the expense of their leaders. On primary night, Brennan's ticket prevailed. But such primaries were the exception rather than the rule by the postbellum period.[47]

Election days in Five Points also became relatively tranquil. By the eve of the war, the ward's new, more peaceful attitude toward elections inspired comments in the press. "The 'Bloody Sixth,' yesterday, did nothing to justify its sanguinary cognomen and character," noted a surprised reporter from the *Times* in 1860. "The election dawned, and grew, and culminated in its precincts as calmly and gently as a Summer cloud. . . . The policemen stood around the polls like shepherds, and, to follow out the pastoral similie, flocks of voters sported and gamboled in their vicinity as inoffensively as lambs." Election-related violence did not disappear completely during the war years. But quarrels tended to be small-scale confrontations rather than the neighborhood-wide free-for-alls of the 1840s and '50s.[48]

Physical intimidation ceased to be a significant factor in Five Points voting primarily because politicians perfected another means—electoral fraud—to control the election results. By 1870, the Sixth Ward had become almost as famous for voter fraud as it had been in the prewar years for political violence.

"EVERY CONCEIVABLE FORM OF FRAUD WAS PRACTICED"

Charges of widespread voter fraud had occasionally surfaced in New York in the antebellum period. During the 1830s and 1840s, party leaders often accused their adversaries of "importing" voters from outside the city and state to cast ballots in important contests. In response to the growing conviction among native-born Americans that immigrant thugs cast multiple ballots or exercised the franchise before receiving their naturalization papers, the state legislature in 1859 enacted one of the nation's first voter-registration laws. Though Republicans felt certain that the new law would limit or eliminate fraudulent voting, politicos merely found new means to improperly influence the outcome of close elections.[49]

This became evident in 1863 with the contest for state Superior Court judge. Tammany nominated city judge John H. McCunn, a native of northern Ireland who had arrived in America as a teenaged sailor and worked as a cabinetmaker before entering the legal profession. Even many Democratic newspapers condemned the nomination, insisting that McCunn was a political hack wholly unqualified for the post. The *Times* labeled him "probably the worst man that ever offered himself as a candidate for a judgeship in any civilized country." Despite the Democratic majority that year, McCunn received 20,000 fewer votes than the other Democratic candidates, and preliminary returns on election night indicated that he had lost the election by a mere handful of votes.[50]

Tammany leaders, not about to let a few dozen ballots stand between them and the judgeship, decided to carry the election by rigging the returns from Five Points. Results had already been released (albeit in preliminary form), so the vote counters altered their tally to make it appear as if a few numerals had simply been transposed or misread in the original returns. Revising the results without changing the total number of votes cast was no mean mathematical feat, but the Sixth Ward polling officials managed to pull it off:

Candidate	Preliminary Tally	Official Returns
Bosworth	311	131
McCunn	200	280
Garvin	334	434
White	21	21
Total	866	866

Whether this scheme was hatched within Sixth Ward Democratic circles or imposed upon Five Pointers by other Tammany officials is impossible to determine. Coordination between the two must have been necessary. How the Sixth Warders managed to slip the changes past Republican ballot inspectors is also uncertain. Democrats might have resorted to bribery, though Matthew Brennan's brother Owen, one of the ward's Republican leaders, may have facilitated the subterfuge. In any case, that swing of 260 votes between McCunn and his nearest rival gave McCunn the election. He would soon play a key role in expanding election fraud to even greater heights.[51]

Over the remainder of the decade, voting fraud would reach levels never seen before or since in New York City. Revising the vote count continued to be a favorite ploy. Tweed later described to investigators how his election inspectors would "count the ballots in bulk, or without counting them announce the result in bulk, or change from one to the other, as the case may have been." Another tactic was to permit those who were ineligible—especially immigrants who had not yet received their naturalization papers—to cast ballots anyway. The most popular method of fraudulent voting, however, was "repeating," finding party loyalists who would cast multiple ballots at each election.[52]

All these strategies were pursued in the postbellum years to an extent and with a shamelessness unprecedented even in New York politics. This was especially true in Five Points. The *New York Tribune* in 1867 singled out the Fourth and Sixth Wards as those with the most fraudulent registrations. With a presidential election at stake the following year, the illegal voting in New York increased further still. "Never in the history of popular suffrage in any country was there so bold, general, well organized and thoroughly executed an attempt made" to carry an election "by frauds . . . as at the Presidential election of 1868," wrote a Republican who subsequently investigated the contest. ". . . Every conceivable form of fraud was practiced, and every crime possible to be committed against the elective franchise, was perpetrated with the most unblushing effrontery." *The Nation* agreed that "election frauds on such an enormous scale have never been witnessed in this country."[53]

Fraudulent naturalizations were one method used to augment the Democratic vote. McCunn naturalized 27,897 people in 1868 and another Tammany judge, George G. Barnard, granted citizenship to 10,070 more. In order to process so many applications, these judges dispensed with all pretense of normal judicial procedure, banning the press from their courtrooms to prevent word of the irregular proceedings from leaking out. Journalists would have found it strange, for example, that a single New

Yorker, Patrick Goff, was able to serve as a witness for 2,162 naturalization applicants in the autumn of 1868, verifying both their date of arrival in the United States and their good character. On three October days alone, the apparently well-known Goff served as a witness for more than 1,000 applicants. Had such judges merely been streamlining the citizenship process to ensure the naturalization of deserving immigrants before the election, one might excuse such behavior. But many of these naturalization documents were generated by Tammany specifically to make repeat voting possible. One court clerk later testified that he brought forty naturalization certificates to Five Points on election day so that repeaters could use them to verify false identities and cast fraudulent ballots. Thousands of certificates were probably issued in the names of nonexistent immigrants, and others were given to immigrants who were not yet eligible.[54]

Voting more than once required registering more than once, and by 1868 Tammany leaders had systematized multiple registration. William H. Hendrick, for example, was hired in that year by Peter Norton (brother of state senator Mike Norton) to join a gang of repeaters operating in the Sixth, Eighth, and Fourteenth Wards. In each ward, the men would visit the saloon of a Tammany leader, who would provide the gang members with the false names, addresses, and voting districts where they should register. Usually these addresses were buildings owned or occupied by the politicos themselves, so that if necessary the ward heelers could testify that the repeaters were their lessees. After registering about three times each in the Eighth and Fourteenth Wards, Hendrick and his partners proceeded to the Sixth Ward, where they visited the Bowery saloon of Alderman Edward Cuddy. From behind the bar, Cuddy produced a ledger book with hundreds of fictitious names and addresses. He gave each repeater a slip of paper with a name and Five Points address to use. They were told that after registering, they should return to Norton's place to receive their pay and be sure on election day to vote at all the places they had registered. Subsequent testimony would reveal that hundreds—and perhaps more than one thousand men—had fraudulently registered in the Sixth Ward for the 1868 elections.[55]

The army of repeaters sent to the polls on election day in 1868 was part of a desperate attempt to carry the state for both Tweed's handpicked gubernatorial candidate, John T. Hoffman, and Democratic presidential candidate Horatio Seymour, who faced almost certain defeat at the hands of Republican war hero Ulysses S. Grant. Many came from outside Five Points to vote illegally in the neighborhood. Edward Cobb of Hester Street, for example, later admitted that for thirty dollars he voted the Democratic ticket fifteen or sixteen times, including at least once at Five Points' Bayard Street polling place. Cobb reported that he saw Cuddy leading gangs of repeaters around the neighborhood that day. In many cases, Five Pointers invaded other districts to cast illicit ballots. Among them was James Clark of Mott Street, who testified later that for eight dollars he voted the Democratic ticket "eight or nine times in the 10th and 7th wards."

But repeating was especially heavy in Five Points. One observer saw men at the polling place on Elizabeth Street just north of Bayard exchanging clothing with each other before going in to vote, either because they had already voted there or because they feared that a poll watcher might remember that they had cast ballots elsewhere earlier in the day. After depositing their ballots, the men went around the corner to the voting booths on Bayard, where a man furnished the repeaters with slips of paper listing the names and addresses they would use there. Others entering the polling place on Baxter Street also exchanged hats and coats with each other before casting their ballots.[56]

Why did Republican election inspectors acquiesce to such blatant fraud? Some were threatened with physical violence; others were drugged; still others had their registration books stolen. Some were probably bribed. And many who protested were simply ignored. In one Five Points election district, the Republican inspector tried many times to challenge voters he did not recognize as neighborhood residents. But his Democratic counterpart would snarl, "'You be damned!' and took the vote and put it in the box." The Republican noted that as the day wore on and the crowds thinned, the Democratic inspectors would look at the registration book, copy down some names, and leave the room momentarily. A few minutes later, in would come a large group to vote upon those very names. Republicans who arrived late in the day to cast ballots often found their names had already been voted upon.[57]

All these facts came out in a congressional investigation in the winter of 1868–69. Yet the glare of public attention did nothing to curb the fraudulent voting. In fact, the number of votes cast in the Sixth Ward continued to escalate suspiciously, even though the subsequent elections were far less important than the 1868 presidential contest:

Comparison of Sixth Ward Population to Votes Cast, 1850–70

	Population	Votes cast	Ratio of votes cast to population
1850	24,696	1,523	1:16
1856	26,469	2,880	1:9
1860	26,696	3,224	1:8
1864	?	3,786	1:6 (estimate)
1865	19,754	2,475	1:8
1866	20,034	3,461	1:6
1867	20,314	3,486	1:6
1868	20,594	5,401	1:4
1869	20,874	6,274	1:3
1870 (May)	21,555	6,350	1:3 (special election for chief justice of the Court of Appeals)

The number of ballots cast in the Sixth Ward increased 80 percent from 1867 to 1869, even though only one tenement was built in the district in that interval and others were torn down to make room for commercial buildings. The cities of Hartford and Providence, each with 50,000 inhabitants, did not cast as many votes in 1869 as did this single New York ward with only 21,000 residents. The 1870 census revealed that more ballots were regularly deposited in one Five Points precinct than there were men, women, boys, *and* girls living there. In other Five Points districts, there were more voters than adult male citizens eligible to cast ballots.[58]

Motivated in large measure by these revelations, Congress included provisions in two 1870 statutes that empowered federal officials to monitor and punish electoral fraud, though they could do so only in balloting for national office. The U.S. Attorney General consequently appointed lawyer John I. Davenport as a U.S. commissioner with wide-ranging powers to prevent and punish fraudulent voting in New York. Legislation enacted in 1871 and 1872 enhanced Davenport's authority. The federal election inspectors who monitored balloting as a result of this legislation significantly diminished the illegal voting that had become so rampant in the Sixth Ward since the war:

Comparison of Sixth Ward Population to Votes Cast, 1865–70

	Population	Votes cast	Ratio of votes to population
Without federal inspections			
1865	19,754	2,475	1:8
1868	20,594	5,401	1:4
1870 (May)	21,555	6,350	1:3
With federal inspections			
1870 (November, Governor)	21,555	3,903	1:6
1870 (November, Congress)	21,555	2,865	1:8

The presence of federal inspectors scared away many repeaters, while others willing to vote repeatedly in the state contest would not do so in the national balloting for fear of arrest.[59]

Although federal legislation may have drastically reduced repeat voting, it did not deter Tammany entirely. Instead, the Democratic machine merely modified its tactics. If Democrats could not bring illicit voters to the polls, they would merely miscount those ballots that *were* cast. As usual, such practices were especially common in Five Points. Only 153 of the 283 registered voters visited the polls at 5 Mott Street on election day in November 1870. Nonetheless, Democratic inspectors announced that 280 votes had been cast—275 for Hoffman (in his bid for reelection as governor) and 5 for his Republican opponent—even though Republican poll watchers swore that at least thirty Republicans had cast ballots. In another Five Points precinct, inspectors reported that Hoffman had received 318 of 319 votes, prompting nine Republicans who had voted for his opponent there to write to the *Sun* asking what had become of their ballots. By focusing their fraud in Five Points, Tammany leaders further sullied the neighborhood's reputation and established it in New Yorkers' minds as the locus of Tammany's electoral crimes.[60]

"MATT. BRENNAN IS *NOT* AN HONEST OFFICIAL"

Though Five Pointers continued to flourish in city politics, their ability to maintain their positions was increasingly dependent on the whims of

"Boss" Tweed. Police Justice Joseph Dowling became an intimate Tweed ally—not a member of the Boss's inner circle like Mayor A. Oakey Hall or Clancy's mentor Peter Barr Sweeny, but an important supporter nonetheless. Dowling's status was reflected in his selection (along with Hall and Sweeny) as a delegate to the Democratic National Convention in 1868. Jourdan, Dowling's right-hand man, was appointed citywide superintendent of police in April 1870. Of the major Five Points politicians, only the Walsh brothers and Brennan remained aloof from Tweed. The Walshes actively opposed the Boss, refusing to cooperate with Tammany as long as Tweed controlled the organization. They were consequently frozen out of political office in the immediate postwar years. Brennan remained faithful to Tammany, though he kept his distance from Tweed. Yet in 1870, seeking a candidate with a reputation for honesty, Tweed acquiesced in Brennan's nomination for county sheriff in return for his endorsement of the Boss's candidates for mayor and comptroller. Brennan and the other Democrats easily carried the election.[61]

When Brennan took office as sheriff in January 1871, Tweed was at the pinnacle of his power. As a state senator representing the district that included Five Points, he had pushed through the legislature a new city charter that further entrenched his power. Tweed collected millions of dollars annually in kickbacks from contractors on city construction projects. He also collected obscene profits from businesses he owned that held city contracts. As president of the Board of Supervisors, Tweed and a fellow supervisor, Five Pointer Walter Roche (after whom the Roche Guard gang of the 1850s had been named), cooperated to demand payoffs from those who sought to have bills brought before that legislative body. Tweed was also assistant city street commissioner, and used that office to secure Roche the post of commissioner of street openings. Venal yet ingratiating, corpulent yet graceful, Tweed by 1871 ruled New York like Lorenzo de' Medici. He dispensed jobs, bribes, and charitable donations—even food and shoes—to ensure a large and varied base of support while simultaneously using electoral fraud to maintain the sham that he and his regime were popularly elected. Few could resist his charms or defy his commands.[62]

Yet in selecting Brennan for the sheriff's post, Tweed had sown the seeds of his own downfall. Brennan's predecessor in the lucrative post, James O'Brien, apparently coveted another term in office. When Tweed spurned O'Brien's efforts to secure the Democratic nomination (supposedly as punishment for O'Brien's treachery in a factional dispute), O'Brien decided to seek revenge and began leaking evidence of Tweed's crimes to the *New York Times*, which printed the revelations in July 1871. Tweed nonetheless stood for reelection to the state senate that fall, staying in the race even after authorities indicted him on civil fraud charges less than two weeks before the election.[63]

Fearing that a policeman arresting the Boss might bring him before Dowling or some other judge "in the Tweed interest," prosecutors gave the warrants for his arrest to Brennan, who dutifully carried out the delicate task of arresting the most powerful man in New York. The forewarned press was on hand when, on October 27, Brennan entered Tweed's office, tapped the apparently bemused Boss on the shoulder, and declared, "You're my man!" Thomas Nast's image of the scene for *Harper's Weekly* contains the only known likeness of Brennan. Despite the apparently cool relations between the two men, Brennan did not make things too unpleasant for Tweed. The sheriff allowed the Tammany leader to begin his detention at a hotel owned by Tweed's son, where the prisoner was given a spacious suite of rooms. Reporters arriving to interview Tweed found him "regaling himself in the apartments of his friend Judge Dowling," who just happened to live in the adjoining suite. The *Times* later charged that Dowling kept several potential prosecution witnesses in jail on trumped-up charges in order to prevent them from testifying against the Tammany chieftain.[64]

Sensing Tweed's vulnerability even before his arrest, Republicans had recruited as his opponent in the senate campaign Cork native Jeremiah O'Donovan Rossa, an Irish freedom fighter who had arrived in New York earlier in 1871 after the British released him and a half dozen other Fenian movement leaders from confinement in Tasmania. Tweed's adversaries believed that the support Rossa might gain from the large Cork and Kerry populations in the Fourth and Sixth Wards could carry the revolutionary to victory, but on election night Tweed was declared the winner. In fact, Rossa apparently outpolled Tweed by 350 votes, but Tammany election officials "counted out" Rossa in order to perpetuate Tweed's reign. The eccentric Rossa eventually became proprietor of a Five Points saloon "whose atmosphere," according to one neighborhood historian, "seethed with hatred of Britain."[65]

Meanwhile, Tweed's empire began to collapse. In December, he was arraigned on criminal charges. Soon thereafter he was expelled from the

Sheriff Brennan, center, arresting Boss Tweed, October 27,
1871. *Harper's Weekly* (November 18, 1871): 1084. Collection of the author.

Tammany Society and forced to resign his municipal offices. After two
years of legal maneuvering, Tweed was finally convicted of fraud in
November 1873 and sentenced to twelve years in prison.[66]

Like all New Yorkers of modest means, Five Pointers viewed Boss
Tweed's demise with mixed emotions. One neighborhood saloonkeeper
recalled a few years later that "the majority of people with whom I talked
believe that the prosecutors of Tweed did wrong" in punishing him so
severely. "Tweed has thousands among the poor today, who bless him. He

kept the poor employed, and they would have done anything for him." Jacob Riis found the same attitude toward the Boss still prevalent twenty years later. Tweed's "name is even now one to conjure with in the Sixth Ward," reported Riis. "He never 'squealed,' and he was 'so good to the poor.'"[67]

Even though these statements probably exaggerated Tweed's popularity in Five Points, neighborhood residents had benefited from the Boss's reign in a variety of ways. Any Democratic leader would have supplied jobs to his most loyal political followers. Con Donoho had done so when Tweed was just a teenager. But under Tweed, such opportunities had expanded significantly. In addition, it was only when Tweed reached the height of his influence that the city's Catholic churches, which for years had sought government subsidies for their parochial schools, finally received assistance. Five Points' Transfiguration parish school received a grant of $11,500 in 1869 and slightly larger sums in each of the next two years before Tweed's fall from grace, when such funding ceased.[68]

With Tweed's indictment, his henchmen came under scrutiny, including his Five Points allies. In February 1872, Roche was arrested for absconding with funds from the bankrupt Bowling Green Savings Bank, of which he was vice president. The *Times* speculated that Roche might have been plundering the Bowling Green to save the Guardian Savings Bank, where the onetime saloonkeeper also served as vice president while Tweed acted as president. Roche had induced many Tammany politicos, including Brennan, to deposit large sums in the Guardian. By early 1874, however, Roche had still not been brought to trial, and he apparently never served any jail time.[69]

Despite his reputation for honesty and relative aloofness from Tweed, Brennan also came under suspicion as the Tweed Ring collapsed. Even before Tweed's indictment, the *Tribune* published a series of reports charging that the sheriff's Ludlow Street jail levied outrageous fees on prisoners, keeping the proceeds for himself and his cronies. Brennan also apparently inflated the bills he submitted to the city for making arrests and seizing goods. In one such case, he charged the city $419. After complaints by the defendant, a judge in November 1872 examined the sheriff's actual expenses and reduced the fee to $19. Month after month, the *Times* published editorials condemning "Brennan's blackmail" and excoriating the Five Pointer for his "career of plunder." One case of "plunder" involved

Monroe Hall, the building that housed Brennan's saloon. In 1863, Brennan had signed a ten-year lease to rent part of the building to the Second District Civil Court for an outrageous $2,800 per year. When Tweed Ring plundering reached its height in 1870, charged the *Times*, Brennan had had the audacity to have the board of aldermen annul that agreement and increase the rent to an astounding $7,500. "MATT. BRENNAN," the *Times* solemnly concluded, "is *not* an honest official."[70]

Brennan tried desperately to maintain his position in city politics and the Democratic party. In theory, Tweed's downfall might have helped Brennan advance, inasmuch as the Boss and his Ring leaders had all either been indicted or fled the country. Yet Brennan was never able to win acceptance from the "reform" wing of the party headed by "Honest John" Kelly either, especially as the press continued to condemn the extravagant fees levied by his sheriff's office. In the fall of 1873, the *Times* reported gleefully that Brennan had failed to get his handpicked choices selected to represent the city at the Democratic state convention. A few weeks later, his candidate for state assembly also lost a primary battle. Brennan himself was denied renomination that fall, as Tammany chose a slate of reform candidates associated with Kelly that included William Walsh as the nominee for county clerk. Brennan would have to serve out his remaining days as sheriff as a political outsider.[71]

In the end, Brennan's involvement with the Ring did land him in jail, though not for the reasons one would expect. Just before Christmas 1873, with only a few days remaining in Brennan's term, Tweed associate Henry W. Genet was convicted of stealing city building supplies and funds by submitting fictitious work vouchers. Genet, whom the *Times* later called "one of the most vulgar, brutal, and defiant of the Ring conspirators," was remanded to the custody of William H. Shields, Brennan's chief deputy and husband of his favorite niece. Shields, as he often did with prominent convicts, allowed the prisoner to enjoy himself in the short interim until his sentencing. A month earlier, Shields had offered the same privilege to the convicted Tweed, who had spent each of the three days before his sentencing with the "Stable Gang" of politicos who congregated at a Five Points livery stable. Shields allowed Genet to attend a gala "going away" party in his honor at which virtually every important city Democrat made an appearance. Before escorting Genet to his sentencing on December 22, Shields allowed him to return home for a last visit with his wife. While the deputy sat unsuspectingly in the parlor, "Prince Hal" escaped out a back window. Within hours, he was on his way to Canada, and from there he set sail for Europe. For allowing Genet to escape, the incensed trial judge fined Shields and Brennan $250 each and sentenced them to thirty days in jail. On January 8, 1874, just a few days after stepping down as sheriff, the humiliated Brennan returned to the Ludlow Street jail he had presided over for three years, this time as a prisoner.[72]

Brennan's ensuing decline was remarkably swift. Breen recalled that Brennan, "a very proud man, was then getting old, and was so deeply mortified by his imprisonment and the abuse he received from the public press that he never recovered his former self. After getting out of prison he kept to his house, and although up to this episode he was one of the most popular men in New York, he never again took any further interest in public affairs."[73]

"AN ERA IN NEW-YORK POLITICS SO ENTIRELY OF THE PAST THAT IT SEEMS LIKE ANCIENT HISTORY"

"Mr. Brennan was the product of an era in New-York politics so entirely of the past that it seems like ancient history," asserted the *Times* when it announced that Brennan had died on January 19, 1879, at age fifty-six. The *Times* was right. Ward primaries were no longer decided by knockdown, drag-out brawls. Polling places were no longer dominated by gangs seeking to prevent certain voters from casting their ballots. Service in the police or fire departments was no longer a prerequisite to political advancement. And gone were the days when Irish Catholics were all but barred from city-wide offices.[74]

The old era of New York politics also seemed a thing of the past because while Brennan died young by modern standards, he had outlived almost all of his Five Points political contemporaries. Yankee Sullivan committed suicide in a San Francisco jail cell in 1855 while in his late forties. Clancy died during the Civil War at thirty-five. Jourdan passed away suddenly in 1870 at thirty-nine, only a few months after becoming the city's police superintendent. McCunn, whose naturalization frauds were just a few of his many crimes, was impeached and removed from office by a unanimous vote of the state senate on July 2, 1872. Literally mortified, McCunn died at age forty-seven just four days later. William Walsh passed away prematurely as well, in March 1878 at age forty-two, soon after completing his term as county clerk. Tweed died in jail a month later at fifty.[75]

Brennan also outlived his former protégé Dowling, who succumbed to kidney failure in 1876 at age fifty. Despite Dowling's connections to the Tweed Ring, New Yorkers eulogized "Old Baldy" with particular fondness. "With the death of 'Joe' Dowling is lost one of the best known Irishmen among us," commented the *Herald*. Breen aptly described the colorful Dowling as "one of the most remarkable characters that has ever appeared in the history of New York politics." Dowling had remained a police justice until about 1874, when the state legislature reorganized the police courts and eliminated his district. He thoroughly enjoyed retirement, traveling extensively in England and on the Continent. While in London, he became the toast of the town after pummeling into submission thieves he caught attempting to plunder the house of the magistrate with whom he was staying. Upon his return to New York, according to one biographer, Dowling "amused himself with speculation in various enterprises, particularly theatres." He also owned about a half-dozen tenements. Dowling appears to have been a successful investor, for at his death he left a fortune estimated to be worth from $150,000 to as much as $500,000 (the equivalent of $2–$7 million today). Nor was it uncommon for once impoverished Five Points politicians to die with such substantial assets. According to the *Times*, Jourdan too left "a large fortune, a portion of which he acquired by inheritance and the remainder by honest industry in his profession." The meaning of the phrase "honest industry" was probably better captured in the famous account of Tammany by George W. Plunkitt, *Plunkitt of Tammany Hall*, in which he explained that politicians reaped fortunes through "honest graft," investment opportunities that depended on insider information available only to the politically well connected.[76]

Brennan was not so lucky. A reform-minded comptroller refused to pay most of his outstanding claims against the city for services rendered as sheriff. Brennan sued, but the courts ruled against him. At the same time, many New Yorkers sued him, claiming that the sheriff or his deputies had overcharged for their services. To pay his legal fees and the judgments against him in these civil suits, Brennan was forced to sell most of his assets—primarily real estate—at depressed prices during the severe recession of 1874 and 1875. As a result, noted the *Times*, "he retired to private life with hardly a competence." According to the *Tribune*, Brennan "died poor."[77]

Remnants of both the brawling and corrupt eras of Five Points politics would persist after Brennan's death. One Five Pointer, in particular, rose to fame by the old rules. Recall the seven-year-old bootblack and newsboy named Tim Sullivan, who in 1870 lived with his mother, four siblings, stepfather, and three boarders in a run-down tenement apartment at 25 Baxter Street just south of the Five Points intersection. Born in New York, Sullivan was the son of Lansdowne immigrants from County Kerry who upon their arrival were among the very poorest of the Five Points poor. Sullivan hustled to earn every possible penny to help his struggling family, because his mother bore Tim's unreliable stepfather four more children after 1870.

Young Tim became quite an entrepreneur. In his various jobs delivering newspapers, he developed a network of contacts among the city's newsboys and periodicals dealers. He often gave orphans and runaways just starting as newsboys their first stack of newspapers for free, both to help the struggling street urchins and win their loyalty. In his teenaged years, he began to work after school in the news plants themselves, but simultaneously became a newspaper distributor as well, because distribution managers knew that his web of newsboys could guarantee the sale of their papers throughout Manhattan. "Every new newspaper that come out, I obtained employment on, on account of my connection with the newsdealers all over the City of New York," Sullivan recalled in 1902. Sullivan's income from these operations must have been significant, because by his late teens he was ready to open his first saloon, and by his early twenties he purportedly had interests in three or four.

Sullivan was also a very popular young man. According to Sixth Ward lore, Sullivan in 1886 came upon a noted "pugilist" beating a woman on Centre Street near the Tombs. When the man refused to heed Sullivan's warning to desist, Sullivan challenged the fighter himself and bested the bully. This battle "is still sweet in the memories of old Sixth warders," commented the *Herald* nearly twenty years later. From that day on, its reporter wrote, the "'young element'" in the district "hailed him as their chief" and "forced Thomas P. Walsh . . . to nominate Mr. Sullivan to the Assembly in 1886." Walsh, who at this point headed the anti-Tammany "County Democracy" in the Sixth Ward, probably needed little persuading to nominate the twenty-three-year-old Sullivan. Leaders of the County Democracy were always looking for popular new personalities who might challenge the Tammany incumbents. "Five Points Sullivan" lived up to Walsh's expectations, defeating his Tammany rival despite his youth and lack of political experience. Sullivan soon began cooperating with Tammany (as did Walsh), and quickly moved up through the ranks. He eventually served in both the state senate and the U.S. House of Representatives.

Sullivan's power in Tammany eventually surpassed even Brennan's. By the turn of the century, he was known as "Big Tim" Sullivan, "the political ruler of down-town New York." Some observers considered him the second most powerful politician in the city, after Tammany "boss" Richard Croker. Sullivan also became quite wealthy. Critics charged that he built his fortune from payoffs extorted from gambling and prostitution syndicates in his district. Sullivan insisted that he had never taken a bribe in his life, and that his substantial income derived from shrewd investments in vaudeville theaters and other legitimate business enterprises. Whatever the case, Sullivan remembered his humble origins and shared his wealth with his less fortunate constituents, giving away thousands of pairs of shoes and Christmas dinners each year.[78]

Still, Big Tim was now the exception rather than the rule. And in many ways, Five Points was also a very different neighborhood. By 1870, it was much less poverty-stricken than it had been in the 1830s and '40s. The "Arch Block," the "Big Flat," and "Gotham Court," all in other neighborhoods, had become the most infamous tenements in the city. "Hell's Kitchen" aroused more fear and dread. And so might the story of Five Points have ended, but for the tremendous influx in the late 1870s and 1880s of Italians and Asians, whose arrival would once again make the neighborhood notorious for disease, crime, and overcrowding.[79]

11

PROLOGUE

"So It Was Settled That I Should Go to America"

On June 5, 1870, a twenty-one-year-old Danish immigrant named Jacob Riis stepped off a trans-Atlantic steamer at the southern tip of Manhattan, anxious to begin a new life in America. The young Dane had been born and raised in Ribe, a town of three thousand inhabitants on the windswept North Sea coast near the Prussian border. Riis's father, a schoolteacher, had supported his family relatively comfortably, yet life was far from easy. Only four of the seventeen children Riis's mother gave birth to survived into their teens. One year the family could not afford to buy overcoats to protect the children from the cold Scandinavian winter. But Riis's childhood years were not especially difficult ones.

Despite his father's prodding, young Jacob took little interest in academic pursuits and he was eventually apprenticed to a carpenter. In his midteens, he fell passionately in love with a twelve-year-old schoolmate named Elisabeth Gortz, but both she and her stepfather (a prosperous lumber merchant) rebuffed the young man's advances. When Riis publicly insulted the stepfather at a town dance, apparently destroying all prospects of winning her affection, he decided to leave Ribe and complete his apprenticeship in Copenhagen.

Four years later, Riis returned to his birthplace and proposed to Elisabeth. The stepfather again rejected him. "I kissed her hands and went out," he recalled years later, "my eyes brimming over with tears, feeling that there was nothing in all the world for me any more, and that the farther I went from her the better. So it was settled that I should go to America." Elisabeth's mother, feeling sorry for the spurned suitor, slipped Riis a photograph of her daughter and a lock of her hair. "I lived on that picture and that curl six long years."

Believing that all the United States was wild and dangerous, Riis upon arriving in New York spent half his savings on a huge pistol, which he strapped to his waist as he strode up Broadway. A policeman, "seeing that I was very green," suggested that Riis leave it at home. Riis had letters of introduction to the Danish consul in New York and an American businessman who had once been saved from a shipwreck near Ribe, but both men were in Europe when he arrived. Rather than await their return, he visited the employment office at the Castle Garden immigration depot, where he signed on to labor at a new ironworks in western Pennsylvania. A few days later, Riis was using his carpenter's skills to construct huts for the company's employees.[1]

When the news reached Pennsylvania in July that Prussia and France had gone to war, Riis precipitously quit his job and returned to New York, hoping to volunteer for the French Army and "take revenge for the great robbery of 1864" in which Prussia had annexed parts of southern Denmark near Ribe. He also hoped that military glory would win him the heart of his beloved Elisabeth. Riis pawned almost everything he owned to finance the journey to New York, arriving with a single cent in his pocket. Much to his chagrin, he discovered that the French were neither accepting volunteers in New York nor paying for their transportation to Europe. Having sold his boots to pay for his lodging, Riis was now completely destitute, and decided to walk northward out of town to look for work. He did odd jobs in exchange for food in Westchester County, sleeping in barns, carts, fields, and on roadsides. When he had saved a bit of money, he returned to New York to try to volunteer again, only to be rebuffed once more. Next, he took work in a New Jersey brickyard, until reading six weeks later of a French volunteer unit being outfitted in New York. He hurried there, but found that the regiment had already sailed for Europe. Entreaties to the French consul also proved fruitless. One day, he was offered work on a steamer sailing imminently for Le Havre, and realizing that this would at least bring him closer to the seat of war, he ran to his boardinghouse to collect his meager belongings. But by the time he returned to the docks, his ship had sailed. Riis sat on the pier and wept.

By this point it was autumn. "The brick-making season was over," he recalled, and "the city was full of idle men." Riis learned firsthand about New York's seasonal labor market. "Homeless and penniless, I joined the great army of tramps, wandering about the streets in the daytime with the one aim of somehow stilling the hunger that gnawed at my vitals, and fighting at night with vagrant curs or outcasts as miserable as myself for the protection of some sheltering ash-bin or doorway. . . . It was under such auspices that I made the acquaintance of Mulberry Bend, the Five Points, and the rest of the slum, with which there was in the years to come to be a reckoning." He spent weeks in the notorious neighborhood, sleeping in the doorways or alleys of the district's worst dwellings, sometimes relocating to a stoop in Chatham Square when Five Points' "utter nastiness" was too much to bear, and subsisting on "meat-bones and rolls" that a sympathetic French cook at Delmonico's would slip him out a rear kitchen window. Wondering how he could improve his circumstances and where he would stay now that it was too cold to sleep outside, Riis contemplated suicide. In the end, however, he decided to seek shelter at a police station house instead. But later that night the police evicted him from his cell for fighting, killed his dog, and put him on a ferry to Jersey City. Riis vowed he would never return to New York.

Out of the metropolis, Riis's prospects finally began to improve. He walked one hundred miles to Philadelphia, "living on apples and an occasional meal earned by doing odd jobs." There the Danish consul fed and clothed him and sent the twenty-one-year-old to a job in western New York near Jamestown. Riis worked making cradles in a furniture shop, as a lumberman felling trees, and on the frozen lakes harvesting ice. He tried to strike out on his own, operating an "express business" in which he hauled goods by wheelbarrow from the nearest ferry to his inland village, but he could not earn enough money to support himself. He was more successful as a trapper, sometimes earning a dollar a day selling muskrat skins, but this too did not last long. Riis did odd jobs on a farm, then moved to Buffalo, where he stacked boards in a lumberyard, made bedsteads, and finished doors in a planing mill. Cheated by his employer, he left town to toil at railroad construction. He returned to Buffalo to work in a shipyard. All this in a single year.

Riis flitted from job to job in part because he yearned to escape manual labor altogether. Thus, when some other Scandinavian woodworkers asked him to promote their furniture as a traveling salesman, he enthusiastically agreed. He did this for a number of years, peddling irons when the furniture makers went bankrupt. He tired of the nomadic salesman's life, however, and returned to New York to enter telegraphy school. But he ran out of money before he could finish.

Riis began looking over the help-wanted ads, and one immediately caught his attention. A small weekly newspaper across the river in Long Island City was seeking a "city editor." Ever since arriving in America, Riis had aspired to be a reporter. This motivation to pursue journalism may have originated with his father, who had once published a small weekly paper in Ribe. Riis saw the reporter's vocation as far more dignified and honorable than the others he had pursued since arriving in the United States. He got the job in Long Island City, not pausing to wonder why he could land it so easily despite his lack of experience. After two weeks, though, he discovered that his employer was penniless, and quit.

By this point, it was the autumn of 1873. A terrible depression had brought business to a virtual standstill, and steady employment was nearly impossible to find. The news that his beloved Elisabeth was engaged—to a dashing cavalry officer, of all things—compounded Riis's misery. He sold books door to door, but often went hungry, until one day at the end of the year he met the principal from his telegraphy school. Perhaps remembering Riis's career goal, the man told him of an opening for a reporter at the New York News Association, a wire service. With a reference from the principal, Riis got the job, which paid ten dollars per week. He never went hungry again.[2]

Five months later, Riis left the wire service to take a position with the *South Brooklyn News*, the organ of some local Democrats. After two weeks, the politicos made him editor (he was the paper's only employee) and raised his salary to twenty-five dollars per week. When the owners captured the fall elections, though, they decided to close their money-losing venture. Riis, inspired by the news that Elisabeth's fiancé had died, induced the journal's proprietors to sell it to him, for $75 down and the remaining $575 when he could raise it. Riis toiled unceasingly to make the paper a success, and his pluck, enthusiasm, boundless energy, and ambition soon began to pay dividends. In half a year he paid off his entire debt, delivering the final installment on June 5, 1875, Elisabeth's birthday. That night "found me sleepless," he recalled, "pouring out my heart to her" in a letter and begging her to marry him. This was his first communication with her since he had left Ribe, other than a perfunctory letter of best wishes he had written after learning of her engagement. "I carried the letter to the post-office myself," Riis remembered, "and waited till I saw it started on its long journey. I stood watching the carrier till he turned the corner; then went back to my work."

When Elisabeth received Jacob's letter, she was still in deep mourning for her man in uniform, whom she had loved passionately. She had always been impressed with Jacob's ardor but had felt little for him. Angered at Riis's impudence and insensitivity, she dashed off another rejection letter and gave it to Riis's mother to forward to her son in America. Mrs. Riis, however, opened the envelope and read the letter. To protect her son from further heartache, she decided not to send it.

Months passed, and with no word from Elisabeth, Riis immersed himself in other pursuits. He became a devout Methodist and was "converted" at one of the group's revival meetings. He also threw himself into his work with even greater energy. No longer dependent on the politicos, Riis criticized them for firing good city employees who did not do the bosses' political bidding. The ward heelers promised Riis patronage if he would toe the party line and secured him a post as court interpreter (which paid $100 per month for very little work) to induce him to find other targets for his editorial barbs. Riis could not stifle his independent spirit for long, however, and after three months he was fired from his sinecure.

Meanwhile, "the summer and fall had worn away, and no word had come from home" from Elisabeth. "Every day when the letter-carrier came up the street, my hopes rose high until he had passed. The letter I longed for never came." Elisabeth, though, began to have second thoughts about Riis. Her fiancé in his dying days had told her that "'if I should die, and some other man who loved you, and who you knew was good and faithful, should ask you to marry him, you ought to accept him, even if you did not love him.' . . . Did he mean Jacob," she wondered, "who had surely proved constant, and like me, had suffered much? He was lonely and I was lonely, oh! so lonely!" After wrestling with her ambivalence for weeks, she finally decided to contact Jacob, telling him "we might write and get acquainted, and get used to the idea of each other, . . . and that if he still would have me, I was willing to go with him to America if he would come for me sometime."

Around November 1, 1874, this letter arrived on Riis's desk. "I think I sat as much as a quarter of an hour staring dumbly at the unopened enve-

lope," he recalled twenty-five years later. He took it home and locked himself in his room before opening it. His screams of joy upon reading it were
so loud that his neighbor knocked at the door to make sure he was all right.
At first, the couple decided that he should not return to Europe for at least
a year. Riis could not restrain himself, however, soon writing that he
would come for her in six months, then five, then four.

In the end, he could not wait even that long. "What had happened was
that just at the right moment the politicians had concluded . . . that they
could not allow an independent newspaper in the ward, and had offered to
buy it outright." Riis sold them the *South Brooklyn News* for five times
what he had paid just a year earlier. His pockets bulging with his newfound
wealth, Riis boarded the very next steamer for Hamburg. He arrived in
Ribe on New Year's Eve 1875, proposing to a surprised and somewhat overwhelmed Elisabeth that same evening. They were married there in March
and soon returned to America.[3]

To say that Jacob Riis was a man of determination and energy is obviously an understatement. Soon he would use that energy as a reformer,
determined to improve the decrepit living conditions of poor New Yorkers,
especially those in Five Points. First through his innovations in the use of
flash photography, then through his groundbreaking book *How the Other
Half Lives*, Riis revived and intensified New Yorkers' concern for Five
Points and its infamous slum housing.

CHAPTER ELEVEN

The Remaking of a Slum

⟨⟩⟨⟩

I F AN IRISH Rip Van Winkle had left his home in Five Points at the beginning of 1850 and returned twenty years later, he would have been astounded by the changes that had taken place during his absence. Standing on the site of the notorious Old Brewery tenement was a Methodist church and mission. Cow Bay had vanished as well, covered over entirely by the huge Five Points House of Industry. The blocks radiating from the Five Points intersection, once inhabited almost exclusively by African Americans and Irish immigrants, were now overwhelmingly Italian. Tenement hallways in that part of the neighborhood, formerly suffused with the aroma of boiling potatoes and cabbage, were now dominated by the scent of garlic and onions.[4]

Perhaps the most significant change in Five Points during the Civil War years was the plunge in its population. The Sixth Ward's population dropped a remarkable 23 percent from 1860 to 1865, from more than 26,000 to just below 20,000. A number of factors contributed to this tremendous decline. The exodus of New Yorkers into the army and navy helped drive up wages for those manual laborers left in the workforce. With substantially rising incomes, many Five Pointers could afford the move to a better neighborhood. New tenement construction uptown and on the Lower East Side, as well as the development of other Irish enclaves, also enabled many to find alternate lodgings. As a result, Five Points by the postwar years was no longer the most densely populated portion of the city. That dubious distinction now fell to the Lower East Side (the area east of the Bowery between Canal and Fourteenth Streets), though its relatively new five- and six-story brick tenements were more spacious and comfortable than the older, more dilapidated buildings in Five Points. Even decades after the war, when tall brick buildings had replaced most of the old wooden tenements, the neighborhood's population never again approached its antebellum levels.[5]

"THE IRISH ELEMENT IS . . . YIELDING ONE STRONGHOLD AFTER ANOTHER TO THE ITALIAN FOE"

Although Five Points was no longer renowned for its overcrowding, New Yorkers continued to think of it as the city's most ethnically diverse neighborhood. The *Tribune* reported in 1885 that Cruz's Boardinghouse on Baxter Street near Franklin "demands a polyglot to run it properly and a polyglot it has. Cruz speaks, or attempts speaking, in English, German, French, Spanish, Danish, Portugese, Chinese, Japanese, Javanese, Manillan, Cochinese, Corean and Hindostan." A rector of Transfiguration Roman Catholic Church likewise boasted of having officiated at a baptism at which "the grandfather was Irish, the grandmother Scotch, the father Chinese, the mother an American, the godfather an Italian, and the godmother a negress. Surely, Europe, Asia, and Africa have come very closely together in this little section of America." The *Herald* in 1878 characterized the large brick tenement at 31 Baxter, once dominated by Lansdowne immigrants, as "a veritable tower of Babel," with "a different language at every door."[6]

New Yorkers' sense of Five Points as a tower of Babel was still somewhat exaggerated. In one generation, from 1855 to 1880, the Irish and German populations in Five Points were reduced by about half, the Italians increased dramatically, and Polish Jews became a more significant presence:

Nativity of Five Points Adult Residents[7]

Place of Birth	Percentage of 1855 Adult Population	Percentage of 1880 Adult Population
Ireland	66%	31%
Italy	3	23
United States	11	22
Poland	2	11
German States	14	7

	Percentage of 1855 Adult Population	Percentage of 1880 Adult Population
England	2	3
China	0	2
Other	1	1

Nevertheless, Five Points had not lost as much of its Irish flavor by 1880 as these figures imply. Fully 80 percent of the native-born Americans living in the district were the children of Irish-born parents.

Ten years later, the Italians had completed their takeover of the neighborhood, as the city's police census of 1890 indicates:

Ethnicity of Five Points Residents, 1890[8]

Ethnicity	Percentage
Italian	49%
Jewish	18
Irish	10
Chinese	5
German	1
Unknown	17

"The Irish element is . . . yielding one stronghold after another to the Italian foe," Riis could write by 1892. "It lost its grip on the Five Points and the Bend long ago."[9]

The physical changes that took place in Five Points after the war were just as striking. The most significant was probably the extension of Worth Street eastward from the Five Points intersection to Chatham Square in 1868. Before the lengthening of Worth Street, Paradise Park and the Five Points intersection had felt closed in and secluded. Connecting the intersection to the hustle and bustle of Chatham Square and the Bowery helped eliminate the sense of dread that visitors felt in that part of the neighborhood. "The extension of Worth Street through the Points . . . to Chatham Street, let the daylight into the slums so effectually, that as many as could of the criminal class therein resident 'got up and dusted,'" noted *Frank Leslie's Illustrated Newspaper.* Twenty years after its completion, New Yorkers still attributed much of the neighborhood's improvement to the Worth Street project.[10]

Whereas the extension of Worth Street improved Five Points, the opening of an elevated railway on the Bowery in 1878 had the opposite effect. The new rail line did speed the movement of passengers from uptown residential neighborhoods to downtown commercial districts. But the mammoth steel girders that supported the tracks plunged the once airy boulevard into darkness, while the noise from the trains (no longer absorbed by the ground) made the Bowery's saloons and dance halls especially inhospitable. The "el" helped transform the Bowery, once the working-class Broadway, into the seedy gathering place for drunks and "bums" for which it is still (unjustly) renowned.[11]

Five Points also changed in less concrete ways in the early postwar years. By 1869, for example, a journalist could declare the Bowery B'hoy "nearly extinct. . . . His crimson shirt, and his oiled locks, and his peculiar slang, and his freedom of pugnacity, and his devotion to the fire-engine are things gone by." The subculture of the "sporting man" persisted to the turn of the century, but by 1880 its adherents no longer congregated in the Sixth Ward. "Twenty years ago it was one of the head-quarters of the gamblers," reminisced one old sport in 1885, "but you find none of these gentry of any importance in the neighborhood now." As African Americans moved out of Five Points in the 1860s, so too did the neighborhood's famous dance halls. Prostitution diminished significantly as well, as brothels relocated to Greenwich Village to be closer to the city's most prosperous commercial and residential districts, now located above Fourteenth Street. By about 1880, most working-class theaters had also moved uptown.[12]

The vacuum created by these departures was filled in part by the influx of large-scale "manufactories." By 1868, a huge paper box factory occupied all of Mission Place and half of the south side of Worth Street between Centre Street and the Five Points intersection. A playing card factory took over much of the north side of Worth on that block. Portions of the neighborhood south of Worth Street and west of Baxter Street became especially popular with manufacturers in this period.[13]

"NO PENCIL CAN FULLY PICTURE ALL ITS HORRORS"

Perhaps the most significant physical change in Five Points in the post–Civil War years was the ongoing transformation of its tenements. In the postwar decades, landlords continued to replace the neighborhood's old wooden tenements with five- and six-story brick structures. The ratio of brick to frame domiciles, which had stood at three to two in 1855, reached about three to one by the mid-1880s.[14]

Many of the changes in Five Points' tenements resulted from postwar legislation. In the spring of 1867, New York State enacted the nation's first building codes, which included a variety of tenement regulations. The statute required landlords to install fire escapes and connect their outhouses to sewer lines, and prohibited them from renting space in basements without a permit from the Board of Health. The law also mandated that every room have a window (though it could face a hallway or another room rather than the outside), that no animals other than dogs or cats live in tenement apartments, and that all inhabited rooms have a minimum ceiling height of eight feet. The Board supplemented these rules with others that placed limits on the number of people who could occupy an apartment, as well as requiring the periodic spraying of disinfectants in and around the outhouses.[15]

A potentially more important change in the city's tenements developed in 1879. State lawmakers were again debating the tenement issue and considering legislation that would limit new buildings to 65 percent of a lot and require that every inhabited room have a window to the outside. Anticipating that these proposals would become law, the trade journal *Plumber and Sanitary Engineer* announced a prize competition for the best tenement floor plan that would satisfy such restrictions. The society awarded first prize to architect James E. Ware, whose winning design became known as the "dumbbell" tenement because the floor plan vaguely resembled a weight lifter's implement. Ware's design replaced the perfectly rectangular buildings of the past with ones that narrowed on the sides so that rooms away from the front and back of the structure could have windows that faced the outside. Rather than open to the street or the yard, these side windows would face narrow airshafts. Ware's floor plan became the standard design for the remainder of the nineteenth century.[16]

Both the design changes and the new regulations significantly improved the lives of many Five Points tenement dwellers. The Board of Health forced landlords to cut 46,000 interior windows citywide, increasing the airflow in the neighborhood's "sleeping closets." The city also conducted tenement inspections, evicting illegal cellar dwellers and spraying disinfectants in the district's yards, basements, and privy vaults. The new laws also resulted in the construction of larger apartments, as virtually all dumbbell flats consisted of three rooms rather than the two-room habitations that builders had typically constructed in the past. Richard W. Gilder, editor of *Century Magazine* and chairman of the city's 1894 tenement commission, testified in 1901 that housing for the poor had improved dramatically during the previous half century as a result of these innovations. He recalled being taken as a boy "into the old Five Points and . . . shown things that no tenement-house commissioner, certainly none of 1900—or 1901—can now see in this city. Sub-cellars occupied by the refuse of humanity; Old Cow Bay; scenes such as exist in the pictures that Dante makes, but not now in reality, certainly, in this city."[17]

Nonetheless, many New Yorkers understood that these minor modifications had by no means solved the "tenement problem." Referring to Ware's award-winning design as well as those of the runners-up, the *Times* asserted that "if the prize plans are the best offered—which we can hardly believe—they simply demonstrate that the problem is insoluble. . . . If one of our crowded wards were built up after any one of these three prize designs, the evils of our present tenement-house system would be increased ten-fold."[18]

This was hyperbole, to be sure, yet subsequent experience proved that the *Times* was not entirely mistaken. The advent of the airshaft exacerbated two already chronic tenement problems: noise and stench. The airshafts became echo chambers that seemingly amplified the sounds of screaming babies, boisterous children, and quarreling adults. Whereas the inhabitants of older tenements could hear sounds from apartments above, below, and next to theirs, now the noise from half the building was transported loudly and clearly into every other flat. Dumbbell dwellers complained just as bitterly about the vile smells that now wafted into their apartments. One woman who lived on the ground floor at the bottom of the airshaft reported that her neighbors constantly threw "garbage and dirty papers and the insides of chickens" into it. Even the contents of chamber pots were occasionally deposited there. Because "the stench is so vile and the air is so foul," and because of the unrelenting noise, dumbbell dwellers almost never opened their airshaft windows.[19]

Safety innovations also failed to dramatically improve tenement life. In 1871, the *Times* observed of Five Points that "there is here and there a fire-escape, but even these in many cases would be entirely useless, being in the rear, where all the smoke and fire would concentrate, and no creature could live one minute." By the 1880s, fire escapes were much more common, but tenants in terribly overcrowded apartments used them for storage, making them virtually useless for emergencies. One tenement dweller likened the fire escapes to "curiosity shops," noting that one found on them "quilts and clothes . . . chairs, tin boxes, ice boxes, dogs, birds, cats, rabbits, jars and bottles of every description, big parrots screeching at each other, canaries singing, and children playing." Bathtubs were also a common sight on fire escapes, as were washtubs and rudely constructed sleeping platforms.[20]

Many tenement problems that had existed before the war persisted in the postbellum years. Although tenements were now more likely to be connected to sewers, their outdoor toilets were still repulsive. "I have the children go to the toilet at school, for I am afraid of sickness," testified one tenement resident at the turn of the century. "It is so horrid for my daughter, that she waits to use the toilet where she works. She hasn't been inside of one here for four or five months." State investigators in 1884 found that many Five Points tenements still had backyard privy vaults "reeking with filth and decomposition," rather than the required sewer connections. Older people still had to descend and climb four, five, or six flights of stairs merely to use the toilet, take out the garbage, or fetch some water. Some refused to risk the steep, pitch-black, often banister-less stairwells more than once or twice a week. Darkness in the hallways remained a problem as well. In 1892, a *Herald* reporter remarked that Bayard Street tenement stairwells were still enshrouded in total darkness even though legislation mandating their illumination had been on the books for more than a decade. "It was necessary," she wrote, "to grope our way to the top by lighting matches on every landing." Lack of tubs and running water above the first floor also meant that bathing was still a rarity. "Many tenants do not bathe more than six times a year, and often less," noted one tenement dweller. The lack of bathing facilities was especially frustrating during the summer, when the tenements once again became virtual brick ovens.[21]

Overcrowding also persisted in the postwar years. The Board of Health had far too few inspectors to enforce the new laws limiting the number of occupants per apartment. Still, Five Points tenements were not as notoriously overcrowded as they had been in the antebellum period. When, in the late 1860s, Charles Loring Brace described finding "a half a dozen families—as we frequently do—occupying one room," he added that such conditions had abounded "formerly in the Five Points," but were now more often found on the Lower East Side.[22]

Nonetheless, appalling overcrowding did persist on some blocks in the postwar years. In the early 1870s, an investigator found in a Baxter Street cellar a fifteen-by-ten-foot room in which at least twenty people slept on the straw-covered floor. Through the straw one could plainly see the filthy floorboards whose "numberless holes . . . show it to be as much the residence of rats, as of men." In another Baxter Street tenement, the same journalist discovered a room sixteen feet square where eighteen people slept. A reporter for *Frank Leslie's* encountered seventeen people (as well as a goat and some chickens) sleeping in a room twelve feet square in a Mulberry Street basement. These were extreme cases, but finding as many as ten or twelve inhabitants in a two-room apartment, especially one occupied by Italians, was not extraordinary.[23]

Fifteen years later, such conditions persisted. One night Riis accompanied the police on their raids of illegally overcrowded dwellings. In a Bayard Street apartment, he found appalling overcrowding:

> In a room not thirteen feet either way slept twelve men and women, two or three in bunks set in a sort of alcove, the rest on the floor. A kerosene lamp burned dimly in the fearful atmosphere, probably to guide other and later arrivals to their "beds," for it was only just past midnight. A baby's fretful wail came from an adjoining hall-room, where, in the semi-darkness, three recumbent figures could be made out. The "apartment" was one of three in two adjoining buildings we had found, within half an hour, similarly crowded. Most of the men were lodgers, who slept there for five cents a spot.

Riis's moving photograph of the scene makes almost palpable the discomfort and misery suffered by men and women crowded into these tiny spaces.[24]

By the 1880s, as immigration increased and affordable housing for the poor became scarce, appalling basement lodging houses once again began to proliferate throughout New York. As in the antebellum period, many of

Jacob Riis, "Lodgers in a Bayard Street Tenement," c. 1888. Collection of the Museum of the City of New York.

these establishments located in Five Points. In 1882, *Frank Leslie's Illustrated Weekly* described one such lodging house at 508 Pearl Street. For twelve cents a night, it reported, one could have a bed on the ground floor. Belowground a bed cost ten cents per night. Another subterranean chamber contained no beds at all—merely narrow canvas strips slung between wooden frames, hammocklike "beds" just wide enough to hold a man. There were two rows of these resting places, one on top of the other. No bedding was provided, and each lodger paid five cents per night. Although *Leslie's* published a print of this room, it assured its readers that

> no pencil can fully picture all its horrors. . . . Imagine these scores
> of beds filled with dirty and degraded men, clothed only in their
> own nakedness; for while the custom of such lodging places is that
> the sleeper shall remove the garments he has worn during the day,

he is furnished no other covering, and depends on the heat furnished by the stove and generated by his fellows to keep him warm. Imagine such a room, where not only is every canvas occupied, but late comers have stretched themselves at full length on the floor, cut off from the outside air as effectually as the closing of every window will permit, while a hot stove pours forth heat, and the odors of damp clothing and long unwashed bodies combine with the breathing of the crowd of occupants to make an atmosphere which almost sickens the visitor who steps inside but for a moment. Imagine all this, and the reader will have a faint idea of a scene, the full horror of which can only be appreciated by one who has actually gazed upon it—and smelled it!

Despite the assertions of Brace and Gilder to the contrary, terrible tenement and lodging house conditions persisted in Five Points throughout the late nineteenth century, and became especially bad after 1880.[25]

"Like a wart growing on the top of a festering sore"

Certain tenements in post–Civil War Five Points became especially notorious. In 1873, for example, the Board of Health announced that "the city's worst tenement" was the building known as "Mulberry Hall" or the "old Baptist Church tenement," a building that covered the rear portion of 5, 7, and 9 Mulberry Street. As the latter nickname implied, the building had originally served as a house of worship. When it was built in about 1809, the sixty-foot-wide and forty-two-foot-deep wooden church had sat well away from the street at the back of a pleasant green lawn and attracted Baptists from all over the city, including some of the city's most prominent citizens.

In about 1850, however, the congregation moved uptown and sold the property. The new owner built six-story brick tenements at the front of the lot, leaving only a fourteen-foot yard between them and the old sanctuary. He converted the church into a tenement, dividing the once airy interior into five floors of living space, though in order to squeeze in that many stories he constructed ceilings just six-and-a-half-feet high.[26]

As soon as they opened, the new tenements at 5–9 Mulberry Street filled to overflowing with famine immigrants, especially those from County Cork. The new front buildings were not especially noisome. Young politicos Tom and William Walsh had moved into number 7 and opened a saloon there. But by the late 1860s, conditions in the old church building in the rear had become scandalously wretched. *Harper's Weekly* found that "the doors are unhinged, the windows broken, the plastering hangs in shreds, [and] the dust and grime of years blackens the walls." Just as bad as the physical dilapidation of Mulberry Hall was the "foul stench" that permeated the building. In 1873, a Board of Health sanitary inspector found that "the walls and floors are saturated with offensive effluvia, the accumulation of years, to such a degree that the air is poisoned by them, and the inmates who are continually exposed to their noxious influence are all pallid, thin, and delicate in appearance." In addition, he noted, "the sewer connection of the privies is clogged, they are full of night-soil, and very offensive. The floor of this place is covered continually with excrement, urine, and rubbish, and is continually wet from the deluge of water used in attempts to keep it clean. . . . The odors from these areas are exceedingly offensive." The malfunctioning toilets inside the building also contributed to the horrible stench.[27]

Mulberry Hall was renowned for the dissipation of its inhabitants. "At night . . . nearly all the adult tenants are drunk," reported the sanitary inspector. The *Times* concurred that "strong fumes of whisky came from many mouths." Many of the alcoholics were not residents of the building, but homeless folk who sought refuge there to sleep off a bender. "Street tramps and drunkards slink in the hallways, especially at night, and sleep upon the floors," noted the *Times*. "Two besotted cases were there when we entered; both were beastly drunk, and lay with their persons exposed, their rags and tatters being covered with vermin, and dabbed in their own vomit."[28]

These conditions contributed to Mulberry Hall's phenomenally high mortality rate. Tenants died so frequently that the Board of Health ordered the building vacated in November 1871. Yet after the owner of the property, Peter Dolan, promised henceforth to lease only half of the building's forty apartments, the board agreed to keep Mulberry Hall open. Even with fewer tenants, the death rate continued to increase, to 9.2 deaths per 100 inhabitants for the year ending in March 1873, nearly four times the citywide rate. Despite repeated efforts by health officials and reformers to close "this repulsive pile," the Old Baptist Church Tenement still housed dozens of Five Pointers in the early 1890s.[29]

Number 65 Mott Street, the oldest tenement in the city, also became notorious in the postwar years. This building, reported the *Times* in 1880, stood out "like a wart growing on the top of a festering sore. It is the crowning glory of tenement-houses." The seven-story front structure was so tall that it "might lead you to take it for a mill or a factory or an over-grown car-stable, or anything but a human habitation." As with Mulberry Hall, the building's accumulation of dirt and grime was most notable. "The filth in it is so thick and deep that it is hanging out of the windows like icicles," insisted the *Times*'s reporter. A year earlier, another repulsed journalist had found that the chicken-rendering plant on the ground floor suffused the apartments with a noxious odor that far surpassed the stench of the typical Five Points tenement. As the *Times* story aptly concluded, "the building is far beyond being a disgrace to the city—that would be mild—and its owner ought to be ashamed of himself; no doubt he is, but he collects the rent regularly."[30]

In 1880, Mulberry Hall and 65 Mott Street were relatively recent additions to the list of the city's worst tenements. But another of Five Points' most decrepit residential complexes—the low, wooden tenements on the east side of Baxter Street just north of the Five Points intersection—had held that status for half a century. "It is a miserable shell, of perhaps 100 feet front, thirty feet depth and two stories high," noted a *Times* correspondent in 1871 of the front buildings stretching from 33 to 39 Baxter, the same tenements filled twenty years earlier with Lansdowne immigrants such as Ellen Holland and Sandy Sullivan. "The roof and floors have sagged down some five feet from the level; the shingles are split and rotten, and admit the rain like a basket; all the timbers are badly decayed, and tremble to the footsteps upon the floors." Conditions in the rear buildings and yards were just as dreadful. "Six goats roam here at will, and four besotted women lay helpless in the dirt," reported the *Times*. "Children of various ages and in all stages of nastiness were numerous, some crying, others shouting, fighting or cursing."[31]

The most infamous tenement on this block would help make Riis's reputation. Just to the north at 47 Baxter, it was known as "Bottle Alley." Though already decrepit before the Civil War, Bottle Alley only earned citywide renown in the postbellum years. In 1866, *Frank Leslie's* featured

Jacob Riis, "Bottle Alley: Mulberry Bend in Its Worst Days," c. 1888. Collection of the Museum of the City of New York.

the alley's tenements in a story on New York's "fever nests." When *Harper's Weekly* decided in 1879 to run a series on "the abodes of the poor," its editors chose Bottle Alley to inaugurate the series.[32]

Peering through the four-and-a-half-foot-wide passageway that ran thirty-five feet under the front building to a filthy, garbage-strewn court-yard, Bottle Alley appeared to lead to a stable. "No one would ever dream that the tumble-down building in the rear was the abode of human beings," reported *Harper's*. The passageway led to a courtyard that was paved with irregularly shaped flagstones. Huge sacks of rags, bones, and discarded paper, collected by the ragpickers living in Bottle Alley, typically filled the small plaza, but over the years heaps of other refuse had accu-mulated as well and spilled into the surrounding apartments. "The vilest filth that ever offended a human nostril covered the paving stones and even the door sills," wrote a reporter in the *New York Tribune* in the summer of 1879. "Besotted women lay as they had fallen."[33]

Inside the rear building, the *Tribune* found that "men and women were huddled together like cattle." The ten-by-fourteen-foot cellar, "a queer hole" according to the *Harper's* account, had housed as many as thirteen— and sometimes even seventeen—persons in recent years. One of the walls consisted of nothing but bare logs, another of "undressed stone. There are no chairs to sit on, only a few rough boxes."

"The two upper floors are not quite so bad," continued the *Harper's* story, "but there are sights to be seen in some of the rooms that baffle description." A staircase and balcony on the front of the building led to the one-room apartments on the top floor. One of these, depicted by the *Harper's* artist, housed five Italian men—one carpenter, one shoemaker, and three street sweepers:

> The floor is destitute of carpet, is sunken in one corner, and is cov-
> ered with grease and dirt. The ceiling and walls are more like those
> of a smoke-house than of a dwelling. There are no closets or
> pantries. The cooking utensils hang about the fire-place, the dishes
> are piled on the table, and the personal effects are crammed into
> canvas bags that hang from pegs against the wall. None of the ves-
> sels used in cooking or serving a meal are ever washed. . . . The
> food is gathered principally from the garbage boxes on the streets
> or from the offal of the markets. . . . The sleeping appointments are
> equally bad. There are no bedsteads. Five filthy-looking mattresses
> spread on boards supported by carpenters' "horses" serve as resting
> places.

The men slept in the same clothes they wore during the day, "boots and all." Theirs was not the only squalid apartment, either. A year later, *Harper's* found a ground-floor apartment in which "the plastered walls, cracked, broken, and grimy, were damp, and sickening to look at. Millions of roaches crawled over the walls and ceiling, and gathered in black clusters over the solitary smoking candle that dimly lighted the room." Ten years later, when Riis featured Bottle Alley in *How the Other Half Lives*, nothing had changed.[34]

"THE WORST SLUM THAT EVER WAS"

The block just north of the Five Points intersection had been notorious for more than half a century, but it lacked a catchy name like Cow Bay, the Arch Block, or Hell's Kitchen by which New Yorkers could identify it. Riis changed all that in 1888 when he began referring to the area bounded by Baxter, Bayard, Mulberry, and Park Streets as "Mulberry Bend." While he may not have coined the term, Riis certainly made it famous. *Frank Leslie's* stated in August 1888 that "the 'Bend' was once the dead-line of the Five Points; now it takes its place as a seat of iniquity, poverty and dirt. It is one of the danger-spots of the town." In November, another magazine maintained that "by all odds the most vicious, ignorant and degraded of all the immigrants who come to our shores are the Italian inhabitants of Mulberry Bend and the surrounding region of tenements." In 1890, *How the Other Half Lives* devoted an entire chapter to "The Bend," and the term became a household word.[35]

Mulberry Street looking north from Bayard Street toward Canal, c. 1901. Dominated by street peddlers, banks, and *padroni,* this image captures the sense of bustle and activity that made Mulberry Street the focal point of Five Points' Italian community. Detroit Photographic Company Collection, Library of Congress.

"Where Mulberry Street crooks like an elbow within hail of the old depravity of the Five Points, is 'the Bend,' foul core of New York's slums," begins Riis's chapter on Mulberry Bend. It is "a vast human pig-sty. There is but one 'Bend' in the world, and it is enough." Standing on Mulberry Street at the Bend, the tenements did not look particularly frightening. Italian vendors dominated the street scene. "Hucksters and pedlars' carts make two rows of booths in the street itself, and along the house is still another—a perpetual market doing a very lively trade in its own queer staples, found nowhere on American ground save in 'the Bend.'" Mixed in with the substantial traders with large hand trucks were a number of female peddlers. "Two old hags, camping on the pavement, are dispensing stale bread, baked not in loaves, but in the shape of big wreaths like exaggerated crullers, out of bags of dirty bedtick." On another portion of the sidewalk, Riis found Italian women "haggling over baskets of frowsy weeds, some sort of salad probably, stale tomatoes, and oranges not above suspicion. Ash barrels serve them as counters."[36]

Little in these descriptions seemed to warrant the extravagant claims of wretchedness for which Mulberry Bend was renowned. The neighborhood was no longer dominated by saloons, junk shops, and second-hand stores. Merchants on or near the Bend sold everything from beds and mattresses to clocks and guns, as well as food and wine. Doctors, midwives, and pharmacists all operated out of storefronts there as well. Riis admitted that the Bend might be "ordinary enough to look at from the street," but behind those brick walls, he insisted, lay three acres "built over with rotten structures that harbored the very dregs of humanity. . . . [It was] pierced by a maze of foul alleys, in the depths of which skulked the tramp and the outcast thief with loathsome wrecks that had once laid claim to the name of woman. Every foot of it reeked with incest and murder. Bandits' Roost, Bottle Alley, were names synonymous with robbery and red-handed outrage."[37]

One of the most appalling features of Mulberry Bend was its death rate. Children living in its cramped, dirty quarters became especially susceptible to contagious diseases such as tuberculosis, measles, and diphtheria, and died from them at horrific rates. Eight children under the age of five living at 61 Mulberry Street died in 1882. Next door at 59½ Mulberry, eleven small children perished that same year. Of the nine youngsters living at that same address in 1888, five died. These were extreme cases, to be sure. Yet the death rate for all ages on Mulberry Bend was about 50 percent above the citywide average, while children under age five died at about three times the citywide rate.[38]

The Bend—and especially its Mulberry Street side—was infamous not merely for squalid tenements but for its "stale-beer dives" as well. "Stale beer" was the term used to describe the dregs left at the bottom of a standard barrel of lager. Enterprising young immigrants—usually Italians—"go out early in the morning and sweep out lager-beer saloons or help the drivers of beer wagons. . . . For this work they receive the dregs found remaining in the cags [kegs] the day before." In order to make this recycled brew more appetizing, Riis noted, the beer was "touched up with drugs to put a froth on it."[39]

Stale-beer cellars abounded in Mulberry Bend. "Every other basement seemed to be a stale beer saloon," noted a *Tribune* reporter who toured the Bend in 1879. By 1880, journalists found "tramps of every nationality," "the lowest of the low," imbibing "these stupefying dregs" in Bottle Alley haunts. But it was Riis, a decade later, who made the Bend's stale-beer dives truly infamous. Accompanying a raiding party of Sixth Ward police officers, Riis found in one such establishment a room about twelve feet square with "hard-trodden mud" on the floor and "shuddering showers of crawling bugs" on the walls. "Grouped about a beer-keg that was propped on the wreck of a broken chair," Riis discovered "a foul and ragged host of men and women, on boxes, benches, and stools. Tomato-cans filled at the keg were passed from hand to hand. In the centre of the group a sallow, wrinkled hag, evidently the ruler of the feast, dealt out the hideous stuff."[40]

The infamous stale-beer dives of one Mulberry Street alleyway, "Bandits' Roost," inspired the creation of Riis's single most famous photo. In Riis's image, the pavement is damp and dotted with puddles. Overflowing ash barrels are visible on the left, while clotheslines heavy with the day's wash filter the afternoon sunlight ominously. Tall tenements, the rear buildings of 57 and 59 Mulberry Street, loom on either side. The people add to the sense of foreboding. In the right foreground stands a neatly dressed young man in bowler hat who would have been recognized by contemporaries as a menacing gang member. Just behind him is an older, bearded figure apparently holding a double-barreled shotgun. Above these two toughs, one of Riis's omnipresent "old hags" leans out a window. Stairs leading to the alley's numerous stale-beer dives are visible as well. Most of Riis's

Jacob Riis, "Bandits' Roost," c. 1888. Collection of the Museum of
the City of New York.

photos inspire pity or disgust at tenement dwellers' wretched conditions,
but his image of Bandits' Roost creates a sense of menace and dread that is
nearly as palpable today as it was in 1888 when Riis first exhibited it.[41]

Most residents of the Bend shunned the stale-beer cellars in favor of
street-level saloons. It was primarily the homeless—the "tramps," as Riis
called them—who patronized stale-beer dives because they could stay in
their seats all night once they made a purchase. In many of these cellars,
beer was the only item for sale. In others, Riis noted, "a cup of 'coffee' and
a stale roll may be had for two cents." These small, dirty subterranean
dens were consequently known as "two-cent restaurants." Yet some cus-

tomers could avoid even this small surcharge. "The men pay the score," explained an indignant Riis. "To the women—unutterable horror of the suggestion—the place is free."[42]

We tend today to suspect Riis of sensationalizing and exaggerating the Bend's conditions, and in fact, not all observers depicted Mulberry Bend in such pejorative terms. *Frank Leslie's* emphasized the positive. "The 'bend' is woefully overcrowded with people and smell," it admitted. Yet the inhabitants "are joyous in squalor and merry in poverty, these lazzaroni. Babies roll on the sidewalk and snooze in the gutter, while the adults enjoy the dreamy *dolce far niente* [pleasant idling] across some ash-barrel or on some sunny wagon-seat." Journalists rarely bothered to describe the many tenement apartments that had been made cheerful and pleasant by their inhabitants. "Some of their homes were low, dark rooms, neglected and squalid," noted one reporter, but others were "clean and picturesque, with bright patchwork counterpanes on the beds, rows of gay plates on shelves against the walls, mantels and shelves fringed with colored paper, red and blue prints of the saints against the white plaster, and a big nosegay of lilacs on the dresser among the earthen pots."[43]

Most accounts of the Bend, however, depicted it in terms that made Riis's assessment seem mild. "Mulberry Bend . . . is an eddy in the life of the city where the scum collects, where the very offscourings of all humanity seem to find a lodgment," wrote one journalist in 1888. "In the great 'dumb-bell' tenements, in the rickety old frame buildings, in the damp, unwholesome cellars, on the sidewalks and in the gutters reeking with filth and garbage, is a seething mass of humanity, so ignorant, so vicious, so depraved that they hardly seem to belong to our species."

After a brief hiatus, Americans once again considered Five Points "the worst slum that ever was."[44]

12

PROLOGUE

"These 'Slaves of the Harp'"

In June 1873, a groundskeeper in Central Park made a startling discovery. Huddled in a secluded corner of the park he found a famished twelve-year-old boy, "with scarcely a rag on him." The boy could speak no English, but his hunger was evident, so the park worker shared his lunch with the unfortunate lad, who ravenously devoured the food. Before the park worker could decide what to do with the poor child, he ran off. The groundskeeper found the boy again the next day, however, and after feeding him again, took him to one of the park's shanty-like huts, where many impoverished New Yorkers lived. There, a Mrs. McMonegal cleaned the boy up, fed him, and found him some decent clothes. During the two weeks that the boy remained with Mrs. McMonegal, he was able, bit by bit, to explain how he had ended up in Central Park alone and famished.

His name was Joseph, and he had been born in Calvello, a desolate, windswept village about ninety miles southeast of Naples in the mountainous Italian region of Basilicata. Joseph had lived with his parents, who were peasant farmers, until age nine, when they handed him over to a stranger who took him aboard a ship with eight other boys from the same region. The man was a *"padrone,"* a labor contractor who had bought the right to the children's labor from their parents. After weeks at sea, they arrived in New York, where the *padrone* sent Joseph onto the streets to play a triangle and beg for money. He slept on a pile of straw on a cellar floor and was fed only small rations of black bread twice a day. Soon he was taught the violin and told not to return each night to his basement home on Crosby Street until he had collected one dollar from passing pedestrians. The *padrone* beat him when he failed to bring home the requisite sum and bound him by his wrists at night so he could not run away. But after living in such conditions for more than two years, Joseph did escape. A few days later, he was found in Central Park and his story, as told to the *Times*, became the talk of the town.[1]

New Yorkers were appalled by Joseph's saga. Explaining the outpouring of sympathy, an editorial noted that "it seemed impossible that the world had given up stealing men from the African coast, only to kidnap children from Italy, and that the auction-block for negroes had been overturned in the Southern States, only to be set up again for white infants in New-York." No slave, the *Times* asserted, "ever narrated cruelties more brutal than has this wretched boy."[2]

Aside from his escape, Joseph's story was not unique. Tiny Italian minstrels, generally ranging in age from six to twelve, had first become fixtures on the thoroughfares of Paris and London. Brought to those capitals in the late 1850s and early 1860s, the children played small harps, violins, and triangles while soliciting donations from passersby. When officials in France and England announced that they would no longer allow *padroni* to victimize the helpless waifs in this manner, many of them brought their tiny charges to New York. In some cases, an entrepreneur purchased the right to a youngster's labor in Italy and accompanied him all the way to the United States. In other instances, a child might be traded two or three times in different countries—once in Italy, another time in France (usually Marseilles), and a third time in the United States—before he began performing on the sidewalks of New York. By the early 1870s there were about a thousand child street musicians, almost all boys, living in the city.[3]

Like Joseph, these children were mostly natives of Basilicata. Residents of this isolated and impoverished southern province had for centuries learned *mestiere per partire*, jobs specifically designed to help them escape Basilicata and earn a living in more prosperous areas—either within Italy or abroad. Learning to play a musical instrument was a *mestiere per partire* especially popular in Basilicata. Yet it was only in the mid-nineteenth century that children began leaving Basilicata to work as musicians. Parents who sold their offspring might appear cruel or heartless, but they often had the youngsters' best interests at heart. By turning their children over to *padroni*, these parents felt they were giving them a chance of escape the crushing poverty of life in Basilicata. Besides, each *padrone* promised to train his charges to become skilled musicians, a trade that in theory would guarantee them a far better income than had ever been within the reach of their parents.[4]

Whatever the parents' motivations, New York's child street musicians lived and worked in appalling circumstances. "Without father or mother, or any relative who might be in the least interested in their welfare," complained the *Times*, "these 'slaves of the harp' have been torn from their homes in Italy, and compelled to support, by the hardest of hard work, a lazy lot of 'padrones' whose only care is to make as much out of the poor children as possible. Half-starved and ragged they are sent into the streets, and should they return at night without a certain sum of money which they have been ordered to make, the poor children are severely punished, and sent to their filthy couches without their supper." Charles Loring Brace, who was intimately familiar with the musicians' circumstances through his work with the Children's Aid Society, noted that the colder the weather, the more likely the *padrone* would force his charges out onto the streets, playing the harp "to excite the compassion of our citizens. . . . I

An Italian street musician and his *padrone. Harper's Weekly* (September 13, 1873): 801. Collection of the author.

used to meet these boys sometimes on winter-nights half-frozen and stiff with cold." One *Times* reporter encountered a boy just five years old, who "trudged along, bearing his cross, in the form of a harp, twice the size of himself" and was crying "dove mia Mama," where's my mother?[5]

After publishing Joseph's tale, the *Times* sent a reporter to uncover the stories of other Italian street musicians. He soon found a small band of the waifs rummaging through some garbage barrels looking for food. The youngest "was regaling himself upon a semi-petrified beef bone. In the other hand he held a piece of bread begrimed with filth. His triangle lay on the ground forgotten." At first, the children refused to talk with the journalist, but they grew more forthcoming after he fed them a meal of meat, bread, and strawberries at his home. The youngest, a six-year-old called Franceschito ("little Francis"), was the triangle player. His *padrone* required him to bring home at least eighty cents each day. A second boy, Rocco, a twelve-year-old from Laurenzano (a small village about five miles west of Calvello), had been in New York for six months. A third youngster, Pietrocito ("little Peter"), also a Laurenzano native, had arrived in New York just six days earlier via Naples and Marseilles. "Their clothing is such as a beggar would scorn," commented the outraged *Times* correspondent. ". . . They are only washed once a month, and in the meantime they never have their clothes off. At the end of the month they receive a clean shirt."

The *padrone* kept his charges in tatters not merely to save money but to elicit the most sympathy from passersby and thus increase the youngsters' income. Aside from an hour of music practice each morning at dawn, the children spent all day and much of the evening on the streets, rain or shine, performing and begging. "Hundreds of . . . young Italian children," the *Times* lamented, "are now suffering the greatest cruelties at the hands of task-masters, or owners, who have purchased them in New-York City, and who cruelly and maliciously beat and ill-treat them daily should they not bring home enough money every night to satisfy their greed."[6]

The extent to which these child street musicians lived in Five Points is unclear. Most of the children described by the *Times* resided on Crosby Street a mile or so north of the notorious neighborhood. Yet little Joseph told the *Times* reporter that many of his fellow musicians lived on Mulberry Street. In 1881, *Harper's Weekly* published an image of a Baxter Street *padrone* whipping a child musician, further evidence that some of these children lived in Five Points. Other accounts of the neighborhood's tenements noted the presence of small violins and harps, indicating that the children inhabiting them probably performed on the streets.[7]

After the *Times* published Joseph's story in mid-1873, an outraged public demanded an end to the virtual enslavement of these poor children. Initial efforts to arrest the *padroni* proved fruitless because prosecutors discovered that the Italians were not violating any laws. That changed in 1874, as the New York legislature enacted a statute making it a crime to receive children under the age of sixteen for the purpose of performing on the street. By the end of the year, the Children's Aid Society could proudly report that the new law had virtually eliminated the sight "of boys of tender age staggering under the weight of the harp, or begging for the harpist." Thus came to an end one of the most cruel forms of child labor New York has ever known.[8]

CHAPTER TWELVE

Italians

⌖

T HE STREETS NEW YORKERS now associate with Little Italy—
Baxter, Mulberry, and Elizabeth—did not become thoroughly Italian
until the 1880s. Before then, Italian immigrants were just a modest presence in Five Points. Both Cow Bay and the block of Baxter Street just north
of the Five Points intersection had become home in the 1850s to many
natives of Italy. In the prewar decade, the majority of the city's Italian
immigrants were either professionals or skilled artisans. But those who
lived in Five Points worked primarily as unskilled day laborers and fruit
peddlers, while the women toiled as ragpickers and the boys as bootblacks.
Like their countrymen in other parts of the city, most of the first Italians
in Five Points were natives of northern Italy, particularly the province of
Liguria and its bustling port capital of Genoa. By 1855, the Italian presence
in Five Points was significant enough to prompt the Children's Aid Society
to establish a special night school there especially for Italian immigrants.[9]

During the 1860s, the neighborhood's Italian population continued to
increase steadily. In 1865, it was sufficient to support three Italian groceries. These establishments, two of which featured billiard tables and
crowded barrooms, served as social hubs for the Italian residents. Growth
in the early 1870s was even more rapid, and soon the Italian "colony"
began spreading south from the Five Points intersection down Baxter
Street. This concentration was the largest in Manhattan, prompting the
editor of the city's Italian-language newspaper to dub Five Points the city's
"Boulevard des Italiens."[10]

Many of the newly arriving immigrants still hailed from Liguria and other northern provinces, but by the early 1870s, large numbers also began arriving in New York from the southern half of the Italian peninsula, especially Campania (the region surrounding Naples) and Basilicata (the region south of Campania). By this point, significant Italian enclaves developed a few miles to the north of Five Points on Thompson, Sullivan, Jersey, Crosby, and Washington Streets. Yet most of the impoverished southern Italians arriving in these years chose to make Five Points their home.[11]

Overpopulation, crop failures, high taxes, desperate poverty, and in the case of Basilicata in particular, fear of malaria, all drove southern Italians from their homeland in the 1870s. Until about 1875, most of these sojourners settled in South America, especially Argentina. But as the American economy revived later in the decade, New York became their preferred destination. Soon, *hare l'America,* to go to America, became a goal of all young Italians, "almost a sign of manhood," notes one historian. Men did, in fact, outnumber women in this early Italian emigration, by a margin of nearly ten to one in the mid-1880s. They came without women in part because they did not intend to relocate permanently. Most hoped merely to save money and return to Italy to pay off family debts, buy a farm, or in some other way improve upon their previously miserable standard of living.[12]

"GROANING OUT THEIR HORRID MUSIC UNDER OUR WINDOWS"

Unlike Irish Five Pointers, who had quickly embraced American foods upon their arrival in America, Italians chose to bring their culinary staples with them. They could find virtually all of their favorite foods in the neighborhood's many Italian groceries. Luigi Peirano's emporium at 98 Park Street carried "a complete assortment of every type of food, specializing in the foods of Genoa and Naples, imported directly. . . . We have olive oil from Lucca and the Ligurian Riviera, parmesan, romano, pecorino, and Swiss and Dutch cheese, dried mushrooms, preserves, salami, rice, flour etc." The store also stocked wines from Italy and California. Italian groceries also sold pasta, of course, though most Italian housewives settling in Five Points continued to make their own by hand. As in Italy, many Italian food shops in Five Points were highly specialized. Pasquale Cuneo's Mulberry Street "salumeria," for example, sold only pork products, including salami, Bolognese mortadella, lard, and numerous varieties of sausage and prosciutto. The Italian press waxed eloquent on the wonderful aromas emanating from Five Points' kitchens, a sentiment never expressed when the Irish dominated the neighborhood. Yet other New Yorkers did not salivate over the thought of Italian cuisine. Still wedded to a meat and potatoes diet, they looked disdainfully upon the Italians' "dirty macaroni."[13]

Some specialties, such as Italian ice cream, were sold on the street. For just one cent, a vendor dished out, "on a bit of brown paper, a small dab of ice-cream, or its mysterious and sticky relative called 'hokey-pokey'; and he finds plenty of cash customers. While ice-cream is sold at such popular prices, even the poorest family need not be without cramps and dyspepsia."[14]

The first Italians in New York became synonymous not merely with certain types of food but with specific occupations as well. Initially, organ-grinding was the vocation most associated with Italian immigrants. Journalist Solon Robinson had complained in the 1850s that New Yorkers were "tormented" by Italians "groaning out their horrid music under our windows, while the grinder and his monkey look anxiously for falling pennies or pea-nuts." As Robinson noted, monkeys were an integral part of the organ-grinder's trade, climbing up building facades to solicit donations from those in upper-story windows. Their antics delighted children, who in turn beseeched their parents for coins. Grinders usually dressed their simian assistants in ornate costumes to attract attention, though they did so with a sense of humor. After the Austro-Italian War of 1866, for example, it became especially popular to dress the monkeys in Austrian officers' uniforms.[15]

New Yorkers associated organ-grinding with Five Points. Nearly one in twenty Italian men living there was an organ-grinder in 1880. Even if he did not live in Five Points, the organ-grinder probably bought or rented his instrument there. An aspiring grinder could rent a hand organ for four dollars per month on Baxter Street, or buy one direct from the manufacturer a block away in Chatham Square. The Chatham Square dealer claimed to have supplied five thousand Italians with the instruments from 1870 to 1890.[16]

Five Pointers also supplied organ-grinders with their monkeys. A *Harper's Weekly* story on "Italian Life in New York" featured a full-page print of a Baxter Street "monkey training school." The "half-grown" monkeys enrolled at the simian academy were taught to doff their hats and shake hands in response to commands in either Italian or English. A properly trained monkey could significantly increase a grinder's income by thoroughly working the crowd for tips and amusing onlookers so that they dug deeper into their pockets for donations. Trained animals were worth twenty to thirty dollars, the equivalent of several months' salary to impoverished Five Pointers.[17]

Consequently, a Five Pointer would go to virtually any length to keep a monkey healthy. An Italian author visiting the neighborhood related with astonishment that "one day, seated on a step of one of the darkest tenements, one could see an Italian lady who, with uncovered breasts, nursed a monkey as if it were a baby. The monkey was sick; and this woman, the wife of an organ-grinder, hoped to restore it with her own milk."[18]

As had been the case with child street musicians, legislation hastened the decline of organ-grinding. "The law forbidding organ-grinders to have monkeys, and the demand for Italian laborers, have made organ-grinding almost a thing of the past," reported *Harper's Weekly* in 1890. This was something of an exaggeration, as the trade persisted well into the twentieth century. But the number of organ-grinders in New York probably declined by two-thirds from the 1870s to 1890. Once Italian boys began to displace Irish youngsters as bootblacks and newsboys, and Italian men gained acceptance as day laborers, few lamented the demise of these musical street trades.[19]

"WE WANT SOMEBODY TO DO THE DIRTY WORK; THE IRISH ARE NOT DOING IT ANY LONGER"

Because they could speak no English, most Italian men turned to *padroni* to find them jobs. The *padroni* supplied manual laborers to construction sites and public works projects inside the city, and to railroad track crews and mining companies outside of it. Employers paid the *padroni*, who deducted a generous fee before turning over the balance to their laborers.

The *padroni* who found employment for adults soon became as notorious as their predecessors who had exploited children. The initial fee they levied for finding work seemed exorbitant, often amounting to one or even two weeks' pay. A newcomer might not receive a dime in wages for quite some time, and if he was laid off before his *padrone* had been paid in full, the laborer would leave the work site without a cent and still be in debt to the contractor. If the job did last, the *padrone* continued to deduct a portion of the worker's salary as long as he was employed. *Padroni* were notorious for laying off workers without cause in order to generate a new round of up-front fees. Some *padroni*, especially those new to the business, actually supervised their charges at the work site. A few even brandished pistols to maintain discipline. The more established *padroni* hired foremen to oversee the laborers and translate the construction boss's orders into Italian. Whether they wanted to stay in New York or journey thousands of miles for work, Italian immigrants quickly learned that Mulberry Street in Five Points was the place to find the *padroni* who could secure them their first jobs in America.[20]

Many successful Five Points *padroni* eventually branched out into "banking," and the district soon became as renowned for its shady Italian banks as it was for its rapacious *padroni*. "Almost every other house in the Italian quarter is a 'bank,'" observed the *Herald* in 1892. Another writer christened Mulberry Street "'the Italian Wall Street,' because of the many banking houses and money exchanges that line that thoroughfare." In the late nineteenth century, there were six and sometimes even ten banks per block on Mulberry Street.[21]

These banks had little in common with typical American depositories of the period. Other financial institutions built imposing offices in order to convey a sense of solid financial stability. The Mulberry Street banks, in contrast, were generally "shabby little affairs, run in connection with lodging houses, restaurants, grocery stores, macaroni factories, beer saloons, cigar shops, etc., but under imposing names, such as Banca Roma, Banca Italiana, Banca Abbruzzese, and the like." They were neither licensed nor regulated and paid no interest whatsoever on their deposits. Anyone, it seemed, could open a Mulberry Street bank. A successful watchmaker began offering banking services in 1891. A wine shop doubled as a bank as well. Most Mulberry Street "bankers" also served as railroad and steamship company agents, and typically transacted more business wiring money to Italy than they did taking in immigrants' hard-earned savings for deposit.[22]

Despite these shortcomings, New York's Italian newcomers were drawn to the Mulberry Street banks. With Italian unification a recent event, immigrants still thought of themselves more as Basilicatans or Neapolitans than

Italians, and the bankers skillfully manipulated the newcomers' regional loyalty to win their confidence. In addition, many believed they had no choice but to make the banks their first stop in New York. Often the bankers' agents in Italy stamped the name and address of a particular Mulberry Street bank on their passports and instructed them to report there for work.[23]

The Italian bankers insisted that their unsavory reputation was unfounded. They paid no interest, they asserted, because they did not put their depositors' funds at risk by investing them. Their fees and commissions were not exorbitant either, they contended, because so many immigrants defaulted on their loans. That the bankers loaned money at all, however, indicates that they *were* investing their depositors' funds. It is also hard to believe that the many bankers who accumulated substantial real estate holdings did not use deposits to purchase tenements or secure mortgages.[24]

One of the most successful bankers in Five Points was Antonio Cuneo. Born in the Piemonte region of northwestern Italy, Cuneo immigrated to New York in 1855. Like many early Italian immigrants, Cuneo first chose self-employment, selling fruit and roasted nuts from a pushcart. Four years later, he managed to acquire a grocery, and as Italian immigrants began arriving in Five Points in greater numbers in the postwar years, he opened a bank. In 1881, he abandoned the grocery business altogether to concentrate on finance and real estate, and soon his office at the corner of Mulberry and Park Streets became one of the best known banks in the neighborhood. By the end of the 1880s, Cuneo boasted that he owned more than $400,000 in property, mostly tenements in or near Mulberry Bend. Despite his wealth and prestige, Cuneo continued to live in Five Points at 101 Park Street well into the 1890s.[25]

Cuneo had chosen the location of his bank wisely, for as *Harper's Weekly* commented in 1890, "the moment an Italian arrives in New York—that is, one of humble means and without friends in the city—he wends his way to Mulberry Street." For most Italians arriving there, Five Points was merely a staging ground. On Mulberry Street the newcomer could exchange some money, locate employment through a *padrone*, write (or hire someone to write) a letter back to Italy reporting his safe arrival in the United States, and regain his bearings while he awaited transportation to his first American job. For most Italian immigrants, this meant an additional journey to Texas, Florida, the Rocky Mountain West, or some other far-flung corner of North America.[26]

Of the Italians who took jobs outside of New York, the vast majority toiled on railroad construction crews. "The typical railroad-builder of a few years ago," noted *Frank Leslie's* in 1882, "was a newly-arrived Irish immigrant, ready to do hard work for moderate pay. [But] the representatives of the Green Isle have been largely supplanted in this work by the sons of Italy." A prominent railroad construction contractor told the *Tribune* in 1887 that "on all the big railroad jobs throughout the West you will find Italians in droves. . . . On some roads they are employed almost exclusively." Although this contractor lamented that the Italians "are not nearly as good workmen as the Irish," they became the preferred source of labor for most railroad construction projects by the mid-1880s.[27]

Many railroad crews were recruited by *padrone* Francesco Sabbia, a Sicilian from Catania who arrived in New York in the late 1870s. Sabbia settled in Five Points and soon opened a grocery and stale-beer dive at 92 Mulberry Street. By the 1890s, he was placing newly arrived immigrants in railroad construction gangs up and down the East Coast. He later opened a bank as well. Unlike Cuneo, who remained throughout his life a pillar of the Italian-American community, Sabbia became the personification of *padrone* greed and exploitation when Progressive Era muckrakers discovered in 1907 that the workers he had supplied to the Florida East Coast Railroad lived as virtual slaves. Despite such horror stories, and various governmental attempts to stamp out the *padroni* by establishing employment offices at Ellis Island, *padroni* remained the primary source of railroad employment for Italians well into the twentieth century.[28]

Mining jobs were also popular among newly arriving Italians. An 1888 edition of *Frank Leslie's* featured a print entitled "Arrival of Contract Laborers for the Coal Mines," which depicted hundreds of Italians marching up Mulberry Street for transportation to a distant site. Many Italians worked the coal mines of Pennsylvania and West Virginia, but thousands of others entered mining in Colorado, Wyoming, and Montana. Italians rarely dominated mining in the same manner as they did railroad construction. Employers often hired a variety of ethnic groups in order to divide the workers and prevent unionization. Mine owners also believed that Italian miners would work harder if they knew that the Slavs or Welshmen working another shaft might out-produce them.[29]

Unlike mining, work on the railroads was not available all year round. In fact, outside the Deep South, most kinds of construction labor ceased each winter. As a result, many of the Italians who had passed through Mulberry Bend on their way to job sites across North America returned to Five Points for the winter. "They come in from the country, the railroad and other work having stopped," reported a labor journal in 1884. "Some of them find odd jobs, but the majority live on their scanty earnings—a piece of bread and an onion for breakfast, about the same for dinner, and maccaroni for supper." An Italian visiting New York found that during the winter thousands of unemployed Italian railroad laborers "fill up the streets of New York, where the young polish shoes and the adults are engaged in work refused by workers of other nationalities—emptying garbage from barges into the sea, cleaning sewage—or they go around with a sack on their shoulders rummaging for bones, etc." Never sparsely populated, Mulberry Bend seemed to burst at the seams each winter as permanent Italian residents took in out-of-work friends and relatives, while commercial boardinghouses filled to overflowing as well.[30]

Many in these trying times turned to mutual aid societies for assistance. Immigrants from virtually every village and town in Italy organized self-help societies in New York whose membership was limited to natives of a particular Italian locale. The groups loaned money to indigent members, helped them find jobs, and organized social gatherings.[31]

Given the cramped quarters and lack of employment opportunities in wintertime, many of the immigrants—both those who lived in New York year-round and those who did not—chose to return to Italy for the season. Italians were the first New York immigrants to partake in this "return migration." Some laborers "go to Italy in the fall and return in the spring, so that during the months of September, October, November and December there is an exodus of over thirty thousand of them," reported a group of Italian bankers and steamship agents. Often these returnees decided to remain in Italy permanently, lured by the prospect of marriage or the ability to purchase land with their newfound American wealth. Most, however, returned to America the following spring, anxious to earn even more money before resettling permanently in Italy. These repeat immigrants frequently brought with them friends or relatives who were drawn to New York by stories of high pay and plentiful job opportunities. Others decided to journey to the United States after seeing the remittances earlier immigrants had sent home to loved ones. To southern Italians whose families had been mired in poverty for centuries, even Five Points streets seemed to be paved with gold.[32]

Although most Italian immigrants merely passed through Five Points on their way to a distant job site, some decided to make the neighborhood their home in America. Even more so than the Irish a generation earlier, these Italians were renowned for clustering in tenements with other immigrants from the same region or village. Unfortunately, the neighborhood's Catholic church did not keep the detailed nativity records for its Italian parishioners that it had for the Irish a generation earlier, so we cannot document the Italians' regional clustering with certainty. Nonetheless, contemporaries were sure that the Italians of Mulberry Bend lived "grouped by 'villages.'" An Italian-American journalist agreed that "in one street there will be found peasants from one Italian village; in the next the place of origin is different and distinct, and different and distinct are manners, customs, and sympathies. Entire villages have been transplanted from Italy to one New York street."[33]

Five Points Italians also found themselves, like the Irish before them, situated initially at the bottom of the city's economic ladder. The vast majority of unskilled Italians living in Five Points toiled as menial laborers on construction sites and public works projects. By the mid-1890s, Italians comprised three-quarters of all New York construction workers and 90 percent of laborers employed by the city. Italian laborers did the same backbreaking and dangerous hauling and excavating that the Irish had once dominated. "We can't get along without the Italians," commented one police officer in 1895. "We want somebody to do the dirty work; the Irish are not doing it any longer."[34]

In Five Points before the Civil War, four of five Irishmen who were not laborers worked in skilled trades. But in 1880, the majority of non-laborer Italians were peddlers or otherwise self-employed on the streets. Many were organ-grinders, but the vast majority peddled fruit. Speaking of the once ubiquitous Irish apple seller, Police Superintendent Thomas Byrnes noted that "twenty years ago you couldn't pass a street corner without finding one; now all the fruit stands are kept by Italians."[35]

Some Italians sold a variety of fruits; others concentrated on one specialty, such as watermelon or lemons. In the winter, when fruit was not readily available, they sold hot chestnuts and peanuts. These fruit vendors actually altered New Yorkers' eating habits. "Italians have put up fruit stands at every available corner where there is a chance of selling their wares, and have learned to arrange their fruits so tastefully as to tempt the passer-by," commented the *Times* in 1895. "It is mainly due to the efforts of the Italians," the journalist concluded, "that fruit eating has become quite universal here." By that point there were said to be ten thousand Italian fruit vendors in New York. Their union, the Society of Italian Fruit Peddlers *(Societá di Frutivendoli Ambulanti)*, usually held its meetings in Five Points.[36]

Italian women also worked for pay. Whereas three-quarters of the neighborhood's Irishwomen had worked either in the needle trades or as domestic servants in 1855, by 1880 only 24 percent of Italian women were employed in those fields. A variety of manufacturing jobs had become available since the Civil War, and many Italian women took jobs in these industries instead. They worked primarily in candy and tobacco factories in 1880, though they made artificial flowers as well. Italian women would eventually dominate artificial flower and paper box making, but Irish-American women (mostly the American-born daughters of immigrants) still held the bulk of these jobs in 1880. By the mid-1890s, many Italian women would move into garment work as well.[37]

New Yorkers in these years especially associated Mulberry Bend women with the "rag picking" trade. "Most of the rag pickers in New York live in the Five Points, and near the Central Park," wrote Virginia Penny in her encyclopedic study of women's work. The term "ragpicker" was something of a misnomer, as those who followed this vocation collected not only rags, but paper, bones, and scrap metal and glass as well. "Some even carry a basket in which they gather waste vegetables or putrid meat, or the trimmings of uncooked meat," explained Penny, "which they feed on themselves, or give to a pet pig, or trade with some neighbor." A ragpicker's life was a hard one. Trudging about the city rummaging through trash barrels and garbage heaps was only the beginning of her work. When she returned home, she had to sort the rags into clean and dirty, washing the latter. She also separated linens from woolens, clean paper from dirty, and white from colored. In the Civil War years, ragpickers generally got two cents per pound for rags and paper, and on a very good day might collect forty pounds. Bones sold for thirty cents a bushel. They sold fat to soapmakers or rendering plants and the metal and glass to junk dealers.

Huge sacks of rags and paper are visible in most of Jacob Riis's photos of Mulberry Bend, indicating the omnipresence of ragpickers in the neighborhood. In the 1850s and '60s, both Irish and Italian Five Pointers followed this line of work. By the 1880s, however, four of five neighborhood ragpickers were Italian.[38]

The employment rate for Italian women was held down by demographics and cultural attitudes. Thirty-five percent of married Irish-American women living in Five Points in 1880 did paid work, versus only 7 percent of married Italian-American women. Most Italian husbands would have been ashamed to let their wives work outside the home. Among unmarried women, 74 percent of Irish Americans worked for pay, versus just half of the Italians. The sample of unmarried Italian women was tiny, however, because there were *very few* unmarried Italian woman in Five Points. Eighty-five percent of Italian women aged eighteen or older were married, whereas only 36 percent of Irish-American women had a spouse. This huge disparity resulted primarily from the differing sex ratios in the two communities. Among adult Five Pointers, Italian men outnumbered women by two to one in 1880, while Irish-American women comprised 53 percent of the neighborhood's adult Hibernian population. Italian men sometimes went to great lengths to find wives. *Padroni* occasionally brought potential brides from Italy to New York, noted one reporter, "and they are disposed of at prices that pay the passage money and a good profit on the venture."[39]

With so few Italian women working outside the home, Italian boys were especially likely to choose employment over school. "Bootblacking," once monopolized by the Irish, eventually became associated with Italian youths. Although they initially had trouble breaking into the Irish bootblacks' close-knit ranks, by 1890 Italians controlled bootblacking completely. An 1894 survey of 484 New York bootblacks found that 473 were Italian Americans. Nonetheless, many more Italian adolescents worked as laborers than as bootblacks.[40]

Irish workers often resented the Italians who displaced them. When Irish sewer diggers went on strike for higher wages during the severe depression of 1874, the contractor dismissed them and hired Italians. The Irish threw rocks at the Italians, seriously injuring two before police drove them off. "They left vowing vengeance," reported the *Times*, "and threatening to murder every Italian who would dare to accept employment in the place of Irishmen." Labor groups condemned all manner of Italian workers—from laborers to barbers—for accepting less than the prevailing American wage during the late nineteenth century.[41]

Labor leaders often cursed Italians' supposed hostility to unions, but many obstacles prevented them from becoming part of the Gilded Age labor movement. The *padrone* system, for example, made it virtually impossible for laborers to seek union membership. But in a few cases Italians in Five Points did aid the cause of organized labor. When New York freight handlers called a strike in 1882, employers brought in Italians to man the piers. A mass meeting was held in Five Points at which Jeremiah Murphy, president of the Freighthandlers Union, asked the Italians not to work as scabs. Consequently, two hundred Italians already hired as replacement workers for the Erie Railroad walked out as well. Many joined the union, which agreed to provide food for the Italian strikers. Yet such cases of interethnic labor cooperation were relatively rare in the late nineteenth century. Much more common were comments like those of a clothing manufacturer who stated that he preferred to hire Italians because while Jews were always striking, the Italians "work along steadily and do not complain."[42]

"THE ITALIANS AS A BODY ARE NOT HUMILIATED BY HUMILIATION"

During the last fifteen or so years of the nineteenth century, religious antagonism between Italian- and Irish-Americans in Five Points became even more intense than workplace hostilities. This animosity developed as a result of Five Points' evolving demographics and the reactions of Irish Catholic leaders to those transformations.

Looking back in 1897 at the changes Five Points had undergone during the previous twenty years, a Catholic priest remembered that the district had once had about thirteen thousand Irish Catholic parishioners. But then

> came the Chinese, who gradually usurped all of Pell and Doyers streets, and Mott street from the Bowery to Pell. Then came the Jews, who not satisfied with Baxter street, settled in Mott, Hester, Bayard, and Chrystie streets. Then came the Italians and they drove the Irish from Mulberry and Park streets and took full possession of the "Bend." Last of all came the manufacturers with

their big factories and dispersed our people from Elm, Leonard, and Franklin streets so that at the end of twenty years we have in our parish limits scarcely eight hundred English-speaking people.[43]

In theory, these changes should not have alarmed the neighborhood's Roman Catholic clergy. There were virtually as many Catholics in the parish in 1890 as there had been two decades earlier, and a truly "catholic" church ought to have welcomed the Italians who replaced the Irish in the Transfiguration pews. But American prelates viewed the Italian newcomers as inferior Christians. "It is a very delicate matter to tell the Sovereign Pontiff how utterly faithless the specimens of his country coming here really are," confided one American bishop to another in 1884. "Ignorance of their religion and a depth of vice little known to us yet, are their prominent characteristics." Even in correspondence with Rome, the Americans found it impossible to conceal their prejudices. "Nowhere among other Catholic groups in our midst," they complained, "is there such crass and listless ignorance of the faith as among the Italian immigrants."[44]

One might imagine that those clergymen who worked directly with the Italians would develop familiarity, respect, and even sympathy for the newcomers, but this was not the case in Five Points. Rev. Thomas F. Lynch, who from 1881 to 1894 served as rector of the parish that encompassed Five Points, often complained about his Italian parishioners. And Lynch's brother Bernard wrote an article for the *Catholic World* that seethed with intolerance and prejudice.

In the article, entitled "The Italians in New York," Bernard Lynch asserted that "the Italians in the jurisdiction of Transfiguration parish . . . come to America the worst off in religious equipment of, perhaps, any foreign Catholics whatever." They do not know the "Apostles' Creed" nor the other basic "elementary truths of religion, such as the Trinity, the Incarnation, and the Redemption." Italians instead focused their energies upon "'devotions,' pilgrimages, shrines, miraculous pictures and images, [and] indulgences," while remaining in "almost total ignorance of the great truths which can alone make such aids of religion profitable." Lynch admitted that some northern Italians arrived in America well educated in the teachings of the church. But most southern Italians, he charged, were not even "well enough instructed to receive the sacraments."

As if these statements were not incendiary enough, Lynch impugned the Italians' character as well. Italians, he wrote, lack "especially what we call *spirit.*" In addition, "they for the most part seem totally devoid of . . . personal independence and manliness. An American or an Irishman will almost starve before asking for charity, and often really does starve. Not so the lower-class Italian. He is always ready to beg." The Transfiguration Italians, Lynch boldly declared, did not have "the qualities fitting them to be good Americans!"[45]

How had relations between Five Points Italians and Irish Catholics sunk to this level? While some of the neighborhood's first Italian immigrants had attended mass at Transfiguration, others had preferred to venture out of the neighborhood to churches run by Italian priests. The first, St. Anthony of Padua, had opened in 1866 a mile and a half north of Five Points at the corner of Bleecker and Sullivan Streets. By 1878, as the Five Points Italian population continued to grow, Transfiguration rector James McGean began allowing his Italian parishioners to hold a separate mass in the church's basement. Italian priests from St. Anthony's officiated at these services. But McGean still sent Italians to St. Anthony's for confessions, baptisms, marriages, and last rites. As the Five Points Italian population continued to increase during the 1880s, Lynch requested that the archdiocese assign him an Italian assistant who could officiate at the Italian masses and administer the sacraments. The first clergyman assigned to this duty arrived in Five Points in the autumn of 1886. A second arrived in 1887. Each Sunday, more than two thousand Italians celebrated mass in the Transfiguration basement.[46]

Not surprisingly, the newcomers resented their banishment to the basement. Transfiguration's Irish Catholic leaders asserted publicly that the Italians preferred worshipping separately. But as New York Archbishop Michael A. Corrigan noted privately in 1885, the Irish clergy had exiled the Italians to the Transfiguration basement because "these poor Italians are not extraordinarily clean, so the [other parishioners] don't want them in the upper church, otherwise they will go elsewhere, and then farewell to the income." Responding to charges that segregating the Italians was insulting the newcomers, Bernard Lynch asserted that "the Italians as a body are not humiliated by humiliation." But the Italians clearly *were* insulted. Complaining of one of the many bigoted comments in Lynch's article, an Italian priest in New Jersey asserted that "there is no other pastor in New York City who would allow his brother to say this, so disparaging a remark," against fourteen thousand of his own parishioners. This was proof, he concluded, that the Irish priests were irrevocably prejudiced against the Italians.[47]

Even Reverend Lynch's request for the permanent assignment of Italian priests to Transfiguration was motivated by selfishness. Lynch appears to have thought that he could better control and monitor the activities of the Italians if they were ministered to by his own assistants rather than by clergymen from St. Anthony's, over whom he exercised no authority. An Italian cleric assigned to Transfiguration complained to the head of his order in Italy that "Your Excellency knows that Fr. Lynch said that here the Italian priests, ours included, must be servants, servants, servants." Another Italian priest informed a superior in Italy that Lynch constantly denigrated him. Poor Italians who dared to enter the upper church and stand to avoid paying pew rent, he added, were scorned and verbally abused by the ushers.[48]

Transfiguration was only the first New York parish in which such animosity developed. Soon, the treatment of Italian Americans by the predominantly Irish-American Catholic hierarchy became a matter of international debate, referred to as "the Italian Problem," and discussed in the highest Catholic councils both in the United States and Rome. Pope Leo XIII believed that the American church leaders were neglecting the Italian immigrants, and perhaps willfully mistreating them as well. Beginning in 1887, he expressed his displeasure both in writing and in audiences with American prelates. He also ordered Bishop Giovanni Scalabrini of Piacenza to begin specially training Italian priests to minister to the Italian immigrants in America.[49]

The American bishops seethed with indignation at this reprimand from Rome. They retorted that the pope and his northern Italian advisers understood neither the depth of the southern Italians' ignorance nor how the United States' multiethnic Catholic population would be splintered if each immigrant group received its own parishes and priests. In a letter to Archbishop Corrigan, Lynch propounded an additional reason for opposing the pope's policy. It was important to keep the Italians in parishes presided over by English speakers, he contended, so that their children "grow up with our (proper) notions of supporting the church." Lynch was not referring merely to financial considerations. Turning over American parishes to Italian priests would make it difficult for Irish-American church leaders to impose their "proper notions" of church practice on the newest generation of American immigrants.[50]

Transfiguration's Italian parishioners sent two petitions to Rome in the spring of 1888 complaining of their treatment by Lynch and their banishment to the church's basement, and asking that the diocese set up a separate Italian parish in their neighborhood. A few months later Corrigan consented to the opening of a Scalabrinian-run church on Baxter Street just north of Canal. Services were held in a storefront on Centre Street for three years until, in September 1891, the Church of the Most Precious Blood opened in the yet unfinished Baxter Street building. Many Five Points Italians happily left Transfiguration to attend services at the new church.[51]

"THE SAINT BELONGED TO THE PEOPLE, NOT TO THE CHURCH"

The support they had received from Rome apparently emboldened the Italians in other ways. For centuries, Italians had organized lavish street processions on important feast days. Archbishop Corrigan had forbidden them from transferring this custom to New York, however, both because he considered it undignified and because these festivals (or *feste*) diverted Catholics' attention from what Irish-American church leaders considered the "true" essence of Catholicity. Yet in 1888, Five Points Italians began ignoring the ban on processions, organizing them first at the Scalabrinian church across Chatham Square on Roosevelt Street, and by 1891 in Transfiguration itself.[52]

The best known religious street celebration in late-nineteenth- and early-twentieth-century New York was the homage to Our Lady of Mount Carmel. The *Madonna del Carmine*, as she was known within the Italian community, was, according to one immigrant, "the Madonna they worship most." The *Festa della Madonna del Carmine* took place not in Five Points but within Manhattan's other "Little Italy" (as these enclaves came to be known in the 1890s), located in East Harlem around 116th Street. Yet devout Five Pointers, especially those from the Campania region surrounding Naples where the *Madonna del Carmine* was most venerated, participated in the mid-July festivities anyway. "Some march barefoot the six miles and over from Mulberry street" to the *festa*, Riis reported, displaying their humility by "choosing the roughest pavements and kneeling on the sharpest stones on the way to tell their beads. Lest there should be none sharp enough, the most devout carry flints in their pockets to put under their knees." Because there were so many Neapolitans in Five Points, July 16 was always keenly anticipated there.[53]

Another famous Italian street *festa* was the one held for St. Rocco, and this celebration *was* associated with lower Manhattan, Transfiguration, and Five Points. Describing the festivities held in Rocco's honor each August 16, Riis observed that his "patronage is claimed by many towns. . . . There were half a dozen independent celebrations going on all day in as many yards, always the darkest and shabbiest, which this saint seems to pick out by a kind of instinct." He wrote in 1899 that "one of my last recollections of the Bend, and one of the very few pleasing ones, is seeing the vilest of the slum alleys, Bandits' Roost, lighted up in honor of 'St. Rocco' a few nights before the wreckers made an end of it. An altar had been

Jacob Riis, "The Feast of San Rocco in Bandits' Roost," c. 1894. Collection of the Museum of the City of New York.

erected against the stable shed at the rear end of it, and made gaudy with soiled ribbons, colored paper, and tallow dips stuck in broken bottle-necks. Across the passageway had been strung a row of beer-glasses, with two disabled schooners for a centerpiece, as the best the Roost could afford."[54]

Riis's photo captures the Five Pointers' humanity as few images ever have. Innocent children excited about the celebration and the accompanying fireworks replace the glowering thugs and withered old "hags" who dominated Riis's better-known image of Bandits' Roost. The care with which the altar has been assembled and decorated also reflects a level of devotion and pride one rarely sees in representations of Five Points. Even the stringing of glass tumblers across the alleyway demonstrates that, in whatever manner they could, the impoverished residents of these notorious tenements used every resource at their disposal to create a festive atmosphere.

The Five Pointers who erected this altar in honor of "San Rocco" were probably natives of Basilicata. People all over Italy venerated Rocco, but the *Tribune* in 1901 aptly characterized him as "the healing saint of Basilicata." Although Basilicatans may not have organized the first of New York's San Rocco celebrations, held in 1888 and 1889 at the Scalabrinian-run church on Roosevelt Street, they were definitely in charge by 1890 when, for the first time, the festival became a grand production. In that year, the Brotherhood of San Rocco of Savoia di Lucania (a small mountaintop village in western Basilicata whose patron saint was Rocco) organized the celebrations with assistance from a Basilicata-wide San Rocco society. A decade later, this *festa* was still associated with this isolated region of southern Italy and this single tiny hilltop village. The *Tribune* noted that the story of Rocco curing people of the bubonic plague "has been handed down from father to son in Basilicata for centuries," and quoted a little girl at the parade who said that that "if he [San Rocco] had not come to Savoia none of us would be alive to-day."[55]

In order to create a celebration befitting their patron saint, the immigrants from Savoia di Lucania called upon the immigrant fraternal societies of neighboring Italian villages. At the 1891 *festa*, for example, music was provided by the Society of San Michele Arcangelo (composed of immigrants from Sant' Angelo le Fratte, just two miles south of Savoia di Lucania on the other side of the Melandro River Valley), the Society of Monte Carmelo (immigrants from Polla, a town five miles southwest of Savoia), and the Society of the Madonna della Pietá (immigrants from Calvello, about fifteen miles east of Savoia). The San Rocco Society band would return the favor by performing when these groups staged *feste* for their patron saints.[56]

The festivities for San Rocco generally began on August 15, the evening before the actual feast day, with a street party, music, "lavish and expensive" fireworks, a parade, and visits to the tenement alley shrines set up for the veneration of San Rocco. The streets near the shrines and churches were "decorated with tricolor banners and, at night, flaming with lights and various pyrotechnic spectacles, crowded with people, [and] gay with happy melodies." Among the preliminary events were competitions to determine which neighborhood residents would have the honor of carrying the statue and banners of San Rocco through the streets the following day.[57]

On the sixteenth, the celebrations reached their climax. Already by 1893 the San Rocco *festa* was important enough to merit inclusion in an Italian-language novel entitled *The Mysteries of Mulberry Street*. The author's description of the festivities, the most vivid we have from these early years, suggests that he was intimately familiar with the proceedings:

Mulberry Street was on holiday: from the windows of the Italian houses hang tapestries, flags, and three-coloured lanterns, and everywhere were garlands of light-bulbs. . . . In the street, the crowd was happy and noisy: women—and among them several were very young and handsome—wore their holiday dresses and brought the gay note of gaudy colours amid the dark suits of the men and the uniforms of the military societies. San Rocco was being celebrated, and the Italians of Mulberry Street wanted to do things properly. Towards 11 a.m., the call of the trumpets was heard and in the distance flags and banners appeared. The crowd thronged the sidewalks to enjoy the parade in honor of San Rocco. A squad of policemen headed the procession, followed by the Conterno Band, and right after by a banner on which San Rocco was painted in oil, with all his wounds and his dog. Two flags, one Italian, the other American, flapped at the banner's sides, thus placing the saint under a double protection. Then came the members of the Società of San Rocco, stern and proud in their blue dresses with golden buttons and stripes, as if the whole world belonged to them.

In the buttonhole of their parade dresses, they had flowers, ribbons, and cockades. After another musical band, a military society paraded, in the uniform of the military engineer corps, with the three colours flapping in the wind; and then came a colossal banner of San Rocco, wounded more than ever, and after it the [societies] of the Carmine, of the Madonna Addolorata, and of other saints like San Cono, Sant'Antonio, etc.[58]

As the parade progressed, spectators pinned dollar bills onto the banners depicting San Rocco. The procession wound slowly and solemnly through virtually every block of both Five Points and the Italian neighborhood north of Canal Street as well.

Although these were the features of virtually every Italian religious *festa*, there was one aspect of the San Rocco celebration that made it unique: wax body parts. Because Rocco was said to have miraculously healed thousands in fourteenth-century Europe during the bubonic plague, the devout looked to him to cure their own ailments. They marched in the parade holding lifelike wax body parts representing their diseased limbs and organs or those of a loved one. Merchants and street vendors did a brisk business in these body parts in the weeks leading up August 16. The procession concluded at a neighborhood church (in the 1890s either Transfiguration or Most Precious Blood), where the images of San Rocco and the tremendous pile of wax body parts would be displayed around the altar while the faithful celebrated mass. That evening the festivities reached their climax. Valuable prizes were raffled off, more fireworks were ignited, and there was music, dancing, and "rivers of beer." Only in the wee hours of the morning did the merriment finally come to an end.[59]

These *feste* were held despite Corrigan's ban. Such prohibitions were difficult to enforce as more and more Italian priests began arriving in New York. In response to inquiries from Corrigan in August 1892, Lynch insisted that "no such procession has ever gone forth from this church." But he reported that just a few days earlier "the procession of St. Donatus (which you forbade) was held . . . with all the noise of a brass band and fireworks in the streets." Lynch walked to Most Precious Blood to investigate and found it gaudily decorated for the celebration. The "Piacenzan priests," Lynch gravely informed the archbishop, "had disobeyed your orders."[60]

Although the Italian immigrants were undoubtedly grateful to the

Scalabrinians for participating in their festivals, the newcomers did not entirely trust the immigrant clergymen either. Back in southern Italy, they had viewed their priests as allies of the landed elite that had impoverished them. This traditional anti-clericalism persisted among the Italians who settled in the United States. In a particularly revealing account of the San Donato *festa* (the same "Donatus" referred to by Lynch), Riis reported that this feast had been organized by immigrants from the town of Auletta, located just six miles west of Savoia di Lucania. He noted that except for the days when the image of St. Donato was being used for the festival, the natives of Auletta left Donato "in the loft of the saloon, lest the priests get hold of him and get a corner on him, as it were. Once [the priest] got him into his possession, he would not let the people have him except upon payment of a fee that would grow with the years. But the saint belonged to the people, not to the church. . . . In the saloon they had him safe."[61]

Banned from the main sanctuary at Transfiguration and denigrated by its Irish-American rector, Five Points Italians thus revived their beloved *feste* as a means of asserting some degree of religious autonomy in their new surroundings. The *feste* may have appeared quaint to American journalists, and sacrilegious to Irish-American church leaders, but they played a major role in helping the newcomers create a distinctly Italian-American community and identity.[62]

Five Points Italians were soon reminded of their precarious status within the New York Catholic community, though, when Most Precious Blood suddenly closed in 1893. The Scalabrinian who had spearheaded the building campaign for the church was a financial incompetent who had borrowed far more to construct it than the parishioners could afford. Both the church and some of the Scalabrinians' other property in New York were soon sold at auction to satisfy creditors.

Italians blamed the Irish-American church leadership. They were convinced that the archdiocese would have loaned money to prevent foreclosure had theirs been an Irish parish. The former parishioners began soliciting money door to door in an attempt to reopen the church, insisting that "unless the church reopens 'Italians will be the *slaves of the Irish as they have been before the church in Baxter St. existed,*' and that they will always remain slaves." A former clergyman from Most Precious Blood told a group gathered to discuss the church's future that "the Irish priests wanted everything and gave no privileges in return."[63]

Given the demands of the pope, Corrigan could not take back Most Precious Blood from the Italian community. Instead, he eventually allowed it to reopen under the auspices of a different Italian Catholic religious order, the Franciscan brotherhood. Meanwhile, a new priest, Thomas McLoughlin, was assigned to Transfiguration in 1894. According to a parish history written during his tenure there, "Father McLoughlin did his best to make the two races coalesce, by compelling the Italians to attend services in the upper church, but found that far better results could be obtained by having the two people worship . . . separately." Although Five Points' southern Italians became disillusioned with the northern Italians who came to dominate Most Precious Blood, they continued to leave Transfiguration for the new parish. Average attendance at Sunday mass at Transfiguration fell from 1,200 in 1894, to 700 in 1897, and to only 350 by 1901. Finally accepting that the parish could not survive as long as its leaders treated 90 percent of the parishioners as second-class citizens, Corrigan in 1901 arranged to transfer control of the parish to the Salesians of Don Bosco, placing "the whole building at the disposal of the Italian Catholics of that neighborhood."[64]

The Salesians immediately appointed an Italian pastor to head Transfiguration and ended the basement masses. They allowed the Italians to place their statues of Saints Rocco, Vittorio, Anthony, and others in the church. Catholic societies dedicated to these saints and others were permitted as well. It had been a long struggle, but the Italians of Five Points finally had a church of their own. By 1901, Italians had dominated most aspects of neighborhood life for more than a decade. The transfer of Transfiguration to Italian control, after years of Irish resistance, symbolized the Irish community's grudging acceptance that the transformation of Five Points into an Italian neighborhood was now complete.[65]

13

PROLOGUE

"The Chinese Devil Man"

QUIMBO APPO WAS ranting again. He had occasional moments of lucidity when he could entertain visitors at the Matteawan State Hospital for the Criminally Insane with stories of the old days in China and California. But at other times, his delusions were monumental. His son was president of the United States. He owned Madison Square Garden and all the laundries in the nation. The Virgin Mary visited him in his cell. He was "King of the World."

These might have been typical ravings for a mental patient, but Quimbo Appo was no ordinary asylum inmate. In the 1850s, Appo had been the best known Chinese immigrant in New York. Journalists had sought him out as a guide to the insular world of the New York Chinese and quoted him at length. He was even patriotic. When his Irish-born wife gave birth to a son on the Fourth of July 1856, he named the boy George Washington Appo. Quimbo Appo was, in short, an "exemplary Chinaman."

Appo's name appeared again in the press in March 1859, but this time as a murder suspect. Over the next two decades, he would be implicated in two more murders and a number of violent assaults. Journalists soon rechristened the exemplary Chinaman "the Chinese devil man." He spent nearly all of the last half century of his life incarcerated, first at the state penitentiary at Sing Sing and later at Matteawan. How had Quimbo Appo fallen so far, so fast?[1]

Appo was born Lee Ah Bow in 1825 on Zhusan, an island off the Chinese coast about fifty miles southeast of Shanghai. Western opium traders frequently visited the island, and it was probably through these contacts that Appo secured passage to California in 1847. His early years in North

America remain something of a mystery. He seems to have stayed in California until 1853, probably prospecting for gold. He eventually made his way to New York and married Catherine Fitzpatrick, a widow who bore him his son George.[2]

In New York, the five-foot three-inch Appo found work as a clerk and "taster" at an upscale tea shop. He may have even owned his own Greenwich Village tea emporium for a while. Virtually every *Times* story on the New York Chinese mentioned him by name. In 1856, the paper's reporter was especially taken with his five-month-old son George, gushing over the "handsome, healthy boy," who was "very sprightly, [and] as white as his mother—a Yankee boy to all appearances." The same journal noted in 1859 that while most Chinese New Yorkers lived in decrepit boardinghouses in the worst neighborhoods, Appo resided in a "first class house."[3]

So it must have come as something of a shock to New Yorkers when they read in their morning papers on March 9, 1859, that Quimbo Appo stood accused of murder. The Appos' life, it turned out, had a darker side. The couple fought frequently about Catherine's heavy drinking, and neighbors in their Fourth Ward tenement at 47 Oliver Street often complained about the noise. On the eighth, when Quimbo returned home from work around 7:00 p.m. to find that his intoxicated wife had prepared him no dinner, he flew into a rage and began beating her. Their landlady, Mary Fletcher, came to Catherine's aid—the two had been drinking together that afternoon to celebrate Fletcher's birthday. The building's other Irishwomen came running to support their friends as well, but Quimbo, determined to teach Catherine a lesson, would not relent. Catherine eventually broke free and fled the room, but Quimbo and the Irishwomen continued to scuffle. He called them drunks; they called him a "China nigger." One of the Irishwomen even pummeled Appo with a "smoothing iron." Finally, as the struggling mass of fists and curses moved from the Appos' apartment into the hallway, Appo drew a knife and stabbed Fletcher in the neck. She collapsed and quickly bled to death. Appo grazed another woman in the head during the struggle and stabbed a third in the arm as he escaped out the tenement door. Police found him a few hours later hiding under a bed in a nearby Chinese boardinghouse. They charged him with murder.[4]

It seemed that Appo's days were numbered. When the police escorted him through the streets of the Fourth Ward to appear at the coroner's inquest, an angry mob of Irish Americans bent on revenge tried to kidnap and lynch him. At his one-day trial a month later, his desultory attorney offered no defense whatsoever, and after only a few minutes of deliberation a jury convicted him of murder. The judge sentenced Appo to hang.[5]

Had Appo killed Fletcher in California, where anti-Chinese sentiment ran deep, he undoubtedly would have perished on the gallows. But native-born New Yorkers in the antebellum years still regarded the Chinese as hardworking, enterprising, and thrifty, whereas hard-drinking Irishwomen were not to be trusted. A sympathetic editorial in the *Times* questioned the competence of Appo's attorney and implied that he had not received a fair trial. Still, no court could condone the use of a deadly weapon against inebriated women, even if one of them wielded a flatiron. An appeals tribunal consequently upheld Appo's conviction. Yet New York's governor commuted his life sentence to ten years, and Appo was released after serving seven years and nine months in Sing Sing.[6]

There was no homecoming celebration to greet Appo on his return to New York sometime after April 1869. Soon after Appo had entered Sing Sing, Catherine and George had left for California, where Catherine's brother lived. During the trip west, Catherine perished, apparently in a shipwreck. George survived, however, and was sent back to New York to await his father's release from prison. The authorities found the three-year-old a home with a poor longshoreman's family, the Allens, in a part of Five Points known as "Donovan's Lane."[7]

In the decade after the Civil War, Donovan's Lane was one of the most notorious addresses in Five Points. It was not an officially recognized thoroughfare, but rather a pair of alleys (one leading west from Baxter Street, the other running north from Pearl Street) that intersected at a decrepit courtyard ringed by four tall and dark rear tenements. "There lived in this Donovan's lane," George remembered years later, "poor people of all nationalities and there were four old tenement houses and a large horse and wagon stable and sheds in the Lane and it was a common sight to see every morning under the wagon sheds at least six to ten drunken men and women sleeping off the effects of the five cent rum bought at 'Black Mike's' saloon." Contemporary accounts confirm Appo's. "This Arcadia of garbage," reported the *Daily Graphic* in early 1873, "is approached from Baxter street by a covered alley, running under a reeking structure that seems impinged with filth and redolent of disease." At the other end were "rambling hovels and Alpine ranges of garbage heaps." Italians dominated one Donovan Lane tenement, Irishwomen another, and Chinese men a third. Authorities probably considered the ethnic mix in Donovan's Lane a perfect match for little George Appo.[8]

When Quimbo was released from prison, he and George, now about twelve, moved to a boardinghouse at the south end of the Sixth Ward near City Hall. Quimbo returned to work as a tea tester, but was jailed a few months later after fighting in a liquor store with a man he claimed was robbing him. George once again moved in with the Allens in Donovan's Lane and started working as a newsboy. But he soon followed his father into a life of crime, falling in with a gang of juvenile pickpockets. Arrested for robbery in early 1871 at age fourteen, he was sentenced by Police Justice Joseph Dowling to duty on the *Mercury*, a prison ship of sorts, where juvenile delinquents learned nautical skills. Appo served about a year aboard the vessel, sailing to ports as far away as Rio de Janeiro and Africa before he jumped ship in New York Harbor in about 1873. He made his way back to Five Points and moved in with his "stepsister," Mary Ann Allen, who had an apartment on Worth Street at the Five Points intersection.[9]

The senior Appo had long since been released from jail, but he could still not control his violent impulses. On the night of August 9, 1871, the apparently homeless Appo was sleeping under a stoop near the entrance to Donovan's Lane when some boys began harassing him. He chased after them, throwing a large stone at them as he pursued. The stone missed the boys and instead hit a Polish Jewish shoemaker in the head as the man stepped out the door of his workshop. The severely injured victim spent three weeks in the hospital recovering. No witnesses could swear to having seen Appo throw the stone, and his trial resulted in a hung jury. But at his retrial he was convicted of assault, and served nearly four years at Sing Sing. Toward the end, he was reunited with George, who was sent "up the river" in

George Appo, from Louis J. Beck, *New York's Chinatown* (New York, 1898): 251.

mid-1874 to begin a thirty-month sentence after police again caught him picking pockets. Quimbo completed his sentence first, in August 1875, but a month later he was arrested yet again for assault and battery. A judge jailed Appo for three more months. When he was released in early January 1876, he supported himself peddling cigars on the streets. But before the end of the month he was incarcerated yet again, this time for "insanity," on the complaint of one of his Baxter Street neighbors. After his release a few months later, he was caught selling tobacco products without the proper excise stamps (he apparently served no jail time for this minor offense).[10]

By this point, fifty-one-year-old Quimbo Appo was clearly a man of conflicting impulses. On one arm, the devout Roman Catholic had a tattoo of the crucifixion; on the other was a Spanish dancing girl and a skull and crossbones. For years, he had heard voices he believed to be revelations, telling him, in the words of a doctor, that "whatever he should consider it right to do would be considered a good act by God Almighty." Given these delusions and his propensity to respond to threats with excessive violence, it was only a matter of time before Appo killed again.[11]

On October 19, 1876, Appo spent the evening at his Five Points boardinghouse playing checkers with another resident, John A. Kelly. Appo won the checkers games and the small bets made on each contest, then retired. Kelly went out for a few drinks and returned to the house between midnight and 1:00 a.m., still fuming over his defeat. He dragged Appo out of bed and began beating his nemesis, finally knocking him down a flight of stairs. The night clerk tried to restrain Kelly, while Appo tried to flee, but Kelly would not relent, landing additional blows each time he managed to reach him. Finally, Appo grabbed a penknife and stabbed the onrushing Kelly through the heart. Appo was charged with manslaughter in the second degree, convicted at a trial two months later, and sentenced to seven years in prison.[12]

At Auburn State Prison, Appo became increasingly delusional, and authorities eventually transferred him to the mental hospital at Matteawan. George, meanwhile, had become a notorious criminal in his own right, first as a thief and later as a counterfeiter. He was also prosecuted three or four times for stabbing men during fights—one of these incidents, over a game of cards, was eerily similar to his father's final crime. George lost an eye when he was shot by one of his counterfeiting victims.

The public would have learned very little about these exploits had George not given detailed descriptions of police corruption to a state investigative committee in 1894, testimony that made him one of the best known criminals in the city. Appo apparently hoped to use his testimony as a springboard to going straight, but such a transformation was not easy. A few months after his committee appearance, an assailant cut George's throat and nearly killed him, an act he interpreted as police revenge for his testimony. Two years later, he complained to the *Times* that he could not find honest work. Employers would not hire him because of his criminal record, but he could not return to a life of crime because his testimony had made him a pariah to his underworld friends. A few weeks after making this statement to the press, George was arrested for a stabbing at the corner of Mott and Chatham Streets, just a hundred feet from the spot where his father had knifed John Kelly. At his trial, the judge declared George insane and sent him to Matteawan, where he was once again reunited with his father, whom he had not seen since Sing Sing twenty years earlier. But whereas Quimbo's dementia continued, George's persecution complex eventually subsided, and he was released in 1899. Though he aspired to be an actor and a poet, George spent the remainder of his life in a variety of menial jobs in New York, Philadelphia, and Trenton. He died in 1930.[13]

In many ways, the Appos' story parallels the changing course of New Yorkers' attitudes toward the city's early Chinese community. Just as they had once viewed Quimbo Appo as an exemplary immigrant, New Yorkers had initially welcomed the city's Chinese newcomers, stereotyping them as hardworking, thrifty, and law-abiding. But during the postbellum years, New Yorkers came to see the Chinese as a threat. They were a depraved race, incapable of restraining their "appetites," just as Quimbo Appo could not restrain his violent impulses. And George's career proved to many that the racial and ethnic mixing typical in Five Points was creating, in the words of one journalist, a "hybrid brood" of "half-breeds" who were especially prone to lives of crime.[14]

The Appos' story also reflects the uneasy ties between Five Points' various ethnic groups. Quimbo Appo, like many of the first Chinese Five Pointers, married an Irishwoman. Yet every one of his murder victims was an Irish American as well. Even his delusions revealed both resentment and affection toward the Irish. On the one hand, he blamed his long incarceration at Matteawan on the "Fenian Party," insisting that Irish-

American Democrats were conspiring with the governor to keep him behind bars. But at the same time, he believed that his own persecution was tied to the oppression of the Irish, telling a doctor in 1885 that "he has been, and is now, suffering for the cause of Ireland and that he must suffer until she is free." The once exemplary Chinaman continued to suffer his personal torment at Matteawan for another twenty-seven years until he died, at age eighty-seven, in 1912.[15]

CHAPTER THIRTEEN

Chinatown

⟨᪣᪣᪣⟩

"HE HEAR HE CAN MAKE MONEY IN NEW-LORK, AND BOYS NO POUND HIM WITH STONES"

TODAY, FIVE POINTS is long gone. The name dropped out of use in the 1890s. The five-way intersection has become three-pointed. Virtually all the Irish, Italians, and Jews have moved away. Only one group from the nineteenth century has stayed—the Chinese. Five Points has become Chinatown.

Before the Civil War, most Chinese New Yorkers had lived in the impoverished, Irish-dominated Fourth Ward to the east of Five Points. Chinese immigrants probably settled in the Fourth Ward because it was located on the waterfront. Many of the first Chinese New Yorkers were sailors—it was not uncommon to find a Chinese cook or steward working on a ship with an otherwise all Caucasian crew. Eventually, a number of boardinghouses opened to accommodate them.

Not all of the early Chinese New Yorkers were sailors. Others worked as street peddlers, in particular selling cheap cigars and rock candy. A few, like Quimbo Appo, found higher-status employment in the tea trade. Some had come to New York after failing to strike it rich in the California gold mines. Others had escaped to New York by way of the Peruvian Chincha Islands, where they had worked as "coolie laborers" in near-slavelike conditions shoveling guano for use as fertilizer. Still others had been tobacco workers in Cuba.[16]

In the years after the Civil War, however, Five Points became a magnet for the New York Chinese. By 1869, the *New York Tribune* could authoritatively call "Baxter st., and its immediate neighborhood, the particular locality of New-York in which all the Chinese live." It is possible that the Irish somehow pushed the Chinese out of the Fourth Ward, for the block on lower Baxter Street on which the Chinese concentrated was remarkable in Five Points for its *lack* of Irish residents, and was instead dominated by Italian and Polish Jewish immigrants. The Chinese may have felt more welcome—or at least less threatened—among the city's other outcast groups on lower Baxter Street than they did in the overwhelmingly Irish Fourth Ward.

Apart from the relocation, New York's Chinese community remained unchanged in 1870. Sailors and cigar sellers still predominated. Most residents continued to live in Chinese-run boardinghouses, where, for three dollars a week, they received a bed, breakfast, and "a good meat supper." And it was still a very small community. "There are not more than 60 or 70 Chinamen regularly living in New-York," asserted the *Tribune* in 1869. A year later, the census recorded only thirty-eight Chinese natives living in Five Points, though the enumerator seems to have skipped some of the seediest Baxter Street tenements where additional Chinese immigrants lived.[17]

From the very beginning, the Chinese in Five Points organized "clubhouses" to foster sociability within their community. A *Daily Graphic* reporter found one such clubroom in early 1873 on an upper floor of a Donovan's Lane tenement. Its members "are very respectable men, chiefly cooks and stewards of ships." Dominoes seemed to be the diversion of choice, although one section of the clubhouse contained writing materials so that members could correspond with loved ones back in China. "The gamesters were sprawled about in all sorts of attitudes, and no professional gambler could have a more inscrutable physiognomy than these phlegmatic, unimpressionable beings. They played and smoked in profound silence." By the end of the year, the *Times* had identified two additional Chinese "mutual benefit" clubs operating in Five Points, one on Baxter Street and another on Mott.[18]

During the 1870s, the Five Points Chinese began to shift from Baxter to Mott Street. Again, it is difficult to determine why. A Chinese boardinghouse already existed on Mott (probably at No. 13) by 1870. A prominent Chinese merchant, Wo Kee, moved his popular general store and boardinghouse from the Fourth Ward to 34 Mott in 1873. Wo Kee may have opted for Mott Street because he found it impossible to secure commercial space near the Chinese residences on lower Baxter, where Jewish clothing merchants virtually monopolized storefront property. But prosperous Chinese merchants instead may have sought to distance themselves from the especially decrepit Baxter Street tenements. In any case, by the mid-1870s, newspaper accounts of the Chinese in New York began referring more and more to Mott Street. In 1880, the *Times* called Mott Street New York's "China Town."[19]

By that point, the city's Chinese population had increased dramatically. Some Chinese had begun filtering into New York after completion of the transcontinental railroad in 1869 facilitated the journey from California. But most of the increase stemmed from the anti-Chinese movement fomented in San Francisco by Denis Kearney. An Irish immigrant, Kearney rose to prominence by founding the California Workingmen's Party, which blamed the Chinese for the massive unemployment that gripped California during the severe depression of the late 1870s. Crying "the Chinese must go," Kearney and his supporters used intimidation and violence to drive the Chinese out of their California workplaces and prevent new employers from hiring Asians. In a typical incident, Kearney led a mob to the mansions of railroad tycoons Leland Stanford and Charles Crocker, threatening to destroy their homes if they continued to employ the Chinese in railroad construction. San Francisco vigilantes led or inspired by Kearney also wrecked numerous Chinese-owned businesses in 1877. Kearney's tactics drove thousands of Chinese Americans from California in that year, and many headed for New York. More left the West Coast in late 1879, after Kearney's party gained control of the San Francisco municipal government and began enacting discriminatory legislation against the Chinese.[20]

By March 1880, newspaper reports expressed alarm at the increasing size of the Mott Street Chinese enclave. The *Tribune* announced that one hundred Chinese had arrived in New York from California in a single day, and that fifty had completed the journey from San Francisco a few days earlier. "They are the vanguard of the immense army of almond-eyed exiles who are about to pour into this city if the situation in the West continues to be serious," intoned the *Herald* ominously. Samuel Weeks, a prominent lower Mott Street landlord, told the *Tribune* that the Chinese "had been leasing all the desirable property in that part of Mott-st., in several cases they had paid large prices for the tenants to leave." Weeks noted that Chinese entrepreneurs preferred to lease entire buildings rather than individual apartments, opening shops on the ground floor while providing dormitories and rooms for socializing above.[21]

With the press having played a prominent role in fomenting the anti-Chinese violence in San Francisco, few of the newcomers were willing to talk to the many journalists who converged on Mott Street to document their influx. But the *Times* managed to locate one new Chinatown resident, laundry operator Wah Ling, who agreed to discuss the surge in Chinatown's population. Using another immigrant who had already lived in New York for several years as an interpreter, Wah told the *Times* that San Francisco was "no good place for Chinaman any more. White man flaid to bling his shirts to iron any more. Chinaman get pounded with stones by boys on stleet. He hear he can make money in New-Lork, and boys no pound him with stones." Wah also cited a price war between rail and steamship companies, which had cut the cost of a transcontinental journey in half, as a factor in his decision to come to New York. Nearly all of the New York Chinese were natives of Guangdong, the South China region best known for the cities of Hong Kong and Canton. The 1880 census recorded 748 Chinese natives living in New York (200 of whom lived in Five Points), but the press insisted that the true figure was closer to 2,000.[22]

Although the Chinese constituted only a tiny proportion of the Five Points population, it seemed to many observers that the Asians had overrun the neighborhood. "Mott Street might be in Pekin instead of Gotham, so Chinese has it become," commented *Frank Leslie's* in a typical 1880 story. ". . . Almond eyes and pig-tails . . . are the order of the day." Like the Irish Lansdowne immigrants before them, the Chinese chose to concentrate on just two of the neighborhood's approximately twenty blocks: Mott Street below Pell and Pell Street between Mott and the Bowery. In 1890, when the New York City Police conducted a census of the neighborhood, 95 percent of the eight hundred or so Chinese they found in Five Points lived on these two blocks. So even though the number of Chinese in the city was still relatively small, noted *Frank Leslie's*, they are "so distinct and so concentrated that [they] form a much more considerable community than double the number of Italians, Hungarians or Polish Jews."[23]

By this point, Mott Street had become as well known in Guangdong as Mulberry Street was in Basilicata and Campania. One Chinese American vividly recalled when the idea of emigrating first dawned upon him. He remembered that when he was a child in China,

> a man of our tribe came back from America and took ground as large as four city blocks and made a paradise of it. . . . The man had gone away from our village a poor boy. Now he returned with unlimited wealth, which he had obtained in the country of the American wizards. After many amazing adventures he had become a merchant in a city called Mott Street, so it was said. When his palace and grounds were completed he gave a dinner to all the people who assembled to be his guests. One hundred pigs roasted whole were served on the tables, with chickens, ducks, geese and such an abundance of dainties that our villagers even now lick their fingers when they think of it. He had the best actors from Hong Kong performing, and every musician for miles around was playing and singing. . . . Having made his wealth among the barbarians this man had faithfully returned to pour it out among his tribesmen, and he is living in our village now very happy, and a pillar of strength to the poor. The wealth of this man filled my mind with the idea that I, too, would like to go to the country of the wizards and gain some of their wealth.[24]

Just as newly arrived Italians always made Mulberry Street their first stop in New York, Chinese immigrants invariably went to Mott Street to find lodging and work in the great metropolis.

Work opportunities abounded. Some Chinese continued to labor as sailors and peddlers. By the 1870s, many Chinese peddlers sold "that peculiar preparation known as Chinese candy," probably a rock candy made from brown sugar. Only a tiny amount of start-up capital was required, as the vendors usually produced the confection themselves.[25]

Most Chinese street peddlers hawked cigars. *Ballou's Pictorial* portrayed a Chinese cigar peddler in its 1855 collage of "New-York Street Figures," and they became especially ubiquitous by the end of the 1860s.

Most had come to the United States via Cuba, where they had worked as indentured servants on sugar plantations before escaping into the tobacco industry. In Manhattan, they bought tobacco remnants from upscale cigar manufacturers, which they rolled into one hundred fifty or more cigars each evening and sold on the street the next day for three cents apiece.[26]

Eventually, many Chinese began working as cigarmakers for the city's Anglo tobacco merchants. "Because of their natural deftness and quickness of finger," Chinese cigarmakers were said to earn even more than the city's well-paid German cigarmakers—as much as twenty-five dollars per week. But their impressive earnings also resulted from their skill at organizing. By 1885, several hundred Chinese tobacco workers had formed a trade union. Several were able to open their own cigar factories. One, operated by Mig Atak on Chatham Street just south of Five Points, employed as many as one hundred workers. New Yorkers continued to associate the Chinese with cigars until almost the end of the century.[27]

By the 1880s, however, New Yorkers began to associate Chinese immigrants more with the laundry trade than with cigarmaking. The Chinese shifted their focus from cigars to shirts in part because laundrywork did not threaten the occupations of white men and therefore would not lead to the labor unrest that had driven them from California. Chinese immigrants also gravitated to laundrywork because the Irish immigrant women who had once taken in laundry were leaving the business as their economic status improved. With demand for laundry services high and competition minimal, laundrywork seemed perfectly suited to the needs of the Chinese.

Operating a laundry required the leasing of retail space, which meant that start-up costs were significantly higher than those for cigar and candy peddlers. One might acquire this capital working in someone else's laundry. It generally took two people to run a "hand laundry"—a washer and a presser. The washer would come in early in the morning and launder the clothes. The presser would report to work at midday and work late into the evening ironing by hand. Often there was so much work that both partners worked sixteen-to-eighteen-hour days.[28]

Another way to obtain funds was to take part in a *whey*, a cooperative loan system Chinese immigrants used to raise seed money for business ventures. Signs posted on Mott Street advertised the organization of these syndicates, which typically involved a ten-dollar contribution from each of twenty participants. Once twenty subscribers had been found, each would write on a slip of paper the interest rate he was willing to pay for one month's use of the two hundred dollars they had collectively pledged. The highest bidder went home that day with the two hundred dollars, minus the agreed-upon interest, which was divided among the remaining participants. At the end of the month, the borrower turned two hundred dollars over to the next-highest bidder, and so on until every man in the *whey* had borrowed the money. Some desperate immigrants paid as much as 40 percent interest to get first crack at the *whey's* funds.[29]

As the Chinatown community matured, immigrants seeking credit relied less on *wheys*, and more on the enclave's Chinese groceries. By 1888, there were nearly thirty Chinese groceries on Mott Street, enjoying the same status in the Chinese community as the Italian banks just a block away on Mulberry Street. Like the Mulberry Street banks, most Chinese groceries played on the newcomers' regional loyalty to attract business. There were several dozen counties within the Guangdong region represented in New York, and arriving immigrants would go straight to the general store run by a native of his county to look for work and lodging.

According to the Chinese-American journalist Wong Ching Foo, if the newcomer "was in any way known in China by any of the . . . men at this headquarters, he is given capital by the storekeeper for whatever business he wished to start, to the limit of two hundred dollars. . . . Most of these storekeepers are old laundrymen who accumulated enough money from the washing business to start these more profitable groceries." Wong reported that these merchants charged no interest on the thousands of dollars they loaned. Instead, the borrower had to promise to buy his supplies from the lender and to pay down his debt in regular installments.[30]

The Chinese groceries on Mott Street served the community not only as a source of credit and supplies, but also, as Wong observed, as "clubs, and general newspaper stations, [and] post-offices." Chinese immigrants typically received mail at a Mott Street grocery rather than at their homes. This custom developed in part because the laundrymen moved frequently, especially before they purchased their own establishment. Certain groceries served as postal drops for particular clans or Chinese counties or towns. Kaimon Chin, a longtime Chinatown resident, recalled in about 1990 that his father's store at 59 Mott became a mail distribution center for the Chins from his village. Sundays were especially busy at the groceries, because that was the only day of the week that Chinese laundries were closed. At the grocery, laundrymen would buy food and laundry supplies for the week, collect their mail, trade gossip and news from back home, and relax over a cup of tea and a game of dominoes. Most Chinese laundrymen in New York eagerly anticipated Sundays, when they could escape their exhausting, isolated workplaces and enjoy the comforting sociability of their favorite Mott Street general store.[31]

Describing Wo Kee's general store, probably when it was still at 34 Mott, a correspondent from the *Sun* reported that "it contains apparently somewhere near a million different things of the most incongruous character." They included

> gigantic pills, roots, herbs, barks, seeds, and such like. There are incense sticks, jade bracelets; strange evolutions of Celestial fancy in the way of ornamentation, like glorified valentines; quaint and pretty tea services; dried shark fins, looking like tangled strips of amber-tinted glue; ducks split, baked in peanut oil, and flattened out dry, so as to look like strange caricatures of dragons; sweetmeats in infinite variety, nuts that nobody but a Chinaman knows the names of, dried mushrooms, opium and pipes for smoking it, tobacco, teas of many kinds, some of them exquisite and much more expensive than any American store sells; silks, fungus-looking black lumps, of which it is guaranteed that a small bit will make the drunkest man immediately sober; sandals and Chinese clothing.[32]

The *Sun's* reporter described Wo Kee tallying customers' purchases with an abacus and making entries into his account books with a camel's-hair brush, leaving readers with the impression that these stores were quaint and old-fashioned. But they were also extremely profitable. By 1885, Wo Kee owned businesses and property in Chinatown worth $150,000. Most of this fortune derived from the export to China of American cutlery, firearms, and fine prints. With headquarters first at 32 Pell Street and then at 9 Doyers, Wong He Cong also exported goods to China, Southeast Asia, and Cuba, while simultaneously becoming, according to the *Herald*, "the foremost wholesale dealer in tea and rice in New York." Journalists estimated his net worth at a million dollars. Such phenomenal success was rare, of course. But through their control of the enclave's venture capital, Chinatown's merchants became the community's most powerful and influential members.[33]

Prominent merchants were able to dominate the Five Points Chinese enclave because relatively few Chinese actually lived in the neighborhood. Laundrymen were scattered throughout the city, living wherever their businesses were located. By the mid-1880s, "China Town" had become a shopping, social, and leisure center for the city's far-flung Chinese residents. "All the Chinese do not live here," observed a *Frank Leslie's* reporter on a visit to Mott Street, "but it is safe to say that all of them are regular and frequent visitors to this centre of Mongolian business, society and dissipation." Those who did make Pell, Doyers, or lower Mott Street their home were primarily merchants and professionals, cigarmakers, those who worked in menial capacities in the district's businesses, and newcomers who had not yet found work or raised capital to start businesses of their own. In 1885, the *Tribune* estimated that 80 percent of New York's Chinese immigrants toiled as laundrymen, but they made up fewer than one in five of the Chinese inhabitants of Five Points.[34]

"DRIVING OUT THE CHINESE"

Like the Italians on Mulberry Street, the Chinese in Five Points lived in both individual apartments and boardinghouses. Boarding facilities must have been especially popular given the overwhelming preponderance of men in the enclave. Like the Irish and Italians before them, enterprising Chinese immigrants in Five Points also tried to lease entire buildings and then sublet the individual apartments. But as the city's Chinese population began to expand rapidly in early 1880, the newcomers found it more and more difficult to find accommodations in Five Points, because many neighborhood landlords refused to rent to them. The Rutgers Fire Company refused to lease its vacant house at 3 Mott Street to Chinese, even when the immigrants offered to pay a large advance on the rent. The owners' representative vowed he would "sooner pull down the building than allow a single Chinaman to live in it." Another Mott Street landlord let his property stand vacant rather than accept $1,000 a year from the Chinese.

According to the press, the Irish in particular sought to stop the Chinese influx into Five Points. "A determined effort is being made by property owners in the upper end of Mott Street to prevent the colony from spreading," reported the *Herald,* describing the portion of the street above Pell where no Chinese had yet settled, "and to all offers of high rents they give a stolid denial. They feel that if the Chinese get sufficient headway they will take possession of that quarter of the city."[35]

Some landlords even began evicting the Chinese from some of the Mott Street buildings they already occupied. On May 7, under the headline "Driving Out the Chinese," the *Times* reported that the Irish Catholic parishioners of Mott Street's Transfiguration Church, resentful of having "to cut their way through an army of 'haythen' on Sunday," had spearheaded the expulsions of the Chinese from their homes. The church "had leased the whole series of tenements from Pell-street to Park, and refused to let to Chinamen on any terms." Many current residents were told to vacate immediately; a few were given until the end of the month. "Other landlords in the vicinity took the cue, although they liked their tenants, and for the last week a wholesale eviction has been going on." Even wealth provided little protection from the evictions, as merchant Wo Kee was forced to relocate his landmark grocery from Mott Street to dark and quiet Park Street. Yet like Wo Kee, most of the expelled Chinese managed to stay in the neighborhood.[36]

A *Times* editorial lashed out at "the Irish proscription of the Chinese colony in this City," complaining that

> . . . hatred of the Chinese springs eternal in the Celtic breast. In fact, the hospitable and generous Irishman has almost no friendship for any race but his own. As a laborer and politician, he detests the Italian. Between him and the German-American citizen there is a great gulf fixed. So, when a little colony of Chinese, scarcely one thousand in number, settles in the midst of what has been an Irish-Catholic quarter, there springs up at once an active enmity against the new-comers. . . . There might have been, at least, an attempt to convert these heathen. . . . But the most natural thing for the Americanized Irishman is to drive out all other foreigners, whatever may be their religious tenets.

But perhaps the *Times* was allowing its own prejudice against the Irish to color its reporting. The newspaper's confession that it would not like "a colony of Chinese occupying the Stewart mansion on Fifth-avenue, or hanging their washing out to dry on the roof of the Union League Club-house," indicates that Irish Catholic Five Pointers were not the only New Yorkers who did not want the Chinese in their neighborhood.[37]

In 1880, the Chinese vice-consul in California sent a telegram to New York's Chinese leaders instructing "the companies and merchants to move to the west side of the city." *Frank Leslie's* reported that the Chinese were scouting out possible locations on Eighth Avenue uptown. But in the end, the Chinese had an even harder time renting property in other parts of town. Chinatown could not be moved. To protect themselves against the whims of Caucasian landlords, however, Chinese Americans began to buy Five Points buildings themselves. By 1883, Wo Kee had managed to move his store back to Mott Street by purchasing 8 Mott for $8,500. Another of the most prominent Chinatown businessmen, Tom Lee, bought 16 Mott at about the same time for $15,000. Other Chinese-American merchants acquired 10 and 12 Mott.[38]

Ironically, Wo Kee upon taking possession of 8 Mott demanded that the occupants pay a 40 percent increase in rent or vacate the premises. The other new Chinese property owners made similar demands and evicted many tenants. Chinese residents of Mott Street held an indignation meet-ing to protest the rent increases and collected funds to fight the evictions in court. Eventually, a compromise was reached. The landlords agreed to adopt procedures already followed in San Francisco, which stipulated that when Chinese bought buildings already occupied by Chinese, the rent would remain unchanged for one year. As the Chinese became Chinatown property owners, all talk of moving the enclave came to an end, as did most efforts to prevent the Chinese from settling in Five Points.[39]

THE GREAT MONGOLIAN
MAGNATE OF MOTT STREET

Unmarried men dominated the Chinese community. The 1880 census taker did not find a single Chinese-born woman in Five Points, and only a small proportion of the men married Caucasian women. As a result, the Chinese-operated businesses that sprang up in Five Points catered largely to its bachelor society.

One staple of a bachelor community is the restaurant, and Mott Street soon became renowned for its "outlandishly quaint Chinese restaurants." During the 1880s and '90s, most Chinese restaurants in Five Points (there were eight in 1888) were located on the second or third floors of Mott Street tenements. They were small establishments that could rarely seat more than a few dozen patrons at a time. The eateries were sparsely decorated, usually adorned with little more than long scrolls on the walls bearing "maxims from philosophers for the entertainment of those who eat." Cooks prepared the food in a kitchen at the rear of the building or in the tenement's basement. Their custom-made wood-burning stoves, with separate stations for roasting, boiling, steaming, and frying, were often imported directly from China.[40]

The Chinese who patronized these first restaurants ate many of the same Cantonese dumplings, soups, and noodle dishes still served on Mott Street today. But in Chinatown's early years, when few Asian vegetables and spices were available in America, the immigrants were forced to improvise with American ingredients to create dishes pleasing to the Cantonese palate. One such dish was "chow chop suey," which Americans typically believe was created for their own edification, when it was actually developed by Chinese-American cooks for their Asian customers. Wong Ching Foo characterized chop suey as "a staple dish for the Chinese gourmand," describing it as "a mixture of chickens' livers and gizzards, fungi, bamboo buds, pig's tripe, and bean sprouts stewed with spices. The gravy of this is poured into the bowl of rice," with a Chinese condiment Wong termed "the prototype of Worcestershire sauce." By the 1890s, Chinese farmers had begun to grow Chinese vegetables on Long Island, but until then, dishes like chop suey remained an integral part of Chinese-American cuisine.[41]

At first, Americans looked upon Chinese cooking with suspicion. But curious Americans soon began to patronize these eateries, and by the 1890s, Caucasians ventured to Chinatown just for the food. "Chow chop sui calls Americans to Chinatown," observed *Frank Leslie's* in 1896. "An American who once falls under the spell of chop sui may forget about all things Chinese for awhile, [but] suddenly a strange craving that almost defies will power arises; as though under a magnetic influence he finds that his feet are carrying him to Mott Street." Other American favorites were "yok-e-man, a strong, palatable soup, containing bits of chicken, pork, and hard-boiled egg," as well as "chow main." Those who visited Five Points for an afternoon or evening of "slumming" could now include an exotic meal to round out the fun. The *Tribune* noted that there was "a free and easy atmosphere about the Chinese eating house which attracts many would-be 'Bohemians.'" The dark and intimate confines encouraged patrons to "loll about and talk and laugh loudly." By the turn of the century, Chinese restaurants had become so popular that they began to open outside Chinatown. Those in Five Points continued to thrive, with some, such as the famous Port Arthur at 7–9 Mott, catering to an exclusively Caucasian clientele.[42]

By contrast, white New Yorkers were almost never granted entrée into another mainstay of Chinatown's bachelor society—its gambling dens. "The Celestial is a shameless and inveterate gambler," remarked George Walling, a former New York chief of police, in the 1880s. "It is a rare thing to find a Chinaman who is not infatuated with games of chance." These might have been the exaggerated comments of a prejudiced outsider, but Wong Ching Foo, who vehemently defended the Chinese community from almost every other criticism hurled its way, admitted that the Chinese were obsessed with games of chance. Stopping the Chinese from gambling, Wong asserted, would be as monumental a task as stopping the annual floods of the great rivers of China.[43]

Two games were especially popular: *fan tan* and *pak ko piu*. In *fan tan*, a large pile of coins was placed on a table. Coins were removed, four at a time, until no more than four were left. Gamblers placed bets on whether four, three, two, or one coin would be left on the table, and those who selected the correct number won three dollars for every one bet, minus a 7 percent commission. Those who were risk-averse could bet on two of the four numbers, and if successful were paid even money. A gambler could even hedge his bet still further. A wager on number 2 "toward" number 1, for example, meant that if 2 was the winning number, the bettor won two dollars for every one wagered, but if 1 was the winner, he merely got back the money he had bet. Just as casinos in Atlantic City and Las Vegas do today, Chinatown's *fan tan* parlors gave their best customers free food, drinks, and lodging in order to keep them at the tables. By 1891, more than a dozen *fan tan* parlors operated in Five Points, in back rooms, basements, and in spaces above some of Mott Street's most prestigious shops.[44]

Pak ko piu was essentially the same "policy" game played in antebellum Five Points. In this lottery, players were given sheets on which eighty

Fan tan players. *Frank Leslie's Illustrated Newspaper* (December 17, 1887): 296. Collection of the author.

Chinese characters appeared. Each gambler marked off a certain number of characters (the number varied from game to game) and submitted his wager (which could be as low as a few cents) with his ticket. The syndicates that operated these games held daily drawings. If the bettor matched five of the characters drawn that day, he won two dollars for every dollar wagered. If he matched six he was paid 20 to 1, seven correct earned him 200 to 1, eight correct 1,000 to 1, and so on, up to as much as 3,000 or 10,000 to 1, depending on the total number of characters drawn. By the early 1890s, about a dozen lottery offices operated on Mott Street where gamblers could lay their *pak ko piu* bets. Walling was told that big winners typically moved back to China with their prize money.[45]

In most Western societies, gambling and alcohol go hand in hand. But visitors to Mott Street invariably noted that they never encountered drunken Chinese. Opium, rather than alcohol, was the stimulant of choice. No journalist considered a story on Chinatown complete without a detailed

description of its many opium dens. "Opium joints" were usually nonde-
script rooms lined with divans set up by the Mott Street merchants who
sold the drug. An 1888 print in *Cosmopolitan* magazine even depicts
bunks for opium smokers in a Chinese barbershop. But some opium dens
operated independently in dark, secluded spaces where heavy users—
opium "fiends"—could spend a day or two sleeping off the soporific effects
of the narcotic.

Preparing the opium for smoking involved an elaborate ritual. First,
the smoker rolled the black opium paste into a small ball ranging from the
size of a pea to that of a marble, and skewered it on the end of a long piece
of metal that resembled a knitting needle. Then he suspended it over the
flame of a small oil lamp and rotated it to heat it evenly until the drug
attained the consistency of a hard pill. Next, the smoker ran the end of the
needle into the small hole on the top of the long wooden opium pipe until
the opium pill became lodged in the top of the hole. Then he removed the
needle, heated the pipe over the flame, and drew in opium smoke through
the pipe's ivory mouthpiece. An experienced smoker might consume the
entire opium pill in one very long breath.[46]

The earliest depictions of Five Points opium dens were rarely judg-
mental. Journalists devoted most of their attention to the process of smoking itself and to conveying the exotic and mysterious nature of the drug,
which was not then illegal. Describing a Donovan's Lane opium den in
1873, a journalist for the *Daily Graphic* reported that "those in the habit of
coming here say that it has a beneficial medicinal effect, and, if only
inhaled in small quantities, animates the spirits and gives energy to the
intellectual powers, at the same time imparting a languor to the body, leaving the mind free from nervous effects." Yet those who smoked too much,
the Chinese admitted, found themselves "for several days in a lethargic,
torpid state, neither caring for nor taking food." Through the early 1880s,
descriptions of Chinatown opium joints took a similarly detached attitude.[47]

But in 1883, New Yorkers began to reassess their stance on both opium
and Chinese gambling. In fact, both Chinese Five Pointers and their non-
Chinese neighbors began to complain about the district's vice industry.
The Chinese objected not to the presence of gambling and opium in their
community, but rather to the control exerted over them by a single man,
Tom Lee.

Few facts about Lee's life can be documented with certainty. He was apparently born Wong Ah Ling in about 1840 in Canton or its environs. He immigrated to California, eventually becoming a labor contractor there. In the mid-1870s he moved to St. Louis, where he operated a cooperage business and become a naturalized American citizen in 1876. After a return visit to China, Lee relocated to Philadelphia, where he was a merchant. He finally settled in New York in 1878, and in 1879 married a Scots-German immigrant, Elsie Kaylor, whom he had met in Philadelphia. They eventually had two sons.[48]

Lee appears to have first settled in New York at 4 Mott Street, where according to some accounts he ran a cigar store. But his business interests were undoubtedly more varied. Lee was "the accredited New York agent of the Six Companies in San Francisco," that combination of powerful families and merchants that controlled the bulk of the Chinese import-export trade in California. Although a relative newcomer to New York, Lee skillfully used the press to promote his image as one of Chinatown's most important residents. In August 1878, the *Herald* reported that Lee hosted a sumptuous Chinese banquet at his Mott Street home to honor attorney Edmond E. Price, who had successfully defended Chinese interests "in a number of cases." Six months later, Price and other white New Yorkers were once again fêted at Lee's expense.[49]

Just what kind of Chinatown interests Price had defended became clearer a few weeks after this second banquet when, in March 1879, police made their first ever raid on a Chinatown vice operation. Nearly fifty officers stormed the grocery and apothecary at 13 Mott—"one of the places which are popularly supposed to abound in pickled rat, edible dog and savory candles"—where they found a *fan tan* game and opium smokers. Thirty-one men were jailed on gambling charges. Appearing for the defense the next day, Price argued that the police had found not a gambling business but merely a social gathering. The judge ordered the men released, commenting that those arrested were only engaged in "some private amusement such as is not uncommon in the best clubs and in private houses."[50]

One writer has surmised that the dismissal of charges in this case resulted from Lee's influence among politically well-connected New Yorkers such as Price. Although there is no evidence to substantiate such speculation, Lee was making significant strides toward increasing his power base in Chinatown. In 1879, thanks to the political connections he was forging, Lee was named a deputy sheriff of New York County. And in the spring of 1880, Lee helped establish Chinatown's first *tong*.[51]

Tongs were secret fraternal associations first created by seventeenth-century Buddhist monks to help organize the overthrow of Manchurian rule in China. When Lee and a few other prominent Chinatown residents filed articles of association for their *tong* in Albany in 1880, they described it as more of a mutual aid society, designed to provide "aid in sickness, poverty, adversity, and affliction." Each of the city's prominent newspapers transliterated the name of Lee's *tong* a bit differently. The *Times* called it the "Lone We Tong." The *Herald* referred to it as the "Loon Ye," while the *Tribune* spelled it "Lung Ye." Whatever the case, Lee's *tong* became one of the most powerful entities in nineteenth-century Chinatown.[52]

Lee soon began demanding payoffs from Chinatown's gambling dens. He would flash his deputy sheriff's badge and insist that without a payment of five dollars per week, the police would close down the establishment. Lee probably also threatened to use his *tong*'s toughs to punish any holdouts. By 1883, virtually every one of Chinatown's two dozen or so gambling resorts made weekly payments to Lee and his Loon Ye Tong minions, netting them thousands of dollars each year.[53]

The victims of Lee's extortion eventually began to balk at making the protection payments. They hired an attorney who filed affidavits with the District Attorney's Office documenting Lee's demands. As a result, Lee's commission as deputy sheriff was revoked, and a grand jury directed the district attorney to file charges. After deliberating for some time about exactly what Lee could be charged with, he was indicted on May 1 for "keeping a gambling establishment" at 17 Mott and "compounding a crime" by taking money from other illegal gambling houses.[54]

Lee responded aggressively. To the press, he argued that the accusations were motivated by Chinese regional jealousies. Nearly all the New York Chinese hailed from the region around Canton, explained the *Times*, but while Lee was from the subdistrict of Sin Ching, those charging him with extortion were natives of Ha Sin Ning. Wong Ching Foo, a Lee ally, told the *Times* that Lee's enemies were "armed to the teeth" and had threatened Lee with "extermination." Yet Lee's men apparently did most of the threatening. They promised death to anyone who testified against

Lee, leaving those who had made statements against him, their attorney complained, "in a state of almost abject terror."[55]

In the days before Lee's gambling trial was scheduled to take place, the other pillar of Chinatown's vice industry—its opium dens—also came under attack. But whereas the fight over *fan tan* was an intra-Chinese battle, the assault on the opium trade was mounted by Five Points' non-Asian residents. Many Irish-American parents had become convinced that Chinese opium joints were corrupting their daughters. The president of Transfiguration's Catholic Young Men's Association, John A. O'Brien, condemned the opium dens as "girl traps." Five Pointers commonly believed that Chinese peddlers, as one eighteen-year-old woman put it, "give girls opium in candy and all sorts of things, until we can't do without it." Another neighborhood resident claimed that "little girls" in their early teens secretly whiled away their days in the dens.[56]

Spearheading this attack was the organizer of the Young Men's Association, Transfiguration assistant pastor James Barry. In early May 1883, Barry stationed surveillance teams on the neighborhood's rooftops. Whenever these units observed a white woman entering one of the suspected opium joints, they notified the police, who would immediately raid the premises and arrest the occupants under the state law, passed just a year earlier, that for the first time made it a misdemeanor both to smoke opium and operate a joint. But the raids did not uncover the expected hordes of opium-crazed girls. The only "girl" found in the joints, identified by Barry as a fourteen-year-old, turned out to be nineteen and was never charged. The association nonetheless claimed that many girls aged ten to fifteen had escaped over backyard fences.[57]

Despite the hysteria whipped up by Barry and fanned by the newspapers, many non-Asian New Yorkers stepped forward to defend the Chinese. An official of the Society for the Prevention of Cruelty to Children called the whole affair "newspaper buncombe. . . . Nothing more is going on in Mott street than has been going on for the past two or three years." Irish women, he asserted, "tempt the Chinamen to immorality as often as they are tempted." A Protestant missionary agreed that "Mott street wickedness is not general."[58]

The stories of the arrested Caucasian women substantiated these claims. Katie Crowley had come to Mott Street to visit her sister—known

"Crazed by Opium" reflects the increasingly prevalent fear that white women were becoming addicted to opium in Five Points' opium dens. *Frank Leslie's Illustrated Newspaper* (May 19, 1883): 204. Collection of the Library of Congress.

as "Chinee Annie" because she had married a Chinese American and lived in Chinatown. Two other white women picked up in the raids were also Irish Americans who had married Chinese men. They admitted smoking opium, but probably had picked up the habit from their husbands. Only the last of the four, apprehended at her brother's behest for "vagrancy," had no apparent kinship ties to the Chinese community. She admitted frequenting opium dens, but insisted she did so only to eat Chinese candy.[59]

Father Barry's campaign against the opium dens was not endorsed even by the head of his own parish, Father Thomas F. Lynch. Barry's crusade "finds no favor with Father Lynch," reported the *Tribune*. "He says that the charges that the Chinese have been debauching large numbers of young girls are grossly exaggerated." In his eighteen months at Transfiguration, Lynch told the *Tribune*, "not a single instance of the ruin of a young girl by a Chinaman had come under his notice." He condemned Barry's attempts to, in the reporter's words, "stir up race hatred against the Chinese." The Chinese, of course, worried about being stigmatized as well. "The trouble," observed Wong Ching Foo after the raids and arrests, "is that the Irish are trying to direct this clamor against the whole [Chinese] race."[60]

The opium raids could not have pleased Tom Lee. The one indicted opium den operator, Ah Chung, admitted selling the drug but said he thought the ten dollars per month he paid Lee was a license fee that made his operation legal. To this point, Lee had been implicated only for taking money from *fan tan* operators. These narcotics-related revelations, coming just days before the start of his trial on the gambling charges, did not bode well. But prosecutors did not file any additional charges against Lee. Furthermore, as his court date approached, his terror campaign seemed to pay dividends, as one after another of the men who had implicated Lee began to recant. At a preliminary hearing held on May 16, the prosecution could muster but a single witness, and with Lee's men ominously filling the courtroom, even he changed his testimony. The charges were eventually dropped and Lee was reinstated as deputy sheriff.[61]

In the future, opium dealers would have to operate more furtively. The opium den proprietors also learned to forestall prosecution by keeping their female clientele to a minimum. And they learned, along with the *fan tan* operators, that the authorities would do nothing to prevent Lee from extorting protection money from them. Until these men could establish some organization of their own to match Lee's Loon Ye Tong, he would remain the "the great Mongolian magnate of Mott Street," the most powerful man in Chinatown and the best known Chinese New Yorker.[62]

"YOUR RELIGION IS GOOD ENOUGH AS FAR AS IT GOES, BUT OURS IS BETTER AND GOES FURTHER"

New Yorkers would continue to associate Mott Street with vice. But fraternal, occupational, and religious organizations became a much more integral part of the Five Points Chinese community. The Chinese made such organizations the focal point of both their business and social lives.

Most of Chinatown's fraternal societies had economic or social agendas. As New York's Chinese population expanded in the 1880s, for example, Chinatown's residents replaced the all-encompassing mutual aid societies of the 1870s with more selective groups organized around family and geographic origins. Village associations, known as *fongs*, rented apartments in Chinatown for use as both social headquarters and lodging houses for homeless or unemployed members. Members traded intelligence on job openings and laundry opportunities, and pooled money to start businesses. They also sent money back to China to finance flood or famine relief, build a new school, or help the village defend itself against bandits.

More consequential than these geographically based groups, however, were the family or surname organizations known as *kung saw*, which limited membership to those with a certain surname, no matter what part of China they had emigrated from. These groups were far more important than the regional bodies, especially for newcomers seeking loans and lodging. The Wong family association, for example, located at 5 Mott Street in a building controlled by a wealthy Wong merchant, played a major role in Chinatown life. Smaller clans often joined forces in order to attain a membership base that could sustain an organization. When one Chinese, Hor Pao, arrived in New York in the late 1870s, he could not find enough clansmen to create a *kung saw*. He and his kin eventually teamed with Lais and Gongs to form the Sam Yip, or Three Family Society.[63]

The press constantly marveled at the number and variety of Chinese mutual aid societies. Among the most important were the laundrymen's organizations. Some catered to laundry owners, regulating the prices that were charged for a given service. Others functioned more like trade unions for their employees—it was even said that the washers and the pressers maintained separate labor organizations. Chinese cigarmakers established unions as well, while Chinatown merchants created a chamber of commerce. Even leisure activities were organized; a *fan tan* society, for example, regulated that game. The Chinese could depend upon one another even in death. A burial society provided for interment in the traditional manner, arranging for the return of its members' remains to China.[64]

Given their penchant for organization, it should come as no surprise that Chinatown's residents created an umbrella group to regulate their myriad societies. This was the Chinese Consolidated Benevolent Association, established around 1883 and modeled after a body of the same name in San Francisco. The association coordinated celebrations for Chinese New Year and adjudicated disputes that could not be settled by the smaller bodies. Each year the heads of the various organizations that constituted this society elected a leader, christened by the press as the "mayor of

Chinatown." Its headquarters—a lavish brick building at 16 Mott—was known as the "Chinese City Hall."[65]

Number 16 Mott also eventually housed Chinatown's most important religious institution, its "joss house." Chinese Americans' religious practices are difficult to characterize, for their Taoist roots had been melded over the centuries with elements of Confucianism, Buddhism, and ancestor worship. Their temples consequently contained images of various popular gods drawn from these traditions. Whether Chinese Americans devoted much attention to religion is also difficult to determine. One immigrant, asked by the *Tribune* about his spiritual views, "laughingly replied that he had left all that at Canton," and American journalists rarely found crowds in Chinatown's places of worship. Nonetheless, these temples were one of the most talked about features of Chinese life in Five Points.[66]

At first, Chinese New Yorkers built makeshift shrines in their club-houses, initially on Baxter Street and later on Mott. By the early 1880s, they had constructed a more formal and elaborate temple in a third-floor apartment at 10 Chatham Square. Americans always referred to the carved deity at the center of these shrines as "joss" (the origin of the term, first coined in California, is not known) and the buildings in which they sat as joss houses. "The joss himself sits in a gorgeous shrine of carved wood, mounted with gold," noted one Caucasian visitor to the Chatham Square sanctuary:

> The setting is most fantastic and bewildering. Birds, dragons, ante-diluvian animals, serpents, crabs and fishes burst out all over the front of the shrine. Almost veiled from view, the joss peers out on the worshipper. He is painted on carved wood, and is as hideous a deity as was ever seen in the most frenzied of opium dreams. In front of the shrine stands a table—a handsome one, with all the appliances of worship upon it. Worship takes the form of burning scented sticks and paper. . . . Before the god an oil lamp burns day and night. . . . On the walls are painted mythological scenes. . . . Handsomely illuminated texts from Confucius in rich frames are everywhere. . . . The costly furnishing of the room, however, is found in the magnificent two-armed ebony chairs, elaborately carved. . . . There are a dozen or more of these chairs in a row. The

great merchants and teachers of the Chinese colony sit in them on feast days and occasions of solemn conclave.

By the end of the 1880s, the Chinese had completed an even more ostentatious temple in the Consolidated Benevolent Association Building at 16 Mott.[67]

New Yorkers were both fascinated by and suspicious of Chinese religious practices. "The Chinese have peculiar ways of showing reverence for their sanctuaries," intoned Transfiguration's Father Thomas McLoughlin. "Namely they sit around and smoke and chat and have a quiet little game; nay right back of the shrine is a room with two bamboo couches where the priests of the temple and their friends 'hit the pipe' to pass away the time." Observing that most who entered the joss house across the street from his church merely lit incense and chanted a few quick prayers before departing, McLoughlin ridiculed the Chinese "go as you please [form of] worship, having no fixed hours, nor fixed days, nor fixed ritual, nor fixed liturgy." The only reason most Chinatown residents attended at all, McLoughlin sneered, was to receive a piece of paper that contained "his fortune for the week, *i.e.*, what were to be his lucky and unlucky days[,] what his lucky numbers [were] in gambling, on what days to buy and sell, etc."

Most Protestants, of course, continued to disparage both religions practiced on Mott Street. "I visited the Joss house in Mott Street last week and saw the pagans bowed down before their idols and offering their incense," commented one minister. "Right opposite, I entered a so-called Christian Temple and there found a lot of Papist idolators bowed down in like manner before their idols of wood and stone."[68]

Catholics were initially unwilling to make efforts to convert the Chinese, but the Methodists of the Five Points Mission actively proselytized in the Chinese-American community. In 1879, they rented prime retail space at 14 Mott Street to house their Chinese mission and placed at its head Moy Jin Kee, a young immigrant whose father was a Methodist minister in Canton. At one of the mission's first Sunday services, an uptown minister told the Chinese in attendance that "your religion is good enough as far as it goes, but ours is better and goes further." Such an approach did not bode well for the mission's success. The next day, Chinatown residents mobbed Moy for disparaging remarks he had apparently made about them to the press. To make matters worse, police arrested him hours later for stealing silks from his former employer. Although the Mott Street mission soon closed, the Methodists did eventually achieve a modicum of success converting Chinese immigrants. Another Protestant organization aimed at the Chinese was started in the 1890s by Baptists on Doyer Street. Known in the neighborhood as "Tom Noonan's Rescue Mission," it became a Chinatown institution, though it focused its proselytizing efforts primarily on Bowery drunks rather than the Chinese.[69]

Unwilling to lose the Chinese to the Protestants by default, Five Points Catholic leaders eventually felt compelled to proselytize in Chinatown as well. When McLoughlin replaced Lynch in the early 1890s, he announced to the press that he would work to convert the neighborhood's Chinese immigrants. But he gave up a few years later, insisting that such efforts were pointless. The Chinese immigrant "comes here for the sole object of making money," explained McLoughlin, "and he has the poorest idea of the spiritual world that it is possible for a human being to have." This last point echoed almost verbatim Lynch's assessment of the Italians a few years earlier. McLoughlin claimed that apparent Protestant success with the Chinese was a sham. "Most of their converts still carry the queue," he noted, "which is a sign that they still hold to their own superstitions."[70]

"A PECULIAR FANCY FOR WIVES OF CELTIC ORIGIN"

New Yorkers considered the Chinese—with their "heathenish" religion, strange foods, opium and gambling dens, and utterly incomprehensible language—more "foreign" than any other immigrants who had ever settled in New York. One potentially threatening aspect of this utterly foreign enclave was its overwhelming domination by men. Just as antebellum Americans had viewed the celibacy of Catholic priests as "unnatural" and speculated endlessly about the "crimes" and "perversions" to which such a life might drive them, postbellum New Yorkers worried about Chinatown's lack of women. This was one of the unspoken subtexts of the panic over the "ruin" of white women in the neighborhood's opium joints. Yet Americans must have realized that they themselves were partly to blame for the scarcity of women in Chinatown. The Chinese Exclusion Act of 1882 had prohibited even most Chinese already in the United States from bringing wives from Asia to New York. The law's sponsors apparently hoped that Chinese men would return to Asia rather than face the possibility of a lifetime without a spouse.

Chinese New Yorkers began instead to marry other immigrants. Even before the Civil War, Americans noticed the propensity of Chinese men to court Irish women, who for more than a generation had suffered from a shortage of potential Irish spouses. By the late 1860s, Chinese-Irish unions were quite common. "These Chinamen have a peculiar fancy for wives of Celtic origin," asserted the *Tribune* in early 1869. A reporter from the *World* who in 1877 toured a Baxter Street tenement housing fifteen Chinese immigrants found that all had Irish wives. With shortages of both Chinese women and Irish men, laws of supply and demand drew these Five Pointers together.[71]

Some Chinese Five Pointers did manage to find Chinese wives. Two spirited their brides across the Canadian border dressed as men. Most of the Chinese women who came to New York unattached were young indentured servants who, when they became old enough, could be "bought" from their "owners" and wed. In 1896, even though he already had two wives in China, forty-six-year-old Hor Poa paid $1,200 to marry sixteen-year-old Gon She, described by one reporter as "the Belle of Chinatown." Another immigrant paid $900 for his bride.[72]

Nonetheless, the majority of Chinese men still married non-Chinese women. Courtship could not have been easy for these couples. Most Chinese New Yorkers spoke very little English, while their mates told the *Times* that "they knew little of the language of their spouses, it was very hard to learn." Many New Yorkers could not fathom why a non-Asian would marry a "Chinaman." When a journalist from the *World* asked two Five Points Irishwomen why they had wed Chinese immigrants, one just laughed, but the other replied indignantly, "Because we liked 'em, of course; why shouldn't we?" The reporter "suggested that it was more in accordance with the nature of things that they should marry white men, whereupon Mrs. Ching Si said that [their husbands] were as white as anybody and a good deal whiter than many of their neighbors, and Mrs. Ah Muk showed her little baby as proof that she was more than content with her lot. . . . 'Joe is his name,' said the proud mother. 'He don't look like a Chinaboy, does he, when he's asleep'?"[73]

Intermarriage is sometimes hailed as a benchmark of assimilation, but anti-Chinese prejudice remained strong, both in Five Points and beyond. This became especially manifest when Congress in 1892 passed the Geary Act. In addition to renewing the ban on Chinese immigration imposed a decade earlier, the Geary Act required Chinese Americans (other than merchants and professionals) to register with the Treasury Department, which would issue them a certificate of residency, including a photograph. Any Chinese caught without this photo identification were to be punished with up to one year's hard labor followed by deportation, unless they could produce a "white witness" to prove that they had been prevented from obtaining the certificate by accident or illness.

The Geary Act inspired unprecedented indignation in Chinatown. Wong Ching Foo condemned it in testimony before Congress, noting that convicts were the only other group forcibly photographed by the American government. A Mott Street laundryman, Fong Yue Ting, organized the Equal Rights League to coordinate the Chinese community's legal challenge to the statute. Many non-Asians also condemned the legislation. *Harper's Weekly* called it "an act of bad faith" and "unintelligent zeal," while the *Times* denounced it as "one of the most humiliating acts of which any civilized nation has been guilty in modern times."[74]

The San Francisco–based Chinese Six Companies coordinated resistance to the Geary Act. It called on Chinese Americans nationwide not to register, asked for one dollar from each immigrant to finance a legal challenge, and hired a prominent expert on constitutional law—attorney Joseph H. Choate—to head their legal team. Choate arranged with federal prosecutors to have Fong Yue Ting and two other laundrymen arrested on May 6, 1893, the first day upon which the Chinese would be liable to deportation. Choate immediately appealed their case to the U.S. Supreme Court, which had already agreed to consider the matter on an expedited basis.

New York's Chinese Americans were stunned when the Court ruled by a five to three vote that the Geary Act was, in fact, constitutional. In their unusually vigorous dissenting opinions, the minority insisted that the law violated the Burlingame Treaty's pledge to grant Chinese immigrants all "the same privileges, immunities, and exemptions" as other immigrants; that its presumption of guilt in the deportation proceedings violated the Fourteenth Amendment's guarantee of due process to all "persons"; and that deportation itself was cruel and unusual punishment. The Court majority, however, insisted that Congress had just as much right to regulate the residence of aliens who had taken no steps to become naturalized as it did to regulate immigration itself. How the Chinese could be expected to apply for naturalization when they were now banned from doing so was not addressed. As to the act's supposed violation of due process, the Court ruled that due process was a right for citizens, but only a privilege for aliens, one that Congress could choose to withhold from them.[75]

The Supreme Court's ruling in *Fong Yue Ting v. the United States* highlighted the importance of naturalization to the legal rights of immigrants in the United States. The handful of Chinese New Yorkers such as Tom Lee who had become citizens before 1882 must have felt both lucky and relieved. But most white Americans found the sight of *any* Chinese immigrant exercising the rights of citizenship appalling. In August 1904, after casting ballots for more than a quarter century in state and national political contests, Tom Lee was arrested for voting illegally. His naturalization papers were invalid, prosecutors declared, because Congress had subsequently stipulated that the Chinese were not eligible for naturalization. Police also arrested Civil War veteran William A. Hang, a Pearl Street cigar manufacturer who had lived in New York for more than forty years, on identical charges. Hang was serving aboard one of David G. Farragut's fourteen gunboats in Mobile Bay when the admiral shouted, "Damn the torpedoes! Full speed ahead." No amount of service to one's country could earn a Chinese immigrant the privileges of citizenship.[76]

Americans rationalized their refusal to naturalize Chinese immigrants on the grounds that the Chinese could never become "true" Americans. Even *Harper's Weekly,* which defended them throughout the Gilded Age, insisted that "the Chinese are the most undesirable of immigrants because, with all their useful qualities, they cannot assimilate socially or politically or morally with Americans." In truth, no Five Points immigrants had ever assimilated to an extent that would have satisfied native-born Americans. The Irish, Germans, Italians, Jews, and Chinese all tended to re-create their Old World culture in New York rather than adopt American habits and values. They socialized mostly with other immigrants from the land of their birth, sang the same songs and played the same games as they had back home, ate much the same food, and complained that American values would ruin their children. While they may not have regretted coming to America, they often pined for their native soil. Italians and Chinese dreamed of returning to their homelands with great riches. The Irish yearned to return to Ireland and liberate it from the British. Only the neighborhood's Jews gave little thought to returning to the "old country."

It was, as ever, their children who assimilated. They were embarrassed by their parents' "foreign" habits and wanted to be like other American kids, speak English without an accent, play baseball, and so on. And to a great extent they achieved these goals. One of Tom Lee's sons became a Methodist minister. The other sold cars in affluent Westchester County. Although Hor Poa's son remained in Chinatown for many years, both as a bookie and a waiter, he eventually started a bowling club, a softball team, and even organized a Chinese-American squad for the Police Athletic League basketball tournament. Sailor William Assing's son, William Junior, became New York's first Chinese-American policeman.[77]

In little more than a decade, Five Points and its reputation had once again changed dramatically. In 1875, it was an Irish-American enclave that had improved markedly since the days of the Old Brewery and Cow Bay. But by 1890, it was an overwhelmingly Italian and Chinese quarter, once again perceived as the most repulsive in the city, an incubator of vice and crime. Protestantism had not saved it after all. But Jacob Riis believed that he could.

14

The End of Five Points

෴

"HIS BOOK IS LITERALLY A PHOTOGRAPH"

HAVING WON the hand of his beloved Elisabeth in Denmark, Jacob Riis returned with her to the United States in 1876 and settled once again in Brooklyn. For a while, he continued to run the *South Brooklyn News*, which he had sold to some local politicos before his betrothal. But without the editorial freedom that came with owning the newspaper, Riis became frustrated and bored, and soon quit the *News* for good. How he achieved fame is quite a story, one that altered the course of Five Points history.

While working at the *News*, Riis had purchased a "stereopticon outfit," the nineteenth-century equivalent of a slide projector. He was fascinated by the "magic lantern," as it was popularly known, and after he left the *News*, he decided to earn a living with it. Riis and a partner would string a canvas screen between two trees in city parks and project onto it images of famous world landmarks, which they interspersed with advertisements for local businesses. During the winter, the slide shows moved indoors to a storefront in downtown Brooklyn. In the spring of 1877, profits began to dwindle, and Riis and his partner hit upon the sideline of publishing the first city directory of Elmira, New York, which they would advertise through the slide shows. But believing that the two strangers had come to town to foment violence during the ongoing nationwide rail strike, the authorities ran them out of town. With a new baby to support, Riis returned to Brooklyn and began to look for work as a reporter.[1]

At first, New York's major dailies scoffed at his résumé, and after weeks of rejection it appeared that he would have to change careers yet again. But suddenly his luck changed. One of the newsmen who had refused to hire Riis was William F. G. Shanks, city editor of the prestigious *New York Tribune* and Riis's neighbor in Brooklyn. Toward the end of 1877, Shanks found himself desperately in need of an extra newsman. He found Riis and hired him as a general assignment reporter on a trial basis.

The work was not what Riis had imagined. His editors stuck him with assignments no other reporters wanted, usually in the farthest-flung corners of the city. Once, he trudged miles through knee-deep snow to cover a disaster on Coney Island, only to be upbraided by Shanks for sloppy reporting. And because he was not part of the permanent staff, the pay was terrible, too little to live on even for the now thrifty Riis. So "after six months of hard grubbing I decided that I had better seek my fortune elsewhere," Riis later wrote. He composed a letter of resignation and left it on Shanks's desk one morning.

When Riis returned that afternoon, he realized that Shanks had been out all day and had not seen his letter. Riis retrieved it, tore it up, and went out to cover his assignment. That evening, rushing downtown to file his story, he came running around a corner in Printing-House Square at full speed and crashed into Shanks, knocking the editor into a snowdrift. The incensed editor asked him why he was careening around corners so recklessly, to which Riis replied that he was hurrying to file his story before deadline. When a somber-faced Shanks summoned Riis into his office the next morning, Riis expected to be fired. Instead, Shanks promoted him to a full-time post as the *Tribune*'s reporter at police headquarters. "It is a place that needs a man who will run to get his copy in," said Shanks. Riis, of course, was thrilled. "Got staff appointment," he telegraphed his wife in Brooklyn. "Police Headquarters. $25 a week. Hurrah!"[2]

Riis flourished on his new beat, which included the fire and health departments in addition to police work. Whereas most reporters covering the police relied on paid informants in both headquarters and the precincts to leak them news, Riis hustled to come up with his own leads, which often led to scoops. For one story, he tracked down all the guests at a party to prove that a series of apparently unrelated illnesses was in fact an outbreak of trichinosis. In another, he was the only reporter to accurately report the conclusion to a celebrated case of grave-robbing, in which thieves stole the body of department store magnate A. T. Stewart and held it for ransom. After a few years, Shanks could boast that Riis had made the *Tribune* police reports "the best in the city."[3]

Police headquarters in those days was located at 300 Mulberry Street, about a mile north of Five Points. When Riis got off work, usually at about dawn, he would walk down Mulberry Street past Mulberry Bend and Five Points to the Fulton Street Ferry. He could have taken a train down the Bowery to the docks, but he preferred to walk and see "the slum when off its guard." Riis knew the Bend well from his days and nights as a homeless immigrant. Soon he made it his special cause, accompanying the police there to capture murderers and tagging along with health inspectors as they hunted for the source of epidemics. He became intimately familiar with Bottle Alley, Bandits' Roost, and the reputation of every tenement in the neighborhood.

Riis began to make shocking slum conditions a leitmotif of his reporting. Most journalists attributed the persistence of slums to the "ignorant" and "backward" immigrants who inhabited them, but Riis assigned some of the blame to the tenement buildings themselves and the greedy landlords who refused to provide adequate light, ventilation, or maintenance. Riis was not above prejudice; greedy Jews, lazy Italians, and sly Chinese filled his writings. He was convinced, however, that tenements actually bred many of the social ills that Americans blamed on immigrants. Exorbitant rents drove tenement dwellers to take in too many boarders, and the resulting overcrowding led to epidemics. Poor ventilation exacerbated the rate of illness. Constant sickness made it impossible for the tenement dwellers to keep steady jobs. Unlike most Americans, Riis knew from his own experience that most impoverished immigrants were not simply too lazy to work.[4]

Riis recalled in his memoirs that on his "midnight trips with the sanitary police . . . the wish kept cropping up in me that there were some way of putting before the people what I saw there. . . . We used to go in the small hours of the morning into the worst tenements to count noses and see if the law against overcrowding was violated, and the sights I saw there gripped my heart until I felt that I must tell of them, or burst, or turn anarchist, or something." He considered publishing drawings, but *Harper's*

Weekly and *Frank Leslie's* had used these for years to little effect. Riis continued to write about the tenements, "but it seemed to make no impression."[5]

His crusade did have *some* impact. In early 1887, Mayor Abram S. Hewitt pressed state lawmakers to finance the construction of small parks in tenement districts. The lack of parks and playgrounds in neighborhoods such as Five Points had been a theme of Riis's slum reporting. "The project is to open up parks in the tenement districts as breathing places," explained the *Times*'s Albany correspondent, "and it is one of Mayor Hewitt's pet schemes." The Small Parks Act was passed and signed into law in May.[6]

That same year, Riis read about the invention of flash photography. Riis excitedly contacted his friend Dr. John T. Nagle, head of the Health Department's Bureau of Vital Statistics and an avid amateur photographer. A few weeks later, Riis, Nagle, and a couple of other photography buffs began to document the filth and overcrowding of New York's most notorious tenements. "I had at last," Riis wrote, "an ally in the fight with the Bend."[7]

A police escort initially accompanied Riis's photographic "raiding party" into the tenements, but as he later recalled, "they were hardly needed. It is not too much to say that our party carried terror wherever it went. The flashlight of those days was contained in cartridges fired from a revolver. The spectacle of half a dozen strange men invading a house in the midnight hour armed with big pistols which they shot off recklessly was hardly reassuring." Soon the amateur photographers who took the photos tired of the late-night work. Riis hired professionals, but they were not fond of the hours Riis kept either. He eventually bought his own camera and—using a frying pan instead of a revolver for the flash powder—began taking the photos himself.[8]

Riis put some of his pictures to practical use immediately. He used his photo of men crammed into bunks in a Bayard Street apartment, for example, to help secure a judgment against the lessee before the city's Board of Health. But his sights were set much higher. "For more than a year," he later wrote, "I knocked at the doors of the various magazine editors with my pictures, proposing to tell them how the other half lived, but no one wanted to know." When *Harper's* offered to take the photos but insisted on hiring "a man who could write" to tell their story, Riis stormed out of the magazine's office. He tried to arrange speaking engagements before city religious groups, but they declined as well. When even his own Brooklyn church, where he was a deacon, refused to hear his "truth-telling," he resigned in disgust.[9]

The only organization that would give Riis a speaking engagement was the New York Society of Amateur Photographers. Remembering the success of his magic lantern shows, he had slides made from his negatives and used them to illustrate the lecture he delivered on January 25, 1888. He turned out to be a gifted public speaker. "Mr. Riis was so ingenious in describing the scenes and brought to his task such a vein of humor," that he often had the audience in stitches, the *Tribune* reported the next day. He brought tears to his listeners' eyes as well, especially with the heart-rending stories of the Bend's defenseless waifs and scrub girls.[10]

About a month later, the minister of the Broadway Tabernacle, a prestigious Congregational church on Broadway just four blocks west of the Bend, consented to let Riis lecture to his parishioners. He again wowed his audience. Invitations quickly followed from some of the most prominent churches in New York and Brooklyn. Soon, he began lecturing to church groups up and down the East Coast. In Buffalo, according to a local journalist, Riis mixed "racy description[s] of the infected district" with "a vein of earnestness that lifted the lecture quite above the level of a mere passing away of the time." Another theme of Riis's lecture, noted the *Washington Post*, was "what [are] we going to do to protect ourselves?" Far-flung audiences were just as troubled by Riis's images as were New Yorkers in part because every American city had its share of impoverished immigrants, and in part because they believed it was their responsibility as good Christians to ameliorate the suffering of the poor. Combining humor with horror, and evoking both pity and outrage, Riis transformed Mulberry Bend and its wretched tenements into a national issue.[11]

Riis also turned to the local press. On February 12, 1888, the *New York Sun* published "Flashes From the Slums," which told the story of Riis's photo expeditions and described the results. As was typical in that era, the story had no byline; though it described Riis in the third person, he was probably its author. But unlike magazines, a newspaper could not usually reproduce actual photographs, so "Flashes From the Slums" featured eleven *drawings* of Riis photos, which significantly lessened their impact.[12]

An editor at Scribner's publishing house who had heard one of Riis's church lectures soon approached him about converting it into an illustrated article. "How the Other Half Lives" appeared in the December 1889 issue of *Scribner's Magazine,* illustrated mostly with drawings based on Riis's photos, but also with nine "halftones," a relatively new process for reproducing photographs in the print media. Some of the halftones look more like drawings than photographs. But others, including an image of homeless children sleeping on the streets and another of children praying at the Five Points House of Industry, are quite vivid and moving.[13]

Both "Flashes From the Slums" and "How the Other Half Lives" are landmarks in the history of photojournalism. Never before had photographs played such a central role in the telling of a news story. In fact, the photos *were* the story. Ever since, journalists have used photos not merely to add color or variety to news reporting, but to document their allegations.

Riis considered these articles an integral part of his "battle with the slum." So he was surprised when, despite their publication, city officials did nothing to clean up Mulberry Bend. Many New Yorkers, including Riis, had assumed that the Bend would be the first site to benefit from the Small Parks Act. Yet in 1890, three years after that act became law, Mulberry Bend stood untouched. "Whether it was that it had been bad so long that people thought it could not be otherwise," Riis later wrote, "or because the Five Points [intersection] had taken all the reform the Sixth Ward had coming to it, or because, by a sort of tacit consent, the whole matter was left to me as the recognized Mulberry Bend crank—whichever it was, this last was the practical turn it took. I was left to fight it out by myself."[14]

Riis soon got the break he had been waiting for. A publisher who read the *Scribner's* article asked him to expand it into a book. He wrote the entire manuscript late at night after his family had gone to bed, completing it in just a few months. "I had had it in me so long that it burst out at last with a rush," he later explained. In November 1890, *How the Other Half Lives* appeared.[15]

In twenty-five short chapters, Riis surveyed the variety of tenement evils that had frustrated reformers for decades. Five Points was featured prominently, especially in chapters on the Bend, stale-beer dives, basement lodging houses, and Chinatown. His thesis, reiterated for years in his police reporting, was that the tenements themselves were the source of the slum problem, incubating disease and crime and perpetuating poverty. He blamed the situation in part on the landlords, who charged exorbitant rents, did little to maintain their buildings, and refused to build better ones. He also blamed the city's political bosses, who did not want to anger powerful property owners by insisting on effective enforcement of the existing laws. But Riis also charged that the immigrants were themselves an obstacle to reform, taking in too many boarders, allowing filth to accumulate in tenement yards, and refusing to demand better housing. "This is true particularly of the poorest" immigrants, he argued. "They are shiftless, destructive and stupid; in a word, they are what the tenements have made them. It is a dreary old truth that those who would fight for the poor must fight the poor to do it."[16]

Riis did not demand new laws, insisting that "the law has done what it could." All he asked was enforcement of the existing statutes. True, property owners could charge lower rents, place agents on the premises full time to make repairs and clean common spaces, and replace their dilapidated buildings with well-ventilated, light-filled "model tenements." But overall, Riis argued, "the landlord has done his share."[17]

The main obstacle to tenement reform, Riis believed, was an apathetic public. "The law needs a much stronger and readier backing of a thoroughly enlightened public sentiment to make it as effective as it might be made," he declared. Noting that a landlord would always try to avoid spending money to improve his property, Riis argued that "nothing short of the strongest pressure will avail to convince him that these individual rights are to be surrendered for the clear benefit of the whole." The tenements threatened not merely impoverished immigrants, Riis concluded, but every American through the crime, disease, and political unrest that the newcomers might spread if conditions were not immediately improved.[18]

How the Other Half Lives quickly became a sensation. The poet James Russell Lowell found it hard to sleep after reading its chilling accounts of decrepit tenements and their destitute inhabitants. Reviewers called it "thrilling," "harrowing," "startling," "a book of immense, shuddering interest," and "a saddening, terrifying book." Many commentators noted the importance of Riis's photos. "His book is literally a photograph," wrote one, while another praised Riis for looking at the tenements "with the unerring eye of the 'Kodak.' His own camera, not the imagination of a draughtsman, has furnished the illustrations."[19]

The book was not merely an exposé but also a call to arms. No human being, wrote the *Chicago Tribune,* could "read it without an instant and unappeasable desire to do something." Soon after its publication, a thirty-two-year-old civil service commissioner named Theodore Roosevelt stopped by Riis's office at police headquarters hoping to meet the author. Finding Riis away from his desk, Roosevelt left his card and scribbled a note on the back saying that he had read Riis's book and "come to help." As Luc Sante has noted,

> very few works of social criticism have ever had an effect as immediate, concrete, and measurable as *How the Other Half Lives.* The worst of the rookeries he describes were torn down. New laws were passed and old ones enforced to ensure minimal standards of hygiene and comfort in multiple-family dwellings. . . . [Homeless shelters] were established; public bathhouses were built. New schools whose design incorporated playgrounds went up one by one. The settlement-house movement was born and flourished. At length, and not without grave difficulties, child-labor laws were enacted, eventually on a national level.

Virtually every tenement problem Riis identified in his book was ameliorated to some extent because of the demands for change inspired by *How the Other Half Lives.*[20]

The notoriety Riis brought to Mulberry Bend made its demise inevitable. With the publication of *How the Other Half Lives,* the pressure to tear it down became too strong to resist. New Yorkers wrote letters to newspapers asking why the plan to build a park there was not progressing. Mulberry Bend property owners did not seriously fight to save their buildings, only for the highest possible compensation.[21]

After squabbling with property owners for two years over assessments and compensation, the city finally set the purchase price at $1.5 million and acquired the lots in the summer of 1894. But the Small Parks Act limited the expenditure to $1 million and the process ground to a halt once more as officials debated how they could legally exceed that sum. Once they cleared that hurdle (by issuing bonds to cover the purchase until the state could appropriate additional funds), demolition began, and was completed in early July 1895.[22]

Even then, the city did not begin work on the park. The huge empty lot became a favorite place for the city's cartmen to leave their hand trucks when not in use. At the end of 1895, several neighborhood children were crushed when they rode one of these carts into one of the cellar holes left amidst the rubble. Fed up with the endless string of delays, Riis filed a complaint against the city for maintaining a nuisance. City workers finally began constructing the park in the summer of 1896. Grand opening festivities took place on June 15, 1897.[23]

Ironically, Riis was not invited. He attended anyway, and got a lump in his throat as it sunk in that his many years of effort had finally borne fruit. Even a policeman chasing him off the grass did not spoil the moment. "The whole battle with the slum had summed itself up in the struggle with this dark spot," he later wrote. If reformers could succeed in having "the wickedest of American slums" torn down and replaced by a park, Riis believed, then there was no doubt that the "battle with the slum" could be won.[24]

According to Riis, quality of life in the neighborhood improved immediately. Five years later, the murder rate in the Sixth Ward had plummeted, and it had not been exported to other parts of the city, where the rate remained flat. "The whole neighborhood has taken a change, and decidedly for the better," a policeman told Riis. The 2,643 residents of the Bend who were displaced when their tenements were razed also improved their lives, said Riis in *The Battle with the Slum*, immediately finding housing in cleaner and safer neighborhoods.* Riis argued that the clearing of Mulberry Bend was such an unmitigated success that it paved the way for other radical improvements in city life. "Every other reform in New York," Riis insisted, could be traced to the successful reformation of Mulberry Bend.[25]

---

* It is impossible to verify Riis's claims concerning the fate of those displaced by the razing of the Bend. One also wonders what happened to other Five Pointers once they left the neighborhood, for the vast majority did not live there for even a decade. Most Irish Five Pointers had names that were too common to allow them to be traced in city directories or census indexes once they left the district. Italian and Chinese names were too often mangled by the census takers and too often left out of city directories to allow them to be tracked down. I was able to identify with certainty in the 1860 city directory only about one in ten Five Pointers who had opened accounts at the Emigrant Savings Bank in the early 1850s. About half still lived in Five Points. Most of the remainder had relocated to immigrant neighborhoods on either the Lower or Upper East Side, but there were a few scattered in nearly every part of the city.

A year after the tenements had been torn down, the *Times* reported that slumming parties no longer found the neighborhood particularly exciting. Five Points "is now a quiet, peaceable little breathing spot," stated a survey of the metropolis in 1899. "The squalor and misery and wretchedness of former times had vanished with the old-time buildings," agreed another writer. Visitors to the Bend saw no evidence of the "plague-spot of old." Even those intimately familiar with the neighborhood concurred with this assessment. "The Five Points no longer lies deep in the shadow of sin as it once did," announced the Children's Aid Society in 1907. Its annual report spoke of "the historical Five Points" as if the neighborhood itself was a thing of the past.[26]

"THE NEW YORK APPROACH"

Five Points was, for all intents and purposes, destroyed with the Bend. All the most notorious tenement complexes in the neighborhood—the Old Brewery, Cow Bay, Bottle Alley, and Bandits' Roost—were now mere memories, replaced by charitable institutions and open space. The stale-beer dives were mostly gone too, as were nearly all of the prostitutes. Other districts were by that point more crowded than Five Points, more crime-ridden, more dilapidated. The disease rate in the neighborhood dropped. By 1900, New Yorkers no longer associated Five Points with any of the vices or maladies that had once made it famous the world over.[27]

Subsequent urban renewal projects reshaped the Sixth Ward still further. Two years after the Bend was razed, the city tore down many tenements on Elm Street (two blocks west of the Bend) in order to widen it for use as a major north/south thoroughfare, rechristened Lafayette Street. In the first years of the twentieth century, the southern end of the ward was completely demolished to make room for the city's new municipal building. By about 1920, most of the tenements and factories between Baxter and Centre Streets had been knocked down to make room for courthouses and state offices. Nearly every Five Points tenement that stood east of Mulberry Street one hundred twenty years ago still stands there today, but not a single building west of Mulberry and south of Bayard remains.[28]

The destruction of Mulberry Bend was not the first instance of "urban renewal" in American history. Bostonians had razed an entire Irish neighborhood, squalid Fort Hill, as part of a redevelopment plan implemented in the late 1860s. But in New York, the clearing of Mulberry Bend began a whirlwind of tenement destruction that, by World War II, had leveled huge swaths of the Lower East Side and many of the city's other notorious tenement complexes, and replaced them with huge public housing projects that in some cases became almost as frightful as the rookeries. New Yorkers became so enamored of tearing down old tenement districts that one historian has referred to it as "the New York approach."[29]

The razing of the worst tenements through such urban renewal programs and the enactment of stricter regulatory laws are generally credited with bringing an end to the privations of the tenement system. From 1867 to 1901, New York enacted a series of increasingly stringent tenement laws that mandated better ventilation and sanitation, improved maintenance, and indoor plumbing. But to what extent did regulation really contribute to the demise of the tenement menace? Despite the stipulations that each room have a window and that stairwells have better lighting, stench continued to overpower tenement residents, and the promised improvements in ventilation never materialized. Lewis Hines's photographs from the years after the enactment of the 1901 legislation reveal crowding just as awful as Jacob Riis had found in the late 1880s and nearly as bad as that which antebellum investigators had uncovered in Cow Bay and the Old Brewery.

Heat also continued to afflict tenement dwellers as well. Filthy hallway toilets replaced filthy outhouses. Tragic fires continued to kill tenement dwellers, despite laws that required the use of "fireproof" materials. Disease also ravaged immigrant slums well into the twentieth century. Scientific advances pinpointing the causes of illness, rather than regulations outlawing tenement crowding and mandating the installation of indoor plumbing, finally brought the tenement death rate under control. Legislation could not eradicate the crime, prostitution, or overcrowding that continued to plague tenement neighborhoods in the first decades of the twentieth century.[30]

Cheap mass transit did not provide relief, either. Elevated trains began operating after the Civil War, and subways were introduced in the early twentieth century. Still, the tenements of Five Points, the Lower East Side, and other immigrant enclaves in Manhattan remained virtually as crowded as ever.

Nor was landlord greed the source of the tenement problem, as two

Civil War–era cases clearly demonstrate. In 1850, a "benevolent Quaker" gentleman named Silas Wood built a "model" tenement in the Fourth Ward just east of the Five Points. Wood hoped to prove that a landlord could reap a reasonable profit while providing a wholesome environment for his tenants. He charged only enough rent to bring in a modest return on his investment and hired as his agent a compassionate neighborhood resident he could count on to treat the tenants fairly. Despite these efforts, the overcrowded building soon became far worse than any other in the neighborhood. In fact, with the razing of the Old Brewery, Wood's tenement, known as Gotham Court, became the single most infamous tenement in postbellum New York.[31]

The case of Gotham Court was not an isolated one. In 1855, the New York Association for Improving the Condition of the Poor constructed its own model tenement half a block north of Five Points, running from Elizabeth to Mott Street just north of Canal. The AICP's structure, known as the "Big Flat," boasted indoor plumbing, a separate, assigned toilet for every family, and reasonable rents. The *Times* declared a year after its opening that it was the "best constructed tenant-house in the City of New-York." Yet within a decade of its construction, the Big Flat had become a den of thieves and a concentration of misery nearly as notorious as Gotham Court.[32]

What then finally brought an end to the miserable tenement conditions that afflicted New York and other large cities for so much of the nineteenth and early twentieth centuries? The only answer left seems to be the end of mass immigration itself. Only in the years after Congress severely restricted immigration did the conditions associated with tenement life— filth, overcrowding, and disease—truly begin to subside. The end of mass immigration dried up the supply of new arrivals who, especially when they lodged in someone else's apartment, exacerbated tenement crowding and overtaxed building facilities. The end of unrestricted immigration also enabled those immigrants already in the United States to find steady, higher-paying work, as they had fewer new arrivals to compete with. After immigration restriction, those tenement dwellers who had adapted to the necessities of urban life were not immediately replaced by newcomers unschooled in these lessons of hygiene and fire safety.

I do not mean to imply that individual immigrants or even any ethnic, racial, or national group should be blamed for the miseries of nineteenth-century tenement life. They had no way of knowing that methods of sanitation that had sufficed in rural Europe or Asia might spread cholera or typhus in an urban setting. Nor could they be blamed for taking in lodgers or sharing apartments with friends and relatives in order to feed hungry family members back home or finance their emigration. The huge number of immigrants pouring into New York, their desperation both to find cheap housing and to save money, and their difficulty adapting to the sanitary requirements of an urban setting all contributed to the inevitability of the tenement conditions found in Five Points. Property owners and sub-landlords may have exacerbated these problems through their greed and prejudice, their failure to maintain buildings, and their toleration of nuisances that brought them greater profits. But life in the tenements for most newly arrived, destitute, and unskilled immigrants would have been miserable no matter what landlords, reformers, and government officials imbued with nineteenth-century notions of laissez-faire might have attempted.

"DOWN THERE IN CHINATOWN"

Mulberry Street remained a center of Italian immigrant life for many years, but most Italians moved north above Canal Street and spread out across Mott and Elizabeth Streets as well. The portion of Little Italy south of Canal became the fringe of the community rather than its core.[33]

Meanwhile, Chinatown was transformed at the turn of the century into an entertainment zone. The two restaurants that heralded this change were the Port Arthur at 7–9 Mott Street and the Chinese Delmonico's on Pell, both of which opened in 1897. These cavernous new halls were luxuriously appointed, decorated with lanterns and dragons, and trimmed with teakwood, mother-of-pearl, and mosaic floors. Mayor William L. Strong himself attended the grand opening of the Chinese Delmonico's, an indication that Chinatown was no longer solely associated with opium dens and gambling parlors.

In the first years of the twentieth century, Chinatown also became renowned for its saloons and nightclubs. The teenaged Harry and Al Jolson helped launch their vaudeville careers there by "busking," traveling from saloon to saloon singing and dancing in return for the nickels and dimes tossed by the patrons. Harry later became a singing waiter at Callahan's dance hall at the corner of Chatham Square and Doyers Street. The teenaged Irving Berlin appeared there as well. He soon became a singing waiter at the Pelham Club, a saloon and nightclub at 12 Pell Street popularly known as "Nigger Mike Saulter's" after its swarthy Jewish proprietor. Another aspiring performer, Jimmy Durante, played ragtime piano at the nearby Chatham Club. Patrons danced far into the night at these dives. "At three o'clock in the morning down there in Chinatown, it was like Broadway and Forty-second Street," Durante recalled.[34]

New York's gangsters soon began to covet a share of Chinatown's nightclub profits. The gang that controlled the downtown area west of the Bowery was the predominantly Italian "Five Pointers." They were Five Pointers in name only, however, drawing members from all over the city, including Brooklynite Al Capone before he relocated to Chicago.

A Jewish mobster, Monk Eastman, headed the gang that controlled the area east of the Bowery. Like the Five Pointers, Eastman's syndicate demanded protection money from many dance halls. Hoping to add a bit of the lucrative Chinatown district to his sphere of influence, Eastman and his gang declared sovereignty over the territory from Nigger Mike's to the Bowery. The Five Pointers resisted, of course, and the shootings and stabbings that resulted took many lives. The district's political leader, Tom Foley, eventually organized a truce over dinner uptown at the Palm Restaurant.[35]

While the Italians and Jews fought over nightclubs, Chinese gangs went to war as well. A new *tong*, the Hip Sing, had grown in the late 1890s to challenge the dominance of Tom Lee's Loon Ye organization, which had demanded protection money from Chinese-operated businesses for decades. The ensuing "tong wars" first drew public attention in 1897, but escalated in the first years of the new century with shoot-outs and stabbings in restaurants, on street corners, even in the Chinese Opera House on Doyers Street. Tom Lee's alarm clock was shot off his night table in 1901, but he escaped unscathed. Dozens were killed and hundreds wounded until a truce was negotiated in 1911, though sporadic violence would continue between the two groups into the 1920s and beyond.[36]

All this fighting was over business, not politics. The neighborhood became a political backwater primarily because its new Italian residents were relatively apathetic, while the Chinese were completely disenfranchised. "Years of oppression and gross neglect had left the peasantry with an almost pathological distrust of government, or more accurately, of all power above them," observed one historian of the Italians' experience before coming to America. As a result, a reporter noted in 1888, Italian New Yorkers had "a certain temperamental indifference to the diversions of politics. They do not naturally care for the petty power and personal aggrandizement that in times of peace make the chief charm of political life under a popular government."[37]

When they did become politically active, the Italians tended, unlike most other Catholic immigrants, to vote Republican. This stemmed primarily from the continuing Irish-Italian religious struggles—Italians no more wanted to be dominated by the Irish in the Tammany hierarchy than in the Catholic hierarchy. The city's first two prominent Italian-American politicians, Congressmen Fiorello La Guardia and Vito Marcantonio, were both Republicans, though they sounded and voted like Democrats. And reflecting the relative political impotence of downtown Italians, both men represented the uptown Little Italy around 116th Street. Irish Americans continued to dominate elective office in Five Points well past World War I.[38]

The immigration restrictions imposed by Congress in the 1920s changed the character of Five Points further still. Chinese immigration, previously limited to merchants, was now cut off altogether, while Italian immigration fell by more than 98 percent from its peak in the decade before the war. Crowding in the neighborhood's tenements soon disappeared. The Mulberry Street labor brokers became superfluous. In the late 1930s and 1940s, New Deal housing programs drew many Italian Americans to the suburbs, especially New Jersey. The Feast of San Rocco moved with them, to Fort Lee and other towns. Five Points was now a quiet district of Italian and Chinese restaurants inhabited primarily by the children of immigrants rather than the immigrants themselves.

Beginning in the mid-1960s, when Congress repealed the discriminatory immigration quotas of the 1920s, a flood of newcomers revitalized the neighborhood. Chinese immigrants, mostly from Taiwan rather than Guangdong, began filling its tenements. A new wave of Italian immigrants arrived as well, but they tended to settle above Canal Street or in Queens and Brooklyn. By the late 1960s, New Yorkers generally referred to the entire Five Points neighborhood as Chinatown, and the area north of Canal as Little Italy. Chinese immigration grew steadily through the 1970s and 1980s. When the People's Republic of China relaxed emigration restrictions, thousands of mainland Chinese began coming to New York as well, especially from the eastern Fujian province. Many came legally, either as part of the yearly quotas or through quota exemptions available to relatives of those already in the United States. But by the late 1980s and early 1990s, many immigrants were paying tens of thousands of dollars to be smuggled into the United States illegally, only to toil in slave-like conditions in brothels, restaurants, or sweatshops to pay off their debts to the smugglers.[39]

TODAY, THE NEIGHBORHOOD once known as Five Points is again a thriving, bustling, crowded immigrant enclave. On the surface, it shares little with the notorious neighborhood of one hundred fifty years ago. The Irish have moved to Queens and the suburbs, though many of their descendants work as police officers and district attorneys in the courthouses along Centre and Pearl Streets. The neighborhood's streets are relatively free of garbage, odor, and crime. The tenements have modern plumbing and decently lit hallways. There are few signs of destitution. New Yorkers do not fear walking its streets, even at night. It is no longer a "slum."

Yet in some ways, life is the same. Immigrant street vendors are everywhere, though today they hawk music CDs and bootleg videos rather than suspenders and razor strops. Food is still the most popular item for sale on the streets, though spring rolls and other Asian delicacies have replaced hot corn and pears in syrup. A Chinese-American woman who has sold Hong Kong egg cakes at the corner of Mott and Mosco (formerly Park) Streets for almost twenty years helps her family make ends meet much as did female Irish apple sellers in the mid-nineteenth century, though in a modern twist she has used her earnings to put two sons through college. Ragpickers no longer scour the district, but some Asians do rummage through garbage bins collecting discarded aluminum cans.[40]

The neighborhood is no longer renowned for its variety of immigrant groups, yet the ethnic mixing that once gave birth to tap dancing is still evident. The Asia-Roma Restaurant on Mulberry Street offers Asian and Italian cooking, as well as a karaoke bar. Immigrants from Thailand and Vietnam began working in the kitchens of the neighborhood's Chinese restaurants in the 1980s, slowly sneaking their native dishes onto the predominantly Cantonese menus. In many cases, these immigrants have now taken over the eateries and converted them into Thai, Vietnamese, and

Malaysian restaurants. Likewise, few of the cooks in lower Mulberry Street's Italian restaurants are still Italians.

A variety of ethnic and regional tensions are still apparent. Some animosity between the Italians and Chinese remains. Italians have charged that when the Chinese buy neighborhood real estate, they evict long-standing Italian tenants. Italian restaurateurs complain that sidewalk sales by Chinese fish and vegetable dealers create a stench that drives away customers. But most of this conflict now takes place north of Canal Street, as the Chinese have spread well above Canal and east of the Bowery. A kind of de facto segregation still persists at Transfiguration Church. Each Sunday, separate masses are held in Cantonese for those from Guangdong, in Mandarin for more recent immigrants from other parts of China, and in English for non-Asians.[41]

Yet intraethnic conflict now overshadows interethnic animosity. Guangdong natives who have lived in Chinatown for decades resent the increasing power of the Fujianese. Their organization, the United Chinese Associations of New York, has in many ways superseded the Consolidated Chinese Benevolent Association, the Guangdong-dominated society that controlled Chinatown's political and cultural landscape from Tom Lee's day until the mid-1990s.[42]

Many of these tensions still manifest themselves through gang warfare. Just as the Roche Guard and the Bowery Boys fought for neighborhood supremacy one hundred fifty years ago, today Chinese gangs such as the Ghost Shadows and the Flying Dragons vie for control, though now they sometimes cross swords with gangs of Vietnamese immigrants as well. In one shoot-out between Chinese gang members in 1991, a stray bullet killed a tourist at the corner of Mulberry and Bayard Streets, the very spot where some of the slain fell during the 1857 Bowery Boy Riot.[43]

These gangs control the district's sex trade, which has revived as the population of single men has again mushroomed. Rather than walk the streets or openly solicit customers in brothel doorways, prostitutes now operate out of the neighborhood's beauty salons, drawing customers through advertisements touting full body massages. Sweatshops have returned to the district as well. Jewish immigrants had sewn clothing in Five Points throughout the nineteenth century, but such operations moved uptown after World War I. Yet with the influx of Chinese immigrants into the neighborhood after 1965, the sweatshops returned, as Chinese immigrants turned out clothing for fashionable retailers and discount chains alike. Illegal immigrants still work in appalling conditions in these garment factories, toiling for more than a dozen hours a day and receiving just a fraction of the wages paid to legal employees.[44]

Finally, the huge influx of immigrants and skyrocketing rents have combined to revive tenement crowding not seen in New York since the heyday of Mulberry Bend. An exposé in the *Times* in 1996 revealed overcrowding just as astounding as that found in the Old Brewery in the 1840s or photographed by Riis in the 1880s. Triple-decker bunk rooms have reappeared. Multiple families again share tiny two-room apartments. The number of laws enacted to prevent and punish such overcrowding has multiplied since Riis published *How the Other Half Lives*, but each successive wave of immigrants nonetheless follows the path of its predecessors.[45]

From 1607 to 2001 and beyond, would-be Americans have arrived from abroad, adjusted to the often harsh realities of their new lives, and set to work. The Five Points story, at a certain level, is common to us all. Koreans arriving in Los Angeles, Mexicans in Houston, West Indians in Miami, Salvadorans in Washington, Arabs in Detroit, and Hmong in Minneapolis all replay its acts and scenes today. There may never again be another slum quite like Five Points, but as long as the United States remains a nation of immigrants, the outline of the Five Points story will never die.

NOTES

To avoid needless repetition, and because almost every newspaper cited in these notes was published in New York, I have left off the place of publication from all New York newspapers. Most of the following references to newspapers date from the Civil War period, so I have followed the customary mode of citation for those papers by listing the date only. In about 1880, however, the size of American newspapers expanded significantly, making reference to page numbers more important. So for most newspaper citations after 1880, I have included the page numbers as well. Finally, all emphasis found in quotations in *Five Points* is contained in the original source.

INTRODUCTION

1. *Frank Leslie's Illustrated Newspaper* (August 16, 1873): 363; J. Frank Kernan, *Reminiscences of the Old Fire Laddies* (New York, 1885), 41; *Church Monthly* (March 1858), quoted in *Monthly Record of the Five Points House of Industry* 2 (June 1858): 34-35.

2. Junius H. Browne, *The Great Metropolis: A Mirror of New-York* (Hartford, 1869), 272.

3. [William M. Bobo], *Glimpses of New-York City, by a South Carolinian* (Charleston, 1852), 93.

4. Herbert Asbury, *The Gangs of New York: An Informal History of The Underworld* (New York, 1928), Alvin F. Harlow, *Old Bowery Days: The Chronicles of a Famous Street* (New York, 1931).

5. Carol Groneman, "The 'Bloody Ould Sixth': A Social Analysis of a New York City Working-Class Community in the Mid-Nineteenth Century" (Ph.D. dissertation, University of Rochester, 1973); George E. Pozzetta, "The Mulberry District of New York City: The Years Before World War One," Robert F. Harney and J. Vincenza Scarpaci, eds., *Little Italies in North America* (Toronto, 1981); Christine Stansell, *City of Women: Sex and Class in New York, 1789–1860* (Urbana, 1982); Richard B. Stott, *Workers in the Metropolis: Class, Ethnicity, and Youth in Antebellum New York* (Ithaca, 1990); Timothy J. Gilfoyle, *City of Eros: New York City, Prostitution, and the Commercialization of Sex, 1790–1920* (New York, 1992); Ronald Bayor and Timothy Meagher, eds., *The New York Irish* (Baltimore, 1996); Luc Sante, *Low Life: Lures and Snares of Old New York* (New York, 1991); Caleb Carr, *The Alienist* (New York, 1994); *Times*, June 15, 1991, p. 11; May 7, 1995, sect. 13, p. 2; J. A. Lobbia, "Slum Lore," *Village Voice*, January 2, 1996, pp. 34–36; Rebecca Yamin, "New York's Mythic Slum," *Archaeology* 50 (March/April 1997): 44–53; Yamin, "Lurid Tales and Homely Stories of New York's Notorious Five Points," *Historical Archaeology* 32 (1998): 74–85; Kenneth T. Jackson, ed., *The Encyclopedia of New York*

City (New Haven, 1995), 414–415; Edwin G. Burrows and Mike Wallace, *Gotham: A History of New York City to 1898* (New York, 1999), 392.

6. See especially Groneman, "'Bloody Ould Sixth'"; Lobbia, "Slum Lore"; and Yamin, "Lurid Tales."

CHAPTER ONE

1. Lewis Tappan, *The Life of Arthur Tappan* (New York, 1871), 194–95; Paul O. Weinbaum, *Mobs and Demagogues: The New York Response to Collective Violence in the Early Nineteenth Century* (Ann Arbor, 1979), 21–24; John A. Garraty and Mark C. Carnes, eds., *American National Biography*, 24 vols. (New York, 1999), 5: 527–28 (Cornish), 21: 311–12 (Tappans).

2. Paul Boyer, *Urban Masses and Moral Order in America, 1820–1920* (Cambridge, MA, 1978), 9; Garth M. Rosell and Richard A. G. Dupuis, eds., *The Memoirs of Charles G. Finney: The Complete Restored Text* (Grand Rapids, 1989), 354.

3. Leonard L. Richards, *"Gentlemen of Property and Standing": Anti-Abolition Mobs in Jacksonian America* (New York, 1970), 115–16; *Sun*, July 7, 1834. For Cox's opposition to colonization, see *American National Biography*, 5: 630.

4. *Evening Post*, July 8, 1834.

5. *Evening Post*, July 10, 12, 1834; Tappan, *Life of Arthur Tappan*, 209–15, 420; "Old Sports of New York," *Leader*, June 16, 1860 (quotation).

6. *Transcript* and *Sun*, July 14, 1834.

7. *Evening Post*, July 12, 1834; *Transcript* and *Sun*, July 14, 1834.

8. *Evening Post*, July 12, 1834; *Transcript* and *Sun*, July 14, 1834.

9. Paul A. Gilje, *The Road to Mobocracy: Popular Disorder in New York City, 1763–1834* (Chapel Hill, 1988), 167; Tappan, *Life of Arthur Tappan*, 214–15; Richards, *"Gentlemen of Property,"* 141–45, 150–54.

10. William Duer, *New-York as it Was During the Latter Part of the Last Century* (New York, 1849), 13–14; *The Old Brewery and the New Mission House at the Five Points, By Ladies of the Mission* (New York, 1854), 16; Alvin Harlow, *Old Bowery Days: The Chronicles of a Famous Street* (New York, 1931), 86, 106–10, 120–21, 142; Rebecca Yamin, ed., "Tales of Five Points: Working-Class Life in Nineteenth-Century New York" (draft report of the Five Points archeological project), 14–23. The Collect covered the area bounded by modern-day Worth, Lafayette, Franklin, and Baxter Streets.

11. Isaac N. P. Stokes, *Iconography of Manhattan Island: 1498–1909*, 6 vols. (1915–28; New York, 1967), 1: 396–97; Duer, *New-York as it Was*, 13–17; Harlow, *Old Bowery Days*, 125–26.

12. Yamin, "Tales of Five Points," 23–31; Harlow, *Old Bowery Days*, 106–10, 114.

13. Charles H. Haswell, *Reminiscences of an Octogenarian, 1816–1860* (New York, 1897), 84. Yamin, "Tales of Five Points," 27, dates the extension of Anthony Street to 1809, based on an undated map in the New-York Historical Society labeled "Opening of Anthony Street."

14. Carol Groneman, "The 'Bloody Ould Sixth': A Social Analysis of a New York City Working-Class Community in the Mid-Nineteenth Century" (Ph.D. dissertation, Uni-

versity of Rochester, 1973), 23–29, 35. These figures are based on those for the entire Sixth Ward, of which the Collect neighborhood composed approximately one-third. I have approximated the figures for the Five Points locale by comparing the wardwide figures with those for native, black, and immigrant residents provided by Groneman. Consequently, these figures should be taken as estimates only. Per capita income is that for 1810, the latest figures available; it too should be considered approximate. For Five Points workers living with their employers, see Elizabeth Blackmar, *Manhattan for Rent, 1785–1850* (Ithaca, 1990), 169, 177–79.

15. I have grossly simplified a very complicated process. For the nuances of this transformation, see Sean Wilentz, *Chants Democratic: New York City and the Rise of the American Working Class, 1788–1850* (New York, 1984).

16. Blackmar, *Manhattan for Rent*, 103–4, 243.

17. Ibid., 173, 193–94, 199, 234.

18. Ibid., 135; Gilje, *Road to Mobocracy*, 208–9.

19. *Report of the Select Committee Appointed to Investigate the Health Department* (1859), quoted in Edward Lubitz, "The Tenement Problem in New York City and the Movement for Its Reform, 1856–1867" (Ph.D. dissertation, New York University, 1970), 95–96.

20. Timothy J. Gilfoyle, *City of Eros: New York City, Prostitution, and the Commercialization of Sex, 1790–1920* (New York, 1992), 31; indictments of October 7 and 10, December 25, 1820, February 13, March 14, May 16, July 16, 31, August 28, December 5, 1821, May 8, June 21, 1822, June 30, 1823, in boxes 7436 and 7437 of the Police Court Papers and in the District Attorney's Indictment Papers, both at the New York Municipal Archives. Gilfoyle kindly brought these indictments to my attention.

21. "CORNELIUS" to the Editor, *Evening Post*, September 21, 1826.

22. *Evening Post*, March 19, 1829.

23. *Minutes of the Common Council of the City of New York, 1784–1831*, 19 vols. (New York, 1917), 17: 587, 652, 760; 18: 19 (quotation).

24. *Evening Post*, May 13, 1830; *Minutes of the Common Council*, 17: 760; Blackmar, *Manhattan for Rent*, 172–76.

25. *Minutes of the Common Council*, 18: 11–12 ("great rent"), 19–20, 632; Haswell, *Reminiscences of an Octogenarian*, 264; John J. Post, *Old Streets, Roads, Lanes, Piers, and Wharves of New York* (New York, 1882), 72, 76; Stokes, *Iconography of Manhattan Island*, 5: 1720; *Mirror*, May 18, 1833, in Frank Moss, *The American Metropolis*, 3 vols. (New York, 1897), 3: 50–51.

26. Charles E. Rosenberg, *The Cholera Years* (Chicago, 1962), 41–42; "A RESIDENT OF THE VICINITY" to the Editors, *Evening Post*, July 23, 1832.

27. *Sun*, May 29, 1834.

28. *Sun*, May 27 and 29, 1834.

29. *Sun*, May 29, 1834.

30. Ibid.

31. The painting is in the collection of Mrs. Screven Lorillard, Far Hills, NJ. The family had once owned a tannery on the shores of the Collect and continued to own rental property

there after the lake was filled in. When a lithographer from the *Manual of the Common Council* (popularly known as *Valentine's Manual*) copied the painting in 1859 for the publication's series of images of old New York, he labeled the work "Five Points in 1827," though Mrs. Lorillard informs me that she can find no such date on the painting today. The *Valentine's Manual* image is the best known portrayal of Five Points, but a comparison of the painting to the lithograph shows that the printmaker made many significant changes. As a result, the painting ought to be relied upon over the better-known print. See *Manual of the Common Council of the City of New York for 1859* (New York, 1859).

32. *An Account of Col. Crockett's Tour to the North and Down East* (Philadelphia, 1835), 48–49; Mark Derr, *The Frontiersman: The Real Life and the Many Legends of Davy Crockett* (New York, 1993), 214–20.

33. *Evening Post*, April 9, 11, 1834; Weinbaum, *Mobs and Demagogues*, 5–9.

34. *Evening Post* and *Sun*, April 11, 1834; *The Diary of Philip Hone, 1828–1851*, Allan Nevins, ed. (New York, 1936), 123.

35. *Sun*, April 11, 1834.

36. Gilje, *Road to Mobocracy*, 140–41; *Diary of Philip Hone*, 122.

37. Ray Billington, *The Protestant Crusade, 1800–1860: A Study of the Origins of American Nativism* (Chicago, 1938), 70–76, 122–25; *Commercial Advertiser*, September 29, October 4, 1834, January 5, March 18, 1835, in Weinbaum, *Mobs and Demagogues*, 55.

38. *Courier and Enquirer* quoted in *Evening Post*, June 25, 1835.

39. Graham Hodges, "'Desirable Companions and Lovers': Irish and African Americans in the Sixth Ward, 1830–1870," in Ronald Bayor and Timothy Meagher, eds., *The New York Irish* (Baltimore, 1996), 115; Michael Kaplan, "The World of the B'hoys: Urban Violence and the Political Culture of Antebellum New York City, 1825–1860" (Ph.D. dissertation, New York University, 1996), 78; Harlow, *Old Bowery Days*, 293; *Evening Post*, June 22, 1835; *Sun*, June 23, 1835.

40. *Evening Post*, June 22, 1835; *Sun*, June 22 and 23, 1835.

41. *Sun*, June 23, 1835; *Courier*, July 2, 1835, in Kaplan, "The World of the B'hoys," 83.

42. *Sun*, June 24 and 25, 1835; *Evening Post*, June 25, 1835.

43. *Sun*, June 24 and 25, 1835; *Evening Post*, June 25, 1835; Hodges, "'Desirable Companions and Lovers,'" 115; *Herald*, February 25, 1836.

44. *Herald*, March 4 and 5, 1836 (quotation from March 5); Asa Green, *A Glance at New York* (New York, 1837), 49; J. Frank Kernan, *Reminiscences of the Old Fire Laddies* (New York, 1885), 39.

45. *Herald*, April 14, 1842 (a "bloody and riotous" ward); *Tribune*, April 12, 1848 (first known description of the ward as the "Bloody Sixth").

46. Charles Dickens, *American Notes* (1842; London, 1985), 80–82.

47. *The Prose Works of N. P. Willis* (1845; Philadelphia, 1849), 582–83; Lydia Maria Child, *Letters from New York*, 2nd ed. (New York, 1844), 26; Fredrika Bremer, *The Homes of the New World*, 3 vols., trans. Mary Howitt (London, 1853), 3: 409; *Clipper*, October 3, 1868, p. 204 (for Dickens's role in popularizing slumming).

48. *Evening Post,* January 30, 1846; [George G. Foster], *New York in Slices: By an Experienced Carver* (New York, 1849), 22; *Times,* April 7, 1856; Lyman Abbott, *Reminiscences* (Boston, 1915), 33; *Herald,* April 12, 1842; *Old Brewery,* 34.

49. [William A. Caruthers], *The Kentuckian in New-York,* 2 vols. (1834; Ridgewood, NJ, 1968), 2: 28; [William M. Bobo], *Glimpses of New-York City, by a South Carolinian* (Charleston, 1852), 97; "Slavery and Freedom," *Southern Quarterly Review* 1 (April 1856): 80; John S. C. Abbott, *South and North* (New York, 1860), 78 (not quoted); unnamed congressman quoted in Francis W. Kellogg, *Speech of Hon. Francis W. Kellogg, of Michigan, in the House of Representatives, June 12, 1860* (Washington, DC, 1860), 14. Though Caruthers's work is a novel, his service as a doctor in Five Points makes his views noteworthy, even though expressed through a fictional character.

50. Kellogg, *Speech of Hon. Francis W. Kellogg,* 14; Hinton R. Helper, *The Impending Crisis of the South* (New York, 1860), 170–73.

51. *Clipper,* October 3, 1868, p. 204.

Chapter Two

1. William Bennett, *Narrative of a Recent Journey of Six Weeks in Ireland* (London, 1847), 127–29.

2. Gerard J. Lyne, "William Steuart Trench and the Post-Famine Emigration from Kenmare to America, 1850–1855," *Journal of the Kerry Archaeological and Historical Society* 25 (1992): 72, 97; Ira A. Glazier, ed., *The Famine Immigrants: Lists of Irish Immigrants Arriving at the Port of New York, 1846–1851,* 7 vols. (Baltimore, 1983–86), 6: 629 (composition of Holland's family). My belief that Ellen Holland must have been in the workhouse by late 1849 is based on the Lansdowne agent's later statement that he chose as the first emigrants those who had been in the workhouse the longest. Because Holland was one of the first to leave under Lansdowne's emigration program, she was probably in the workhouse by 1849.

3. Descriptions of famine conditions in this prologue are based on the sources listed below in notes 34–36 and 47–48.

4. *Herald,* March 17, 1851; Lyne, "Post-Famine Emigration from Kenmare to America," 102–4.

5. *Tribune,* March 19, 1851; *Herald,* March 23, 1851.

6. *Evening Post,* May 17, 1849 (hogs).

7. Accounts 5479 and 9445, Test Books and Account Ledgers, Emigrant Savings Bank Collection, New York Public Library.

8. Advertisement in *Tribune,* March 18, 1854; Ned Buntline, *The Mysteries and Miseries of New York* (New York, 1848), 84; "A Voice from Cow Bay," *Vanity Fair,* January 21, 1860, in Edward Lubitz, "The Tenement Problem in New York City and the Movement for Its Reform, 1856–1867" (Ph.D. dissertation, New York University, 1970), 73–74; *New York Illustrated News* (February 18 and 25, 1860): 216–17, 233; George G. Foster, *New York by Gas-Light* (1850; Berkeley, 1990).

9. Robert Ernst, *Immigrant Life in New York City, 1825–1863* (1949; Port Washington, NY, 1965), 20; Richard B. Stott, *Workers in the Metropolis: Class, Ethnicity, and Youth in Antebellum New York* (Ithaca, 1990), 72.

10. Citizens' Association, *Report of the Council of Hygiene and Public Health* (New York, 1865), cxxi; Ernst, *Immigrant Life*, 193. My figures on Five Points' immigrant population come from a random sample of families taken from the 1855 New York State manuscript census. Approximately one in ten families from the Five Points neighborhood was sampled. I defined the Five Points "neighborhood" as the area bounded by Centre, Canal, Bowery, Chatham, and Pearl Streets. The total number of individuals in the sample is 1,407, of whom 400 were born in the United States. Of those eighteen or older, 97 of 851 were born in the United States. I utilized city directories to determine which portions of the 1855 census covered those blocks. Given that it is sometimes difficult to determine exactly when the census taker has left or entered the neighborhood, a few families may have been inadvertently included in or excluded from my sample. All the statistics in the following paragraphs are taken from this sample unless otherwise noted—1855 New York State manuscript census, Old Records Division, New York County Clerk's Office.

11. *Five Points Monthly* (December 1864), in Pamela Haag, "The 'Ill-Use of a Wife': Patterns of Working-Class Violence in Domestic and Public New York City, 1860–1880," *Journal of Social History* 25 (1992): 455; *Times*, April 11, 1860 ("every nationality").

12. I have assumed that if both husband and wife had lived in New York for the same number of years, they emigrated together. The percentage of married couples that emigrated together can be determined because the 1855 census takers asked New Yorkers how long they had lived in their city of residence. Some immigrants, however, might have reunited someplace else in North America before coming to New York. But comparing the dates of emigration listed in the Emigrant Savings Bank records to the "years in New York" answer in the census for families documented in both sources, I found that in 95 percent of these cases, the "years in New York" figure matched the date of emigration. For the percentage of immigrants arriving with other family members, see Glazier, *Famine Immigrants*, passim.

13. Families 62, 66, 73, 101, 151, 284, 292, 329, and 680, second division, third electoral district, Sixth Ward, 1855 New York census; marriage of James Tucker, August 7, 1860, marriage register, Church of the Transfiguration, 29 Mott Street, New York.

14. Religion is not listed in the census, but I determined the subjects' religion by examining their first and last names. In most cases, the names were quite distinct. Jewish families tended to name their children Abraham, Isaac, Jacob, Moses, Yetta, Sarah, and Deborah. Christians chose names such as Christian, Christine, Frederick, Catharine, August, Hildebrand, etc. Surnames such as Levy, Cohen, Isaacs, and Abraham were considered indications of Jewish roots, whereas names such as Von Glahn were considered indications of Christian ties. In cases where neither the surnames nor the given names indicated the religious background with certainty, these persons were classified as "unknown." The religious background of six families out of forty-five could not be determined by this method.

15. Accounts 924, 2130, 2281, 2487, 3527, 3626, 3847, 5367, 5948, 6199, 6709, and 7242, 8440, 9414, and 9569, Emigrant Savings Bank Test Books.

16. Accounts 450, 451, 1245, 1723, 2501, 2608, 2723, 2725, 3135, 3173, 3191, 3538, 3580, 3616, 3652, 4260, 4740, 4780, 5134, 5192, 5230, 5731, 6077, 7171, 7204, 8970, 9263, 10021, and 10864, Emigrant Savings Bank Test Books.

17. Carol Groneman, "'The Bloody Ould Sixth': A Social Analysis of a New York City Working-Class Community in the Mid-Nineteenth Century" (Ph.D. dissertation, Uni-

versity of Rochester, 1973), 35; *Commercial Advertiser,* August 23, 1849; *Tribune,* June 5, 1850 (quotation); *Times,* April 7, 1860; J. Frank Kernan, *Reminiscences of the Old Fire Laddies* (New York, 1885), 41.

18. Dwellings 63–74, 82–87, first division, third electoral district, dwellings 6–73, second division, third electoral district, dwellings 16–26, fourth election district, dwellings 135–61, fifth election district, dwellings 94–113, sixth election district, Sixth Ward, 1855 New York census.

19. I refer to Irish Catholics rather than all Irish because the source for my Irish nativity figures is the marriage records of Five Points' Roman Catholic Church of the Transfiguration, which from 1853 to 1860 recorded the place of birth of virtually every person married at the church. My figures probably approximate the county origins of all Five Points Irish fairly accurately, because although there were undoubtedly *some* Irish Protestants in the neighborhood, there were not many. This is confirmed by an analysis of the Emigrant Savings Bank Test Books, which also list place of birth and whose depositors included Protestants and Jews as well. Of the Five Pointers in the Transfiguration register, 173 were from Sligo, 142 from Cork, 141 from Kerry, 59 from Galway, 56 from Limerick, 52 from Tipperary, 42 from Mayo, 36 from Leitrim, 40 from Roscommon, 30 from Waterford, 27 from Kilkenny, 19 from Dublin (city and county), 17 from Tyrone, 16 from Donegal, 15 from Fermanagh, 15 from Clare, 15 from Longford, 14 from Meath, 14 from Louth, 13 from Queen's, 12 from Westmeath, 12 from King's, 12 from Cavan, 10 from Monaghan, 9 from Wexford, 9 from Armagh, 9 from Derry, 8 from Kildare, 7 from Carlow, 3 from Down, 3 from Wicklow, and none from Antrim.

20. Accounts 1005, 2661, 3787, 5419, and 6433, Emigrant Savings Bank Test Books.

21. Eighty-seven of the 173 Sligo natives listed in the Transfiguration marriage register for 1853–60 had been born either in the parish of Ahamlish (Palmerston's estate) or Drumcliff (the parish owned almost exclusively by Gore Booth). Seventy-nine percent of the Kerry natives married there in those years were natives of Kenmare, Tuosist, or Bonane parishes, all owned primarily by Lansdowne.

22. *Irish University Press Series of British Parliamentary Papers,* "Colonies, Canada" series (Shannon, 1969), 17: 469–70 (hereafter cited as *IUP-BPP, Colonies, Canada*); David Fitzpatrick, "Emigration, 1801–70," in *Ireland Under the Union, 1: 1801–70,* vol. 5 of *A New History of Ireland* (Oxford, 1989), 592.

23. House of Commons, "Poor Inquiry (Ireland), Appendix D, Containing Baronial Examinations Relative to Earnings of Labourers, Cottier Tenants, Employment of Women and Children, Expenditure," *Sessional Papers, Reports from Commissioners, 1836,* 31: 13, and supplement p. 38.

24. Commons, "Poor Inquiry (Ireland), Appendix D," 31: 13–14, 77, 85, 95; "Poor Inquiry (Ireland), Appendix F, Containing Baronial Examinations Relative to Con Acre Quarter or Score Ground, Small Tenantry, Consolidation of Farms and Dislodged Tenantry, Emigration," *Sessional Papers, Reports from Commissioners, 1836,* 33: 6–7, 41–42, 224; *Evidence Taken Before Her Majesty's Commissioners of Inquiry into the State of the Law and Practice in respect to the Occupation of Land in Ireland* [Devon Commission], No. 616 (1845), 20: 203–8, 223–25.

25. House of Commons, "Poor Inquiry (Ireland), Appendix E, Containing Baronial Examinations Relative to Food, Cottages and Cabins, Clothing and Furniture, Pawnbroking and Savings Banks, Drinking," *Sessional Papers, Reports from Commissioners, 1836,* 32: 7–8.

26. Ibid., 32: 7; "Poor Inquiry (Ireland), Appendix D," 31:108 (Christmas); *Evidence Taken Before her Majesty's Commissioners of Inquiry*, 20: 919.

27. Jonathan Binns, *The Miseries and Beauties of Ireland*, 2 vols. (London, 1837), 1: 50; "Poor Inquiry (Ireland), Appendix D," 31: 13–14. Binns was an "assistant agricultural commissioner" involved in the 1836 Irish Poor Inquiry.

28. Binns, *Miseries and Beauties of Ireland*, 1: 49–50; "Poor Inquiry (Ireland), Appendix E," 32: 7–8, 25, 58, supplement p. 213; Kevin Danaher, *The Year in Ireland* (Cork, 1972), 163–66 ("hungry July").

29. William S. Trench, *Realities of Irish Life* (London, 1868), 112–13; Lyne, "Post-Famine Emigration from Kenmare," 66; Commons, "Poor Inquiry (Ireland), Appendix D," 31: 52 (quotation); Henry D. Inglis, *Ireland in 1834: A Journey Throughout Ireland During the Spring, Summer, and Autumn of 1834*, 2nd ed., 2 vols. (London, 1835), 1: 209–13.

30. Commons, "Poor Inquiry (Ireland), Appendix E," 32: 41.

31. Inglis, *Ireland in 1834*, 209–13; Michael Doheny, *The Felon's Tracks* (1849; Dublin, 1951), 244; Binns, *Miseries and Beauties of Ireland*, 2: 333–34; Commons, "Poor Inquiry (Ireland), Appendix E," 32: 58, 90, supplement p. 213.

32. "Poor Inquiry (Ireland), Appendix E," 32: 70, supplement p. 213.

33. "Poor Inquiry (Ireland), Appendix F," 33: 148 ("extremely wretched"); "Poor Inquiry (Ireland), Appendix D," 31: 15 (early marriage); Trench, *Realities of Irish Life*, 112–13 (early marriage); *Evidence Taken before Her Majesty's Commissioners of Inquiry*, 20: 912 (early marriage), 919 ("face of the globe," not Lansdowne's fault); Binns, *Miseries and Beauties of Ireland*, 2: 336–37.

34. [Sixth] Marquis of Lansdowne, *Glanerought and the Petty-Fitzmaurices* (London, 1937), 127; Trench, *Realities of Irish Life*, 113–14; Kenmare Relief Committee to the Lord Commissioners of Her Majesty's Treasury, August 22, 1846, in *Irish University Press Series of British Parliamentary Papers*, "Famine" series (Shannon, 1970), 6: 94–95 (hereafter cited as *IUP–BPP, Famine*).

35. Mr. Gill to Mr. Russell, February 25, 1847, in *IUP–BPP, Famine*, 7: 550; Bennett, *Narrative of a Recent Journey of Six Weeks in Ireland*, 132. For more on conditions in Tuosist, see *IUP–BPP, Famine*, 2: 835, 838, 843–50, 852; 3: 336; Lyne, "Post-Famine Emigration from Kenmare," 124–25.

36. O'Sullivan Diary, c. March 1847, in Lyne, "Post-Famine Emigration from Kenmare," 125; O'Sullivan to Trevelyan, "February, 1847," in *IUP–BPP, Famine*, 7: 524; Bennett, *Narrative of a Recent Journey of Six Weeks in Ireland*, 127–29.

37. James R. Stewart and Joseph Kincaid to Palmerston, December 24, 1845 (BR 146/7/57), February 6, 1846 (BR 144/10/30), Broadlands Papers, University of Southampton. See also [Stuart] Maxwell to Stewart, November 5, 1845, Widow O'Farrel to Kincaid, November 10, 1845, Dr. West to Stewart or Kincaid, n.d. [March 1846], in Desmond Norton, "Landlords, Tenants, Famine: Letters of an Irish Land Agent in the 1840s," manuscript in the possession of the author (hereafter cited as Norton manuscript). The letters quoted from Norton's manuscript are apparently in his possession, and I sincerely appreciate his sharing their contents with me.

38. *Sligo Champion*, October 10, 1846; Kincaid to Palmerston, August 6, 1846, BR148/3/5/1, undated newspaper clipping BR148/3/20/2, enclosed in letter dated December 9, 1846,

Broadlands Papers; Dr. West to Kincaid, December 13, 1846, Norton manuscript; Captain Flude to Charles Trevelyan, December 20, 1846, in Cecil Woodham-Smith, *The Great Hunger: Ireland, 1845–1849* (1962; New York, 1991), 160.

39. *Sligo Champion*, March 20, 1847; Captain O'Brien to Lieut.-Colonel Jones, March 2, 1847, in *IUP–BPP, Famine*, 7: 204.

40. Captain O'Brien to Lieut.-Colonel Jones, March 2, 1847, in *IUP–BPP, Famine*, 7: 204 (block quotation); undated newspaper clipping ("a waste") in BR148/3/17/2, Broadlands Papers; letter with illegible signature to Sir Robert Gore Booth ("actually starving"), January 13, 1847, reel 1, microfilm 590, series H/8/1, Lissadell Papers, Public Records Office of Northern Ireland; S. H. Cousens, "The Regional Variation in Mortality During the Great Irish Famine," *Proceedings of the Royal Irish Academy* 63, section C, no. 3 (February 1963): 130; Joel Mokyr, *Why Ireland Starved* (London, 1983), 267. Just about the only thing that Cousens and Mokyr agree upon is Sligo's status as one of the leaders in excess mortality during the famine years.

41. Michael and Mary Rush to "Dear Father and Mother," September 6, 1846, in *IUP–BPP, Colonies, Canada*, 17: 100–101. Although the Rushes did not live on either the Palmerston or Gore Booth estate, their desperate situation must have been similar to that of Ahamlish and Drumcliff residents.

42. Lynch to Kincaid, December 18, 1846, Norton manuscript; Kincaid to Palmerston, March 23, 1847, BR146/9/3, Broadlands Papers. A much more detailed account of the Palmerston emigration program can be found in my "Lord Palmerston and the Irish Famine Emigration," *The Historical Journal* (June 2001).

43. Marianna O'Gallagher and Rose Masson Dompierre, *Eyewitness Grosse Isle 1847* (Sainte-Foy, Québec, 1995), 349, 352, 357–58; A. L. Buchanan to S. Wolcott, June 11, 1847, BR146/9/8/2 (wreck), copy of letter from Chief Emigrant Agent at Québec enclosed in Lord Elgin's Despatch No. 76 "of 11th Aug. 1847," BR 146/9/10 (emigrants well supplied), "Passengers Sent out from Lord Palmerston's Estate to Quebec April 1847," BR146/9/4, Broadlands Papers; John C. McTernan, *Memory Harbour: The Port of Sligo, Its Growth and Decline and Its Role as an Emigration Port* (Sligo, 1992), part II, 32; *IUP–BPP, Emigration*, 10: 15 (overall mortality rate); *IUP–BPP, Colonies, Canada*, 17: 471–77 (Palmerston and Gore Booth mortality).

44. M. H. Perley to John S. Saunders, September 2, 18 (quotation), 1847, Dr. W. S. Harding to [the Lieutenant-Governor?], September 13, 1847, in *IUP–BPP, Colonies, Canada*, 17: 300, 318, 321–22; *Sligo Champion*, September 11, 18, 1847; *New Brunswick Courier* in McTernan, *Memory Harbour*, part II, 30; Adam Ferrie, *Letter to the Rt. Hon Earl Grey . . . Embracing a Statement of Facts in Relation to Emigration to Canada* (Montreal, 1847), 7–11.

45. Stewart and Kincaid to Palmerston, December 3 and 16, 1847, in *IUP–BPP, Colonies, Canada*, 17: 351–53; Stewart to Kincaid, n.d. (marked "1847"), Norton manuscript; Gore Booth testimony, June 2, 1848, in *IUP–BPP, Emigration*, 5: 266; testimony of Joseph Kincaid, June 21, 1847, in ibid., 4: 143–66.

46. Letter of Michael Brennan, et al., October 27, 1847, in *New Brunswick Courier*, November 6, 1847, in Elizabeth Cushing, et al., *A Chronicle of Irish Emigration to St. John, New Brunswick, 1847* (St. John, 1979), 50; Gore Booth emigrants quoted in Fitzpatrick, "Emigration, 1801–70," in *New History of Ireland*, 5: 597.

47. Lansdowne, *Glanerought and the Petty-Fitzmaurices*, 127; Ommanney to the Commissioners, March 5, 26, April 1, 1848, in *IUP–BPP, Famine*, 3: 335, 339–40.

48. Unknown writer to "My dear William," February 27, 1849, O'Sullivan to Poulett Scrope, April 30, 1849, *The Nation*, December 12, 1857, all in Lyne, "Post-Famine Emigration from Kenmare," 72, 97, 100–101. The mortality figure is based on Lansdowne, *Glanerought and the Petty-Fitzmaurices*, 128–29, which cites Trench as saying that 5,000 had died in the Kenmare "union" (relief district) by the time he became agent in early 1850. The Lansdowne estate made up about one-third of the Kenmare union, thus my upper estimate that about one-third of that figure had died.

49. Trench, *Realities of Irish Life*, 122–24.

50. Ibid., 124–25; Lyne, "Post-Famine Emigration from Kenmare," 89 (poorhouse figures), 102–3 (*Cork Examiner*), 136–37.

51. Lyne, "Post-Famine Emigration from Kenmare," 136–37; Trench, *Realities of Irish Life*, 124–26. For some of the Lansdowne ships, see Glazier, *Famine Immigrants*, 6: 619–20, 626–27, 662–63, 644–49, 7: 16–19, 84–85.

52. Lyne, "Post-Famine Emigration from Kenmare to America," 104–5, 112–13; Maxwell to Stewart and Kincaid, November 27, 1847, in *IUP–BPP, Colonies, Canada*, 17: 353–54 (food supply).

53. *Tribune*, March 19, 1851; *Herald*, March 22 (*Robert Peel*'s arrival), 23 (editorial), 1851.

54. *Dublin Review*, n.s., 12 (January–April 1869), 4–17, *Tralee Chronicle*, February 26, 1869, Eugene O'Connell to the *Freeman's Journal*, November 20, 1880, in Lyne, "Post-Famine Emigration from Kenmare to America," 120–22; Charles Russell, *"New Views on Ireland," Or, Irish Land: Grievances: Remedies*, 3rd ed. (London, 1880), 47; Lansdowne, *Glanerought and the Petty-Fitzmaurices*, 129.

Chapter Three

1. *The Old Brewery, and the New Mission House at the Five Points, By Ladies of the Mission* (New York, 1854), 43; *National Police Gazette* in Edward Van Every, *Sins of New York as "Exposed" by the Police Gazette* (1930; New York, 1972), 282–83; Solon Robinson, *Hot Corn: Life Scenes in New York Illustrated* (New York, 1854), 209.

2. *National Police Gazette* in Van Every, *Sins of New York*, 282–83; *Old Brewery*, 49; "The Five Points," *National Magazine* 2 (1853): 169.

3. Herbert Asbury, *The Gangs of New York: An Informal History of the Underworld* (New York, 1928), 15–16, 19; Fredrika Bremer, *The Homes of the New World*, 2 vols., trans. Mary Howitt (New York, 1853), 2. 602.

4. *Tribune*, June 19, 1850; unidentified newspaper quoted in *Old Brewery*, 48; Joel H. Ross, *What I Saw in New York* (Auburn, NY, 1851), 96; *The Prose Works of N. P. Willis* (1845; new ed. in one vol., Philadelphia, 1849), 582–83.

5. Dwellings 23 and 24, Sixth Ward, 1850 United States manuscript census, National Archives. Dwelling 24 must be the Old Brewery because one of the inhabitants listed, John Burke, is described as a longtime resident of the building in Ross, *What I Saw in New York*, 92–94. That dwelling 23 was also part of the Old Brewery, perhaps with a separate entrance, is based on my comparison of its residents listed in the census with the 1850–51 New York City directory.

6. Ross, *What I Saw in New York,* 92–94; Bremer, *Homes of the New World,* 2: 602.

7. *The Eleventh Annual Report of the New York Association for Improving the Condition of the Poor* (New York, 1854): 23.

8. "Manhattan Record of Assessment," Sixth Ward, 1860 (which describes height and dimensions of buildings), and blocks 161–65 and 199–202, "Block and Lot Folders," New York City Housing Department Papers, both at New York Municipal Archives; William Perris, *Maps of the City of New York. Surveyed under the Direction of the Insurance Companies of Said City* (New York, 1853 and 1857).

9. [George G. Foster], *New York in Slices: By an Experienced Carver* (New York, 1849), 23; *Report of the Select Committee Appointed to Investigate the Health Department* (1859), 31, in Edward Lubitz, "The Tenement Problem in New York City and the Movement for Its Reform, 1856–1867" (Ph.D. dissertation, New York University, 1970), 95–96; John H. Griscom, *The Sanitary Condition of the Laboring Population of New York* (1845; New York, 1970), 8; Citizens' Association, *Report of the Council of Hygiene and Public Health* (New York, 1865), 77.

10. *Times,* July 1, 1859; *Morning Courier and New-York Enquirer,* January 13, 1847; *Report of the Select Committee Appointed to Investigate the Health Department* (1859), 31, in Lubitz, "The Tenement Problem," 95–96.

11. *Report of the Select Committee Appointed to Investigate the Health Department* (1859), 31, in Lubitz, "The Tenement Problem," 95–96.

12. Election districts 3–6, Sixth Ward, 1855 New York State manuscript census, Old Records Division, New York County Clerk's Office (percentage of brick tenements and proportion of Five Pointers living in them); "Report of the Select Committee Appointed to Examine into the Condition of Tenant Houses in New-York and Brooklyn," *Documents of the Assembly of the State of New-York, Eightieth Session—1857* (Albany, 1857), doc. 205, pp. 17–18; Richard Plunz, *A History of Housing in New York City: Dwelling Type and Social Change in the American Metropolis* (New York, 1990), 13.

13. "Report . . . into the Condition of Tenant Houses in New-York and Brooklyn," 18–19; *Report of the Select Committee Appointed to Investigate the Health Department* (1859), 66, in Lubitz, "Tenement Problem," 63–64; Lawrence Veiller, "Back to Back Tenements," in Robert W. DeForest and Lawrence Veiller, eds., *The Tenement House Problem,* 2 vols. (1903; New York, 1970), 1: 293.

14. *Harper's Weekly* 1 (February 21, 1857): 114–15; *Monthly Record of the Five Points House of Industry* 2 (November 1858): 150.

15. *Tribune,* June 5, 1850; *Sixteenth Annual Report of the New York Association for the Improvement of the Condition of the Poor* (New York, 1859): 37; Lubitz, "Tenement Problem," 541. The figures on inhabitants per apartment were derived by surveying the Perris insurance maps and New York City Department of Housing "Block and Lot" records to identify buildings most likely to have the neighborhood's standard two-room apartments, and then determining the number of residents by consulting the 1855 New York State manuscript census in conjunction with the city directories.

16. *Thirteenth Annual Report of the Children's Aid Society* (1866): 28; John Morrow, *A Voice from the Newsboys* (New York, 1860), 39.

17. *Thirteenth Annual Report of the Children's Aid Society* (1866): 28.

18. George Ellington [pseud.], *The Women of New York; Or, The Under-World of the Great City* (New York, 1869), 600–603 ("same bare floors"); *Times,* June 20, 1859. This *Times* story, which describes tenements in the First and Fourth Wards, is the only one I know of that details antebellum tenement decoration. Many tenements in those wards, especially the Fourth, were as bad as those at Five Points, which is why I believe it is a useful source despite its lack of reference to Five Points itself. For the archeological items found in Five Points, see the project's Web site: *http://r2.gsa.gov/fivept/fphome.htm,* and Rebecca Yamin, "Lurid Tales and Homely Stories of New York's Notorious Five Points," *Historical Archaeology* 32 (1998): 74–85. The artifacts are currently stored in the basement of the World Trade Center, but their ultimate destination, in a museum or archive, has not yet been determined.

19. Second division, third election district, Sixth Ward, 1855 New York census. The 1855 census taker for this portion of the neighborhood distinguished between boarders and lodgers in his enumeration. Females accounted for just 35 percent of boarders but made up 60 percent of the lodgers.

20. Account 4739, Emigrant Savings Bank Test Books, New York Public Library; families 140 and 156, second division, third election district, Sixth Ward, 1855 New York census.

21. Account 3307, Emigrant Savings Bank Test Books, dwelling 54, second division, third electoral district, Sixth Ward, 1855 New York census; dwelling 288, p. 215, Sixth Ward, 1850 United States census.

22. The *Tribune* (June 5, 1850) did not state precisely what proportion of these Sixth Ward cellar dwellers lived in the Five Points neighborhood. Given that the Five Points district made up about one-third of the ward, and that it was the most impoverished portion of the ward with the largest population of poor people likely to seek cellar accommodations, it seems reasonable to estimate that half of the cellar population lived in Five Points.

23. Samuel Prime, *Life in New York* (New York, 1847), 179–80; *Times,* July 1, 1859; *Tribune,* June 5, 13, 1850; Griscom, *Sanitary Condition,* 10.

24. *Times,* July 1, 1859; *Tribune,* June 13, 1850; family 63, fourth election district, Sixth Ward, 1855 New York census; [James D. Burn], *Three Years Among the Working-Classes* (London, 1865), 5–6.

25. *Twenty-third Annual Report of the New-York Ladies' Home Missionary Society* (1867): 28; *Herald,* September 18, 1892, p. 11; "Report . . . into the Condition of Tenant Houses in New-York and Brooklyn," 23; "Tenement Evils as Seen by the Tenants," in DeForest and Veiller, eds., *Tenement House Problem,* 1: 394 (not quoted). Many of the quotations in this section are from the late nineteenth century rather than the Civil War era. I have used such quotations in this section because many aspects of tenement life, especially from the perspective of the tenant, were not recorded in the antebellum years.

26. DeForest and Veiller, eds., *Tenement House Problem,* 1: 414.

27. Charles H. Haswell, *Reminiscences of an Octogenarian, 1816–1860* (New York, 1897), 332; James Ford, *Slums and Housing, with Special Reference to New York City: History, Conditions, Policy* (Cambridge, MA, 1936), 1: 95; *Plumber and Sanitary Engineer* (December 15, 1879), 26; *Times,* March 22, 1880; folder 200/27, "Block and Lot Folders," New York City Housing Department Papers. As mentioned earlier, a typical tenement with the dimensions found in the front building at 65 Mott had four apartments on each floor, while the rear tenements had two per floor. We know from the census that groceries

occupied the front spaces of the first floor in the front building in 1860, while in 1903 the entire first floor was set aside for commercial purposes. If the grocers took up only the front of the ground floor, this would have left room for thirty-six apartments. If the groceries occupied the entire first floor, that would have left space for thirty-four apartments. Dwellings 40 and 41, third district, Sixth Ward, 1860 United States census. Tax assessment records from the 1850s list the owner of 65 Mott Street as "J. Weeks," possibly the Jacob Weeks who still owned the property in 1903. If that is the case, then Weeks was probably not responsible for the construction of the building nearly eighty years earlier. "J. Weeks" was probably the brother of Samuel Weeks, who in 1860 owned 47 and 49 Mott among other properties, and son of the "Mrs. Weeks" who owned 37 Mott.

28. *Times*, March 28, 1856; Griscom, *Sanitary Condition*, 7.

29. Asa Green, *A Glance at New York* (New York, 1837), 169, 174–75.

30. *Tribune*, December 15, 1848, June 5, 1850, September 19, 1865; *Report of the Council of Hygiene*, 76.

31. Owen Kildare, *My Old Bailiwick* (New York, 1906), 227; DeForest and Veiller, eds., *Tenement House Problem*, 1: 388, 394–95.

32. DeForest and Veiller, eds., *Tenement House Problem*, 1: 388, 394–95.

33. Ibid., 1: 294; *Report of the Council of Hygiene*, 80; Eugene P. Moehring, *Public Works and the Patterns of Real Estate Growth in Manhattan, 1835–1894* (New York, 1981), 96; *Sixteenth Annual Report of the New York Association for Improving the Condition of the Poor*, 50; *Report of the Select Committee Appointed to Investigate the Health Department* (1859), 66, in Lubitz, "Tenement Problem," 64–66.

34. *Monthly Record of the Five Points House of Industry* 4 (April 1860): 17.

35. DeForest and Veiller, eds., *Tenement House Problem*, 1: 387; Griscom, *Sanitary Condition*, 18; *Report of the Council of Hygiene*, 73. The green fluid quotation describes a yard at 49 Elizabeth Street, a half block north of the area I have defined as Five Points, but typical of yards in the Five Points district as well.

36. Philip Wallys, *About New York: An Account of What a Boy Saw in his Visit to the City* (New York, 1857), 63; *Report of the Council of Hygiene*, 77; *Sixteenth Annual Report of the New York Association for Improving the Condition of the Poor*, 50, 52; *Annual Report of the City Inspector* (1842), 188–97, (1856), 157, in Carol Groneman, "The 'Bloody Ould Sixth,': A Social Analysis of a New York City Working-Class Community in the Mid-Nineteenth Century" (Ph.D. dissertation, University of Rochester, 1973), 182.

37. *Subterranean*, February 13, 1847, in Christine Stansell, *City of Women: Sex and Class in New York, 1789–1860* (Urbana, 1982), 58; DeForest and Veiller, eds., *Tenement House Problem*, 1: 390–94; Owen Kildare, *My Mamie Rose* (New York, 1903), 19.

38. [Burn], *Three Years Among the Working-Classes*, 302–3; James D. McCabe, *Lights and Shadows of New York Life* (Philadelphia, 1872), 403; Kildare, *My Mamie Rose*, 15, 23, 38–39; Charles Loring Brace, *The Dangerous Classes of New York and Twenty Years Work Among Them*, 3rd ed. (New York, 1872), 204–05.

39. *Voice from the Old Brewery: The Organ of the Five Points Mission* 1 (August 1, 1861): 29; *Monthly Record of the Five Points House of Industry* 1 (June 1857): 64 ("cried and cried"); *Five Points Monthly* 3 (February 1856): 24–25; *Tribune*, November 23, 1864.

40. Kildare, *My Mamie Rose*, 15; *Harper's Weekly* 23 (August 9, 1879): 629; 27 (June 30, 1883): 401, 410; 29 (August 1, 1885): 491, 496; *Frank Leslie's Illustrated Newspaper* (August 12, 1882): 390 (quotations), 392–93; (July 23, 1887): 373.

41. Lubitz, "Tenement Problem," 217; *Times*, February 4, 6, 7, 1860; *Harper's Weekly* 4 (April 7, 1860): 211.

42. *Report of the Council of Hygiene*, 73; *Herald*, June 10, 1863.

43. *Old Brewery*, 104.

44. William F. Barnard, *Forty Years at the Five Points: A Sketch of the Five Points House of Industry* (New York, 1893), 2; *Monthly Record of the Five Points House of Industry* 1 (January 1858): 219; Robinson, *Hot Corn*, 209, 307. Maps of the Collect Pond seem to show that water covered the ground that would eventually become Cow Bay, so the story describing the origin of its name may be apocryphal.

45. *Monthly Record of the Five Points House of Industry* 1 (May 1857): 20, 22; (June 1857): 68; (October 1857): 165; (January 1858): 225; *Commercial Advertiser*, August 23, 1849; George G. Foster, *New York by Gas-Light* (1850; Berkeley, 1990), 125; Robinson, *Hot Corn*, 209, 307; Ross, *What I Saw in New York*, 96; dwellings 105–15, pp. 26–28, Sixth Ward, 1850 United States census; dwellings 82–87, third election district, Sixth Ward, 1855 New York census. Although neither the 1850 nor the 1855 census takers appears to have entered all of the Cow Bay tenements, the census does accurately reflect the continuing African-American exodus from the neighborhood.

46. *Old Brewery*, 199; *Express* in Samuel B. Halliday, *The Lost and Found; or Life Among the Poor* (New York, 1859), 211–12 (this tour is also described in the *Times*, July 1, 1859).

47. Robinson, *Hot Corn*, 70.

48. Ibid., 212–13; *Monthly Record of the Five Points House of Industry* 1 (June 1857): 70.

49. "Report . . . into the Condition of Tenant Houses in New-York and Brooklyn," 18; *Evening Post*, May 17, 1849.

50. "Report . . . into the Condition of Tenant Houses in New-York and Brooklyn," 18. I cannot document that Honora Moriarty and her daughters were Lansdowne immigrants, but their surname and residence in a building particularly dominated by emigrants from that estate make it likely that the identification is accurate.

51. *Times*, July 1, 1859; *Express* in Halliday, *Lost and Found*, 207–8; *New York Illustrated News* (February 18, 1860): 216; account 6524, Emigrant Savings Bank Test Books; Ira A. Glazier, ed., *The Famine Immigrants: Lists of Irish Immigrants Arriving at the Port of New York, 1846–1851*, 7 vols. (Baltimore, 1983–86), 6: 647; family 227, p. 136, second district, Sixth Ward, 1860 United States census.

52. Dwelling 31, second division, third electoral district, Sixth Ward, 1855 New York census; accounts 4983, 5800, 6773, and 7504, Emigrant Savings Bank Test Books; wedding of Daniel Haley, October 14, 1857, marriage register, Transfiguration Church.

53. For these calculations, I only considered buildings with four or more apartments. The sample blocks include two with large German populations (the east side of Centre from Worth to Leonard Streets and the east side of Mott Street from Canal to Pell) and three that were more heavily Irish (the east side of Mulberry from Canal to Bayard, the west side of Mulberry from Park to Bayard, and the east side of Baxter from Park to Bayard).

Source for composition of all sample blocks is the 1855 New York State census, except Mulberry from Canal to Bayard, which is from the 1860 census.

54. Dwellings 12–30, fourth election district, dwellings 45–57, 117–31, fifth election district, Sixth Ward, 1855 New York census; dwellings 24–52, third district, Sixth Ward, 1860 United States census.

55. Dwelling 39, second division, third election district, dwellings 67 and 68, fourth election district, dwellings 83–87 (Cow Bay), 138–40 (Park Street), 147–49 (Mulberry Street), fifth election district, Sixth Ward, 1855 New York census.

56. Marriage register, Transfiguration Church; William Bennett, *Narrative of a Recent Journey of Six Weeks in Ireland* (London, 1847), 129–30; 119 of the 185 residents identified on these blocks in the Transfiguration marriage records were natives of Kerry. Ninety-four of those 119 had been born on the Lansdowne estate.

57. Emigrant Savings Bank Test Books; marriage register, Transfiguration Church.

58. "Report . . . into the Condition of Tenant Houses in New-York and Brooklyn," 17–18, 28; *Monthly Record of the Five Points House of Industry* 3 (March 1860): 248–49; 4 (April 1860): 12–14; Robinson, *Hot Corn,* 212–13.

59. *Tribune,* April 1, 1856, November 29, 1864; DeForest and Veiller, eds., *Tenement House Problem,* 1: 408; *Report of the Select Committee Appointed to Investigate the Health Department* (1859), 31, in Lubitz, "Tenement Problem," 32–33, 133; *Monthly Record of the Five Points House of Industry* 3 (March 1860): 248–50; *Times,* November 8, 1853 ($8.50), July 2, 1871; 1860 and 1870 Manhattan Records of Real Estate Assessment, New York Municipal Archives.

60. Griscom, *Sanitary Condition,* 6; Brace in *Times,* January 22, 1853.

61. *Times,* March 31, 1856. In 1847, two Five Points property managers, the Osborn brothers, paid $35 in taxes, $6.50 in insurance, $26 for painting, $35 for masonry work, $50 for carpentry, $21 for wallpapering, and $7 for glass installation at 70 Mott. Other miscellaneous repairs brought the total expenses for the year to $200.66. This left a net income of less than $100, which if the property was worth $3,000 or so, represented a 3 percent rate of return, not an outrageous profit. Expenses, however, did not usually consume so large a proportion of the landlord's income. At 79 Orange Street, for example, the Osborns recorded just $5.38 spent on repairs in 1847; they also spent $41.84 for taxes and insurance, $13.56 to evict a tenant, and $15.74 in commissions to the carpenter they hired to collect the rents. Subtracting these figures from the $437.65 in rent collected leaves $361.13. Of that total, the Osborns took $200 for managing the property for the year, leaving the owner, Cornelius Van Rensselaer, $161.13 in profit for the year. If the property was worth $3,000, that amounted to a return on assets of about 5½ percent. If the owner still paid mortgage interest on this property, then these profits would be reduced further—Charles F. Osborn Account Book, George L. Osborn Account Book, New York Public Library.

62. Charles F. Osborn Account Book, George L. Osborn Account Book; *Doggett's New York City Directory for 1848–49* (New York, 1848), 182, 408; *Doggett's New York City Directory for 1849–1850* (New York, 1849), 149, 231, 302; *Doggett's New York City Street Directory for 1851,* 262; 1850 United States manuscript census, Sixth Ward, pp. 204 (McDermott), 221 (Trainor), 225 (Hall). The Osborn account books refer to this building first as 66 Mott and later as 70 Mott because the block was renumbered sometime in late 1848 or early 1849.

63. *Tribune,* April 7, 1856, April 15, 1859; *Express* in Halliday, *Lost and Found,* 214. See also the *Courier and Enquirer* in *Times,* December 1, 1851.

64. *Herald,* January 30, February 17, 1858.

65. Isaac N. P. Stokes, *Iconography of Manhattan Island, 1498–1909,* 6 vols. (1915–28; New York, 1967), 5: 1859; *Times,* March 9 and October 13, 1853; *Express* in Halliday, *Lost and Found,* 212.

66. Barnard, *Forty Years at the Five Points,* 13.

CHAPTER FOUR

1. For a list of working-class New York memoirs, see Richard B. Stott, *Workers in the Metropolis: Class, Ethnicity, and Youth in Antebellum New York* (Ithaca, 1990), 279–83. The closest thing to a Five Points memoir, though it says very little about Five Points itself, is the autobiography of pickpocket George Appo in the Society for the Prevention of Crime Papers, Columbia University, much of which was reprinted in Timothy J. Gilfoyle, "A Pickpocket's Tale: The Autobiography of George Appo," *Missouri Review* 16 (1993): 34–77. For Appo's story, see Chapter Thirteen.

2. John Morrow, *A Voice from the Newsboys* (New York, 1860), 15–26.

3. Ibid., 26.

4. Ibid., 26–35.

5. Ibid., 36–41.

6. Ibid., 49, 54.

7. Ibid., 61–85. Johnny's memoir does not mention the House of Industry in connection with Willie's adoption, but for the links between the two programs see Chapter Eight.

8. Morrow, *Voice from the Newsboys,* 96–111.

9. Ibid., 100–17.

10. Notes on the back of a photo of the gravestone of John Morrow, Box 16, Peter J. Eckel Newsboy Collection, Department of Rare Books and Special Collections, Princeton University Library; Record of Deaths in the City of Brooklyn, 1861, p. 66, New York Municipal Archives.

11. John McCormack, for example, who had toiled as a laborer in County Tipperary until his emigration in May 1851, held the same menial status in Five Points five months later. See account 1247, Emigrant Savings Bank Test Books, New York Public Library; Ira A. Glazier, ed., *The Famine Immigrants: Lists of Irish Immigrants Arriving at the Port of New York, 1846–1851,* 7 vols. (Baltimore, 1983–86), 7: 193.

12. My calculation of the current value of Healy's $700 in savings is based on John J. McCusker, "How Much Is That in Real Money?" *Proceedings of the American Antiquarian Society* 101 (1991): 327–32, which suggests a multiplier of 16 to convert dollar amounts from the 1850s into 1991 dollars. All subsequent estimates of the current value of nineteenth-century monetary figures are based on McCusker's work.

13. "Passengers Sent out from Lord Palmerston's Estate to Quebec April 1847," BR146/9/4, Broadlands Papers, University of Southampton; account 3976, Emigrant Savings Bank

Test Books. Healy's movements through the city can be traced in *Doggett's New York City Directory for 1850–1851* (New York, 1850), 229; *Rode's New York City Directory for 1850–1851* (New York, 1850), 233; *Trow's New York City Directory for 1855–56* (New York, 1855), 375; *Trow's New York City Directory for 1856–57* (New York, 1856), 368; *Trow's New York City Directory for 1857–58* (New York, 1857), 369–70; and *Trow's New York City Directory for 1858–59* (New York, 1858), 357. He can also be found listed in dwelling 107, sixth election district, Sixth Ward, 1855 New York State manuscript census, Old Records Division, New York County Clerk's Office, and in family 95, dwelling 15, third district, Sixth Ward, 1860 United States manuscript census, National Archives. This Owen Healy should not be confused with a second saloonkeeper of the same name who lived on Cherry Street. See account 26110, Emigrant Savings Bank Test Books.

14. All percentages have been rounded to nearest whole number except those under one, which are rounded to nearest tenth of a percent. Five Points employment statistics are based on my 1855 census sample, whose composition is described in Chapter Two, note 10. "All New York" categories adapted from Robert Ernst, *Immigrant Life in New York City, 1825–1863* (1949; Port Washington, NY, 1965), 214–18, and Stott, *Workers in the Metropolis*, 92.

   The occupational categories are made up of the following vocations: "Professionals" includes physicians, clergymen, lawyers, and architects. "Business owners" includes manufacturers, merchants, hotel and boardinghouse keepers, restaurateurs, "proprietors," clothiers, dry goods dealers, shopkeepers, wine merchants, grocers, and food and liquor dealers. It is impossible, through the census, to determine whether a "grocer" or "saloon keeper" actually owned his or her own business or merely worked in someone else's. For the sake of consistency, all grocers and saloonkeepers have been placed in this category. "Petty entrepreneurs" includes peddlers and ragpickers. "Lower-status white-collar workers" were overwhelmingly clerks, but this category also includes a few salesmen, government workers, actors, and male teachers. The "Skilled workers" category is composed of assayers, bakers, blacksmiths, bleachers, boilermakers, brass workers, brewers and distillers, bricklayers, burnishers, butchers, cabinetmakers, carpenters, carvers, caulkers, chandlers, coach and wagon makers, confectioners, coopers, coppersmiths, dyers, factory workers, furriers, glassmakers, glaziers, guilders, gunsmiths, hatters, ironworkers, jewelers, leather workers, locksmiths, masons, mechanics, musical instrument makers, oil, paint, and paper makers, painters, plasterers, plumbers, polishers, potters, precious metal workers, precision instrument makers, printers, refiners, roofers, sailmakers and riggers, sawyers, shipbuilders, shoemakers, stonecutters, tailors, textile workers, tobacco workers, turners, upholsterers, varnishers, and weavers. "Unskilled workers" are defined as cartmen, chimney sweeps, hostlers and grooms, laborers, policemen (so classified because people from any occupational category took these jobs when offered), porters, sailors, waiters, and watchmen. Finally, "Difficult to classify" includes adult students, authors, conductors or other railroad employees, drovers, expressmen, farmers, financiers, fishermen, florists, gamblers, gardeners, gentlemen, hunters, scavengers, speculators, superintendents, and undertakers. For the women, "Needle trades" include cap makers, dressmakers, mantilla makers, milliners, seamstresses, "tailoresses," vest makers, and wigmakers. "Servants" includes servants, cooks, and nurses. Some better versed in the nuances of the antebellum trades or labor history in general may quibble with my placement of certain workers in certain groups, or even the categories themselves. I believe, however, that these groupings suffice for the purpose of drawing general comparisons between Five Pointers and the rest of the New York population.

15.

Percentage of Male Workers in Various Skilled Occupations, 1855

	Percent of All Workers		Percent of Skilled Workers	
	Five Points	*All New York*	*Five Points*	*All New York*
Tailors	14 %	8 %	29 %	17 %
Shoemakers	5	4	11	9
Glaziers	3	0.1	6	0.1
Carpenters	3	5	5	10
Machinists	2	1	4	2
Blacksmiths	2	2	3	4
Musicians	2	0.5	3	1
Brass finishers	1	0.3	3	0.6
Painters	1	2	3	5
Printers	1	1	3	3
Bakers	1	2	2	5
Cabinetmakers	1	2	2	5
Coopers	1	1	2	1
Plumbers	1	1	2	1
Bricklayers/Masons	0.5	2	1	5
Cigarmakers	0.3	1	0.5	3
Shipbuilders	0	1	0	2

Source: "Five Points" figures based on 1855 New York census; "All New York" figures adapted from Ernst, *Immigrant Life in New York City*, 214–18, and Stott, *Workers in the Metropolis*, 92.

16.

Occupational Distribution of Male Workers by Nativity (or, for Jews, Ethnicity), 1855

	Five Points				All New York
	Irish	*German*	*U.S.-born*	*Jews*	
Professionals	0.4%	0%	0%	0%	2%
Business owners	3	7	0	6	14
Low-status white-collar	3	7	0	0	9
Petty entrepreneurs	1	3	0	6	1
Skilled workers	34	75	61	88	47
Unskilled workers	58	4	39	0	22
Difficult to classify	1	4	0	0	5

Source: "Five Points" figures based on 1855 New York census; "All New York" figures adapted from Ernst, *Immigrant Life in New York City*, 214–18, and Stott, *Workers in the Metropolis*, 92.

17. *The Eighteenth Annual Report of the New York Association for Improving the Condition of the Poor* (New York, 1861): 21–23; *Tribune*, July 9, 1845; Carol Groneman, "The 'Bloody Ould Sixth': A Social Analysis of a New York City Working-Class Community in the Mid-Nineteenth Century" (Ph.D. dissertation, University of Rochester, 1973), 99; Edith Abbott, "Wages of Unskilled Labor in the United States, 1850–1900," *Journal of Political Economy* 13 (June 1905): 363.

18. Groneman, "'Bloody Ould Sixth,'" 97–99.

19. *Tribune*, July 9, 1845; Stott, *Workers in the Metropolis*, 119.

20.

Deposits in Five Pointers' Bank Accounts by Month, 1852–54

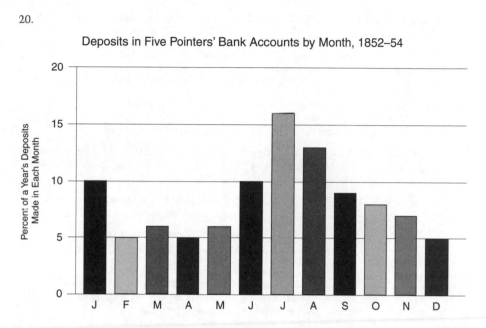

Source: Accounts 300, 319, 347, 375, 396, 450, 451, 461, 472, 528, 572, 643, 685, 710, 722, 738, 740, 776, 789, 817, 866, 897, 906, 924, 927, 945, 987, 1015, 1017, 1022, 1024, 1049, 1063, 1104, 1185, 1235, 1245, 1247, 1258, 1270, 1310, 1314, 1319, 1322, 1333, 1360, 1373, 1380, 1387, 1400, 1444, 1445, 1669, 1710, 1760, 1875, 1885, 1935, 2072, 2075, 2116, 2165, 2250, 2260, 2265, 2270, 2281, 2287, 2320, 2332, 2335, 2378, 2403, 2405, 2406, 2440, 2464, 2467, 2639, 2661, 2663, 2674, 2709, 2723, 2977, 2978, 2995, 3035, 3067, 3093, 3155, 3204, 3424, 3461, 3543, 3580, 3597, 3651, 3666, 3735, 3805, 3830, 3914, 3976, 4069, 4120, 4134, 4137, 4163, 4188, 4191, 4201, 4203, 4205, 4228, 4248, 4255, 4260, 4277, 4336, 4344, 4382, 4383, 4386, 4408, 4409, 4427, 4454, 4456, 4497, 4516, 4525, 4529, 4536, 4542, 4544, 4572, 4592, 4602, 4617, 4654, 4735, 4737, 4738, 4739, 4740, 4745, 4751, 4774, 4780, 4808, 4820, 4838, 4873, 4888, 4960, 4976, 4983, 5036, 5098, 5115, 5134, 5137, 5138, 5152, 5155, 5172, 5192, 5209, 5225, 5230, 5240, 5243, 5245, 5249, 5266, 5276, 5286, 5290, 5303, 5304, 5354, 5360, 5367, 5394, 5403, 5409, 5419, 5433, 5454, 5479, 5514, 5583, 5607, 5612, 5631, and 5649, Emigrant Savings Bank Test Books and Account Ledgers. See also Cormac O'Grada, "Immigrants, Savers, and Runners: The Emigrant Industrial Savings Bank in the 1850's," Center for Economic Research Working Papers Series (1988), no. 2.

21. Virginia Penny, *The Employments of Women: A Cyclopaedia of Woman's Work* (Boston, 1863), 110; Greeley, *Recollections,* and *Five Points Monthly Record* in Stott, *Workers in the Metropolis,* 112–17, 164 (quotations); "Report of the Committee to Examine into the . . . Commissioners of Emigration," *Documents of the Assembly of the State of New-York, Seventy-fifth Session, 1852* (Albany, 1852), doc. 34, 176–77; *Harper's Weekly* (July 4, 1857): 418–19.

22. *Nineteenth Annual Report of the New York Association for Improving the Condition of the Poor* (New York, 1862): 22. The *Manual of the Corporation of the City of New York for 1858* (New York, 1858), 336–37, lists three licensed pawnshops and twenty-six

licensed second-hand shops in the Five Points district. Many other second-hand shops operated without licenses.

23. *British Mechanic's and Labourer's Hand Book* and John White, *Sketches from America,* in Stott, *Workers in the Metropolis,* 128, 131–32, 140; [James D. Burn], *Three Years Among the Working-Classes in the United States During the War* (London, 1865), 11.

24. United States Senate, Committee on Education and Labor, *Report of the Senate Committee Upon Relations Between Labor and Capital* (Washington, D.C., 1885), 1: 413–14; Stott, *Workers in the Metropolis,* 140; Groneman, "'Bloody Ould Sixth,'" 105.

25. Sean Wilentz, *Chants Democratic: New York City and the Rise of the American Working Class, 1788–1850* (New York, 1984), 119; *Tribune,* September 26 ("pot boiling"), November 15, 1845, July 26, 1850 ("half-starved").

26. *Tribune,* June 10, 1850, March 20, 21, 29, 31, 1854; *Herald,* July 23 and 25, November 14, 1850, October 3, 1853; Robert Crowe, *Reminiscences of Robert Crowe, the Octogenerian* [sic] *Tailor* (New York, 1901), 26.

27. *Tribune,* September 5, 9 (quotation), 1845, May 8, 1850, May 27, 1853; Ernst, *Immigrant Life,* 79, 215.

28. Dwelling 57, third electoral district, second division, Sixth Ward, 1855 New York census; J. D. Eisenstein, "The History of the First Russian-American Jewish Congregation," *Publications of the American Jewish Historical Society* 9 (1901): 68.

29. [William M. Bobo], *Glimpses of New-York City, by a South Carolinian* (Charleston, 1852), 118 ("suspenders"); Alvin F. Harlow, *Old Bowery Days: The Chronicles of a Famous Street* (New York, 1931), 173–74 ("sha-a-d"); account 1828, Emigrant Saving Bank Test Books and Account Ledgers; Hyman Grinstein, *The Rise of the Jewish Community of New York, 1654–1860* (Philadelphia, 1945), 411.

30. Ernst, *Immigrant Life,* 86; Junius H. Browne, *The Great Metropolis: A Mirror of New-York* (Hartford, 1869), 98–99; William H. Bell Diary, October 9, 1850, New-York Historical Society.

31. Browne, *Great Metropolis,* 277; George G. Foster, *New York by Gas-Light* (1850; Berkeley, 1990), 126; "Autobiography of George Appo," typescript, pp. 1–3, Society for the Prevention of Crime Papers, Columbia University; *Evening Post,* January 21, 1854; Harlow, *Old Bowery Days,* 377.

32. *Tribune,* May 8, 13, 14 (quotation), 1850; John F. Maguire, *The Irish in America* (London, 1868), 232–33. For neighborhood construction accidents, see *Tribune,* December 4, 1850; *Herald,* November 5, 1853.

33. *Irish-American,* July 30, 1853 (Coogan quotation); Stott, *Workers in the Metropolis,* 102, 120; *Monthly Record of the Five Points House of Industry* 1 (June 1857): 61; 2 (April 1959): 274; *Annual Report of the New-York Ladies' Home Missionary Society* (1868): 8; entry of December 15, 1856, Adoption Case Histories, Five Points Mission Records, United Methodist Church Archives, Drew University.

34. *Herald,* June 11, 1853 (Mulberry Street shirt sewer); *Tribune,* June 8, 1853; *Times,* March 1, 1855.

35. Wirt Sikes, "Among the Poor Girls," *Putnam's Magazine,* n.s. 1 (April 1868): 433; accounts 1875 and 12057, Emigrant Savings Bank Test Books.

36. Accounts 3652 and 4542, Emigrant Savings Bank Test Books; *Tribune*, March 27, 1851.

37. *Tribune*, June 8, 1853; Sikes, "Among the Poor Girls," 436.

38. *Herald*, October 9, 1850, June 11, 1853; *Times*, February 24, 27, 1855.

39. *Herald*, October 7, 1851 ("caprice"), June 11, 1853; *Tribune*, March 27, 1851, March 22, 1853.

40. *Tribune*, September 3, 1845, June 8, 1853; *Herald*, June 11, 1853 ("Song of the Shirt").

41. [George G. Foster], *New York in Slices: By an Experienced Carver* (New York, 1849), 53; *Tribune*, June 8, 1853 (quotation); Christine Stansell, *City of Women: Sex and Class in New York, 1789–1860* (Urbana, 1982), 118. Many Five Points women became seamstresses because the work could be done at home while caring for one's children.

42. *Tribune*, November 6, 1845; account 2405, Emigrant Savings Bank Test Books and Account Ledgers. Naylan listed her address as 32 Orange Street when she opened her account, but it is very unlikely that she worked at that address. She was probably one of the domestics who commuted to work.

43. [Bobo], *Glimpses of New-York City*, 187; *Tribune*, November 6, 1845.

44. *Frank Leslie's Illustrated Newspaper* (March 13, 1880): 27; John F. Maguire, *The Irish in America* (London, 1868), 315, 317–18.

45. *Tribune*, November 6, 1845; statement of Ann Kelly, April 10, 1859, reel 75, New York County District Attorney's Indictment Papers, New York Municipal Archives.

46. Carl N. Degler, "Labor in the Economy and Politics of New York City, 1850–1860: A Study of the Impact of Early Industrialism" (Ph.D. dissertation, Columbia University, 1952), 124–25; *Tribune*, September 16–17, 1845; *Times*, March 2, 1859.

47. *Irish-American*, May 28, 1853 (including quotation from *Sun*), May 16, 1857; *Herald*, May 13, 1853; Degler, "Labor in the Economy," 137–38; Ernst, *Immigrant Life*, 67.

48. Account 2320, Emigrant Savings Bank Test Books; dwellings 87 and 92, fourth election district, Sixth Ward, 1855 New York census; *Doggett's New York City Street Directory for 1851* (New York, 1851), which lists, alphabetically by street, the proprietors of many Five Points businesses; Bell Diary, October 9, 1850.

49. William Burns, *Life in New York, In Doors and Out of Doors* (New York, 1851), unpaginated; *Irish-American*, February 24, 1850; accounts 1017, 1049, 2579, 3035, Emigrant Savings Bank Test Books; family 467, fifth election district, Sixth Ward, 1855 New York census.

50. Solon Robinson, *Hot Corn: Life Scenes in New York Illustrated* (New York, 1854), 44; *The Diary of George Templeton Strong*, ed. Allan Nevins, 5 vols. (New York, 1952), 2: 149; Harlow, *Old Bowery Days*, 176.

51. Robinson, *Hot Corn*, 44–47, 104–11; *Tribune*, October 10, 1853; *Diary of George Templeton Strong*, 2: 148.

52. George Ellington [pseud.], *The Women of New York; Or, The Under-World of the Great City* (New York, 1869), 605–6 ("brisk business"); Samuel Halliday, *The Lost and Found; or Life Among the Poor* (New York, 1859), 118–23; *The Old Brewery and the New Mission House at the Five Points, By Ladies of the Mission* (New York, 1854), 168–69.

53. "C.L.B." (Charles Loring Brace) in *Times*, March 12, 1853; Foster, *New York by Gas-Light*, 115–19; *Irish-American*, February 17, 1850.

54. Edward W. Martin [pseud. for James D. McCabe], *The Secrets of the Great City* (Philadelphia, 1868), 261–64; Owen Kildare, *My Mamie Rose* (New York, 1903), 45–51; "C.L.B." in *Times*, March 12, 1853; Morrow, *Voice from the Newsboys*, 128–32; *Frank Leslie's Illustrated Newspaper* (December 29, 1855): 43; *Times*, October 16, 1902; family 79, sixth election district, Sixth Ward, 1870 United States manuscript census (identified as Sullivan in Daniel Czitrom, "Underworlds and Underdogs: Big Tim Sullivan and Metropolitan Politics in New York, 1889–1913," *Journal of American History* 78 [1991]: 539–40).

55. *Sun*, April 17, 1889, p. 1 (Sullivan); Martin, *Secrets of the Great City*, 264–65; Browne, *Great Metropolis*, 425–33; Charles L. Brace, *The Dangerous Classes of New York and Twenty Years Work Among Them*, 3rd ed. (New York, 1872), 205; *Seventh Annual Report of the Children's Aid Society* (1860): 15–16.

56. *Third Annual Report of the Children's Aid Society* (New York, 1856): 26; Philip Wallys, *About New York: An Account of What a Boy Saw in His Visit to the City* (New York, 1857), 43–44, 51–52; Stansell, *City of Women*, 50–51; Morrow, *Voice from the Newsboys*, 37–38, 41; Browne, *Great Metropolis*, 95; *Seventh Annual Report of the Children's Aid Society* (New York, 1860): 5; Groneman, "'Bloody Ould Sixth,'" 127.

57. *Evening Post*, November 18, 1854; *Tribune*, February 3, 1855.

58. *Tribune*, February 3, 8, 16, 20, 1855; *Eleventh Annual Report of the New-York Ladies' Home Missionary Society* (New York, 1855), 8–9; *Irish-American*, December 23, 1854, January 20, 1855; *Eleventh Annual Report of the New York Association for Improving the Condition of the Poor* (New York, 1854), 37; *Twelfth Annual Report of the New York Association for Improving the Condition of the Poor* (New York, 1855), 42.

59. *Fourteenth Annual Report of the New-York Ladies' Home Missionary Society* (New York, 1858), 8; *Monthly Record of the Five Points House of Industry* 1 (November 1857): 171 (not quoted); *Herald*, October 21, 1857; *Fifteenth Annual Report of the New York Association for Improving the Condition of the Poor* (New York, 1859), 30.

60. *Irish-American*, June 9, 1855.

61. Gerard J. Lyne, "William Steuart Trench and the Post-Famine Emigration from Kenmare to America, 1850–1855," *Journal of the Kerry Archaeological and Historical Society* 25 (1992): 92–94; William S. Trench, *Realities of Irish Life* (London, 1868), 126–27.

62. Catharine Bradley to "My dear Uncle John," October 6, 1847, Eliza Quin to her parents, January 22, 1848, in *Irish University Press Series of British Parliamentary Papers*, "Emigration" series (Shannon, 1969), 5: 125, 128 (hereafter cited as *IUP-BPP, Emigration*).

63. "Bridget Rooney to her father Pat Rooney," January 15, 1848, BR146/10/13, Pat McGowan to his parents, December 21, 1847, BR146/10/13, Broadlands Papers.

64. Eliza Quin to her parents, January 22, 1848, in *IUP-BPP, Emigration*, 5: 128; Pat McGowan, to his parents, December 21, 1847, BR146/10/13, Broadlands Papers.

65. *Irish-American*, July 30, 1853.

66. Oscar Handlin, *Boston's Immigrants: A Study in Acculturation* (Cambridge, MA, 1959), 55; Kerby A. Miller, *Emigrants and Exiles: Ireland and the Irish Exodus to North America* (New York, 1985), 295–99, 326. For a recent dissent from the standard interpretation, see Joseph P. Ferrie, "Up and Out or Down and Out? Immigrant Mobility in the Antebel-

lum United States," *Journal of Interdisciplinary History* 26 (1995): 33–55, and Joseph P. Ferric, *Yankeys Now: Immigrants in the Antebellum United States, 1840–1860* (New York, 1999).

67. One in seven Five Pointers getting married at the neighborhood's Catholic church was a Kerry native; more than 75 percent of them had once lived on the Lansdowne estate. Given that about two-thirds of the neighborhood's 14,000 residents in 1855 were Irish natives or their children, and that nearly all of them were Catholics, one can estimate that roughly 1,000 Five Points inhabitants were former Lansdowne tenants. If we take the size of the average Lansdowne nuclear family to be four persons, then their 153 accounts could represent 60 percent of the 1,000 Lansdowne emigrants living in Five Points, but because a few persons opened more than one account, I put the figure at 50 percent instead.

    The Lansdowne account numbers are 776, 987, 1235, 2250, 2639, 3067, 3424, 3461, 3666, 3735, 4163, 4277, 4408, 4409, 4542, 4737, 4738, 4739, 4745, 4774, 5115, 5155, 5303, 5304, 5433, 5479, 5735, 5763, 5800, 5953, 6143, 6144, 6468, 6473, 6474, 6524, 6605, 6623, 6773, 6797, 6805, 6975, 7014, 7061, 7085, 7193, 7225, 7358, 7464, 7504, 7524, 7525, 7596, 7660, 7705, 7747, 7759, 7912, 8060, 8528, 8592, 8675, 8687, 8923, 9102, 9130, 9150, 9201, 9202, 9203, 9212, 9276, 9304, 9358, 9359, 9438, 9445, 9561, 9572, 9611, 9732, 9776, 9785, 9860, 9923, 10010, 10153, 10164, 10222, 10267, 10292, 10368, 10411, 10465, 10524, 10576, 10646, 10647, 10693, 10712, 10727, 10747, 10754, 10804, 10835, 10836, 10876, 10885, 11113, 11218, 11236, 11342, 11368, 11390, 11455, 11488, 11500, 11552, 11560, 11566, 11650, 11730, 11754, 11807, 11808, 11873, 11895, 11910, 11971, 11979, 11998, 12001, 12036, 12040, 12041, 12046, 12053, 12057, 12084, 12120, 12215, 12240, 12259, 12309, 12310, 12311, 12316, 12317, 12344, 12419, and 12420.

68. Accounts 4737, 4738, 4739, and 4745, Emigrant Savings Bank Test Books.

69. Accounts 1235, 3424, 7464, 12046, and 12419, Emigrant Savings Bank Test Books.

70. Accounts 5479 and 9445, Emigrant Savings Bank Test Books and Account Ledgers. The highest balance achieved by the Lansdowne immigrants in their bank accounts was, on average, $200. The highest balance achieved by non-Lansdowne Five Pointers was, on average, $234.

71. [Burn], *Three Years Among the Working-Classes*, 14–15; *Church Monthly* (March 1858), in *Monthly Record of the Five Points House of Industry* 2 (June 1858): 34–35; Eliza Quin to "Dear Parents," January 22, 1848 (written from the Sixth Ward Hotel), in *IUP-BPP, Emigration*, 5: 128.

CHAPTER FIVE

1. Thomas L. Nichols, *Forty Years of American Life*, 2 vols. (London, 1864), 2: 159; Sherlock Bristol, *The Pioneer Preacher: Incidents of Interest, and Experiences in the Author's Life* (1887; Urbana, 1989), 66–67.

2. *Times*, January 14, 1885; Nichols, *Forty Years of American Life*, 2: 159.

3. *Clipper*, January 24, 1885; Nichols, *Forty Years of American Life*, 2: 159.

4. Nichols, *Forty Years of American Life*, 2: 159; Bristol, *Pioneer Preacher*, 66–67.

5. *Times*, January 14, 1885; *Clipper*, January 24, 1885; Nichols, *Forty Years of American Life*, 2: 159–61 (quotation); Matthew P. Breen, *Thirty Years of New York Politics Up-to-Date* (New York, 1899), 307–8; *National Police Gazette*, February 7, 1885, p. 5, and *Frank Leslie's Illustrated Weekly* 59 (January 24, 1885): 380. Most biographies refer to Rynders's customhouse post as that of "weigher," but I have utilized the title listed in *Doggetts'*

New York City Directory because it was probably provided by Rynders himself— *Doggetts' New York City Directory for 1847–48* (New York, 1847), 356.

6. *Evening Post,* January 25, 27, 1845; *Times,* January 14, 1885.

7. *The Nation* (November 4, 1875): 288; Richard B. Stott, *Workers in the Metropolis: Class, Ethnicity, and Youth in Antebellum New York* (Ithaca, 1990), 239; Breen, *Thirty Years,* 233.

8. New York Board of Aldermen, *Documents* 25 (1858), doc. 6, pp. 53–54, 161, 171; J. Frank Kernan, *Reminiscences of the Old Fire Laddies* (New York, 1885), 23–24 (Matthew Brennan), 501 (Fitzgerald); *Times,* October 30, 1884, p. 5 (Owen Brennan); *Manual of the Corporation of the City of New York for 1855* (New York, 1855), 168.

9. William M. Ivins, *Machine Politics and Money in Elections in New York City* (1887; New York, 1970), 13–14, 25; *Manual of the Corporation of the City of New York for 1856* (New York, 1856), 225; "A Policeman" in *Tribune,* October 20, 1856.

10. Ivins, *Machine Politics,* 9–11; Breen, *Thirty Years,* 39–43.

11. Kernan, *Reminiscences,* 47.

12. Ibid., 47–48; John Doggett, Jr., ed., *The New York City Directory for 1842* (New York, 1842), 100.

13. Kernan, *Reminiscences,* 50; *Proceedings of the Board of Aldermen* 18 (1839–40): 324, 410; 21 (1841): 269. For extra hiring at election time, see *Tribune,* March 13, 1846.

14. Ivins, *Machine Politics,* 20; Kernan, *Reminiscences,* 49.

15. Kernan, *Reminiscences,* 49–50. On the influence of money and fighters in securing nominations citywide, see *Herald,* October 29, 30, 1850, March 10, 1855; Breen, *Thirty Years,* 40–43.

16. Kernan, *Reminiscences,* 48–50.

17. *Tribune,* April 12, 1848; *Manual of the Corporation of the City of New York for 1849* (New York, 1849), 319; *Herald,* November 6, 1850 ("free indulgence"). See also *Harper's Weekly* (November 13, 1858): 724 (for an image of a Five Points polling place); *People v. James H. Lally, et al.,* April 27, 1841, New York County District Attorney's Indictment Papers, New York Municipal Archives; [George G. Foster], *New York in Slices: By an Experienced Carver* (New York, 1849), 49. Whig fighters sometimes instigated polling place brawls as well, though such cases were rare after 1845. See Tom Quick, "Old Sports of New York," *Leader,* June 16, 1860.

18. *Freeman's Journal,* October 27, 1849 ("grossest caricatures"); *Aurora,* April 11, 1842, in *Walt Whitman of the New York Aurora,* ed. Joseph J. Rubin and Charles H. Brown (State College, PA, 1950), 68; *Herald,* April 11, 1842; *Tribune,* April 12, 1842; Edwin G. Burrows and Mike Wallace, *Gotham: A History of New York City to 1898* (New York, 1999), 630–31.

19. *Walt Whitman of the New York Aurora,* 58–59, 67–68.

20. *Herald,* April 14, 1842. The *Herald's* account of this contest is not completely consistent. While its detailed story on the fourteenth implied that Shaler was the regular nominee, its election coverage the previous day stated that Ferris had won the endorsement of the primary meeting. And I have found no evidence that Donoho ever served as the ward's collector.

21. *Herald,* April 14, 1842.

22. *Walt Whitman of the New York Aurora,* 77, 78, 80; *Tribune,* April 12 ("most savage"), 13, 1842; *Herald,* April 14, 1842.

23. *Herald,* April 14, 1842 (first quotation); *Walt Whitman of the New York Aurora,* 77; *Manual of the Corporation of the City of New York for 1842–43* (New York, 1842), 74 (Donoho's victory). Donoho later petitioned the board of aldermen for compensation "for damage done to his premises, on the evening of the 12th of April instant, by a mob"— *Proceedings of the Board of Aldermen* 22 (1842): 441.

24. *The Diary of Philip Hone, 1828–1851,* ed. Allan Nevins (New York, 1936), 596. If true, Whitman's statement that Mike Walsh and the Spartans attacked those speaking against the Maclay Act at a public meeting in City Hall Park further complicates an assessment of the rioters' motivations—*Walt Whitman of the New York Aurora,* 58.

25. Kernan, *Reminiscences,* 50–51; *Herald,* April 11, 1849. Biographical details of Kelly's early life are not readily available, in part because his name is so common. He first appears in a city directory as a Five Points saloonkeeper in 1843 at 74 Bayard Street. He also served as a Sixth Ward school commissioner in 1847. John Doggett, Jr., ed., *The New-York City and Co-Partnership Directory* (New York, 1843), 189; *Manual of the Corporation of the City of New York for 1847* (New York, 1847), 231 (which lists his address as 78 Bayard).

26. *Herald,* September 26, 27 (letter to the editor correcting erroneous report of Foote's victory), 1849.

27. I was able to identify the address and occupation of 52 of the 68 Foote nominees and 46 of the 62 Kelly nominees in the 1849–50 or 1850–51 New York directories.

Occupational Distribution of 1849 Sixth Ward Democratic Primary Nominees

	Percentage of Foote Ticket	*Percentage of Kelly Ticket*
Lawyers	6%	9%
Liquor dealers	58	48
Other merchants	15	11
Clerks (mostly govt. jobs)	10	11
Artisans	10	15
Unskilled	0	7
Difficult to categorize	2	0

The "Other merchants" category for Kelly includes two bakers who seem to own their own bakeries, while the Foote "Merchant" category includes an agent, a boardinghouse keeper, and a hotel proprietor. The "Unskilled" category includes a laborer, a "bill poster," and a "carman." The "Difficult to categorize" nominee was James "Jumps" Hogan, who according to Brennan kept a "policy [lottery] office" on Centre Street. The tickets can be found in the *Herald,* September 26, 1849.

28. *Herald,* October 17, 19, 21 (all quotations), 24, 1849. Ridaboek's status as a coal dealer is from his testimony in a trial reported in the *Times,* January 20, 1853, by which point he served on the influential Tammany general committee.

29. *Herald,* October 17, 19, 21, 24, 1849; *Irish-American,* October 28 (quotation), November 4, 1849.

30. *Herald,* October 15, 17, November 7, 1849; *Clarion,* November 5, 1849.

31. *Tribune*, October 31, November 1, 1849; *Herald*, October 31, November 1, 3, 1849.

32. *Clarion*, November 5, 1849; *Herald*, November 7, 1849; *Tribune*, November 8, 1849 ("uproarious"); *Manual of the Corporation of the City of New York for 1850* (New York, 1850), 409 (official returns).

33. *Tribune*, December 1, 1849.

34. *Leader*, October 6, 1860 (quotation); *Times*, November 18, 1869. The various obituaries and biographical sketches upon which this description of Brennan's early life is based contradict each other in many details. In such cases, I have relied on the *Leader*, whose editor John Clancy was Brennan's close friend. For Brennan's older brother Timothy, see *Times*, December 4, 1881, p. 7. I have inferred that Brennan's mother was widowed around the time of his birth because his father's last listing in the city directory is in the 1821–22 edition, in which he is listed as living at 13 Ferry Street. After a hiatus of a few years in which the family does not appear in the directory, Hannah is listed as a "huckster" living at Old Slip—*Longworth's American Almanac* (New York, 1821), 90.

35. *Times*, January 20, 1879; *Herald*, January 20, 1879 ("coffee, cakes"); *Tribune*, January 21, 1879 ("fleet of foot").

36. *Doggett's New York City Directory for 1844–45* (New York, 1844), 48; *Doggett's New York City Directory for 1845–46* (New York, 1845), 50; *Times*, January 20, 1879.

37. *Leader*, November 22, 1862.

38. *Manual of the Corporation of the City of New York for 1848* (New York, 1848), 100.

39. *Herald*, January 20, 1850; *Tribune*, May 9, 1850; [Wendell P. Garrison], *William Lloyd Garrison, 1805–1879: The Story of His Life*, 3 vols. (New York, 1885–89), 3: 285–300; Kernan, *Reminiscences*, 53–54.

40. Kernan, *Reminiscences*, 53–54; *Manual of the Corporation of the City of New York for 1851* (New York, 1851), 345–46; *Herald*, November 8, 1850 (election results by ward). Rynders won 967 votes in the Sixth Ward, while the two Democratic candidates for assistant alderman, the highest ward-wide office up for grabs that year, captured 1,328 votes between them. One cannot be sure that the events described by Kernan took place in 1850, though given Rynders's appearance in that year's race for assembly, my inference that Kernan is describing the 1850 primary is probably accurate. Alvin F. Harlow, *Old Bowery Days: The Chronicles of a Famous Street* (New York, 1931), 302–3, implies that the events described by Kernan took place before 1849 and attributes the anti-Irish rhetoric used by Rynders in fomenting the Astor Place Riot to resentment against the Irish inspired by this electoral defeat, but there is no evidence I know of to substantiate Harlow's dating.

    Newspapers reported Rynders's nomination at Tammany Hall without comment (see *Herald*, October 10, 1850), so my assessment of how he captured the nomination despite the opposition of Sixth Ward voters cannot be confirmed either. Evidence of growing Irish-American resentment toward Rynders's attempts to influence Sixth Ward politics before the fall of 1850 can be found in the *Irish-American*, February 24, 1850. Following the lead of Breen, who asserted that Rynders "had long ruled the Sixth Ward with a rod of iron," many historians have erroneously stated that Rynders did for a time control Sixth Ward politics. But Kernan's account is the only one not contradicted by contemporary evidence (Breen would have been a young child in 1850). Breen, *Thirty Years*, 518–19; Lloyd Morris, *Incredible New York* (New York, 1951), 32; Herbert Asbury, *The Gangs of New York: An Informal History of the Underworld* (New York, 1928), 43. Rynders attributed his defeat in the race for assembly to "money circulating somewhere in the Third ward. If our side had had it, I might, perhaps, tell you a different story"— *Herald*, November 6, 1850.

41. Brennan became captain on November 20, 1851—*Manual of the Corporation of the City of New York for 1852* (New York, 1852), 101. Barr's role in Brennan's appointment is mentioned in the *Times*, January 20, 1879. The statement in one of Brennan's obituaries that he had served as ward assessor before becoming police captain appears to be untrue, as he did not serve in that capacity (according to the *Manual of the Corporation*) in either 1850 or 1851.

42. Ivins, *Machine Politics*, 13–14; *Manual of the Corporation of the City of New York for 1855*, 168; *Tribune*, November 1, 1856 (quotations); *Leader*, October 9, 1858.

43. *Herald*, November 3, 5, 6, 8, 1854 (all advertisements except election results on the eighth). Brennan captured 2,823 votes, to 1,854 for "Captain Kissner" of the Fourteenth Ward police, 1,145 for John McGrath, and 353 for Whig David W. Clark—*Manual of the Corporation of the City of New York for 1855*, 368–69, 379.

44. *Leader*, November 22, 1862; *Herald*, January 20, 1879; John Ridge, "The Hidden Gaeltacht in Old New York," *New York Irish History* 6 (1991–92): 17. Brennan can be found in the 1860 federal census in the Sixth Ward, fourth district, dwelling 265, where he is listed as a thirty-nine-year-old police justice with $14,000 in real property, $1,000 in personal property, along with his thirty-three-year-old wife Margaret (also a New York native, who owned $2,000 in real estate), five children aged nine, seven, five, three, and one, and two servants. State Democrats realized that victory in 1856 was virtually impossible, and it is likely that Brennan would not have received the nomination for prison inspector had the party had a realistic chance to carry the contest.

45. *Herald* and *Times*, May 14, 1876; *Manual of the Corporation of the City of New York for 1849*, 87.

46. *Leader*, July 2, 1864.

47. Ibid. (first two quotations); *Times*, July 2, 1864 ("graceful and polished writer"); *Doggett's New York City Directory for 1850–51* (New York, 1850), 101.

CHAPTER SIX

1. Charles Dickens, *American Notes* (1842; London, 1985), 80–83.

2. Marian Hannah Winter, "Juba and American Minstrelsy," Paul Magriel, ed., in *Chronicles of the American Dance* (New York, 1948), 42–43 (including *Herald* quotation); Edward LeRoy Rice, *Monarchs of Minstrelsy* (New York, 1911), 48; Michael B. Leavitt, *Fifty Years in Theatrical Management* (New York, 1912), 33–34; Marshall and Jane Stearns, *Jazz Dance: The Story of American Vernacular Dance* (New York, 1968), 44–45; *Illustrated London News*, August 5, 1848.

3. *Walt Whitman of the New York Aurora*, ed. Joseph J. Rubin and Charles H. Brown (State College, PA, 1950), 21; Mathews quoted in Richard B. Stott, *Workers in the Metropolis: Class, Ethnicity, and Youth in Antebellum New York* (Ithaca, 1990), 251; Diarmund O'Muirithe, *A Seat Behind the Coachman: Travellers in Ireland, 1800–1900* (Dublin, 1972), 64.

4. Rice, *Monarchs of Minstrelsy*, 40 ("greatest jig dancers"); Winter, "Juba," 39, 47, 52 (other quotations).

5. Winter, "Juba," 39.

6. Cornelius Mathews, *A Pen-and-Ink-Panorama of New-York City* (New York, 1853), 124; *Walt Whitman of the New York Aurora*, 18; Junius H. Browne, *The Great Metropolis: A Mirror of New-York* (Hartford, 1869), 129–30; [William M. Bobo], *Glimpses of New-York City, by a South Carolinian* (Charleston, 1852), 162.

7. Charles H. Haswell, *Reminiscences of an Octogenarian, 1816–1860* (New York, 1897), 360; Browne, *Great Metropolis*, 165–66; *Clipper*, October 21, 1860 (Worden House); Alvin F. Harlow, *Old Bowery Days: The Chronicles of a Famous Street* (New York, 1931), 381, 415–16, 535.

8. Harlow, *Old Bowery Days*, 175; *Morning Express*, July 6, 1857 ("coffee and cake saloon").

9. George G. Foster, *New York by Gas-Light* (1850; Berkeley, 1990), 192–93; J. Frank Kernan, *Reminiscences of the Old Fire Laddies* (New York, 1885), 43–44 (all quotations).

10. Davis S. Reynolds, *Walt Whitman's America: A Cultural Biography* (New York, 1995), 103–4; Richard H. Thornton, *An American Glossary*, 2 vols. (London, 1912), 1: 58–60; [Bobo], *Glimpses of New-York*, 164 (long quotation); [George G. Foster], *New York in Slices: By an Experienced Carver* (New York, 1849), 43–47; Harlow, *Old Bowery Days*, 196; Haswell, *Reminiscences*, 270–71 (final quotation).

11. Foster, *New York by Gas-Light*, 170, 171, 173; [Foster], *New York in Slices*, 45 (final quotation only); *Tribune*, October 4, 1848 (not quoted).

12. Foster, *New York by Gas-Light*, 175–76. Abram C. Dayton, *The Last Days of Knickerbocker Life in New York* (1880; New York, 1897), 219.

13. Foster, *New York by Gas-Light*, 169, 175; Mathews, *Pen-and-Ink-Panorama*, 137–38; Haswell, *Reminiscences*, 270–71.

14. John Ripley, "Account of the Astor Place Riot" (1897), quoted in Sean Wilentz, *Chants Democratic: New York City and the Rise of the American Working Class, 1788–1850* (New York, 1984), 300; Harlow, *Old Bowery Days*, 189, 296–97.

15. Harlow, *Old Bowery Days*, 206; Stott, *Workers in the Metropolis*, 225.

16. *Times*, January 14, 1885 (which defines the sporting man as "a combination of gambler, horseman and politician"); Owen Kildare, *My Mamie Rose* (New York, 1903) and *My Old Bailiwick* (New York, 1906).

17. *Clipper*, October 21, 1860 (quotations), January 24, 1885 (Arena); Kernan, *Reminiscences*, 42–43.

18. *Clipper*, October 21, 1860; Kernan, *Reminiscences*, 42–43.

19. *Walt Whitman of the New York Aurora*, 36; Matthew P. Breen, *Thirty Years of New York Politics Up-to-Date* (New York, 1899), 71; Mathews, *Pen-and-Ink-Panorama*, 95–96.

20. Firemen may have exaggerated their occupational status when they were surveyed. "Return of the Engine, Hose, Hook and Ladder, and Hydrant Companies" (a broadside) and *Annual Report of the Chief Engineer of the Fire Department* (New York, 1858), both in New York Board of Aldermen, *Documents* 12 (1845), doc. 16, p. 361; 25 (1858), doc. 6, pp. 53–54, 161, 171; Kernan, *Reminiscences*, 862–81.

21. "Return of the Engine, Hose, Hook and Ladder, and Hydrant Companies," in New York Board of Aldermen, *Documents* 25 (1858), doc. 6, pp. 53–54, 161, 171.

22. Account 2378, Emigrant Savings Bank Test Books and Account Ledgers, New York Public Library; family 680, second division, third electoral district, and family 375, fifth election district, Sixth Ward, 1855 New York census, Old Records Division, New York County Clerk's Office; *Trow's New York City Directory for 1858–59* (New York, 1858), 364, 806; marriage of James Tucker to Maria Quinn, August 7, 1860, marriage register, Church of the Transfiguration, 29 Mott Street, New York.

23. Charles Townsend Harris, *Memories of Manhattan in the Sixties and Seventies* (New York, 1928), 36; [James D. Burn], *Three Years Among the Working-Classes in the United States During the War* (London, 1865), 108–9; William H. Bell Diary, July 24, 1851, New-York Historical Society; report of Chief Alfred Carson in New York Board of Aldermen, *Documents* 17 (1850), part II, doc. 57, pp. 930–32, 945–48.

24. Harlow, *Old Bowery Days*, 193.

25. Mathews, *Pen-and-Ink-Panorama*, 99–100; John T. Ridge, *Sligo in New York: The Irish from County Sligo, 1849–1991* (New York, 1991), 16, 20; *Irish-American*, March 20, 1852 (Brennan Guard), August 15, 1857. That the Sarsfield Guard captain, John R. Boland, operated a saloon at that address is documented in *Doggett's New York City Street Directory for 1851* (New York, [1851]), 290.

26. Edward K. Spann, "Union Green: The Irish Community and the Civil War," in Ronald H. Bayor and Timothy J. Meagher, eds., *The New York Irish* (Baltimore, 1996), 194; Ridge, *Sligo in New York*, 14, 15, 18 (quotation).

27. Carol Groneman, "Working-Class Immigrant Women in Mid-Nineteenth Century New York: The Irish Woman's Experience," *Journal of Urban History* 4 (1978): 267; *OUA*, April 7, 28, 1849; Tyler Anbinder, "'Boss' Tweed: Nativist," *Journal of the Early Republic* 15 (Spring 1995): 109–16; Luc Sante, *Low Life: Lures and Snares of Old New York* (New York, 1991), 253.

28. The group sold the tenement at some point between 1892 and 1905. Craig S. Wilder, "The Rise and Influence of the New York African Society for Mutual Relief, 1808–1865," *Afro-Americans in New York Life and History* 22 (July 1998): 7–9; Kernan, *Reminiscences*, 41; John J. Zuille, *Historical Sketch of the New York African Society for Mutual Relief* (New York, [1892?]), 16; Samuel R. Scottron, "New York African Society for Mutual Relief— Ninety-Seventh Anniversary," *Colored American Magazine* 9 (December 1905): 685–90.

29. Ridge, *Sligo in New York*, 13; John T. Ridge, "Irish County Societies in New York, 1880–1914," in Bayor and Meagher, eds., *New York Irish*, 275–79; Robert Ernst, *Immigrant Life in New York City, 1825–1863* (1949; Port Washington, NY, 1965), 122.

30. Ridge, *Sligo in New York*, 14 (including *Irish-American* quotation), 18; *Irish-American*, February 17, 1850.

31. Ridge, *Sligo in New York*, 17–20; *Irish-American*, August 3, 31, December 28, 1850, February 22, 1851; Ridge, "Irish County Societies," 278.

32. Harlow, *Old Bowery Days*, 234–56; Reynolds, *Walt Whitman's America*, 104; *Herald*, August 29, 1836, in Timothy J. Gilfoyle, *City of Eros: New York City, Prostitution, and the Commercialization of Sex, 1790–1920* (New York, 1992), 110; Mathews, *Pen-and-Ink-Panorama*, 187; Browne, *Great Metropolis*, 430; Foster, *New York Naked*, quoted in Peter G. Buckley, "To the Opera House: Culture and Society in New York City, 1820–1860" (Ph.D. dissertation, State University of New York at Stony Brook, 1984), 161.

33. Haswell quoted in Harlow, *Old Bowery Days*, 382–85.

34. Harlow, *Old Bowery Days*, 260, 265–67, 385; *The Diary of Philip Hone, 1828–1851*, Allan Nevins, ed. (New York, 1936), 273.

35. Harlow, *Old Bowery Days*, 206; Stott, *Workers in the Metropolis*, 223–25; *Herald*, April 26, 1848 (on the popularity of the Mose series).

36. Richard Moody, *Ned Harrigan: From Corlear's Hook to Herald Square* (Chicago, 1980), 72, 241; *Frank Leslie's Illustrated Newspaper* (January 17, 1874): 316; *Herald*, February 20, 1874; Herbert Asbury, *The Gangs of New York: An Informal History of the Underworld* (New York, 1928), 244; Sante, *Low Life*, 91. The *Herald* and *Frank Leslie's Illustrated Newspaper* placed the theater at 17 and 19 Baxter Street respectively.

37. *Doggett's New York City Street Directory for 1851.* Sometimes the distinction between a saloon and a grocery was imperceptible. Some of the "grocers" listed in the directory were labeled saloonkeepers in the census, and vice versa.

38. "Report of the Select Committee Appointed to Examine into the Condition of Tenant Houses in New-York and Brooklyn," *Documents of the Assembly of the State of New-York, Eightieth Session—1857*, doc. 205 (Albany, 1857), 25–26; *Clipper*, October 3, 1868, p. 204 (all but final quotation); Charles Loring Brace, *The Dangerous Classes of New York and Twenty Years Work Among Them*, 3rd ed. (New York, 1872), 207; [Foster], *New York in Slices*, 79, 82, 84; *Tribune*, August 10, 1846.

39. *Monthly Record of the Five Points House of Industry* 1 (January 1858): 224–25; Foster, *New York by Gas-Light*, 128–29.

40. Family 128, fifth election district, Sixth Ward, 1855 New York state census; *Times*, January 22, 1853; *Monthly Record of the Five Points House of Industry* 1 (January 1858): 224–25; 3 (March 1860): 249; *Doggett's New York City Directory for 1849–50* (New York, 1849), 112; *Longworth's New York City Directory for 1840–41* (New York, 1840), 185 (which describes the establishment as a "tavern" rather than a grocery). That 1,000 people per day patronized Crown's is based on *Monthly Record of the Five Points House of Industry* 3 (March 1860): 249, which reported that on Sunday, January 22, 1860, 1,054 people entered Crown's Grocery and the saloon "directly opposite" in a five-hour stretch from 10:00 a.m. to 3:00 p.m. Of these, 1,054, 547 went into the "saloon" and 507 went into "Crown's." I suspect that the "saloon" was merely the entrance to the barroom of Crown's itself. But even if this was not the case, if 507 went into Crown's in five hours, it seems safe to assume that more than 1,000 would enter the grocery during the course of an entire business day.

41. Stott, *Workers in the Metropolis*, 218–19; Breen, *Thirty Years*, 251–52, 255. Ethnicity of saloon and grocery operators is based on an examination of surnames in *Doggett's New York City Street Directory for 1851*, supplemented by information from the 1855 New York manuscript census. I found twenty-four grocers who were obviously Irish Americans, forty-four with German-American surnames, and twenty-nine whose last names did not clearly indicate a certain ethnicity. Among saloonkeepers, eighty-seven were Irish, twenty were German, and forty could not be securely identified.

42. *Sun*, May 29, 1834; Sante, *Low Life*, 105; Walsh in Edward K. Spann, *The New Metropolis: New York City, 1840–1857* (New York, 1981), 348. Brace, *Dangerous Classes*, 64–65; William Hancock, *An Emigrant's Five Years in the Free States of America* (London, 1860), 76, in Stott, *Workers in the Metropolis*, 220; Harlow, *Old Bowery Days*, 379; *Clipper*, October 3, 1868, p. 204; J. H. Green, *Report on Gambling in New York* (New York, 1851), 85–89.

43. John F. Maguire, *The Irish in America* (London, 1868), 287.

44. Charles Stelzle, *A Son of the Bowery: The Life Story of an East Side American* (New York, 1926), 47–48; Carl Wittke, *We Who Built America*, in Edward M. Levine, *The Irish and Irish Politicians* (Notre Dame, 1966), 117; Breen, *Thirty Years*, 231.

45. Leon Beauvallet, *Rachel and the New World: A Trip to the United States and Cuba* (New York, 1856), 274; *Tribune*, October 12, 1863; Green, *Report on Gambling*, 93. "Rachel" was Elisa Rachel Félix, the most famous French actress of the 1840s and '50s. Beauvallet was an actor and aspiring playwright in the troupe that toured the United States with her.

46. Dickens, *American Notes*, 79; Foster, *New York by Gas-Light*, 87; Green, *Report on Gambling*, 73–74 ("wait upon the players"); account 5735, Emigrant Savings Bank Test Books.

47. *National Police Gazette*, October 11, 1845, May 30, 1846 (Moses); *Tribune*, February 27, 1855; Green, *Report on Gambling*, 45–46; *Clipper*, October 3, 1868; Ann Fabian, *Card Sharps, Dream Books, and Bucket Shops: Gambling in Nineteenth-Century America* (Ithaca, 1990), 136–50; F. Norton Goddard, "Policy: A Tenement House Evil," in Robert W. DeForest and Lawrence Veiller, eds., *The Tenement House Problem*, 2 vols. (1903; New York, 1970): 2: 27–31.

48. Kernan, *Reminiscences*, 41–42; *Monthly Record of the Five Points House of Industry* 1 (October 1857): 146–47.

49. Foster, *New York by Gas-Light*, 143; Kernan, *Reminiscences*, 42, 44; *Monthly Record of the Five Points House of Industry* 1 (October 1857): 146–47; *Tribune*, October 12, 1863.

50. *Clipper*, October 21, 1860 ("Uncle Pete's"), October 3, 1868 ("great mogul"); John Doggett, Jr., ed., *The New-York City and Co-Partnership Directory* (New York, 1843), 367; Foster, *New York by Gas-Light*, 145. It is possible that Williams's place later relocated to 51 Orange, for in 1852 "Pete Williams 51 Orange" is listed among a number of saloonkeepers operating without a license. Unlike the others on the list, however, Williams was never charged—New York County District Attorney's Indictment Papers, April 22, 23, 24, 1852, New York Municipal Archives. He may have moved after a fire destroyed his previous establishment. See Foster, *New York by Gas-Light*, 140–41.

51. *The Prose Works of N. P. Willis* (1845; new ed. in one vol., Philadelphia, 1849), 582–83; Dickens, *American Notes*, 80–83; Foster, *New York by Gas-Light*, 141; *Monthly Record of the Five Points House of Industry* 1 (October 1857): 148; *Clipper*, October 21, 1860.

52. Foster, *New York by Gas-Light*, 142–43; *Monthly Record of the Five Points House of Industry* 1 (October 1857): 149. For other descriptions of Williams's place, see *Harper's Weekly*, February 21, 1857; [Bobo], *Glimpses of New-York City*, 96; Samuel Prime, *Life in New York* (New York, 1847), 175.

CHAPTER SEVEN

1. *Tribune*, October 20, 1856; *Clipper*, July 9, 1864.

2. Ed James, *The Life and Battles of Yankee Sullivan* (New York, n.d.), 3–5.

3. Ibid., 3–12, 21; *Times*, June 30, 1854; George Foster quoted in Richard B. Stott, *Workers in the Metropolis: Class, Ethnicity, and Youth in Antebellum New York* (Ithaca, 1990), 234.

4. James, *Life and Battles of Yankee Sullivan*, 11; *Times*, May 14, 1876 (obituary of another Five Pointer mentioning sparring match at Monroe Hall); *Tribune*, April 12, 1842; *Herald*, September 26, 27, October 21, November 1849. For the 1842 riot, see Chapter Five.

5. James, *Life and Battles of Yankee Sullivan*, 13–19 ("*must fight*"); *Clipper*, November 17, 1860 ("pride of Chatham Square"), July 9, 1864.

6. Ed James, *Life and Battles of Tom Hyer* (New York, n.d.), 7–12; *Herald*, February 8 ("urchins") and 9 (other quotations), 1849; Wallace Shugg, "'This Great Test of Man's Brutality': The Sullivan-Hyer Prizefight at Still Pond Heights, Maryland, in 1849," *Maryland Historical Magazine* 95 (2000): 47–63.

7. James, *Life and Battles of Tom Hyer*, 12–14; *Clipper*, July 9, 1864 ("native boys").

8. James, *Life and Battles of Tom Hyer*, 14–18 (quotations); James, *Life and Battles of Yankee Sullivan*, 18–20.

9. *Clipper*, July 9, 1864; William L. Riordan, *Plunkitt of Tammany Hall*, ed. Terrence J. McDonald (Boston, 1994), 95.

10. James, *Life and Battles of Tom Hyer*, 20–24; *Doggett's New York City Street Directory for 1848–49* (New York, 1848), 393; *Doggett's New York City Directory for 1849–50* (New York, 1849), 220; *Times*, June 30, 1856 (Sullivan), June 27, 1864 (Hyer); *Tribune*, March 10, 1855. James places the Branch Hotel at 40 Bowery, but the city directories show that it was located at no. 36.

11. William F. Barnard, *Forty Years at the Five Points: A Sketch of the Five Points House of Industry* (New York, 1893), 2; *Herald*, February 17, 1858; "The Five Points," *National Magazine* 2 (1853): 169.

12. John Francis Richmond, *New York and Its Institutions, 1609–1872* (New York, 1872), 477–78; [Foster], *New York in Slices*, 23; letter of L. M. Pease in *Times*, November 19, 1852; Foster, *New York by Gas-Light*, 122; *Evening Post*, January 30, 1846.

13. Locations of brothels based on a list compiled by Professor Timothy Gilfoyle, Loyola University of Chicago, in the possession of the author. Gilfoyle's inventory is based primarily on criminal indictments. See, for example, indictments of September 21, 1841 (charging inhabitants of 139 Anthony Street), April 15, 1850 (142 Anthony and 34 Orange), February 21, 1851 (50, 62, 67, and 71 Cross), May 23, 1851 (151 Anthony and 6 Little Water), January 23, 1852 (145 Anthony and 89 Cross), April 22, 1852 (163 Anthony and 33, 35, 36½, 40, and 41 Orange), April 23, 1852 (143, 149, and 157 Anthony, and 92 Cross)—New York County District Attorney's Indictment Papers, New York Municipal Archives.

    These records must be used with some caution. Not every person indicted was necessarily guilty, though notations on the indictment papers indicate that most were convicted, pled guilty, or promised to abandon the premises (thus implying guilt). In addition, it was possible to be charged with conducting a "disorderly house" that was merely a raucous saloon rather than a brothel. I accept Gilfoyle's contention, however, that the vast majority of those charged with this offense promoted prostitution. That most of those indicted for "keeping a disorderly house" responded by vacating the premises also implies that these were brothels. If those under indictment were only operating loud saloons, they could have merely asked their customers to be quieter. One might also argue that prosecution for prostitution over the course of two decades does not prove that these buildings housed brothels *simultaneously*. But brothel keepers were generally only prosecuted for keeping a "disorderly" house of prostitution. As a result, indictments were relatively rare, and were only handed up when neighbors repeatedly complained about persistent disturbances in the bordellos. So indictments probably underestimate the pervasiveness of prostitution in Five Points.

14. Christine Stansell, *City of Women: Sex and Class in New York, 1789–1860* (Urbana, 1982), 183; Marilynn Wood Hill, *Their Sisters' Keepers: Prostitution in New York City, 1830–1870* (Berkeley, 1993), 49 (eleven-year-old); deposition of Mary O'Daniel, December 19, 1851, in indictment of Bridget McCarty, January 20, 1852, New York County District Attorney's Indictment Papers; *Herald,* October 6, 1853 (Hoffman); case of Elizabeth Dayton in Gilfoyle, *City of Eros,* 66; *Pease v. Mangin,* August 1, 1855, Box 7953, Police Court Cases, New York Municipal Archives; William W. Sanger, *The History of Prostitution* (1859; New York, 1937), 452.

15. Gilfoyle, *City of Eros,* 39; Sanger, *History of Prostitution,* 475–77; *Annual Report of the Trustees of the Five Points House of Industry* (1855): 20–24. Sanger found that 947 of the 2,000 prostitutes surveyed had children. Of these, 357 (38%) were single, 357 were married (though the majority of these were separated or had been abandoned), and 233 (25%) were widows.

16. *Times,* March 2, 1859.

17. Depositions of Mary O'Daniel, Ellen Cable, and Bridget McCarty, in indictment of Bridget McCarty, January 20, 1852, New York County District Attorney's Indictment Papers; *Herald,* February 7, 1852.

18. *Clipper,* October 3, 1868; Gilfoyle, *City of Eros,* 164–65, 352; Patricia Cline Cohen, *The Murder of Helen Jewett: The Life and Death of a Prostitute in Nineteenth-Century New York* (New York, 1998), 98. A brothel still operated at 3 Franklin as late as 1851. See William H. Bell Diary, February 21, 1851, New-York Historical Society.

19. Gilfoyle, *City of Eros,* 173; William H. Bell Diary, February 6, 1851; *Herald,* April 10, 1841; Matthew H. Smith, *Sunshine and Shadow in New York* (Hartford, 1868), 490–93; George Ellington, *The Women of New York* (New York, 1869), 203–5.

20. Foster, *New York by Gas-Light,* 122; *The Prose Works of N. P. Willis* (1845; new ed. in one vol., Philadelphia, 1849), 582–83; Robert F. Lucid, ed., *The Journal of Richard Henry Dana, Jr.,* 3 vols. (Cambridge, MA, 1968), 1: 232–33; Walt Whitman, *New York Dissected,* ed. Emory Holloway and Ralph Adimari (New York, 1936), 6, 217–18, in Reynolds, *Whitman,* 228; [Foster], *New York in Slices,* 23.

21. Lucid, ed., *Journal of Richard Henry Dana, Jr.,* 1: 119–21, 232–33. The question of how many prostitutes worked in Five Points is impossible to answer with any certainty. In 1860, by which point religious institutions had managed to chase a significant number of brothels from the neighborhood, a careful survey found 180 prostitutes living in the area bounded by Centre, Leonard, Orange, Bayard, Mulberry, Chatham, and Pearl Streets. One imagines that a decade earlier, as destitute and rootless immigrants flooded the neighborhood, double that number could have worked in Five Points, while prostitutes residing elsewhere would have brought their customers to houses of assignation in the district as well—*Monthly Record of the Five Points House of Industry* 4 (April 1860): 16.

22. Foster in Gilfoyle, *City of Eros,* 59; Sanger, *History of Prostitution,* 491, 600–601; Stansell, *City of Women,* 122–23; letter of Henry R. Remsen, et al., in *Times,* October 15, 1853.

23. Sanger, *History of Prostitution,* 488–89.

24. Ibid.; Foster, *New York by Gas-Light*, 130.

25. Sanger, *History of Prostitution*, 484, 523; Ellington, *Women of New York*, 183–84; Gilfoyle, *City of Eros*, 55–56, 60–61.

26. Hill, *Their Sisters' Keepers*, 102, 104, 183.

27. Gilfoyle, *City of Eros*, 71–73, 351–52.

28. Indictments of March 14, 1842, September 14 and October 9, 1843, New York County District Attorney's Indictment Papers.

29. *Advocate of Moral Reform* 9 (August 15, 1843): 127; *Herald*, April 7, September 14, 1849, October 6, 1853; indictments of May 16, 23, 1851, New York County District Attorney's Indictment Papers; *Times*, May 23, 24, 1855.

30. *Evening Post*, September 21, 1826 ("CORNELIUS" to the Editor), March 19, 1829.

31. *Times*, July 4 (White), 13 (McCasken), 1857; *William Tracy v. Maria Gorman alias Carey*, indictment of March 26, 1853, New York County District Attorney's Indictment Papers.

32. *Herald*, February 25, 1850; William H. Bell Diary, October 10, 1850, May 2, 1851.

33. William H. Bell Diary, February 7, April 2–3, 1851; Sante, *Low Life*, 310; "Autobiography of George Appo," typescript, pp. 1–3, Society for the Prevention of Crime Papers, Columbia University; Stansell, *City of Women*, 50. For the stories of children forced to steal by alcoholic parents in order to finance their liquor habits, see John Morrow, *A Voice from the Newsboys* (New York, 1860), 27–36, and Edward W. Martin [James D. McCabe], *The Secrets of the Great City* (Philadelphia, 1868), 192–96.

34. *National Police Gazette* in Edward Van Every, *Sins of New York as "Exposed" by the Police Gazette* (1930; New York, 1972), 285; *Herald*, August 19, 1849; *Monthly Record of the Five Points House of Industry* 2 (September 1858): 97–99.

35. *Herald*, February 22, 25, 1850; *Times*, February 1, 1853; account 3347, Emigrant Savings Bank Test Books, New York Public Library (Dowdican).

36. William H. Bell Diary, November 28, 1850, May 3, 1851; indictment of January 23, 1852, New York County District Attorney's Indictment Papers.

37. *Herald*, July 12, 1849 (Peterson), February 12, 1852 (Wilson); *National Police Gazette* in Van Every, *Sins of New York*, 284 (Rice and Moran); *Times*, February 11, 1852 (Wilson), July 13, 1857 (Gannon).

38. *Times*, January 22, 1853 (Adams and Tucker), December 14, 1872.

39. *Times*, July 1, 1859 ("banging his wife"); *Tribune*, August 6, 1850; *The Old Brewery and the New Mission House at the Five Points, By Ladies of the Mission* (New York, 1854), 154–55.

40. *People v. George Holberton, et al.*, February 11, 1852, New York County District Attorney's Indictment Papers; *Herald*, January 27, February 12, 19, 1852. For the other rape case, see *National Police Gazette* in Van Every, *Sins of New York*, 284.

41. *Herald*, January 12, 1841, October 27, 29, 1849. The press did not report any resolution to the Rafferty case, and there is no indication of an indictment in the District Attorney's Papers.

42. *Annual Report of the New-York Ladies' Home Missionary Society* (1867): 27–28, (1870): 12; entries of September 26, 1856 and June 13, 1860, Adoption Case Histories, Five Points Mission Papers, United Methodist Church Archives, Drew University.

43. Graham Hodges, "'Desirable Companions and Lovers': Irish and African Americans in the Sixth Ward, 1830–1870," in Ronald H. Bayor and Timothy J. Meagher, eds., *The New York Irish* (Baltimore, 1996), 114.

44. *Times,* June 14, November 23, 24, 1853, November 28, 1863 (another liquor-related murder). For a previous case of "skylarking," see *Tribune,* October 18, 1849.

45. *Evening Post,* September 14, 1846; *Herald,* January 6, 1868; *Times,* January 6, February 18–21, March 10–11, 1868.

46. *Herald,* April 19, May 2, 1851; William H. Bell Diary, May 1–2, 1851.

47. *Herald,* January 17–19, April 20, May 5–8, 11, June 16–17, 1859; *Times,* February 12, 1863; Nelson J. Waterbury to Horatio Seymour, December 26, 1864 (on Matthew Brennan's use of political pressure to get the Glasses pardoned), Seymour Papers, New-York Historical Society; *Manual of the Corporation of the City of New-York for 1858* (New York, 1858), 102 (Glass as foreman).

48. *Tribune,* March 16, 22, 1855, January 30, 1857.

49. Annual Report of Fire Chief Alfred Carson in New York Board of Aldermen, *Documents* 17, part II, no. 57 (September 3, 1850): 930–32; Tom Quick, "Old Sports of New York," in *Leader,* September 1, 1860.

50. Denis T. Lynch, *The Wild Seventies,* 2 vols. (1941; Port Washington, NY, 1971), 1: 9–13. See also *Irish-American,* August 19, 1849; *Tribune,* March 18, 1854; *Herald,* November 3, 1849, February 25, 1852.

51. Board of Aldermen, *Documents* 23 (1856), doc. 16, pp. 4–11; *Manual of the Corporation of the City of New York for 1870* (New York, 1870), 96–97.

52. *Old Brewery,* 94; "Autobiography of George Appo," 1–3; *Tribune,* June 13, 1850 (alcoholics living in cellar boarding establishments); *Herald,* June 10, 1863.

53. Entries of September 20 (Bertram), October 18, 20, 1856, Adoption Case Histories, Five Points Mission Papers; Ellington, *Women of New York,* 604–5.

54. Entry of August 7, 1856, Adoption Case Histories, Five Points Mission Papers; Samuel B. Halliday, *The Lost and Found; or Life Among the Poor* (New York, 1859), 126–29; Chas. J. Wood to "Dear Friend," April 8, 1877, in *Twenty-fourth Annual Report of the Children's Aid Society* (1876): 65.

55. *Monthly Record of the Five Points House of Industry* 1 (June 1857): 66–67 ("mother was dead"); 2 (April 1859): 277–81; Martin, *Secrets of the Great City,* 192–96.

56. *Monthly Record of the Five Points House of Industry* 1 (February 1858): 255–56; *Twenty-third Annual Report of the New-York Ladies' Home Missionary Society* (1867): 7; Kildare, *My Mamie Rose* (New York, 1903), 24. Also see Browne, *Great Metropolis,* 277.

57. *Annual Report of the Metropolitan Board of Health [for] 1866* (New York, 1867), 135 (quotation); Hasia Diner, *Erin's Daughters in America: Irish Immigrant Women in the Nineteenth Century* (Baltimore, 1983), 113; Pat McGowan to his parents, December 21, 1847, BR146/10/13, Broadlands Papers, University of Southampton; John F. Maguire, *The Irish in America* (London, 1868), 282–85.

58. *Minutes of the Common Council of the City of New York, 1784–1831*, 19 vols. (New York, 1917), 17: 421; Foster, *New York by Gas-Light*, 121; [Bobo], *Glimpses of New-York City*, 95, 97; *Herald*, February 19, 1852.

CHAPTER EIGHT

1. David H. Donald, *Lincoln* (New York, 1995), 237–38.

2. Andrew A. Freeman, *Abraham Lincoln Goes to New York* (New York, 1960), 1–21, 58–66 (quotation p. 17).

3. Francis F. Browne, *The Every-Day Life of Abraham Lincoln* (New York, 1886), 323; William F. Barnard, *Forty Years at the Five Points: A Sketch of the Five Points House of Industry* (New York, 1893), 69.

4. Henry J. Raymond, *History of the Administration of President Lincoln* (New York, 1864), 42–43.

5. *Times*, July 10, 1897, p. 12; Denise Bethel, "Mr. Halliday's Album," *Seaport* 28 (Fall 1994): 16–21; Massachusetts Commission on Hours of Labor, *Reports of the Commissioners on the Hours of Labor* (Boston, 1867), 102 (quotation).

6. Samuel B. Halliday, *The Lost and Found; or Life Among the Poor* (New York, 1859), 118–23. When Halliday's book was reprinted in 1861 the title was changed to *The Little Street Sweeper*, a decision that reflected the appeal of Mullen's story.

7. Halliday, *Lost and Found*, 53–55, 123 (quotation); Bethel, "Mr. Halliday's Album," 16–21.

8. Donald, *Lincoln*, 238–40; *Tribune*, February 28, 1860. For Hyer's presence in Chicago, see Murat Halstead, *The Caucuses of 1860: A History of the National Political Conventions of the Current Presidential Campaign* (Columbus, OH, 1860), 141.

9. *Frank Leslie's Illustrated Newspaper* (August 16, 1873): 363 ("no church"); David Clarkson, *History of the Church of Zion and St. Timothy, 1797–1894* (New York, 1894), 60 ("idolatrous"); *Tribune*, February 19, 1855; Graham Hodges, "'Desirable Companions and Lovers': Irish and African Americans in the Sixth Ward, 1830–1870," in Ronald Bayor and Timothy Meagher, eds., *The New York Irish* (Baltimore, 1996), 111–12; *Times*, April 11, 1860 ("peculiar repulsiveness").

10. Hyman B. Grinstein, *The Rise of the Jewish Community of New York, 1654–1860* (Philadelphia, 1945), 472–74.

11. Ibid., 50–52, 54–55, 295.

12. Ibid., 50–52, 295.

13. Ibid., 62–64, 172, 341, 345. A "seatholder" was allowed to attend services but could not vote for the officers of the congregation.

14. Ibid., 50, 472–77; J. D. Eisenstein, "The History of the First Russian-American Jewish Congregation," *Publications of the American Jewish Historical Society* 9 (1901): 63–65; Barnard, *Forty Years at the Five Points*, 8.

15. Christine Stansell, *City of Women: Sex and Class in New York, 1789–1860* (Urbana, 1982), 69; *Advocate of Moral Reform* 5 (September 9, 1839): 130; Carroll Smith Rosenberg, *Religion and the Rise of the American City: The New York City Mission Movement, 1812–1870* (Ithaca, 1971), 206–7.

16. Rosenberg, *Religion*, 206–7, 247–48, 251, 255; *Annual Report of the New York Association for Improving the Condition of the Poor* 3 (1846): 15–20.

17. *Monthly Record of the Five Points House of Industry* 1 (1857): 114; *Times*, April 11, 1860; *Tribune*, January 16, 1855.

18. *Annual Report of the New-York Ladies' Home Missionary Society of the Methodist Episcopal Church* 1 (1845): 13; *The Old Brewery, and the New Mission House at the Five Points, By Ladies of the Mission* (New York, 1854), 36 (quoting their annual report of 1848).

19. *Old Brewery*, 36, 38; entry of July 1,1851, New-York Ladies' Home Missionary Society of the Methodist Episcopal Church Board Minute Book (hereafter cited as Board Minute Book), Five Points Mission Records, United Methodist Church Archives, Drew University.

20. Letter of Henry R. Remsen, et al., in *Times*, October 15, 1853 ("gin shop"); *Annual Report of the New-York Ladies' Home Missionary Society* 32 (1876): 6–8; family 1069, fifth election district, Sixth Ward, 1855 New York State manuscript census, Old Records Division, New York County Clerk's Office; *Five Points Monthly* (March 1854): 4, in Isaac J. Quillen, "A History of the Five Points to 1890: The Evolution of a Slum" (M.A. thesis, Yale University, 1932), 49 (Lenox); entry of April 1,1851, Board Minute Book, Five Points Mission Records.

21. Letter of L. M. Pease in *Times*, November 19, 1852.

22. *Times*, December 15, 1853.

23. *Times*, November 19, 1852.

24. *Times*, November 19, 1852 (quotation), October 15, 1853; Barnard, *Forty Years at the Five Points*, 14–15; *Monthly Record of the Five Points House of Industry* 2 (1858): 77–78. The dates Pease gives for the commencement of these activities differ in his various accounts. Those used here seem most consistent with other contemporary evidence.

25. *Times*, November 19, December 21 (Pease to the editor), 1852; entry of September 3, 1850, Board Minute Book, Five Points Mission Records.

26. Entries of March 4 (quotation) and June 6, 1851, Board Minute Book, Five Points Mission Records; *Times*, November 19, 1852, October 15, 1853; Rosenberg, *Religion*, 232–33; *Old Brewery*, 40–41; *Annual Report of the New-York Ladies' Home Missionary Society* 7 (1851): 9–10. Although Carroll Smith Rosenberg states in *Religion and the Rise of the American City*, 233, that she used the "Five Points House [of Industry] Archives" for her work, I was not able to track down the current location of these papers.

27. Entry of February 3, 1852, Board Minute Book, Five Points Mission Records; *Old Brewery*, 42, 64, 80, 214–22; John Francis Richmond, *New York and Its Institutions, 1609–1872* (New York, 1872), 480; *Times*, January 28, 1853; *Gleason's Pictorial Drawing-Room Companion* 4 (January 15, 1853): 40.

28. *Times*, October 11, 16, 1852; *Freeman's Journal*, October 16, 1852. *Old Brewery*, 63, states that the city *did* contribute $1,000 toward the project, but I could find no record of any such expenditure in the Common Council records.

29. *Old Brewery*, 64; *Tribune*, June 18, 1853; *Monthly Record of the Five Points House of Industry* 2 (1859): 210; 8 [really 9] (April 1866): 185; Barnard, *Forty Years at the Five Points*, 19–22; *Times*, February 7, 1870.

30. *Freeman's Journal*, October 15, 1853; *Tribune*, June 18, 1853; *Old Brewery*, 77; *Annual Report of the New-York Ladies' Home Missionary Society* 12 (1856): 8–9; 23 (1867): 30–31.

31. *Monthly Record of the Five Points House of Industry* 2 (May 1858): 8; *Times*, November 19, 1852, October 4, 1853.

32. Edward K. Spann, *The New Metropolis: New York City, 1840–1857* (New York, 1981), 78; *Tribune*, December 15, 1848 (Tyng and Griscom's House of Industry); *Freeman's Journal*, February 5, March 4, 1848; Brace, *Short Sermons to News Boys* (New York, 1866), 9–10; [New York] *Christian Advocate and Journal* (December 8, 1853): 194, (February 22, 1855): 30 (quotation). Charles Fourier was an early nineteenth-century French critic of capitalism who advocated the establishment of agricultural communes.

33. Rosenberg, *Religion*, 229–30, 234; Benson J. Lossing, *History of New York City* (New York, 1884), 632; *Monthly Record of the Five Points House of Industry* 1 (1857): 37; 2 (1858): 116–17; *Annual Report of the New-York Ladies' Home Missionary Society* 24 (1868): 7; 26 (1870): 11; 28 (1872): 10–11; 35 (1879): 8.

34. *Times*, December 21, 1852 ("soup-room"), October 15, 1853 ("the room so stank"); Charles Loring Brace, *The Dangerous Classes of New York and Twenty Years Work Among Them*, 3rd ed. (New York, 1872), 132, 143; [New York] *Christian Advocate and Journal* (December 8, 1853): 194.

35. Entries of May 6, July 1, 1851, November 14, 1854, December 2, 1856, Board Minute Book, Five Points Mission Records; Pease to the Editor, October 3, 1853, in *Times*, October 4, 1853.

36. *Freeman's Journal*, October 15, 1853; *Times*, October 4, 13, 1853.

37. *Herald*, October 10, 1853 (story written by Pease); A. Stonelake to the Editor, *Tribune*, October 24, 1853; *Freeman's Journal*, October 15, 1853.

38. *Times*, October 13, 1853; Benjamin M. Adams to the Editor, *Tribune*, October 13, 1853; entry of October 7, 1856, Board Minute Book, Five Points Mission Records; *Annual Report of the New-York Ladies' Home Missionary Society* 20 (1864): 7; Rev. Thomas P. McLoughlin, "The Passing Away of Tony Gimp," *Catholic Youth* (1899), in Peter P. McLoughlin, *Father Tom: Life and Lectures of Rev. Thomas P. McLoughlin* (New York, 1919), 85.

39. *Old Brewery*, 80; *Monthly Record of the Five Points House of Industry* 1 (1857): 179; 2 (1859): 250; Rosenberg, *Religion*, 237; *Annual Report of the New-York Ladies' Home Missionary Society* 12 (1856): 8–9.

40. *Times*, May 9, 1866; *Annual Report of the New-York Ladies' Home Missionary Society* 24 (1868): 7; Lossing, *History of New York City*, 631.

41. *Old Brewery*, 88.

42. *Voice from the Old Brewery*, May 1, 1869. By 1857, even the House of Industry emphasized the religious motivation behind its distribution of food and clothing. "We call our entire work a mission work, even to feeding the hungry and clothing the naked," stated its *Monthly Record*. "Nothing but illness . . . will be accepted as an excuse for the absence of any individual" from morning or evening prayer services. Such statements, so unlike Pease's earlier remarks, suggest that the organization began to change significantly after he left Five Points in early 1857 to take charge of the House of Industry's Westchester County farm—*Monthly Record of the Five Points House of Industry* 1 (1857): 125–26.

43. *America As I Found It. By the Mother of Mary Lundie Duncan* (New York, 1852), 87–88.

44. "Five Points Mission: Historical Presentation," Five Points Mission Records. For the shoe club, see *Voice from the Old Brewery*, passim.

45. *Times*, December 20, 1852; Jacob A. Riis, *How the Other Half Lives: Studies Among the Tenements of New York* (1890; New York, 1971), 151.

46. *Irish-American*, February 25, October 14 ("Publicola"), 1854; *Freeman's Journal*, October 15, 1853.

47. Entries of September 20, October 18, 1856, Adoption Case Histories, entry of January 6, 1857, Board Minute Book, Five Points Mission Records; Francis E. Lane, *American Charities and the Child of the Immigrant* (Washington, DC, 1932), 88; *Monthly Record of the Five Points House of Industry* 1 (1858): 228–29.

48. *Monthly Record of the Five Points House of Industry* 1 (1857): 3–5, 127.

49. Entry of October 7, 1856, Board Minute Book, Five Points Mission Records; *Monthly Record of the Five Points House of Industry* 1 (1857): 125–27; Barnard, *Forty Years at the Five Points*, 34; Rosenberg, *Religion*, 234–35.

50. *Monthly Record of the Five Points House of Industry* 1 (1858): 252–54, 265.

51. *Annual Report of the Trustees of the Five Points House of Industry* (1855): 15–18; *Monthly Record of the Five Points House of Industry* 1 (1857): 15; Halliday, *Lost and Found*, 95–96.

52. *Tribune*, November 22, 1856. For the Children's Aid Society adoption efforts, see Miriam Z. Langsam, *Children West: A History of the Placing-Out System of the New York Children's Aid Society, 1853–1890* (Madison, 1964).

53. Entry of July 1, 1856, Board Minute Book, Five Points Mission Records; *Belleville Weekly Democrat*, April 17, 1858, quoted in Marilyn I. Holt, *The Orphan Trains: Placing Out in America* (Lincoln, 1992), 99–100; *Voice from the Old Brewery* 1 (June 1, 1861): 24; John Morrow, *A Voice from the Newsboys* (New York, 1860), 95–98; Langsam, *Children West*, 27; Brace, *Dangerous Classes*, 241. The mission and House of Industry never released figures on the precise number of children they gave up for adoption.

54. *Monthly Record of the Five Points House of Industry* 2 (1859): 235–36; *Annual Report of the New-York Ladies' Home Missionary Society* 23 (1867): 31; entries of November 8, 23, 1856, Adoption Case Histories, Five Points Mission Records.

55. *Annual Report of the Children's Aid Society* 8 (1861): 11–12; Adoption Case Histories, Five Points Mission Records; *Monthly Record of the Five Points House of Industry*, passim.

56. *Annual Report of the Trustees of the Five Points House of Industry* (1855): 15–16; entry of August 15, 1856, Adoption Case Histories, Five Points Mission Records.

57. Solon Robinson, *Hot Corn: Life Scenes in New York Illustrated* (New York, 1854), 52–75 and ff. (quotation p. 54). Mission officials groused that Maggie was never really as wild as Pease claimed, but the life story of the Maggie they describe is so different from that of Robinson's "Wild Maggie" that they must be different children—*Old Brewery*, 182–90.

58. Entries of September 16, 1856, January 29, 1857, Adoption Case Histories, Five Points Mission Records.

59. Entries of July 25, December 5, 1856, Adoption Case Histories, Five Points Mission Records.

60. Entries of August 20, October 14, 1856, Adoption Case Histories, Five Points Mission Records; *Monthly Record of the Five Points House of Industry* 2 (1858): 66–67.

61. *Annual Report of the Trustees of the Five Points House of Industry* (1855): 16–18.

62. *Monthly Record of the Five Points House of Industry* 1 (1857): 136–42.

63. Morrow, *Voice from the Newsboys,* 91–92.

64. *Annual Report of the Trustees of the Five Points House of Industry* (1855): 20–24.

65. *Monthly Record of the Five Points House of Industry* 1 (1857): 87–90.

66. Ibid., 212–14.

67. *Irish-American,* April 23, 1859.

68. *Irish-American,* November 14, 1863; *Freeman's Journal,* May 2, 1863; "Public Charities," *Catholic World* 17 (1873): 3–7, in Langsam, *Children West,* 52; Brace, *Dangerous Classes,* 234–35.

69. Lane, *American Charities and the Child of the Immigrant,* 118; Holt, *Orphan Trains,* 62–63, 99–100; Langsam, *Children West,* 56, 65; Brace, *Dangerous Classes,* 268.

70. Clarkson, *History of the Church of Zion and St. Timothy,* 60–63; John G. Shea, *The Catholic Churches of New York City* (New York, 1878), 693–96; *Transfiguration Church: A Church of Immigrants, 1827–1977* (New York, 1977), 9; Jay P. Dolan, "Urban Catholicism: New York City, 1815–1865" (Ph.D. dissertation, University of Chicago, 1970), 313–17; Dolan, *The Immigrant Church: New York's Irish and German Catholics, 1815–1865* (Baltimore, 1975), 47–51 (quotation).

71. *Freeman's Journal,* February 20, 1847; Holt, *Orphan Trains,* 106–7, 112–13; Langsam, *Children West,* 48; John F. Maguire, *The Irish in America* (London, 1868), 512–14.

72. *Evening Post,* February 7, 1854; *Old Brewery,* 64; *Gleason's Pictorial Drawing-Room Companion* 4 (January 15, 1853): 48; *America As I Found It,* 90–91.

73. *Annual Report of the New York Association for Improving the Condition of the Poor* 16 (1859): 39; *Harper's Weekly,* February 21, 1857; *Times,* February 7, 1870; *Monthly Record of the Five Points House of Industry* 1 (October 1857): 151; 3 (March 1860): 250; *Voice from the Old Brewery* 1 (February 1, 1861): 5; *Seventeenth Annual Report of the New-York Ladies' Home Missionary Society* (1861): 7–8.

74. *Times,* February 7, 1870; Timothy L. Smith, *Revivalism and Social Reform in Mid-Nineteenth Century America* (New York, 1957): 169–70.

75. John W. Pratt, "Boss Tweed's Public Welfare Program," *New-York Historical Society Quarterly* 45 (1961): 396–411.

CHAPTER NINE

1. *Express, Tribune, Times,* and *Herald,* July 6, 1857; Lyman Abbott, *Reminiscences* (Boston, 1915), 35.

2. *Times,* March 8, 1878 (William), June 26, 1899, p. 2 (quotation).

3. New York City Board of Aldermen, *Documents* 25 (1858), doc. 6, p. 53 (Walsh as assistant foreman).

4. *Trow's New York City Directory for 1859–60* (New York, 1859), 881; *Trow's New York City Directory for 1860–61* (New York, 1860), 889; *Trow's New York City Directory for 1861–62* (New York, 1861), 884; p. 927, district two, Sixth Ward, 1860 United States manuscript census, National Archives. For conditions in these tenements, see Denis T. Lynch, *The Wild Seventies*, 2 vols. (1941; Port Washington, NY, 1971), 2: 293–95; *Times*, July 2, 1871, August 27, 1873; *Harper's Weekly* 17 (September 13, 1873): 796.

5. *Leader*, November 27, 1858 (William), January 3, 1863 (Tammany general committee); *Irish-American*, November 19, 1859 (William); *Manual of the Corporation of the City of New York for 1862* (New York, 1862), 57 (street inspector); *Times*, June 26, 1899, p. 2 (superintendent of markets); Frank Moss, *The American Metropolis*, 3 vols. (New York, 1897), 3: 52 (quotation). The polling place for this district was, by 1860, located at the same address as Walsh's saloon. Although the *Herald* stated that the voting station there was located in a butcher shop, it was undoubtedly placed at that address to allow Walsh to monitor the voting—*Herald*, November 7, 1860.

6. William's break with Tammany apparently began in 1864, when he had a falling-out with Brennan and ran for Congress against the Tammany nominee, Brennan confidant Morgan Jones—*Times*, March 8, 1878.

7. *Times*, March 8, 1878, June 26, 1899, p. 2; Matthew P. Breen, *Thirty Years of New York Politics Up-to-Date* (New York, 1899), 529–31; *Trow's New York City Directory for the Year Ending May 1, 1871* (New York, 1870), 1257.

8. *Times*, June 26, 1899, p. 2.

9. *Times*, December 23 ("pothouse," p. 4), 24 ("inevitably become," p. 4), 25 (p. 4), 26 (p. 9), 1886.

10. *Times*, December 25, 1886, p. 4, April 13, 1888, p. 5.

11. *Times*, November 1, 1915, p. 11; *Herald*, June 26, 1899, p. 4 (quotation); John A. Garraty and Mark C. Carnes, eds., *American National Biography*, 24 vols. (New York, 1999), 22: 563.

12. *Times*, June 26, 1899, p. 2.

13. *Times*, June 26 (quotation, p. 2), 30 (p. 14), 1899.

14. *Herald*, October 26, November 4, 1853 (political advertisements in which Kerrigan is identified as head of the movement to defeat the regular Democratic nominee for council from the twelfth district), October 17, 1860; *Times*, August 8, 1887, p. 2 (quotations), November 3, 1899, p. 7; *Irish-American*, October 29, 1853; Florence E. Gibson, *The Attitudes of the New York Irish Toward State and National Affairs, 1848–1892* (New York, 1951), 58.

15. *Times*, March 23, 1855, August 8, 1887, p. 2 (dominated board of councilmen).

16. *Herald*, January 10, 30, 1856, November 2, 1899; *Tribune*, January 30, 1856.

17. *Herald*, December 3, 1852, January 20, June 7, 1853; statement of Schell, December 13, 1852, in indictment of December 23, 1852, New York County District Attorney's Indictment Papers, New York Municipal Archives; *Times*, January 20, 24, 1853; *Irish-American*, October 29, 1853; Gibson, *Attitudes of the New York Irish*, 58; family 424,

dwelling 85, fourth election district, Sixth Ward, 1855 New York State manuscript census, Old Records Division, New York County Clerk's Office. For Mathews's status as a sporting man, see *Times,* January 14, 1885, and Ned James to the Editor, *Clipper,* January 24, 1885. Gilmartin may have been one of the many Five Pointers who had emigrated from North Sligo. That surname, not a common one in New York at the time, was very prominent among the Palmerston and Gore Booth immigrants, and is still common today in Ahamlish and Drumcliff.

18. *Times,* November 5–6, 1856; *Citizen,* November 15, 1856 ("regular running street fight"); *Tribune,* November 5, 1856; *Herald,* November 5, 1856; testimony of William A. Smith ("Mulberry St. Boys"), July 6, 1857, reel 89, New York County Coroner Inquests. In Ireland in the 1850s, the term "Molly Maguires" referred to members of a secret anti-British society who pledged allegiance to a mythical woman who symbolized their struggle against injustice. The term was later adopted by Irish labor activists in Pennsylvania coal-mining regions.

19. Jerome Mushkat, *Fernando Wood: A Political Biography* (Kent, OH, 1990), 41–75; *Leader,* September 14, 1856; *Irish-American,* October 26, 1850, November 4, 1854, November 15, 1856, October 24, 1857 (for Wood's popularity with the Irish).

20. *Irish-American,* July 11, 1857; *The Diary of George Templeton Strong,* ed. Allan Nevins, 5 vols. (New York, 1952), 2: 342; *Times,* May 1, 1857; *Harper's Weekly* (January 31, 1857): 65.

21. Tyler Anbinder, *Nativism and Slavery: The Northern Know Nothings and the Politics of the* 1850s (New York, 1992), 143–45; *Irish-American,* August 9, 1856; *Tribune,* July 6, 1857 (quotation).

22. *Citizen,* November 22, 1856 (quotation); *Irish-American,* January 31, 1857, August 14, 1858 (quotation); *European,* December 6, 1856; *Irish News,* June 19, 1858; *Tribune,* February 1, 1850; Robert Ernst, *Immigrant Life in New York City, 1825–1863* (1949; Port Washington, NY, 1965), 164; Edwin G. Burrows and Mike Wallace, *Gotham: A History of New York City to 1898* (New York, 1999), 838–39.

23. *Tribune,* July 4, 6, 1857; *Herald,* July 4, 1857; testimony of Joseph Souder, July 10, 1857, reel 89, New York County Coroner Inquests; *Times,* July 6, 1857.

24. Herbert Asbury, *Gangs of New York,* 113, quoted in Paul S. Boyer, *Urban Masses and Moral Order in America, 1820–1920* (Cambridge, 1978), 69; *Diary of George Templeton Strong,* 2: 346; *Times,* July 11, 13 (final quotation), 1857.

25. "UN QUI SAIT" to the Editor, July 11, 1857 ("beat all the new policemen") in *Times,* July 13, 1857; testimony of William A. Smith ("hooting & cheering"), Richard Quinn, July 6, 1857, microfilm roll 89, New York County Coroner Inquests (Smith's and Quinn's testimony is paraphrased in the *Times,* July 7, 1857); testimony of Josiah McCord in *Herald,* July 6 ("Bowery boys"), 7 (for 40 Bowery as Mathews's headquarters), 10 (testimony of Metropolitan Police Sergeant Joseph Souder on Florentine), 1857; *Morning Express,* July 6, 1857 ("coffee and cake" and Mathews); *Tribune,* July 6, 1857 (final two quotations).

26. American Republican Party General Executive Committee Minute Book, New-York Historical Society; *Herald,* October 29, 1854 ("reform" nominations); family 363, dwelling 64, second division, third electoral district, Sixth Ward, 1855 New York census (previous white native-born male head of household was a twenty-two-year-old sailor in family 211); *Trow's New York City Directory for 1855–56* (New York, 1855), 292. While it cannot be *proven* that the "reform" slate was the Know Nothing ticket, given Florentine's

father's affiliation and the Know Nothing tendency to use this ploy in 1854, this seems the most logical explanation. For this tactic, see Anbinder, *Nativism and Slavery*, 52–53.

27. Testimony of William Y. Taft, July 8, 1857, reel 89, New York County Coroner Inquests; *Tribune*, July 6, 1857.

28. *Tribune*, July 6, 1857.

29. *Tribune* and *Herald*, July 6, 1857; Abbott, *Reminiscences*, 33 ("blood streaming").

30. *Morning Express and Tribune*, July 6, 1857; *Clipper*, January 24, 1885 (on Mathews and Kerrigan as sporting men).

31. Marcus Horbalt [*sic*] to the Editor, July 7, 1857, in *Times*, July 8, 1857; *Herald*, July 7 (testimony of Charles Francis), 10 (Molony to the Editor), 1857; account 8355, Emigrant Savings Bank Test Books, New York Public Library (Roche).

32. Testimony of Thomas Harvey, July 6, 1857, reel 89, New York County Coroner Inquests; *Morning Express*, July 8, 1857.

33. *Annual Report of the Chief Engineer of the Fire Department* (New York, 1858), in Board of Aldermen, *Documents* 25 (1858), doc. 6, pp. 53, 171; *Leader*, October 31, 1857 (Horbelt as election inspector); *Manual of the Corporation of the City of New York for 1858* (New York, 1858), 102; family 904, dwelling 144, fifth election district, Sixth Ward, 1855 New York census (Horbelt); *Trow's New York City Directory for 1856–57* (New York, 1856), 701 (Roche).

34. *Herald* ("busily engaged") and *Morning Express*, July 6, 1857.

35. *Morning Express* and *Herald*, July 6, 1857.

36. Abbott, *Reminiscences*, 34; Robert F. Lucid, ed., *The Journal of Richard Henry Dana, Jr.*, 3 vols. (Cambridge, 1968), 2: 823–24.

37. *Tribune* and *Times*, July 6, 1857; Joshua Brown, "The 'Dead Rabbit'-Bowery Boy Riot: An Analysis of the Antebellum New York Gang" (M.A. thesis, Columbia University, 1976), 24–27.

38. *Herald* and *Times*, July 6, 1857. The press occasionally referred to Kerrigan and Mathews's followers as the "Atlantic Boys" because many of them belonged to Atlantic Hose Company No. 14.

39. *Times* and *Tribune*, July 6–7, 1857; *Evening Post*, July 6, 1857; Brown, "'Dead Rabbit'-Bowery Boy Riot," 165–69. Brown lists twelve killed in the riot, but I believe that one of those he lists as killed—William "Fatty" Walsh—is actually Thomas Walsh or his brother William, both of whom survived the riot. No Walsh was found in any of the coroner's reports. But Brown does not include among the dead Metropolitan Thomas Sparks, who died as a result of injuries sustained at the hands of the mob on Chatham Street in the early morning hours of the Fourth. Consequently, I believe the figure of twelve killed is accurate.

40. *Herald*, July 10, 1857; *Times*, July 8, 10, 13 (Clancy quotation), 17 (Gallagher quotation), 1857; *Citizen*, August 1, 1857; testimony of policeman James Irving, July 8, 1857, testimony of policeman Thomas Dutcher, July 10, 1857, statements of prisoners Edward Doyle, Patrick Mooney, Patrick McBride, Thomas McGaraghy, and Barney Gallagher, July 9, 1857, reel 89, New York County Coroner Inquests. The outcome of the case of Owen Gilmartin, who demanded a jury trial, could not be determined.

41. For the Astor Place death toll, see Edward K. Spann, *The New Metropolis: New York City, 1840–1857* (New York, 1981), 237–38; Peter G. Buckley, "To the Opera House: Culture and Society in New York City, 1820–1860" (Ph.D. dissertation, State University of New York at Stony Brook, 1984), 3.

42. Burrows and Wallace, *Gotham*, 839; William D'Arcy, *The Fenian Movement in the United States: 1858–1886* (Washington, DC, 1947), 159–66, 244–48.

43. *Citizen*, July 18, 1857. That a large number of the Roche Guard hailed from lower Mulberry is indicated by both the location of Roche's original saloon and the addresses given by those questioned by the coroner in the death of William Cahill. The questioning indicated the coroner's belief that these men were active members of the Roche Guard. The *Times* identified these men as John Roche (probably William's brother) of 5 Mulberry; Philip Murphy of 9 Mulberry; Thomas White of 11 Mulberry; Michael Finane of 6 Mulberry; and Patrick Lane, whose address was not given—*Times*, July 7, 1857.

44. *Irish-American*, July 18, 1857; *Herald*, July 6, 1857.

45. *Tribune*, July 6, 1857; testimony of Louis B. Pike, July 8, 1857, reel 89, New York County Coroner Inquests.

46. *Journal of Richard Henry Dana, Jr.*, 2: 824–25; *Times*, July 7, 1857.

47. *Times*, July 20, 1857.

48. *Manual of the Corporation of the City of New York for 1858*, 143, 438; *Herald*, May 14, 1876 (Dowling); *Times*, October 10, 1870 (Jourdan).

49. *Manual of the Corporation of the City of New York for 1859* (New York, 1859), 116 (Kerrigan's clerkship).

50. *Leader*, July 2, 1864.

51. *Leader*, October 2, 1858. In his listing of Sixth Warders who had held citywide office, Clancy did not include Andrew H. Mickle, elected mayor in 1846. Mickle, a Protestant, had been born in a Five Points tenement with pigs in both the basement and attic, but married the daughter of his employer, a successful tobacco dealer. Mickle later took over the business and died a millionaire. By the time he became mayor, he had not lived in the Sixth Ward for decades, explaining why Clancy did not include him in his account of Sixth Warders who had held important city offices—Harlow, *Old Bowery Days*, 302.

52. *Leader*, November 6, 1858 ("too Irish"); *Irish-American*, August 14 (*Dispatch* quotation), October 23 ("claims of the Sixth Ward"), 1858.

53. Clancy captured 38,077 votes, while his Republican opponent received 30,092. John Kelly, running for sheriff at the head of the Democratic ticket, won about 1,000 more votes than Clancy—*Manual of the Corporation of the City of New York for 1859*, 413.

CHAPTER TEN

1. *Herald*, December 13, 14, 1860.

2. *Manual of the Corporation of the City of New York for 1859* (New York, 1859), 116 (Kerrigan's clerkship); *Herald*, October 17, 1860.

3. *Herald*, October 17, 1860.

4. Ibid.

5. Philip Foner, *Business and Slavery: The New York Merchants and the Irrepressible Conflict* (Chapel Hill, 1941), 294–95.

6. *Tribune*, December 17, 1860; *Herald*, January 19, 22, 23, 1861; *Times*, January 19, 22, 24, 1861, January 16, 1862 (size of Kerrigan's regiment).

7. William H. Russell, *My Diary North and South* (Boston, 1863), 507–8.

8. The account of Kerrigan's service and court-martial is based on his service records and on court-martial II/680, both in Record Group 153, National Archives. Sketchy accounts of the trial can be found in *Tribune*, December 11, 12, 18, 20, 21, 1861, and *Times*, January 16, 1862. For Kerrigan's arrest, see *Congressional Globe*, 37th Congress, 3rd Sess., 1545; *Herald*, March 4, 1863.

9. *Times*, August 8, 1887, p. 2 ("dare-devil"); William D'Arcy, *The Fenian Movement in the United States: 1858–1886* (Washington, DC, 1947), 159–66; *Herald*, June 5–7, 1866.

10. D'Arcy, *Fenian Movement*, 244–48; *Times*, November 3, 1899, p. 7.

11. John S. Reynolds, *Reconstruction in South Carolina, 1865–1877* (1905; New York, 1969), 152–53.

12. *Herald*, November 2, 1899 ("never uttered"); *Times*, November 3, 1899, p. 7 ("syndicate").

13. *Irish-American*, October 29, 1853, January 31, 1857; *Day Book*, November 11, 1857.

14. *Freeman's Journal*, July 22, 1843, October 6, 1860.

15. *Freeman's Journal*, July 22, 1843 (O'Connell quotation); *Irish-American*, August 12, 1849 (quotation), May 17, 1851, June 11, 1853.

16. *Freeman's Journal*, July 22, 1843; *Irish-American*, January 31, 1857.

17. *Irish-American*, January 9, 1858; *Leader*, October 9, November 6, 1858 (on Douglas), March 12, 1859 (Ivy Green).

18. *Herald*, November 7, 1860.

19. *Irish-American*, January 26, February 16 (quotation), 1861; *Leader* quoted in Jerome Mushkat, *Tammany: The Evolution of a Political Machine, 1789–1865* (Syracuse, 1971), 327; *Times*, April 16, 1861.

20. *Herald*, January 23, 1861; *Irish-American*, April 27, 1861; *Eighteenth Annual Report of the New York Association for Improving the Condition of the Poor* (1861): 17; *Voice from the Old Brewery* 1 (August 2, 1861): 35; *Twenty-first Annual Report of the New-York Ladies' Home Missionary Society* (New York, 1865): 9.

21. Robert Crowe, *Reminiscences of Robert Crowe, the Octogenerian* [sic] *Tailor* (New York, 1901), 26; M. R. Werner, *It Happened in New York* (New York, 1957), 196; Edward Lubitz, "The Tenement Problem in New York City and the Movement for Its Reform, 1856–1867" (Ph.D. dissertation, New York University, 1970), 319.

22. *Herald*, November 4 (quotation), 6, 1861; *Times*, July 23, 1896, p. 5 (Stacom); military service file of John Stacom, National Archives; *Supplement to the Official Records of the Union and Confederate Armies, Part II—Record of Events*, 80 vols. (Wilmington, NC, 1997), 44: 695 (Petersburg). For the Sixth-ninth Regiment, see *Irish-American*, June 4, July 6, 1861; Edwin G. Burrows and Mike Wallace, *Gotham: A History of New York City*

to 1898 (New York, 1999), 870–71; Joseph G. Bilby, *The Irish Brigade in the Civil War: The 69th New York and Other Irish Regiments of the Army of the Potomac* (1995; Conshohocken, PA, 1998), 11–17.

23. *Leader* and *Tribune,* July 2, 1864; Mushkat, *Tammany,* 330–32; Florence E. Gibson, *The Attitudes of the New York Irish Toward State and National Affairs, 1848–1892* (New York, 1951), 117.

24. *Leader,* June 28, 1862, quoted in Mushkat, *Tammany,* 342; *Times,* November 15, 20, 21, 23, 1862; *Official Proceedings of the Democratic Republican Nominating Convention of Tammany Hall, Which Nominated Matthew T. Brennan for the Office of Comptroller of the City of New York . . . November 20, 1862* [New York, 1862].

25. *Leader,* November 22, 1862; *Times,* November 23, 29, 1862; *Herald,* November 26, 28 ("at all qualified"), 29, December 3, 1862. Brennan captured about 30,000 votes, while his running mate for corporation counsel, John E. Develin, received 33,000—*Times,* December 3, 1862.

26. *Leader,* January 10, 1863; Board of Aldermen, *Documents* 25 (1858), doc. 6, p. 171; *Times,* July 16, 1894, p. 5. Walsh by this point lived just across the Bowery in the Fourth Ward on Madison Street (the aldermanic district included portions of both wards), but his ties to Five Points remained strong with his brother Tom still a political force on lower Mulberry Street.

27. *Times,* November 20, 1863, October 10, 1870, May 14, 1876. Although both Jourdan and Dowling were good fighters, Jourdan was said to have had "the greater coolness in times of bodily peril." Once when Dowling and Jourdan went in plainclothes to capture two noted Sixth Ward thieves, they were attacked in a dark room with iron bars. Dowling drew his pistol, but Jourdan knocked his arm away, insisting on capturing the thieves alive. After a long hand-to-hand struggle, the policemen overpowered the thieves with their pistol butts, but not before the policemen were left "with blood streaming from head and face." The two officers "dragged their equally disfigured captives . . . into a hack, where, exhausted and almost senseless, the four brutally beaten contestants rested from their labors and mingled their blood until they reached the station house. . . . From the encounter resulted Dowling's premature and excessive baldness. He was about as nearly scalped as mortal man ever was, and from that day, instead of having a thick and heavy head of hair, his poll shone like a polished billiard ball." In his years on the bench Dowling was consequently known as "old Baldy"—*Herald,* May 14, 1876.

28. *Herald,* November 6, 1861; Robert Ernst, *Immigrant Life in New York City, 1825–1863* (1949; reprint, Port Washington, NY, 1965), 291 (Hughes).

29. *Tribune,* April 8, 1863; *Leader* in James F. Richardson, *The New York Police: Colonial Times to 1901* (New York, 1970), 131; *Irish-American,* passim late 1862–early 1863.

30. Edward K. Spann, "The Irish Community and the Civil War," in Ronald Bayor and Timothy Meagher, eds., *The New York Irish* (Baltimore, 1996), 203–4; *Tribune,* April 14, 1863; Albon P. Man, Jr., "Labor Competition and the New York Draft Riots of 1863," *Journal of Negro History* 36 (1951): 398–400. The April strikers found only ten African Americans at Pier Nine and "a few" at the other East River docks, confirming that no sweeping replacement of Irish Americans by African Americans had occurred. The original culprit in the misrepresentation of this incident seems to have been Emerson D. Fite, *Social and Industrial Conditions in the North During the Civil War* (1910; Williamstown, MA, 1976), 189–90. None of the contemporary descriptions of the June strike that I was able

to locate mentioned black workers replacing white strikers. See *Tribune*, June 8, 9, 15, 20, 1863, and *Herald*, June 9, 16, 1863.

31. *Day Book* quoted in Spann, "Irish Community," 203; *Irish-American*, July 4, 1863.

32. *People v. Denis P. Sullivan*, December 9, 1862, New York County District Attorney's Indictment Papers, New York Municipal Archives; *Herald*, November 30, December 1, 1862; *Times*, February 11–15, 1863.

33. Burrows and Wallace, *Gotham*, 887–88; *Irish-American*, May 16, 1863; *Herald*, July 14, 1863.

34. *Irish-American*, July 25, 1863.

35. *Leader*, November 7, 1863; Luc Sante, *Low Life: Lures and Snares of Old New York* (New York, 1991), 353; Richard O'Connor, *Hell's Kitchen: The Roaring Days of New York's Wild Side* (New York, 1958), 16.

36. Adrian Cook, *The Armies of the Streets: The New York City Draft Riots of 1863* (Lexington, KY, 1974), 213–16; Iver Bernstein, *The New York City Draft Riots* (New York, 1990), 28, 31–36; *Tribune*, July 18, 1863; *Leader*, July 18, November 7, 1863.

37. Cook, *Armies of the Streets*, 256–68.

38. *Herald*, July 14 ("Mr. Crook") and 17, 1863; David M. Barnes, *The Draft Riots in New York* (New York, 1863), 14, 42–44 (all other quotations). The most recent account of the riots to repeat the erroneous story of the mission's burning is Burrows and Wallace, *Gotham*, 890.

39. *Herald*, July 17, 1863; districts 5–11, Sixth Ward, 1870 United States manuscript census, National Archives. For Five Points' importance as a residence for African-American sailors on shore leave, see W. Jeffrey Bolster, *Black Jacks: African American Seamen in the Age of Sail* (Cambridge, MA, 1997), 185.

40. Sixth Ward draft statistics based upon the list of draftees published in the *Herald*, August 26, 1863, supplemented and corrected by Register of Drafted Men, Fourth Congressional District of New York, Entry 1589, Record Group 110, National Archives. Five Pointers did not respond to the draft much differently from other New York Irish Americans. In the August 1863 draft in the Fourth Ward, the district demographically most similar to the Sixth Ward, 50% of the draftees failed to report, 40% were exempted, 2% paid the commutation fee, 7% hired substitutes, and not a single drafted man entered the army. Upstate, the draft produced far more recruits. In the Ontario county seat of Canandaigua, for example, fully 24% of those drafted paid the commutation fee, hired a substitute, or enlisted—Register of Drafted Men, Entry 1589 (Fourth Ward), Descriptive Roll of Drafted Men, Entry 2194 (Canandaigua), Record Group 110, National Archives. For Nealis, see *Times*, February 12–15, 1863.

41. Boyle's service record can be found in the papers of the Eighteenth New York Cavalry Regiment, National Archives. The movements of his unit can be traced in *Supplement to the Official Records of the Union and Confederate Armies, Part II—Record of Events*, 41: 600–602; Frederick H. Dyer, *Compendium of the War of the Rebellion*, 3 vols. (1908; Dayton, OH, 1978), 1: 380.

42. *Times*, December 2, 1863; *Irish-American*, December 12, 1863.

43. *Irish-American*, October 8, 1864.

44. *Irish-American,* October 15 ("own aggrandizement"), November 5 (block quotation), 1864.

45. *Herald,* November 17, 19 (quotation), 1866.

46. *Leader, Times, Herald,* and *Tribune,* July 2, 1864. The press offered widely divergent accounts of the cause of Clancy's death. The *Herald* reported that he had succumbed to Bright's disease, a chronic inflammation of the kidneys, while the *Times* attributed his death to "a brain fever caused by a sunstroke received at Lake Mahopac on the 20th of last month."

47. William M. Ivins, *Machine Politics and Money in Elections in New York City* (1887; New York, 1970), 19; Matthew P. Breen, *Thirty Years of New York Politics Up-to-Date* (New York, 1899), 516–17. Brennan told a congressional committee in 1868 that he lived at 84 White Street and voted in the Sixth Ward, but admitted he almost always slept at his "summer residence" on "the Bloomingdale Road." By 1869, he had given up any pretense of still residing in the Sixth Ward, listing the location of his residence as 105th Street and Broadway in the city directory—*New York Election Frauds,* 40th Congress, 3rd Sess. House Report No. 31 ([Washington, DC]: 1869), 442; *Trow's New York City Directory for 1869–70* (New York, 1869). I have not been able to identify with certainty the year in which this primary took place, but a story on the front page of the *Times,* February 26, 1872, implies that it was in 1871.

48. *Times,* November 9, 1859, November 7, 1860; *Herald,* November 7, 1860.

49. *Testimony Relating to the Great Election Frauds of 1838* (New York, 1840); *Irish-American,* October 2, 1858, February 12, April 23, June 25 (quotation), 1859. For one of the few antebellum references to significant voter fraud in Five Points, see *Herald,* December 9, 1858.

50. *Times,* November 7, 1863; John I. Davenport, *Election and Naturalization Frauds in New York City, 1860–1870,* 2nd ed. (New York, 1894), 49–56; Albie Burke, "Federal Regulation of Congressional Elections in Northern Cities, 1871–1894" (Ph.D. dissertation, University of Chicago, 1968), 71.

51. Davenport, *Election and Naturalization Frauds,* 49–56.

52. Ibid., 92–93, 117–23, 274–75 (quotation). To be naturalized legally, an immigrant had to have resided in the United States for five years and to have declared his or her intention to become an American citizen at least two years before seeking naturalization. Those who had emigrated before their eighteenth birthday did not have to make the advance declaration, and those honorably discharged from the American armed forces could become citizens both without the prior declaration and after only one year of residence in the United States. In all cases the prospective citizen had to provide witnesses who could confirm that the applicant met these prerequisites and was "of good moral character." Political parties in New York had offered, since at least the 1840s, to pay the fees and in other ways facilitate the naturalization process for immigrants, hoping of course that the grateful new citizens would cast their first ballots for their benefactors.

53. *Tribune,* November 5, 1867; Davenport, *Election and Naturalization Frauds,* 107; *The Nation* 7 (November 5, 1868): 362.

54. Davenport, *Election and Naturalization Frauds,* 123, 141; *Times,* October 24, 1868; Burke, "Federal Regulation of Congressional Elections," 47; *Frank Leslie's Illustrated Newspaper* (November 13, 1869): 141.

55. Davenport, *Election and Naturalization Frauds*, 176–78, 242; *New York Election Frauds*, report p. 436, testimony pp. 239, 244, 248–50 (all references refer to "report" pages rather than the separately paginated "testimony" section, unless otherwise noted).

56. *New York Election Frauds*, 505–6, 626–27; Davenport, *Election and Naturalization Frauds*, 180.

57. *New York Election Frauds*, testimony pp. 409–11.

58. Davenport, *Election and Naturalization Frauds*, 246, 286; *Times*, November 9, 1864; *The Nation* 9 (September 8, 1870): 147.

59. Davenport, *Election and Naturalization Frauds*, 256–59, 284, 343; Burke, "Federal Regulation of Congressional Elections," 17, 25.

60. Davenport, *Election and Naturalization Frauds*, 341–43; Gustav Lening, *The Dark Side of New York Life and Its Criminal Classes: From Fifth Avenue Down to the Five Points* (New York, 1873), 288 (Five Points' reputation for voter fraud).

61. *Official Proceedings of the National Democratic Convention* (New York, 1868): 36; *Times*, April 13, 1870 (Jourdan); *Tribune*, March 8, 1878 (Walsh); *Herald*, January 20, 1879 (Brennan). Brennan could not have been on terribly bad terms with Tweed, as both Matthew Brennan and his brother Owen accepted memberships in the Americus Yacht Club that Tweed established in Greenwich, Connecticut. See Leo Hershkowitz, *Tweed's New York: Another Look* (New York, 1977), 123.

62. Alexander B. Callow, *The Tweed Ring* (New York, 1966), 23 (Board of Supervisors); *Times*, February 14, 1872 (street openings).

63. On O'Brien's failure to receive renomination, see Hershkowitz, *Tweed's New York*, 155.

64. *Harper's Weekly* (November 18, 1871): 1084 ("You're my man"); *Tribune*, October 28, December 16, 1871 (other quotations); *Times*, February 26, 1872.

65. *O'Donovan Rossa's Prison Life* (New York, 1874), 431–32, 436; Denis T. Lynch, *The Wild Seventies*, 2 vols. (1941; Port Washington, NY, 1971), 1: 135; Joseph I. C. Clarke, *My Life and Memories* (New York, 1925), 106; John Devoy, *Recollections of an Irish Rebel* (1929; Shannon, 1969), 328–29; Alvin Harlow, *Old Bowery Days: The Chronicles of a Famous Street* (New York, 1931), 417.

66. Tyler Anbinder, "William M. Tweed," *American National Biography*, 24 vols. (New York, 1999), 22: 60–62.

67. Breen, *Thirty Years*, 304, 512, 555 (quotation); Jacob A. Riis, *The Battle with the Slum* (New York, 1902), 5.

68. *Times*, August 10, 1870, October 30, 1875 (both describe funds received by Transfiguration).

69. *Times*, February 14, March 11, 1872, January 3, 1874.

70. *Times*, June 15, 25, October 3 (quoting *Tribune*), November 8, December 21, 1872, August 27, 1873.

71. *Times*, June 21, September 26, October 21, 1873.

72. Breen, *Thirty Years*, 504–11; *Times*, December 23, 1873, February 5, 1878, November 12, 1881, September 7, 1889 (Genet's obituary); *Herald*, January 20, 1879; Hershkowitz,

Tweed's New York, 262–63. Genet gave himself up in February 1878 and eventually served eight months behind bars.

73. Breen, *Thirty Years*, 504–5; *Times*, January 20, 1879.

74. *Times*, January 20, 1879.

75. *Times*, October 11, 14, 1870, July 3, 7, 1872, March 8, 1878. The *Times* obituary erroneously states that McCunn died at age fifty-seven, but it accurately lists his date of birth as 1825.

76. *National Cyclopedia of American Biography*, 63 vols. (New York, 1893–), 3: 391 ("amused himself"); *Tribune*, May 15, 1876; *Herald*, May 14, 1876; *Times*, May 14, 1876; Breen, *Thirty Years*, 523–24.

77. *Times* and *Herald*, January 20, 1879; *Tribune*, January 21, 1879.

78. Daniel Czitrom, "Underworlds and Underdogs: Big Tim Sullivan and Metropolitan Politics in New York, 1889–1913," *Journal of American History* 78 (1991): 539–42 ("political ruler"); *Times*, April 30, 1887 ("Five Points Sullivan"), October 16, 1902, p. 3; *Herald*, April 18, 1889, p. 7, October 16, 1902, p. 5, May 19, 1907, magazine sect., part 1, pp. 1–2 (quotations); *Sun*, April 18, 1889, p. 5.

79. For postwar comment on improving conditions in Five Points, see Whitelaw Reid, *After the War: A Southern Tour* (London, 1866), 356; Edward W. Martin [pseud. for James D. McCabe], *The Secrets of the Great City* (Philadelphia, 1868), 189; Junius H. Browne, *The Great Metropolis: A Mirror of New-York* (Hartford, 1869), 272, 523; and Edward Crapsey, *The Nether Side of New York; or, the Vice, Crime and Poverty of the Great Metropolis* (New York, 1872), 155.

Chapter Eleven

1. Jacob A. Riis, *The Making of an American* (1901; New York, 1936), 1–25.

2. Riis, *Making of an American*, 26–79, 98–102. That Riis cried on the pier, not mentioned in *Making of an American*, is taken from his handwritten outline for the book, found in his papers at the Library of Congress.

3. Riis, *Making of an American*, 80–112.

4. *Monthly Record of the Five Points House of Industry* 13 (April–May 1870): 300–301 (expansion that eliminated Cow Bay).

5. John I. Davenport, *Election and Naturalization Frauds in New York City, 1860–1870*, 2nd ed. (New York, 1894), 15, 17 (population and density statistics); *Herald*, September 18, 1892, p. 11 (Lower East Side tenements).

6. *Tribune*, June 21, 1885, p. 9; Rev. Thomas P. McLoughlin, "In Darkest Chinatown," *Donahue's Magazine* (November 1897), in Peter P. McLoughlin, *Father Tom: Life and Lectures of Rev. Thomas P. McLoughlin* (New York, 1919), 102; *Herald*, November 30, 1878.

7. The 1880 Five Points adult population figures are based on a random sampling of Five Points residents age seventeen and older from the 1880 United States manuscript census, National Archives. Five Points is defined (as it has been throughout this book) as the area bounded by Canal Street to the north, the Bowery and Chatham Square to the east, Pearl Street to the south, and Centre Street to the west. Children have been excluded from this

calculation because they inflate the figures for U.S. natives. For the method used to compile the 1855 figures, see Chapter Two, note 10.

8. Election districts 18–27, Sixth Ward, 1890 Police Census, New York Municipal Archives. The federal manuscript census of 1890 was destroyed by fire. Ethnicity was determined by examining first and last names. The police figures probably exaggerate the decline of Five Points' Irish population to some extent because many of the residents whose surnames did not definitively reveal their ethnicity were probably Irish Americans.

9. Jacob A. Riis, *The Children of the Poor* (New York, 1892), 67–68.

10. Isaac N. P. Stokes, *Iconography of Manhattan Island: 1498–1909*, 6 vols. (1915–28; New York, 1967), 3: 1012; John J. Post, *Old Streets, Roads, Lanes, Piers, and Wharves of New York* (New York, 1882), 76; *Frank Leslie's Illustrated Newspaper* (August 16, 1873): 363; Viola Roseboro, "The Italians of New York," *Cosmopolitan* 4 (January 1888): 404. The Worth Street project had been contemplated for years—see *Tribune*, January 21, 1854.

11. Alvin Harlow, *Old Bowery Days: The Chronicles of a Famous Street* (New York, 1931), 387–88.

12. Junius H. Browne, *The Great Metropolis: A Mirror of New-York* (Hartford, 1869), 137; J. Frank Kernan, *Reminiscences of the Old Fire Laddies* (New York, 1885), 64.

13. The rise of large-scale manufacturing in Five Points can be seen in the Perris insurance maps of 1857, 1875, and 1884.

14. Building material comparison based on Perris insurance maps of 1855 and 1884.

15. Lawrence Veiller, "Tenement House Reform in New York City, 1834–1900," in Robert W. DeForest and Lawrence Veiller, eds., *The Tenement House Problem*, 2 vols. (1903; New York, 1970), 1: 94–96; Edward Lubitz, "The Tenement Problem in New York City and the Movement for Its Reform, 1856–1867" (Ph.D. dissertation, New York University, 1970), 514–18, 521, 529.

16. DeForest and Veiller, eds., *Tenement House Problem*, 1: 99–100; Richard Plunz, *A History of Housing in New York City: Dwelling Type and Social Change in the American Metropolis* (New York, 1990), 24–27.

17. Jacob A. Riis, *How the Other Half Lives: Studies Among the Tenements of New York* (1890; New York, 1971), 13; *Harper's Weekly* (July 12, 1873): 603, 606; *Frank Leslie's Illustrated Newspaper* (September 20, 1884): 65, 70; *Tribune*, July 15, September 10 (p. 8), 1884; *Proceedings of the New York State Conference of Charities and Correction* (1901), in Roy Lubove, *The Progressive and the Slums: Tenement House Reform in New York City, 1890–1917* (Pittsburgh, 1962), 89 (Gilder quotation).

18. *Times*, March 16, 1879.

19. "Tenement Evils as Seen by the Tenants," in DeForest and Veiller, eds., *Tenement House Problem*, 1: 386, 388 (quotation), 397, 407–8, 413 (quotation).

20. *Times*, July 2, 1871; DeForest and Veiller, eds., *Tenement House Problem*, 1: 394.

21. DeForest and Veiller, eds., *Tenement House Problem*, 1: 385, 414–15; "Report of Tenement-House Commission," February 17, 1885, *Documents of the Senate of the State of New-York, 108th Session, 1885* (Albany, 1885), vol. 5, doc. 36, p. 100; *Herald*, September 18, 1892, p. 11.

22. Charles Loring Brace, *The Dangerous Classes of New York and Twenty Years Work Among Them*, 3rd ed. (New York, 1872), 223.

23. Gustav Lening, *The Dark Side of New York Life and Its Criminal Classes: From Fifth Avenue Down to the Five Points* (New York, 1873), 17–19; *Frank Leslie's Illustrated Newspaper* (July 5, 1873): 271; *Times*, July 2, 1871. Because overcrowding was now a crime, tenement dwellers had an incentive to underreport the number of boarders they took in. As a result the census, which so vividly documented the overcrowding of the 1850s, is an unreliable guide to postwar conditions.

24. Riis, *How the Other Half Lives*, 58–59.

25. *Frank Leslie's Illustrated Newspaper* (March 18, 1882): 55–57.

26. Riis, *How the Other Half Lives*, 11; Denis T. Lynch, *The Wild Seventies*, 2 vols. (1941; Port Washington, NY, 1971), 2: 293–95; *Times*, August 27, 1873. Why the owner was allowed to build such low ceilings, despite the 1867 law, is unclear. Perhaps the old building, as an existing structure, did not have to meet the new requirements.

27. *Harper's Weekly* 17 (September 13, 1873): 796; *Times*, July 2, 1871 ("foul stench"), August 27, 1873 (remaining quotations).

28. *Times*, July 2, 1871, August 27, 1873.

29. *Times*, January 20, November 23, 1871, August 27, 1873; Jacob A. Riis, *The Battle with the Slum* (New York, 1902), 16 ("repulsive pile").

30. *Times*, March 22, 1880; *Plumber and Sanitary Engineer* (December 15, 1879): 26; folder 200/27, "Block and Lot Folders," New York Municipal Archives. According to the *Plumber and Sanitary Engineer*, the buildings at 65 Mott were the first erected in New York specifically for use as tenements.

31. *Times*, July 2, 1871 (quotation); *Herald*, December 26, 1869; *Tribune*, July 8, 1879.

32. *Frank Leslie's Illustrated Newspaper* (September 15, 1866): 405; *Harper's Weekly* 23 (March 22, 1879): 226–27.

33. *Harper's Weekly* 23 (March 22, 1879): 226–27; 24 (February 28, 1880): 142; *Tribune*, July 8, 1879.

34. *Frank Leslie's Illustrated Newspaper* (September 15, 1866): 405; *Harper's Weekly* 23 (March 22, 1879): 226–27; 24 (February 28, 1880): 142; *Tribune*, July 8, 1879; Riis, *How the Other Half Lives*, 54.

35. "Flashes from the Slums," *Sun*, February 12, 1888, p. 10; *Frank Leslie's Illustrated Newspaper* (August 11, 1888): 415; Allan Forman, "Some Adopted Americans," *American Magazine* 9 (November 1888): 46–47; Riis, *How the Other Half Lives*, 49–60. The first published use of the term "Mulberry Bend" that I have found is in a January 1888 article by Viola Roseboro, in which she describes her "unusually careful examination [of] Mulberry Street, particularly the part known as the 'Bend.'" See "The Italians of New York," *Cosmopolitan* 4 (January 1888): 397.

36. Riis, *How the Other Half Lives*, 50.

37. Riis, *Battle with the Slum*, 39–40; advertisements in *Il Progresso*, September 4, 1889, August 1, 1891 (for Mulberry Bend businesses).

38. Riis, *How the Other Half Lives*, 52–54; Page Smith, *The Rise of Industrial America* (New York, 1984), 367; "Report of Tenement-House Commission," February 17, 1885, in *Documents of the Senate, 108th Session*, vol. 5, doc. 36, pp. 233–35.

39. Riis, *How the Other Half Lives*, 47, 62; *Tribune*, July 8, 1879.

40. *Tribune*, July 8, 1879; *Harper's Weekly* 24 (February 28, 1880): 142; Riis, *How the Other Half Lives*, 61.

41. *Sun*, February 12, 1888, p. 10.

42. Riis, *How the Other Half Lives*, 62.

43. *Frank Leslie's Illustrated Newspaper* (August 11, 1888): 415; Charlotte Adams, "Italian Life in New York," *Harper's Monthly Magazine* 62 (April 1881): 681.

44. Forman, "Some Adopted Americans," 46–47 (first quotation); Riis, *The Making of an American*, 181 ("worst slum"); I[gnatz] L. Nascher, *The Wretches of Povertyville: A Sociological Study of the Bowery* (Chicago, 1909), 67.

CHAPTER TWELVE

1. *Times*, June 17, 1873.

2. *Times*, June 18, 1873.

3. *Times*, February 1, 1869; John E. Zucchi, *The Little Slaves of the Harp: Italian Child Street Musicians in Nineteenth-Century Paris, London, and New York* (Montreal, 1992), 39.

4. *Times*, June 17, 19, 1873; Zucchi, *Little Slaves of the Harp*, 114–15. Basilicata specialized in the production of these small harps. Photos of child street musicians playing harps, violins, and triangles in Basilicata, London, and America can be found in Giulia Rosa Celeste, *L'Arpa Popolare Viggianese nelle Fonti Documentarie* (Viggiano, Italy, 1989), 108–14.

5. *Times*, June 20, 1873 ("where's my mother"), June 4, 1874 ("slaves of the harp"); Charles Loring Brace, *The Dangerous Classes of New York and Twenty Years Work Among Them*, 3rd ed. (New York, 1872), 195. This child's comment may have indicated that his parents, rather than a *padrone*, forced him to work on the streets.

6. *Times*, June 17 (final quotation), 19 (all other quotations), 1873; *Eco d'Italia*, July 23, 1869; *Frank Leslie's Illustrated Newspaper* (March 22, 1873): 28.

7. Zucchi, *Little Slaves of the Harp*, 191. Horatio Alger wrote one of his early dime novels about an Italian child street musician, based largely on accounts of their lives provided by the head of the Children's Aid Society's Five Points Italian School. See *Phil the Fiddler, or the Story of a Young Street-Musician* ([New York], 1872).

8. *Times*, August 1, 20, 27, December 16, 1873; Zucchi, *Little Slaves of the Harp*, 125; *Twenty-second Annual Report of the Children's Aid Society* (1874): 33; Jacob A. Riis, *The Children of the Poor* (New York, 1892), 148–50. The "Padrone Act" did not prevent parents from sending their own children into the streets to play music, and consequently some Italian youngsters continued to perform for money on New York's sidewalks. But those who examined Italian life in New York in the 1880s and '90s agreed that "since the abolishment of the *padrone* system one sees few child-musicians." Charlotte Adams, "Italian Life in New York," *Harper's Monthly Magazine* 62 (April 1881): 684.

9. Second division, third election district, Sixth Ward, 1855 New York State manuscript census, Old Records Division, New York County Clerk's Office; George E. Pozzetta, "The Mulberry District of New York City: The Years Before World War One," in Robert F. Harney and J. Vincenza Scarpaci, eds., *Little Italies in North America* (Toronto, 1981), 9, 11, 29; Brace, *Dangerous Classes*, 196–98; *Third Annual Report of the Children's Aid Society* (New York: 1856): 17–18; *Fourth Annual Report of the Children's Aid Society* (New York: 1857): 15–17; *Seventh Annual Report of the Children's Aid Society* (1860): 15–16.

10. *Tenth Annual Report of the Children's Aid Society* (1863): 28 ("colony"); *Twelfth Annual Report of the Children's Aid Society* (1865): 29; John I. Davenport, comp., *The Registered Voters of the City of New York* (New York: 1877), 43, 706 (showing a marked increase in the number of Italian voters since 1874); *Eco d'Italia*, October 29, 1869.

11. Robert F. Foerster, *Italian Emigration of Our Times* (Cambridge, MA, 1919), 38; *Twenty-ninth Annual Report of the Children's Aid Society* (1881): 32–33; G. Florenzano, *Della Emigrazione Italiana in America* (Naples, 1874), 140; *Times*, December 13, 14, 1872, June 17, 18, 19, 1873, April 4, 1885, p. 8 (Jersey Street).

12. George E. Pozzetta, "The Italians of New York City, 1890–1914" (Ph.D. dissertation, University of North Carolina, 1971), 40–54; *Tribune*, April 13, 1890, p. 17 (Argentina); Dino Cinel, *The National Integration of Italian Return Migration, 1870–1929* (New York, 1991), 123 (quotations); *Frank Leslie's Illustrated Newspaper* (August 11, 1888): 415; George J. Manson, "The 'Foreign Element' in New York City. V—The Italians," *Harper's Weekly* 34 (October 18, 1890): 817.

13. *Eco d'Italia*, October 22, 1869 (waxed eloquent), April 15, 1881, and April 26, 1883 (advertisements for neighborhood businesses); Brace, *Dangerous Classes*, 194 ("dirty macaroni").

14. *Frank Leslie's Illustrated Newspaper* (August 29, 1885): 27.

15. Solon Robinson, *Hot Corn: Life Scenes in New York Illustrated* (New York, 1854), 213; *Tribune*, May 12, 1883; Denis T. Lynch, *The Wild Seventies*, 2 vols. (1941; Port Washington, NY, 1971), 2: 287–88.

16. Brace, *Dangerous Classes*, 194; Adams, "Italian Life in New York," 682; Manson, "'Foreign Element,'" 818; Edwin Winslow Martin [pseud. James D. McCabe], *The Secrets of the Great City* (Philadelphia, 1868), 124–25; Sixth Ward, 1880 United States manuscript census, National Archives.

17. Adams, "Italian Life in New York," 681–82.

18. My translation of Adolfo Rossi, *Un Italiano in America* (Milan, 1892), 64.

19. Manson, "'Foreign Element,'" 818.

20. Ibid., 817; Viola Roseboro, "The Italians of New York," *Cosmopolitan* 4 (January 1888): 400–402; *Herald*, September 18, 1892, p. 11; Rossi, *Un Italiano in America*, 67–68; Edwin Fenton, *Immigrants and Unions, A Case Study: Italians and American Labor, 1870–1920* (New York, 1975), 95–135; Gunther Peck, *Reinventing Free Labor: Padrone and Immigrant Workers in the North American West, 1880–1930* (New York, 2000); Humbert Nelli, "The Italian Padrone System in the United States," *Labor History* 5 (1964): 153–67.

21. *Herald*, September 18, 1892, p. 11; E. Idell Zeisloft, ed., *The New Metropolis* (New York, 1899), 523; Jacob A. Riis, *How the Other Half Lives: Studies Among the Tenements of New York* (1890; New York, 1971), 52.

22. John Koren, "The Padrone System and the Padrone Banks," *United States Bureau of Labor, Special Bulletin No. 9* (March 1897): 126. For the watchmaker and the wine shop, see advertisements in *Il Progresso*, September 4, 1889, August 1, 1891.

23. Pozzetta, "Italians of New York City," 329–36; Pozzetta, "Mulberry District of New York City," 16–17.

24. Giovanni Lordi, et al., to the Editor, *Herald*, September 25, 1892, p. 13.

25. *Il Progresso*, September 4, 1889, April 2, 1893; Pozzetta, "Mulberry District of New York City," 10; *Trow's New York City Directory for the Year Ending May 1, 1893* (New York, 1892), 301.

26. Manson, "'Foreign Element,'" 817; Pozzetta, "Mulberry District of New York City," 15; *Fifty-fifth Annual Report of the Children's Aid Society* (1907): 94–95.

27. *Frank Leslie's Illustrated Newspaper* (October 14, 1882): 123–24; *Tribune*, January 23, 1887, p. 9.

28. Pete Daniel, *The Shadow of Slavery: Peonage in the South, 1901–1969* (Urbana, 1972), 103–06; Pozzetta, "Mulberry District of New York City," 14–15, 31; *Times*, October 10, 1895, p. 25 (Ellis Island alternatives to *padrone*).

29. Charlotte Erickson, *American Industry and the European Immigrant, 1860–1885* (Cambridge, MA, 1957), 111; *Frank Leslie's Illustrated Newspaper* (August 11, 1888): 412–13.

30. *John Swinton's Paper*, January 20, 1884, p. 1; my translation of Rossi, *Un Italiano in America*, 64.

31. Pozzetta, "Italians of New York City," 243–48; Pozzetta, "Mulberry District of New York City," 19–20.

32. Giovanni Lordi, et al., to the Editor, *Herald*, September 25, 1892, p. 13; *Tribune*, April 13, 1890, p. 17; *Frank Leslie's Illustrated Newspaper* (May 1, 1880): 139; Pozzetta, "Italians of New York City," 172–75; Cinel, *National Integration of Italian Return Migration*, 128–34, 141–49, 186.

33. Jacob A. Riis, *The Making of an American* (1901; New York, 1936), 178 ("grouped by villages"); Alberto Pecorini, "The Italians in the United States," *Forum* 45 (January 1911), quoted in Pozzetta, "Italians of New York City," 96; Pozzetta, "Mulberry District of New York City," 18. This clustering was even well known in Italy. See Umberto Bosco, et al., *Basilicata* (Milan, 1965), 43. For Italian housing patterns north of Five Points in the early twentieth century, see Donna R. Gabaccia, *From Sicily to Elizabeth Street: Housing and Social Change Among Italian Immigrants, 1880–1930* (Albany, 1984).

34. *Tribune*, June 2, 1895, p. 26 (quotation); Roseboro, "Italians of New York," 399.

**Male Residents of Five Points Subdivided by
Occupational Category and Ethnicity, 1880**

	Italians	*Irish*	*Polish Jews*	*All Men*
Professionals	0%	0%	1%	0.5%
Business owners	3	6	9	5
Lower-status white-collar	2	6	8	9
Skilled manual workers	9	31	51	31
Peddlers/Street traders	24	11	25	14
Factory workers	4	1	0	2
Unskilled workers	56	39	1	34
Difficult to classify	2	8	5	5

Comparison of 1880 Italian and 1855 Irish Occupation Distribution
Among Five Points Residents

	1880 Italians	*1855 Irish*
Professionals	0%	0.4%
Business owners	3	3
Lower-status white-collar	2	3
Skilled manual workers	9	34
Peddlers/Street traders	24	1
Factory workers	4	0
Unskilled workers	56	58
Difficult to classify	2	1

The source for these employment figures and all those that follow is the 1880 United States manuscript census. I would have preferred to use the 1890 census, but the manuscript returns were destroyed by fire many years ago. I chose not to utilize the 1900 census because by that point Mulberry Bend had been razed, which altered the character of the neighborhood. For the source of the 1855 figures, see Chapter Two, note 10.

35. *Tribune,* June 2, 1895, p. 26.

36. Adams, "Italian Life in New York," 677; *Times,* October 6, 1895, p. 25; *Il Progresso,* August 17, 1890; Manson, "'Foreign Element,'" 818.

37. Adams, "Italian Life in New York," 678 (artificial flowers); *Times,* October 6, 1895, p. 25 (garment work). Women's occupations in 1880 broke down as follows:

Female Residents of Five Points
Subdivided by Occupational Category and Nativity, 1880

	Italians	*All Women*	*Irish*
Teachers/Sales clerks	0%	4%	3%
Domestic servants	16	19	17
Peddlers and Street trades	26	11	10
Manufacturing	34	24	26
Needle trades	8	19	11
Take in boarders	16	16	13
Miscellaneous	0	8	6

Comparison of 1880 Italian and 1855 Irish
Female Occupational Distribution in Five Points

	1880 Italians	*1855 Irish*
Teachers/Sales clerks	0%	0%
Domestic servants	16	29
Peddlers and Street trades	26	0
Manufacturing	34	0
Needle trades	8	47
Take in boarders	16	15

For long-term patterns in female Italian employment citywide, see Kathie Friedman-Kasaba, *Memories of Migration: Gender, Ethnicity, and Work in the Lives of Jewish and Italian Women in New York, 1870–1924* (Albany, 1996), and Miriam Cohen, *Workshop to Office: Two Generations of Italian Women in New York City, 1900–1950* (Ithaca, 1993).

38. Virginia Penny, *The Employments of Women: A Cyclopaedia of Woman's Work* (Boston, 1863), 467; *Times*, January 22, 1853; Lynch, *Wild Seventies*, 1: 60–62; *Monthly Record of the Five Points House of Industry* 1 (January 1858): 227; Robinson, *Hot Corn*, 194–98, 202–4, 213–19, 223–24; *Herald*, November 5, 1853.

39. J. Gilmer Speed, "The Mulberry Bend," *Harper's Weekly* 36 (April 30, 1892): 430.

40. George Ellington, *The Women of New York* (New York, 1869), 605; Howard R. Weisz, *Irish-American and Italian-American Educational Views and Activities, 1870–1900: A Comparison* (New York, 1976), 407; Pozzetta, "Italians of New York City," 310–11; Foerster, *Italian Emigration*, 335; *Times*, November 15, 1896, p. 15.

41. *Times*, June 10, 1874, October 6, 1895, p. 25.

42. Erickson, *American Industry and the European Immigrant*, 119–20; *World*, July 12, 1882, p. 1; *Times*, October 6, 1895, p. 25. For the view that the Italians' aversion to organized labor in this period has been overstated, see Donna Gabaccia, "Neither Padrone Slaves nor Primitive Rebels: Sicilians on Two Continents," in Dirk Hoerder, ed., *"Struggle a Hard Battle": Essays on Working-Class Immigrants* (DeKalb, 1986), 95–117.

43. Rev. Thomas P. McLoughlin, "In Darkest Chinatown," *Donahue's Magazine* (November 1897), in Peter P. McLoughlin, *Father Tom: Life and Lectures of Rev. Thomas P. McLoughlin* (New York, 1919), 95.

44. Bishop Thomas A. Becker to Archbishop James Gibbons, December 17, 1884 (photocopy), Box 1, Records of the St. Raphael Society, Center for Migration Studies, Staten Island, NY; Becker and Archbishop James Gibbons to Rev. Simeoni, in Stephen M. DiGiovanni, *Archbishop Corrigan and the Italian Immigrants* (Huntington, IN, 1994), 29.

45. Bernard J. Lynch, "The Italians in New York," *Catholic World* 47 (April 1888): 68–70; Thomas F. Lynch to Archbishop Corrigan, March 26, 1888, file C-19, microfilm roll 12, Papers of the Archdiocese of New York, Archives of the Archdiocese of New York. Bernard Lynch's comments, while distasteful, were nonetheless typical of this period. Just a few months after his article was published, an editorial in *Frank Leslie's* asserted that "of the 40,000 Italian immigrants who have landed at Castle Garden since the 1st of January last, probably not one out of ten was a desirable addition to the population of the country." They lack "that feeling of self-respect and personal independence which is desirable in a free, governing people. We cannot become enthusiastic in contemplating a manhood that would prefer driving a shoebrush to a plane, or turning the crank of a hand-organ to digging a ditch or paving a street."—*Frank Leslie's Illustrated Newspaper* (July 14, 1888): 343.

46. Lynch to Archbishop Michael A. Corrigan, March 26, 1888, file C-19, microfilm roll 12, and "A Short History of the Spiritual Work Done for Italians in the Roman Catholic Church of the Transfiguration," undated MS in the handwriting of Rev. Thomas F. Lynch, Transfiguration parish history file, series D, Papers of the Archdiocese of New York; Mary Elizabeth Brown, *Churches, Communities, and Children: Italian Immigrants in the Archdiocese of New York, 1880–1945* (New York, 1995), 51; Lynch, "The Italians in New York," 71.

47. DiGiovanni, *Archbishop Corrigan and the Italian Immigrants*, 60, 241; Lynch, "The Italians in New York," 72.

48. Father Francesco Zaboglio to Giovanni Scalabrini, June 28, 1888, in Silvano M. Tomasi, *Piety and Power: The Role of the Italian Parishes in the New York Metropolitan Area,*

1880–1930 (New York, 1975), 79; Marcellino Moroni to Cardinal Giovanni Simeoni, May 16, 1888, in DiGiovanni, *Archbishop Corrigan and the Italian Immigrants,* 99–101.

49. DiGiovanni, *Archbishop Corrigan and the Italian Immigrants,* 63–65; *Times,* January 3, 1889, p. 5. See also Grace Abbott, "Leo XIII and the Italian Catholics in the United States," *American Ecclesiastical Review* 1 (February 1889): 41–45, and Henry J. Browne, "The 'Italian Problem' in the Catholic Church of the United States, 1880–1900," United States Catholic Historical Society, *Historical Records and Studies* 35 (1946): 46–72.

50. Lynch to Corrigan, March 26, 1888, file C-19, microfilm roll 12, Papers of the Archdiocese of New York.

51. DiGiovanni, *Archbishop Corrigan and the Italian Immigrants,* 98–99, 129, 135–36, 143, 145, 241.

52. Tomasi, *Piety and Power,* 143; Robert A. Orsi, *The Madonna of 115th Street: Faith and Community in Italian Harlem, 1880–1950* (New Haven, 1985), 55–59.

53. Jacob A. Riis, "Feast-Days in Little Italy," *Century Magazine* 58 (August 1899): 496–98.

54. Ibid., 495.

55. *Tribune,* August 17, 1901; Denise M. DiCarlo, "The History of the Italian *Festa* in New York City: 1880's to the Present" (Ph.D. diss., New York University, 1990), 85–94; *Il Progresso,* August 16–19, 1890.

56. *Il Progresso,* August 16, 1891. Although press reports tended to focus on the part of the *festa* that took place on upper Mott Street outside the Five Points district, the head of the *festa* in 1890 was Gabriele Isola, probably the same man listed in the city directory as living at 14 Baxter Street near the Five Points intersection—*Il Progresso,* August 19, 1890; *Trow's New York City Directory for the Year Ending May 1, 1893,* 692.

57. *Il Progresso,* August 17, 1890, August 16, 1891, August 16, 1892.

58. Bernardino Ciambelli, *I Misteri di Mulberry Street* (New York, 1893), translated in Mario Maffi, *Gateway to the Promised Land: Ethnic Cultures on New York's Lower East Side* (New York, 1995), 113–14.

59. *Il Progresso,* August 16, 1891, August 18, 1896 ("rivers of beer"); *Tribune,* August 17, 1902, part II, p. 5.

60. Lynch to Corrigan, August 10, 1892 (photocopy), Transfiguration folder, Box 1, Italian-Americans and Religion Collection, Center for Migration Studies.

61. Riis, "Feast-Days in Little Italy," 493.

62. For more on Italian religious *feste,* see *Tribune,* July 18, 1904, p. 5; *Times,* July 12, 1903.

63. DiGiovanni, *Archbishop Corrigan and the Italian Immigrants,* 129, 135–36, 143, 145; Most Precious Blood parish history file, series D; Lynch to Corrigan, January 23 ("slaves of the Irish"), February 3 ("no privileges"), 1894, file G-5, roll 15, Papers of the Archdiocese of New York.

64. DiGiovanni, *Archbishop Corrigan and the Italian Immigrants,* 144–48, 165–70; *Souvenir History of Transfiguration Parish—Mott Street* (New York, 1897), 44, quoted in Tomasi, *Piety and Power,* 77; McLoughlin, *Father Tom,* 80; [Corrigan] to Rev. T. J. Campbell, November 2, 1893, file G-6, roll 16, and McLoughlin to Corrigan, November 10, 1898,

August 28, 1901, February 28, 1902, Transfiguration parish history file, series D, Papers of the Archdiocese of New York.

65. *Transfiguration Church: A Church of Immigrants, 1827–1977* (New York, [1977]), 16–17.

CHAPTER THIRTEEN

1. John Kuo Wei Tchen, *New York Before Chinatown: Orientalism and the Shaping of American Culture, 1776–1882* (Baltimore, 1999), 90, 284–85.

2. Ibid., 91; *Times*, October 22, 1876, p. 2. The various accounts of Appo's early life differ in many of the particulars. When in doubt I have relied upon information provided by Professor Timothy Gilfoyle of Loyola University of Chicago, who thoroughly studied the life of Quimbo Appo for "A Pickpocket's Tale: The Autobiography of George Appo," *Missouri Review* 16 (1993): 34–77, as well as for his forthcoming book on the history of crime in New York.

3. *Times*, December 26, 1856, June 20, 1859; *Trow's New York City Directory for 1855–56* (New York, 1855), 37; *Trow's New York City Directory for 1857–58* (New York, 1857), 36. Tchen identifies a Bowery tea clerk mentioned in an 1854 magazine article as Appo, but there is no evidence that the immigrant described in the passage is actually him. It appears likely that Appo did not yet live in New York in 1854. E. W. Syle to the Editor, *Spirit of the Missions* 19 (August 1854): 325; Tchen, *New York Before Chinatown*, 91.

4. *Times*, March 9, 10, April 12, 1859; Tchen, *New York Before Chinatown*, 159–62.

5. *Times*, March 10, April 12, 13, 1859.

6. *Times*, March 9, 10, April 12, 13, November 10, 1859, October 22, 1876; *Herald*, October 18, 25, 1859; *Tribune*, November 2, 1859; *Brother Jonathan*, May 19, 1860 (sentence commuted); Tchen, *New York Before Chinatown*, 160–61. Tchen mistakes the appeals process for a "second trial." The clerks in the Old Records Division, New York County Clerk's Office, can no longer locate the writ that details the appeals case.

7. *Times*, October 22, 23, 1876; "Autobiography of George Appo," typescript, pp. 1–3, Society for the Prevention of Crime Papers, Columbia University. Much of this memoir is reprinted in Gilfoyle, "A Pickpocket's Tale." The available sources provide contradictory evidence as to Appo's release date. According to Gilfoyle, Sing Sing's records indicate that he was still there in April 1869. I suspect that he was paroled sometime later that year.

8. "Autobiography of George Appo," pp. 1–3; *Daily Graphic*, March 18, 1873 (quotations); *Frank Leslie's Illustrated Newspaper* (March 16, 1872): 5, (July 5, 1873): 271.

9. "Autobiography of George Appo," pp. 1–3; Gilfoyle, "A Pickpocket's Tale," 42–45. Newspaper articles, all written years later, provide contradictory information concerning Quimbo's second arrest. Neither Gilfoyle nor I could find any information concerning it in the District Attorney's Papers.

10. "Autobiography of George Appo," pp. 1–3; Gilfoyle, "A Pickpocket's Tale," 42–45; *People v. Appo*, December 13, 1871, District Attorney's Papers, and arrests of September 20, 1875 and January 31, 1876 ("Charles Gimbo"), First District Police Court Docket Books, both at New York Municipal Archives; *Times*, September 30 ("notorious"), December 15 (p. 6), 16 (p. 6), 19 (p. 2), 1871, October 21–23, 1876; *Herald*, August 10, 1871, January 5 (p. 11), 6 (p. 11), 1872. My dating of Appo's release from prison for his various crimes is based on prison records uncovered by Gilfoyle that I have not examined.

11. Tchen, *New York Before Chinatown*, 285–88.

12. *Times*, October 21 (p. 1), 22 (p. 2), 25 (p. 10), December 21 (p. 6), 22 (p. 6), 1876; Tchen, *New York Before Chinatown*, 285–88.

13. Gilfoyle, "A Pickpocket's Tale," 37–38; *Times*, August 6 (p. 2), 7 (p. 8), 8 (p. 12), 28 (p. 8), September 4 (p. 8), 1880, June 17 (p. 3), July 11 (p. 9), 12 (p. 17), 1896, June 15, 1899 (p. 3). Information on George Appo's last years was provided to me by Gilfoyle.

14. Louis Beck, *New York's Chinatown* (New York, 1898), 250, 259–60, quoted in Gilfoyle, "A Pickpocket's Tale," 37.

15. Tchen, *New York Before Chinatown*, 284.

16. *Times*, December 26, 1856, June 20, 1859; Tchen, *New York Before Chinatown*, 74–86.

17. *Tribune*, January 4, 1869; *Daily Graphic*, March 18, 1873; *Harper's Weekly* 18 (March 7, 1874): 222; Tchen, *New York Before Chinatown*, 236; Sixth Ward, 1870 United States manuscript census, National Archives.

18. *Daily Graphic*, March 18, 1873; *Times*, December 26, 1873, February 16, 1874.

19. *Times*, December 26, 1873, March 22, 1880; *Sun*, February 16, 1874; *World*, January 30, 1877; Tchen, *New York Before Chinatown*, 225, 232–33, 236–37.

20. Arthur Bonner, *Alas! What Brought Thee Hither? The Chinese in New York, 1800–1950* (Cranbury, NJ, 1997), 41–42; John A. Garraty and Mark C. Carnes, eds., *American National Biography*, 24 vols. (New York, 1999), 12: 421–22.

21. *Herald*, March 3, 1880; *Tribune*, March 4, 1880, p. 8.

22. *Times*, March 4, 6, 1880, both p. 8; *Herald*, March 6 (p. 3), 7 (p. 8), 1880; *Frank Leslie's Illustrated Newspaper* (March 27, 1880): 55; Sixth Ward, 1880 United States manuscript census.

23. *Frank Leslie's Illustrated Newspaper* (March 27, 1880): 55, (June 30, 1888): 324; districts 18–27, Sixth Ward, 1890 Police Census, New York Municipal Archives.

24. David M. Katzman and William M. Tuttle, Jr., eds., *Plain Folk: The Life Stories of Undistinguished Americans* (Urbana, 1982), 168–69. For the regional origin of the New York Chinese, see Bonner, *Alas! What Brought Thee Hither?*, 67.

25. *Harper's Weekly* 12 (September 19, 1868): 604; Tchen, *New York Before Chinatown*, 233–34.

26. Junius H. Browne, *The Great Metropolis: A Mirror of New-York* (Hartford, 1869), 97–98; *Tribune*, January 4, 1869, June 21, 1885, p. 9; Tchen, *New York Before Chinatown*, 227–28.

27. *Tribune*, June 21, 1885, p. 9; *Frank Leslie's Illustrated Newspaper* (January 28, 1888): 398; *Times*, March 6, 1880; Bonner, *Alas! What Brought Thee Hither?*, 67; Tchen, *New York Before Chinatown*, 227–28.

28. The best descriptions of the laundryman's working conditions are Renqui Yu, *To Save China, To Save Ourselves: The Chinese Hand Laundry Alliance of New York* (Philadelphia, 1992), 8–30, and Paul C. P. Siu, *The Chinese Laundryman: A Study of Social Isolation* (New York, 1987).

29. Wong Ching Foo, "The Chinese in New York," *Cosmopolitan* 5 (October 1888): 298.

30. Ibid., 298–300.

31. Ibid., 301; Mary Lui, "Groceries, Letters, and Community: The Local Store in China-town's 'Bachelor Society,'" *Bu Gao Ban* [New York Chinatown History Museum] 8 (Winter 1991): 1–4.

32. *Sun*, March 7, 1880.

33. Bonner, *Alas! What Brought Thee Hither?*, 71; *Herald*, August 2 (quotation, p. 9), November 7, 1894.

34. The *Tribune* asserted that New York's Chinese population in 1885 consisted of 4,500 laundrymen, 300 cigarmakers, 200 sailors, 200 gamblers, 300 unemployed looking for places to start laundries, and 100 merchants. It is difficult to verify the *Tribune's* figures with the census because Chinatown was just beginning to expand rapidly as the 1880 census was conducted, and the Chinese were just beginning to turn to laundrywork in large numbers. The 1890 census returns were destroyed in a fire. A sample of the 1880 census reveals the following occupational breakdown among Five Points Chinese Americans: 38% cigarmakers, 24% merchants and professionals, 14% laundrymen, 10% cooks, 5% sailors, and the remainder in miscellaneous or difficult to classify occupations. *Tribune*, June 21, 1885, p. 9; *Frank Leslie's Illustrated Newspaper* (June 30, 1888): 324; Sixth Ward, 1880 United States manuscript census.

35. *Herald*, March 3, 5, 1880; *Times*, March 6, 1880, p. 8; *Sun*, March 7, 1880 (not quoted).

36. *Times*, May 6, 1880, p. 8; *Evening Post*, May 10, 1880.

37. *Times*, May 7, 1880, p. 4; *Evening Post*, May 10, 1880; Thomas F. Lynch to Archbishop Corrigan, May 4, 1889, Transfiguration parish history file, series D, Papers of the Archdiocese of New York.

38. *Herald*, March 5, 1880, p. 8; *Frank Leslie's Illustrated Newspaper* (March 27, 1880): 55; *Sun*, March 7, 1880; *Times*, April 7, 1883, p. 8.

39. *Times*, April 7, 1883, p. 8, April 12, 1883, p. 8. Although the *Times* reported that Lee bought 18 Mott, city real estate records indicate that he actually purchased 16 Mott. But he did lease 4 and 18 Mott in their entirety. See lots 3, 9, and 10, block 162, "Block and Lot Folders," New York Municipal Archives.

40. *Frank Leslie's Illustrated Newspaper* (June 30, 1888): 324; Wong, "Chinese in New York," 304.

41. Wong, "Chinese in New York," 304; George Walling, *Recollections of a New York Chief of Police* (New York, 1887), 430–31; Rev. Thomas P. McLoughlin, "In Darkest Chinatown," *Donahue's Magazine* (November 1897), in Peter P. McLoughlin, *Father Tom: The Life and Lectures of Rev. Thomas P. McLoughlin* (New York, 1919), 100–101 (on Chinese vegetables).

42. *Frank Leslie's* and the *Tribune* quoted in Bonner, *Alas! What Brought Thee Hither?*, 97, 105; E. Idell Zeisloft, ed., *The New Metropolis* (New York, 1899), 271.

43. Walling, *Recollections of a New York Chief of Police*, 423; Wong, "Chinese in New York," 305.

44. Wong, "Chinese in New York," 306; Steward Culin, "The Gambling Games of the Chinese in America," *University of Pennsylvania Series in Philology, Literature and Archaeology* 1, no. 4 (1891): 1–5; Bonner, *Alas! What Brought Thee Hither?*, 62–64; Walling,

Recollections of a New York Chief of Police, 426; Frank Moss, *The American Metropolis*, 3 vols. (New York, 1897), 2: 427–29.

45. Moss, *American Metropolis*, 2: 427–29; Wong, "Chinese in New York," 306; Culin, "Gambling Games of the Chinese," 6–11; Bonner, *Alas! What Brought Thee Hither?*, 66; Walling, *Recollections of a New York Chief of Police*, 423–25. A block away on Mulberry Street, Italian Five Pointers gambled as well. They had their own numbers game, called *lotto*, while Italian newsboys were especially fond of craps. George E. Pozzetta, "The Mulberry District of New York City: The Years Before World War One," in Robert F. Harney and J. Vincenza Scarpaci, eds., *Little Italies in North America* (Toronto, 1981), 25–26; *Forty-eighth Annual Report of the Children's Aid Society* (1900): 67.

46. *Herald*, December 26, 1869; *Times*, March 22, 1880; Walling, *Recollections of a New York Chief of Police*, 418–22; Wong, "Chinese in New York," 308–11.

47. *Daily Graphic*, March 18, 1873; *Harper's Weekly* 18 (March 7, 1874): 222; *Times*, August 11, 1878, p. 5; *Frank Leslie's Illustrated Newspaper* (May 12, 1883): 181, 190; (May 19, 1883): 204, 206.

48. *Tribune*, September 28, 1904, p. 3, January 11, 1918, p. 13; *Herald*, January 11, 1918; *Times*, April 2, 1882, p. 2.

49. *Herald*, August 11, 1878, February 5, 1879, April 25, 1883, p. 10.

50. *Daily Graphic*, March 26, 1879.

51. Bruce Edward Hall, *Tea That Burns: A Family Memoir of Chinatown* (New York, 1998), 59; Bonner, *Alas! What Brought Thee Hither?*, 42–45, 61–62; *Times*, April 25, 1883, p. 8.

52. *Times*, April 28, 1880, p. 1; *Tribune*, October 18, 1885, p. 9; *Herald*, April 25, 1883, p. 10; *Sun*, January 31, 1881.

53. *Times*, April 25, 1883, p. 8; *Herald*, April 25, 1883, p. 10.

54. *Times*, April 25 (p. 8), 26 (p. 8), May 3 (p. 3), 1883. The affidavits can be found in *People v. Tom Lee, et al.*, folders 1098 and 1101, Box 103, Court of General Sessions Indictment Papers, New York Municipal Archives.

55. *Times*, April 24 (p. 8), 26 (p. 8), May 17 (pp. 2 and 4), 1883; *Herald*, April 25, 1883, p. 10.

56. *Herald*, May 11 (p. 3, "little girls"), 12 (p. 9, "girl trap"), 1883; *Frank Leslie's Illustrated Newspaper* (May 12, 1883): 190 ("can't do without it").

57. *Frank Leslie's Illustrated Newspaper* (May 19, 1883): 206; *Herald*, May 11, 1883, p. 3; *Sun*, May 11, 1883; *Tribune*, May 11, 13, 1883; arrests of May 10, 11, 12, pp. 257, 260, 262, First District Police Court Docket Books, New York Municipal Archives; Augustine E. Costello, *Our Police Protectors: The History of the New York Police from the Earliest Period to the Present Time* ([New York], 1885), 517 (full text of 1882 opium law).

58. *Herald*, May 11 (p. 3, "buncombe"), 12 (p. 9), 14 (p. 8, "not general").

59. *Herald*, May 11 (p. 3), 13 (p. 11), 1883; *Tribune*, May 13, 1883 (p. 5).

60. *Tribune*, May 12, 1883; *Herald*, May 11, 1883, p. 3. In internal archdiocese correspondence, Lynch complained that the Young Men's Association organized its own "promiscuous balls" and that the group continued to tell the press that it was associated with Transfiguration even though "they have been cut off from the church for the past two years"—Lynch to Archbishop Corrigan, May 16, 1886, file C-9, reel 9, Papers of the Arch-

diocese of New York. Chinese Americans sometimes complained to the police about the opium dens. See Capt. John McCullagh to Police Superintendent William Murray, June 30, 1887, Box 87-HAS-30, Abram S. Hewitt Mayoral Papers, New York Municipal Archives.

61. *Tribune,* May 12, 1883; *Herald,* May 12, 1883, p. 9; *Times,* May 17, 1883, pp. 2 and 4; Ah Chung affidavit in *People v. Ah Chung,* May 15, 1883, folder 1091, Box 102, *People v. Tom Lee et al.,* May 1, 1883, folders 1098 and 1101, Box 103, Court of General Sessions Indictment Papers. Ah Chung was tried and acquitted. The *Times*'s statement that charges against Lee were dropped on May 16 is contradicted by the indictment records. It is unclear whether the Ah Chung who implicated Lee after his arrest in the opium raids is the same person as the "Ar Chun" who filed an affidavit in the gambling case, or the "Ah Chum" who was the only witness called at Lee's hearing. The *Herald* and *Frank Leslie's* named Wo Kee (sometimes referred to by this point as "Sam Kee") as the leader of the Chinatown forces opposing Lee. See *Frank Leslie's Illustrated Newspaper* (May 12, 1883): 190.

62. Allen S. Williams, *The Demon of the Orient and His Satellite Fiends of the Joints: Our Opium Smokers as They Are in Tartar Hells and American Paradises* (New York, 1883), 12, 32 ("magnate").

63. Peter Kwong, *Chinatown, New York: Labor and Politics, 1930–1950* (New York, 1979), 39–41; Hall, *Tea That Burns,* 58–59; *Times,* August 1, 1883, p. 8 (Wong society).

64. Bonner, *Alas! What Brought Thee Hither?,* 39–40.

65. *Times,* December 8, 1884, p. 3; Bonner, *Alas! What Brought Thee Hither?,* 82.

66. *Tribune,* January 4, 1869.

67. *Times,* December 26, 1873; Walling, *Recollections of a New York Chief of Police,* 429–30; Wong, "Chinese in New York," 308.

68. McLoughlin, "In Darkest Chinatown," 91–93.

69. *Sun,* May 12 (quotation), 13, 1879; *Times,* April 25 (p. 3), May 5 (p. 8), 28 (p. 8), 1879; Bonner, *Alas! What Brought Thee Hither?,* 110.

70. *Herald,* December 2, 1894; McLoughlin, "In Darkest Chinatown," 96.

71. *Times,* December 26, 1856; *Yankee Notions* (March 1858): 65; *Tribune,* January 4, 1869; *Herald,* December 26, 1869; *World,* January 30, 1877; Wong, "Chinese in New York," 308. It is possible that the press exaggerated the extent of these Chinese-Irish marriages. The census documents eighty-two Chinese-white couples living in Five Points in 1900, and of these, only one in seven involved an Irish immigrant. But Chinese-Irish unions may have been more common in the immediate postwar years. Record of Marriages, p. 362, Five Points Mission Records, United Methodist Church Archives, Drew University; Mary Ting Li Lui, "Contested Relations: Interracial Marriages and Families in New York City's Chinatown, 1880–1910," paper presented at the Fourteenth National Conference of the Association for Asian American Studies, April 1997, pp. 3–9.

72. *Times,* December 9, 1890, p. 3; *Tribune,* February 15, 1885, p. 12; *Herald,* March 3, 1885, p. 10; Hall, *Tea That Burns,* 105–11; Lui, "Contested Relations," 14.

73. *Times,* June 20, 1859; *World,* January 30, 1877.

74. Lucy E. Salyer, *Laws Harsh as Tigers: Chinese Immigrants and the Shaping of Modern Immigration Law* (Chapel Hill, 1995), 47–55 (including *Times* quotation); Charles J.

McClain, *In Search of Equality: The Chinese Struggle Against Discrimination in Nineteenth-Century America* (Berkeley, 1994), 201–13; *Harper's Weekly* (April 16, 1892): 362.

75. *Times*, March 18 (p. 1), May 11 (p. 11), 16 (p. 9), 22 (p. 11, for the dissenting opinions as unusually "vigorous"), 1893; Salyer, *Laws Harsh as Tigers*, 47–58; McClain, *In Search of Equality*, 201–13; *Fong Yue Ting v. United States*, 149 U.S. 698 (1893). Without the budget to deport the tens of thousands who failed to register, Secretary of the Treasury John G. Carlisle ordered Customs and Internal Revenue agents not to enforce this provision of the act. I have not been able to determine whether Fong Yue Ting and his co-defendants were actually deported after the Supreme Court's ruling. The *Times* reported that "the three Chinamen . . . will probably be sent out of the country at an early date unless some expedient be devised to circumvent the law," but apparently never followed up on the story—*Times*, May 16, 1893, p. 9.

76. *Times*, August 17, 1904, p. 7; *Tribune*, September 28, 1904, p. 3.

77. *Harper's Weekly* (April 16, 1892): 362; *Herald*, January 11, 1918, p. 10 (Lee); Bonner, *Alas! What Brought Thee Hither?*, 48; *Tribune*, September 10, 1884, p. 8 (Assing); Hall, *Tea That Burns*, 209 (Hor Poa). On second-generation Italian-American teenagers' desire to assimilate, see Viola Roseboro, "The Italians of New York," *Cosmopolitan* 4 (January 1888): 404, who notes that an immigrant's daughter was anxious "to sink her foreign extraction and be considered an American." On the same phenomenon among second-generation Irish Americans, see *Irish-American*, April 30, 1858, and Thomas D'A. McGee, *A History of the Irish Settlers in North America*, 6th ed. (Boston, 1855), 236. I had hoped to be able to say more about assimilation in Five Points, but there is very little evidence concerning this issue in the neighborhood's documentary record.

Chapter Fourteen

1. Jacob A. Riis, *The Making of an American* (New York, 1901), 113–24.

2. Ibid., 124–29.

3. Ibid., 130–43.

4. Ibid., 152–53; James B. Lane, *Jacob A. Riis and the American City* (Port Washington, NY, 1974), 29–44. Those who blamed the immigrants for tenement conditions reasoned that their American homes were an improvement over their European abodes, and that the newcomers therefore felt no compulsion either to maintain them properly or to complain about landlord abuses. As one observer put it in the 1880s, the tenements were "an upward step in evolution so far as many foreigners are concerned. . . . Indeed, in the last analysis, many of the worst social conditions we see are really stages of an upward advance"—Henry D. Chapin, "Preventable Causes of Poverty," *Forum* 7 (1889): 415–23, in David Ward, *Poverty, Ethnicity and the American City, 1840–1925: Changing Conceptions of the Slum and the Ghetto* (New York, 1989), 63.

5. Riis, *Making of an American*, 173. Riis wrote (p. 178) that "my scrap-book from the year 1883 to 1896 is one running comment on the Bend." This scrapbook is in the Riis Collection, Manuscripts Division, Library of Congress.

6. *Times*, April 21 (p. 8), 30 (p. 5, quotation), May 14 (p. 5), 1887; *World*, April 21, 1887, p. 10; Allan Nevins, *Abram S. Hewitt: With Some Account of Peter Cooper* (1935; New York, 1967), 504–5.

7. Riis, *Making of an American,* 174–77. For the dating of Riis's first tenement photographs to 1887, I have relied on Maren Stange, *Symbols of Ideal Life: Social Documentary Photography in America, 1890–1950* (New York, 1989), chap. 1.

8. Riis, *Making of an American,* 173–75.

9. Ibid., 192–93.

10. *Tribune,* January 26, 1888, p. 10; Riis, *Making of an American,* 193.

11. Stange, *Symbols of Ideal Life,* 5–6; *Evening Post,* February 28, 1888; Riis, *Making of an American,* 193.

12. *Sun,* February 12, 1888, p. 10. One newspaper, the *Daily Graphic,* had begun printing photos using the halftone process in March 1880, but New Yorkers considered that journal a scandal sheet rather than a serious newspaper.

13. Riis, *Making of an American,* 193–94; Jacob A. Riis, "How the Other Half Lives: Studies Among the Tenements," *Scribner's Magazine* 6 (December 1889): 643–62.

14. Riis, *Making of an American,* 177. Five Pointers were discussing the plans to tear down Mulberry Bend by the spring of 1888. See Thomas F. Lynch to Michael Corrigan, March 26, 1888, C-19, roll 12, Archives of the Archdiocese of New York. In his *Iconography of Manhattan Island,* Isaac Stokes states that plans for the park were submitted in 1889, but I could not find the *Tribune* article he cites. See Isaac N. P. Stokes, *Iconography of Manhattan Island: 1498–1909,* 6 vols. (1915–1928; New York, 1967), 5: 2000. For an earlier proposal to tear down part of the Bend, see "Report of Tenement-House Commission," February 17, 1885, in *Documents of the Senate of the State of New-York, 108th Session, 1885* (Albany, 1885), vol. 5, doc. 36, pp. 3–5, 7–15.

15. Riis, *Making of an American,* 196–97, 199 (quotation).

16. Jacob A. Riis, *How the Other Half Lives: Studies Among the Tenements of New York* (1890; New York, 1971), 214.

17. Ibid., 211–12.

18. Ibid., 212.

19. Lowell to Riis, November 21, 1890, in Riis, *Making of an American,* 199; *Press,* November 23, 1890; *The True Nationalist,* November 29, 1890; *Chicago Times,* December 20, 1890; *Boston Times,* November 30, 1890; *The Critic,* December 27, 1890; *The Independent,* January 1, 1891, all in Riis Scrapbook, Riis Collection.

20. *Brooklyn Times,* November 29, 1890; *Chicago Tribune,* December 13, 1890, both in Riis Scrapbook, Riis Collection; Riis, *Making of an American,* 212; Luc Sante, Introduction to Penguin Books edn. of *How the Other Half Lives* (New York, 1997), xi.

21. *Times,* July 17, 1891, p. 8, October 7, 1892, p. 10, January 21 (p. 9), 28 (p. 10), May 20 (p. 9), 1893.

22. Stokes, *Iconography of Manhattan Island,* 5: 2018; *Times,* December 7, 1894, p. 2, January 22 (p. 9), June 7 (p. 7), 20 (p. 3), 1895.

23. *Times,* December 21, 1895, p. 14, June 23, 1896, p. 9, June 16, 1897, p. 7; Jacob A. Riis, *The Battle with the Slum* (New York, 1902), 269–70.

24. *Times,* June 16, 1897, p. 7; Riis, *Battle with the Slum,* 264 (quotation), 268; Riis, *Making of an American,* 183; Riis, "The Clearing of Mulberry Bend: The Story of the Rise and Fall of a Typical New York Slum," *Review of Reviews* 12 (August 1895): 172.

25. Riis, *Battle with the Slum,* 286–87, 289 (quotation), 307–9, 355 (quotation); James Ford, *Slums and Housing, with Special Reference to New York City: History, Conditions, Policy,* 2 vols. (Cambridge, MA, 1936), 1: 201.

26. *Times,* November 15, 1896, magazine p. 15; E. Idell Zeisloft, ed., *The New Metropolis* (New York, 1899), 522–23; Charles Hemstreet, *When Old New York Was Young* (New York, 1902), 194; *Fifty-fifth Annual Report of the Children's Aid Society* (1907): 107.

27. Gwendolyn Berry, *Idleness and the Health of a Neighborhood: A Social Study of the Mulberry District* (New York, 1933), 4–7; Walter Laidlaw, ed., *Population of the City of New York, 1890–1930* (New York, 1932); Pozzetta, "Mulberry District of New York City," 28.

28. *Times,* September 19, 1891, p. 1 (municipal building), June 26 (p. 3, Elm Street), November 7 (magazine, p. 6), 1897; Harlow, *Old Bowery Days,* 508.

29. Walter M. Whitehill, *Boston: A Topographical History* (Cambridge, MA, 1968), 174–75; Joel Schwartz, *The New York Approach: Robert Moses, Urban Liberals, and Redevelopment of the Inner City* (Columbus, OH, 1993).

30. See Ford, *Slums and Housing;* Roy Lubove, *The Progressive and the Slums: Tenement House Reform in New York City, 1890–1917* (Pittsburgh, 1962); and Ward, *Poverty, Ethnicity and the American City,* passim.

31. *Evening Post,* August 20, 1850; *Times,* July 1, 1859; Riis, *How the Other Half Lives,* 32.

32. *Times,* March 28, 1856; Robert W. DeForest and Lawrence Veiller, eds., *The Tenement House Problem,* 2 vols. (1903; New York, 1970), 1: 87; Robert H. Bremmer, "The Big Flat: A History of a New York Tenement," *American Historical Review* 64 (1958): 54–62. The only "model tenement" built in Five Points was the one constructed in the 1850s at 34 Baxter Street. "Filthy," "wretched," and "impregnated with the effluvia" from the commodes, this tenement suffered the same fate as the Big Flat and Gotham Court. Architect John Sexton owned the property and probably designed it as well. See *Monthly Record of the Five Points House of Industry* 3 (March 1860): 249–50; "Report of the Select Committee Appointed to Examine into the Condition of Tenant Houses in New-York and Brooklyn," *Documents of the Assembly of the State of New-York, Eightieth Session— 1857* (Albany, 1857), doc. 205, p. 28; Manhattan Records of Real Estate Assessment, Sixth Ward, 1860, New York Municipal Archives (for Sexton as owner); *Times,* February 20, 1904, p. 9 (Sexton's obituary).

33. Donna R. Gabaccia, *From Sicily to Elizabeth Street: Housing and Social Change Among Italian Immigrants, 1880–1930* (Albany, 1984).

34. Bruce Edward Hall, *Tea That Burns: A Family Memoir of Chinatown* (New York, 1998), 119–21; Alvin Harlow, *Old Bowery Days: The Chronicles of a Famous Street* (New York, 1931), 483–84; Philip Furia, *Irving Berlin: A Life in Song* (New York, 1998), 18; Gene Fowler, *Schnozzola: The Story of Jimmy Durante* (New York, 1951), 19–21.

35. Herbert Asbury, *The Gangs of New York: An Informal History of the Underworld* (New York, 1928), 272–95; Harlow, *Old Bowery Days,* 501–3; Luc Sante, *Low Life: Lures and Snares of Old New York* (New York, 1991), 234.

36. Asbury, *Gangs of New York*, 299–324; *Herald*, January 11, 1918, p. 10; Hall, *Tea That Burns*, 132–61.

37. Pozzetta, "The Italians of New York City," 27 (quotation), 373–75; Viola Roseboro, "The Italians of New York," *Cosmopolitan* 4 (January 1888): 400, 402–3.

38. Riis, *Battle with the Slum*, 186–87; *Tribune*, September 21, 1894, p. 4; *Times*, October 6, 1895, p. 25.

39. See Hsiang-Shui Chen, *Chinatown No More: Taiwan Immigrants in Contemporary New York* (Ithaca, 1992); Ko-Lin Chin, *Smuggled Chinese* (Philadelphia, 1999); Peter Kwong, *The New Chinatown* (New York, 1987); and Gwen Kinkead, *Chinatown: Portrait of a Closed Society* (New York, 1992).

40. "The Egg-Cake Lady of Mosco Street," *Times*, December 11, 1994, sect. 13, p. 4.

41. *Times*, April 26, 1974, p. 39, July 13, 1980, sect. 4, p. 6, May 7, 1995, sect. 13, p. 6.

42. *Times*, June 22 (sect. 13, p. 1), November 20 (p. B3), 1997.

43. *Times*, December 28, 1981, p. A1, February 14, 1998, p. B6; *Daily News*, July 5 (p. 22), 6 (p. 16), 1998.

44. *Times*, February 6 (p. A1), March 12 (sect. 1, p. 1), 1995, July 8 (p. A15), November 12 (sect. 14, p. 9), 2000; *Daily News*, November 8, 1999, p. 14.

45. *Daily News*, November 10, 1995, p. 7; *Times*, October 6, 1996, sect. 1, p. 1.

SELECT BIBLIOGRAPHY

Five Points is based overwhelmingly on the writings of those who saw the neighborhood firsthand. Because so much misinformation about the district and its inhabitants has spread over the years, I always attempted to verify stories found in historical works by consulting the contemporary record. Consequently, my notes do not reflect how much valuable material I found in the writings of other historians. What follows is a list of the works, other than newspapers, that I relied upon most heavily for re-creating the Five Points story:

ARCHIVAL SOURCES

Archives of the Archdiocese of New York, Yonkers, NY
  Most Precious Blood and Transfiguration Parish History Files
Church of the Transfiguration, 29 Mott Street, New York
  Marriage Registry
Columbia University
  "Autobiography of George Appo." Society for the Prevention of Crime Papers
Five Points Archaeology Project
  Artifacts currently housed in the basement of the World Trade Center. A permanent location for storage and display has not yet been determined. See http://r2.gsa.gov/fivept/fphome.htm
Library of Congress,
  Jacob A. Riis Collection
National Archives
  Manuscript Returns of the 1850, 1860, 1870, 1880, and 1900 federal censuses.
  Register of Drafted Men, Fourth Congressional District, Entry 1589, Record Group 110
New York County Clerk's Office, Old Records Division
  Manuscript Returns of the 1855 New York State Census
New-York Historical Society
  William H. Bell Diary
New York Municipal Archives
  1890 New York Police Census
  Housing Department "Block and Lot" Folders
  Manhattan Records of Real Estate Assessment
  New York County District Attorney's Indictment Papers
New York Public Library
  Charles F. and George L. Osborn Account Books
  Emigrant Savings Bank Collection
United Methodist Church Archives, Drew University, Madison, NJ
  Five Points Mission Records

Published Sources and Dissertations

Alland, Alexander. *Jacob A. Riis: Photographer and Citizen*. New York, 1974.

Asbury, Herbert. *The Gangs of New York: An Informal History of the Underworld*. New York, 1928.

Barnard, William F. *Forty Years at the Five Points: A Sketch of the Five Points House of Industry*. New York, 1893.

Barnes, David M. *The Draft Riots in New York*. New York, 1863.

Bayor, Ronald, and Timothy Meagher, eds. *The New York Irish*. Baltimore, 1996.

Bethel, Denise. "Mr. Halliday's Picture Album." *Seaport* (Fall 1994): 17–21.

Blackmar, Elizabeth. *Manhattan for Rent, 1785–1850*. Ithaca, 1990.

[Bobo, William M.] *Glimpses of New-York City, by a South Carolinian*. Charleston, 1852.

Bonner, Arthur. *Alas! What Brought Thee Hither! The Chinese in New York, 1800–1950*. Cranbury, NJ, 1997.

Boris, Eileen. *Home to Work: Motherhood and the Politics of Industrial Homework in the United States*. New York, 1994.

Boyer, Paul. *Urban Masses and Moral Order in America, 1820–1920*. Cambridge, 1978.

Brace, Charles Loring. *The Dangerous Classes of New York and Twenty Years Work Among Them*. 3rd ed. New York, 1872.

Breen, Matthew P. *Thirty Years of New York Politics Up-to-Date*. New York, 1899.

Bremmer, Robert H. "The Big Flat: A History of a New York Tenement." *American Historical Review* 64 (1958): 54–62.

Brown, Mary Elizabeth. *Churches, Communities, and Children: Italian Immigrants in the Archdiocese of New York, 1880–1945*. New York, 1995.

Browne, Henry J. "The 'Italian Problem' in the Catholic Church of the United States, 1880–1900." United States Catholic Historical Society, *Historical Records and Studies* 35 (1946): 46–72.

Browne, Junius H. *The Great Metropolis: A Mirror of New-York*. Hartford, 1869.

Burrows, Edwin G., and Mike Wallace. *Gotham: A History of New York City to 1898*. New York, 1999.

Czitrom, Daniel. "Underworlds and Underdogs: Big Tim Sullivan and Metropolitan Politics in New York, 1889–1913." *Journal of American History* 78 (1991): 536–58.

Davenport, John I. *Election and Naturalization Frauds in New York City, 1860–1870*. 2nd ed. New York, 1894.

DeForest, Robert W., and Lawrence Veiller, eds. *The Tenement House Problem*. 2 vols. New York, 1903.

Dickens, Charles. *American Notes*. London, 1842.

DiGiovanni, Stephen M. *Archbishop Corrigan and the Italian Immigrants*. Huntington, IN, 1994.

Dolan, Jay P. *The Immigrant Church: New York's Irish and German Catholics, 1815–1865*. Baltimore, 1975.

Ernst, Robert J. *Immigrant Life in New York City, 1825–1860*. New York, 1948.

Five Points House of Industry. *Annual Reports*.

——. *Monthly Record of the Five Points House of Industry*.

Foster, George G. *New York by Gas-Light*. New York, 1850.

——. *New York in Slices: By an Experienced Carver, Being the Original Slices Published in the N.Y. Tribune*. New York, 1849.

Gilfoyle, Timothy J. *City of Eros: New York City, Prostitution, and the Commercialization of Sex, 1790–1920*. New York, 1992.

——. "A Pickpocket's Tale: The Autobiography of George Appo." *Missouri Review* 16 (1993): 34–77.

Gilje, Paul A. *The Road to Mobocracy: Popular Disorder in New York City, 1763–1834.* Chapel Hill, 1988.

Glanz, Rudolf. "Vanguard to the Russians: The Poseners in America." *YIVO Annual of Jewish Social Science* 18 (1983): 1–38.

Gorn, Elliott J. *The Manly Art: Bare-Knuckle Prize Fighting in America.* Ithaca, 1986.

Grinstein, Hyman B. *The Rise of the Jewish Community of New York, 1654–1860.* Philadelphia, 1945.

Griscom, John H. *The Sanitary Condition of the Laboring Population of New York.* New York, 1845.

Groneman, Carol. "The 'Bloody Ould Sixth': A Social Analysis of a New York City Working-Class Community in the Mid-Nineteenth Century." Ph.D. diss., University of Rochester, 1973.

——. "'She Earns as a Child; She Pays as a Man:' Women Workers in a Mid-Nineteenth-Century New York City Community." In Milton Cantor and Bruce Laurie, eds., *Class, Sex, and the Woman Worker.* Westport, CT, 1977.

——. "Working-Class Immigrant Women in Mid-Nineteenth Century New York: The Irish Woman's Experience." *Journal of Urban History* 4 (1978): 255–73.

Hall, Bruce Edward. *Tea That Burns: A Family Memoir of Chinatown.* New York, 1998.

Halliday, Samuel B. *The Lost and Found; or Life Among the Poor.* New York, 1859.

Harlow, Alvin F. *Old Bowery Days: The Chronicles of a Famous Street.* New York, 1931.

Hill, Marilynn Wood. *Their Sisters' Keepers: Prostitution in New York City, 1830–1870.* Berkeley, 1993.

Holt, Marilyn I. *The Orphan Trains: Placing Out in America.* Lincoln, NE, 1992.

Ivins, William M. *Machine Politics and Money in Elections in New York City.* New York, 1887.

James, Ed. *The Life and Battles of Tom Hyer.* New York, n.d.

——. *The Life and Battles of Yankee Sullivan.* New York, n.d.

Kaplan, Michael. "The World of the B'hoys: Urban Violence and the Political Culture of Antebellum New York City, 1825–1860." Ph.D. diss., New York University, 1996.

Kernan, J. Frank. *Reminiscences of the Old Fire Laddies.* New York, 1885.

Langsam, Miriam Z. *Children West: A History of the Placing-Out System of the New York Children's Aid Society, 1853–1890.* Madison, 1964.

Lubitz, Edward. "The Tenement Problem in New York City and the Movement for Its Reform, 1856–1867." Ph.D. diss., New York University, 1970.

Lubove, Roy. *The Progressive and the Slums: Tenement House Reform in New York City, 1890–1917.* Pittsburgh, 1962.

Lynch, Bernard J. "The Italians in New York." *Catholic World* 47 (April 1888): 67–73.

Lyne, Gerard J. "William Steuart Trench and the Post-Famine Emigration from Kenmare to America, 1850–1855." *Journal of the Kerry Archaeological and Historical Society* 25 (1992): 51–137.

Manson, George J. "The Foreign Element in New York City. V: The Italians." *Harper's Weekly* 34 (October 18, 1890): 817–20.

Mathews, Cornelius. *A Pen-and-Ink-Panorama of New-York City.* New York, 1853.

McLoughlin, Peter P. *Father Tom: The Life and Lectures of Rev. Thomas P. McLoughlin.* New York, 1919.

McTernan, John C., *Memory Harbour, The Port of Sligo: An Outline of Its Growth and Decline and Its Role as an Emigration Port.* Sligo, 1992.

Morrow, John. *A Voice from the Newsboys.* New York, 1860.

Nelli, Numbert. "The Italian Padrone System in the United States." *Labor History* 5 (1964): 153–67.

New York Election Frauds. House Report No. 31, 3rd Session, 40th Congress. Washington, DC, 1869.

The Old Brewery and the New Mission House at the Five Points, By Ladies of the Mission. New York, 1854.

Peck, Gunther. *Reinventing Free Labor: Padrone and Immigrant Workers in the North American West, 1880–1930.* New York, 2000.

Penny, Virginia. *The Employments of Women: A Cyclopaedia of Woman's Work.* Boston, 1863.

Perris, William. *Maps of the City of New York, Surveyed Under the Direction of the Insurance Companies of Said City.* New York, 1853–75.

Plunz, Richard. *A History of Housing in New York City: Dwelling Type and Social Change in the American Metropolis.* New York, 1990.

Pozzetta, George E. "The Italians of New York City, 1890–1914." Ph.D. diss., University of North Carolina at Chapel Hill, 1971.

——. "The Mulberry District of New York City: The Years Before World War One." In Robert F. Harney and J. Vincenza Scarpaci, eds., *Little Italies in North America.* Toronto, 1981.

"Report of the Select Committee Appointed to Examine into the Condition of Tenant Houses in New-York and Brooklyn." *Documents of the Assembly of the State of New-York, Eightieth Session—1857.* Document 205. Albany, 1857.

Reynolds, David S. *Walt Whitman's America: A Cultural Biography.* New York, 1995.

Richards, Leonard L. *Gentlemen of Property and Standing: Anti-Abolition Mobs in Jacksonian America.* New York, 1970.

Ridge, John T. *Sligo in New York: The Irish from County Sligo, 1849–1991.* New York, 1991.

Riis, Jacob A. *The Battle with the Slum.* New York, 1902.

——. *The Children of the Poor.* New York, 1892.

——. "The Clearing of Mulberry Bend: The Story of the Rise and Fall of a Typical New York Slum." *American Review of Reviews* 12 (August 1895): 172–78.

——. "Feast-Days in Little Italy." *Century Magazine* 58 (August 1899): 491–99.

——. "How the Other Half Lives: Studies Among the Tenements." *Scribner's Magazine* 6 (December 1889): 643–62.

——. *How the Other Half Lives: Studies Among the Tenements of New York.* New York, 1890.

——. *The Making of an American.* New York, 1901.

——. *Out of Mulberry Street: Stories of Tenement Life in New York City.* New York, 1898.

Robinson, Solon. *Hot Corn: Life Scenes in New York Illustrated.* New York, 1854.

Roseboro, Viola. "The Italians of New York." *Cosmopolitan* 4 (January 1888): 396–406.

Rosenberg, Carroll Smith. *Religion and the Rise of the American City: The New York City Mission Movement, 1812–1870.* Ithaca, 1971.

Sanger, William. *The History of Prostitution.* New York, 1859.

Sante, Luc. *Low Life: Lures and Snares of Old New York.* New York, 1991.

Shugg, Wallace. "'This Great Test of Man's Brutality': The Sullivan-Hyer Prizefight at Still Pond Heights, Maryland, in 1849." *Maryland Historical Magazine* 95 (2000): 47–63.

Spann, Edward K. *The New Metropolis: New York City, 1840–1857.* New York, 1981.

Stansell, Christine. *City of Women: Sex and Class in New York, 1789–1860.* Urbana, 1982.

Stokes, Isaac N. P. *Iconography of Manhattan Island, 1498–1909.* New York, 1915–28.

Stott, Richard B. *Workers in the Metropolis: Class, Ethnicity, and Youth in Antebellum New York.* Ithaca, 1990.

Tchen, John Kuo Wei. *New York Before Chinatown: Orientalism and the Shaping of American Culture, 1776–1882.* Baltimore, 1999.

Ward, David. *Cities and Immigrants: A Geography of Change in Nineteenth Century America.* New York, 1971.

——. *Poverty, Ethnicity and the American City, 1840–1925: Changing Conceptions of the Slum and the Ghetto.* New York, 1989.

Wilder, Craig S. "The Rise and Influence of the New York African Society for Mutual Relief, 1808–1865." *Afro-Americans in New York Life and History* 22 (July 1998): 7–9.

Wilentz, Sean. "Crime, Poverty, and the Streets of New York City: The Diary of William H. Bell, 1850–1851." *History Workshop* 7 (1979): 126–55.

Winter, Marian Hannah. "Juba and American Minstrelsy." In Paul Magriel, ed., *Chronicles of the American Dance*. New York, 1948.

Wong Ching Foo. "The Chinese in New York." *Cosmopolitan* 5 (October 1888): 297–311.

Yamin, Rebecca. "Lurid Tales and Homely Stories of New York's Notorious Five Points." *Historical Archaeology* 32 (1998): 74–85.

——. "New York's Mythic Slum." *Archaeology* 50 (March–April 1997): 44–53.

Zucchi, John E. *The Little Slaves of the Harp: Italian Child Street Musicians in Nineteenth-Century Paris, London, and New York.* Montreal, 1992.

Zuille, John J. *Historical Sketch of the New York African Society for Mutual Relief.* New York, [1892?].

ACKNOWLEDGMENTS

This book might never have been written were it not for beef *lo mein*. As a teenager, I used to travel with my friends from my home in the suburbs north of New York City down to Chinatown to have lunch. There I fell in love with the *lo mein* served at Hop Shing at 9 Chatham Square. We sometimes saw the managers of our suburban Chinese restaurant eating there, confirming our belief that we had found the best and most authentic Chinese eatery in New York. After leaving New York for college, I returned to the city for graduate school in the mid-1980s and again often found myself on the downtown express headed to Chinatown for my fix of *lo mein* and steamed shrimp dumplings.

After graduate school, I moved west to teach at the University of Wyoming and published my first book, a study of the anti-Catholic, anti-immigrant Know Nothing party of the 1850s. Although I had planned to continue writing about Civil War–era politics, the Know Nothings sparked my fascination with immigrants. Having spent years studying the newcomers from the nativist point of view, I now wanted to hear the immigrants tell their own story. The infectious enthusiasm that my students in Wyoming brought to the study of their immigrant heritage inspired me as well.

But I still needed a focus for my new book. I did not want to write another narrow monograph on a single ethnic group, so many of which told the same story: We came, we suffered, we were discriminated against, we persevered, we triumphed. I mentioned my dilemma to reference librarian *extraordinaire* Beth Juhl on a visit to New York, and she suggested that I trace the history of a single block in an immigrant enclave. A block was too small, I decided, but a single *neighborhood* seemed to fit my requirements perfectly.

How I decided upon Five Points as that neighborhood I do not remember. My Wyoming colleague Ron Schultz may have suggested it. We had plenty of time to discuss such things during our 136-mile-a-day round-trip commute from Fort Collins, Colorado, to Laramie. That no modern historian had published anything substantial about the district despite its notoriety in the nineteenth century made it an attractive topic. When I discovered that my beloved Hop Shing was *in* the neighborhood, my mouth began to water and my mind was quickly made up. I would write the history of Five Points.

In the eight years since, many friends, colleagues, and institutions have provided the guidance and assistance that made this book possible. Grants from George Washington University and the Irish American Cultural Institute, as well as a Fellowship for University Teachers from the National Endowment for the Humanities, funded my research and helped me extend my 1998 sabbatical to a full year. Ken Cobb at the New York Municipal Archives led me to a number of important sources, as did the head of the Five Points archaeology project, Rebecca Yamin, and Marion Casey of New York University. When I decided to trace the stories of the neighborhood's Kerry and Sligo immigrants back to their native land, Peter Gray of the University of Southampton; Cormac O'Grada and Desmond Norton of University College, Dublin; and Gerard Lyne of the National Library of Ireland helped me identify the appropriate Irish sources and critiqued drafts of that once-colossal chapter.

As the manuscript began to take shape, other historians offered important suggestions, including Kevin Kenny of Boston College; Kerby Miller of the University of Missouri; Elliott Gorn at Purdue University; Patrick Williams at the University of Arkansas; Tony Kaye of the Freedmen and Southern Society Project; Howard Gillette at Rutgers University, Camden; Josh Brown of the American Social History Project; and independent scholar Mary Elizabeth Brown. Countless others offered research advice or answered e-mail queries. Mark Santangelo and Anne McLeer were indefatigable research assistants. Tim Gilfoyle of Loyola University of Chicago generously shared with me his prodigious research on prostitution, Tom Lee, and Quimbo and George Appo. His reading of Chapters Seven and Thirteen saved me from dozens of errors. My George Washington University colleague Richard Stott read the entire manuscript and offered valuable advice at every stage of this project. His wide-ranging knowledge of working-class history in general, and New York City history in particular, has helped improve my understanding of Five Points in countless ways. I am very lucky to have him as a colleague and friend.

Once I began to seek a publisher, I got superb advice from my agent Jill Grinberg. Long before I found Jill, I met my editor, Bruce Nichols. When I first described the Five Points project to Bruce in 1993, he told me he was not interested. But because of his interest in my next project, a history of immigrant life in New York City from the first Dutch settlers to the present, he took me to lunch anyway and stayed in touch. When I met him at a conference six years later and told him he really ought to read the first eight chapters, he agreed, and finally did become interested. In the two years since, he has improved the manuscript in numerous ways, making me a better writer and *Five Points* a much better book. I am also indebted to the terrific production team at The Free Press, especially Ann Adelman, Juanita Seidel, Maria Massey, Steve Friedeman, and David Frost.

In the end, though, it was my dear friends and family members who made *Five Points* possible. Jordana Pomeroy was there from the beginning of the project and forced me to visit even the most remote portions of the Lansdowne immigrants' homelands in County Kerry. Marianne Szegedy-Masak, Matt and Anne Canzonetti, and Katy Bohlmann helped me in countless ways, and all read the book's early chapters. Katy was an especially valuable companion when I decided to visit the native villages of my young Italian street musicians in Basilicata. I owe a great deal to my parents, Madeline and Stephen Anbinder; my father gave the manuscript his typically thorough stylistic critique. Lisa Rein read most of the manuscript in its final stages and worked particularly hard at helping me craft the chapter prologues. I am extraordinarily grateful for her contributions and don't know how I would have completed the book without her.

But more than anything else, I have looked forward to completing *Five Points* so I could dedicate it to my children, Jacob and Dina. They bring me more joy than I could have ever imagined possible, and it is with my unbounded love that I dedicate this book to them.

INDEX